The Security of the
Caspian Sea Region

Stockholm International Peace Research Institute

SIPRI is an independent international institute for research into problems of peace and conflict, especially those of arms control and disarmament. It was established in 1966 to commemorate Sweden's 150 years of unbroken peace.

The Institute is financed mainly by the Swedish Parliament. The staff and the Governing Board are international. The Institute also has an Advisory Committee as an international consultative body.

The Governing Board is not responsible for the views expressed in the publications of the Institute.

Governing Board

Ambassador Rolf Ekéus, Chairman (Sweden)
Dr Catherine Kelleher, Vice-Chairman (United States)
Dr Alexei G. Arbatov (Russia)
Dr Willem F. van Eekelen (Netherlands)
Dr Nabil Elaraby (Egypt)
Sir Marrack Goulding (United Kingdom)
Professor Dr Helga Haftendorn (Germany)
Professor Ronald G. Sutherland (Canada)
The Director

Director

Dr Adam Daniel Rotfeld (Poland)

sipri

Stockholm International Peace Research Institute
Signalistgatan 9, SE-169 70 Solna, Sweden
Cable: SIPRI
Telephone: 46 8/655 97 00
Telefax: 46 8/655 97 33
E-mail: sipri@sipri.se
Internet URL: http://www.sipri.se

The Security of the Caspian Sea Region

Edited by
Gennady Chufrin

sipri

OXFORD UNIVERSITY PRESS
2001

OXFORD

UNIVERSITY PRESS

Great Clarendon Street, Oxford OX2 6DP

Oxford University Press is a department of the University of Oxford.
It furthers the University's objective of excellence in research, scholarship,
and education by publishing worldwide in

Oxford New York

Athens Auckland Bangkok Bogotá Buenos Aires Calcutta
Cape Town Chennai Dar es Salaam Delhi Florence Hong Kong Istanbul
Karachi Kuala Lumpur Madrid Melbourne Mexico City Mumbai
Nairobi Paris São Paulo Singapore Taipei Tokyo Toronto Warsaw
and associated companies in Berlin Ibadan

Oxford is a registered trade mark of Oxford University Press
in the UK and certain other countries

Published in the United States
by Oxford University Press Inc., New York

© SIPRI 2001

First published 2001

All rights reserved. No part of this publication may be reproduced,
stored in a retrieval system, or transmitted, in any form or by any means,
without the prior permission in writing of SIPRI or as expressly permitted by law,
or under terms agreed with the appropriate reprographics rights organizations.
Enquiries concerning reproduction outside the scope of the above should be sent to
SIPRI, Signalistgatan 9, SE-169 70 Solna, Sweden

You must not circulate this book in any other binding or cover
and you must impose the same condition on any acquirer

British Library Cataloguing in Publication Data
Data available

Library of Congress Cataloguing-in-Publication Data
Data available

ISBN 0-19-925020-0

Typeset and originated by Stockholm International Peace Research Institute
Printed in Great Britain on acid-free paper by
Biddles Ltd., Guildford and King's Lynn

327.17209475
Se 269
cop.2

SSHEL

Contents

Preface   *xi*

Acknowledgements   *xiv*

Acronyms and abbreviations   *xv*

1. Introduction   1
Gennady Chufrin
    I.   The changing Caspian security environment   1
   II. Time limits and research objectives   7
  III. The structure of this volume   7
Figure 1.1. Map of the Caspian Sea region   6

Part I. The Caspian security environment

2. The new geopolitical situation in the Caspian region   11
Lena Jonson
    I.   Introduction   11
   II. The Russian factor in the Caspian region   13
  III. International engagement   16
  IV. The energy field—parallel systems evolving?   22
   V. The security field—parallel systems evolving?   26
  VI. Prospects for the future   31

3. Energy reserves, pipeline routes and the legal regime in the   33
Caspian Sea
John Roberts
    I.   The energy reserves and production potential of the Caspian   33
   II. Caspian pipelines: the carriage of Caspial oil and gas to   44
       market
  III. The Caspian Sea legal regime   64
  IV. The Turkish Straits issue   67
Figure 3.1. Caspian oil and gas pipelines, existing, under construction   46
       and proposed

4. The Caspian Sea: threats to its biological resources and   69
environmental security
Igor Zonn
    I.   Introduction   69
   II. Threats to the Caspian's biological resources   70
  III. Environmental problems   74
  IV. Future scenarios   80
Table 4.1. Sturgeon catches in the Caspian Basin   72

5. Major trends in military expenditure and arms acquisitions by the   83
states of the Caspian region
Mark Eaton
    I.   Introduction   83
   II.   Iran   85
  III.   The South Caucasus   88
  IV.   Central Asia   97
   V.   Multilateral security cooperation   111
  VI.   Conclusions   114
Table 5.1.   Military expenditure in the Caspian Sea region, in local   84
            currencies, 1995–2000
Table 5.2.   Military expenditure in the Caspian Sea region, in US   85
            dollars, 1995–2000
Table 5.3.   Military expenditure as a percentage of gross domestic   86
            product, 1995–2000

Part II. National perspectives on security in the Caspian Sea region

6. Russia's national security interests in the Caspian region   119
Vitaly Naumkin
    I.   Introduction   119
   II.   The southern direction of Russia's national security   119
  III.   Russia's interests   120
  IV.   Will the Caspian come to rival the Persian Gulf?   123
   V.   Is there a conflict of interests between Russia and the USA?   126
  VI.   Oil, development and security   128
 VII.   Russia's Caspian policy becomes more active   132

7. US policy towards the Caspian region: can the wish-list be realized? 136
Amy Jaffe
    I.   Introduction: the underpinning of US policy towards the   136
         Caspian
   II.   Oil as a driving factor: myths and realities   140
  III.   Natural gas: equal export troubles for US policy   144
  IV.   US strategic interests: what is at stake?   145
   V.   Russia and the USA: a cooperative framework?   147
  VI.   US policy change expected   147
 VII.   Conclusions   149

8. Turkey's objectives in the Caspian region   151
Ali Karaosmanoglu
    I.   Introduction   151
   II.   Energy and the economy   152
  III.   The environmental risks of oil transport   154
  IV.   The geopolitics of pipelines   156

V.   Cooperation with Russia   159
VI. Multilateralism and Western orientation   161
VII. Turkey's internal and external constraints   163
VIII. Conclusions: future trends   164

9. The evolving security role of Iran in the Caspian region   166
Mehrdad M. Mohsenin
I.   Introduction   166
II.   The legal status of the Caspian Sea   169
III. Oil and gas transport routes   171
IV.   Iran's policy in the Caspian Sea   173

10. Azerbaijan's strategic choice in the Caspian region   178
Sabit Bagirov
I.   Introduction   178
II.   Strengthening political and economic relations with the   179
      West
III. The policy of balanced relations with Russia, Turkey and   182
      Iran
IV.   The delimitation of sea frontiers on the Caspian Sea   188
V.   A diversified system of oil and gas pipelines   190
VI.   Conclusions   194

11. The choice of independent Georgia   195
Alexander Rondeli
I.   Introduction   195
II.   Recent political developments   197
III. Georgian foreign policy   200
IV.   Georgia, Russia and the West   203
V.   Georgia's choice   208
VI.   Conclusions   211

12. Kazakhstan's security policy in the Caspian Sea region   212
Konstantin Syroezhkin
I.   The concept of national security   212
II.   The development of a new balance of forces   215
III. Social and economic reforms in Kazakhstan as a   220
      precondition of its national security
IV.   New challenges and new approaches   226
Table 12.1. Immigration to and emigration from Kazakhstan   223

13. Turkmenistan's quest for economic security   231
Najia Badykova
I.   Introduction   231
II.   The role of energy resources in the political and economic   231
      security of Turkmenistan

III. The major competitors and partners of Turkmenistan 234
IV. The trans-Caspian gas pipeline 236
V. Existing pipelines 238
VI. The legal status of the Caspian Sea 241
VII. Conclusions 242

14. Turkmenistan and Central Asian regional security 244
Murad Esenov
I. Introduction 244
II. The neutrality concept 245
III. The Taliban connection 246
IV. The reality of Turkmenistans's neutrality 252

Part III. The changing conflict dynamics in the Caspian Sea region

15. The conflict in Nagorno-Karabakh: its impact on security in the 257
Caspian region
Dina Malysheva
I. Introduction 257
II. The positions of the contending parties 259
III. The positions of the regional countries 264
IV. The stand of the Western countries 271
V. Attempts at mediation 273
VI. The danger of armed conflict 275
VII. Scenarios for conflict resolution 277
VIII. Conclusions 279

16. The Georgian–Abkhazian Conflict 281
Alexander Krylov
I. Introduction 281
II. The post-war situation 286
III. The position of Russia 290
IV. The position of the West 292
V. Conclusions 294

17. The glitter and poverty of Chechen Islam 295
Aleksei Malashenko
I. Introduction 295
II. The influence of Islam on events in Chechnya 296
III. The aims of the Chechen leaders in appealing to Islam 298
IV. The failure of the 'Salafite project' 304
V. External influences 308

18. Radical Islam as a threat to the security of the Central Asian   311
states: a view from Uzbekistan
Farkhad Khamraev
    I.   Introduction   311
   II. Threats to security   313
  III. The future of security relations in Central Asia   318

Part IV. Competition and cooperation in the Caspian Sea region

19. The Caspian Sea region: towards an unstable future   325
Gennady Chufrin
    I.   Introduction   325
   II. The regional states   325
  III. Non-regional actors   331
  IV. Global powers   336
   V. Russian–US interaction in the Caspain region   341

Appendix. Chronology of defence and security-related declarations   345
and agreements involving the countries of the Caspian region,
1991–2001
Mark Eaton

About the authors   358

Index   361

Preface

This book is the result of a two-year SIPRI project on the Security of the Caspian Sea Region directed by Gennady Chufrin and launched after the completion of two previous studies which resulted in two books: *Russia and Europe: The Emerging Security Agenda* (Oxford University Press, 1997), edited by Vladimir Baranovsky; and *Russia and Asia: The Emerging Security Agenda* (Oxford University Press, 1999), edited by Gennady Chufrin. The present volume analyses the political, economic, security and social issues and events prominent throughout the region during the decade following the breakup of the Soviet Union and offers alternative scenarios for its future development.

The authors contributing to the volume come from 12 different countries, including all five of the Caspian littoral states—Azerbaijan, Canada, Georgia, Kazakhstan, Iran, Russia, Sweden, Turkey, Turkmenistan, the UK, the USA and Uzbekistan. Most of the contributors are from academic and research institutions, while others represent the government and business sectors. All have a unique knowledge of regional affairs. The study also benefited from the rich intellectual contribution made by the participants at the international conferences and workshops organized within the framework of the project and held in Stockholm, Almaty and Moscow.

The book takes an innovative approach to exploring regional issues, concentrating on an analysis of the geopolitical environment. Energy issues are an important aspect but are treated mainly as they relate to conflicting trends in the political, security and social developments in the region. The volume addresses such specific issues as the national political and security interests in the region during the post-Soviet period of the littoral and the major outside countries, including the USA, members of the European Union, China and Turkey. The economic security of the Caspian states and the role of energy resources in influencing the overall security situation in the region is also analysed. Finally, the changing conflict dynamics in the region are presented, as are the prospects for international interaction in the region in the 21st century.

The contributors come to the conclusion that the likelihood of the Caspian Sea region remaining a zone of conflict and instability for the foreseeable future is very high. However, it is in the interests of the international community to control these tendencies, opening the door to possible cooperation between Russia and the USA, whose roles are central to the political and economic future of the region.

In addition to analysing these issues, the volume contains valuable data on major trends in arms acquisitions and military spending by regional governments, on regional energy resources, on existing and proposed energy pipelines, and on the biological resources of the Caspian Sea.

Eve Johansson of the SIPRI editorial staff contributed her keen skills to editing the volume. I would also like to express my gratitude to the John D. and Catherine T. MacArthur Foundation for their generous financial support.

Adam Daniel Rotfeld
Director of SIPRI
June 2001

The Security of the Caspian Sea Region

Advisory Committee

Ambassador Rolf Ekéus (Chairman, SIPRI Governing Board)
Professor Aleksei Malashenko (Moscow Carnegie Centre)
Dr Adam Daniel Rotfeld (Director, SIPRI)
Dr Harold Saunders (Kettering Foundation, Dayton, Ohio)
Professor Daniel Tarschys (Stockholm University)

Acknowledgements

The Advisory Committee of the project defined the concept of this study after intensive and exciting brain-storming meetings. The ideas of its members were essential to finalizing the framework and goals of the research.

The successful completion of such a broad and complex research project depended on the cooperation and intellectual input of many people with very diverse knowledge and experience. The study was truly international in nature: the contributors to this volume were from academic and government organizations and the private sector in 12 countries. In addition scholars, politicians, government officials and businessmen from several countries contributed their ideas at various stages of the project.

Several research institutions cooperated directly with SIPRI in helping to organize the conferences and workshops held within the framework of the project. I am grateful for the invaluable support provided by the Institute for Strategic Studies under the Office of the President of the Republic of Kazakhstan and its Director, Maulen Ashimbayev, as well as by the Russian Centre for Strategic Research and International Studies and its President, Professor Vitaly Naumkin. I would also like to express my gratitude to the Kettering Foundation, and to Dr Harold Saunders personally, for helping to organize the workshop on US–Russian Interaction in the Caspian Region within the framework of the Dartmouth Conference Regional Conflict Task Force.

Several members of the SIPRI staff also contributed a great deal to the success of this project. Mark Eaton rendered effective research assistance throughout the project. Elizabeth Sköns, Petter Stålenheim and Evamaria Loose-Weintraub provided valuable information on military expenditures; Nicholas Chipperfield, Pieter T. Wezeman and Siemon D. Wezeman contributed their expertise on arms transfers; and Shannon Kile helped formulate the main goals and framework of the project at its initial stages. Eve Johansson applied her exceptional editorial skills to editing the entire manuscript—a task made more difficult since most of the chapters were written by non-English speakers. Anna Helleday and Monica Möllerström handled the day-to-day financial aspects of the project and provided support in planning project conferences; Billie Bielckus drew the maps; and Gerd Hagmeyer-Gaverus and Sten Wiksten provided computer support.

Finally, I would like to acknowledge the generous financial support of the John D. and Catherine T. MacArthur Foundation, without which the implementation of the project would not have been possible.

Gennady Chufrin
Project Leader
June 2001

Acronyms and abbreviations

ACG	Azeri–Chirag–Guneshli
ACV	Armoured combat vehicle
AIFV	Armoured infantry fighting vehicle
AIOC	Azerbaijan International Operating Company
APC	Armoured personnel carrier
BG	British Gas
BP	British Petroleum
BSEC	Black Sea Economic Cooperation
BTC	Baku–Tbilisi–Ceyhan
CASCO	Caspian Sea Cooperation Organization
CAU	Central Asian Union
CBM	Confidence-building measure
CentrasBat	Central Asian Battalion
CFE	Conventional Armed Forces in Europe
CIPCO	Caspian International Petroleum Company
CIS	Commonwealth of Independent States
CNPC	China National Petroleum Corporation
CPC	Caspian Pipeline Consortium
CPF	Collective Peacekeeping Force (Tajikistan)
ECO	Economic Cooperation Organization
EIA	Energy Information Administration (USA)
EPA	Environmental Protection Agency (USA)
EU	European Union
FBS	Federal Border Service (Russia)
FMF	Foreign Military Financing programme (US)
GDP	Gross domestic product
GNP	Gross national product
GUAM	Georgia, Ukraine, Azerbaijan and Moldova
GUUAM	Georgia, Ukraine, Uzbekistan, Azerbaijan and Moldova
IEA	International Energy Agency
IMET	International Military Education and Training programme (US)
IMF	International Monetary Fund
IMO	International Maritime Organization
IMU	Islamic Movement of Uzbekistan
INOGATE	Interstate Oil and Gas Transport to Europe
KFOR	Kosovo Force
KKK	Korpedze–Kurt-Kui (gas pipeline)
KPO	Karachaganak Petroleum Operating group
KTI	Kazakhstan–Turkmenistan–Iran (prospective oil pipeline)

MBT	Main battle tank
MEP	Main export pipeline
MRD	Motor Rifle Division
MRL	Multiple rocket launcher
NAOC	North Apsheron Operating Company
NBC	Nuclear, biological and chemical
NIOC	National Iranian Oil Company
NKAR	Nagorno-Karabakh Autonomous Region of Azerbaijan
NKR	Nagorno-Karabakh Republic
OIC	Organization of the Islamic Conference
OKIOC	Offshore Kazakhstan International Operating Company
OPEC	Organization of the Petroleum Exporting Countries
OSCE	Organization for Security and Co-operation in Europe
PFP	Partnership for Peace
PKK	Kurdish Workers' Party
SAM	Surface-to-air missile
SOCAR	State Oil Company of the Azerbaijan Republic
TCGP	Trans-Caspian Gas Pipeline
TMG	Turkmengas State Gas Company
TMN	Turkmenneft State Oil Company
TPAO	Turkish Petroleum Corporation
TRACECA	Transport Corridor Europe Caucasus Asia
UAE	United Arab Emirates
UTO	United Tajik Opposition

Units of measurement

b/d	Barrels/day
bbl	Billion barrels
bcm	Billion cubic metres
btoe	Billion tonnes of oil equivalent
mb/d	Million barrels/day
mt/y	Million tonnes/year
tcm	Trillion cubic metres

Conventions

m.	Million
b.	Billion (thousand million)
..	Data not available or not applicable
–	Nil or a negligible amount
( )	Uncertain figure
[ ]	SIPRI estimate
$	US dollars, unless otherwise indicated

1. Introduction

Gennady Chufrin

I. The changing Caspian security environment

Following the breakup of the Soviet Union, the Caspian Sea region has risen from relative obscurity to considerable prominence in international affairs. For the purposes of this study the region is defined as consisting of the Caspian Sea littoral states (Azerbaijan, Iran, Kazakhstan, Russia and Turkmenistan) and their immediate neighbours in the South Caucasus (Armenia and Georgia)[1] and Central Asia (Kyrgyzstan, Tajikistan and Uzbekistan).[2] Its political landscape has been fundamentally transformed over the past decade.

Major international actors have also become increasingly interested not only in maintaining relationships with their traditional partners in the region—Iran and Russia—but also in forging gainful relationships with the former Soviet republics that emerged as new sovereign states in the Caspian Sea Basin. The growing interest in these new states among the international community is stimulated by two groups of factors.

The first are geo-strategic considerations. The new sovereign Caspian states occupy central positions in the heartland of the Eurasian continent and on the traditional trade routes between Europe and Asia. The concrete national strategies these states will follow have become of intense interest to the major extra-regional powers (the USA, China and the European Union member states among them) and have induced them to start formulating their own policies in the Caspian Sea region—policies which may not only be reactive but also actively influence political, economic and security developments there to their own advantage.

Second, the widespread international interest in the Caspian Sea region is motivated by the large reserves of oil and natural gas that are believed to lie there. Since no comprehensive geological surveys of the Caspian seabed and maritime region have been carried out since the Soviet era, it is difficult to state with certainty the exact size of these reserves. Estimates of recoverable oil reserves range from 40–60 billion barrels to as high as 100 and even 200 billion barrels; those for natural gas range between 10 and 20 trillion cubic metres.

These estimates are clearly influenced by political and economic interests; in particular, those offered by the newly independent littoral states are made to attract the foreign investment that is needed to turn the oil and gas potential of

---

[1] The South Caucasus, sometimes called the Transcaucasus, is defined for the purposes of this book as consisting of Armenia, Azerbaijan and Georgia.

[2] Central Asia is defined for the purposes of this book as consisting of Kazakhstan, Kyrgyzstan, Tajikistan, Turkmenistan and Uzbekistan.

the region into a major sustainable source of economic prosperity. However, whichever estimates are correct, it is widely accepted that the Caspian region's recoverable oil and natural gas reserves are exceeded in size only by those of the Middle East and western Siberia.

Among the many factors influencing the regional security environment are disputes among the littoral states over the Caspian Sea legal regime and the division of the Caspian Sea energy resources into national economic zones and sectors. The legal regime which currently governs the exploitation of the Caspian oil and gas resources is based on the Soviet–Iranian treaties of 1921 and 1940 and no longer reflects the geopolitical changes in the area after the breakup of the Soviet Union. Although the need to establish a new legal regime for the Caspian Sea is recognized by all the littoral states, efforts to do this have run into serious difficulties because of these countries' radically differing approaches to the proposed regime.

In addition to determining the legal status of the Caspian Sea and the ownership of hydrocarbon deposits, the littoral states confront another contentious issue, namely, determining the routes for transporting the oil and gas extracted from the Caspian region to outside consumers. The dispute over this issue has emerged as perhaps the single most important cause of growing international political tensions in the Caspian area. The basic conflict of interests derives from the fact that by the end of the 1990s essentially all Caspian oil and gas pipelines (with the exception of a gas pipeline from Turkmenistan to Iran and an oil pipeline from Azerbaijan to Georgia) run through Russia. While Russia wishes to retain its pre-eminent position in having oil and gas pipelines passing mainly across its territory, the landlocked Caspian states want to escape their near-total dependence on Russia.

The energy potential of the Caspian Sea region is another factor behind the interest of the extra-regional actors. This is particularly true of the USA, which is actively promoting the construction of oil and gas export pipelines across the Caspian Sea and the South Caucasus. Ukraine, a major East European country which is experiencing a very acute shortage of energy resources and trying for strategic reasons to reduce its overdependence on Russian oil and gas, also actively supports the creation of a transport corridor that would connect the Caspian region with Europe across Ukrainian territory. The controversies over oil and gas transport routes from the Caspian Sea region are further complicated by Turkish threats to impose restrictions on tanker traffic passing through the Bosporus and Dardanelles, ostensibly for environmental safety reasons. Other countries, such as China or the European Union (EU) member states, are also pursuing increasingly active policies in the region, motivated by their growing energy requirements and their assessments of the new strategic situation that is taking shape in the Caspian region. China's degree of self-sufficiency in energy is declining rapidly and it takes a particularly close interest in getting permanent access to the energy resources of the Caspian Sea region. This has become a high-priority task in its foreign policy, strongly influencing other aspects of its strategy in the Caspian Sea region.

All this means that the Caspian energy resources and access to them from the outside world are major factors that have a direct impact on the security situation in the Caspian Sea region.

Apart from energy-related factors, the regional security environment has been dramatically influenced in the 1990s by the general political, social and economic developments in the former Soviet republics of the South Caucasus and Central Asia. Being in the process of intensive, often conflictual nation-building, they have been confronted with a wide range of challenges and threats to their security, domestic as well as external. Their very confused domestic situations have been exacerbated by the continuing economic and social crisis in the post-Soviet states as well as by the hardening struggle for the succession to power from the former Soviet elite which is now in power to the next generation. If with this generational change more aggressive nationalistic regimes are established in one or more of the new sovereign Caspian states then the security situation in the region will most likely become more tense and potentially explosive.

The volatility of the security situation in the Caspian Sea region has been intensified by developments connected with the numerous ethno-political conflicts going on there which seriously threaten the national security and territorial integrity of regional states. In addition, regional stability is potentially jeopardized by the growing influence of militant Islamic ideologies. This is especially true in the wake of the successes of the Taliban movement (which also has a strong ethnic character) in neighbouring Afghanistan and in the light of the growing influence of radical Islam in the Russian North Caucasus, the South Caucasus and Central Asia.

The cumulative impact of these developments has been largely negative for stability in the Caspian Sea region. Together, they are driving the region in the direction of increased confrontation and are generating rising interstate as well as intra-state tensions. The growing conflict potential in the region arises from the nexus of complex regional disputes with the increasing involvement of outside powers. In particular, there is an emerging tendency towards military buildup which can be observed at different levels—national, regional and international. This is manifested in the Caspian states' programmes to build national armed forces and to modernize their military equipment holdings as well as in the growing transfers of arms to the region from outside sources. Over the five years 1995–99 defence expenditure for the entire region (excluding Russia) in constant 1998 prices rose by 23 per cent, in the South Caucasus subregion by 19.2 per cent, in the Central Asian subregion by 36.5 per cent, and in Iran by 18.4 per cent.[3] In spite of a lack of transparency concerning regional arms imports, it can be concluded that there was a significant increase in transfers to the Caspian region during the latter half of the 1990s as almost 70 per cent of arms deliveries to the newly independent states of the Caspian region during the 1990s originated between 1995 and 1999.[4] During the same period Armenia,

[3] SIPRI military expenditure archive.
[4] Figures calculated from the SIPRI arms transfer archive.

Iran and Kazakhstan emerged among the world's leading recipients of conventional weapons. To modernize their armed forces, the Caspian states were increasingly importing more sophisticated weaponry, including up-to-date combat aircraft, battle tanks and anti-aircraft and missile systems.

Although all the post-Soviet countries in the South Caucasus and Central Asia joined the Russia-centred Commonwealth of Independent States (CIS), for some of them their role in the CIS has become more formal than active with the passage of time. The crisis of cooperation between them on military and security affairs resulted in Azerbaijan, Georgia and Uzbekistan in 1999 terminating their membership in the CIS Treaty on Collective Security (the Tashkent Treaty of 1992). During 1999 Russia was compelled to withdraw its border guards from Georgia and Kyrgyzstan and to agree to close two of its military bases in Georgia by 1 July 2001. Turkmenistan, another CIS member state, although not a party to the Tashkent Treaty, also contributed to the trend of decreasing military and security cooperation among the post-Soviet states in the Caspian region when, also in 1999, it decided not to prolong its earlier agreement with Russia on the joint guarding of Turkmenistan's state borders.

Driven by the perceived changes in their national interests, the Central Asian and South Caucasus states have been searching simultaneously for new national and collective responses to emerging security challenges, and this has resulted in the formation of new political alignments and formal alliances in the region. Most prominent among these was the strengthening of the political and military ties of most of these states with the Western countries and NATO. It resulted in the development of their cooperation with Turkey and the USA within the framework of the NATO Partnership for Peace (PFP) programme which, starting in 1997, included joint military exercises in the Caspian Basin. Kazakhstan, although continuing as a party to the Tashkent Treaty, in its military doctrine regarded increased cooperation with NATO as an important element of its national security system which it wished to develop with an enlarged number of security partners. Not only did Kazakhstan join the PFP programme; in 1999 it organized on its soil the first bilateral military exercises with the USA. Uzbekistan did the same. Azerbaijan and Georgia took an even more resolute step towards the West by openly favouring joining NATO, and even before that stage was reached Azerbaijan indicated its readiness to deploy a NATO military base on its soil, justifying this by the need to ensure the safety of oil pipelines crossing its territory in a southerly direction.

Apart from strengthening their ties with NATO, the post-Soviet Caspian states were forming alliances that are alternatives to the CIS among themselves or with some other post-Soviet states. One of those is GUUAM, originated by Georgia, Ukraine, Azerbaijan and Moldova in 1997 and joined by Uzbekistan in 1999. Its goals included the promotion not only of political and economic but also of military cooperation among the members of the group. Another subregional group is the Central Asian Union (CAU), established by Kazakhstan, Kyrgyzstan and Uzbekistan in 1994. Tajikistan joined in 1999. Although the main declared goal of the CAU is to promote economic cooperation among its members, its founders announced that they intend to expand this cooperation to the political and military spheres as well.

The security situation in the region is strongly affected by the policies of major international actors. Competing with each other for political and economic influence in the region, they risk turning it into another area of international confrontation. Relations between Russia and the USA, both of which regard the Caspian Sea Basin as important for their national interests, have been developing recently along the lines of a 'zero-sum game'.

Russia retains strong national interests in the Caspian Sea region, most of which until relatively recently was part of the Soviet Union, and continues to have considerable influence on economic, political and military developments there, although this influence has been waning over the past decade. It views the growing role of NATO in the region with deep apprehension, perceiving it as further threatening its own national interests. As a consequence, after a decade of erratic misrule under President Boris Yeltsin, the new Russian leadership under President Vladimir Putin declared its intention to pursue a more consistent and vigorous policy aimed at protecting Russia's interests in the Caspian Sea region and at stopping and reversing its strategic retreat from the region.[5] New initiatives were launched aimed at expanding economic cooperation with regional countries and strengthening military and security ties with them.

In its 'revivalist' policy Russia is strongly challenged by the USA. Its policy in the region during the 1990s shifted from an originally benevolent but fairly passive support for the sovereignty of the newly independent states there to a more active engagement in regional affairs on an array of political, economic and security issues.

In 1997–99, in order to encourage a pro-Western orientation on the part of the Caspian countries and to address threats to their independence by possible Russian neo-imperialism, the US Congress approved legislation, including the Silk Road Strategy Act of 1999, which called on the US Government to support the development of democracy and creation of civil societies in those states as well as actively to assist their economic development, including the construction of trans-Caspian and trans-Caucasus energy pipelines.[6] The USA has also been actively expanding its influence in Caspian region security affairs through the promotion of the PFP programme and individual military cooperation programmes with regional countries. Apart from competing with Russia in the region, the USA has continued energetically to pursue a dual containment policy towards Iran, another Caspian littoral state, trying to minimize its role in the use and transport of Caspian energy resources and to weaken its political role in the region.

---

[5] 'Kontseptsiya vneshney politiki Rossiyskoy Federatsii' [Foreign policy concept of the Russian Federation], *Diplomaticheskiy Vestnik,* no. 8 (2000), p. 8.

[6] US House of Representatives, Silk Road Strategy Act, 1999, HR 1152, 3 Aug. 1999.

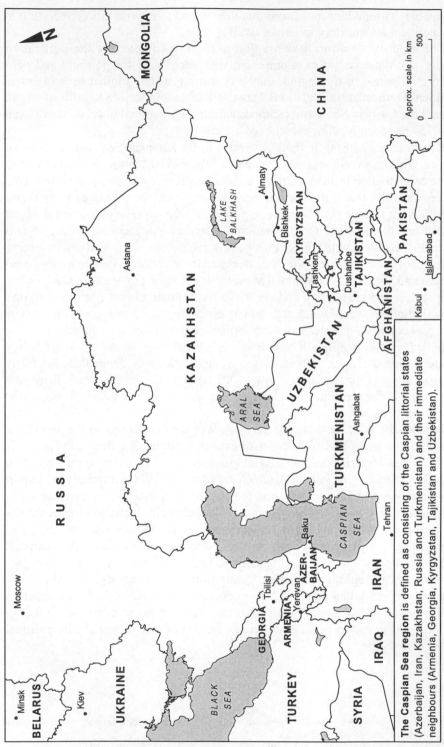

The Caspian Sea region is defined as consisting of the Caspian littorial states (Azerbaijan, Iran, Kazakhstan, Russia and Turkmenistan) and their immediate neighbours (Armenia, Georgia, Kyrgyzstan, Tajikistan and Uzbekistan).

Figure 1.1. Map of the Caspian Sea region

In spite of the USA's opposition, the breakup of the Soviet Union and the emergence of new Caspian sovereign states have increasingly brought Iran to the forefront of regional politics and accelerated its transformation into an important regional power competing for political and economic influence in the Caspian Sea region. Iran's position has become pivotal in settling the future of the Caspian Sea legal regime and proposed hydrocarbon transport routes.

Turkey has also become more actively involved in the Caspian region. The region is growing in importance as a source to meet Turkey's increasing energy requirements. Interrelated with these long-standing strategic interests in the region is Turkey's desire to lay down a transit route for Caspian energy resources across its own territory. In addition, it seeks to use its historic, cultural and ethno-linguistic ties to many of the Caspian countries to enhance its political influence there.

Taking into account the great divergence in the national interests of the various local and international actors in the Caspian Sea region and their highly competitive policies in pursuit of those interests, the future of peace and stability in the region is now in serious doubt. Whether these actors succeed in accommodating their respective interests in the region and move towards cooperation or whether they allow their differences to continue to destabilize the situation there is increasingly important for the state of regional and international security and calls for the analysis of different future political scenarios.

II. Time limits and research objectives

This study, which started in February 2000 and covered events in and around the Caspian region until mid–2001, set out with the following research objectives: (a) to assess the diverse and often conflicting interests of different parties in the Caspian Sea region, focusing on the strategic competition over the exploitation of oil and gas reserves there; this includes a comprehensive analysis of the national interests and policies of the Caspian littoral states as well as those of major extra-regional countries; (b) to examine the incipient threat of the militarization of the Caspian region; (c) to explore the main local conflicts in the region and their increasing linkages to wider security-related controversies there; (d) to analyse the multi-faceted political role played by Islam in the region and to assess its implications for regional security; and (e) to examine different policy options aimed at the de-escalation of existing tensions in the Caspian region and at the establishment there of an atmosphere of growing trust and international cooperation.

III. The structure of this volume

The study consists of four parts.

The first part examines the changing security setting in the Caspian Sea region. It describes the principal geopolitical changes which have taken place there in the wake of the breakup of the Soviet Union. This part also evaluates the region's energy and biological wealth, threats to the regional environment, problems related to oil and gas transport routes, and the controversy over the Caspian Sea legal regime.

The second part explores the national perspectives of the littoral states and of the major outside powers on security in the Caspian Sea region. It analyses their evolving—and often competing—economic and strategic interests in the region and the impact of these conflicts of interests on the security environment there. Particular attention is given to analysing the shifting patterns of political alignments in the region in the larger context of the potential collision and convergence of interests between Russia and the United States.

The third part analyses threats and challenges to regional stability posed by the fully or partially unresolved conflicts in the Caspian Sea region which have developed from inter-ethnic, inter-confessional and inter-clan contradictions. Special attention is paid to the impact of militant Islam on regional stability. These conflicts are also examined in the context of the growing rivalry among the littoral states and their immediate neighbours over various political and economic issues in the Caspian Sea region.

The fourth part summarizes the findings of the study and offers conclusions from them.

Part I
The Caspian security environment

2. The new geopolitical situation in the Caspian region

Lena Jonson

I. Introduction

The Caspian region has been undergoing radical change since the breakup of the Soviet Union. It is becoming internationalized to an extent not seen before, and a major reconfiguration of power and influence is taking place. Russia's reduced role and diminishing influence in the Caucasus and in Central Asia since 1991 together with the determined efforts of the states of the region to diversify their relations with the outside world have opened the doors for external actors to engage in the region. The prospects for the exploitation of oil and gas in the region have raised the stakes of external actors.

The purpose of this chapter is to analyse the new geopolitical situation and the impact of the growing international involvement in the Caspian region in an effort to identify trends for the future. The focus is on the distribution of power and influence in the region as reflected in the evolving patterns of cooperation in the fields of energy and security.

The new geopolitical situation as it developed during the 1990s can be characterized briefly as follows: (*a*) a process of Russian retreat from the Caucasus and Central Asia in the economic, political and military fields; (*b*) an increasing involvement by external actors (both state and non-state); and (*c*) increased competition between Russia and external state actors, first and foremost the USA.

A reduced Russian role and increased international cooperation have been regarded by the states of the region as a prerequisite if they are to strengthen their independence. 'Attempts by the Caspian countries, assisted by foreign actors, to weaken their dependence on this Russian-dominated infrastructure (and on each other) are at the heart of Caspian geo-politics.'[1] Tension in the region following from the larger international engagement has been interpreted by several observers as an unwelcome but unavoidable consequence of a geopolitical situation which is understood mainly in terms of strategic rivalry. Russia's relations with the West deteriorated after the 1994 decision by NATO to enlarge to the east and in 1999 reached their lowest point of the post-cold war era, further confirming Russia's understanding in geo-strategic terms of the intentions and motives behind Western engagement in the Caspian region.

Energy and security are key issues determining the future strategic setting of the Caspian region. The structures and arrangements which evolve today with

---

[1] McCarthy, J., 'The geopolitics of Caspian oil', *Jane's Intelligence Review*, July 2000, p. 21.

regard to the exploitation and transport of the energy resources in the region and in response to conflicts and threats to security may be decisive for tomorrow's patterns of cooperation, friendship and dependence. The country or group of countries which can assist the Caucasian and Central Asian states with regard to their energy and security needs will play an important role in the region in the future.

So far Russia has dominated the energy field and no serious alternatives to Russian pipeline outlets exist except on the drawing board. There is, however, an intense political struggle over routes, shares and influence. The exploitation of energy resources and the future routes of pipelines from the oil and gas fields in the Caspian Basin for export to external markets will to a great extent determine the future development of the Caspian region. The energy factor is vital to economic development and wealth but also to the future geopolitical configuration of the region. The outcome of the rivalry between different pipeline options will determine not only the pattern of foreign policy orientation and cooperation in the region but also the influence and position of regional powers. The extent to which powers such as China, Iran, Russia, Turkey and the USA are able to strengthen their influence in the Caucasus and Central Asia depends on what they can offer these states in the energy field.

The embryos of parallel security arrangements for responding to conflicts and crises are in the making in the Caspian region, and the outcome of this process is still unknown. The security of Central Asia and the Caucasus is vulnerable, and local dynamics threaten to overturn pipeline schemes and projects. Weak states, severe social and economic conditions, ethnic and regional divisions, crime and extremism threaten to build up a situation which could erupt in violence, with possible repercussions on the regional level. The question how the security of the region can be guaranteed is as important as the energy issue. The arrangements for security cooperation that evolve will determine not only the future security in the region but also the position and influence of regional powers. Thus, the energy and security issues are closely interconnected.

The parallel drawn by many observers in Russia and in the West between the Russian–Western competition of today in the Caspian region and the 'Great Game' of the 19th century between Russia and Great Britain is an oversimplification. It reflects one important aspect of the new situation—a clash of interests between Russia and outside powers—but also distorts the picture and overlooks important differences between the centuries. First, this approach underestimates the fact that the main sources for change are to be found in the internal dynamics of the region rather than in the influence of external actors. Second, it overlooks the fact that there is a multiplicity of non-state actors which act independently from the state actors. Third, it represents a 'zero-sum' approach, which emphasizes rivalry and excludes the possibility of a 'win–win' outcome. As a result, signs of evolving international cooperation in the region may be dismissed and possibilities missed for joining forces to respond to common challenges. The zero-sum approach, whereby an advance for one actor is regarded a loss for the other, is strong in the Russian tradition of foreign policy thinking. It has also played a significant role in Western thinking. These aspects are discussed throughout this chapter and evaluated in the concluding section.

The behaviour of the states in the Caspian region very much confirms the basic assumptions of the realist school of thought—that states always seek to increase their security and international influence. The realist school provides the basic assumption in this chapter as to how states behave. This will not, however, prevent us from borrowing the assumption of the constructivist school that international cooperation can change the basic parameters of a region and that the search for a win–win solution is therefore worthwhile.

Section II of this chapter analyses the Russian factor in the Caspian region. Section III gives an overview of the external actors and their stakes, interests and policies. Sections IV and V analyse the impact of international engagement on energy and security arrangements in the region, and the final section presents some tentative conclusions with regard to the trends and prospects for the geopolitical change in the region.

II. The Russian factor in the Caspian region

The great powers, whether Britain and Russia during the 19th century or Russia and the USA today, have often perceived the Caucasus and Central Asia as a single strategic entity.[2] The question can, however, be asked in what sense a single and separate Caspian region exists. With regard to security the independent Caucasian and Central Asian states have not been as interdependent as might have been assumed, since they are both parts of the former Soviet empire. The Caucasian states' security has been to a great extent shut off from developments in Central Asia, and vice versa.[3] They are therefore analysed here as two subregions or security complexes. The energy issue may slowly change this as pipeline projects connect the states and contribute to pose new, common problems. These include different aspects of security, from safe transport to environmental issues. The orientation of the Caucasian and Central Asian states and their search for active participation in international security arrangements also contribute to make them more interdependent in security matters.

The major changes in the Caspian region during the 1990s followed from the internal dynamics of the former Soviet Union—for example, the centrifugal force after the dissolution of the empire. The Caspian states define themselves and their foreign policy in relation to Russia. As Russia failed to attract them into functioning cooperation in a commonwealth, they were moving away from Russia. As the Russian factor weakened, new dividing lines appeared in the region.

[2] See, e.g., Maksimenko, V., 'Central Asia and the Caucasus: geopolitical entity explained', *Central Asia and the Caucasus* (Luleå), no. 3 (2000).

[3] Jonson, L. and Allison, R., 'Central Asia: internal and external security dynamics', eds R. Allison and L. Jonson, *Central Asian Security: The New International Context* (Brookings Institution: Washington, DC, 2001).

The number of Russia's allies in the region shrank during the latter half of the 1990s. Azerbaijan, Georgia and Uzbekistan were the most determined in the search for closer cooperation with Western states. Neutral Turkmenistan went its own way, while Kazakhstan and Kyrgyzstan remained fairly close to Russia. Tajikistan, torn by civil war, was totally dependent on Russia, as was Armenia. At the end of the 1990s Russia was left with the Commonwealth of Independent States (CIS), where all the Caucasian and Central Asian states were formal members but did not actively participate, and the 1992 Treaty on Collective Security (the Tashkent Treaty), in which, in the Caucasus and Central Asia, only four of the seven original member states remained.[4] When Georgia, Ukraine, Azerbaijan and Moldova in November 1997 created GUAM, and Uzbekistan joined them in April 1999 to form GUUAM, two major political groups seemed to be in the making.

During the first half of the 1990s Russia tried a policy of integrating all the Caucasian and Central Asian states into the CIS structures, but in 1996 this policy had to be revised. Instead policy became diversified with regard to individual CIS member states. Priority was given to those with which strong links could be developed, and a stronger emphasis on bilateral relations followed. As a consequence Armenia developed as a Russian stronghold in the Caucasus, and Kazakhstan and Tajikistan became Russia's key partners in Central Asia. Azerbaijan, Georgia and Uzbekistan played a subordinate role in Russian policy and distanced themselves from Russia. This trend was clearly demonstrated when these states withdrew from the Tashkent Treaty in April 1999.

In the economic field a similar process was going on. The volume of trade between Russia and the CIS member states fell. Russia remained the largest trading partner of most of the states in the region but on a much lower level. For all the Caspian CIS member states (except Tajikistan) the share of other CIS countries in their trade (both import and export) fell during the 1990s. The share of CIS countries in Russia's total foreign trade fell from 54.6 per cent in 1991 to 18.7 per cent in 1999 and the share of non-CIS members increased.[5] Russian capital investment plays a minor role in the region except in the energy sector.[6]

Towards the end of the 1990s Russia seemed to be in a process of retreat not only outside its borders but also on its own territory. The Khasaviurt Agreement of 31 August 1996, which ended the first Chechnya war (1994–96), resulted in a Russian military retreat from the republic. Russia lost control and Chechnya became de facto independent. Instability, crime and terrorism expanding on an increasing scale from the territory of Chechnya into neighbouring republics and

[4] Armenia, Kazakhstan, Kyrgyzstan and Tajikistan. On the membership of the Tashkent Treaty see the appendix in this volume. The text of the treaty was published in *Izvestiya*, 16 May 1992.

[5] Grinberg, R. S. *et al.*, 'Sodruzhestvo nezavisimykh gosudarstv: sostoyanie i perspektivy razvitiya' [Commonwealth of Independent States: current state and development prospects], Paper prepared for an international conference on 'Sodruzhestvo nezavisimykh gosudarstv: sostoyanie i perspektiv' [The CIS: current state and prospects], Moscow, 30–31 Mar. 2000.

[6] Yudanov, Yu., 'Tsentral'naya Aziya: novy favorit inostrannykh investorov' [Central Asia: new favourite of foreign investors], *Mirovaya Ekonomika i Mezhdunarodnye Otnosheniya*, nos 3–4 (2000).

regions threatened to undermine the federation as the federal centre was incapable of responding to the challenge. When in August 1999 the crisis in Dagestan erupted after Chechen rebels together with Dagestani Islamists took control of a few villages on Dagestani territory close to the border with Chechnya and proclaimed the goal of creating a Chechen–Dagestani Islamic state, this was considered a serious threat to Russia's territorial integrity: if the Chechen conflict were to spread to Dagestan it would threaten to reduce the Russian coastline along the Caspian Sea. Moreover, the first Chechnya war, which broke down the social and economic structures and contributed to turmoil in the North Caucasus, threatened Russia's pipeline for the transport of oil from Baku to its Black Sea port of Novorossiysk as well as the transport and communication lines from Russia to the South Caucasus.

Russia's fear that the USA would fill the power vacuum left by Russia infected its relations with the USA in the region. Deteriorating Russian–US relations on the European scene in the late 1990s also had a direct impact on the degree of tension in the Caspian region. After the NATO intervention in Kosovo in April 1999 Russia feared that NATO's new Strategic Concept would imply a risk for NATO intervention in conflicts also in the Caspian region. The Russian reaction was reflected in the new doctrinal documents signed in the spring of 2000—the military doctrine, the national security doctrine and the foreign policy concept.[7] Russia's second military campaign in Chechnya, initiated in September 1999, indicated a new determination to take control of developments in the region but at the same time reflected the long-term trend of a decline in influence.

When Vladimir Putin came to power—first as prime minister in August 1999, then as acting president in December 1999 and as elected president in March 2000—Russian policy became more active in an effort to counter the trend of rapidly diminishing influence in the Caspian region.

As prime minister, Putin initiated the campaign in Chechnya, indicating a new determination to act and capacity to mobilize. This was followed up by a more active policy on CIS territory. The fight against terrorism became a platform for Russian initiatives in developing security cooperation first of all with Central Asian states. Putin took a more active stance on the issue of the transport of Caspian energy and requested a more active engagement by Russian companies in the oil and gas sectors of the Caspian in order to counter foreign/Western investment, projects and proposals. The Russian Government initiated more active diplomacy in mediating in the frozen conflicts of the South Caucasus (in Abkhazia, Nagorno-Karabakh and South Ossetia). As a result of a new awareness that multilateral CIS cooperation had come to a definite stand-

[7] The new military doctrine as approved by President Putin on 21 Apr. 2000 was published in *Nezavisimaya Gazeta*, 22 Apr. 2000. An unofficial translation into English was released by BBC Monitoring on 22 Apr. 2000. Presidential Decree no. 24 of 10 Jan. 2000 revising the national security concept and the full text were published in *Krasnaya Zvezda*, 20 Jan. 2000. An English translation is available in *Military News Bulletin*, vol. 9, no. 2 (Feb. 2000), pp. 1–12; and excerpts in English were published in *Arms Control Today*, Jan./Feb. 2000, pp. 15–20. The new foreign policy concept was published in *Diplomaticheskiy Vestnik*, no. 8 (Aug. 2000), pp. 3–11.

still, Russia explicitly put more emphasis on developing bilateral relationships, as was evident at the CIS summit meetings in January and June 2000.[8] The government clearly gave priority to winning back those CIS states which were on their way to leaving the Russian orbit and were considered by the USA as strategic key states in the Caspian region—Azerbaijan and Uzbekistan. Uzbekistan has the largest population in the region, the strongest army and a capacity to influence its neighbours. Azerbaijan is a small state without comparable strength but is nevertheless regarded as a key to the gate for the West into the Caspian Sea; a pro-Moscow government there would change the geopolitical balance in the region.

In 1998 Russia's position had started to change on the issue of the legal division of the Caspian Sea.[9] Russia's June 1998 agreement with Kazakhstan on the division of the north Caspian Sea into national sectors was followed by a Russian suggestion in June 2000 of an interim solution dividing the seabed into national sectors while preserving general use of the sea's waters and surface.[10] This stronger support for the principle of national sectors in 2000 was perceived by several Russian commentators as part of an effort to approach Azerbaijan.

Some critics considered Putin's new policy in the Caspian region counterproductive. The policy was formulated by the Russian Security Council in the spring of 2000; officials in the Ministry of Foreign Affairs remained sceptical.[11] Observers commented that the tougher Russian policy, its concentration on anti-terrorism and its emphasis on Azerbaijan and Uzbekistan could result in a backlash by undermining the support of Russia's traditional allies.

The response initiated by Putin in late 1999 was a clear effort to turn the tide and win back influence. The Russian Government reacted as if the Caspian region were part of a zero-sum game and tried its best to win that kind of game.

III. International engagement

The international actors in the Caspian region can be divided into state actors (states or organizations of states) and non-state actors (companies, associations or criminal groups). The policies of the states engaging in the Caspian region can be explained by their stakes and interest in the energy resources of the region, their national security concerns and their strategic concerns.

---

[8] See, e.g., Suvorov, A., 'After a long and severe illness', *Kommersant-Vlast*, 30 May 2000, pp. 31–32; and *Former Soviet Union 15 Nations: Policy and Security*, no. 6 (2000), pp. 36–37.

[9] See also chapter 3, section III in this volume.

[10] *Jamestown Monitor*, vol. 6, issue 112 (9 June 2000).

[11] Vladimir Stupishin, the first Russian Ambassador to Armenia (1992–95), claims that Russia is now carrying out a campaign aimed at improving relations with Azerbaijan and Uzbekistan at the expense of the interests of its closest allies in the South Caucasus and Central Asia—Armenia and Kazakhstan. According to Stupishin, not only could this result in the end of the CIS; it also fundamentally contradicts Russia's strategic tasks in Central Asia and the Caucasus. He considers there is a serious risk that Moscow's policy will harm Russian–Armenian relations, that this is the fault of officials who do not understand Russia's interests, and that it is a victory for US diplomacy which has led Russia to believe the words of Zbigniew Brzezinski about the special role of Azerbaijan and Uzbekistan. A key role in this strategy was played by former Secretary of the Security Council Sergey Ivanov, and the Special Representative of the President for the Caspian Region, Viktor Kalyuzhny. Dzhilavyan, A., 'Erevan razdelyaet bol' Moskvy' [Yerevan shares Moscow's anguish], *Nezavisimaya Gazeta*, 17 Aug. 2000, p. 4.

Stakes and interests

The energy resources in the Caspian region explain to a great extent the engagement by state actors, even if not all external powers have a direct and urgent
need for energy from the region. The Caspian oil reserves are estimated at
40–60 billion barrels, only 4–6 per cent of proven global reserves. Unproven
deposits may be three times this amount, thereby making the Caspian fields
more than twice as great as those of the North Sea.[12] Russia has large deposits
of its own and for it considerations other than energy demand therefore play the
major role.[13] To the USA and Europe, Caspian energy is important in order to
diversify the supply of energy. The European Union (EU) countries plan to
import large volumes of gas from Russia; so does Turkey for its expanding
industry. Iran has energy of its own. To China, however, oil and gas from the
Caspian region will be crucial in the future in guaranteeing the economic
development of the underdeveloped and unstable Xinjiang region and securing
the industry along the Chinese coast.

As the costs of exploitation and transport of the Caspian's resources will be
high, the question whether investment will be profitable or not depends on
prices on the international oil market. Producers in the Middle East cast a wary
look at the Caspian region and may influence the profitability of extracting
Caspian oil. As pointed out by Edward L. Morse, 'The oil producers of the
Middle East have absolutely no interest in seeing Caspian oil coming onto the
world markets'.[14] This adds to the uncertainty over how the planned projects
will be financed.

China, Iran, Russia and Turkey have direct national security concerns in the
region as they all have borders with states in the region and share national
minorities with Caucasian and/or Central Asian states. Russia has a large
diaspora in the countries of the region but fears most of all the effects on its
own security of instability in the Caspian region spilling over its more or less
transparent borders. The turmoil in Chechnya is perceived as closely connected
with the growth of irredentism in other parts of the Caspian region, and most
recently in Central Asia. Russia regards and will regard the Caspian region as a
major concern for its national security.

In July 1997 US Deputy Secretary of State Strobe Talbott stated in a speech
that what happened in the Caspian region 'matters profoundly' to the USA.[15] In
the US debate this statement has since been questioned and it has been argued

[12] See also chapter 3 in this volume.

[13] Goldman, M. I., 'Russian energy: a blessing and a curse', *Journal of International Affairs*, vol. 53,
no. 1 (fall 1999).

[14] Morse, E. L., 'A new political economy of oil?', *Journal of International Affairs* (Columbia
University), vol. 53, no. 1 (fall 1999). Morse continues: 'Both Iran and Iraq are opening themselves to
foreign investment with the intention, once sanctions are lifted, of raising their production levels'.
However, their intention clearly is to attract the capital that is now flowing elsewhere, especially to the
Caspian countries. Iran and Iraq together hold some 205 billion barrels of oil, roughly 20% of the world's
total reserves and possibly as much as 10 times more than those of the Caspian region.

[15] 'A farewell to Flashman: American policy in the Caucasus and Central Asia', Address by Deputy
Secretary of State Strobe Talbott at the Paul H. Nietze School of Advanced International Studies, Johns
Hopkins University, 21 July 1997, URL <http://www.sais-jhu.edu/pubs/speeches/talbott.html>.

that the USA has no direct national security concerns in the Caspian region. Nevertheless, the USA and European states are concerned about security in the Caspian region and as members of international organizations they share with Russia and the Caspian states an interest in and a responsibility to maintain peace and democracy. This mainly explains their engagement in conflict resolution by the Organization for Security and Co-operation in Europe (OSCE) and the United Nations. The more Western companies invest in the energy and the economies of the region, the higher the stakes and the more to secure.

Strategic concerns play a major role for Russia. It regards close relations with the states of the Caucasus and Central Asia as crucial for its international status, and views with deep concern US and Western actors filling the 'power vacuum' created by its own retreat. From Russian analysis of the intentions behind the main state actors in the Caspian region it is evident that the geopolitical school of thought has been going through a renaissance in Russia. In extreme form the ideas of John Halford Mackinder of a 'Eurasian Heartland' and a strategic rivalry to control it are often referred to in Russian analysis.[16]

Strategic concerns also play a role in US foreign policy thinking. Emphasis has been given to restraining Russian influence in order to strengthen the independence of the Caspian states. Arguments put forward by influential analysts, among them Zbigniew Brzezinski, to the effect that Russia's influence on the Eurasian continent must be balanced by strong independent states suit US strategic considerations.[17] The USA's focus on Azerbaijan and Uzbekistan follows from the perception of them as key states in such a strategic balancing of Russian influence.[18]

China, Iran and Turkey have so far remained minor actors in the Caspian region since the breakup of the Soviet Union and their possible strategic concerns have played a subordinate role. The main strategic concerns of China and Iran have been reflected mainly in efforts to prevent the USA as an 'outsider' from shifting the strategic balance in the region.

Policies

The most drastic change in the geopolitical situation of the Caspian region is the considerable engagement of the USA, which has raised the concern of China, Iran and Russia.

[16] Clover, C., 'Dreams of the Eurasian heartland: the reemergence of geopolitics', *Foreign Affairs*, vol. 78, no. 2 (Mar./Apr. 1999).

[17] Brzezinski, Z., 'A geostrategy for Eurasia', *Foreign Affairs*, vol. 76, no. 5 (Sep./Oct. 1997). See also references to geopolitical theories in, e.g., Jones, S. A., 'Introduction', eds G. K. Bertsch *et al.*, *Crossroads and Conflict: Security and Foreign Policy in the Caucasus and Central Asia* (Routledge: New York and London, 2000); and Schilling, W., 'The return of geopolitics in the Caucasus and Central Asia', *Aussenpolitik*, no. 2 (1998) (in English).

[18] See the recommendation to the US Government in 1996 by the US scholar Frederick Starr to make Uzbekistan an anchor of US policy in Central Asia. Starr, S. F., 'Making Eurasia stable', *Foreign Affairs*, vol. 75, no. 1 (Jan./Feb. 1996). The focus on Azerbaijan is described by James MacDougall in his article 'Novaya stadiya politiki SshA v Kaspiyskom basseyne' [New stage of US policy in the Caspian Basin], *Tsentral'naya Aziya*, no. 5 (1997).

In the years immediately after the breakup of the Soviet Union the USA lacked a clear policy towards the Caspian region except for general support for the newly independent states, but in 1994 the US Government became more aware of its policy priorities. A Russia-first approach still dominated, but it soon became evident to the USA that its strategic objectives in the region were not only to create conditions in which the Caucasian and Central Asian states were strengthened as independent states but also to hold back and reduce Russian influence.[19] The private sector had early discovered the Caspian region, and US companies took the lead in the international consortia which emerged in Azerbaijan and Kazakhstan during the first half of the 1990s. The US commitments to multiple pipelines followed from its backing the Baku–Ceyhan option in February 1995, which was intended to prevent first Russia but also Iran from dominating future pipeline decisions.

However, it was not until 1997 and the second administration of President Bill Clinton that US strategic objectives in the Caspian region were formulated. In March 1997 then National Security Adviser Sandy Berger singled out the region as one of the priorities to US policy and stressed Washington's intention to step up its involvement in the Caucasus and Central Asia. The July 1997 speech by Deputy Secretary of State Talbott followed.[20] By active engagement in the Caspian region, in energy issues as well as security matters, the USA sent a clear signal to the world that priority would be given to increasing US influence there even over safeguarding the US 'partnership' with Russia.[21]

Together with Turkey the USA formed an axis into the Caspian region consisting of Western-oriented states. When Uzbekistan in April 1999 joined GUAM an East–West belt of states was created which all became important in US policy in the region. Kazakhstan also played an important role in US strategy in the Caspian region, but its geographical location and large Russian population set certain limits to any foreign policy orientation away from Russia.

Turkey is sensitive to developments above all in the South Caucasus. While its relations with Azerbaijan and Georgia developed in the 1990s, relations with Armenia were cut off as a result of the Nagorno-Karabakh conflict. Turkey's expectations in 1991 that its cultural and linguistic affiliation with the states of the region would enable it to assert leadership in a broad pan-Turkic community, and thereby pave the way for a new international role for Turkey, were not realized. As a result Turkey had to lower its profile.[22] It did not manage to create for itself a substantial political role; instead its economic presence

[19] MacDougall (note 18); and Bremmer, I., 'Oil politics: America and the riches of the Caspian Basin', *World Policy Journal*, vol. 15, no. 1 (1998).

[20] 'A farewell to Flashman' (note 15).

[21] Goble, P., 'Central Asia: Analysis from Washington. A jump too far?', Radio Free Europe/Radio Liberty (RFE/RL), *RFE/RL Report*, 2 Sep. 1997, quoted by Cornell, S., *Beyond Oil: US Engagement in the Caspian Region*, Working Papers no. 52 (Department of East European Studies/Department of Peace and Conflict Research, Uppsala University: Uppsala, Jan. 2000). See also Blank, S., 'The US and Central Asia', eds Allison and Jonson (note 3).

[22] Winrow, G., 'Turkey and Central Asia', eds Allison and Jonson (note 3); and Winrow, G., *Turkey and the Caucasus: Domestic Interests and Security Concerns* (Royal Institute of International Affairs: London, 2000).

expanded. Turkish business only had the capacity for small and medium-sized projects and could therefore assist only on the margins of major reconstruction projects. Nevertheless, Turkey's role in future plans for oil and gas export from the Caspian makes it a key country for the future. The construction of the Blue Stream underwater pipeline for Russian gas across the Black Sea to Turkey and, if it is ever realized, the trans-Caspian gas pipeline from Turkmenistan across the Caspian to Baku and further to Ceyhan would make Turkey the key partner in two rival gas transport projects.[23] The plans for an oil pipeline from Baku to Ceyhan give Turkey a central role with regard to Caspian oil.[24] A member of NATO, Turkey has increased its military and security cooperation with states of the region, primarily Azerbaijan and Georgia. However, its independent influence in the region remains limited. Its role is subordinate to the USA's and will remain so in spite of the ambitions of individual Turkish politicians.

Like Turkey, Iran never lived up to the great expectations of growing influence in the Caspian region in 1991. Contrary to the fears in the early 1990s that it would export its revolution, Iran in 1993 took on a low profile and a pragmatic and cautious policy in which regional stability had first priority. Iran is deeply concerned about regional stability, especially in the Caucasus, fearing ethnic separatism in its own country. It has a large Azeri minority (more Azeris live in Iran than in Azerbaijan proper).[25] This has contributed to a strong Iranian interest in maintaining close relations with Russia and encouraged it to accept Russia's strategic interests in the region, and this has hindered the expansion of Iranian influence in the region.[26] Iran has developed its relations in the region by providing technical and financial assistance, supporting regional integration, expanding cultural links, and facilitating the efforts of Kazakhstan and Turkmenistan to develop alternative transit routes for oil and gas.[27] As a littoral state Iran participates in deciding the future legal status of the Caspian Sea. It has remained a defender of the condominium principle in favour of equal sharing of the Caspian Sea between the littoral states.[28]

Iran could have developed into a key state for the export of Caspian gas to Turkey had not the USA maintained its policy of isolating it internationally and effectively locked it out from influence in the Caspian region. Nevertheless, Iran is becoming an important economic partner in the region, especially to Turkmenistan but also to Armenia. Its engagement in conflict resolution has

[23] The projected gas pipeline would run under the Black Sea from Izobil'noye in Russia to Samsun and Ankara in Turkey. See chapter 3, figure 3.1 in this volume.

[24] With a daunting cost estimate of nearly $2.5 billion, the 1080-mile Baku–Ceyhan pipeline plan has been more popular with statesmen than with businessmen, as its appeal is much more geopolitical than commercial. Even the combined diplomatic weight of the United States and Turkey has failed to overcome the Western oil companies' commercial doubts about supporting this 'pipeline dream'. Giragosian, R., 'Massive Kashagan oil strike renews geopolitical offensive in Caspian', *Central Asia–Caucasus Analyst* (Johns Hopkins University, Paul E. Nitze School of Advanced International Studies, Central Asia–Caucasus Institute), 7 June 2000.

[25] Herzig, E., 'Relations to the south: Iran and Afghanistan', eds Allison and Jonson (note 3).

[26] Sokolsky, R. and Charlick-Paley, T., *NATO and Caspian Security: A Mission Too Far?*, Report MR-1074-AF (RAND Corporation, Santa Monica, Calif., 1999).

[27] Herzig (note 25).

[28] See also chapters 3 and 9 in this volume.

helped to improve its image in the region. It helped Russia broker the diplomatic settlement in the Tajik civil war and has tried to mediate in the dispute between Armenia and Azerbaijan over Nagorno-Karabakh.

China is situated far from the Caspian but is concerned about stability in Central Asia because it has long borders with Kazakhstan, Kyrgyzstan and Tajikistan, and shared national minorities along these borders. Agreements on borders and demilitarization with Russia and the Central Asian states since 1996 have reduced tension between China and these states.[29] Instead, the issue of separatism in the Xinjiang Autonomous Region of China and fear of the spread of radical Islamism have moved high on the Chinese security agenda. The presence of Uighur minorities in Kazakhstan, Kyrgyzstan and Tajikistan creates a link between Xinjiang and these states and further to Afghanistan, where the Taliban regime is considered the main source of instability in the wider region.[30] The Central Asian states' achievement of independence provides China with major new economic opportunities.[31] China's increasing need for energy for its economic development causes it to look to the Caspian region for energy supply.[32] Its interest in maintaining regional stability has made China recognize Russia's interests in the Caspian region. China's own influence there is as yet very limited. What role it will play for the states of the eastern Caspian region if Russian influence diminishes further in the future remains an open question.

The USA's policy of isolating Iran since 1979 created a basis for Iranian–Russian cooperation. The US advance in the Caspian region and its more assertive behaviour awoke China and created a basis also for a Chinese–Russian rapprochement on the issue of countering US influence in the region; but there have been no signs of an anti-US alliance.

Even if China and Iran in the very long term can exercise substantial influence in the Caspian region, for the present Russia and the USA have developed into the main contenders in the region. The way in which they relate to each other and respond to challenges in the region will therefore be decisive in the near future. Russian–US relations are a major determinant of stability in the Caspian region. In the context of competition and rivalry in the Caspian region the relations between the main contenders are crucial. Mixed signals and misperceptions of purposes and intentions may create a tense climate with a destabilizing impact on the region. This is very much the case where energy and security issues are concerned.

[29] See, e.g., Nosov, M., 'Russian–US relations in Asia–Pacific', ed. G. Chufrin, SIPRI, *Russia and Asia: The Emerging Security Agenda* (Oxford University Press: Oxford, 1999), p. 357.

[30] According to the 1989 Soviet census figures there were 185 301 Uighurs in Kazakhstan, 36 779 in Kyrgyzstan and 35 762 in Uzbekistan. Olcott, M. B., 'Russia–Chinese relations and Central Asia', ed. S. W. Garnett, *Rapprochement or Rivalry? Russia–China Relations in a Changing Asia* (Carnegie Endowment for International Peace: Washington, DC, 2000), p. 395.

[31] Guangcheng Xin, 'China and Central Asia', eds Allison and Jonson (note 3).

[32] Andrews-Speed, P. and Vinogradov, S., 'China's involvement in Central Asian petroleum: convergent or divergent interests?', *Asian Survey*, vol. 40, no. 2 (Mar./Apr. 2000); Burles, M., *Chinese Policy Toward Russia and the Central Asian Republics* (RAND Corporation: Santa Monica, Calif., 1999); and Guangcheng Xin (note 31).

IV. The energy field—parallel systems evolving?[33]

Azerbaijan, Kazakhstan and Turkmenistan regarded the energy factor as the key to independence and wealth, and their governments started to look for investors to exploit the energy deposits and for alternatives to the Russian outlets for the export of oil and gas to foreign markets. Russia maintained its monopoly of the pipelines transporting oil and gas to the outside world up to the end of the 1990s, but the new deposits of oil and gas in the Caspian Basin increased the demand for larger transport capacity. In 1998 the small connection which opened for Turkmen gas to Iran, linking Korpedze to the Iranian pipeline system in Kurt-Kui, indicated that alternative options would appear in the future. At the same time small volumes of Kazakh oil were exported by rail to China or by ship to Iran. In April 1999 the Baku extension to Supsa at the Georgian Black Sea coast became operational.

None of these routes provided a serious challenge to Russia's dominance of the transport system. Nevertheless, they demonstrated a new situation for Russia in the Caspian region energy sector. External interest in Caspian energy in the mid-1990s resulted in memoranda and projects for pipeline options in all geographical directions. Then in November 1999 at the OSCE Summit Meeting in Istanbul, when the presidents of Azerbaijan, Georgia, Kazakhstan, Turkey and Turkmenistan, in the presence of the US President, signed a memorandum and the Baku–Ceyhan pipeline project became the main alternative option, the Russian dominance of oil outlets was seriously threatened.

Even if Russia dominated the existing pipeline systems it could not guarantee an outlet for increased exports of Kazakhstan's and Azerbaijan's oil in the future.

Since Soviet times Russia has provided Kazakhstan with a route for oil from Atyrau in Kazakhstan to Samara in Russia and a connection to Russia's huge export pipeline, but disputes over quotas and prices have hampered cooperation. In order to deal with increasing production at the Kazakh Tengiz field, the international Caspian Pipeline Consortium (CPC), of which Russia is a major member, took on the task of constructing a new pipeline from Tengiz to Novorossiysk. Work was delayed, mainly because of the Russian side and much to the detriment of the Kazakh side, but began in earnest in November 1999 and the pipeline was completed in 2001. It provides Kazakhstan with a major outlet for its oil, thereby securing Russian territory for the transfer of at least a major part of Kazakh oil in the future.

Since Soviet times Russia has also provided Azerbaijan with an outlet for its oil at Novorossiysk. As Russia lost control over Chechnya it also lost control of the pipeline extension from Baku to Novorossiysk, which runs across Chechen territory. An important purpose of the two Chechnya wars was to secure federal control not only over the republic but also of the pipeline. When the second Chechnya campaign was initiated in September 1999, a bypass was built across

---

[33] On the alternative pipeline routes see chapter 3 in this volume, particularly figure 3.1.

Dagestan which became operational in the spring of 2000. Russia plans to upgrade the extension and to make the Chechnya transit operational again, but the situation in the North Caucasus makes it difficult for it to guarantee safe delivery of oil. As long as the Baku–Novorossiysk route is seriously challenged by instability in North Caucasus, Russia's role in the transport of South Caspian oil is seriously threatened.

With regard to the transport of gas Russia completely dominates the pipeline system and Turkmenistan, the main producer in the region, is thus completely dependent on it. The export of gas requires permanent structures, and for Turk-menistan Russia remained the only option with the extension from Dauletabad in eastern Turkmenistan over Chardzhou to Russia. A dispute between Russia and Turkmenistan over quotas, tariffs and prices resulted in Turkmenistan tem-porarily stopping its deliveries in 1997. Several alternative options for the construction of new outlets for gas have been discussed. As long as the USA prevents Western companies from participating in building a gas pipeline across Iranian territory, Russia does not have to fear competition from an Iranian pipeline. However, a rapprochement between Iran and the USA would pave the way for the export of Turkmen gas across Iran to Turkey. If a trans-Caspian gas pipeline is ever constructed from Turkmenistan to Baku and further to Ceyhan, as was agreed in a second memorandum signed in November 1999, Turkmeni-stan will become a main competitor to Russia's own Blue Stream project.

When Putin became Russian Prime Minister a more determined effort was launched to counter Russia's loss of influence in the Caspian region. In April 2000 in the Russian Security Council Putin stated that Russia should be more active in the region and requested more active participation in the exploitation of the Caspian energy resources and coordination of the activities of the companies involved, the government and the ministries. The post of Special Representative of the Russian President in the Caspian region was created with the responsibilities of coordinating policy and dealing with all foreign policy issues concerning the region, including the legal division of the Caspian Sea, and the former Minister for Energy, Viktor Kalyuzhny, was appointed. Efforts to coordinate state and corporate policies were considered crucial.[34]

The bypass across Dagestan was the result of the renewed Russian effort in 1999 to counter the Baku–Ceyhan proposal, as was the launching in earnest of the CPC pipeline from Tengiz in Kazakhstan to Novorossiysk. In the spring of 2000 Russia also increased the quota of Kazakhstani oil being pumped to the north from Atyrau to Saratov, evidently aiming to reduce Kazakhstan's interest in connecting to the Baku–Ceyhan oil pipeline in the future.[35] However, when

---

[34] Shakhov, D., 'Moscow toughens its positions in Caspian region', 20 May 2000, URL <http://www.transcaspian.ru/chi/web/eng/29.html>. According to Shakhov tension and clashes between the state and companies and between companies are common. For the time being the government decides whether a company may join a consortium or not and whether it may develop an oil or any other deposit or not. Apart from Transneft such companies as Unified Energy Systems (UES), Gazprom and Lukoil now nego-tiate with officials from the Ministry of Foreign Affairs and Ministry of Environment on an increasingly regular basis.
[35] Shakhov (note 34).

new oil deposits were found at Kazakhstan's Kashagan field in the summer of 2000, Kazakh Prime Minister Kassymzhomart Tokayev stated that Kazakhstan still maintained an interest in the Baku–Novorossiysk and Baku–Ceyhan options.[36]

In the autumn of 1999 Putin also initiated discussions on an increase of Russian imports of Turkmen gas. Russia wanted to consolidate its leverage over Turkmen gas exports by buying 49 billion cubic metres (bcm) of Turkmen gas annually for the next 30 years. A document of intent was signed in May 2000 whereby Russia was to increase its purchases of Turkmen gas by 10 bcm each year from 2001 to a level of 60 bcm by 2004. The sides would continue negotiating over the prices and the payment mechanism during the year.[37] Analysts commented that if they agreed on pricing the proposal for a trans-Caspian gas pipeline to Turkey would definitely be shelved.[38] Nevertheless, Turkmen President Saparmurat Niyazov in May 2000 declared his country's continuing interest in maintaining several pipeline options.

It therefore remains unclear what pipelines will be constructed in the future. Even if Russia during 2000 demonstrated that it had not lost the battle for the future transport of oil and gas from Kazakhstan and Turkmenistan, the prospects of it securing the Baku–Novorossiysk pipeline seemed more limited, even with the bypass across Dagestan. The second Chechnya war seemed unlikely to bring stability to the North Caucasus in the near future. Instead Russia again risked becoming trapped in Chechnya and threatened by the spread of the war into neighbouring territories.

Parallel pipeline systems for Caspian oil and gas may be in the making and, as alternative routes are constructed, Russian dominance in the region is being undermined.

The memorandum signed in 1997 on the construction of an eastern 3000-km oil pipeline from the Kazakh oil fields to Xinjiang in China and on to the Chinese coast may not be realized in the near future for financial reasons. However, it reflects China's role as an economic actor in Central Asia. In 1997 the China National Petroleum Company was allowed to buy a 60 per cent share in the Kazakh oil company in Aktyubinsk and to develop the oilfield at Uzen. China is also becoming a major trade partner for Kazakhstan and Kyrgyzstan. The infrastructure of highways, railways and air communication under construction will increase China's trade with the Central Asian states[39] and may pave the way for a drastic increase in China's economic role in the region as soon as the pipeline is operational and energy cooperation is fully developed.

Iran's role with regard to outlets is so far limited but, as mentioned above, it provides alternative outlets for small volumes of oil and gas. Through swap arrangements for oil and the gas pipeline connection that was built in 1998 and connects the Turkmen and Iranian systems, Iran assists Turkmenistan with

[36] *Nezavisimaya Gazeta*, 16 June 2000, p. 4. See also *Jamestown Monitor*, vol. 6, issue 104 (26 May 2000).

[37] *Jamestown Fortnight in Review*, 26 May 2000.

[38] McCarthy (note 1).

[39] Olcott (note 30).

outlets. Like China, Iran is actively engaging in the economic field and its trade is increasing especially with Armenia and Turkmenistan.

It is an interesting question how far companies in the energy field will follow their commercial interests and how far they will follow political interests as defined by their governments. While the answer may be clear with regard to Chinese and Iranian companies, as state interests will prevail over commercial interests, the situation is different for Western companies. British and US companies play a major role here.[40] The US Government may be able to prevent US companies from investing in pipeline systems in Iran, but it cannot force them to invest in non-profitable objects. Moreover, similar cost-benefit analysis seems increasingly to apply to the Russian side.

The main Russian companies involved are Gazprom, Lukoil, Rosneft and Yukos, with important interests in the exploitation of resources in the Caspian. The most active is Lukoil, which is a partner in several international consortia in the South Caspian.[41] In the spring of 2000 Lukoil further intensified its activities in the exploitation of Azerbaijan's resources in the South Caspian. In August 2000 it was joined by the Belarussian–Russian oil company Slavneft.[42]

The Russian side is by no means monolithic. Since the early 1990s Russia has spoken with several voices on policy in the Caspian. Companies pursue their own interests, which have not always been in line with those of the government. Lukoil provides an example. In 1993–94 intergovernmental agreements were signed about cooperation in the oil sector with the participation of Lukoil where the term 'Azerbaijani sector' was used contrary to the Russian Foreign Ministry's declared view that it did not accept the principle of 'national sectors'. From about 1996 Russia's policy towards its neighbours became more integrated, constructive and ready to compromise. The shift of the Russian position with regard to the division of the Caspian Sea has been explained by Lukoil's interests in the South Caspian resources and Azerbaijani deposits, which put the Russian Government under pressure to adapt its position. Thus, the Russian companies represent a dynamic which may contribute to change the character of the strategic–political competition between state actors in the Caspian region into a mainly commercial competition between companies.

In a long-term perspective it is demand for energy from the Caspian region that will determine the directions of the pipelines and several major routes may therefore be constructed. Turkey's expanding industry may require not only Russian but also Turkmen gas in the future. China, which is in desperate need

[40] British-based multinationals, notably BP, Shell and British Gas, are among the biggest investors in Caspian oil and gas projects, especially in Azerbaijan and Kazakhstan. McCarthy (note 1). BP heads the Azerbaijan International Operating Company (AIOC). Evans, M., 'The Caucasus and the Black Sea', *RUSI Journal*, Apr. 2000, pp. 55–60. US companies also play a large role. There is an unusually high US component in licence terms and supply contracts of the oil industry; virtually all the supply contracts to develop the area have a US component. Morse (note 14).

[41] Zhiznin, S. Z. and Rodionov, P. I., 'Energeticheskaya diplomatiya v Kaspiysko-Chernomorskom regione: gazovye aspekty' [Energy diplomacy in the Caspian–Black Sea region: gas aspects], *Diplomaticheskiy Vestnik*, no. 6 (June 2000), pp. 79–87.

[42] Memorandum signed by the State Oil Company of the Azerbaijan Republic (SOCAR) and Slavneft on projects on the deposit at Guneshli. Gadzhizade, A., 'Nashli drug druga' [Found each other], *Nezavisimaya Gazeta*, 15 Aug. 2000, p. 5.

of gas and oil, will try to find the capital necessary for investments in new pipelines from Central Asia, possibly even regardless of commercial calculations. An expanding South Asian market may need direct access to Caspian energy even across Afghanistan if turmoil and war in that country come to an end. This means that, even if not all options are realized in the future, the energy factor may contribute in the long run to integrate the countries of the Caspian region into parallel and partly overlapping networks in different geographical directions.

V. The security field—parallel systems evolving?

Even if Russia has lost its earlier role as a security guarantor in the Caspian region, it remains the major state offering security assistance. Nevertheless, as it withdraws its troops from Central Asia and the Caucasus it has not succeeded in replacing its former military presence with a viable security system embracing the states of the Caspian region, and other security arrangements have therefore evolved. Thus, since the early 1990s the international community, first and foremost the UN and the OSCE, have engaged in conflict resolution in the region. Since the mid-1990s NATO and NATO-led cooperation, as in the Partnership for Peace (PFP) programme, have played the major role. It remains unclear what security arrangements will prevail in the future. A decisive question is who will provide security assistance in responding to the new challenges to the countries of the region.

A Russia-based security system

The elements of a Russia-based security system are the Tashkent Treaty, various CIS agreements, and bilateral agreements between Russia and individual states of the Caspian region. The Tashkent Treaty, which now includes six countries (Armenia, Belarus, Kazakhstan, Kyrgyzstan, Russia and Tajikistan) does not include Azerbaijan, Georgia, Turkmenistan or Uzbekistan. Turkmenistan, which is neutral, never joined the treaty, and in April 1999 the other three chose not to extend their participation. No viable structures were constructed on the basis of the treaty and bilateral agreements between Russia and individual states therefore complemented the treaty.

During the 1990s Russia tried to create structures within the CIS framework for dealing with internal threats to the security of the member states. However, when Russia suggested the creation of permanent troops and mechanisms for conflict prevention and peacekeeping the other CIS states remained reluctant. They did not agree to set up a permanent CIS peacekeeping force or to give CIS bodies the power and responsibility to decide on the use of force. Only in two of the four conflicts on former Soviet territory (Abkhazia and Tajikistan) did a CIS mandate exist for the Russian peacekeeping troops.

Since August 1999, when Chechen rebels intruded into Dagestan and Uzbek Islamists forced their way into Kyrgyzstan, heading for Uzbekistan from Tajikistan, the Putin Government has made the common fight against terrorism the linchpin of security cooperation with Central Asian and Caucasian states. The Tashkent Treaty was activated in support of Kyrgyzstan and Russia provided military assistance, weapons, equipment and military advisers to Kyrgyzstan; however, no soldiers were sent.[43] At the CIS Council of Defence Ministers meeting in September 1999 Putin announced the establishment of an 'anti-criminal coalition' in order to handle extremists 'everywhere from the Caucasus to the Pamir'.[44] A series of joint command-and-staff exercises for anti-terrorism combat followed with Kyrgyzstan, Russia, Tajikistan and Uzbekistan participating. The CIS summit meeting in January 2000 decided to work out an inter-state programme of joint measures to combat extremism, terrorism and organized crime.[45] The CIS summit meeting in June 2000 adopted a programme on the fight against extremism, terrorism and organized crime and decided to set up an anti-terrorism centre. In May 2000 the agenda of the Tashkent Treaty was adapted from its earlier focus on external threats of a traditional, military kind to a focus on international terrorism and separatism. In October 2000 a general decision was taken to create a common force, which would function as a joint rapid-deployment force in anti-terrorist operations.[46] Russia thus made the fight against terrorism into the platform for vitalizing CIS military and security cooperation, especially in Central Asia. Yet the Central Asian states remained as reluctant to delegate power to the centre as they had proved to be in earlier discussions within the CIS and among the parties to the treaty. The CIS members' different interpretations of what constitutes a terrorist threat also indicated complications for the future anti-terrorist struggle.

Combating international terrorism and extremism became a main theme of Putin's rapprochement with Uzbekistan. As a consequence of events in Kyrgyzstan, Russia and Uzbekistan returned to military and security cooperation both between themselves and with other CIS states. Agreements were signed when Putin visited Uzbekistan in December 1999 and May 2000 envisaging cooperation between the two countries' defence ministries and armed forces in strengthening military security, developing and producing military equipment and armaments, training military personnel, and the joint struggle against international terrorism.[47] Without returning to the Tashkent Treaty, Uzbekistan from the autumn of 1999 began to participate in joint exercises and training with Russia and the other parties to the treaty. The fear of radical Islamism and terrorism thus seemed to influence the geopolitical balance in the region.

---

[43] *Jamestown Fortnight in Review*, no. 18 (Oct. 1999).

[44] Golotyuk, Yu., 'Rossiya ne speshit otkryt' "vtoroy front"' [Russia is not in a hurry to open a 'second front'], *Izvestiya*, 22 Sep. 1999, p. 3.

[45] Ostankino Radio Mayak, Moscow, 26 Jan. 2000, in BBC Monitoring, International Reports, 26 Jan. 2000.

[46] The Russian proposal of Nov. 1999 to create 'joint rapid-deployment anti-terrorist forces' under the Tashkent Treaty was not endorsed by the CIS member states. ITAR-TASS, reported in *Jamestown Monitor*, vol. 5, issue 206 (5 Nov. 1999).

[47] ITAR-TASS (Moscow), 11 Dec. 1999; and Reuters, 11 Dec. 1999/BBC Worldwide Monitoring, 11 Dec. 1999.

It remains to be seen whether this rapprochement between Russia and Uzbekistan is sustainable. There is much to suggest that Uzbekistan's policy towards Russia is of a pragmatic turn, which means that Uzbekistan does not intend to harm its good relations with the West. Uzbekistan did not join the CIS anti-terrorism centre and President Islam Karimov has urged the UN and the OSCE to take a more active stance on the anti-terrorism issue.[48]

An international community-led security system

The embryo of an international community-led security system in the Caucasus and Central Asia developed rapidly in the 1990s but reached an impasse at the end of the decade. The UN and the OSCE contributed in monitoring and mediating in the conflicts in Azerbaijan (Nagorno-Karabakh), Georgia (Abkhazia and South Ossetia) and Tajikistan. They influenced Russian policy by providing standards and rules of conduct for Russian peacekeeping missions. Even if the conflicts in the Caucasus remain frozen, and so far a peace agreement has been signed only in Tajikistan, the participation of the UN and the OSCE has contributed to internationalize the conflicts and to bring the states concerned into the international community. The OSCE also played a role in the Chechnya conflict from 1995 to 1998, when its mission withdrew from Chechnya because of the security situation there. The Assistance Group for Chechnya in April 1995 was given a broad mandate and the head of the group was instrumental in facilitating the negotiation process which led to the 1996 Khasaviurt agreement and an end to the first Chechnya war.[49]

A NATO-based security system

The embryo of a NATO-based security system developed mainly during the late 1990s. In 1994 all the Caucasian and Central Asian states (except Tajikistan) joined the PFP programme, and since then the major part of their security cooperation with Western states has developed under the umbrella of the PFP. All the Caspian states (including neutral Turkmenistan) declared a great interest in further developing their individual programmes with the PFP. Armenia,

---

[48] In Oct. 2000 Uzbek President Karimov and the visiting Turkish President issued a joint statement calling for the establishment of a Central Asian anti-terrorist centre under UN auspices. As observers commented, the proposal seemed designed to counterbalance the plan for a Russian-led anti-terrorist centre, which Uzbekistan had declined to join. The 2 presidents also decided to create a consultative mechanism of their law enforcement, military and intelligence agencies to prevent and investigate acts of terrorism and agreed on the 'need to settle regional security issues in coordination with the UN, the Organization for Security and Co-operation in Europe and NATO'. The phrase signifies Uzbek rejection of Russia's latest plan for a 'regional group of forces' under its own leadership within the framework of the Tashkent Treaty. *Jamestown Monitor*, no. 197 (23 Oct. 2000).

[49] The OSCE Assistance Group was given a mandate to carry out its tasks in conjunction with the Russian federal and local authorities and in conformity with the legislation of the Russian Federation. Skagestad, O. G., 'How can the international community contribute to peace and stability in and around Chechnya?', eds L. Jonson and M. Esenov, *Chechnya: The International Community and Strategies for Peace and Stability* (Swedish Institute of International Affairs: Stockholm, 2000).

Russia's stronghold in the Caucasus, in early 2000 also announced an increased interest in participating in the PFP.[50]

In fact much of what is understood as PFP cooperation does not formally constitute PFP activities but is part of bilateral cooperation between a NATO member and individual Caucasian or Central Asian states—what NATO officials call 'in the spirit of PFP'.[51] The PFP offers individual programmes for states to develop cooperation to the degree they themselves want, and most PFP member states perceive PFP cooperation as the first step towards an application for membership of NATO. Of the countries in the Caspian region only Georgia, through President Eduard Shevardnadze, has declared its intention to join NATO and to apply for membership in 2005 at the latest.[52] Subregional organizations have indicated an interest in developing security cooperation on the local level and also within a PFP framework. The Central Asian Battalion (CentrasBat), created in 1996 by Kazakh, Kyrgyz and Uzbek units, has held annual exercises since 1997 with US troops participating within the PFP programme.[53] Russia participated in the exercises in 1997, 1998 and 2000. In early 1999 the GUUAM states—those most willing to cooperate with the PFP and NATO—agreed in principle on setting up a peacekeeping unit for the South Caucasus.

NATO Secretary General Lord Robertson visited the region in July 2000 to discuss among other issues the fight against terrorism. He urged the Central Asian states 'to take advantage of what NATO has to offer through the Partnership for Peace because there are a lot of doors that would open to them'.[54]

The USA has tried not to be left behind in the field of anti-terrorism. The Central Asian tour by Madeleine Albright in April 2000 was the first by a US Secretary of State since James Baker visited the area in 1992. Regional security and the fight against terrorism were high on the agenda and Albright promised US financial help for this purpose to Kazakhstan, Kyrgyzstan and Uzbekistan.

While the Caucasus is considered almost a neighbour of NATO, Central Asia is not. In spite of official US statements indicating a will to guarantee the security of Caspian states, there is no support in Congress for sending US troops.[55] Influential reports have warned the USA and NATO of the risks of over-committing themselves in the Caspian region. Neither would be able, critics argue, to live up to the expectations of the states of the region if a serious threat to security did develop, and they warned about the consequences for NATO itself of a major NATO engagement in the Caspian area.[56] The same may hold

---

[50] Foreign Ministry spokesman Ara Papian said that Armenia's participation has been minimal and this situation required correction.

[51] Bhatty, R. and Bronson, R., 'NATO's mixed signals in the Caucasus and Central Asia', *Survival*, vol. 42, no. 3 (autumn 2000), pp. 129–45.

[52] ITAR-TASS World Service, 10 Apr. 2000/Reuters, 10 Apr. 2000.

[53] On CentrasBat see also chapter 5, section V in this volume.

[54] Reuters, 'NATO urges better mutual ties in Central Asia, with West', 5 July 2000.

[55] 'If you go to a senior Pentagon official, or the great majority of congressmen, and suggest the deployment of US troops to the Caspian region—to bases or as peacekeepers, let alone in conflict—they look at you as if you had sprouted a very large pair of hairy ears.' Lieven, A., 'The (not so) Great Game', *National Interest*, no. 58 (winter 1999–2000).

[56] Sokolsky and Charlick-Paley (note 26); and Blank (note 21).

true for the EU, which by 2003 will set up a rapid reaction force for conflict prevention and crisis management. However, there is no general interest among EU or NATO members in engaging militarily or deploying troops in violent conflicts on former Soviet territory. There is rather a great disparity of views as to how far it is in the interest of NATO as an organization or of its individual members to engage in areas far away from NATO's traditional geographical area.[57]

Security threats

The issue of terrorism activated China as well as Turkey. China increased its participation in the 'Shanghai Five', which has developed since the 1996 agreements between Russia, China and its Central Asian neighbours. In July 2000 the group was renamed the Shanghai Forum, Uzbekistan joined as an observer and it was decided to set up an anti-terrorism centre in Bishkek.[58] China delivered weapons to Uzbekistan for fighting terrorists in 1999 and 2000 and in September 2000 signed an agreement on military cooperation with Uzbekistan. In Central Asia the approach to China is ambivalent, but many regard China as an increasingly important actor in the fight against terrorism. It shares the fears of the Central Asian leaders in this regard and was thus stimulated to develop security cooperation with Kazakhstan, Kyrgyzstan and Uzbekistan. Turkey's interest in also playing a role was reflected when in October 2000 the Turkish and Kyrgyz presidents decided to create an expert group to combat international terrorism. The Turkish delegation brought with it a donation for non-lethal military equipment to the Kyrgyz armed forces. This was the third Turkish donation on such a scale since the 1999 incursion of Islamist insurgents into Kyrgyzstan.[59]

A main question for the future will be who is prepared to take on the task of assisting in the fight against terrorism in a region with weak states and a high potential for conflicts. The security of the Caspian region is to a great extent a question of non-traditional, non-military threats, which require a different kind of response from the military one. The roots of the new terrorist threats can be found in the severe social and economic conditions, and measures for economic development and political reform are therefore decisive. However, if such measures are not taken, conflicts may develop which really will require a military response.

VI. Prospects for the future

During the 1990s the trend of a Russian retreat and a larger international engagement, which were clearly reflected in the fields of energy and security, changed the geopolitical situation in the Caspian region. Vladimir Putin's

---

[57] Bhatty and Bronson (note 51).

[58] In June 2001 Uzbekistan became a full member of the forum and the name of the organization was changed to the Shanghai Cooperation Organization. For details see chapter 5, section V in this volume.

[59] The donation was worth $2.5 million. *Jamestown Monitor*, issue 197 (23 Oct. 2000).

policy for turning the trend seemed at first to be successful, but this success may prove to have been more symbolic than real. In the South Caucasus the trend of a Russian retreat continues in spite of Russian efforts to reinterpret the agreement on troop withdrawal from Georgia signed at the OSCE Summit Meeting in Istanbul in November 1999.[60] Putin made a major counter-offensive on the issue of the exploitation and transport of Caspian energy but was not able to put an end to plans for alternative outlets. He seemed more successful with regard to security in Central Asia as, during his first year, he returned Uzbekistan to military and security cooperation with Russia and strengthened the cooperation of Kazakhstan and Kyrgyzstan within the Tashkent Treaty. Yet the Central Asian states remained as reluctant to join permanent defence structures as before. As long as Russia is unable to make an economic breakthrough in relations with Caspian states it seems difficult for it to really turn the trend.

The states of the Caspian region are vulnerable as they are weak and in deep economic, social and political trouble. There is great potential for conflict and tension within them. If Russia is not able to guarantee security in the region or to provide the vehicle for economic development, the question is what other state or states would be prepared to fill that vacuum. The influence of the USA in the region has increased drastically since the mid-1990s, but many observers have questioned whether it would be prepared to take on a major role to guarantee security in the South Caucasus or Central Asia. A long-term US influence can only be guaranteed if it is part of a multilateral framework. NATO's role, however, is growing rather as providing a larger framework for subregional cooperation than as offering direct military assistance in the event of conflict. While NATO may contribute to stability in the South Caucasus it can hardly be expected to play a major role in the event of a serious conflict in Central Asia.

Among the regional powers, the prospects for Turkey will remain limited to the South Caucasus. Iran is important for regional stability but has so far developed no contacts in the security field, instead concentrating on economic relations. The day US sanctions against Iran are lifted, a gas pipeline to Turkey across Iranian territory may become a reality and Iran may emerge as a major economic partner of the Caspian states.

If Russia continues to withdraw from Central Asia China may in the long term play a larger role in security. Uighur separatism and the spread of radical Islam are causing China serious concern as regards security in Central Asia and Afghanistan. A resurgent China may therefore in the future take on a larger engagement in Central Asian security, which would inevitably be considered a strategic threat by Russia. China's economic relations with Central Asia have a tendency to increase and when the Kazakh–Chinese oil pipeline is completed the Chinese economy will play a central role in Central Asian economic development.

Clashes of interest and competition for influence between state actors have followed the redistribution of power and influence in the region. This has given

---

[60] Jonson, L., 'Russia, NATO and the handling of conflicts at Russia's southern periphery: at a crossroads?', *European Security*, vol. 9, no. 4 (winter 2000). See also chapter 5, section III in this volume.

nourishment to a zero-sum understanding of the situation and the present ideas of a Great Game. However, the conclusion of this chapter is rather that there is such a variety of actors and interests on all sides involved in the Caspian region that no clear-cut picture of any strategic game can be seen. What on the surface seems to be a zero-sum game is much more complicated.

As pointed out above, neither Russia nor other states engaging in the region act as monolithic actors. The Russian Government has encouraged Russian state bodies and private companies to engage in the Caspian region in an effort to counter Western influence. However, differing interests within the Russian state, between the state and the companies and between the companies often result in contradictory behaviour. Russian companies increasingly look for commercial solutions and may themselves constitute a strong lobby on issues in the Caspian region. The same could be said on the Western side. Are Western companies ready to accept political decisions on investments if they are not financially attractive?

Energy is a field where Russia and Western interests may clash, but it also opens the most promising prospects for future cooperation between external actors and the Caspian states. It may provide the dynamic for economic and political reforms in the Caspian states by securing investment. The security field also opens the way for international cooperation.[61] China has joined Russia and Central Asian states in the Shanghai Forum in response to terrorism. There are multilateral and bilateral forums for dealing with the situation in Afghanistan: the 'Six Plus Two' group for discussions with the warring Afghan factions, which includes Afghanistan's neighbours plus Russia and the USA, is an example of a multilateral forum, while the talks initiated in August 2000 between Russia and the USA on terrorism and Afghanistan are an example of bilateralism. The UN and the OSCE in 2000 increased their efforts on these issues. In the field of security there is a great need for joint international efforts in order to stabilize the Caspian region, and there are signs that such efforts may develop.

The geopolitical situation in the Caspian region continues to change, and whether external powers and the states of the region are able to respond to the challenges of the ongoing transformation in the region and take the chances for international cooperation will be crucial for the future.

---

[61] See, e.g., Allison, R., 'Structures and frameworks for security policy cooperation', eds Allison and Jonson (note 3).

3. Energy reserves, pipeline routes and the legal regime in the Caspian Sea

John Roberts

I. The energy reserves and production potential of the Caspian

The issue of Caspian energy development has been dominated by four factors.

The first is *uncertain oil prices*. These pose a challenge both to oilfield developers and to the promoters of pipelines. The boom prices of 2000, coupled with supply shortages within the Organization of the Petroleum Exporting Countries (OPEC), have made development of the resources of the Caspian area very attractive. By contrast, when oil prices hovered around the $10 per barrel level in late 1998 and early 1999, the price downturn threatened not only the viability of some of the more grandiose pipeline projects to carry Caspian oil to the outside world, but also the economics of basic oilfield exploration in the region. While there will be some fly-by-night operators who endeavour to secure swift returns in an era of high prices, the major energy developers, as well as the majority of smaller investors, will continue to predicate total production costs (including carriage to market) not exceeding $10–12 a barrel.

The second is the *geology and geography of the area*. The importance of its geology was highlighted when two of the first four international consortia formed to look for oil in blocks off Azerbaijan where no wells had previously been drilled pulled out in the wake of poor results.[1] The geography of the area involves the complex problem of export pipeline development and the chicken-and-egg question whether lack of pipelines is holding back oil and gas production or vice versa. Suffice it to say that at present both the proposed main export pipeline (MEP) project from Azerbaijan via Georgia to Turkey and actual development at the offshore Azeri–Chirag–deepwater Guneshli (ACG) field complex are continuing to suffer significant delays.

The third factor is the *pipeline issue*. The problem of how to carry Caspian oil to the Black Sea has been cracked; the question how to get it out of the Black Sea has yet to be resolved. In Kazakhstan on 22 November 2000 the Caspian Pipeline Consortium (CPC)[2] announced that it had completed laying the last stretch of its pipeline from the oil terminal at Atyrau on the northern Caspian in Kazakhstan to the Russian Black Sea port of Novorossiysk.[3] The first commer-

---

[1] See below in this section.

[2] The members of the CPC are: Russia (24% of the equity); Kazakhstan (19%); the Chevron Caspian Pipeline Consortium Co. (15%); Lukarco BV (12.5%); Rosneft-Shell Caspian Ventures Ltd (7.5%); Mobil Caspian Pipeline Co. (7.5%); Oman (7%); Agip International (NA) NV (2%); BG Overseas Holdings Ltd (2%); Kazakhstan Pipeline Ventures LLC (1.75%); and Oryx Caspian Pipeline LLC (1.75%).

[3] Caspian Pipeline Consortium, 'Pipeline system in last lap to completion', Press release, 22 Nov. 2000.

cial deliveries of crude via the new line should be loaded on ship at Novo-rossiysk around early July 2001. Other oil pipeline projects, notably the proposed Baku–Ceyhan pipeline, remain subject to delay.

Finally, where gas is concerned, the *ability of the Turkish Government to develop a coherent energy import policy* is likely to prove crucial. There may be room for two major pipelines to carry gas to Turkish markets from the former Soviet republics at the same time, but in all probability the start of major construction work on the first new line from the former Soviet republics is likely to mean a postponement of plans to develop a second. It currently looks as if substantial work constructing the technically complex Blue Stream project to bring gas from Russia and Kazakhstan to Turkey via a sub-sea line across the Black Sea has started, while work is proceeding on upgrading existing lines in Azerbaijan for a realistic project to carry smaller volumes of Azerbaijani gas to Turkey as early as 2002, with substantial volumes to flow from about 2005 onwards. A major project to bring large volumes of Turkmen gas to Turkey via a trans-Caspian line that would also transit Azerbaijan and Georgia is foundering in the face of these two projects.

The size of Caspian reserves

The extent of the Caspian Basin's reserve base is still unknown: post-Soviet exploration is only just starting to yield results in terms of proven additions to previously identified reserves of oil and gas. It is, however, possible to make some reasonable estimates that the oil and gas resources of the Caspian region are significantly higher than, and may even be double, those of the North Sea, while falling far short of those in the Persian Gulf—some 40–60 billion barrels (bbl) of oil, or 4–6 per cent of world proven recoverable oil reserves (currently estimated at 1034 bbl), and 10–15 trillion cubic metres (tcm), or 7–10 per cent of world proven recoverable gas reserves (currently estimated at 146 tcm).[4]

Such figures, which represent the contemporary consensus, are in sharp contrast to the hyperbole which has surrounded the issue of the Caspian resource base in recent years. Thus in mid-1997 the US State Department was distributing documentation which cited unnamed analysts as estimating that the region's resource base might contain as much as 200 bbl of 'implicitly' recoverable reserves, the equivalent of almost one-fifth of the world's proven reserves at that time.[5] At this stage some Russian circles were taking an equally pessimistic view. Russian financial analyst Oleg Timchenko wrote in 1998, following the failure of one Western group to find oil off the Azerbaijan coast, that: 'The moral of this story is that the Caspian is not really a "sea of oil", not every well is going to be successful and there is considerable risk involved in what might appear sometimes to be a low-risk region in which to operate'.[6] Politics rather than geophysical analysis was probably responsible for both conclusions. The

[4] *BP Statistical Review of World Energy*, June 2000.
[5] US Department of State, Draft memorandum on the Caspian, distributed in May 1997.
[6] Timchenko, O., 'Russia morning comment', United Financial Group, Dec. 1998.

USA wanted to talk up the opportunities for Caspian hydrocarbon investment; Russia was at that time seeking to play down Caspian prospects.

Since then, things have changed in two key respects. Much more is known about the underlying resource base of the Caspian. There has been at least one major gas discovery in the southern Caspian, off Azerbaijan, and at least one major oil find in the northern Caspian, off Kazakhstan. In addition, Russia appears to have made a significant discovery off its Caspian coast. The international oil market has fluctuated wildly, with very low prices forcing international companies to take a highly cautious approach to the development of Caspian reserves, and more recently relatively high prices encouraging them to find to new ways to bring their produce to market.

However, one underlying factor has not changed. The attractiveness of the Caspian to international companies is not so much a function of its absolute size as of its availability. Caspian reserves may largely be sited in a cluster of countries which are landlocked and which require considerable political ingenuity if output is to be transported to international markets in a cost-effective way; but most are at least potentially available for exploitation on a production-sharing basis by Western companies. The Persian Gulf probably possesses approximately 10–15 times as much oil as the Caspian, but almost all this oil is only available for exploitation by the national oil companies of the host countries. The Caspian is not a new Middle East, and it is not the ultimate panacea for any concerns about long-term global energy supplies, but it is exciting in its own right, attracting a foreign investment programme which over the next 15–20 years will probably average approximately $4–5 billion a year for exploration, production and transport of the region's oil and gas reserves.

Production plans

The Caspian region's likely production profile changes every year. Actual oil production in the four core Caspian states, Azerbaijan, Kazakhstan, Turkmenistan and Uzbekistan, in 1999 totalled just 59.3 million tonnes—equivalent to approximately 1.25 million barrels/day (mb/d) and accounting for some 1.7 per cent of total world output.[7] Gas production amounted to 88 billion cubic metres (bcm), or 3.8 per cent of total world production.[8] There are several major programmes already in hand which will increase both oil and gas production substantially, so it is not unrealistic to anticipate a doubling of both oil and gas output by 2010, with further increases to follow. Precise rates of growth remain elusive, because of (a) the interaction of production rates and export facilities (the pipeline question); (b) erratic political approaches to energy development, notably in Turkmenistan; (c) oil price volatility; and (d) the fact that production profiles from 2005 on will naturally depend in great part on exploration taking place now and in the next several years.

[7] *BP Statistical Review of World Energy* (note 4).
[8] *BP Statistical Review of World Energy* (note 4).

Azerbaijan

In April 2000, when Azerbaijan's crude oil output was running at 272 000 barrels/day (b/d), Natiq Aliyev, President of the State Oil Company of the Azerbaijan Republic (SOCAR), spoke in Almaty of raising production to some 60 million tonnes per year (mt/y) (1.2 mb/d) by 2010.[9] This appeared to reflect an anticipated slowing down in the expansion of production at the giant ACG field complex by the Azerbaijan International Operating Company (AIOC),[10] since in December 1999 he had spoken of oil export volumes ranging from 1.4 to 2.4 mb/d by 2010.[11] More important for Azerbaijan's immediate economic prospects is the fact that its total oil production is unlikely to exceed 400 000 b/d, and it seems unlikely that overall output will approach the 1.0 mb/d level before around 2007–2008. This is of considerable significance with regard to the related construction of an MEP to carry large volumes of Azerbaijani oil to European and Mediterranean markets.

As of May 2000, Azerbaijan had signed no fewer than 19 contracts with international companies or consortia to develop specific prospects on a production-sharing basis, and in June 2000 the principles of a 20th accord were agreed. Further agreements were under negotiation in the autumn of 2000. Most of the agreements signed are for offshore development, although four of the confirmed contracts and the remaining unconfirmed deal concern development of onshore fields or prospects. If all 19 confirmed contracts proved successful, they would require an estimated $50 billion for 13 of the extant offshore contracts and $4.9 billion for the four confirmed onshore contracts.[12]

However, two projects which, had they proved successful, would have involved investments of several billion dollars have already been dissolved. These were the Pennzoil-led group, which sought to develop the Karabakh prospect, and the Amoco-led group, which secured the concession for the Dan Uludzu prospect. Both groups pulled out after test drilling failed to disclose oil in commercial quantities, although a faint prospect remains that there could yet be a revival of the Dan Uludzu field, since gas was found on-site and development of the nearby Shah Deniz field could make gas production from Dan Uludzu viable on an ancillary basis.

Even though it is now over six years since the AIOC was formed to sign the 'Contract of the Century' for the development of the unitized ACG fields in September 1994, it is still early days in terms of the assessment of post-Soviet additions to Azerbaijan's proven energy reserves. At ACG, the AIOC was, and is, dealing with fields proven in Soviet times. What has been discovered is a

---

[9] Natiq Aliev, presentation to the World Economic Forum's Eurasia Economic Summit in Almaty, Apr. 2000. Information on the World Economic Forum can be found at URL <http://www.weforum.org>.

[10] As of Mar. 2001, the AIOC comprised: BP (34.1367%); Unocal (10.048%); Lukoil (10%); SOCAR (10%); Statoil (8.5633%); ExxonMobil (8.0006%); Turkish Petroleum (6.75%); Devon Energy (4.8175%); and Itochu (3.9203%).

[11] *Middle East Energy Report*, issue 63 (May 2000).

[12] Spearhead Exhibitions, 'Caspian oil and gas, 2001', URL <http://caspianoilgas.co.uk/brochure.htm>. See also chapter 10 in this volume.

vast gas field—Shah Deniz. While corporate sources at British Petroleum (BP), which operates the field, have been cautious, indicating reserves of about 400 bcm, after success with two test wells Azerbaijani officials from President Heidar Aliyev downwards have proclaimed their belief that the field contains as much as 1 tcm of gas. In any respect, the proven volumes (which BP has yet to incorporate into its own tallies of Azerbaijani and Caspian reserves) were deemed large enough by BP to warrant an immediate start on development of a gas export system to Turkey. The current goal, under a contract signed with Turkey in March 2001, is for exports to start at roughly 2–3 bcm/y in 2004, rising quickly to 6.6 bcm/y in 2007 and to remain at that level until 2015.[13]

Kazakhstan

Two developments have inspired the Kazakh authorities—the discovery of oil at Kashagan in the summer of 2000 and the impending opening of the CPC oil export line from Tengiz to Novorossiysk. Current production is fairly modest. The country's oil and condensate output in 2000 is expected to reach 34 million tonnes (equivalent to 680 000 b/d averaged over the year), reflecting increased production at Tengiz, Karachaganak and a number of lesser fields. By comparison, output in 1999 was 30 million tonnes (600 000 b/d) and in 1998 26 million tonnes (520 000 b/d).

What the leaders of Kazakhstan (and of the other Caspian republics) want is to be producers on a Persian Gulf scale. President Nursultan Nazarbayev declared in April 2000 that output could rise to no less than 400 mt/y (8.0 mb/d) by 2015: 'We think that by 2015 we shall be producing 400 million tonnes of oil a year or about the same as Saudi Arabia'.[14] This was a considerable advance on the previous Kazakh assertion, made by the President of Kazakhoil, Nurlan Balgimbayev, at the summit meeting of Turkic nations in Baku earlier that month, that Kazakh output might reach 200 mt/y (4 mb/d) by 2015.

Nazarbayev was speaking amid intense speculation over the discoveries at Kashagan. The presence of oil and gas was confirmed by Kashagan's operator, the Offshore Kazakhstan International Operating Company (OKIOC), following completion of the field's first well, Kashagan West. Official reports made it clear that a formal declaration of the estimated reserves would have to await completion of a second well, Kashagan East, which would not take place until 2001.[15] The expectation, however, is that the OKIOC is dealing with a truly gigantic field which shares the same structural indications as the nearby giant onshore Tengiz field and may well prove to be even more extensive.

While Nazarbayev's comparison with Saudi Arabia may seem outrageous at first hearing, there is at least a rough logic to his assessment. The three-year seismic programme conducted by the OKIOC and its forebears in the mid-

---

[13] *East European Energy Report*, issue 115 (Mar. 2001).

[14] President Nursultan Nazarbayev, Address to the World Economic Forum's Eurasia Economic Summit in Almaty, 29 Apr. 2000 (note 9).

[15] Press releases by constituent companies of the OKIOC, issued 24 July 2000.

1990s yielded at least three major prospects, of which Kashagan is simply the most hopeful. It is theoretically possible for Kazakhstan's output to rise to approximately 8.0 mb/d if several conditions obtain. All three major offshore prospects would have to yield output of 1 mb/d, while as much as 2.0 mb/d would have to be forthcoming from the clutch of lesser offshore prospects identified in the seismic survey. Tengiz output would have to proceed on track, or even further, peaking not at 700 000 or 800 000 b/d but, as some have suggested it might, at 1.2 mb/d,[16] while Karachaganak would have to meet its existing target for sustainable production of 700 000–800 000 b/d.

Other existing onshore fields, such as Texaco's North Buzachi or the major fields at Uzen, Mangystau and Aktyubinsk, would have to secure sufficient investment to ensure their recovery so that non-Tengiz onshore production could climb to close to 2.0 mb/d. This is not impossible but remains highly improbable. One important element in considering projected output levels is the Kazakhstan Government's continuing preparedness to force foreign companies to dedicate specific volumes to the home market by means of placing limits on export volumes. Thus in December 1999 the government capped oil exports for 2000 at 22 million tonnes.

Turkmenistan

Turkmenistan's proven reserves are as yet relatively modest. According to BP Amoco, they amount to some 500 million barrels of oil and 2.86 tcm of gas.[17] While the country's oil reserves are relatively small—although useful for a country with only 4.5 million people and low per capita income—its gas reserves are of world class, accounting for about 2.5 per cent of global proven reserves of 141.33 tcm. Turkmen officials themselves say that their country has much more substantial reserves than those currently considered proven accor- ding to Western standards. In early 1999 the Ministry of Oil and Gas said that the country possessed some 2.1 billion tonnes (15.3 bbl) of proven oil reserves and 11.5 billion tonnes (84 bbl) of what it termed possible oil reserves. For gas, it listed 4.0 billion tonnes of oil equivalent (btoe) in proven reserves and 16.0 btoe in possible reserves, the equivalent of 4.44 bcm and 17.76 bcm, respectively.[18]

Turkmenistan is aiming to produce some 200 000 b/d of oil and gas conden- sate in 2000, as against 150 000 b/d in 1999. While this is a big increase, and while there are certainly additional reserves waiting to be found and developed, it seems highly unlikely that the government will be able to meet its target, set out in a 10-year economic development programme adopted in July 1999, of expanding oil output to 600 000 b/d by 2010. No one really doubts the country's hydrocarbons potential; the principal doubts all concern the lack of a coherent government policy.

[16] Personal communication to the author by a senior adviser to the President of Kazakhstan.
[17] BP Statistical Review of World Energy (note 4).
[18] See chapter 13 in this volume.

Where gas is concerned, the issue is not so much discovering fresh reserves (although this is to be expected) as exploiting proven deposits. Both Exxon-Mobil and Royal Dutch/Shell remain well placed with regard to both exploration and eventual development, but the timing of actual development (and of specific contracts covering prospective development on a production-sharing basis) remains dependent on the creation or re-establishment of sustained export outlets. In time, ExxonMobil may yet come to play a highly significant role as both potential developer and export facilitator; but its gas ambitions are, at least in large part, focused on export markets to the east and the prospect of a Turkmenistan–China/Japan gas line. Such a line, although the subject of some serious studies by a group including both Exxon and Japan's Mitsubishi, is not likely to materialize for another 10 years or so.

In oil, ExxonMobil naturally looks westwards, since its substantial onshore Turkmen concessions lie close to the Caspian coast. Throughout 2000, Shell was reported to be close to signing a formal agreement for development of major gas deposits in central Turkmenistan, which would serve as the basis for a major export project. In May 2000, the government disclosed that Shell had chosen to develop the Malay block, which Oil and Gas Minister Regepbay Arazov said 'has the potential to produce and export 30 bcm/y'—in other words, enough to meet the entire commitment for gas sales to Turkey and Southern Europe envisaged in the context of the proposed Trans-Caspian Gas Pipeline (TCGP) project.[19]

Almost all of what the Ministry of Oil and Gas considers to be the country's 2.1 billion tonnes of oil reserves are found in the Caspian area, as are the 11.5 billion tonnes of what it terms possible reserves. However, only a handful of fields are in fact operational and the country's first offshore round of exploration in 1997–98 was a disaster. The second round, in the spring of 2000, likewise yielded few positive results. A handful of companies are already operating, notably Malaysia's Petronas and Dragon Oil from the United Arab Emirates (UAE)—both offshore—together with ExxonMobil which, with the British company Lasmo, has some significant but geologically complex onshore fields. Together with the Turkmenneft State Oil Company (TMN), which is responsible for all indigenous oil and gas operations in the Caspian region, these producers accounted for the lion's share of Turkmenistan's 1999 oil output of 140 000–150 000 b/d. Some oil is also produced in the Amu Darya Basin of eastern Turkmenistan, which is the responsibility of the Turkmengas State Gas Company (TMG). In 1998, TMG accounted for 13.3 per cent of total oil output of 127 400 b/d.

The development of energy resources in Turkmenistan is held back by doubts about the government's ability to honour contractual agreements. It has been embroiled in two significant disputes with oil companies—with the Netherlands' Larmag in the area now operated by Dragon and, more seriously, with Argentina's Bridas, over development of both oil and gas fields. In part these

---

[19] *East European Energy Report*, issue 104 (May 2000).

disputes reflected poor bargaining by Turkmenistan when the agreements were first concluded, so they were extremely generous to the foreign companies, but the bottom line after seven years of wrangling and international court cases is simply that Turkmenistan's word is not necessarily trusted. Only the very big corporations, which might be said to have more to offer Turkmenistan than it has to offer them, can take on the authoritarian policies of President Saparmurat Niyazov. His unwillingness to make or to honour long-term commitments has also had considerable repercussions with regard to the development of export pipelines—another factor which has held back field development.

As of early 2001, however, it appears that Niyazov is pinning his country's hopes on a revival of gas sales to Ukraine, via Russia, rather than on the long-proposed TCGP project aimed at supplying gas to Turkey. The current policy certainly has some merits, since the Russian giant Gazprom is currently short of supplies to meet its own export commitments and has therefore been willing to let Turkmenistan make use of its gas pipeline system (at a price) to supply customers such as Ukraine, with which it has cash payment problems.

In October 2000, the presidents of Turkmenistan and Ukraine reached agreement on the delivery over 14–15 months of 35 bcm of gas, with subsequent increases to take deliveries to 50 bcm/y by 2010.[20] However, the agreement does have considerable drawbacks. Just over half of the payment will be by barter and, with Ukraine still owing $315.5 million for Turkmen gas supplied in the first five months of 1999, the omens for smooth implementation of the contract do not look good. However, Turkmenistan has one important card to play: for once it has the possibility of negotiating for sales of gas either to Russia itself or to hard-cash markets served via Russia as a result of potential Gazprom shortfalls. That President Niyazov himself feels that he is now negotiating with Russia from a position of some strength was evident in comments he made in September 2000, when he said that he was now only interested in supplying Russia with gas under contracts to last for just two or three years, instead of a 30-year agreement which Turkmenistan had previously been seeking. Agence France-Presse quoted Niyazov as saying: 'We will sell gas to Russia but long-term agreements can lead to arguments so we will sell gas for a maximum term of two, three years'.[21] Turkmenistan had previously, in August 2000, concluded what was termed at the time a preliminary agreement to sell Russia 50 bcm/y for 30 years, with provision also for onward delivery of projected gas supplies to Ukraine.

Uzbekistan

Uzbekistan enjoyed the most integrated economy of the Central Asian republics in Soviet times and in the first years of independence was able to make good

[20] Synovitz, R., 'Ukraine: gas deal with Turkmenistan reveals Russian influence', 4 Oct. 2000, Radio Free Europe/Radio Liberty, 5 Oct. 2000, URL <http://www.rferl.org/nca/features/2000/10/05102000190034.asp>.

[21] East European Energy Report, issue 109 (Oct. 2000).

use of its indigenous resources, including the technical skills of its population. This, however, was essentially a rationalization of existing resources; there was no accompanying expansion of investment. In energy terms, this meant that both oil and gas production were substantially increased in the 1990s, but the absence of any real economic reform has left the country's energy industry lagging in terms of foreign investment. The government is currently trying to remedy this with its newly introduced 'open doors' policy aimed at encouraging direct foreign investment in Uzbek hydrocarbons.

It will be some time before the results of this change of policy become apparent, and in the absence of more wide-ranging economic reform the outlook is not particularly bright. The (admittedly conservative) BP estimates for the country are that it possesses 0.6 bbl of oil and condensate and 1870 bcm of natural gas. However, the government, citing 'estimates by specialists', in July 2000 sought to attract potential investors by asserting that the country's energy reserves totalled 5.78 billion tonnes (42 bbl) of oil and gas condensate and 5095 bcm of natural gas.[22] It did not say whether these were proven recoverable reserves or reserves in place, and much more independent analysis (not to mention seismic survey work and drilling) will be required before such figures can be validated. Nevertheless, even on the BP estimates, Uzbekistan has some 1.3 per cent of proven global gas reserves, making them a world-class resource.

As for production, oil output rose three-fold between 1989 and 1999, from 65 000 to 190 000 b/d. Gas output also rose, although not so spectacularly, from 38.3 to 51.9 bcm over the same period. This was enough to turn Uzbekistan from a net importer to a net exporter of hydrocarbons. It is currently exporting a modest 6 bcm/y of gas to its neighbours—Kazakhstan, Kyrgyzstan, Russia and Tajikistan—and approximately 1 mt/y (20 000 b/d) of refined oil products. However, by the late 1990s the production increases had stalled and international companies were walking away. In 1998 both Enron and Unocal pulled out of the country. One major reason was severe currency restrictions. The government currently appears to realize that it lacks the resources to effect a major further increase itself, with the state energy company, Uzbekneftegas, anticipating only that output in 2010 will reach 240 000 b/d. With some 70 per cent of the country's production coming from just one field (Kokdumalak in the Bukharo-Khivi region) the Uzbek authorities are naturally looking for a much more wide-ranging exploration programme as part of their revamped approach to foreign investment in oil and gas. In particular, they are looking to develop prospects on the Ustyurt plateau and in the Aral Sea region.

The Russian Caspian

The Russian Caspian essentially consists of four regions—the onshore republics of Kalmykia, Dagestan and Chechnya and the offshore regions of the north-east Caspian Sea. The US Energy Information Administration (EIA) estimates

[22] From an Uzbek government document presented to Financial Times Energy, July 2000.

Russia's Caspian reserves at some 2.7 bbl.[23] This appears to be based on Soviet-era data. Over the next year or two more reliable information, particularly concerning the region's offshore potential, should become known as results from Lukoil's drilling at the Severny prospect are made public—and come under further scrutiny. There are proven gas reserves in the region but their volume is disputed. The EIA cites no figure for these in its latest Caspian assessment.[24]

Actual production is minimal. Oil production totalled a mere 11 000 b/d in 1999, down from 144 000 b/d in 1990. Similarly, gas output fell to just 0.8 bcm in 1999, from 6.1 bcm in 1990. Russia is pursuing an essentially nationalist approach to oil and gas development in both onshore and offshore areas along its Caspian coastline before starting to plan the development of offshore resources. In essence, Russian companies will develop those areas that Moscow considers to be the Russian sector, although there may be a role for Western firms in this development as Russian companies which have bid for offshore work have acknowledged that lack of capital makes it sensible for them to secure foreign participation. How large a stake might then be made available to foreign companies remains to be seen. General Russian policies that will also affect Caspian development include access to export pipelines—a critical issue for foreign investors in the Russian energy sector. Other key issues (affecting all of Russia, not just its Caspian regions) include clarification of the legal framework governing foreign companies' operations in Russia, with particular reference to the implementation and regulation of production-sharing agreements.

In December 1997 Lukoil won a tender for Russian companies to exploit part of the Caspian Sea shelf. However, it may not have the cash to carry out full oilfield development, particularly if it has indeed made a major discovery at Severny. This may be why three of Russia's energy giants, Lukoil, Gazprom and Yukos, announced on 25 May 2000 that they were joining up to form the Caspian Oil Company to prospect for oil in what they termed a 13 000 km^2 area of Russian Caspian waters.[25] In March 2000, Lukoil announced that it had struck oil in its Severny/Khvalynsky field in the northern Caspian.[26] Its first well, it said, had pointed to the presence of at least 300 million tonnes (2.2 bbl) of reserves, a size which, even if this referred to reserves in place, would still make it a major discovery. However, the Lukoil announcement was followed by reports that it might in fact have found more gas than oil, and by June the company was saying only that the first well's results had 'suggested the presence of commercial hydrocarbon reserves' without attaching specific figures. At the same time, Lukoil was reported to have started drilling a second well, usually a minimum requirement to determine even the approximate size of a field's proven reserves.[27] Similarly, initial suggestions that Lukoil was

[23] US Energy Information Administration, 'Caspian Sea region tables and maps', June 2000, URL <http://www.eia.doe.gov/emeu/cabs/caspgrph.html>.

[24] US Energy Information Administration (note 23).

[25] *East European Energy Report*, issue 105 (June 2000).

[26] *East European Energy Report* (note 25).

[27] *East European Energy Report* (note 25).

looking to produce the first oil from the field by 2004 and that it hoped to produce as much as 300 000 b/d by 2008 currently look decidedly premature.

There has been some foreign company involvement in Russian Caspian energy development but it appears to be mainly confined to service companies. In 1996 JKX was negotiating a joint venture to develop the InchkeMore field off the coast of Dagestan in partnership with two of Russia's oil majors, Lukoil and Rosneft, and with the local Dagneft.

Iran

In August 2000, following a study based on seismic analysis rather than actual drilling, Iran announced that it believed it possessed up to 3 bbl of recoverable reserves in the Caspian[28]—a useful figure, if marginal by comparison with the country's 90 bbl of proven reserves in and around the Persian Gulf. The deputy head of the National Iranian Oil Company (NIOC), Mehdi Mir-Moezzi, said on 21 August 2000 that 'preliminary seismic studies show that we have 10 bbl of in-place crude in our 20 per cent of the Caspian Sea, of which 2.5 to 3 bbl are recoverable'. The preliminary studies to which he referred were the outcome of a two-year study by the Royal Dutch/Shell group and Lasmo under a 1998 agreement which grants the companies exclusive rights to four development blocks should oil be discovered. The NIOC also announced that estimated recovery costs would be around $5–7 per barrel, which lies within the industry's normal range, and that it was discussing plans for a tender covering construction of a semi-submersible rig for Caspian activity.[29]

The NIOC official's comments should perhaps be viewed in the light of the Caspian Sea dispute. His mention of 'our 20 per cent of the Caspian Sea' raises questions concerning the precise locations of the hydrocarbon indications reported in the seismic survey. Iran's neighbours have not agreed that it should have a 20 per cent share of the sea; and, while Iran might expect to secure some 15–16 per cent of the sea on the basis of boundary lines agreed according to the principle of equidistance, if a straight line from its most northerly coastal points on the eastern and western coasts of the Caspian were to form the basis of a settlement—as appeared to be the case in the Soviet era—Iran would only control some 12 per cent of Caspian waters. A key question is whether Shell and Lasmo confined their operations to areas of the sea where Iran's exploration rights would not be likely to be challenged under any partition agreement.

Immediately before the signing of the 1998 agreement, the Foreign Ministry of Azerbaijan formally protested to the British and Dutch governments that the agreement with Shell and Lasmo affected a part of what it termed the Azerbaijani sector of the sea.[30] The Caspian finds will provide some additional impetus for Iran's drive to secure foreign investment for upstream oil and gas

---

[28] *East European Energy Report*, issue 108 (Sep. 2000).
[29] *East European Energy Report* (note 28).
[30] Radio Free Europe/Radio Liberty, *Iran Report*, vol. 2, no. 5 (1 Feb. 1999).

development, but the core of Iranian activities will continue to be its fields further south, in and around the Persian Gulf.

II. Caspian pipelines: the carriage of Caspian oil and gas to market

The 1990s were filled with speculation as to how Caspian oil and gas could be carried to hard-currency markets. The first decade of the 21st century should see real progress in that regard, although it will probably be slower than the Caspian producer governments would like.

Oil pipelines

There are at present three significant oil export pipelines in operation with a combined capacity of well under half-a-million barrels of oil a day. These will be dwarfed with completion in the summer of 2001 of the CPC's 560 000-b/d line from the giant Tengiz oilfield in Kazakhstan to Novorossiysk.

The three existing lines are:

1. *Atyrau–Samara*. This is a 280 000-b/d capacity Soviet-era line which runs from the Kazakh terminal at Atyrau to the Russian Urals refinery at Samara and then connects with Russia's main East–West Druzhba system.

2. *Baku–Novorossiysk*. This Soviet-era line runs from the oil terminals outside the port of Baku to Novorossiysk through southern Russia. It has a nominal capacity of 180 000 b/d, but Western oil men in Baku consider that the Russian section, part of which was re-routed in 1999–2000 to avoid Chechnya, still limits throughput from Azerbaijan to approximately 50 000 b/d.

3. *Baku–Supsa*. This line, opened in late 1998 with first deliveries in March 1999, runs from Baku to the Georgian Black Sea port of Supsa. It currently has a capacity of 115 000 b/d but work has begun on doubling capacity to 230 000 b/d.

These are not the only ways by which Caspian oil reaches international markets. There is considerable export by rail (some reports estimate it as high as 240 000 b/d), with deliveries sometimes as far afield as China and Finland, and barges use the Volga–Don canal system to carry Caspian, and especially Kazakh, oil to international markets. A 'swaps' system with Iran is also operational, although at a much lower level than might have been expected: oil from Kazakhstan, Turkmenistan and Azerbaijan goes by tanker or barge to Iran's Caspian ports, while Iran makes available an equivalent volume (or value) of oil in the Gulf.

Apart from the CPC's Tengiz–Novorossiysk line, two other essentially new projects are already physically under way which will add to capacity. These are:

5. *Neka–Tehran*. This line involves the construction of a new pipeline within Iran from the Caspian port of Neka to a refinery just outside Tehran which will enable swaps traffic to increase to 390 000 b/d.

6. *Dyubendi–Batumi*. This line runs from the Azerbaijani oil terminal at Dyubendi to the Georgian port of Batumi and should have an initial capacity of 70 000 b/d, perhaps rising later to 140 000 b/d. It is being developed by Chevron to handle Kazakh crude from the Tengiz field which will first be shipped across the Caspian from the Kazakh port of Aktau. In due course it will probably handle output from Texaco's North Buzachi field.

However, all this capacity barely exceeds 1.2 mb/d, and as such major fields as Tengiz, Karachaganak and the ACG complex approach full production—let alone Kashagan and some 100 smaller fields which would be capable of exporting—significant increases in pipeline capacity will be required. There are two main prospects in this regard, and two other serious contenders.

The two advanced proposals, both aimed at carrying Caspian crude to European and Mediterranean markets, are:

1. *Expansion of the CPC line*. This would take the Tengiz–Novorossiysk line up to a capacity of 1.3 mb/d.

2. *Baku–Ceyhan*. This would be a brand-new 1.0 mb/d-capacity line from Baku to the Turkish Mediterranean port of Ceyhan. The AIOC, which is developing the ACG complex, is obliged under its 1994 contract to help the Azerbaijani authorities choose a route for what is officially termed the MEP and which is intended to carry ACG crude to market. This is the route preferred by the Azerbaijani Government (and by the US and Turkish governments) for the MEP and the AIOC member companies are trying to develop a viable Baku–Ceyhan project, but they have not yet secured full financing.

The two serious contenders are:

1. *Kazakhstan–Turkmenistan–Iran (KTI)*. This would run along the eastern coast of the Caspian and link the oilfields of north-western Kazakhstan with the oil markets on northern Iran, via the western region (and oilfields) of Turkmenistan. Its rationale would be to take advantage of the opportunities offered by Iranian swaps to limit actual construction costs and provide a system for, in effect, increasing Caspian/Iranian exports to Asia–Pacific markets.

2. *Expansion of Baku–Supsa*. This would increase capacity to at least 500 000 b/d. It is under consideration as a possible route for Azerbaijan's main export pipeline. A new or substantially enlarged Baku–Supsa line could be either an alternative to the Baku–Ceyhan line or the first stage of a system that would eventually end at Ceyhan.

Various other oil pipeline proposals, although they may have been discussed at various times at quite senior levels, remain ideas that are not likely to lead to serious project work for many years, if at all. These proposals include:

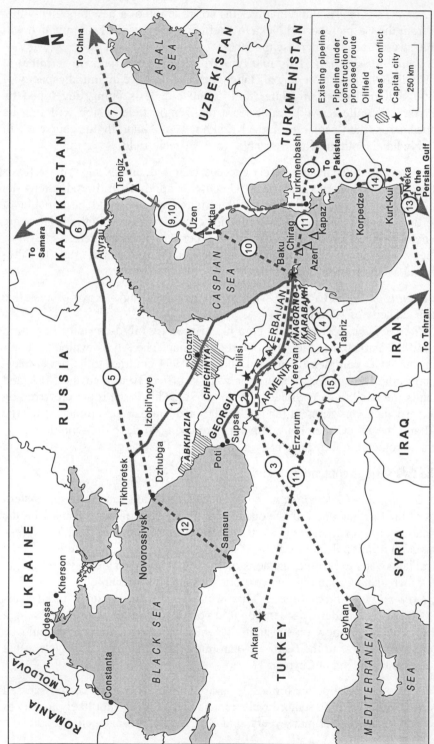

Figure 3.1. Caspian oil and gas pipelines, existing, under construction and proposed

Notes:
1. The Baku–Novorossiysk oil pipeline, operational.
2. The Baku–Supsa 'early oil' pipeline, operational since early 1999.
3. The Baku–Ceyhan oil pipeline project designated MEP route in a series of agreements signed in Istanbul in November 1999 by Azerbaijan, Georgia, Turkey and the USA.
4. The Baku–Tabriz oil pipeline project, possible Azerbaijani oil export option, studied by Total.
5. Atyrau–Novorossiysk (the CPC project) oil pipeline, scheduled to be operational in 2001.
6. Atyrau–Samara, the Druzhba system oil pipeline (operational).
7. Tengiz–China oil line project, under study and not likely to be operational for several years.
8. The Turkmenistan–Pakistan–Central Asian oil pipeline, with possible tie-in from Kazakh fields; unlikely in the near future.
9. Tengiz/Uzen–Kharg. Preliminary oil pipeline proposal by Total.
10. The Trans-Caspian (Tengiz–Uzen–Aktau–Baku) oil pipeline project. It would be a de facto extension of Azerbaijan's MEP.
11. The Trans-Caspian Gas Pipeline (TCGP) project.
12. The Blue Stream gas pipeline from Russia to Turkey, scheduled to be operational in 2001.
13. The Neka–Tehran oil pipeline project which could constitute major element in the 'swaps'/pipeline export system from the Caspian to the Persian Gulf.
14. The Korpedze–Kurt-Kui (KKK) gas pipeline, operational since 1997.
15. The Tabriz–Erzurum gas pipeline, scheduled to be operational in 2001.

1. *Baku–Novorossiysk*. This is officially the third of the three alternative routes for Azerbaijan's planned MEP (the others being Baku–Ceyhan and Baku–Supsa). At various times the Russian authorities have proposed a full upgrade of this line to perhaps a capacity of 1.0 b/d, which would in effect require construction of an entirely new line.

2. *Kazakhstan–China*. The governments of Kazakhstan and China signed a memorandum of understanding in 1997 which provided for the rapid start of work on such a project, but it was only in late 2000 that the Chinese committed themselves even to a feasibility study. This line may eventually be built, but not for some time.[31]

3. *The Central Asian Oil Pipeline* (CAOP), also known as a trans-Afghan line. Detailed studies on the construction of such a line, with a capacity of up to 1.0 mb/d, were carried out by Unocal in 1996–97. The project makes good sense in terms of delivery to a port in Pakistan, but the political situation in Afghanistan makes it unlikely that it will in fact be built.

What has changed during the first years of post-Soviet enthusiasm for Caspian projects is that various ambitious schemes are now being seen in a much colder and more sceptical light than heretofore. Thus Unocal has itself

[31] China appears to have twice committed itself to carrying out a feasibility study. In 1997, a study was included in the memorandum of understanding agreed with the China National Oil Company for oilfield development, although the following year one Western oil man, just back from Kazakhstan, told the author that what China considered to be a feasibility study would in Western terms be considered no more than a preliminary pre-feasibility study. In late 2000, after a period of considerable Kazakh concern at developments concerning China's proposed energy projects in Kazakhstan, a Chinese delegation was reported to have agreed to carry out what would presumably be a proper feasibility study.

abandoned its plans for gas and oil pipelines from Turkmenistan to Pakistan via Afghanistan, even though its former junior partner, the Saudi Delta Oil company, is still seeking to pursue the project with some UN backing. Prospects for oil or gas lines to China—an oil line from western Kazakhstan, and a gas line from Turkmenistan via Kazakhstan—are similarly still a long way off.

As of early 2001, the following specific proposals, or general approaches, for resolving the Caspian export conundrum continue to merit serious attention: (a) the *CPC oil pipeline from Tengiz to Novorossiysk*; and (b) the westward line, the *MEP from Azerbaijan to either Ceyhan or Supsa*. It is also worth keeping an eye on the planned gas connection to Turkey from Azerbaijan, since the two countries agreed in March 2001 that this would follow the same route through the Caucasus as the Baku–Ceyhan oil pipeline.

This list is not intended to exclude other major potential developments, notably the construction of a trans-Caspian oil pipeline or developments outside the immediate region, such as a line from Burgas in Bulgaria to the northern Greek port of Alexandroupolis, or a connector from Odessa in Ukraine to the Druzhba oil pipeline system in Poland. At this stage, however, they remain ideas for the future and their implementation will largely depend on how the current dilemma of securing Kazakh and Azerbaijani oil exports to the outside world is realized.

The status of the CPC

The CPC is the project that ought to have been built in the mid-1990s—it was first proposed in 1992[32]—but is clearly a case of better late than never. After years of waiting, the project for a 1580-km pipeline between Kazakhstan's giant oilfield at Tengiz and a new terminal to be built near Novorossiysk is now being implemented.[33] Pipelaying was completed in late 2000 and oil was scheduled to arrive in Novorossiysk in July 2001 for loading onto tankers. The project essentially involves laying 745 km of new pipeline between Novorossiysk and the Russian city of Komsomol'skaya; inspecting, renovating and upgrading to Western standards some 800 km of pipeline laid in the last years of the Soviet Union between Komsomol'skaya and Tengiz; a new crossing of the Volga; and a new offshore terminal near Novorossiysk.

The pipeline will have a first-phase capacity of 28.5 mt/y (567 000 b/d) but further expansion is taken for granted, with three subsequent phases due to raise capacity to 67 mt/y (1.35 mb/d). However, the speed of further expansion remains unclear. Prolonged wrangling between the consortium's partners in the run-up to their key agreement of 25 November 1998 led to a cap of $2236 million being placed on first-phase spending. This limited the finance available to build in expansion options from the start, and at the time appeared to indicate that the CPC's partners might even be contemplating abandoning

[32] Roberts, J., *Caspian Pipelines* (Royal Institute of International Affairs: London, 1996).
[33] 'Three steps forward, two steps back', *Middle East Energy Report*, issue 39 (30 Apr. 1999).

plans for the second, third and fourth phases. As of 2001 the CPC is still talking about eventual capacity of 67 mt/y but has produced no timetable for this.

The issue is particularly important for Kazakhstan, which anticipates using some 21 mt/y of initial first-phase (28.5 mt/y) capacity, and would have been expected to secure some 50 mt/y of the eventual 67 mt/y capacity. However, Kazakhstan received good news in October 2000 when a $900 million contract was signed under which CCC–Saipem, a Greek Palestinian and French joint venture, is to build a 635-km connecting pipeline to link the giant gas/condensate field of Karachaganak to the CPC line. A spokesman for the Karachaganak Petroleum Operating (KPO) group (a joint venture including Agip, British Gas, Texaco and Lukoil) said that this will enable the KPO group to increase output of condensate from 4 mt/y (80 000 b/d) in 2000 to 11 mt/y (220 000 b/d) by 2003.[34] The principal companies involved in the project are Fluor Daniel, the overall supervisor; a Franco-Russian joint venture, Starstroi, which groups France's Bouygues and Spie-Capag and the local Kuban-neftegastroi and Stavropoltruboprovodstroi; and two pipe suppliers, Chicago Bridge and Iron and the local Volzhskiy Pipe Works.

One important issue is whether the line's main advantage may now have been lost. CPC agreements provide for a fixed tariff of $25 per tonne ($3.425 per barrel) for oil shipped through the line, with roughly 40 per cent of all income, once the line's construction costs have been met, distributed as dividends, 30 per cent going to the governments of Russia and Kazakhstan as transit fees and only 20 per cent being set aside for operating costs. In other words, it is viewed by the governments not simply as a mechanism for ensuring export earnings by carrying oil to hard-cash markets but as a revenue mechanism in its own right. Throughput costs for Kazakh oil from Tengiz including the $25 tariff are estimated at $30 per tonne, while oil from Kumkol would have to pay approximately $38 per tonne. Moreover, the costs for delivery from Novorossiysk have to be added to these figures.

What the CPC project does prove at long last is that a large-scale pipeline transiting Russia, while primarily serving non-Russian Caspian producers, is feasible—even if such projects appear unusually prone to delays. However, the CPC is now being built in a competitive environment, so its owners are less able to count on artificially high transit fees, and this may affect post-first phase expansion. In particular, the CPC will have to compete with what is now becoming a proven oil export corridor—the Baku–Supsa line from the Caspian to the Black Sea. And, with oil already flowing into Georgia along that line, an even more ambitious alternative presents itself—Baku–Ceyhan.

Baku–Ceyhan

As of early 2001, most AIOC member companies, together with the governments of Azerbaijan, Georgia and Turkey, the three countries through which the line would pass, have agreed to pursue the option of developing a Baku–

[34] 'Karachaganak pipeline contract signed', *East European Energy Report*, issue 109 (Oct. 2000).

Ceyhan line with a capacity of approximately 50 mt/y.[35] At the time of writing, in March 2001, a preliminary $20 million engineering study commissioned by the Baku–Ceyhan sponsors' group and begun in December 2000 was half-way through its work. The key issue was whether the group would then commission a $120 million detailed engineering study for the route. A decision on the detailed study was due in the summer of 2001 and, if approved, would almost certainly lead almost seamlessly into actual construction. A series of major bilateral and multilateral agreements necessary for the line's construction and operation have been signed, notably the three host-nation agreements. The governmental commitment to pursue the project was epitomized by Azerbaijan's willingness to forgo transit revenues in order to ensure Georgia's agreement to a tariff structure based on no more than $2.58 per barrel. (Azerbaijan, of course, stands to secure its return from the project through the sale of its own oil, whereas for Georgia, which is expected to be more of a recipient than a supplier of crude oil from the pipeline, transit income is vital.)

Nonetheless, the Baku–Ceyhan pipeline remains the most complex of all the prospective pipeline projects in the region to evaluate. The proposal is straight-forward—construction of a line of between 1800 and 2000 km (depending on the precise route chosen) to link the Azerbaijani terminal of Sangachali, just south of Baku, with the Turkish Mediterranean port of Ceyhan. The advantages of such a line are considerable. It would serve exporters not only in Azerbaijan but also in Kazakhstan—indeed, the current proposals are predicated on a substantial input of Kazakh oil.[36] It obviates the need for oil tankers to pass through the delicate ecosystem of the Turkish Straits (the Bosporus, the Sea of Marmara and the Dardanelles) for at least Azerbaijani, if not for Russian, crude oil exports. Ceyhan is a deep-water port that can service 300 000-tonne super-tankers, whereas the Bosporus is limited to tankers of around 100 000–150 000 tonnes. In addition, navigation of supertankers in the Aegean Sea involves considerable environmental hazards.[37] Ceyhan itself is located on as isolated a stretch of Mediterranean coast as can be found anywhere in modern Europe, thus minimizing the environmental impact. Politically, the line has very strong backing indeed, not least from the Turkish and US governments.

[35] For a full analysis of the finely poised question whether BP and its co-sponsors would indeed move on to actual construction of the Baku–Ceyhan line and on its interrelationship with the gas pipeline between Azerbaijan and Turkey, see Roberts, J., *Energy Economist*, issue 233 (Mar. 2001) and *East European Energy Report*, issue 114 (Feb. 2001). These articles were written a few weeks before the 12 Mar. 2001 agreement on Azerbaijani gas sales to Turkey and accompanying governmental comments that for almost 1000 km, from the Baku area to near the eastern Turkish city of Erzurum, the Baku–Ceyhan oil pipeline and the line to carry Azerbaijani gas to Turkey would follow the same route.

[36] The exact capacity of the line and the respective volumes of Azeri and Kazakh crude remain undecided. A capacity of 1.0 mb/d (50 mt/y) is the figure most often cited, but Turkey was initially contemplating a 900 000 b/d (45 mt/y)-capacity line, while corporate studies have been carried out for a range of volumes. At least 400 000 b/d would probably come from Azerbaijan and Kazakhstan, and perhaps as much as 50 000–100 000 b/d could also be expected from Turkmenistan so long as its dispute with Azerbaijan over the development of fields in the central–south Caspian is laid to rest. Whether Azerbaijan or Kazakhstan would be expected to fill the rest of the line's capacity remains in doubt.

[37] See also section IV below.

Proponents of the Baku–Ceyhan scheme have to yet to answer a set of related questions: (a) who will finance the considerable costs of the line; (b) when such finance will be forthcoming; (c) who will supply the oil volumes required to justify its construction; and (d) when that oil will be available. While there are no clear answers to these questions, there are some key pointers.

The pipeline's most ardent proponents, the governments of Turkey and the USA, both hope to see the pipeline built and operational by October 2004. In September 2000 most of the AIOC's member companies duly came together to set up a sponsors group to develop the Baku–Ceyhan line, thus ensuring that finance would be made available for the detailed engineering study on which, corporate sources said, work was due to begin before the end of 2000. The study was expected to be ready by mid-2001 and, participants in the project say, this timetable will allow the sponsors group to judge whether it can begin raising capital for the project.[38] However, it appeared clear to some senior officials in AIOC member companies that actual construction work on the project, even assuming that all goes well and that finance can be secured in the first half of 2001, would not start until well into 2002 at the earliest, making it highly unlikely that the October 2004 target date would be met.

There are major issues to be faced in terms of availability of oil to fill the pipeline. Its capacity would be 1 mb/d. Azerbaijan is slated to provide some 400 000–500 000 b/d, but the line would only come into operation once Azerbaijan was already exporting some 250 000–300 000 b/d by other routes (at least 200 000 b/d via Supsa and a further 50 000–100 000 b/d via Novorossiysk). In addition, Iran is likely to import some Azerbaijani output in the form of product from the Baku refinery and may import some by barge to its Caspian ports. Baku–Ceyhan can thus only come into its own once Azerbaijan's output reaches approximately 750 000–800 000 b/d—a volume not likely to be reached until around 2008–2010. Already it has become clear that the AIOC is postponing a major expansion of output capacity at its ACG concession until the prospects for the Baku–Ceyhan route (or some other MEP) become clearer.

Then there is the question whether the Baku–Ceyhan route should be considered as a means of providing an integrated solution to the question of oil exports from all, or most, of the Caspian region. Turkish proposals for the Baku–Ceyhan line initially focused on the provision of facilities to transport some 25 mt/y from Azerbaijan and a further 20 mt/y from Kazakhstan. The assumption is now that if the line is to be of 50 mt/y, Kazakhstan will have to provide half the input.

Kazakhstan's leaders regularly show interest in exporting their country's oil through the Baku–Ceyhan line but they have not yet proved willing to commit specific volumes of oil to it, and such a commitment is crucial to the project's viability. In November 1999, after signing a framework agreement on the Baku–Ceyhan line during the Summit Meeting of the Organization for Security and Co-operation in Europe (OSCE) in Istanbul, President Nazarbayev said that

[38] Author's notes, Sep. 2000.

Kazakhstan was in no position to promise the volumes of oil the pipeline's backers require. He also declared: 'The Baku–Ceyhan pipeline cannot take place without oil from Kazakhstan'.[39]

When US Ambassador-at-Large Stephen Sestanovich, Special Adviser to the Secretary of State, visited the Caspian region in December 2000 this was widely seen as a US attempt to secure a firm throughput commitment from Kazakhstan, but it appears to be reluctant to make such a commitment, at least at present. Visiting Baku after bad weather thwarted a planned meeting with President Nazarbayev, Sestanovich was reported to have expressed approval for what was termed the Kazakhstani Government's stated interest in exporting oil via Baku–Ceyhan and he suggested that the line might then be renamed the Aktau–Baku–Ceyhan line in honour of this proposed trans-Caspian element.[40] However, interest is not the same thing as commitment. A joint press release issued in Almaty merely referred to Kazakh backing for increased tankerage of Kazakh oil from Aktau to Baku.

In a way, Kazakhstan's real response was made in a different fashion. While Sestanovich was speaking in Baku, the Kazakh Foreign Ministry was issuing an announcement that it was holding talks with prominent international oil companies on quite another oil export pipeline project—the proposed KTI line.[41]

On the commercial side, the issues are enormous. The AIOC has estimated that transport costs for crude oil shipment to Supsa are likely to be about half of those required for shipment via Ceyhan. Transport represents a major element in overall Caspian production and delivery costs, while pipelines also provide an opportunity for countries to secure transit royalties. The AIOC estimates that its oil costs about $5 per barrel to produce, with transport costs of $2–4 per barrel (to Supsa) taking the total to $7–9 per barrel. According to various sources, in March 1999 Tengizchevroil was paying $30 per tonne ($4.1 per barrel) to transport oil from Aktau in Kazakhstan to Batumi in Georgia, via tanker to Dyubendi in Azerbaijan, pipeline to the Azerbaijan–Georgian railhead, and then rail to Batumi.[42] In 1998 Tengizchevroil exported 1.8 million tonnes by this route, with expectations of similar amounts for 1999. Previous indications were that in 1997–98 it was costing Chevron as much as $56 a tonne ($7.67 a barrel) to get its oil from Tengiz to Batumi. For its part, Georgia hopes to gain $6 million per year from the dispatch through the Baku–Supsa line of some 100 000 b/d and 'up to US$365 million a year, though probably not before 2005' if a full-scale Baku–Supsa line is chosen as the MEP. Similarly, for a Baku–Ceyhan line, it was reported that 'Ankara could raise tariffs to industry levels, earning as much as $357 million a year'.[43]

[39] 'Kazakh stand over Azeri oil pipeline project', *Business Digest*, 24 Nov. 1999.

[40] Turan (Baku), 6 Dec. 2000.

[41] Reuters (Astana), 'Kazakhs in talks to develop oil pipeline to Iran', 6 Dec. 2001.

[42] See, e.g., Caspian Times News Archive, 'Tengizchevroil halts cross Caspian crude shipments', 19 Feb. 1999, URL <http://www.caspiantimes.com/html/states/azerbaijan/admin/azeriF.shtml>. This cites a cost for transport across Azerbaijan and Georgia of $4.30 a barrel, equivalent to $31.39 a tonne of crude.

[43] Recknagel, C., '1998 in review: slump in prices could delay Caspian oil boom', Radio Free Europe/ Radio Liberty, Prague, 17 Dec. 1998.

Until 1996 it was commonly anticipated that construction of a Baku–Ceyhan line would cost approximately $2.5 billion. In 1998 the US company Amoco, one of the partners in the AIOC, commissioned a feasibility study from Fluor Daniel. This estimated the cost at $3.2 billion for a line capable of carrying 50 mt/y (1.0 b/d). By late 1998, the AIOC was asserting that the cost could be as much as $3.7 billion, compared to $1.8 billion for a similarly sized Supsa line and $2.5 billion for an MEP from Baku to Novorossiysk. Contemporary Turkish estimates that a line would cost approximately $2.2 billion were attributed by the AIOC to key differences concerning technical specifications, the route the line would take between Georgia and Ceyhan, and allowance for contingencies.[44]

As soon as there is a formal announcement that the line will definitely be built—in other words, that there is cash available to build it—then the Baku–Ceyhan route will become vulnerable to alternative proposals. In particular, Russia could suddenly decide that it will become a much better partner in terms of providing facilities for Caspian exports via Russian pipelines. An announcement by Moscow that it was prepared to transport an additional 15–20 mt/y of Kazakh crude via the Druzhba system would go far to pre-empt any Kazakh commitment of oil volumes to the Baku–Ceyhan project, since new connections to Druzhba would be both cheaper and quicker to build than Baku–Ceyhan. Similarly, construction of a prospective pipeline to Iran would be a much easier, and shorter, alternative to Aktau–Baku–Ceyhan.

It is the prospect of effective alternatives that haunts the Baku–Ceyhan project. It needs firm commitments of Kazakh throughput if it is to be viable. The Government of Kazakhstan, meanwhile, seems determined to view the Baku–Ceyhan route as just one alternative among many; but the Baku–Ceyhan route is not simply an alternative project—it is unique in that it is the only major pipeline scheme with a real prospect of commercial support that would enable Caspian producers to pipe their oil to market along a purely commercial system that bypassed both Iran and Russia.

It is not that pipelines through Iran or Russia do not inherently make sense—in fact they make excellent sense and should be exploited—but a key element in ensuring that they are operated on an essentially commercial basis and are not subjected to political pressures from the Iranian or Russian governments is the competition posed daily by a significant alternative. In practice this means a route to the West, through the South Caucasus or, in other words, Azerbaijan's proposed MEP. The Baku–Ceyhan route is the logical first choice—but only if Kazakhstan makes a firm and formal commitment of oil to the project. Similarly, the timing of such a project will be determined by the timing of such a commitment. If no commitments prove forthcoming from Kazakhstan in 2002, the prospects are that the member companies in the Baku–Ceyhan sponsors' group will cast their eyes increasingly on a cheaper, if less perfect, alternative—Baku–Supsa.

[44] 'Azerbaijan "faces loss" if Turkey pipeline is chosen', *Financial Times*, 24 Nov. 1998.

Baku–Supsa

In October 1995 Supsa was chosen, along with Novorossiysk, as one of the twin outlets for 'early oil' produced by the AIOC. Ironically, at the time, because of Georgia's doubtful political stability, it was regarded as the weaker candidate and was only added in because of political pressure from the Turkish and US governments. Now Novorossiysk is, in practice if not in theory, out of the running as a Black Sea candidate for an MEP terminal.

Supsa presents a strong case since a line can be constructed either by building a completely new line or by expanding the early oil pipeline completed in early 1999 and, in effect, gradually transforming it into a de facto MEP. The history of the Baku–Supsa route to date provides some indication that the latter course remains quite likely. In 1995, the Baku–Supsa early oil line was to have been a medium-cost project estimated at $236 million essentially based on linking disparate stretches of existing pipeline and having a capacity of 100 000 b/d. By 1996, with a realization that considerable stretches of new line would be required, orders were placed for extra pumping stations to take capacity up to at least 200 000 b/d, with costs put at $315 million. In 1998, with the discovery that virtually no existing pipe could really be integrated into the system, anticipated costs escalated to $590 million, but it also seemed clear that the capacity of what would be in effect a brand-new line for 90 per cent of its length could easily reach 300 000 b/d, even though the highest level the AIOC publicly envisaged was 230 000 b/d. Indeed, in 2000, with the line constantly working at or close to its initial 115 000 b/d capacity, work began to secure at least a doubling of capacity to 230 000 b/d.

As of early 2001, the question naturally emerges whether the existing pipeline will simply end up as one pipe of an eventual twin-pipe system. Since the AIOC and its Georgian affiliate, the Georgian Pipeline Company, already possess rights of way all the way from Sangachali to Supsa, construction of an MEP along this route would offer no real challenge, whether financial or political, that has not already been met in developing the original early oil line. Moreover, since it is in effect the AIOC itself that is developing the existing Baku–Supsa line and operating the new Supsa terminal, it would expect to have similar responsibility for, and control over, an MEP on the Baku–Supsa route.

Baku–Supsa vs Baku–Ceyhan

In 1997 two of the AIOC's most senior officials, Terry Adams (then president) and Greg Rich (then president of the pipeline group), declared, according to a rapporteur: 'International politics will influence the final choice of a main export pipeline. To the extent that political considerations contradict commercial considerations, a question arises as to who should pay the shortfall for a "sub-optimal solution"'.[45]

[45] Adams, T., 'Great power politics and the Azerbaijan oil pipeline: an update', Address to the Washington Institute for Near East Affairs, Washington, DC, 19 Feb. 1997.

At that time the issue of whether Azerbaijan's MEP should terminate at Supsa or Ceyhan was finely poised. In 1998 it appeared to this author that the oil companies clearly preferred the Supsa option but that the US and Turkish governments wanted Ceyhan. Thus in November 1998 Adams' successor as AIOC President, John Leggate, commented on Baku–Ceyhan: 'We understand the importance of this route. Nevertheless, not a single company supporting it has suggested it would participate in financing the project'.[46] He was speaking, of course, at a time when oil prices were falling and the AIOC was slowing down its development programme. It now seems likely that the ACG complex will not be producing at its intended Phase One level of 400 000 b/d until 2004 at the earliest. The question is whether the existing early oil systems—as developed, modified or expanded between 1996 and 2004—will be able to handle this level. It looks as if they might so long as there is some real improvement of the Baku–Novorossiysk line to add to Baku–Supsa's increased capacity.

The weakness of the Baku–Ceyhan route is that it seems that it cannot be developed in phases—at least, this does not appear to make sense if the line is built directly between Baku and Ceyhan, with a crossing into Turkey from central south Georgia. One possibility does still exist for a phased development—the construction of an initial line to Supsa, primarily to serve the AIOC, and an onward extension to Ceyhan as and when the next round of Azerbaijan joint ventures starts to yield results, or when output from the Kashagan field is such that the Kazakh authorities, and especially the companies actually developing Kashagan, feel capable of making a realistic throughput commitment to a Ceyhan line.

The Baku–Supsa route is not an ideal solution in the way, perhaps, that the Baku–Ceyhan route is, but it has one advantage: it would be a much easier project to implement in an era of low or volatile oil prices, since a 50 mt/y line to Supsa would probably cost approximately $1.6 billion as against perhaps double that amount for a line to Ceyhan. In addition, a two-step solution provides an opportunity to test the demand for oil traffic through the Bosporus, since rising oil demand within the Black Sea region itself may well diminish some of Turkey's worst fears. Moreover, the fact that oil development in both Azerbaijan and Kazakhstan is running somewhat slower than expected at the very least delays the need for a full-scale system to Ceyhan, with all the costs implied.

As of early 2001, it looks very much as if the oil companies have swung behind the US and Turkish governments and are serious in their attempts to probe and if possible prove the practicality of the Baku–Ceyhan line. However, senior officials in at least some of the AIOC member companies still hold to the Baku–Supsa route as a fallback position, to be brought into play should Baku–Ceyhan fail to materialize.

---

[46] *International Herald Tribune*, 30 Nov. 1998, quoted in Radio Free Europe/Radio Liberty, *RFE/RL Caucasus Report*, 1 Dec. 1998.

Baku–Novorossiysk

The oil companies in the AIOC have officially three routes under serious consideration. The third is the Baku–Novorossiysk line.

This is a route fraught with difficulties. It entails a transit of the troubled Russian republic of Dagestan, although since Russia completed its 'Grozny Bypass' project in April 2000 it no longer runs through the war-torn territory of Chechnya. During the past five years the Baku–Novorossiysk line has been repeatedly subjected to interruptions, either as a result of physical warfare in Chechnya or because of tariff disputes.

Although it has been operational in its present form for five years, the actual capacity of the Baku–Novorossiysk line remains unknown. The original Soviet design specification, when the line carried oil to Baku for refining rather than from Baku for exporting, was 9 mt/y (180 000 b/d) for the section between Baku and Grozny and 15 mt/y (300 000 b/d) for the section between Grozny and Tikhoretsk in southern Russia, where it joins a much larger oil export system. The AIOC upgraded the section of the line from Baku to the Russian border to at least 100 000 b/d capacity but generally limited actual throughput to no more than 50 000 b/d because it was uncertain whether Russia's Transneft had carried out sufficient repairs to the line within Russia to ensure that it could carry more than this.[47] In practice most of the oil shipped north by this route is supplied by SOCAR, which has a 1996 contract calling for, at present, some 2.3 mt/y (46 000 b/d) to be shipped through the line. SOCAR's inability or reluctance to ship oil north prompted a fierce set of exchanges in mid-2000, with Russia demanding that SOCAR pay some $29 million in penalties.

Although Transneft has put forward the concept of using the Baku–Novorossiysk route as an MEP, the cost is estimated at anything up to $2 billion for a route that would be longer than the Baku–Supsa line but would still only carry Caspian oil to a Black Sea terminal and not to a deep-water port such as Ceyhan. In addition, because it transited Russia (and bearing in mind the problems and delays encountered by the CPC in developing its pipeline across Russia), it is highly unlikely that the international oil companies would secure the same degree of control over the line as they have managed to secure in both Azerbaijan and Georgia for the Baku–Supsa early oil line.

Iranian swaps and proposals for a Kazakhstan–Turkmenistan–Iran oil pipeline

Iran is now making a major effort to become a transit route for Caspian oil exports. A realistic programme of limited pipeline construction and an imaginative use of swap arrangements should eventually ensure a steady flow of oil from Kazakhstan and Turkmenistan, and perhaps from Azerbaijan as well. However, the scale of such flows remains uncertain. At the same time, Kazakh-

---

[47] In Dec. 1999, when a landslide damaged the Baku–Supsa line, the AIOC was reported to have pumped some 75 000 b/d along the Novorossiysk line for a 2-week period, but this was when the Chechen section of the line was out of action and when rail transport was being used to bypass the breakaway republic. *Platt's Commodity News*, 3 Dec. 1999.

stan is now seriously looking at the prospects for constructing an oil pipeline to link Kazakhstan, Turkmenistan and Iran.

Several factors appear to favour the eventual development of a coherent system of oil swaps and pipeline deliveries that would ensure a substantial flow of Caspian oil (or Iranian oil swapped for Caspian oil) into Asian markets. First, the government of President Mohammad Khatami in Iran is lobbying hard for a large-scale swap system that would eventually take Kazakh and Turkmen crude to the Gulf by means of at least one reversed pipeline across Iran. Second, Iran is actually building a new line which would be a major element of any hybrid scheme to transport Caspian exports to the south on a large scale. Third, in December 2000 the Kazakh Foreign Ministry announced that it had held talks with three leading international oil companies during which it had asked them to conduct a feasibility study for the KTI oil pipeline project.[48] Fourth, China may become a more important player than expected if plans for major Caspian exports to Iran, or via Iran to Asian markets, gather speed.

The structure currently envisaged by the Iranian Ministry of Oil and Gas is based on an initial period of swaps, with Kazakh and Turkmen oil imports serving Tehran and other north Iranian cities. Despite low oil prices, Iran demonstrated its commitment to such a programme in January 1999 with the award of a $350 million contract to an Iranian company, Mapna, to build a new 325-km oil pipeline from the Caspian port of Neka to the refinery serving Tehran. However, financial problems delayed the start of actual construction work until October 2000. There seems to have been an assumption when the project was originally tendered that foreign investment funds would be available. Iran's apparent reliance on external funding for such a basic project indicated that in 1999 it could not afford to finance such a scheme out of its own resources, in contrast to the situation in 1995–97 when it paid for the $200 million gas line from Korpedze in Turkmenistan to Kurt-Kui in Iran (the KKK line) without recourse to foreign funding.

Under the Iranian proposals crude oil from Iran's Caspian neighbours would be tankered across the Caspian to Neka, piped to Tehran, and then used either in Tehran or in one of Iran's other three central or northern refineries, at Isfahan, Arak and Tabriz. Iran would pay for the oil in kind, handing over its own crude at Gulf terminals, notably Kharg Island, for export on behalf of the Caspian suppliers. Iran envisages this as the first stage of a programme which would then be expanded by means of a second, 350 000 b/d-capacity line from the Caspian to Tehran, although perhaps starting from another Caspian port such as Bandar Anzali.

Although the Iranians themselves generally accept that there is a limit of approximately 700 000 b/d on the capacity of northern Iran to absorb Caspian supplies, some Iranian officials have talked of as much as 810 000 b/d being brought to northern Iran for local use by means of coastal pipelines to the Tehran area. This figure appears to be a reflection of the potential capacity of

[48] Reuters (Astana), 'Kazakhs in talks to develop oil pipeline to Iran', 6 Dec. 2001.

the Neka–Tehran line now under construction, the proposed new line from the Caspian to the capital, and an existing line from Neka to Tehran, which has a nominal capacity of approximately 100 000 b/d but is apparently limited to 40 000 b/d along some stretches.

Looking beyond this, Iran has pondered the option of a direct oil pipeline connection with Kazakhstan and Turkmenistan, with direct transport of this oil to the Gulf being effected by reversing one of the two pipelines currently used to carry Caspian crude inland (and uphill) from the Gulf to Tehran, one of which passes through Arak and the other through Isfahan. Were both the Gulf–Tehran pipelines to be reversed (an idea mulled over by some Western analysts, but unlikely to find favour with Tehran because it might change Iranians' perceptions of their country's energy security), the Iranians estimate that their country could serve as the end-user for up to 810 000 b/d of Caspian crude and as a direct transit system for a further 810 000 b/d.[49]

The step-by-step nature of this project is one of its greatest assets. Because it can be developed in phases, it limits initial costs while also enabling those costs to be recovered quickly. However, it should be noted that previous swap arrangements with Kazakhstan have promised much more than they have actually delivered, partly because the Iranians themselves appeared to have doubts about one agreement they signed and partly because of quality problems concerning the input of Kazak crude into Iranian refineries.

The Neka–Tehran pipeline should also serve some Azerbaijani exports, but while Azerbaijan does already export some oil to Iran (mainly in the form of refined product) the opening of the Baku–Supsa line in 1999 means that its pressures are not quite so great. France's Total has occasionally proposed a pipeline to carry Azerbaijani crude direct to the Tabriz refinery, while in the summer of 2000 Iran also proposed development of a direct oil pipeline from Azerbaijan to Iran.

As long as the Iranians and their suppliers are able to implement this step-by-step approach smoothly, there is a very real prospect of the eventual development of a full-scale oil pipeline system extending from the Kazakhstan oilfields of the north-western Caspian to the Gulf.

The Kazakhstan–China oil pipeline

In 1997 the China National Petroleum Corporation (CNPC) signed an agreement with Kazakhstan which committed it to various projects including an oil pipeline eastwards from the Uzen oilfield on the Caspian to China. This was an initiative which owed much to China's own need for external oil supplies and, in effect, constituted a reserve addition scheme by the CNPC. It may also have reflected a growing worry in Beijing concerning the prospects for development of the Tarim Basin in Xinjiang. In these circumstances the scheme must be

---

[49] The Iranian swap option was presented in some detail by the Deputy Minister for Oil and Gas, Ali Majedi, at the Adam Smith Institute's Pipeline Conference in Vienna in Mar. 2000. Similar presentations have been made at subsequent international conferences, most notably by senior Iranian officials attending the World Economic Forum's Eurasia Economic Summit meeting in Almaty in Apr. 2000.

taken very seriously indeed. Actual construction is not likely to start for several years, and by that time it is possible that an alternative system for delivering Kazakh crude oil to Chinese markets may be operational.

The confirmed discovery of large volumes of oil at Kashagan in 2000 naturally prompted some changes in Chinese and Kazakh thinking concerning this project, but these were relatively straightforward and do not as yet appear to have had a significant impact on the way in which officials of the two countries and their respective state oil concerns view the projected pipeline. Originally it was to have started at Atyrau. It would then pass through Kenkiyak and Kumkol to reach the Karakoin station of the existing Omsk–Chardzhou pipeline. From there it would run north of Lake Balkhash to cross the border between Kazakhstan and China near the town of Druzhba. Since the discoveries at Kashagan, it appears that the Kazakhs, at least, view the proposed line as an export system for oil from their giant offshore field, and there is no real reason for the Chinese to differ from this point of view.

The total length of the pipeline in Kazakhstan would be 2600–2900 km, depending on the final route chosen downstream of Karakoin. In 1998 two alternatives were under discussion—construction of a new line on the most direct alignment from Karakoin to Druzhba, and reversal of the 427 km-long Atasu–Karakoin section of the existing Omsk–Chardzhou pipeline, with new line construction in this area starting at Atasu.

Nominal capacity appears to have been set at 20 mt/y, the throughput guaranteed by the CNPC. This was mentioned in the original 1997 discussions, in further talks in 1998 and again in a Kazakh statement in October 2000. In conducting its promised feasibility study, the CNPC will find itself confronting some very complex questions that throw doubt on the project—at least as long as it remains focused on construction of such a limited-capacity line.

There are four interrelated issues which will determine the viability of the project: (a) the length of the line in practice—in other words, taking into account its extension into China itself; (b) the volume of throughput required to make a success of the line throughout its length (if normal commercial considerations predominate); (c) the volumes of oil available in Kazakhstan to fill the line; and (d) the question whether the Chinese Government and the CNPC will take a strictly (or at least predominantly) commercial approach to their evaluation of the project.

A 20 mt/y-line appears to be far too small to be economic. Commercial economic considerations would be expected to require the construction of a line with considerably greater capacity, probably of 45–50 mt/y. This is largely because the length of the line on which the two countries are negotiating in fact only represents about half of the system that would actually have to be built, since China's requirement is for oil to serve its industrial areas possibly as far away as its main oil markets on or near its eastern and southern coasts.

It should be noted, however, that there are potential non-commercial reasons why both countries may be prepared to pursue the project with this capacity even if they are not necessarily assured of a commercial rate of return. Energy security is a potentially important consideration for both that could prompt them to require less than full commercial viability. The Kazakh authorities are particularly keen on the project because it includes the construction of an internal West–East oil pipeline link which would bring oil from Kazakhstan's westerly Caspian or near-Caspian fields to the industrial east. This would enable the country to reduce its dependence on energy imported from or via Russia. Germany's ILF Consulting Engineers, together with KazNipiNeft, in 1995 carried out a feasibility study for a domestic pipeline from Atyrau via Kenkiyak to Karakoin, with ILF coming to the conclusion that it made best sense if it was part of a larger pipeline system connecting to China.

For its part, the Chinese Government may be prepared to adopt a less than fully commercial approach to the project because it has the potential to yield a sustained supply of crude oil which does not have to transit any third country. Even so, the question how much oil Kazakhstan will be able to supply to fill the line remains crucial.

Whether the projected Kazakhstan–China oil pipeline is implemented will depend, *inter alia*, on whether the next few years witness a further acceleration of the commercialization of CNPC thinking, or whether Chinese Government concerns about energy security in an era when it is a net oil importer continue to dominate its strategic thinking. Security concerns on the part of producers and the need for high-quality oil could provide an opportunity for Russian and/or Caspian exports, since oil from the Middle East, the most obvious alternative, tends to be heavier and more sour than Caspian oil. The absence of intervening transit states and the promise of finance from a credible, creditworthy partner, the CNPC, should aid the project.

If commercial thinking predominates in an atmosphere in which there is still concern about energy security, the CNPC might start considering the development of export systems via Iran. If pure commercial thinking does triumph, one element worth bearing in mind is that CNPC officials in 1998 expressed their willingness to cooperate with Turkmenistan on an oil line down the Caspian coast to Iran. On the one hand, this could provide an opening for Turkmenistan to pursue possible oil sales eastwards along the proposed Kazakhstan–China oil pipeline. On the other hand, the development of a coastal line constitutes, in effect, full or partial construction of the KTI line that was discussed by the Kazakh Government and leading Western oil companies in December 2000. If such a line were built soon, and if the Iranian swap option worked smoothly, Kazakh oil would reach Far Eastern markets, including China, by a much cheaper route than the proposed Kazakhstan–China pipeline.

Once again, the fate of one proposed pipeline project remains intimately bound up with the fate of another.

Gas pipelines

The question how best to secure gas exports from the Caspian region to the outside world depends on the interplay between a number of complex factors concerning the start, middle and end of the energy chain.

The factors are the following. From a supply perspective, there is the willingness of Turkmenistan, the country with the greatest reserve potential, to create a satisfactory business environment that would encourage major gas projects rather than discourage investors. From a transit perspective, there are the willingness of Russia's Gazprom and its Itera associate to use its existing network to facilitate gas exports at commercial rates, and the ability of Turkmenistan to cooperate with its neighbours, notably Azerbaijan and Iran, in developing transit routes. Finally, from a demand perspective, there are the short- to medium-term requirements of Turkey and the long-term demands of the global gas market.

Existing gas pipelines

At present, the following gas pipelines are in existence.

1. *The Gazprom system.* This is the Soviet-era main gas line system which connects Turkmenistan, Uzbekistan and Kazakhstan with Russia, and, beyond Russia, with an array of markets from the new states of the Caucasus to Ukraine, Central Europe and beyond.

2. *The trans-Balkan line.* This connects the old Soviet system with Turkey via Romania and Bulgaria and is the main route for current Turkish imports of Russian gas. A major expansion of this line, initially intended to increase capacity from 6 bcm/y to 10 bcm/y, was completed in the final months of 2000, with officials from GazExport, a Gazprom subsidiary, saying in late 2000 that as of early January 2001 the line's capacity would 14 bcm/y.[50]

3. *Korpedze–Kurt-Kui.* The 200-km KKK line was built by Iran in 1997 to link the Turkmen gas fields around Korpedze, on the eastern shore of the Caspian, with the Iranian gas distribution system at Kurt-Kui. Its capacity is approximately 10–12 bcm/y but deliveries to date have not exceeded 3 bcm/y.

4. *Tabriz–Erzurum.* This is a new line intended to carry Iranian gas to Turkey from the north-eastern Iranian city of Tabriz to the eastern Turkish city of Erzurum. The 272-km Iranian section has been completed and the line is due to enter service in July 2001 with completion of the 302-km Turkish section. Connections from Erzurum onwards are under construction.

Under construction are the following:

1. *Blue Stream.* This line, from Izobil'noye in southern Russia to Ankara via a sub-sea pipeline across the Black Sea from Dzhubga to Samsun, is progressing so well that Russian Prime Minister Mikhail Kasyanov declared in October 2000 that first deliveries of gas through the line could take place as early as the

---

[50] 'Turkey set for massive rise in gas imports', *East European Energy Report*, issue 110 (Nov. 2000).

autumn of 2001.[51] Blue Stream is the most important of the current gas line projects. The first phase, currently under way, requires laying an 8 bcm/y-capacity pipe at depths of up to 2150 m for approximately 384 km across the Black Sea. A second line will then be laid along a roughly parallel course. A third line has occasionally been discussed. The sub-sea section of the line is costed at approximately $1.7 billion, with financing coming, *inter alia*, from Italy's SACE and a variety of other export credit agencies.

2. *Erzurum to Ankara and Konya*. Turkish companies are currently building a set of lines which will connect the eastern city of Erzurum with both Ankara and Konya in south-central Turkey. This system was originally intended to bring Iranian gas to central, southern and western Turkey but, with active plans for an line to bring Azerbaijani gas to Turkey, Turkish officials during most of 2000 envisaged using it primarily for the transport of gas from Azerbaijan.

Under consideration are:

1. *Baku–Erzurum*. BP has begun engineering studies for a system that would use existing gas lines in Azerbaijan and eastern Georgia, together with some new construction in Georgia and Turkey, to carry Azerbaijani gas to Turkey by early 2003, or even late 2002. This is an ambitious target, but the project is being pursued very seriously indeed.

2. *The Trans-Caspian Gas Pipeline* (TCG1). This is intended to carry some 16 bcm/y of Turkmen gas to Turkey and a further 14 bcm/y through Turkey to markets in Southern and Central Europe, and would involve a sub-sea crossing of the Caspian and transit across Azerbaijan and Georgia to Erzurum in eastern Turkey. It was under very active consideration for much of 1998 and 1999, but in 2000 one of its principal backers signalled its inability to pursue the project in the face of the somewhat erratic attitudes towards major project development of Turkmenistan's President Niyazov. The project is not dead but is most certainly dormant.

3. *The trans-Iranian gas pipeline*. Proposals for a major gas line to carry Turkmen gas to Turkey and Europe via Iran were under active consideration in the early 1990s and, indeed, President Niyazov somewhat prematurely held a ceremony in 1994 which supposedly marked the start of construction of the line. In fact, nothing has yet been built unless the KKK line is considered part of a larger line (which it could well become in the future). At present, both Shell and Total are considering the possibility of such a line. However, for Shell, which is perhaps the better placed of the two because it also has an agreement covering gas field development within Turkmenistan, it is just one option of three, the others being the TCGP (in which it is now the sole active partner) and improved connections via Russia and the Gazprom network.

4. *The trans-Afghan gas pipeline*. The development of a gas export system to serve not only Turkmenistan but Uzbekistan and Kazakhstan as well, and with its core section running from Chardzhou in Turkmenistan to Pakistan's Sui gas

---

[51] 'Turkey set for massive rise in gas imports' (note 50).

fields, was pursued with vigour by Unocal in the mid-1990s, but in 1997, acknowledging the problems of building such a line in the face of continued turmoil in Afghanistan and against the wishes of the US Government, Unocal pulled out. Its junior partner of that era, the Saudi-backed Delta Oil group, remains committed to the project, while the UN also sees such a line as one of the few prospects for weaning Afghanistan's economy off its dependence on drug exports.

5. *A gas line to China and Japan.* Although Mitsubishi and subsequently the US company Exxon have for some years been considering a gas line from Turkmenistan across Kazakhstan and China to the Yellow Sea, this is not likely to be realized until about the year 2010. The project was first broached by Mitsubishi in talks with the CNPC and the Kazakh and Turkmen authorities in the early 1990s. This led to a protocol between China and Turkmenistan stating their intention to build a 6000-km pipeline to the eastern coast of China, with onward facilities to take gas to Japan. In 1995 Exxon, which is developing fields in Xinjiang in western China, joined forces with Mitsubishi to begin a feasibility study. One key question that will have to be addressed is the cost of either constructing a liquefaction plant on the Chinese coast—Lianyungang is mentioned as a site—and acquiring a tanker fleet to ferry the gas as liquefied natural gas (LNG) to Japan, or constructing a further 900-km undersea link. Overall project costs are currently put at approximately $12 billion.

In terms of customer requirements in the Caspian gas context, the role of Turkey is crucial, simply because it is the nearest major market in need of gas and, for geopolitical considerations, is particularly well disposed to purchasing its gas from the Caspian states. Turkey's demand for natural gas is increasing rapidly. It stood at just 2.9 bcm/y in 1989 but had risen to 12.0 bcm/y in 1999. The Turkish Government and Botas, the state pipeline company, have produced estimates that demand could reach 27 bcm in 2010 and 50 bcm in 2015.

As for the Far East, the Chinese market alone is expected to double or even triple between 1995 (when it was 16.7 bcm/y) and 2010. Although Asia continues to consume large volumes of fuel oil (currently comprising 24 per cent of total oil demand), this will decline with continued conversion to natural gas. The share of fuel oil in total demand is projected to drop to 18 per cent by 2010. The World Bank has estimated that gas from Central Asia could be piped the 6000 km to China at a cost of some $106 per thousand cubic metres, as long as volumes of approximately 27–28 bcm/y are envisaged. This would compete with domestic coal prices of $120 per thousand cubic metres of gas equivalent. For Japan, however, the cost would be considerably higher in view of the need to transport Central Asian gas across the Yellow Sea as LNG or under it by pipe.

The International Energy Agency (IEA) argued in 1998 that Japan's interest in Central Asian gas supplied via China 'is probably more an expression of long-term thinking about security of supply rather than a declaration of intent to support such a project in the near future'.[52] It added that importing Russian gas via a regional centre such as Irkutsk was probably a more economic long-term option.

III. The Caspian Sea legal regime

As of early 2001, it looks very much as if all five Caspian littoral states are beginning to move steadily in the direction of a solution to the vexed question of the status of the Caspian. The issue is often presented as a need to agree on whether the Caspian is a sea—which can therefore be partitioned—or a lake, which should be shared by the littoral states. In fact, the question whether it is a sea or a lake has relatively little bearing on the underlying questions whether or not the Caspian's hydrocarbon resources are to be partitioned up between the five littoral countries and, if so, how that division should be effected.[53] All five countries now openly favour partition of at least the sub-sea resources—in other words, its known or presumed oil and gas reserves—but substantial disagreement remains on how to put that division into effect. There also appears to be general agreement that some kind of common regime needs to be established for the sea itself to protect fisheries (notably the caviar-bearing sturgeon) and to ensure a reversal of severe environmental degradation.[54]

Azerbaijan and Kazakhstan, spurred on by the prospect of discoveries of hydrocarbons close to their coastlines (or in what they term their national sectors), have long favoured the principle of partition. Turkmenistan, which had hitherto favoured common development of resources in most of the sea (all the countries have acted as if they own at least a 12-mile coastal zone), in 1997 began considering the prospect of partition. Russia, buoyed by the discovery of oil at the Severny field off the Dagestan coast, has likewise moved away from a concept of common development to one of outright division, as has Iran. But the five states are not necessarily in agreement with each other on how any partition should be effected.

Russia has made two key proposals in this regard. On the one hand, it has pushed for a division of sub-sea resources rather than of the sea itself; on the other, it has argued for this partition to be effected on the basis of what it terms a 'modified median line'. In doing so, Russia has dropped its 1997 proposal for national sectors extending out as far as 45 miles into the Caspian, with all resources lying beyond such a line to be developed on behalf of all five states, in favour of the extension of national sectors that would together cover the whole of the sea. (Although the absence of a general agreement on the partition

---

[52] International Energy Agency, 'Caspian oil and gas: the supply potential of Central Asia and TransCaucasia', Paris, May 1998.

[53] At its simplest, the argument is that, since the Caspian has no outlet to the rest of the world's seas, it is technically a lake, albeit one of enormous size. If it is a lake, the question then arises whether it can be partitioned. This is not common practice, but it has occurred in the Great Lakes of both North America and Central Africa.

[54] On the fisheries and environmental aspects, see chapter 4 in this volume.

of the Caspian's sub-sea resources makes it incorrect to talk about individual national sectors of the sea, such language is common in all five littoral states.)[55]

The modified median line controversy

The first proposal has secured widespread backing in the region because it makes practical sense—there really is a need to develop a common regime for handling actual maritime issues of the Caspian Sea—but the second is more controversial. The use of a median line—a line running at an equal distance from the acknowledged coastal baselines of the states in question—is increasingly becoming the most common way of settling maritime boundary disputes. By a modified median line, Russia is saying that it favours the principle of equidistance in principle but that in practice, where a field has already been developed by a country or where a field found by one country spills over the median line and into waters which might be held to belong to another state, the line should be modified to keep the field intact.

Kazakhstan and Russia both appear prepared to determine their maritime, or rather sub-sea, boundaries on this basis, and in January 2001 President Aliyev of Azerbaijan similarly endorsed the proposal.[56] Turkmenistan has not yet signalled a formal response to Russian initiatives aimed at securing a general Caspian agreement on the basis of modified median lines, while Iranian statements on the Caspian run directly counter to this idea.

Turkmenistan's position is relatively straightforward: before it commits itself to any general settlement it wants to know just where the dividing line will be between its own waters—or, rather, the sub-sea reserves under those waters—and those of Azerbaijan. In this context the problem is that Azerbaijan's historical legacy as the centre for the old Soviet oil industry in the Caspian led to oil exploration and attempts by the Government of Azerbaijan to get concessions in waters lying beyond any likely median line. One such field, called Serdar by Turkmenistan and Kyapaz by Azerbaijan, is disputed by the two countries. Turkmenistan also disputes Azerbaijan's right to include all or part of the Azerbaijani field (and sometimes the Chirag field as well) in its major 1994 agreement with the AIOC for development of the unitized ACG complex. In January 2000 SOCAR reported that Turkmenistan had warned the AIOC that it had no legal right to develop the Azerbaijani and Chirag fields.[57] Despite a major three-year effort by the US Government to get Azerbaijan and Turkmenistan to resolve their boundary issue (and ensure the smooth development of the TCGP project), the two countries are still at odds over this issue.

[55] It would, of course, still be incorrect to talk of national sectors of the Caspian Sea if any actual partition agreement were in strict fact to relate solely to the seabed and to whatever lies underneath the seabed. However, to take such a line might be deemed too pedantic.

[56] ITAR-TASS, 9 Jan. 2001, in 'Russia, Azerbaijan issue statement on need for consensus on carving up Caspian', Foreign Broadcast Information Service, Daily Report–Central Eurasia (FBIS-SOV), FBIS-SOV-2001-0109, 9 Jan. 2001.

[57] 'Regional pipelines: TCP talks enter crucial phase', Middle East Energy Report, issue 57 (2 Feb. 2000).

Iran changes tack

Iran has on the one hand changed its policy dramatically while on the other hand it is holding out for a settlement that would require substantial modification to likely median lines.

Iran was the last supporter of the concept of joint development along condominium lines of the bulk of the Caspian's offshore hydrocarbon resources. It then moved towards a position that favoured the equal division of the Caspian's sub-sea resources, with each state securing exactly 20 per cent of the seabed. However, in March 2000 Deputy Foreign Minister Morteza Sarmadi declared that Iran would back any partition to which the other four states might agree— as long as Iran secured a 20 per cent stake at the southern end of the sea. His comments came just four days after Kazakh Foreign Minister Yerlan Idrisov said in Astana that five-party talks on the Caspian had not yielded 'much of a breakthrough' and that Iran had not responded to Kazakh questions concerning Iran's views on how an equal 20 per cent division might be effected.[58]

While Sarmadi's comments opened up the possibility of a general agreement on how to approach the Caspian Sea question, they continued to muddy the waters concerning the specific bilateral boundary agreements that are necessary to put a five-party accord into effect. The reason is that on normal median line principles Iran can expect to secure no more than 15–16 per cent of the sea. This is more than the 12 per cent of the sea which lies south of a straight line drawn between its two most northerly positions on the Caspian's east and west coasts, Astara and Gasankoff, but is still far short of 20 per cent. The logical assumption is that Iran is simply pressing a maximal demand and that it will settle for less. However, simply by presenting a claim for 20 per cent, Iran is ensuring that negotiations with both Azerbaijan and Turkmenistan for bilateral sub-sea boundary lines are likely to prove extremely tense, since any expansion of de facto Iranian waters would be at their expense. As noted above, Azerbaijan and Turkmenistan are already in dispute over where their common boundary might run.

The same seems to be true of Kazakhstan and Russia. When Russia's Special Envoy for Caspian Sea Affairs, Deputy Foreign Minister Viktor Kalyuzhny, visited Baku in July 2000, he was reported as saying that Kazakhstan and Russia were disputing the ownership of four fields. In further talks in Baku in January 2001 the heads of state of both Russia and Azerbaijan sought to stress the prospects for resolution of this dispute, notably by saying that they endorsed a call by Turkmenistan's President Niyazov for a summit meeting to be held in late February or in March 2001 to resolve the issue of the Caspian's status.[59] The presidential talks in Baku also signalled a further change in Russia's position. In July Kalyuzhny had proposed to Natiq Aliyev, President of SOCAR, that the Caspian littoral states should jointly develop oil and gas deposits whose ownership was disputed. Turan, the Azerbaijani news agency, reported that he

[58] 'Tehran changes tack on the Caspian', *Middle East Energy Report*, issue 60 (13 Mar. 2000).
[59] 'Russia, Azerbaijan issue statement on need for consensus on carving up Caspian' (note 56).

specifically mentioned the Kyapaz/Serdar field. Azerbaijan rejected this proposal.

The joint statement signed on 9 January 2001 by Russian President Vladimir Putin and President Aliyev of Azerbaijan recorded agreement on the principle of the modified median line, with the waters of the Caspian remaining available for common use. However, the statement then said that each littoral state would have exclusive rights to the mineral resources in its sector of the sea. This phrasing was taken as meaning that Russia had abandoned its July 2000 approach.[60]

IV. The Turkish Straits issue

One common problem confronting any oil pipeline terminating on the Black Sea coast is the onward transmission of oil. The Turkish Straits are narrow, the Bosporus having four major bends in just 30 km and being just 700 metres wide at the Kandili narrows. In addition the Straits are crowded with thousands of small boats crossing between the European and Asian shores each day. As well as being a thoroughfare for traffic heading into or out of the Black Sea, they are thus also a hive of shore to-shore activity. The Straits are capacity-constrained, although just what the technical upper limits on safe transit of oil tankers might be remains a matter of dispute. Two factors need to be considered: (*a*) the size of vessels using the Straits; and (*b*) their handling.

Most tanker traffic through the Straits has in recent years consisted of fairly small (by global standards) vessels of between 5000 and 10 000 tonnes. The Straits could handle vessels of up to 100 000 tonnes, or indeed up to 150 000 tonnes as long as they do not draw more than 18 metres of water. Travelling individually through the most problematic section of the Straits—the Bosporus—Turkish pilots allow 2 hours and 40 minutes for a large tanker (any vessel of 10 000 tonnes or more) to travel from the Black Sea to the Sea of Marmara or vice versa. If a strict convoy system were operated, with perhaps a 15- or 20-minute interval between tankers, throughput would no doubt be vastly increased, but it would add to Turkey's very real fears of another incident like the collision between a freighter and an oil tanker which killed 29 seamen in 1994. The danger of a fire in the confined waters of the Bosporus and of it spreading to the Old City of Istanbul or to the historic wooden mansions along the shore remains very real to most citizens of Istanbul.

In addition, the 1936 Convention Regarding the Regime of the Straits (the Montreux Convention) specifies that passage through the Straits shall be without taxes or charges and 'without formalities', which means that any measures to regulate traffic which the Turkish authorities might seek to introduce can be challenged. A traffic-calming scheme introduced by Turkey in 1994 seems to have worked, in that ships passing the Straits obey it, but a

[60] 'Putin, Aliyev narrow differences on Caspian division', *Eurasianet Turkmenistan Daily Digest*, 10 Jan. 2001, URL <http://www.eurasianet.org/resource/turkmenistan/hypermail/news/0008.html>.

strong legal challenge can be made if Turkey seeks to restrict passage on safety grounds. Thus the handling of vessels using the Straits requires consensus.

After contracting hugely after the breakup of the Soviet Union, traffic through the Straits is now increasing again. The IEA has noted that it was 60 mt/y in the late 1980s and early 1990s, but had slipped to 37.5 mt/y in 1991/92.[61] The latter figure is still commonly cited by Turkish officials as their baseline for Bosporus transit oil traffic although, as the IEA further noted, in 1995 such traffic through the Turkish Straits had recovered to between 60 and 70 mt/y.

The IEA/Energy Charter team estimate the maximum capacity of the Turkish Straits at 75–90 mt/y. This figure is probably too low: the introduction of a convoy system and the replacement of small tankers with medium-sized vessels of up to 100 000 b/d could increase capacity somewhat. However, the underlying point is sound: the Turkish Straits cannot be expected to cope with the kind of volumes that will probably require passage out of the Black Sea by 2010 or indeed, if the IEA's capacity estimates are correct, in 2005. Moreover, while large tankers are more efficient, they also bring with them much greater consequences should something go wrong.

In 2010 oil flows from the new Caspian states and Russia are expected to reach between 140 and 195 mt/y. The recent Kashagan discovery makes the larger estimate probable, and this in turn implies an increase in Caspian inflows of approximately 135 mt/y over Soviet peak levels and of 157.5 mt/y over the post-Soviet levels commonly used by Turkey as its baseline for Bosporus traffic.

Such figures are, of course, the prime justification for the proposed Baku–Ceyhan pipeline or for any of the other 'Bosporus bypass' schemes. Apart from the Baku–Ceyhan line, however, these projects all have one significant weakness: they are posited on the piping of oil to one shore of the Black Sea and its carriage by tanker across the Black Sea before the oil is once again pumped onshore and carried by pipe to its next destination. This flaw affects such proposals as the proposed line from Burgos in Bulgaria to Alexandroupolis in northern Greece; the proposals for lines through the Balkans to Vlorë in Albania or Trieste in Italy; and purely internal Turkish lines such as a planned bypass across Thrace from Kiyikoy to Ibrikbana.

All these projects either have serious backers or have been seriously studied at one time or another. They are made viable because of the Turkish Straits problem, but were that to disappear, or to be seen to be about to disappear, with the start of work on a Baku–Ceyhan line, the *raison d'être* for these Bosporus bypasses would disappear. At the same time, if the Baku–Ceyhan line were to secure financing and be given a definite green light, then the prospects that Turkey would adopt a reasonably flexible attitude to the issue of oil traffic through the Turkish Straits in the interim would be vastly improved.

[61] International Energy Agency and the International Energy Charter Secretariat, 'Black Sea oil and gas', Paris, 2000.

4. The Caspian Sea: threats to its biological resources and environmental security

Igor Zonn

I. Introduction

The Caspian Sea is the world's largest inland sea. Physiographically it is unique. It is the most productive body of water in the world[1] and the only one that preserves the geno-fund of the sturgeon, the source of almost all the black caviar produced. About 10 million people live around the Caspian Sea and the occupations of many of them are connected with the sea, and first of all with fishing. By virtue of its oil and gas potential the Caspian has a place among the major world centres of hydrocarbon production. The rivers of the largest water catchment area in the world discharge into it from the industrial and production regions of the littoral states. This fact accounts for the periodic fluctuations of the sea level and for the nature and scale of pollution of the sea.

As for the water body itself, there has always been a conflict between the use of its principal natural resources—biological resources (fishing of valuable fish species, first and foremost the sturgeon)—and the exploitation of hydrocarbons (the development of shelf and offshore oil and gas fields). This conflict has become especially acute since the breakup of the Soviet Union, as a result of which the legal status of the Caspian Sea changed, regulation of the exploitation of the sea's resources has broken down, and the geopolitical interests of five different states conflict. These interests are those connected with military and political security, with shipping, with the exploitation of biological and mineral resources, and with environmental security. The newly independent states in the Caspian region link their prospects of socio-economic development with the implementation of hydrocarbon projects financed by other major countries.

Hydrocarbons can be considered both a direct and an indirect source of many environmental problems in the region, but also as a means, and sometimes the only means, of solving those problems. The existing and planned exploitation of the hydrocarbon resources in the Caspian is fraught with risk to the integrity of its ecosystem, and this risk is multiplied many times because the Caspian is an inland sea. Threats to the natural environment include fluctuations in the sea level, surge effects, the increasing salinity of groundwater, industrial pollution, loss of biodiversity and other factors.

Trans-border environmental problems could give rise to conflicts here. They include a sharp reduction in and deterioration in the quality of commercial fish

[1] Measured as the quantity of all animals and other living organisms living in the sea per volume of water. The productivity of the Caspian Sea is 1.2 tonnes per km^3.

stocks, particularly sturgeon; water pollution from land, coastal and marine sources; accidents at coastal plants and accidents in the course of the extraction and transport of oil and gas in and across the sea; cross-border air pollution, including emissions from gas condensate plants; and the environmental consequences of military action.

The crisis and even impending catastrophe that are becoming visible in the Caspian ecosystem are reminiscent of the environmental problems in the nearby Aral Sea and have aroused great anxiety all over the world. The suggested division of the Caspian Sea into national sectors and uncontrolled development of its hydrocarbon resources could make matters worse.

Hitherto in the system of national interests of the Caspian littoral states—in the first place Azerbaijan, Kazakhstan and Turkmenistan—the environmental importance of the territories under their control has been somewhere in the background. Their deliberate overstating of their hydrocarbon resources and of the profits to be expected from their exploitation, and the struggles over rights to ownership of the energy potential and the right to determine the future routes for the transport of hydrocarbons to the world market, have contributed to the neglect of environmental issues. This makes it very difficult and at times even impossible to formulate a coordinated regional policy in the field of nature conservation and rational management of the resources of the sea.

Control over international projects to develop the hydrocarbon resources will also be especially significant for the improvement of the environmental situation in the Caspian region. National and international environmental security will require a system of coordinated state and interstate mechanisms, actions and guarantees based on each and every state observing general principles and norms of international law to guarantee the efficient solution or elimination of environmental problems of regional or global significance.

II. Threats to the Caspian's biological resources

Throughout its history the Caspian Sea has been a very important source of biological resources. They make up a single ecosystem and are the result of the interplay of many natural and man-made factors—the flow of fresh water into the sea, the hydrological and hydro-chemical regimes[2] of the sea, feeding productivity,[3] natural and artificial reproduction of fish, the toxicological situation and fishing in the region.

The Caspian is important as a region for the seasonal migration, moulting and hibernation of birds which fly there from almost the whole territory of the former Soviet Union and from the Mediterranean. Roughly 10–12 million birds find a temporary habitat in the region on their annual migrations. About 3–3.5 million birds winter on the Caspian, settling in wetlands on river deltas. Most of these wetlands are nature reserves and included in the list of wetlands

---

[2] A hydro-chemical regime is defined as changes in the chemical composition of water in a water body over time.
[3] Feeding productivity is defined as the amount of biogenic elements consumed by fish.

of international importance under the Ramsar Convention of 1971.[4] The Caspian also preserves the only marine mammal of northern origin, the Caspian seal (*Phoco caspica*). It has been hunted since ancient times. In recent decades the population of the Caspian seal has been in a poor state because of a reproduction crisis: according to recent estimates the population is now only 420 000 head. It is no accident that in 1996 the World Conservation Union named the Caspian seal as being a vulnerable species.[5] However, the most important of the Caspian's biological resources is its fish stocks—about 123 fish species and subspecies. Their composition has been determined by the historical evolution of the sea: isolated from the other oceans of the world, it incorporates species originating in both the north and the south (the Mediterranean).

Intensive solar radiation and a rich inflow of biogenic elements have contributed to the high productivity of the Caspian. Total fish resources in the Caspian Sea are estimated at 2 900 000 tons. Here are found purely marine species (53 species, accounting for 43.5 per cent of the total fish stocks of the sea), such as herring, sand smelt and bullhead; river species (42 species, or 34.4 per cent of Caspian fish stocks), such as pike, various kinds of carp, loach and so on; migratory fish (18 species, or 14.7 per cent), such as sturgeon and salmon; and anadromous fish (9 species, or 7.4 per cent), such as some kinds of carp, perch and sheatfish.[6] It is believed that the Caspian Sea is able to produce 500 000–590 000 tons of fish annually, provided no overfishing is allowed.

The Caspian is biologically unique because, together with the rivers that flow into it—first and foremost the Volga—it contains the world geno-fund of the sturgeon and is the world's only repository of a diversity of species of sturgeon. It includes six species and one subspecies—the great sturgeon, *Acipenser nudiventris* (the spiny sturgeon), the sterlet, the Russian sturgeon, the Persian sturgeon, the North Caspian stellate sturgeon, and the South Kura stellate sturgeon.[7] Until recently catches of sturgeon in the Caspian Sea accounted for up to 82 per cent of total world catches.

The fresh, shallow water in the northern Caspian is especially significant. The inflow of river water rich in food, uniquely favourable conditions for spawning and the growth of fry, and the limited role of carnivorous predators make the region a kind of kindergarten for the most valuable fish species. It is not accidental that in the 1970s an area of the Caspian Sea lying to the north of 44°12' N.L. was declared a nature reserve.

---

[4] World Conservation Monitoring Centre, *Directory of Wetlands of International Importance* (Ramsar Convention Bureau: Gland, 1990).

[5] The International Union for Conservation of Nature and Natural Resources/World Conservation Union defines as vulnerable those species that are 'facing a high risk of extinction in the wild in the medium-term future'. See the IUCN Internet site at URL <http://www.redlist.org>.

[6] Kaznacheev, Ye. N., *Ryby Kaspiyskogo Morya: Opredelitel'* [Fish of the Caspian Sea: determinant] (Russian Food Ministry: Moscow, 1981), p. 16.

[7] Ivanov, V. P., *Biologicheskiye Resursy Kaspiyskogo Morya* [Biological resources of the Caspian Sea] (Caspian Fishery Research Institute: Astrakhan, 2000), p. 12.

Table 4.1. Sturgeon catches in the Caspian Basin
Figures are in thousand tons.

Years	Russia	Kazakhstan	Azerbaijan	Turkmenistan	Iran	Total
1940	3.6	1.3	2.2	0.4	0.5	8.0
1950	11.0	0.1	2.4	–	0.8	14.3
1960	7.4	1.6	1.1	–	1.5	11.6
1970	10.7	5.2	0.2	–	2.5	18.6
1980	16.7	8.1	0.3	–	1.5	26.6
1990	11.7	1.9	0.1	–	2.6	16.3
1995	2.00	0.58	0.16[a]	0.18[a]	1.5	4.42
1997	1.14	0.48	0.13[a]	0.10[a]	1.5	3.35
1998	0.96	0.53	0.09[a]	0.06[a]	..	1.64

[a] Includes sturgeon quota catches in the Volga Delta.
– Nil or a negligible figure.
.. Data not available.

Source: Ivanov, V. P., *Biologicheskiye Resursy Kaspiyskogo Morya* [Biological resources of the Caspian Sea] (Caspian Fishery Research Institute: Astrakhan, 2000).

The sturgeon are valuable among other things for their caviar, an expensive delicacy in high demand on the world market. However, diminishing catches in the Caspian have led to a drop in caviar production. In 1989 the Soviet Union produced 1365.6 tons of black caviar and Iran 282 tons. By the late 1990s Russia produced only 40 tons per year, other new sovereign Caspian states (excluding Turkmenistan) 34.8 tons, and Iran about 150 tons. Already, even before full-scale production of hydrocarbons in the Caspian Basin has begun, the situation of the sturgeon in the Caspian Sea is catastrophic—so much so that some experts speak in terms of the Caspian losing its fishery significance.

The Caspian sturgeon has faced crisis more than once. In the late 19th and early 20th centuries, the sturgeon wealth of the Caspian was almost destroyed by overfishing. Only the regulation of fish catches by government decree helped to avoid catastrophe. Then in the mid-20th century, as a result of the construction of hydroelectric plants on practically all the rivers of the Caspian Basin, many natural spawning grounds were destroyed. That crisis was overcome by setting up a powerful system of fish farming of sturgeon, a complete ban on offshore fishing for sturgeon and the introduction of single fishing rules. The present crisis is connected with the breakup of the USSR and heavy pollution of the Caspian Sea. It is now practically impossible to regulate and control sturgeon fishing, and the new sovereign littoral states neglect mutually agreed quotas and scientific recommendations on fishing.

While diplomats and politicians discuss the problem of the division of the Caspian Sea, criminal structures—the 'sturgeon caviar mafia'—have already divided the coast between themselves irrespective of national borders, and as ordinary people are not concerned with high ideals but are trying to survive in difficult economic conditions, widespread non-regulated fishing, or poaching, has started not only in the rivers but in the sea as well. The poaching catches are 11 to 13 times higher than the scientifically validated catches.[8] Especially great are offshore catches. Poaching has become common in all the new Caspian littoral countries and even in Iran. As participants on a Cousteau Society Expedition observed: 'Given the equation: one sturgeon = one month of wages, poaching will be a vocation for many years to come'.[9]

At present over 90 per cent of the populations of the great sturgeon, white salmon and Caspian salmon, up to 27 per cent of the population of the Russian sturgeon and 53 per cent of the population of the stellate sturgeon are maintained by fish farming.[10] The main burden of the cost of maintaining the populations of the valuable fish species in the Caspian has always been and still is born by Russia. In 1999 alone the total release of sturgeon juveniles grown to a viable stage at fish farms in Russia was about 50–60 million.

Caviar is usually obtained from fish that were spawned and grown in a natural habitat. However, it is these that are caught first when they go to spawn in rivers where the major commercial catches are made. The populations of sturgeon of natural origin are therefore shrinking. Today the legal catches of Russian fishermen are insufficient even to provide fish farms with sturgeon species for getting caviar for fish farming and for commercial production of fish products and black caviar.

Pollution of the sea results in morphogenetic deviations in fish—changes in size, weight and age parameters—and morphological, physiological and bio-chemical anomalies. Under the cumulative effect of constant long-term pollution the sturgeon develop a degradation in muscular tissue called myopathy and total desorption of caviar. In the early 1990s these were demonstrated in 60 per cent of sturgeon. Moreover, through the food chain toxic matters can reach the human organism, damage its genetic system and, in the final run, cause hereditable disease and cancer.

In the light of this, and in spite of quotas on sturgeon catches being established in the littoral countries, the problem of the rational management of sturgeon in the Caspian basin is becoming the problem of the maintenance and reproduction of sturgeon resources, including its species composition.

As the legal status of the Caspian Sea still remains unresolved, no agreement on the preservation and use of the Caspian's bio-resources has as yet been signed. The critical condition of the sturgeon makes it urgent for Russia to suggest a tentative moratorium on sturgeon fishing, a simultaneous increase in the scale of fish farming and adoption of a federal act On the State Monopoly on Production and Sale of Caviar and Sturgeon Fish Products.

[8] Ivanov (note 7), p. 83.
[9] Equipe Cousteau, 'La Caspienne: rapport d'expedition, mai–août 1998' [The Caspian: report of an expedition, May/Aug. 1998], p. 70.
[10] Ivanov (note 7), p. 15.

Depletion of biological resources and its economic effects

The development of Caspian oil and gas will affect fishing first of all because drilling began in the northern Caspian, in the areas where the sturgeon spawn and fatten and on their migration routes. Fishermen are losing their traditional fishing areas, the migration cycles of fry and mature fish are broken, and eco-systems in some sea areas are deteriorating because of pollution. According to Brandon's estimates the Caspian littoral countries will lose about $6 billion every year as a result of the reduction in sturgeon fishing alone.[11] In addition, the revenue of the caviar business would be reduced by 90 per cent: its annual turnover is estimated at $10 billion.

The market value of other commercial fish species and Caspian sea animals is also considerable. The annual catch of seals is worth $2.3 million, of pike-perch $14.4 million, of sea roach $13 million and of common carp $2.1 million.[12]

III. Environmental problems

The ecology of the Caspian Sea depends to a great extent on the state of the environment in its water catchment area. That area in turn abounds in environmental problems which are the result of the economic orientation of each region in the Caspian basin—of the sea itself, of the coastal territories and of the rivers that flow into the sea.[13] Among these problems are: (a) the quantitative and qualitative depletion of natural resources (including bio-resources) involved in economic cycles; (b) the degradation of natural and man-made ecosystems; (c) the deteriorating living conditions and health of the population; (d) pollution of the marine environment; and (e) the degradation of water ecosystems. This last is one of the key environmental issues.

At the end of the Soviet period 'the general environmental situation in the Caspian Sea basin, which was accompanied by a drastic worsening of the sanitary–toxic and fishery situation, could be referred to as pre-crisis'.[14] In 1992 the Volga Basin and the coastal territories of the Caspian Sea were termed 'ecological catastrophe zones'.[15] The major sources of pollution in the Caspian are pollutants flowing in with river waters (overland run-off); the disposal of untreated industrial and agricultural waste water, and municipal and domestic effluent from cities and settlements in the coastal zone; sea and river navigation; oil and gas production on land and in the shelf zone; oil transport by sea;

[11] Brandon, S., 'Oil on troubled waters', *Focus Central Asia*, no. 22 (30 Nov. 1995), pp. 12–16.

[12] Tolboyev, M. O. and Andurakhmanov, G. M., *Problemy Obespecheniya Ekologicheskoy Bezopasnosti Prikaspiyskogo Regiona* [Problems of environmental security in the Caspian region] (Dagestan Scientific Center: Makhachkala, 1997), pp. 64–68.

[13] Zonn, I. S., 'Ecological consequences of oil and gas development', eds W. Asher and N. Mirovitskaya, *The Caspian Sea: A Quest for Environmental Security* (Kluwer Academic Publishers: Dordrecht and London, 2000), pp. 65–77.

[14] Russian State Committee for Nature Protection, 'Sokhraneniye biologicheskogo raznoobraziya v Rossii' [Preservation of biological diversity in Russia], Moscow, 1997.

[15] Russian Ministry of the Environment, 'O sostoyanii okruzhayushchey sredy Rossiyskoy Federatsii v 1992 godu' [On the state of the environment in the Russian Federation in 1992], Moscow, 1993.

secondary pollution in the course of dredging work; and the air- and water-borne transfer of pollutants from other regions.

The inflow of pollutants with river waters is measured using an integral index of a number of natural and technogenic factors[16] which include the scale and duration of floods, observation of established fishing quotas, and the effects of industrial, domestic and agricultural waste water containing over 1000 chemical compounds. Every year the Caspian Sea receives 40–45 km³ of waste water— 23–25 km³ from the Volga and 17–20 km³ from other rivers. If these were distributed evenly over the sea surface, then every year the waste water would add 10–11 cm to the depth of the sea.[17]

In considering the pollution of the Caspian in general, the following features must be kept in mind. On the one hand, the uneven distribution of the sources of pollution along the perimeter of the sea leads to uneven pollution of its different parts. On the other hand, as currents going along the seashore are of a cyclonic nature, the pollution of one part of the sea invariably leads to pollution of other parts. It should also be noted that pollutants accumulate in the surface layer, localize in the transitional zones—between the water and the atmosphere and between the water and the sediments at the bottom—and tend to move towards marginal (peripheral) areas of the sea. In other words, the areas of the sea which are biologically most significant are the most heavily polluted.

Chemical pollution is of higher priority and is most dangerous because it involves a high level of oil hydrocarbons, chlorine–organic compounds, heavy metals and radionuclides. The leading pollutant in the Caspian basin is hydrocarbons, the average level of which exceeds by 150–200 per cent the level admissible for waters exploited for fishing. Fortunately, in the Caspian Sea no other harmful substances exceed their maximum admissible levels for fishing, except in individual cases of local pollution, one-time releases and technogenic accidents. Every year 20–30 one-time releases are registered, and the number of technogenic accidents is constantly growing.

The main polluters are first and foremost oil production and underwater oil pipelines near the Apsheron Peninsula (Azerbaijan) and the Mangyshlak Peninsula (Kazakhstan). From the late 19th century Azerbaijan pioneered the development of shelf and offshore oilfields, and it was the first to suffer from pollution of its waters. The first major shelf oilfield, Neftyanye Kamni, opened and developed in the late 1940s, produced 10 million tonnes of oil annually. When oil platforms appeared in the sea this was considered a great achievement of Soviet science and engineering: only a few scientists predicted the negative environmental implications, no critical comments about the further development of offshore oil production in the Caspian were published in the press, and the opinions of biologists were tabooed.

The Baku Bay is one of the most polluted in the Caspian Sea. Biologically it is dead. There are bottom deposits 8–10 metres thick of oil wastes, accumulat-

---

[16] Technogenic factors are any man-made impact associated with the use of technical facilities.

[17] Butayev, A. M., Kaspiy: Status, Neft', Uroven' [The Caspian: status, oil, level] (Promstroyinvest: Makhachkala, 1999), p. 220.

ing about 200 million tonnes of toxic substances in concentrations that exceed the maximum admissible levels by 100 times.[18] Vast areas of water are covered with an oil film that stops oxygen dissolving in the water, so that the flora and fauna of the sea are damaged. According to Brandon, near the Neftyanye Kamni oilfield the oil film covers an area of over 800 km^2.[19] In 1996 on the Russian shore the level of oil hydrocarbons in the lower reaches of the Terek River exceeded the admissible level more than 500 times.[20] This was connected with the military campaign in Chechnya.

New oil- and gas-producing centres—Tengiz (Kazakhstan) and Cheleken (Turkmenistan)—are going the same way as Apsheron. The environmental situation there largely repeats that in the western Caspian, but it is even more aggravated because the oil there has a higher content of sulphur and mercaptan. Such oil requires special de-mercaptanation before it is pumped via a pipeline. Spillages of such oil into the sea entail serious environmental problems. Complex stratum conditions (high temperature and pressure) will require additional expenditure on the trouble-free operation of oil wells. What can now be seen near the Azerbaijani coast will be seen in the very near future over the whole area of the Caspian Sea if the further development of the region's oil and gas riches progresses without strict observance of ecological standards in exploration and production. In this context even the standards of the US Environmental Protection Agency (EPA) applied by Western companies will not be adequate for oil projects because they are not intended for inland water bodies.[21]

In spite of all this, and notwithstanding catastrophic local pollution of some areas of the sea, in general the level of pollution of the Caspian is low. The northern Caspian is assessed as moderately polluted. Where water purity is concerned, an important role is played by the reservoirs on the Volga and other rivers, which act as artificial settling basins (without which it would be impossible to maintain any biological diversity in the deltas of Caspian rivers), by the sediments at the Caspian bottom, and by various physico-chemical and biochemical self-purification processes which take place in the heated top layers of the sea. The above-zero temperatures of surface water that are observed in the middle and southern Caspian even in winter accelerate chemical reactions and this in turn facilitates the rapid year-round decomposition of many pollutants. (Pollution increases with the increase of river flow.)

The environmental problems in the Caspian Sea are made even more acute by the constantly varying sea level and the high natural seismicity in the region.

[18] Guyl, A. K., 'Investments to improve Baku Bay will repay', *Caspian Energy*, no. 2(5) (summer 2000), pp. 62–63.

[19] Brandon (note 11).

[20] Saipulayev, I. M. and Guruev, M. A., 'Zagryazneniye vodnyh obyektov Severnogo Dagestana nefteproduktami' [Pollution of water bodies in North Dagestan with oil products], *Melioratsiya i Vodnoye Khozyaistvo*, no. 3 (1997), pp. 41–43.

[21] Cox, R. and Norman, D., 'The Great Environmental Game: whether the oil resourse development in the Caspian will lead to environmental catastrophe?', *Caspian Sea Bulletin*, no. 6 (1999), pp. 50–59.

Fluctuations of the Caspian Sea level

Since 1978 the Caspian has been in a state of transgression:[22] a rise of over 2.5 metres in the sea level has led to coastal land disappearing under water at a rate of 1–2 km a year, surges when surge waves up to 2–3 metres high reached as far as 20 km inland, the erosion and migration of river beds accompanied by breaching of embankments, abrasion of the bank at a rate of up to 10 metres a year, an overall rise of the groundwater table and submersion of land. Tidal events make their contribution to the pollution of the sea by washing in coastal wastes.

In recent years the sea level has stabilized, but any further rise of the sea level in the oil-producing regions will lead to emergency situations—the flooding of drilling sites in low-lying coastal areas, the breaching of dams and embankments around drilling sites, the breaking of on-field pipelines, and pollution of groundwater, which will in turn pollute the sea.

Seismicity and trans-Caspian pipelines

The southern Caspian and the greater part of the middle Caspian are at great risk from earthquakes, yet the construction of underwater pipelines across the Caspian in these regions is still being planned. One pipeline would carry up to 20 million tonnes of oil annually from the Tengiz field in Kazakhstan either via Uzen, Adjikuil and Baku to Ceyhan or via Kianli to Baku and Ceyhan. In addition a gas pipeline across the Caspian from Turkmenistan to Azerbaijan, Georgia and Turkey is planned.[23] This last project, which has been actively lobbied for by the USA and Turkey, is still on the agenda (although Turkmenistan was trumped by the Russian company Gazprom when the latter embarked on construction of Blue Stream, a gas pipeline from Russia via the Black Sea to Turkey). The idea of a gas pipeline across the Caspian and on to the Black Sea, from Turkmenistan to Azerbaijan, Georgia and Ukraine, also appeared recently.

According to Russian seismologists, the construction of oil pipelines over the Caspian seabed involves the danger of accidents and oil spills as a result of underwater earthquakes. In the long run this could have very serious environmental and socio-economic consequences.[24] There are also many mud volcanoes in the seabed. Especially dangerous environmentally are the oil and gas fields that contain hydrogen sulphur (such as the Tengiz field). A strong earthquake could release millions of tons of hydrocarbons containing hydrogen sulphur to the surface and into the atmosphere under a pressure of 1000 atmospheres, causing global catastrophe.[25] The serious environmental

---

[22] Sea transgression is defined as rising of the sea level.

[23] See chapter 3, figure 3.1 in this volume.

[24] *Caspian Sea Bulletin*, no. 5 (1998), pp. 50–51.

[25] Vostokov, Ye. N., 'Destabilizatsiya prirodnoy sredy Kaspiyskogo regiona v svyazi s osvoyeniem toplivno-energeticheskikh resursov' [Destabilization of the natural environment in the Caspian region in connection with development of fuel and energy resources], Russian Ministry of Natural Resources, Moscow, 1997.

consequences in the long term of the relatively local impact of hydrogen sulphur are seen in the example of the Astrakhan (Aksaraisky) gas condensate plant.[26]

The President of Kazakhstan, Nursultan Nazarbayev, has commented on the likely consequences of the construction of underwater pipelines: 'As the Caspian Sea, being an autonomous water body, is not connected with the World Ocean and the pollutants that build up on its bottom gradually poison the local ecosystem, then . . . the construction of oil pipelines over the sea bed is, of course, potentially dangerous and risky. If you like, this is one more reason why we, in Kazakhstan, do not overestimate the role of seabed pipelines'.[27] Similar statements are often heard from senior officials in other Caspian countries as well. But this does not mean that if such pipelines become geopolitically and commercially viable they will not be constructed.

The Russian Government is in principle against the construction of any pipelines over the Caspian seabed. In this it is vigorously supported by Iran. This was reflected in a joint statement of the foreign ministers of Russia and Iran in 1998: 'The parties voiced their objections against construction of pipelines for transit of oil and gas over the Caspian seabed which may cause irreparable damage to ecology of this water body'.[28]

The position of Russia was stressed once more by the head of the Foreign Ministry's working group on the Caspian Sea, Andrey Urnov:

Their [the pipelines'] construction must wait until all the Caspian states arrive at some common stand on the new legal status of the Caspian Sea and at least until issues of the environmental safety of the Caspian are settled. The unique Caspian ecosystem and its biodiversity are very vulnerable because of the inland location of this body of water. In such a situation it is very important to develop measures to minimize damage to the marine environment, in particular as a result of accidents on pipelines for technogenic or natural reasons, all the more so as the planned routes cross areas with very active geo-dynamics. Such measures should be coordinated among the 'five' [Caspian littoral states], because in the event of an accident to a pipeline the interests of each coastal state will be harmed.[29]

Russian officials probably brought the subject of ecology to the fore not because they were so concerned about the environment of the Caspian Sea, but for political reasons, since they felt that if a pipeline was constructed over the seabed Russia would lose control over energy flows from the region. However, the construction of a safe oil pipeline in this area is practically impossible. An absolutely safe line would cost an enormous amount of money and mean that the transport of any, even the cheapest, oil was not feasible.

[26] Zonn, I., *Kaspiy: Illyuzii i Real'nost'* [The Caspian: illusion and reality] (Edel-M: Moscow, 1999), pp. 323–24.

[27] *Caspian Sea Bulletin*, no. 1 (2000), p. 7.

[28] *Caspian Sea Bulletin*, no. 2 (1998), p. 2.

[29] Urnov, A., 'O mezhdunarodno-pravovom statuse Kaspiyskogo morya' [On the international legal status of the Caspian Sea], *Caspian Sea Bulletin*, no. 3 (2000), pp. 11–14.

Taking into account the conflict potential of the Caspian region, the possibility of 'technological terrorism' choosing sea platforms or oil pipelines as targets in order to damage the natural environment cannot be ignored. Oilfields and oil pipelines were used as objects of terrorism during the Iraqi invasion of Kuwait in 1990 and during the first and second Chechen wars.[30]

The large-scale transport of oil by tanker over the Caspian also greatly increases the risk of oil pollution. Such transport has already started between Aktau (Kazakhstan) and Dyubenty (Azerbaijan): the KazTransoil company plans to carry 1 million tons of oil by tanker annually. Since delivery of Azerbaijani oil via the Baku–Novorossiysk pipeline stops from time to time, the possibility is being discussed of transporting oil from Aktau across the sea to Makhachkala (Russia), from where it will be re-loaded into the recently built pipeline via Tikhoretsk which bypasses Chechnya. As specialists assert, it is impossible to prepare Tengiz oil for safe transport as it has high sulphur and mercaptan content and easily erodes metal. Thus, no one is insured against possible accidents and oil spills. For the Caspian Sea as a land-locked ecosystem a small-scale oil spill is enough to trigger the 'death' of the sea.

In recent years thousands of small launches and outboard motor boats have appeared on the Caspian and become a serious source of pollution of the water with petroleum products. Another significant pollution source is waste water from ships in such major Caspian ports as Makhachkala, Turkmenbashi, Baku and Aktau. The planned expansion of these ports, the construction of new ships and an increase in the number of large ships, tankers and barges for the transport of crude oil and oil products are potential sources of pollution as well, and they create a serious risk of accidents. To the sources of pollution should be added the naval military facilities being established in new Caspian littoral states. Kazakhstan has already received high-speed gunboats from the USA, Azerbaijan has received similar boats from Turkey, and Turkmenistan has been given US financial assistance to build up its naval capability.

Finally, the Caspian has a strong chance of becoming the most important segment of the North–South and East–West transcontinental transport systems, the development of which is expected to bring considerable benefits for the Caspian states—the transport corridor from the Russian Caspian Sea port of Olya (in the Astrakhan Region) to Iran and India. The strategic goal of this project is to redirect part of the cargo traffic away from TRACECA, the Transport Corridor Europe Caucasus Asia, an EU project to revive the ancient Silk Road which is planned to bypass Russian territory and goes against Russia's interests.

[30] Zonn, I. S. and Zonn, S. V., 'Ob ekologicheskikh posledstviyakh voyennoy aktsii v Chechenskoy respublike' [On ecological consequences of the military action in the Chechen Republic], *Ecology and Noospherology* (Kiev), vol. 3, nos 1–2 (1999), pp. 96–109.

Biological pollution

Apart from chemical pollution, there is biological pollution: foreign organisms from ballast water from tankers enter the Caspian waters from the Azov–Black Sea basin along the Volga–Don shipping canal. Not long ago near the Turkmen coast jellyfish (*Aurelia aurita*), comb-jellies (*Mnemiopsis leidyi*) and plankton (*Penilia avirostris*) were found. One of these intruders, the sea gooseberry, can propagate extensively in the Caspian and damage the catch of plankton-eating fish, particularly sprat: the sea gooseberries compete with sprat for food and can deprive the end-users of a cheap protein product.[31] In four to six years the sprat that are currently worth $300 000 per annum could completely loose their commercial fishing significance. Moreover, the Caspian seal feeds mostly on sprat, and the disappearance of sprat could decimate the population or even lead to the complete extinction of the Caspian seal. Increased volumes of transport between the Caspian and other seas in connection with increased oil and gas output can therefore indirectly facilitate biological pollution.

IV. Future scenarios

The Caspian Sea has always been a zone of important Russian national interests. Today its significance for Russia's economy and security is even greater. A deepening political, socio-economic and ecological crisis in the Caspian basin constitutes a serious threat to the national security of Russia and its interests. To withstand it Russia needs to have a more active policy in the region, particularly because the legal status of the Caspian is still unsettled—a fact which makes the resolution of the problems over the use of Caspian natural resources and of the associated environmental problems all the more difficult.

The Russian Government has been trying to find an acceptable agreement on the legal status of the sea that would take into consideration not only Russian interests but also the interests of other Caspian countries, that is, to establish a legal status of the sea that would enable all the littoral states to use the natural resources of the region efficiently.[32] The introduction in May 2000 of the office of Special Envoy of the Russian President for Caspian affairs has facilitated negotiations on the issue.

Today the positions of the littoral states on the legal status of the Caspian Sea differ significantly. The division of the sea into sectors will not satisfy either the political or the economic interests of Russia. The Caspian is a unique bio-

---

[31] *Mnemiopsis leidyi* came to the Black Sea from the Sea of Marmara in 1987 and devoured an enormous amount of zooplankton. Its total mass reached 1 million tons. This affected the catches of plankton-eating fish. Catches dropped from 160 000–190 000 tons per annum in the period 1980–91 to 15 000 tons in 1996.

[32] The foreign policy concept of the Russian Federation adopted in 2000 states that 'Russia will seek such status of the Caspian Sea that will facilitate mutually beneficial cooperation of all Caspian states in management of the regional resources on a just basis and taking into consideration mutual legitimate interests'. 'Kontseptsiya vneshney politiki Rossiyskoy Federatsii' [Foreign policy concept of the Russian Federation], *Diplomaticheskiy Vestnik*, no. 8 (Aug. 2000), p. 8.

system, and if each littoral state sets its own rules and arrangements in bio-resource management this will only accelerate the depletion of these resources. Taking into account existing realities, in July 2000 Viktor Kalyuzhny, Deputy Foreign Minister and Special Envoy of the Russian President for Caspian Affairs, put forward the concept of 'sovereign use of mineral deposits'—the division of the seabed in such a way as to entitle each country to exploit the natural deposits available in its own zone. It is suggested that disputed deposits be developed jointly on a 50 : 50 basis: the 'other' side that raises a claim to mineral deposits should compensate half of its costs to the country that is already developing these deposits. The idea is not to divide territory but to redistribute resources between countries. Under this proposal the waters of the Caspian Sea would remain in common use—the principle of 'common water'. This will make it easier to settle environmental and bio-resource issues of the sea. These ideas were reflected in the declaration signed by the presidents of Russia and Kazakhstan in 1998.[33]

However, while discussions about the legal status of the Caspian Sea are going on, its sturgeon population is being destroyed, its biodiversity is shrinking and the ecosystem is degrading. This affects the quality of life of the population in the region. The longer the solution of this problem is delayed, the greater is the responsibility to future generations to preserve the unique bio-resources of the Caspian. Anxious for the fate of the Caspian Sea, the Russian Academy of Sciences in 2000 addressed the scientific communities in other Caspian littoral states in connection with the intensive development of hydrocarbons in the shelf areas. It suggested that an organization of the Caspian littoral states be set up as soon as possible with the aim of the integrated development of natural resources and environmental protection. These ideas were supported and further developed by the presidents of Russia and Kazakhstan when in October 2000 they launched a joint proposal to establish a single strategic centre for the development of the Caspian by the five littoral states. Among the functions of this centre should be monitoring of the environmental condition of the sea.[34]

In the context of ensuring the environmental security in the Caspian region, Russia should direct its efforts to solving two interconnected strategic tasks. First, nature conservation and nature management must be improved within the framework of Russian policy in this region as an instrument to counteract the attempts of some countries to reduce the role of Russia in the region and its influence on the political and economic situation. Second, all necessary measures must be taken to preserve the marine environment and the ecosystem of the Caspian because, in the long run, the biological resources of the sea, unlike its mineral resources, are renewable and with proper management they can serve people as long as possible.

---

[33] *Diplomaticheskiy Vestnik*, no. 12 (2000), pp. 20–23. On current debates about the legal status of the Caspian Sea see also chapter 3 in this volume.
[34] Romanova, L. and Tesyomnikova, Ye., 'Putin otstaivaet rossiyskiye interesy na Kaspii' [Putin defends Russian interests in the Caspian], *Nezavisimaya Gazeta*, 10 Oct. 2000.

A weighted approach to the management of all kinds of natural resources of the Caspian, agreed on by all the littoral states, is not only the correct one from the legal point of view: there is practically no alternative if the long-term interests of all the littoral states are taken into consideration. US President John Kennedy once said in his address to the Canadian Parliament: 'Geography has made us neighbours. History has made us friends. Economics has made us partners. Necessity has made us allies'.[35] These words can be usefully applied to the Caspian Sea region and the countries located there.

[35] Carrol, J. E., *Environmental Diplomacy: An Examination and a Prospect of Canadian–US Trans-boundary Environmental Relations* (University of Michigan Press: Ann Arbor, Mich., 1983), p. 1.

5. Major trends in military expenditure and arms acquisitions by the states of the Caspian region

Mark Eaton

I. Introduction

Official budgets of the newly independent states of the South Caucasus, Central Asia[1] and Iran clearly show that defence spending has increased in the region since 1995.[2] However, inconsistent reporting and coverage of defence budgets by regional countries are the norm and available data are often unreliable, seldom reflecting the actual military/security environment of the region. For example, paramilitary forces possessing military capabilities and performing defence-related tasks are not usually funded through defence budgets but by interior ministries. The evolving national security doctrines of a number of regional countries see international terrorism and political and religious extremism as the main threats to national security, resulting in increased priority being given to the development of interior ministry forces during the latter half of the 1990s. In this chapter these forces and their sources of funding are considered independently of the regular armed forces. Armed non-state groups are also active in the region and the secret nature of their sources of funding and equipment makes it difficult to reach reliable conclusions about their military capability and their impact on security in the region.

Arms transfers to the countries of the region increased during the second half of the 1990s, with Armenia, Iran and Kazakhstan emerging among the world's leading recipients of conventional weapons. Since 1998 several countries, including NATO member states (the Czech Republic, France, Germany, Turkey and the USA), plus China and Ukraine, have entered the traditionally Russian-dominated market. To modernize their armed forces countries of the region are importing more sophisticated weaponry as well as repairing existing weapons, concluding military–technical cooperation agreements with regional and extra-regional states, and developing indigenous scientific and industrial defence capabilities. The development and capabilities of their national armed forces are also strongly influenced by: (*a*) foreign financial aid, which in the case of Georgia significantly supplements the national defence budget; (*b*) the presence

---

[1] This chapter focuses on developments in Iran; the South Caucasus, comprising Armenia, Azerbaijan and Georgia; and Central Asia, comprising Kazakhstan, Kyrgyzstan, Tajikistan, Turkmenistan and Uzbekistan.

[2] See chapter 1 in this volume; and tables 5.1 and 5.2 for figures. Unless otherwise stated, the SIPRI arms transfers and military expenditure projects are the source for the data in this chapter.

Table 5.1. Military expenditure in the Caspian Sea region, in local currencies, 1995–2000

Figures are in local currency at constant 1998 prices and exchange rates.

	1995	1996	1997	1998	1999	2000
Armenia (b. dram)	21.2	21.7	30.5	33.3	[36]	[45]
Azerbaijan (b. manats)	248	305	353	376	435	494
Georgia (m. lari)	[55]	[76]	[95]	[69]	[68]	[54]
Kazakhstan (b. tenge)	10.8	16.3	17.9	19	17.2	[18.8]
Kyrgyzstan (m. soms)	251	314	482	491	808	[1 016]
Tajikistan (m. roubles)	(713)	(3 977)	(10 713)	(13 562)	[17 070]	..
Turkmenistan (b. manats)	15.1	158	440	436	582	850
Uzbekistan (m. soms)	(3 355)	(6 900)	[13 700]	..	[34 860]	..
Iran (b. rials)	4 457	6 499	8 540	10 050	11 342	15 618

Note: Figures represent budget data and actual expenditure, as available.

( ) Uncertain figure.

[ ] SIPRI estimate.

Source: SIPRI military expenditure database.

of foreign military forces in several Commonwealth of Independent States (CIS) countries; (*c*) participation in international military exercises and training programmes (under CIS, NATO and US auspices); and (*d*) participation in bilateral and multilateral defence, security and military agreements and cooperation.

The newly independent states of the Caspian Sea region are going through a period of transition. Their economies are in the initial stages of development and their foreign and defence policies are still taking shape. However, despite a lack of economic resources in these countries, defence budgets continue to increase as a result of ongoing conflicts (in Afghanistan, Chechnya and the Ferghana Valley), unresolved conflicts (in Abkhazia, Nagorno-Karabakh and South Ossetia), and numerous emerging threats to regional stability including international terrorism, religious and political extremism, and drug trafficking. This chapter argues that the resulting national efforts to modernize armed forces are increasingly being supplemented by external aid in the form of monetary loans and grants, arms transfers and military training, and participation in international security arrangements. Admittedly, US/NATO aid up to now has been small in comparison to Russian aid, especially in arms transfers. However, it is significant as it represents a new set of influential actors contributing to the military capability of regional states and competing with Russia for political influence with them. The role of China in the military affairs of regional states is also increasing and cannot be overlooked.

This increased international engagement could lead to both cooperation and confrontation between these external actors, especially Russia and the West. Moreover, the emerging threats to regional security and stability which moti-

Table 5.2. Military expenditure in the Caspian Sea region, in US dollars, 1995–2000
Figures are US $m. at constant 1998 prices and exchange rates.

	1995	1996	1997	1998	1999	2000
Armenia	255	220	272	273	[293]	[370]
Azerbaijan	329	338	378	406	513	569
Georgia	[212]	[211]	[246]	[173]	[143]	[108]
Kazakhstan	753	814	760	752	629	[608]
Kyrgyzstan	136	130	161	149	180	[185]
Tajikistan	(61.8)	(66.5)	(95.3)	(84.2)	[83.1]	..
Turkmenistan	377	363	550	466	504	646
Uzbekistan	(414)	(553)	[642]	..	[982]	..
Iran	4 580	5 189	5 821	5 737	5 432	7 144

Notes: Figures represent budget data and actual expenditure, as available.
( ) Uncertain figure.
[ ] SIPRI estimate.
Source: SIPRI military expenditure database.

vate much of the increased engagement show few signs of disappearing in the
near future.

II. Iran

Among the Caspian states (excluding Russia) Iran is unique by virtue of its long
history as an independent state with capable and experienced armed forces and
its more developed economy, which accommodates significant spending on
defence. Its relative military strength, combined with its cultural, political, economic and strategic interests in the region, makes it an important actor in the
Caspian geopolitical environment. The 513 000-strong active armed forces plus
the 40 000 Ministry of the Interior forces and the estimated 200 000 'Popular
Mobilization Army' volunteers far outnumber the forces of Iran's neighbours in
the South Caucasus and Central Asia. They are also much better armed. The
major conventional weapons at the disposal of Iran's armed forces include:
1135 battle tanks; 440 armoured infantry fighting vehicles (AIFVs);
590 armoured personnel carriers (APCs); 1950 towed artillery pieces;
664 multiple rocket launchers (MRLs); 6500 mortars; 100 attack helicopters;
291 combat aircraft; and numerous missile defence systems.[3] These forces
benefit from Iran's higher defence expenditures. Significantly, the defence
budget for 2000 of 15.6 billion rials ($7.14 billion at constant 1998 prices and
exchange rates) was 55.7 per cent more than the 1995 budget. Many countries
are also concerned that Iran may be conducting extensive research on nuclear,
biological and chemical (NBC) weapons; however, this section will focus on
Iran's conventional capabilities.

[3] International Institute for Strategic Studies, *The Military Balance 2000/2001* (Oxford University
Press: Oxford, 2000), pp. 139–40.

Table 5.3. Military expenditure as a percentage of gross domestic product, 1995–2000

	1995	1996	1997	1998	1999	2000
Armenia	4.1	3.3	3.8	3.5	[3.6]	[4.3]
Azerbaijan	2.3	2.2	2.2	2.3	2.6	2.7
Georgia	[2.3]	2.0	2.1	[1.4]	[1.2]	..
Kazakhstan	1.1	1.1	1.1	1.1	0.9	[0.8]
Kyrgyzstan	1.6	1.3	1.6	1.4	1.7	[1.6]
Tajikistan	(1.1)	(1.3)	(1.7)	(1.3)	[1.3]	..
Turkmenistan	(2.3)	(2.0)	(4.0)	(3.1)	(3.4)	[3.9]
Uzbekistan	(1.1)	(1.2)	[1.4]	..	[1.7]	..
Iran	2.5	2.8	3.1	3.1	2.7	..

Notes: Figures are based on budget data and actual expenditure, as available.
( ) Uncertain figure.
[ ] SIPRI estimate.
Source: SIPRI military expenditure database.

As few countries are willing to supply it with weapons, Iran focuses on the development of its indigenous arms industry, especially regarding missile production technology. Particularly worrying to the West is the development by Iran of the Shahab-3 missile, equipped with a North Korean engine and with a range of 1300–1500 km. According to Iranian defence officials, larger Shahab-4 and Shahab-5 missiles are currently in production. Although Iran maintains that the missiles have only defensive applications, the West, led by the USA, fears their offensive potential, particularly since they could possibly reach targets in Israel, Saudi Arabia and Turkey.[4] Iran allegedly produces numerous other conventional weapons domestically, including main battle tanks (MBTs), AIFVs, various surface-to-air and anti-tank missile systems, fighter aircraft and attack helicopters, and several types of naval vessel.[5]

In the five-year period 1996–2000 Iran imported weapons worth $816 million (in constant 1990 US dollars), mainly from three countries—Russia, China and North Korea.[6] Since 1990 Russia has provided Iran with 34 fighter and 12 bomber aircraft, 126 battle tanks, 85 infantry fighting vehicles, 800 anti-tank missiles, surface-to-air missile (SAM) systems, 3 submarines and other weapons. Russian transfers will probably increase following the December 2000 decision by Russia to withdraw from the 1995 Gore–Chernomyrdin memorandum banning such transactions.[7] Bilateral ties were strengthened

---

[4] 'Iran now able to deploy Shahab-3', *Jane's Defence Weekly,* 22 Mar. 2000, p. 15; 'Iran forms five units for Shahab ballistic missiles', *Jane's Defence Weekly,* 12 July 2000, p. 16; and BBC World Service, 'Iran says missile for defence only', 18 July 2000, URL <http://news.bbc.co.uk/hi/english/world/americas/newsid_837000/837655.stm>.

[5] Cordesman, A., *Iranian Arms Transfers: The Facts* (Centre for Strategic and International Studies: Washington, DC, 2000), pp. 7–8.

[6] SIPRI arms transfers database, Mar. 2001. The dollar amount is based on SIPRI trend-indicator values, not actual prices paid. On the sources of arms transfers to Iran see Cordesman (note 5).

[7] Hagelin, B. *et al.*, 'Transfers of major conventional weapons', *SIPRI Yearbook 2001: Armaments, Disarmament and International Security* (Oxford University Press: Oxford, 2001), p. 327.

further on 12 March 2001 when Russian President Vladimir Putin and Iranian President Mohammad Khatami signed the Treaty on the Foundation of Relations and Principles of Cooperation in Moscow.[8] Some of the military–technical assistance Iran is hoping to receive from Russia includes battle tanks, armoured vehicles, and spare parts and components for Soviet-made MiG-29 and Su-24 fighter aircraft. Iran is also interested in obtaining Russian-made S-300 air defence systems.[9] Over the four years 1997–2000 Iran domestically produced 75 battle tanks under a licence issued by Russia in 1996 and, according to US officials, Russia is also contributing to the development of Iran's domestic weapon production capabilities with training, testing equipment and some missile components.[10]

Russia is not the only CIS country engaged in supplying weapons to Iran. Iran imported 12 SAMs from Ukraine in 1993 and ordered 12 transport aircraft from the latter in 1997.

China passed Russia as Iran's primary arms supplier in the late 1990s as a result of US pressure on President Boris Yeltsin's government and Iran's financial problems during this period.[11] Since 1995 China has supplied Iran with fighter and transport aircraft, anti-ship cruise missiles, missile-launching systems and other weapons. It has also contributed to Iran's indigenous arms production capacity. As early as June 1985, in the midst of the Iraq–Iran War, Iran signed missile technology agreements with China. China also allegedly helped Iran develop infrastructure for developing, building and testing ballistic missiles. Press reports since 1995 allege that Iran has received advice and technology, including missile-guidance technology, testing materials and training, from China for the further development of its ballistic missile programme.[12]

North Korea's military relations with Iran focus mainly on missile technology. During the 1990s North Korea transferred a substantial number of missiles and missile-launching systems to Iran, and in the 11-year period 1988–98 Iran produced 100 MRLs under a North Korean licence. North Korea has also been accused of providing engines for the development of Iran's long-range missiles since the early 1990s.[13]

US legislation and political and diplomatic pressure have led most Western countries to refuse to export conventional weapons to Iran. Still, NATO member France transferred 6 aircraft to Iran in 1996 and an additional 6 may have

[8] 'Iran set for first batch of Mi-8 derivatives', *Jane's Defence Weekly*, 19 Apr. 2000, p. 28; ITAR-TASS (Moscow), 'Klebanov: Russia withdraws from agreement banning arms trade with Iran', in Foreign Information Broadcast Service, *Daily Report–Central Eurasia (FBIS-SOV)*, FBIS-SOV-2000-1124, 29 Nov. 2000; and Interfax (Moscow), 12 Mar. 2001, in 'Russia signs treaty on bilateral relations, cooperation with Iran', FBIS-SOV-2001-0313, 13 Mar. 2001.

[9] IRNA (Tehran), 13 Mar. 2001, in 'Iran: Russia to sell tanks, armoured vehicles to Iran', Foreign Broadcast Information Service, *Daily Report–Near East and South Asia (FBIS-NES)*, FBIS-NES-2001-0313, 14 Mar. 2001.

[10] 'Third Iranian Shahab test "a fizzle"', *Jane's Intelligence Review*, vol. 12, no. 11 (Nov. 2000), p. 5.

[11] Cordesman (note 5), p. 5.

[12] Katzman, K., *Iran: Arms and Technology Acquisitions* (Library of Congress, Congressional Research Service: Washington, DC, 5 May 2000), pp. 10, 12.

[13] Katzman (note 12), pp. 14–16.

been delivered. Fellow NATO country the Netherlands delivered 8 transport ships to Iran, although delivery of these vehicles ended in 1991. However, between 1992 and 1995 Iran produced 5 transport ships under the terms of a licence issued by the Netherlands. In the period 1994–95, before it joined NATO, Poland supplied Iran with 104 battle tanks.

Of the non-NATO countries, Brazil and Pakistan transferred a total of 50 trainer aircraft to Iran in the period 1989–91, and Romania transferred 150 battle tanks to Iran in 1989–90.

Although Iran's cultural, economic, political and strategic interests are also focused to the south, it has significant interests in the South Caucasus and Central Asia.[14] Its economic interests in the Caspian Sea region are focused primarily on the transport of oil and gas. It is competing with Russia and Turkey for the chance to transport oil and gas, mainly from Azerbaijan, Turkmenistan and Kazakhstan, across its territory and to the outside world. It argues that the southern route is the most financially viable option because the necessary infrastructure (pipelines, ports and refineries) is largely in place and there are links to the outside world on the Persian Gulf.[15] Iran's desire to serve as a transit for Caspian oil and to establish other forms of economic cooperation with regional countries, its relative economic and military strength, and its growing involvement in regional affairs therefore make it a crucial factor in the security environment of the Caspian Sea region as a whole.

III. The South Caucasus

Among the newly independent states of the Caspian region the distinction between Western-oriented and Russian-oriented security and defence policies is most clear in the countries of the South Caucasus. Armenia and Azerbaijan are increasing their defence spending, presumably on the basis of the threats they perceive, including threats from each other. While Armenia consolidates its ties with Russia, Azerbaijan and Georgia are moving closer to the Western security orbit, maintaining and developing certain ties with Russia but also supplementing and even replacing them with new security links with NATO and bilateral cooperation with its member states, particularly the USA and Turkey. They rely on these new ties for financial aid, arms transfers, training and other aspects of the development of their national armed forces.

Armenia

Armenia's defence spending increased by 45 per cent in the six-year period 1995–2000 because of perceived threats from neighbouring Azerbaijan and Turkey. Its 2000 defence budget of 45 billion dram ($370 million at constant 1998 prices and exchange rates) accounted for 4.3 per cent of gross domestic

[14] On Iran's cultural, economic, political and strategic interests in the Caspian region see chapter 9 in this volume.

[15] See chapter 3 in this volume.

product (GDP)—an increase from 3.6 per cent of GDP in 1999. Armenia's armed forces include 41 300 active servicemen, with a potential reserve of 210 000 persons with military experience. The army is equipped with 102 battle tanks, 168 AIFVs, and numerous surface-to-surface and surface-to-air missile systems. The air section of the army possesses 60 fighter and other aircraft. The 15 000–20 000 troops in Nagorno-Karabakh (including capproximately 8000 Armenian nationals) are armed by Armenia and allegedly possess 316 pieces of equipment including battle tanks, armoured combat vehicles (ACVs) and artillery.[16]

To ensure national security, Armenian policy makers believe that ties must be developed with both Russian/CIS and US/NATO security structures, although cooperation with Russia remains a top priority.[17] Armenia's defence ties with Russia are based on the 29 August 1997 Treaty of Friendship, Cooperation and Mutual Assistance. Under the agreement the two countries agree to cooperate in matters of defence and to 'consult immediately' on the joint use of military facilities and mutual military assistance if either is threatened.[18] They have also agreed to increase cooperation between their defence industries and educational institutions. For Armenia, this means obtaining Russian-made weapons at lower cost and free training for its officers in Russian military schools.[19] According to a March 2000 protocol Russia may maintain a military presence in Armenia for 25 years, and on 27 September 2000 ties were further enhanced with the signing of three military cooperation agreements by the Armenian and Russian defence ministers—on joint planning of military activities, on the regulations governing the Russian military presence in Armenia, and on permitting Armenian and Russian military aircraft to fly in each other's airspace.[20]

Approximately 3100 Russian troops guard Armenia's western borders with Turkey, and Russia provides 50 per cent of the funding for this force. Armenian servicemen benefit from the training they receive as members of this force.[21] Russia's 127th Motor Rifle Division (MRD) is also stationed in Armenia at the military bases in Gyumri and Yerevan. It includes 4100 Russian personnel equipped with a squadron of MiG-23s and several MiG-29s, 74 tanks, 181 armoured fighting vehicles and 84 artillery pieces. Both Armenian and Russian troops use these weapons.[22] In April 2001 the decision was made to

[16] The Military Balance 2000/2001 (note 3), pp. 84–87.

[17] Snark (Yerevan), 26 July 2000, in 'Armenia ready to step up cooperation with NATO, even given ties with Russia', Foreign Broadcast Information Service, Daily Report–Central Eurasia (FBIS-SOV), FBIS-SOV-2000-0726, 27 July 2000.

[18] Olcott, M. B., Åslund, A. and Garnett, S. W., Getting It Wrong: Regional Cooperation and the Commonwealth of Independent States (Carnegie Endowment for International Peace: Washington, DC, 1999), p. 102.

[19] Jane's Intelligence Review, vol. 12, no. 5 (May 2000), p. 12.

[20] 'Russia to keep base in Armenia', Jane's Defence Weekly, 22 Mar. 2000, p. 11; and Snark (Yerevan), 29 Sep. 2000, in 'Armenian, Russian defence ministers sign accords on strengthening co-operation', FBIS-SOV-2000-0929, 2 Oct. 2000.

[21] 'Russia to keep base in Armenia' (note 20); and Snark (Yerevan), 2 Dec. 1999, in 'Russian border guard service on Armenia–Turkey border', FBIS-SOV-1999-1206, 7 Dec. 1999.

[22] Olcott, Åslund and Garnett (note 18), p. 101; and Sokolsky, R. and Charlick-Paley, T., NATO and Caspian Security: A Mission Too Far?, Report MR-1074-AF (RAND Corporation: Washington, DC, 1999), p. 18, fn. 14.

further integrate the Armenian and Russian armed forces with the creation of a joint military unit which, according to representatives of the CIS Treaty on Collective Security of 1992 (the Tashkent Treaty), will 'play a large part in ensuring security' in the South Caucasus.[23] In March 1999 the two countries signed an 'Instruction on joint actions by the air defence forces of the Russian Federation and the Republic of Armenia'.[24] According to this agreement, if Armenian airspace is violated the commander of Russia's military base is empowered to determine the appropriate response in agreement with Armenia's military.[25] To facilitate air defence cooperation Russia announced its intention to transfer 8 additional MiG-29 fighter jets and an S-300V anti-aircraft missile air defence system to its Gyumri base. One of the most sophisticated systems of its kind, the S-300V is capable of downing aircraft, helicopters, non-strategic ballistic tactical missiles and cruise missiles at a range of 200 km and an altitude of 30 km.[26] Armenian Defence Minister Serzh Sarkisian confirmed in October 2000 that 76 APCs and infantry fighting vehicles would be transferred to the Gyumri base from the Russian military base at Akhalkalaki in Georgia.[27] Russia also allegedly transferred to Armenia conventional weapons worth an estimated $1 billion between 1993 and 1996. According to reports, Armenia received these weapons free of charge apart from some minor transport costs. In fact, Russian officials claim that the deal cost Russia $70 million.[28]

Armenia is also enhancing its ties with NATO and its member countries. In 1994, the first year of NATO's Partnership for Peace (PFP) programme, Armenia only participated in 11 exercises and seminars, but in 2000–2001 it plans to participate in 75.[29] Bilateral Armenian–US relations were enhanced with the signing on 24 July 2000 of an agreement for the transfer of US technical equipment worth $300 000 to Armenia's border forces. The equipment to be transferred includes detection devices for NBC weapons.[30] In December 2000 the US Department of Defense agreed to grant Armenia an additional $1.3 million for the training and equipping of its border guards and customs.[31] NATO member Greece hosts Armenian servicemen in its military academies, has agreed to help Armenia create and finance a battalion for participation in

[23] 'Armenia, Russia agree to create joint military contingent', Radio Free Europe/Radio Liberty (RFE/RL), *RFE/RL Newsline*, 17 Apr. 2001. On the membership of the Tashkent Treaty see the appendix in this volume. The text of the treaty was published in *Izvestiya*, 16 May 1992.

[24] Noyan Tapan (Yerevan), 30 Mar. 1999, in 'Russia, Armenia sign air defence accord', FBIS-SOV-1999-0331, 4 Apr. 1999.

[25] Interfax (Moscow), 15 Apr. 1999, in 'Air-defence system begins operations in Armenia', FBIS-SOV-1999-0415, 19 Apr. 1999.

[26] *Obshchaya Gazeta* (Moscow), 11 Feb. 1999, in 'Moscow view on Armenia air defense deal', FBIS-SOV-1999-0219, 22 Feb. 1999.

[27] 'Russia to close its South Georgian base this month', *RFE/RL Newsline*, 9 Oct. 2000; and 'Russia to withdraw tanks from Georgia to Armenia', *RFE/RL Newsline*, 19 Oct. 2000.

[28] Anthony, I. (ed.), SIPRI, *Russia and the Arms Trade* (Oxford University Press: Oxford, 1998), pp. 12–13; and *Sovetskaya Rossiya*, 3 Apr. 1997, in 'Armenia, Russia: Rokhlin details arms supplied to Armenia', FBIS-SOV-97-067, 9 Apr. 1997.

[29] 'NATO official wraps up Armenia visit', *RFE/RL Newsline*, 31 July 2000; and Snark (Yerevan), 15 Aug. 2000, in 'Armenian diplomat says Yerevan ready to expand cooperation with NATO', FBIS-SOV-2000-0816, 17 Aug. 2000.

[30] 'US to provide Armenia with border control equipment', *RFE/RL Newsline*, 25 July 2000.

[31] 'US military unveils aid program for Armenia', *RFE/RL Newsline*, 12 Dec. 2000.

NATO peacekeeping missions, and has donated medical and other supplies to its armed forces. Further agreements were reached on 28–30 August 2000 on training for Armenian officers in Greek institutions and on enhancing military–technical relations between the two countries' defence industries.[32]

Armenia has also established military ties with other countries. In 1999 it reportedly received 8 Typhoon missiles from China. The missiles have a maximum range of 60 km and are considered sophisticated offensive weapons. The alleged transfer aroused sharp international criticism, not least from Azerbaijan. Prospects for increasing military cooperation have recently been discussed between defence and internal security committees from both countries.[33]

Azerbaijan

Azerbaijan's defence expenditure rose by 73 per cent in the six-year period 1995–2000. The increase was motivated by ongoing tensions with Armenia over Nagorno-Karabakh and the desire to develop its military capacity. The 2000 defence budget of 494 billion manats ($569 million at constant 1998 prices and exchange rates) accounted for 2.7 per cent of GDP. Defence also consistently accounts for a high percentage of central government expenditure.[34] The country's armed forces include 72 100 active personnel and 575 700 potential reserves equipped with 220 battle tanks, 135 AIFVs, 282 artillery pieces and over 60 SAM systems. The air force has 92 combat and other aircraft, and 35 attack and other military helicopters, as well as 100 SAM systems. In addition, Interior Ministry paramilitary forces number around 15 000 (10 000 militia and 5000 border guard) and are equipped with battle tanks, AIFVs and other weapons.[35] Significantly, combined spending on defence and public order and safety accounted for approximately 22 per cent of central government expenditure in 1999, while health care and education accounted for only 4 per cent.[36]

In February 1999 Azerbaijan decided to leave the Tashkent Treaty. However, emerging threats to regional security and stability may bring it closer to its fellow CIS partners. On 1 October 2000 it concluded three agreements on enhancing multilateral cooperation against terrorism in the North Caucasus

[32] 'Armenian, Greek army chiefs vow to boost strategic partnership', *RFE/RL Caucasus Report*, 31 Aug. 2000; Snark (Yerevan), 31 Aug. 2000, in 'Armenia, Greece unanimous on all issues: Armenian chief of staff', FBIS-SOV-2000-0831, 1 Sep. 2000; and Interfax (Moscow), 16 Jan. 2001, in 'Greece to finance Armenian battalion for participation in NATO peacekeeping missions' (Presidential Bulletin for 16 Jan. 2001), FBIS-SOV-2001-0116, 18 Jan. 2001.

[33] Interfax (Moscow), 18 May 1999, in 'Azerbaijan protests Chinese missiles to Armenia', FBIS-SOV-1999-0518, 19 May 1999; and Snark (Yerevan), 20 Feb. 2001, in 'Armenia to develop military cooperation with China', FBIS-SOV-2001-0221, 22 Feb. 2001.

[34] See tables 5.1, 5.2 and 5.3; and International Monetary Fund, *Government Finance Statistics Yearbook 1999* (IMF: Washington, DC, 1999), pp. 38–40. The trend of increasing defence expenditure will probably continue in 2001 as spending is expected to reach 539.5 billion manats, or 13% of central government expenditure. 'Azerbaijan to increase military spending', *RFE/RL Newsline*, 9 Mar. 2001.

[35] *The Military Balance 2000/2001* (note 3), pp. 86–87.

[36] *Government Finance Statistics Yearbook 1999* (note 34), pp. 38–40.

within the 'Borzhomi Four' (Armenia, Azerbaijan, Georgia and Russia).[37] Bilateral relations with Russia were enhanced with the signing on 9 January 2001 of the Baku Declaration by Russian President Putin and President Heidar Aliyev. The declaration calls for the development of closer military and military–technical cooperation between the two countries.[38]

Azerbaijan receives most of its weapons from CIS member countries. In 1992 and 1993 it reportedly received over 1700 weapons from Russia and Ukraine, including battle tanks, APCs, fighter aircraft, artillery systems and helicopters.[39] These may have included the confirmed transfer of 6 fast attack boats from the Russian Navy in 1992 and approximately 150 battle tanks from Ukraine in 1993–94. Armenian officials claim that Ukraine also transferred arms to Azerbaijan illegally, citing the suspected transfer of 16 fighter aircraft, 100 battle tanks, 2600 rockets, and an unspecified number of semi-active, laser-guided aerial bombs and surface-to-air anti-radar missiles.[40] Kazakhstan also reportedly transferred 8 MiG-25 fighter aircraft to Azerbaijan in 1998.[41]

At the same time, Azerbaijan is enhancing its ties with NATO and its member countries. President Aliyev signed the PFP Framework Document on 4 May 1994 and Azeri armed forces personnel have since participated in numerous PFP exercises and training programmes.[42] In the spring of 1999 Azerbaijan accepted an invitation to contribute a platoon to the NATO Kosovo Force (KFOR).[43] Calls have also been made for even closer ties with the alliance, as some Azerbaijani officials support hosting a NATO base—either US or Turkish—and eventual full membership in NATO. Azerbaijani Foreign Minister Vilayet Guliyev has made statements to this effect but points out that such issues will only be considered when the country's armed forces are brought into line with NATO standards.[44]

Bilateral relations between Azerbaijan and the USA were enhanced with the signing on 28 September 1999 of an agreement pledging cooperation in the counter-proliferation of NBC weapons. Under this agreement the US Department of Defense and Customs Service train and equip Azerbaijani officials 'in techniques of preventing, deterring, and investigating incidents involving the

---

[37] Interfax (Moscow), 1 Oct. 2000, in 'Russia, Armenia, Azerbaijan, Georgia to intensify cooperation in combating terrorism', FBIS-SOV-2000-1001, 3 Oct. 2000.

[38] ITAR-TASS (Moscow), 9 Jan. 2001, in 'Russian, Azeri presidents issue declaration on strategic cooperation', FBIS-SOV-2001-0109, 10 Jan. 2001.

[39] US Library of Congress, Federal Research Division, 'Azerbaijan: a country study', Mar. 1994, URL <http://lcweb2.loc.gov/frd/cs/aztoc.htm>.

[40] 'Ukraine helps Azeris build-up, says Armenia', *Jane's Defence Weekly,* 12 Mar. 1997, p. 3.

[41] *The Military Balance 2000/2001* (note 3), p. 49.

[42] United States European Command, 'Peaceshield 99 concludes on 14 Aug. in Ukraine', 15 Aug. 1999, URL <http://www.eucom.mil/exercises/99/peaceshield99.htm>; and 'Azerbaijan wants closer NATO co-operation', *RFE/RL Newsline,* 2 May 2000.

[43] ITAR-TASS World Service (Moscow), 2 Mar. 1999, in 'Azerbaijan to contribute to NATO force in Kosovo', FBIS-SOV-1999-0302, 3 Mar. 1999.

[44] Interfax, 10 Feb. 2000, in 'Possibility of future NATO bases exists: Azerbaijani minister', URL <http://www.eurasianet.org/resource/azerbaijan/hypermail/200002/0020.html>; and Interfax (Moscow), 30 Mar. 1999, in 'Azerbaijan reportedly considering NATO base', FBIS-SOV-1999-0330, 31 Mar. 1999.

proliferation of weapons of mass destruction and related materials'.[45] Financial aid from Turkey increased following the signing of the Azerbaijani–Turkish agreement on cooperation in the military field on 10 June 1996.[46] In July 1999 Turkey granted Azerbaijan $3.45 million for the modernization of its armed forces and to cover costs related to the dispatch of its NATO battalion.[47] Turkey also agreed to train Azerbaijan's servicemen in its military academies and both countries are working to enhance cooperation between their respective defence industries.[48] On 17 July 2000, the Turkish Navy transferred a fighter boat to Azerbaijan's navy—in the words of Taner Balkis, the Logistic Head of Turkey's naval forces, 'to protect the rights of Azerbaijan, a good friend and an ally, in the Caspian Sea'. Following talks between defence representatives of the two countries in late February 2001, an intergovernmental Agreement on Free Military Assistance and a Protocol on Financial Assistance between the Azerbaijani Defence Ministry and the General Staff of the Turkish Armed Forces were signed under which Azerbaijan's military will receive $3 million in financial assistance from Turkey.[49]

Georgia

Georgia is the only country in the South Caucasus to have reduced its defence expenditure, in spite of unresolved conflicts in Abkhazia and South Ossetia and instability throughout Georgia. Its 2000 defence budget of 54 million lari ($108 million at constant 1998 prices and exchange rates) was its lowest in real terms since independence. Defence spending remains low because Georgia's economy is failing and it has few domestic sources of revenue. However, defence still places a significant burden on the national economy, accounting for 9 per cent of central government expenditure in 1998. Combined with spending on public order and safety, defence accounted for 20 per cent of total central government expenditure in 1998, compared to 8.7 per cent for education and health.[50] Georgia also increasingly relies on foreign aid for the development

[45] US Department of Defense, 'US and the Republic of Azerbaijan sign WMD counterproliferation agreement', 6 Oct. 1999, URL <http://www.defenselink.mil/news/Oct1999/b10061999_bt467-99.html>.

[46] Turan (Baku), 1 Nov. 1996, in 'Azerbaijan: protocols signed with visiting Turkish military delegation', FBIS-SOV-96-214, 5 Nov. 1996.

[47] Interfax (Moscow), 24 July 1999, in 'Turkey to help Azerbaijan bolster defence', FBIS-SOV-1999-0724. 26 July 1999; and Sariibrahimoglu, L., 'Turkish aid for forces in Georgia and Azerbaijan', Jane's Defence Weekly, 4 Aug. 1999, p. 6.

[48] 'Azerbaijan, Turkey sign co-operation agreement', RFE/RL Newsline, 6 Apr. 2000; and Turan (Baku), 20 Sep. 2000, in 'Azerbaijan, Turkey sign military co-operation agreement', FBIS-SOV-2000-0920, 26 Sep. 2000.

[49] Anatolia (Ankara), 17 July 2000, in 'Turkey delivers Turkish fighter boat to Azerbaijani Navy with ceremony', FBIS-SOV-2000-0717, 19 July 2000; 'Turkish firms close deals in Azerbaijan', Defense News, 2 Oct. 2000, p. 2; and Turan (Baku), 28 Feb. 2001, in 'Azeri defence minister, Turkish military delegation discuss cooperation', FBIS-SOV-2001-0301, 2 Mar. 2001.

[50] Government Finance Statistics Yearbook 1999 (note 34), pp. 167–68. It is not clear if the decision to cut Georgia's armed forces personnel by 19% will affect defence spending. Jane's Defence Weekly, 5 July 2000, p. 2.

of its armed forces, receiving $20 million from foreign sources in 1999 in the form of military supplies and officer training in several countries.[51]

Although Georgia left the Tashkent Treaty in 1999 it still cooperates with its CIS neighbours on certain military issues (training in Russian and Ukrainian military schools and bilateral security agreements).[52] However, in general Georgia is actively loosening its CIS ties, particularly with Russia. At the Organization for Security and Co-operation in Europe (OSCE) Summit Meeting in Istanbul in November 1999, Russia promised to reduce the number of its weapons based in Georgia by 31 December 2000 and to close its bases at Gudauta and Vaziani by 1 July 2001.[53] The future of its bases at Akhalkalaki and Batumi is yet to be determined. In addition, several Russian tanks, armoured vehicles and artillery batteries will be destroyed at the Tbilisi tank repair facility.[54] Georgia wants all four Russian bases closed by 31 December 2002, while Russia is hoping to keep a limited force there for a further 25 years.[55]

Abkhazia opposes the closure of the Gudauta base. Abkhazia does maintain a public army: because of a lack of resources to support a regular army, the local population makes up the main part of the army as each citizen can legally bear and bequeath arms. Military instruction is given to the adult population, young people are trained in 'active-service units' and weapons are obtained as war booty from Georgia and, according to Abkhazian President Vladislav Ardzinba, from unnamed foreign suppliers.[56] The continuing presence of Russian forces in Abkhazia is seen by the Abkhaz authorities as a security guarantee against a Georgian military being developed with significant international aid.[57]

Georgia relies on external sources for most of its weapons. It has a modest indigenous arms industry, and the Tbilisi Aircraft Works (TAW) announced in July 1998 that it would begin producing modified Su-25 fighter jets and air-to-air missiles. However, the extent to which this facility supplies Georgia's armed

---

[51] ITAR-TASS (Moscow), 29 Jan. 2000, in 'Georgia got $20 million in military aid in 1999', FBIS-SOV-2000-0129, 31 Jan. 2000.

[52] 'Georgia got $20 million in military aid in 1999' (note 51); and 'Georgia, Russia sign security agreement', *RFE/RL Newsline,* 16 June 2000.

[53] 'Russia begins withdrawing military hardware from Georgia', *RFE/RL Newsline,* 2 Aug. 2000; 'Russia begins Georgia pullout', *Jane's Defence Weekly,* 16 Aug. 2000, p. 8; Interfax (Moscow), 22 Nov. 1999, in 'Russia to cut military presence in Georgia by end 2000', FBIS-SOV-1999-1122, 23 Nov. 1999; and Iprinda (Tbilisi), 26 Oct. 2000, in 'Russia completes third stage of hardware withdrawal from southern Georgian base', FBIS-SOV-2000-1026, 30 Oct. 2000. According to Georgia's Foreign Minister Iraliy Menagarishvili, Russia fulfilled its obligation to withdraw certain amounts of military hardware from its bases in Georgia by the end of 2000. ITAR-TASS (Moscow), 8 Jan. 2001, in 'Georgian official: Russia honours weapons withdrawal accords', FBIS-SOV-2001-0108, 9 Jan. 2001.

[54] 'Last post for Russians in Georgia', Institute for War and Peace Reporting's Caucasus Reporting Service, no. 48 (8 Sep. 2000), URL <http://www.iwpr.net/idex.p15?archive/cau/cau-20009_48-02-eng.txt>.

[55] Interfax (Moscow), 4 Aug. 2000, in 'Georgia: Russian military begins withdrawal from bases 4 Aug', FBIS-SOV-2000-0804, 7 Aug. 2000.

[56] *Vremya MN* (Moscow), 8 Aug. 2000, in 'Ardzinba on Russian military withdrawal, other Abkhazia issues', FBIS-SOV-2000-0809, 14 Aug. 2000.

[57] Iprinda (Tbilisi), 7 Sep. 2000, in 'Georgia: Abkhaz military objects to withdrawal of Russian base', FBIS-SOV-2000-0907, 8 Sep. 2000.

forces with weapons is unclear.[58] Russia transferred 5 battle tanks to Georgia in 1993 and allegedly another 100 tanks, 100 personnel carriers and 6 military launches in 1996.[59] In October 1997 Georgian and Russian defence officials signed a protocol for the transfer to Georgia of 4 Russian warships.[60] It is unclear if Georgia's armed forces benefited materially from the negotiated handover of 10 Russian military installations in January 1998 and the departure of Russian border guards in November 1999. According to bilateral agreements Georgia was entitled to 50 per cent of the weapons and facilities of the departing Russian border forces.[61] CIS member Ukraine has also allegedly transferred weapons to Georgia, including 10 fighter aircraft and 2 naval patrol craft in the period 1997–99.[62]

Georgia has been receiving aid from NATO and its member countries for training and equipment for its fledgling border guard and armed forces.[63] Ties with the alliance were strengthened with the participation of a Georgian battalion in KFOR. Georgian troops have participated in numerous NATO-sponsored military exercises and Georgia intends to host a major PFP exercise in 2001.[64] The August 2000 visit to the Georgian Black Sea port of Poti by the US Navy surveillance frigate *Hawes* and the on-site presence of NATO inspectors during the withdrawal of Russian weapons from Georgia were seen by some Russian officials as evidence of NATO's intention to extend its southern flank.[65] Georgian President Eduard Shevardnadze and Defence Minister David Tevzadze support Georgia's applying for NATO membership by 2004–2005. However, the country's armed forces will require significant restructuring to be brought into line with NATO standards, and according to Shevardnadze US aid is crucial in this regard.[66]

In 1998 a team of Georgian and US experts established a 'resource management study programme' to plan for the most efficient development of Georgia's armed forces. The USA financed the programme at an estimated cost of $500 000 and has also agreed to grant Georgia $1.35 million for the purchase of

[58] Feinberg, J., *The Armed Forces in Georgia, March 1999* (Center for Defense Information: Washington, DC, 1999), p. 25.

[59] 'Nadibaidze on "coup", Russo-Georgian military ties', Open Media Research Institute (hereafter OMRI), *OMRI Daily Digest*, 24 June 1996.

[60] Interfax (Moscow), 16 Oct. 1997, in 'Russia: Russia to give Georgia four warships', Foreign Broadcast Information Service, *Daily Report–Central Eurasia, Military Affairs (FBIS-UMA)*, FBIS-UMA-97-289, 20 Oct. 1997.

[61] 'Russian guards to quit Georgia', *Jane's Defence Weekly*, 25 Aug. 1999, p. 11; and Interfax (Moscow), 8 Jan. 1998, in 'Georgia: Ten Russian military sites to be transferred to Georgia', FBIS-SOV-98-008, 12 Jan. 1998.

[62] International Institute for Strategic Studies, *The Military Balance 1999/2000* (Oxford University Press: Oxford, 1999), pp. 46.

[63] Olcott, Åslund and Garnett (note 18), pp. 90–91.

[64] Darchiashvili, D., 'Georgia courts NATO, strives for defense overhaul', *Eurasia Insight*, 26 July 2000, URL <http://www.eurasianet.org/departments/insight/articles/eav072600.shtml>.

[65] ITAR-TASS (Moscow), 3 Aug. 2000, in 'Georgia: visiting US frigate seen as extension of NATO surveillance', FBIS-SOV-2000-0803, 4 Aug. 2000; and ITAR-TASS (Moscow), 7 Aug. 2000, in 'Georgia: NATO officers arrive to inspect former Russian military facilities', FBIS-SOV-2000-0807, 8 Aug. 2000.

[66] Interfax, 15 Mar. 2000, in 'Georgia to apply for NATO membership in 2005: Shevardnadze', URL <http://www.eurasianet.org/resource/georgia/hypermail/200003/0032.htm>; and 'Georgia restructures for NATO bid', *Jane's Defence Weekly*, 12 Apr. 2000, p. 12.

military communications equipment and over $20 million for the development of its border force.[67] To further bolster Georgia's border force the USA agreed to supply it with 6 military helicopters, 2 patrol boats and communications equipment. It also plans to cover part of the cost (up to $10 million) associated with the Russian military withdrawal from Georgia.[68] Under the US Foreign Military Financing (FMF) and the International Military Education and Training (IMET) programmes, Georgian armed forces personnel receive free and subsidized training.[69] The armed forces of the two countries also participate in bilateral military exercises.[70]

Other NATO member countries provide military aid to Georgia. Britain has joined the USA in offering to help finance the Russian military withdrawal from Georgia and donated two naval vessels in 1999.[71] Turkey granted $9.3 million to Georgia's armed forces in 1998 and 1999 to modernize military and communications facilities and equipment, build training facilities for the Georgian military academy, and acquire computers and navigational equipment. In 1998 it donated a vessel to Georgia's navy and in the spring of 2000 offered an additional grant of $4 million to bring its 11th Motor Infantry Division up to NATO standards and to fund the opening of a NATO office there.[72] Under a 15 April 1998 Georgian–Turkish 'memorandum of understanding on military cooperation', Georgian officers receive free training in Turkey.[73] The two countries also participate together in bilateral and multilateral military exercises, and on 30 October 2000 a Turkish Air Force unit arrived in Georgia to repair the Marneuli Military Airport, south of Tbilisi.[74] According to Turkish Foreign Minister Ismail Cem, Georgian–Turkish military cooperation will continue in the future, particularly in the joint protection of energy pipelines.[75] Germany and the Czech Republic host Georgian armed forces personnel at their military colleges.[76] Georgia also received (or is in the process of receiving) a

[67] ITAR-TASS World Service (Moscow), 19 May 1998, in 'Georgia: US military to draw up defense programme', FBIS-UMA-98-139, 21 May 1998; 'Georgia, US sign defense agreement', RFE/RL Newsline, 25 Mar. 1998; and ITAR-TASS (Moscow), 28 Apr. 2000, in 'US to help Georgia improve border control', FBIS-SOV-2000-0428, 2 May 2000.

[68] 'US to help Georgia improve border control' (note 67); and Interfax (Moscow), 18 July 2000, in 'Russia, US to confer on funding arms withdrawal from Georgia', FBIS-SOV-2000-0718, 19 July 2000.

[69] Darchiashvili (note 64); and ITAR-TASS World Service (Moscow), 9 Apr. 1999, in 'Georgia develops military cooperation with US', FBIS-SOV-1999-0410, 15 Apr. 1999.

[70] 'Joint US–Georgia naval exercise', Jane's Defence Weekly, 16 Aug. 2000, p. 8.

[71] The Military Balance 2000/2001 (note 3), p. 50.

[72] 'Turkey allocates further grant for Georgian military', RFE/RL Newsline, 19 Apr. 2000.

[73] ITAR-TASS World Service (Moscow), 15 Apr. 1998, in 'Georgia: Georgian, Turkish officials sign military accord', FBIS-UMA-98-105, 17 Apr. 1998.

[74] Hürriyet (Istanbul), 27 Sep. 2000, in 'Turkey, Georgia to carry out joint military exercises 29 Sep.', FBIS-SOV-2000-0927, 28 Sep. 2000; and Milliyet (Ankara edn), 8 Nov. 2000, in 'Turkish air force team makes repairs to Georgian military airport', FBIS-SOV-2000-1108, 14 Nov. 2000.

[75] Anatolia (Ankara), 25 July 2000, in 'Turkey's Cem takes up Baku–Ceyhan, East–West corridor with Georgian counterpart', FBIS-SOV-2000-0725, 26 July 2000.

[76] ITAR-TASS, 29 Jan. 2000, in 'Georgia got $20 million in military aid in 1999', FBIS-SOV-2000-0129, 31 Jan. 2000.

Lindau Class minesweeper from Germany and 120 battle tanks from the Czech Republic.[77]

Non-NATO members and numerous international organizations also contribute to the development of Georgia's armed forces. Romania announced in February 2000 that it would donate an anti-submarine vessel to the Georgian Navy, and agreed to exchange ordnance destruction equipment with Georgia and to establish a military education exchange programme.[78] Estonia has offered to train Georgian border guards, police and personnel from other forces.[79] The Council of Europe offered $1.06 million for the development of Georgia's border forces and the European Union (EU) plans to grant equipment, vehicles and fuel for Georgia's checkpoints on the Chechnya border.[80]

IV. Central Asia

In Central Asia the distinction between Western- and Russian/CIS-oriented governments is much less striking than in the South Caucasus. Most Central Asian countries are developing new defence ties with Russia while at the same time enhancing links with NATO through participation in the PFP programme and bilateral agreements with its member states. They are generally increasing their defence expenditures (or have announced plans to do so) and are receiving military aid in the form of money and weapons from many old and new partners. Defence cooperation is also emerging between these governments and several Asian neighbours, including China, India and Pakistan. All of this bilateral and multilateral cooperation is motivated by the emerging threats to regional security—international terrorism, religious and political extremism, and drug trafficking—which show few signs of receding in the near future.

Kazakhstan

Kazakhstan's army of 45 000 active personnel is equipped with 930 battle tanks, 1343 ACVs, 1010 artillery pieces, 145 mortars and 12 surface-to-surface missile systems, among other weapons. In addition, 2680 battle tanks, 2428 ACVs and 6900 artillery pieces remain in storage. The 19 000 air force/defence personnel possess 180 fighter and other aircraft (plus 75 in storage), several military helicopters, 147 SAM systems and S-300 air defence systems.[81] These forces were allocated 18.8 billion tenge in 2000 ($608 million at constant 1998 prices and exchange rates)—a decrease of 3 per cent from the previous year.

---

[77] On 4 Oct. 2000 Georgia received 12 of the tanks it had ordered from the Czech Republic. The tanks cost *c.* $330 000 and were paid for using money from a $5.5 million Turkish grant. 'Georgia takes delivery of Czech army tanks', *RFE/RL Newsline,* 5 Oct. 2000.

[78] 'Romanian corvette for Georgia', *Jane's Defence Weekly,* 23 Feb. 2000.

[79] Baltic News Service (Tallinn), 22 Aug. 2000, in 'Estonia to train Georgia border-guard, police officers', FBIS-SOV-2000-0823, 24 Aug. 2000.

[80] 'Council of Europe allocates funds for Georgian border guards', *RFE/RL Newsline,* 18 July 2000; and 'EU to help upgrade security on Georgian–Chechen border', *RFE/RL Newsline,* 7 Sep. 2000.

[81] *The Military Balance 2000/2001* (note 3), p. 171.

However, based on the fear of regional instability and the desire to combat international terrorism, religious extremism and other threats, defence expenditure is expected to double as a share of GDP in 2001. Defence officials announced in early 2001 that Kazakhstan plans to spend at least 25 billion tenge on defence in 2001, an increase of over 6 billion tenge from 2000.[82]

Significant defence-related forces are not reflected in Kazakhstan's defence budget. Spending on public order and security (including that on *c*. 20 000 Interior Ministry troops) amounted to 32.2 billion tenge in 1999—6.8 per cent of central government expenditure and nearly double the amount allocated for defence.[83] According to the February 2000 National Military Doctrine, these interior security forces now have an anti-terrorism function, namely, to locate and destroy militant formations on Kazakh territory.[84] The establishment of a 1200-strong military headquarters in the south of Kazakhstan and the decision to increase the number of checkpoints along Kazakhstan's borders by 25 per cent should be reflected in future defence budgets. Additional funds will be needed to man and equip these checkpoints, as well as for the unspecified number of reservists called up by the Kazakh Government following the incursions of Islamic militants into Kyrgyzstan and Uzbekistan in the autumn of 2000.[85]

Kazakhstan's ongoing military reforms are motivated by the emerging threats to national security and currently emphasize the creation of modern and professional armed forces. Reforms include increasing military unit size, creating rapid-response units, increasing overall mobility and increasing budget allocations to the military in 2001. By February 2001 a mobile reaction force to be sent to assist regional countries in times of emergency was almost completely formed. Inter-agency military exercises have been held involving units from the armed forces, special services and border troops to increase coordination in anti-terrorist/extremist operations. Local populations have been organized into Sarbazy (Warriors) detachments and have been trained to aid the authorities in their operations. Finally, according to defence officials, 'tens of millions of dollars' will be spent to modernize weapons beginning in 2002.[86]

Kazakhstan supplements these national efforts with cooperation within the CIS and bilaterally with Russia. Dozens of military-related treaties and agree-

[82] 'Kazakhstan to increase defence budget', *RFE/RL Newsline*, 19 May 2000; and 'Kazakh defense officials detail spending, arms exports', *RFE/RL Newsline*, 15 Jan. 2001.
[83] International Monetary Fund, *Staff Country Reports: Republic of Kazakhstan*, no. 00/29 (IMF: Washington, DC, Mar. 2000), p. 120; and *The Military Balance 2000/2001* (note 3), p. 171.
[84] Makarenko, T., 'Central Asia commits to military reform', *Jane's Intelligence Review*, Sep. 2000, pp. 30–31.
[85] Interfax (Kazakhstan)/BBC Monitoring, 'Kazakhs setting up 1200-strong military headquarters in south', 9 Aug. 2000, URL <http://www.eurasianet.org/resource/kazakhstan/hypermail/200008/0018.html>; Interfax (Kazakhstan)/BBC Monitoring, 'Kazakhs to increase border control check points to "effectively" combat drugs', 29 June 2000, URL <http://www.eurasianet.org/resource/kazakhstan/hypermail/200006/0040.html>; and 'Kazakhstan bolsters troop numbers', *Jane's Defence Weekly*, 13 Sep. 2000, p. 14.
[86] Makarenko (note 84); Xinhua (Beijing), 9 Feb. 2001, in 'Kazakhstan setting up rapid reaction force', FBIS-SOV-2001-0209, 13 Feb. 2001; and 'Defence Ministry plans upgrade of equipment, arms', *RFE/RL Newsline*, 20 Feb. 2001.

ments form the basis of Kazakh–Russian military and security ties. The 1992 Kazakh–Russian Treaty on Friendship, Cooperation and Mutual Assistance provides for Russian assistance in the development of Kazakhstan's armed forces. Other significant agreements include the Treaty on Military Cooperation signed on 28 March 1994, the 20 January 1995 Declaration on the Expansion and Deepening of Russian–Kazakh Cooperation, 16 agreements signed on 26 January 1996 regarding joint communications, air defence and defence industry collaboration, and the July 1998 Declaration on Eternal Friendship and Alliance Oriented Toward the 21st Century.[87] Kazakh armed forces personnel receive free instruction at Russian military academies under these and other agreements.[88] The two countries also signed an intergovernmental agreement on the joint use of air defence testing facilities under which Kazakh armed forces personnel may participate in CIS air defence exercises.[89]

Kazakhstan inherited a significant defence industry from the Soviet Union. It comprised 3 per cent of the USSR's defence industry and employed 75 000 workers, and significant production continues today.[90] Between 1996 and 2000 Kazakhstan ranked 21st among the world's suppliers of major conventional weapons. The Chairman of the Defence Industry Committee within the Ministry of the Economy, Industry and Trade, Bekbulat Baigarin, stated that arms worth $20 million would be exported in 2000.[91] However, it is unclear to what extent Kazakhstan's national armed forces benefit from these indigenous sources of arms. Between 1996 and 2000 Kazakhstan ranked 37th among countries receiving conventional weapons. Russia is its primary supplier of weapons and has transferred MiG-29, Su-25 and Su-27 fighter aircraft and numerous SAM systems, among other weapons, to the republic.[92] In September 1999 then Russian Prime Minister Putin signed an edict for the transfer to Kazakhstan of part of Russia's weapons quota under the 1990 Treaty on Conventional Armed Forces in Europe (the CFE Treaty), including 50 tanks, 200 armoured vehicles, 100 artillery pieces, 15 fighter aircraft and 20 helicopter gunships.[93] Russia also contributed to Kazakhstan's air defence with the transfer of two highly advanced S-300 anti-aircraft missile systems and Su-27 fighter aircraft in the

---

[87] On Kazakh–Russian military ties, see Aben, E., 'Kazakhstan–Russian relations today: the pros and cons', *Central Asia and the Caucasus* (Luleå), no. 3 (2000), pp. 18–28; and Alexandrov, M., *Uneasy Alliance: Relations Between Russia and Kazakhstan in the Post-Soviet Era, 1992–1997* (Greenwood: London, 1999).

[88] ITAR-TASS (Moscow), 26 Jan. 1996, in 'Russia, Kazakhstan sign military co-operation agreements', FBIS-SOV-96-019, 30 Jan. 1996.

[89] Interfax (Moscow), 31 July 2000, in 'Russia, Kazakhstan to share testing grounds for air defense exercises', FBIS-SOV-2000-0731, 1 Aug. 2000.

[90] US Library of Congress, Federal Research Division, 'Kazakhstan: a country study', Mar. 1996, URL <http://lcweb2.loc.gov/cgi-bin/query/r?frd/cstdy:@field(DOCID+kz0058)>.

[91] 'Kazakhstan to acquire Russian arms', *RFE/RL Newsline*, 14 Feb. 2000. Kazakhstan exported major conventional weapons worth *c.* $194 million between 1996 and 2000. SIPRI arms transfers database, Mar. 2001. The dollar amount is based on SIPRI trend-indicator values, not actual prices paid.

[92] Kazakhstan imported conventional weapons valued at $648 million (at constant US dollars and 1990 prices) between 1996 and 2000. SIPRI arms transfers database, Mar. 2001. The dollar amount is based on SIPRI trend-indicator values, not actual prices paid.

[93] 'Russia's CFE arms go to Kazakhstan', *Defense News*, 11 Oct. 1999, p. 2.

period 1999–2001. One S-300 system protects the capital, Astana, while another covers the southern border of Kazakhstan and the CIS.[94]

Since Russian transfers are often made to pay its debt to Kazakhstan or as donations, only a small share of Kazakhstan's defence spending should be devoted to weapon procurement.[95] Presidents Nursultan Nazarbayev of Kazakhstan and Vladimir Putin of Russia reaffirmed their intention to promote their defence and military–technical cooperation in the summer of 2000, and advised their respective governments 'to form national sections within the Inter-State Commission for Military–Economic Cooperation of the CIS charged with jointly drawing up proposals for the further integration of enterprises of the military–industrial complex'.[96]

While developing cooperation with its principal strategic partner, Russia, Kazakhstan also seeks to establish links with diverse partners, including the USA. Its armed forces personnel receive training in US institutions under the IMET programme and joint seminars have been held on risk assessment and the creation of a national security strategy.[97] The USA finances the conversion of nuclear and other military-related facilities in Kazakhstan with funds from US military threat reduction programmes, and with US aid the missile control facilities at the Sary-Shagan military test site have been converted for civilian satellite communications operations.[98] The US–Kazakh Defense Cooperation Plan for 2000 provided for continuing IMET training for Kazakh servicemen, the Central Asian Battalion (CentrasBat) peacekeeping exercises and other forms of military cooperation.[99] Kazakhstan may also receive US assistance for the development of its mobile rapid-reaction forces.[100] To further facilitate bilateral cooperation, in mid-2000 US Secretary of State Madeleine Albright pledged $3 million for the development of Kazakhstan's military.[101] The contribution of an armed patrol boat to Kazakhstan's fledgling navy in 1997 also revealed a developing relationship between the two countries.[102]

Kazakhstan has established military and security ties with other NATO members. In late 1999 Turkey granted it an interest-free loan of $700 000 for

[94] Interfax (Moscow), 10 Jan. 2000, in 'Kazakhstan starts receiving Russian military hardware', FBIS-SOV-2000-0110, 11 Jan. 2000; Interfax (Moscow), 15 Mar. 2000, in 'Russia to complete supplying Kazakh S-300 AA system in Apr.', FBIS-SOV-2000-0315, 16 Mar. 2000; and Interfax (Mosocw), 2 Mar. 2001, in 'Russia supplying weaponry to Kazakhstan to pay off debt', FBIS-SOV-2001-0303, 5 Mar. 2001.

[95] 'Donated Russian planes ready to put to use in Kazakhstan', New Europe, 7–13 Feb. 1999, p. 35; and Interfax (Moscow), 14 Feb. 2000, in 'Russia to supply military products to Kazakhstan for debts', FBIS-SOV-2000-0214, 16 Feb. 2000.

[96] ITAR-TASS (Moscow), 20 June 2000, in 'Putin, Nazarbayev agree on cooperation in defense', FBIS-SOV-2000-0620, 21 June 2000.

[97] Hitchens, T., 'Kazakhstan, US work to improve military relations', Defense News, 4–10 Mar. 1996, p. 25; and 'US, NATO conduct training courses in Kazakhstan, Uzbekistan', RFE/RL Newsline, 29 June 1999.

[98] Interfax (Moscow), 27 Oct. 1999, in 'US helps Kazakhstan convert defense facilities', FBIS-SOV-1999-1028, 20 Nov. 1999.

[99] On CentrasBat, see section V below.

[100] Office of the US Assistant Secretary of Defence (Public Affairs), 'US and Kazakhstan sign "Defense Cooperation Plan for 2000"', Washington, DC, 20 Dec. 1999, press release no. 580–99; and 'Kazakhstan, USA sign co-operation pact', Jane's Defence Weekly, 5 Jan. 2000, p. 4.

[101] Davis, A., 'Tighter security for Central Asia', Jane's Defence Weekly, 3 May 2000, p. 14.

[102] 'SeaArk Marine delivers patrol boat to Kazakhstan', Defense News, 21–27 July 1997, p. 3.

the modernization of its military communications systems, and in July 2000 it agreed to grant an additional $1 million to Kazakhstan's Ministry of Defence. Bilateral talks have also focused on the training of Kazakh military personnel in Turkey and jointly combating terrorism, among other military-related issues.[103]

A Chinese donation of communications equipment and other items to Kazakhstan's armed forces is symbolic of the interests shared by both countries. According to Chinese Defence Minister Chi Haotian China and Kazakhstan plan to intensify joint efforts in the fight against separatism, international terrorism and religious extremism.[104]

Kyrgyzstan

Kyrgyzstan's defence spending increased by 36 per cent over the six years 1995–2000. Its year 2000 defence budget of 1016 million soms ($185 million at constant 1998 prices and exchange rates) accounted for 1.6 per cent of GDP. Presumably the most recent spending increases are motivated by the Islamic incursions into Kyrgyzstan.

With 9000 active personnel and 57 000 reserves, equipped mainly with outdated ex-Soviet weapons, Kyrgyzstan's armed forces are the weakest in Central Asia. This does not include the self-defence units being formed in southern Kyrgyzstan, manned by local residents and trained to repel invasions by extremist forces.[105] Officials have also announced plans to strengthen border security with the creation of four new frontier posts in the Batken Oblast staffed by 800 personnel and to establish an anti-terrorist centre in Kyrgyzstan in cooperation with the other Shanghai Forum countries (China, Kazakhstan, Russia and Tajikistan).[106] These initiatives, if carried through, should be reflected in future defence budgets.

Since it gained independence Kyrgyzstan's closest strategic partner has been Russia. While addressing the Assembly of Peoples of Kyrgyzstan on 30 June 2000, President Askar Akayev called Russia Kyrgyzstan's principal past, present and future strategic partner.[107] Many defence and military–technical agreements have been planned and signed by the two states in recent years, and Kyrgyzstan's relations both with Russia and within the Tashkent Treaty focus

---

[103] Interfax (Moscow), 24 Dec. 1999, in 'Kazakhstan: Turkey to give aid for military defense', FBIS-SOV-1999-1224, 27 Dec. 1999; 'Turkish loan to Kazakhstan', *Jane's Defence Weekly*, 12 Jan. 2000, p. 13; and 'Kazakh, Turkish presidents aim to expand co-operation', *RFE/RL Newsline*, 20 Oct. 2000.

[104] 'China to allocate aid to Kazakhstan's armed forces', *RFE/RL Newsline*, 3 May 2000; and Interfax, 2 May 2000, in 'China to give aid to Kazakh armed forces', URL <http://www.eurasianet.org/resource/kazakhstan/hypermail/200005/0003.html>.

[105] *The Military Balance 2000/2001* (note 3), p. 172; Interfax, 16 May 2000, in 'Self-defense units being formed in southern Kyrgyzstan', URL <http://www.eurasianet.org/resource/kyrgyzstan/hypermail/200005/0028.html>; and Interfax (Moscow), 14 June 2000, in 'Kyrgyzstan: Security chief says ready to deal with Islamic fighters', FBIS-SOV-2000-0614, 15 June 2000.

[106] 'Kyrgyzstan creates four new frontier posts', *RFE/RL Newsline*, 3 Feb. 2000; 'Kyrgyzstan increases border defenses', *RFE/RL Newsline*, 18 Feb. 2000; and Kyrgyz Radio First Programme/BBC Monitoring, 'Plans for anti terrorism centre in southern Kyrgyzstan pushing ahead', 18 Sep. 2000, URL <http://www.eurasianet.org/resource/kyrgyzstan/hypermail/200009/0057.html>. On the Shanghai Forum see section V below.

[107] 'Kyrgyz President terms Russia "main strategic ally"', *RFE/RL Newsline*, 3 July 2000.

primarily on cooperative defence of the CIS southern borders against international terrorism and extremist threats to stability.[108]

Russia assumed the primary responsibility for defending Kyrgyzstan's border with China until January 1999, when it stopped funding its forces stationed there. In July 1999 Kyrgyzstan began guarding border areas formerly under Russian control; however, cooperation in this area continues as Russian military advisers remain in Kyrgyzstan, while Kyrgyz border guards receive training in Russian schools.[109] Over 440 Kyrgyz armed forces personnel were enrolled in Russian military schools as of November 1998, numerous joint air defence exercises have been held to facilitate bilateral cooperation, and the Russian Federal Border Service (FBS) began a training course for its Kyrgyz counterparts in early 2001.[110]

Kyrgyzstan's defence budgets are primarily devoted to the development of its border forces, and the development of the general armed forces therefore suffers.[111] However, military–technical cooperation with Russia may contribute to the modernization of Kyrgyzstan's weapons and other equipment. Officials have discussed the possible repair and modernization of Kyrgyz weapons at Russian facilities.[112] The Kyrgyz contribution to the joint air defence system with Russia is being modernized thanks to military–technical cooperation with the Russian Ministry of Defence and Kyrgyzstan has also received modern border control technology from the Russian Ministry of Atomic Energy.[113] Significantly, during the signing of the July 2000 Declaration of Eternal Friendship and a 10-year economic cooperation agreement by presidents Putin and Akayev, both leaders stressed that bilateral defence and military–technical cooperation and the further integration of CIS security structures will remain a priority in future relations between the two countries.[114]

When Islamist forces attacked Kyrgyzstan's Batken Oblast in August 1999, the parties to the Tashkent Treaty and Uzbekistan sent Kyrgyzstan aid in the form of heavy-calibre machine-guns and grenade launchers, ammunition and

[108] ITAR-TASS (Moscow), 12 Apr. 2000, in 'Kyrgyzstan pledges anti-terrorism cooperation with Russia', FBIS-SOV-2000-0412, 13 Apr. 2000; and ITAR-TASS (Moscow), 10 Oct. 2000, in 'Russian, Kyrgyz legislators agree to counter terrorism jointly', FBIS-SOV-2000-1010, 12 Oct. 2000.

[109] Smith, D. L., *Breaking Away from the Bear* (US Army War College Strategic Studies Institute: Carlisle, Pa., Aug. 1998), pp. 15–16; 'Kyrgyzstan, Russia sign border control accord', *RFE/RL Newsline*, 20 July 1999; Sköns, E. *et al.*, 'Military expenditure', *SIPRI Yearbook 1999: Armaments, Disarmament and International Security* (Oxford University Press: Oxford, 1999), p. 291; and ITAR-TASS (Moscow), 15 Jan. 1999, in 'Russia: Russia to continue helping guard Kyrgyz borders', FBIS-UMA-99-015, 21 Jan. 1999.

[110] ITAR-TASS (Moscow), 23 Nov. 1998, in 'Russia: Russia, Kyrgyzstan to sign military cooperation deal', FBIS-SOV-98-327, 24 Nov. 1998; Interfax (Moscow), 12 Jan. 1999, in 'Russia: Russia, Kyrgyzstan to sign defense cooperation accord', FBIS-SOV-99-012, 13 Jan. 1999; and Kyrgyz Press International News Agency (Bishkek)/BBC Monitoring Service, 4 Feb. 2001, in 'Russia, Turkish military specialists help Kyrgyzstan train officers', URL <http://www.eurasianet.org/resources/kyrgyzstan/hypermail/200102/0011.html>.

[111] Smith (note 109), p. 17.

[112] 'Russia: Russia, Kyrgyzstan to sign military cooperation deal' (note 110).

[113] Interfax (Moscow), 27 July 2000, in 'Russia: Kyrgyz President confirms strategic partnership with Russia', FBIS-SOV-2000-0727, 28 July 2000.

[114] 'Kyrgyz, Russian presidents sign eternal friendship declaration', *RFE/RL Newsline*, 28 July 2000.

other technical equipment.[115] To facilitate this military–technical assistance a special department was established within CIS headquarters responsible for analysing the conflict and rendering military assistance to Kyrgyzstan's armed forces.[116] When the incursions resumed in August 2000, Russian Defence Minister Igor Sergeyev announced that Russia intended to provide Kyrgyzstan with military–technical aid, presumably in the form of weapons.[117] Kazakhstan also offered to send weapons and troops if necessary, while Belarus offered surveillance systems and other military equipment.[118]

NATO and its member countries also provide military and military–technical assistance to Kyrgyzstan's armed forces. Kyrgyz units participate regularly in PFP exercises and during NATO Secretary General Lord Robertson's July 2000 visit to Kyrgyzstan the enhancement of Kyrgyzstan's cooperation with NATO dominated the discussions.[119] Kyrgyz and US servicemen have participated in several bilateral military exercises and both armed forces have agreed to hold regular joint exercises.[120] In addition, during her visit to Central Asia in April 2000 US Secretary of State Albright promised a grant of $3 million to enhance the military capability and combat readiness of Kyrgyzstan's armed forces and border guards. The first instalment of this aid ($1 million-worth) reached Kyrgyzstan in December 2000.[121] The US State Department announced in early 2001 that the USA would provide an additional $5.49 million in equipment, training and services over the next few years.[122] NATO member Turkey trains Kyrgyz servicemen, has granted $210 000 to Kyrgyzstan for the purchase of modern communications equipment, and in December 1999 agreed to fund logistical and military–technical assistance for over 3000 Kyrgyz armed forces personnel.[123] Turkey also offered to provide additional funding to Kyrgyzstan's armed forces following the Islamic incursions in August 2000.[124]

[115] ITAR-TASS (Moscow), 20 Sep. 1999, in 'Russia to supply arms to Kyrgyz Government', FBIS-SOV-1999-0920, 23 Sep. 1999; Interfax (Moscow), 2 Oct. 1999, in 'CIS countries to give military help to Kyrgyzstan', FBIS-SOV-1999-1002, 4 Oct. 1999; and ITAR-TASS (Moscow), 8 Oct. 1999, 'Russia sending first batch of weapons to Kyrgyzstan', FBIS-SOV-1999-1008, 13 Oct. 1999.

[116] ITAR-TASS (Moscow), 3 Sep. 1999, in 'Department for aid to Kyrgyzstan set up at CIS HQ', FBIS-SOV-1999-0903, 7 Sep. 1999.

[117] ITAR-TASS (Moscow), 7 Sep. 2000, in 'Sergeyev: Russia to render military aid to Central Asia', FBIS-SOV-2000-0907, 8 Sep. 2000.

[118] 'Kazakhstan signals readiness to help Kyrgyzstan fight Islamic militants', RFE/RL Newsline, 13 Sep. 2000; and 'Belarus agrees to provide Kyrgyzstan with military assistance', RFE/RL Newsline, 11 Oct. 2000.

[119] Interfax (Moscow), 19 Jan. 1998, in 'Uzbekistan: NATO exercises to be held in Uzbekistan, Kyrgyzstan', FBIS-SOV-98-019, 21 Jan. 1998; ITAR-TASS (Moscow), 25 Sep. 1998, in 'Kyrgyzstan: Kyrgyzstan to host NATO manoeuvres 26–28 Sep.', FBIS-SOV-98-268, 28 Sep. 1998; and Kabar (Bishkek)/BBC Monitoring, 'Security in Central Asia of "serious" concern: NATO chief in Kyrgyzstan', 6 July 2000, URL <http://www.eurasianet.org/resource/kyrgyzstan/hypermail/200007/0005.html>.

[120] Kabar (Bishkek)/BBC Monitoring, 'Krygyz and US guards hold three-day military exercises', 15 June 1999; and Vecherny Bishkek/BBC Monitoring, US–Kyrgyz military exercises underway', 4 May 2000, URL <http://www.eurasianet.org/resource/kyrgyzstan/hypermail/200005/0006.html>.

[121] Kabar (Bishkek)/BBC Monitoring, 'US–Kyrgyz officials issue joint statement', 17 Apr. 2000, URL <http://www.eurasianet.org/resource/kyrgyzstan/hypermail/200004/0028.html>; and 'US presents Kyrgyzstan with defense equipment', RFE/RL Newsline, 8 Dec. 2000.

[122] Kabar (Bishek)/BBC Monitoring, 'US security experts discuss border security in Kyrgyzstan', 8 Feb. 2001, URL <http://www.eurasianet.org/resource/kyrgyzstan/hypermail/200102/0021.html>.

[123] US Library of Congress, Federal Research Division, 'Kyrgyzstan: a country study', Mar. 1996, URL <http://lcweb2.loc.gov/frd/cs/kgtoc.html>; Anatolia (Ankara), 12 Dec. 1999, in 'Turkey to extend

Emerging threats to regional stability have also resulted in Kyrgyzstan establishing ties with other regional governments. For instance, China granted Kyrgyzstan's border force 15 million yuan (*c.* $1.6 million) in material assistance by Jan. 2001 and expressed its desire to increase bilateral cooperation against international terrorist and separatist/extremist threats.[125]

Tajikistan

Tajikistan's defence spending increased by 34.5 per cent in the five-year period 1995–99. It fell slightly in 1998 and 1999 (in constant 1998 US dollars) after the conclusion of the Peace and National Reconciliation Accord in June 1997 ending the six-year civil war, but this trend will probably be reversed because of growing tension on Tajikistan's border with Afghanistan and throughout the region. The 1999 defence budget amounted to 17 billion Tajik roubles— $83 million at constant 1998 prices and exchange rates, or 9.4 per cent of central government expenditure and 1.3 per cent of GDP—while spending on defence and law enforcement and judicial bodies combined accounted for 19.2 per cent of central government expenditure.[126]

Tajikistan's closest strategic partner is Russia and their bilateral relations are based on the Treaty of Friendship, Cooperation and Mutual Assistance of 25 May 1993. Regular meetings are held between their presidents, the leaders of their respective parliaments, and several ministries and agencies which coordinate the foreign policies of the two states and strengthen bilateral defence cooperation.[127] Bilateral ties were enhanced with the signing of two agreements on 16 April 1999, the Treaty of Alliance and Cooperation between the Republic of Tajikistan and the Russian Federation Oriented to the 21st Century, and the treaty on the status and conditions of the Russian military presence on the territory of Tajikistan. Under these agreements Russian troops may remain in Tajikistan for 25 years and assume the status of a military base.[128]

Russia assumed the primary financial and manpower burden of the CIS Collective Peacekeeping Force (CPF) in Tajikistan and observed and mediated the peace talks between the Tajik Government and the United Tajik Opposition (UTO).[129] Tajikistan's meagre armed forces (*c.* 6000 active personnel) rely on

military aid to Kyrgyzstan', Foreign Broadcast Information Service, *Daily Report–West Europe (FBIS-WEU)*, FBIS-WEU-1999-1212, 13 Dec. 1999; and 'Turkey to support Kyrgyzstan's military', *RFE/RL Newsline*, 14 Dec. 1999.

[124] Reuters (Ankara), 'Turkey offers Uzbeks, Kyrgyz aid against rebels', 2 Sep. 2000.

[125] Kabar (Bishkek)/BBC Monitoring, 'Kyrgyz border guards get Chinese aid, more in the pipeline', 1 June 2000, URL <http://www.eurasianet.org/resource/kyrgyzstan/hypermail/200006/0006.html>; and 'China provides equipment for Kyrgyzstan's armed forces', *RFE/RL Newsline*, 8 Jan. 2001.

[126] See tables 5.1, 5.2 and 5.2; and International Monetary Fund, *Republic of Tajikistan: Recent Economic Developments*, IMF Staff Country Report no. 00/27 (IMF: Washington, DC, Mar. 2000), pp. 72–73.

[127] Olimova, S., 'Tajikistan–Russia: from "divorce" to integration', *Journal of Social and Political Studies*, no. 3 (2000), p. 37.

[128] Olimova (note 127), pp. 38–39; and Novichkov, N., *Jane's Defence Weekly*, 14 Apr. 1999.

[129] Zviagelskaya, I., 'The Tajikistan conflict', *SIPRI Yearbook 1999* (note 109), p. 74. Despite the decision to end the mandate of the CIS peacekeeping force in Tajikistan, the 201st MRD will remain. 'CIS defence ministers meet in Tajikistan', *RFE/RL Newsline*, 27 Oct. 2000.

cooperation with Russian forces to achieve national security and stability. Russia's 8200-strong 201st MRD and 14 500 FBS personnel assist Tajikistan's armed forces and border guards in protecting the Tajik–Afghan border, among other tasks.[130] Following the August 2000 incursions into Kyrgyzstan by Islamic militants the Russian border force moved to tighten security by building additional posts, increasing observations and planting landmines along the Afghan–Tajik border.[131]

Military cooperation with Russia benefits Tajikistan's armed forces in numerous ways. Specialized training companies composed of Russian instructors and Tajik servicemen have been created and Tajik servicemen also receive training and experience in their positions in the Russian forces in Tajikistan.[132] Hundreds of Tajik armed forces personnel attend Russian military academies every year (c. 500 in March 2000) and the armed forces of the two countries participate in regular military exercises, both bilaterally and within the CIS. According to Tajik and Russian officials, military/security cooperation of this sort will increase in the future.[133]

The two countries signed a protocol on 10 November 2000 under which Russia agreed to rebuild Tajikistan's weapon factories destroyed during its civil war.[134] Taking into account the extensive military-related contacts that Russia and Tajikistan have had in recent years and their common concerns about the threat to regional stability posed by political and religious extremism, international terrorism and drug trafficking, Russian arms exports to Tajikistan may increase in the future. Fellow CIS member Belarus allegedly transferred 5 Mi-24 and 10 Mi-8 combat helicopters to Tajikistan's air force, and plans are reportedly under way to transfer additional Su-25 fighter jets.[135]

Tajikistan has received little financial or military–technical assistance from non-CIS countries. It is the only regional state not participating in the PFP programme and, according to President Imomali Rakhmonov, will seek to increase military cooperation with regional states and push for more comprehensive cooperation within the Tashkent Treaty.[136] Clearly the country depends on defence cooperation with its CIS and Tashkent Treaty partners. As for other regional countries, China has agreed to grant $700 000 in technical support to

[130] The Military Balance 2000/2001 (note 3), p. 176.
[131] ITAR-TASS (Moscow), 29 Aug. 2000, in 'Russian border guards reinforce Tajik–Afghan border', FBIS-SOV-2000-0829, 30 Aug. 2000; and 'Russians guarding Tajikistan worried by Taleban advances', International Herald Tribune, 4 Oct. 2000, p. 6.
[132] Interfax (Moscow), 18 June 1998, in 'Tajikistan: Tajik President favours stronger military ties with Russia', FBIS-SOV-98-169, 22 June 1998.
[133] ITAR-TASS (Moscow), 11 Mar. 2000, in 'Russian Air Force commander visits Tajikistan', FBIS-SOV-2000-0311, 13 Mar. 2000; and Voice of the Islamic Republic of Iran/BBC Monitoring, 'Tajik–Russian military cooperation to be stepped up, Putin tells Tajik paper', 10 July 2000, URL <http://www.eurasianet.org/resource/tajikistan/hypermail/200007/0003.html>.
[134] 'Russia to help rebuild Tajikistan's military–industrial complex', RFE/RL Newsline, 13 Nov. 2000.
[135] The Military Balance 2000/2001 (note 3), p. 176.
[136] ITAR-TASS World Service (Moscow), 3 Apr. 1999, in 'Tajik President backs extending CIS security treaty', FBIS-SOV-1999-0403, 5 Apr. 1999.

Tajikistan's armed forces. Iran has also agreed to supply Tajikistan with weapons and technical equipment.[137]

Turkmenistan

Turkmenistan's armed forces of approximately 17 500 active personnel are equipped with 690 battle tanks, 1770 armoured vehicles, numerous artillery and missile defence systems, and 243 combat aircraft (with another 172 in storage).[138] Between 1995 and 2000 spending on these forces increased by 71 per cent. The 2000 defence budget was 850 billion manats ($646 million at constant 1998 prices and exchange rates)—3.4 per cent of GDP. Turkmenistan's defence spending as a share of GDP has consistently ranked among the highest in Central Asia and the Caspian region as a whole. Allegedly, some military-related expenditures are not included in its defence budgets.[139] Additional funding may also be needed if plans to increase armed forces personnel to 40 000 and to develop a national navy are initiated.[140]

A joint Turkmen–Russian force guarded Turkmenistan's 2300-km border with Iran and Afghanistan until November 1999, when the 1993 Turkmen–Russian treaty regulating the Russian presence there expired. Turkmenistan's servicemen benefited from military–technical assistance and training provided by Russia, and since the expiry of the 1993 agreement Turkmenistan has guarded its borders with Afghanistan and Iran independently.[141] Despite the failure of plans to institute joint command of Russian and Turkmen armed forces, bilateral agreements have been concluded with Russia on the joint use of naval facilities at Krasnovodsk (in Turkmenistan) and joint naval exercises.[142] Turkmenistan also participates in the Caspian Sea Flotilla under Russian command.[143] The two countries have agreed to establish a joint air force training facility, and Russian and Turkmen leaders have expressed a desire to enhance bilateral cooperation further, particularly in the fields of defence and military technology.[144] In addition, Russia, Azerbaijan and Ukraine among the CIS countries host Turkmen armed forces personnel at their military academies.[145]

According to available sources Turkmenistan has not received arms transfers in recent years. In return for fuel Russia agreed in late 1994 to provide material

---

[137] 'China to provide technical assistance to Tajik military', *RFE/RL Newsline,* 14 July 2000; and IRNA (Tehran), 8 Mar. 2001, in 'Iran's defense minister in Dushanbe for military agreement', FBIS-SOV-2001-0308, 12 Mar. 2001.

[138] *The Military Balance 2000/2001* (note 3), pp. 176–77.

[139] See tables 5.1, 5.2 and 5.3; and Sköns *et al.* (note 109), p. 291.

[140] 'The 1999–2000 world defence almanac', *Military Technology,* vol. 24, no. 1 (2000), p. 219.

[141] *Rossiyskaya Gazeta,* 28 Jan. 1995, in 'Treaty on Turkmenistan joint border force', FBIS-SOV-95-023, 19 Nov. 1995; and 'Turkmenistan, Russia reach compromise on border guards', *RFE/RL Newsline,* 7 July 1999.

[142] Smith (note 109), pp. 31–32.

[143] *The Military Balance 2000/2001* (note 3), p. 169.

[144] Smith (note 109), p. 31; and ITAR-TASS (Moscow), 20 June 2000, in 'Putin, Nazarbaev agree on cooperation in defence', FBIS-SOV-2000-0620, 21 June 2000.

[145] Smith (note 109), p. 30; 'Ukraine to provide military assistance to Turkmenistan', *New Europe,* 16 Nov. 1996, p. 40; and 'Training offer to Turkmenistan', *Jane's Defence Weekly,* 29 Mar. 2000, p. 22.

and technical support for the development of Turkmenistan's armed forces, although information on subsequent transfers is either non-existent or not available.[146] It nevertheless seems reasonable to conclude that arms imports, or at least the repair of existing weapons, will be necessary if plans move ahead to increase the number of armed forces personnel on active duty and to form a national navy. Over 40 of Turkmenistan's Su-25 combat aircraft are being refurbished in Georgia at the TAW facility at a cost of $1 million per aircraft. This is to be subsidized by Georgia for repayment of its debt to Turkmenistan (primarily for natural gas imports in 1992–96).[147] Ukraine has also agreed to provide technical maintenance and repair for additional Turkmen weapons.[148]

Turkmenistan's armed forces participate in multilateral military exercises within the PFP programme and its military personnel attend NATO-financed courses on planning and drafting budgets, the use of communications, computer and information systems, and medical training. In addition, Turkey and the USA host Turkmen military personnel at their military academies.[149] President Saparmurat Niyazov also supports a greater role for the UN in mediating a resolution to the Afghan conflict, determining the status of the Caspian Sea, and ensuring the security of regional oil and gas pipelines.[150]

Turkmenistan has also sought military cooperation with China, Iran and other neighbours: for example, its forces personnel receive training in Pakistan.[151]

Uzbekistan

The armed forces of Uzbekistan include approximately 59 100 personnel equipped with 350 MBTs, 295 AIFVs, 379 APCs and hundreds of artillery pieces. Much of the 2000 tanks (T-64), 1200 ACVs and 750 artillery pieces transferred to Uzbekistan by the former Soviet Union in 1991 remains in storage. The air force has 135 combat aircraft and 42 attack helicopters, as well as SAM systems, at its disposal.[152] In 1999 spending on these defence forces amounted to 34.8 billion soms ($982 million at constant 1998 prices and exchange rates)—1.7 per cent of GDP and a vast increase, by 137 per cent,

[146] Interfax (Moscow), 27 Dec. 1994, in 'Gas for arms deal signed with Russia', FBIS-SOV-94-248, 27 Dec. 1994.

[147] ITAR-TASS (Moscow), 7 Aug. 1999, in 'Tbilisi plant to repair warplanes for Turkmenistan', FBIS-SOV-1999-0808, 9 Aug. 1999; and 'Georgia to repair Turkmen jet fighters', RFE/RL Newsline, 8 July 1999.

[148] 'Ukraine to provide military assistance to Turkmenistan', New Europe, 16 Nov. 1996, p. 40.

[149] ITAR-TASS (Moscow), 20 Aug. 1997, in 'Turkmenistan: Niyazov approves partnership within NATO PFP program', FBIS-SOV-97-232, 21 Aug. 1997; Interfax (Moscow), 11 May 1999, in 'Turkmenistan to sign agreement with NATO program', FBIS-SOV-1999-0511, 12 May 1999; Turkmen Press News Agency (Ashkhabad)/BBC Monitoring, 'Turkmenistan to step up NATO partnership activities', 11 May 1999, URL <http://www.soros.org/turkstan/omri/0103.html>; and Smith (note 109), p. 30.

[150] 'Turkmen President calls for increased UN role in guarding pipelines', RFE/RL Newsline, 25 Aug. 2000.

[151] Smith (note 109), pp. 30–33; Interfax (Moscow), 10 Sep. 1999, in 'Turkmenistan for military cooperation with China', FBIS-SOV-1999-0910, 13 Sep. 1999; and 'Turkmen President remains lukewarm on CIS', RFE/RL Newsline, 16 May 2000.

[152] The Military Balance 2000/2001 (note 3), p. 177.

since 1995. Significantly, the 17 000–19 000 internal security forces are not funded as part of the defence budget.[153]

The government has also initiated a process of extensive military reform. The reforms envisage the creation of mobile, well-equipped and well-trained armed forces and focus on training, reforming military command structures and modernizing armaments. To promote inter-agency compatibility and efficiency anti-terrorist exercises have been held involving participants from the military, the interior ministry and the border guard force. President Islam Karimov has also announced the creation of a new border defence unit. However, it is unclear what the ultimate scale of these reforms will be or how they will be reflected in future defence budgets.[154]

Russia remains Uzbekistan's most important strategic partner. This is in spite of Uzbekistan's increasing military cooperation with the West and its decision to withdraw from the Tashkent Treaty and join GUUAM in early 1999.[155] Describing the evolving bilateral relationship in December 1999, then Russian Prime Minister Putin stated: 'We are coming to a qualitatively new level of relations in security matters. We are ready by joint efforts to put a barrier to the spread of terrorism and extremism'.[156] In the same month the two countries concluded a Treaty on the Further Deepening of All-Round Cooperation in the Military and Military–Technical Spheres that calls for enhanced cooperation against international terrorism and in the development, production and delivery of advanced weapons.[157] Military and military–technical agreements were signed during President Putin's official visit to Uzbekistan in May 2000.[158]

Uzbekistan was frustrated with the failure to implement these agreements and with delays in the delivery of Russian arms, mainly because of its own failure to meet its payment obligations. These issues were addressed when President Karimov made a state visit to Moscow on 3–5 May 2001. The two states signed a protocol on exchanging instruments of ratification of the December 1999 agreement and agreed to create working groups within their national security systems to implement and regulate the military–technical cooperation called for in the agreement. Uzbekistan also offered to pay for future Russian aid with exports of cotton, gas, fruit and vegetables (at prices 30 per cent below average international prices).[159]

[153] *The Military Balance 2000/2001* (note 3), p. 177.

[154] Makarenko (note 84), p. 32; and 'Uzbekistan reforms military, upgrades border guards', *RFE/RL Newsline*, 15 Jan. 1999.

[155] On GUUAM see chapter 1 in this volume and section V below.

[156] ITAR-TASS (Moscow), 11 Dec. 1999, in 'Further on Russian–Uzbekistan military cooperation deal', FBIS-SOV-1999-1211, 13 Dec. 1999.

[157] Interfax (Moscow), 18 May 2000, in 'Russia: Putin informs Duma of Uzbek military agreement', FBIS-SOV-2000-0518, 19 May 2000.

[158] ITAR-TASS (Moscow), 2 June 2000, in 'Putin, Uzbek President discuss accords by telephone', FBIS-SOV-2000-0602 , 5 June 2000.

[159] Uzbek Television first channel (Tashkent)/BBC Monitoring Service, 'Uzbekistan, Russia agree to set up military cooperation groups', 6 May 2001, URL <http://eurasianet.org/resource/uzbekistan/hypermail/news/0007.html>; and Tkachuk, T., 'Rossiya–Uzbekistan: nastupayet epokha potepleniya' [Russia–Uzbekistan: a phase of warming begins], *Nezavisimaya Gazeta,* 5 May 2001.

In June 2000 the Russian and Uzbek defence ministers, Igor Sergeyev and Lieutenant-General Yuriy Akmazov, signed an additional agreement on the joint use of Russian weapon testing facilities, and on 19 June 2000 Uzbek and Russian officials agreed to initiate joint anti-aircraft defence duty. Uzbekistan thus joined Armenia, Belarus, Kazakhstan, Kyrgyzstan and Russia in the CIS Integrated Air Defence System and received advanced communications equipment for the continuous exchange of information.[160] Uzbek servicemen train in Russian military academies and the armed forces benefit from participating in CIS military exercises.[161]

According to Uzbek officials, current reforms will require the import of modern weaponry, the repair and modernization of existing stockpiles and increased military–technical cooperation with foreign states.[162] Russian assistance will be crucial in this regard. Between 1995 and 1997, Russia transferred 120 APCs to Uzbekistan, and it announced the transfer of 50 additional APCs in 2000.[163] In 1999 Russia and other CIS states supplied weapons to Uzbekistan's armed forces fighting Islamic rebels, and renewed attacks in August 2000 led Russia to offer $30 million in additional weapons, including armoured vehicles, Mi-8 helicopters, and other weapons and communications equipment. Uzbekistan subsequently accepted the Russian offer of military–technical aid.[164] Agreements have also been drafted for the repair of Uzbek weapons by Russian firms and the joint manufacture of explosives.[165] CIS member Ukraine supplied small amounts of weapons and military equipment to Uzbekistan in 1999 and offered additional military–technical assistance in the autumn of 2000. In addition, over 40 of Uzbekistan's battle tanks have been modernized in Ukrainian facilities, and preparations are under way to have several armoured vehicles repaired there.[166]

The unstable security environment and the perception in Tashkent that Russia regards Uzbekistan as a 'buffer zone' between itself and unstable southern regions has led to the development of defence and security ties with NATO and its member countries, mainly within the PFP programme. Uzbek Army detach-

[160] Interfax (Moscow), 20 June 2000, in 'Russia, Uzbekistan begin joint anti-aircraft defense service duty', FBIS-SOV-2000-0620, 21 June 2000. Akmazov was replaced as Uzbekistan's Defence Minister by Maj.-Gen. Kadyr Gulomov in the autumn of 2000. 'Uzbekistan dismisses defence minister', *Jane's Defence Weekly*, 11 Oct. 2000, p. 28.

[161] ITAR-TASS (Moscow), 3 Oct. 2000, in 'Uzbekistan to train army officers in Russian academies', FBIS-SOV-2000-1003, 6 Oct. 2000; and Interfax (Moscow), 28 Mar. 2000, in 'CIS joint command exercises begin in Tajikistan', FBIS-SOV-2000-0328, 29 Mar. 2000.

[162] *Vatanparvar* (Tashkent), 23 May 2000, in 'Uzbek Deputy Defense Minister outlines plans for re-equipping forces', URL <http://www.eurasianet.org/resource/uzbekistan/hypermail/200006/0003.html>.

[163] *The Military Balance 1999/2000* (note 65), p. 158; and ITAR-TASS (Moscow), 20 Apr. 2000, 'Russian Arzamas plant to supply 50 APCs to Uzbekistan', FBIS-SOV-2000-0420, 24 Apr. 2000.

[164] Agence France-Presse, 30 Aug. 2000, in 'Russia to send 30 million dollars of arms to Uzbekistan', URL <http://www.russiatoday.com/news.php3?id=194396&section=CIS>; and Saradzhyan, S., 'Uzbekistan seeks Russian arms for border clashes', *Defense News*, 18 Sep. 2000, p. 8.

[165] 'Uzbekistan, Russia sign new military cooperation agreements', *RFE/RL Newsline*, 27 June 2000.

[166] 'Ukraine on the world arms market', *National Security and Defence*, no. 5 (2000), p. 66; *Kommersant*, 'Russian paper gives details of Uzbek armed forces reform plans', 7 Sep. 2000, URL <http://www.uzland.uz/2000/09_09.htm#army>; and 'Ukraine, Turkey offer to help combat threat to Central Asia', *RFE/RL Newline*, 4 Sep. 2000.

ments trained in the US states of Louisiana in 1995 and North Carolina in 1996, and US forces have participated in exercises in Uzbekistan.[167] The USA and Uzbekistan have concluded a military–technical agreement and for several years Uzbekistan's armed forces have received much-needed development aid under the FMF programme.[168] In April 2000, Secretary of State Albright pledged $3 million to Uzbekistan for the development of its border force. She also informed President Islam Karimov during the United Nations Millennium Summit in New York in September 2000 that the USA was prepared to offer political, moral and material assistance to Uzbekistan's armed forces in their fight against regional extremist forces.[169]

Germany has provided training to Uzbek Army and Air Force personnel and over $26 million in medical and other military-related supplies to Uzbekistan's armed forces. Turkey offered Uzbekistan financial aid immediately following the August 2000 Islamic incursions and agreed to train Uzbek counter-terrorism teams in its military academies.[170] Under a 16 October 2000 military cooperation agreement the two countries further agreed to jointly fight international terrorism and other criminal activities, and discussed the possible transfer of Turkish arms and other military equipment to Uzbekistan's armed forces.[171] A joint defence cooperation commission has been established with France, and Greece hosts Uzbek armed forces personnel at its military academies. Uzbek military and government officials also participate in military exercises, courses and seminars held in several other NATO countries.[172]

Western countries have been much less active in supplying arms to Uzbekistan. Nevertheless, in the spring of 2000 the USA announced plans to transfer 12 military transport vehicles to Uzbekistan. The transfer is to be financed by a US Government grant.[173] Talks between NATO and Uzbek officials have also focused on NATO military supplies to Uzbekistan.[174]

Cooperation has also been established with other regional countries. In August 2000 China announced that $365 000 in military aid would be granted to Uzbekistan's armed forces. Shortly thereafter, Chinese Vice-President Hu Jintao stated that China planned to increase its cooperation with Uzbekistan in

[167] Pikulina, M., *Uzbekistan in the Mirror of Military Security: A Historical Preface to Current Events* (Royal Military Academy, Conflict Studies Research Centre: Sandhurst, Nov. 1999), p. 11; and Interfax (Moscow), 9 June 1997, in 'Uzbekistan: Joint command exercises with United States completed', FBIS-UMA-97-160, 10 June 1997.

[168] Finnegan, P., 'US, Uzbekistan move to boost defense ties', *Defense News,* 3–9 Nov. 1997, p. 4.

[169] 'Tighter security for Central Asia', *Jane's Defence Weekly,* 3 May 2000, p. 14; and 'Uzbek President says US ready to help wipe out banned Islamic movement', *RFE/RL Newsline,* 12 Sep. 2000.

[170] Interfax (Moscow), 11 Apr. 1997, in 'Uzbekistan: troops begin long-term military training program in Germany', FBIS-SOV-97-101, 14 Apr. 1997; Reuters (Ankara), 'Turkey offers Uzbeks, Kyrgyz aid against rebels', 2 Sep. 2000; and Anatolia (Ankara), 18 Sep. 2000, in 'Uzbek counter terrorism teams to be trained in Turkey', FBIS-WEU-2000-0918, 25 Sep. 2000.

[171] Interfax, 16 Oct. 2000, in 'Uzbekistan, Turkey, to join forces against terrorism, crime', URL <http://eurasianet.org/resource/uzbekistan/hypermail/200010/0026.html>.

[172] Athens News Agency (Internet), 19 Nov. 1998, in 'Greece: Greek–Uzbek military cooperation agreement signed', FBIS-WEU-98-323, 20 Nov. 1998; 'Uzbekistan, France co-operate further', *Jane's Defence Weekly,* 19 July 2000, p. 16; and Pikulina (note 167), p. 11.

[173] 'USA approves sale to Uzbekistan', *Jane's Defence Weekly,* 15 Mar. 2000, p. 4.

[174] 'Russian paper gives details of Uzbek armed forces reform plans' (note 166).

several fields, including the joint fight against 'national separatism, international terrorism, religious extremism and other cross-nation crimes'.[175]

V. Multilateral security cooperation

Some semblance of cooperation and coordination appears to be returning to security relations between CIS countries following a period when some states in the Caspian region distanced themselves from CIS security structures. It appears that, despite the withdrawal of Azerbaijan, Georgia and Uzbekistan from the Tashkent Treaty, the idea of military and security cooperation within CIS structures has been given a new lease on life. This is primarily due to the emerging threats to regional security—international terrorism, religious and political extremism, drug trafficking and other criminal activities—which regional countries are finding increasingly difficult to control unilaterally.

The Tashkent Treaty

The remaining parties to the Tashkent Treaty—Armenia, Belarus, Kazakhstan, Kyrgyzstan, Russia and Tajikistan—have drawn closer together because of the emerging threats. On 24 May 2000 their leaders signed nine documents on multilateral cooperation against international terrorism and political and religious extremism. To facilitate cooperation the signatories are able to buy Russian-made weapons at below-market prices. Cooperation within the treaty was further consolidated on 11 October 2000 with the signing in Bishkek of an agreement on the establishment of a rapid-reaction force that could be deployed to conflict areas on the territories of the signatories.[176] In addition, the Integrated Air Defence System involving all the parties to the Tashkent Treaty plus Uzbekistan is being given higher priority in the security policies of participating countries, particularly in Central Asia.[177]

Regional unrest has led to several agreements being concluded between Tashkent Treaty and other CIS countries. On 16 March 2000 CIS defence ministers signed 10 agreements primarily focused on cooperation in peacekeeping and counter-terrorism, and on 8 September 2000 CIS interior ministers signed a three-year programme on joint measures against international terrorism, extremism, drug trafficking and other criminal activities. The CIS prime ministers have also approved plans to establish an anti-terrorist centre in Moscow to enhance multilateral cooperation.[178] Similarly, CIS military training exercises

[175] 'Uzbekistan, China discuss military cooperation', *RFE/RL Newsline*, 28 Aug. 2000; and Xinhua (Beijing), 25 Aug. 2000, in 'PRC Vice President Hu Jintao discusses cooperation with Uzbek Defense Minister', Foreign Broadcast Information Service, *Daily Report–China (FBIS-CHI)*, FBIS-CHI-2000-0825, 28 Aug. 2000.

[176] 'Signatories to the CIS Collective Security Treaty to boost co-operation', *RFE/RL Newsline*, 25 May 2000; and 'CIS security pact signatories agree to create joint force', *RFE/RL Newsline*, 12 Oct. 2000.

[177] Saradzhyan, S., 'CIS treaty bears fruit in form of common air defense', *Defense News*, 9 Oct. 2000, p. 44.

[178] 'CIS defence ministers sign accords', *Jane's Defence Weekly*, 29 Mar. 2000, p. 14; Interfax (Moscow), 8 Sep. 2000, in 'Interior ministers of 11 CIS countries sign agreement on fight against terror-

are increasingly focusing on joint operations against terrorist and extremist groups.[179]

NATO

Apart from Tajikistan, all the former Soviet republics in the Caspian region are members of the PFP and participate in armed forces development activities limited mainly to officer training, military exercises and military reform. Azerbaijan and Georgia, in particular, are the recipients of an increasing amount of NATO aid, partly through the PFP but also in the form of arms transfers. In March 2001 the foreign and defence ministers of Azerbaijan made statements favouring the deployment of a Turkish or NATO military base in Azerbaijan.[180] Soon afterwards Georgia announced that Turkish military aircraft would receive free access and service at its Marneuli airport.[181] As mentioned above, both Azerbaijan and Georgia have expressed interest in membership of NATO. Most of the regional states favour increasing military cooperation with NATO, but not at the expense of similar cooperation with Russia.

The Shanghai Forum

Originally an arena for resolving border disagreements and developing regional confidence-building measures (CBMs), the Shanghai Forum (founded in 1996 by China, Kazakhstan, Kyrgyzstan, Russia, and Tajikistan: Uzbekistan received observer status in July 2000 and became a full member in June 2001) is expanding the scope of its agenda to deal with contemporary security issues. The determination of the Shanghai Forum countries to enhance interaction and cooperation in the fight against international terrorism, religious extremism and national separatism was reflected in both the Astana Communiqué of 30 March 2000 and the declaration adopted following the Dushanbe summit meeting in July 2000.[182] At the summit meeting in Shanghai in June 2001 the participants adopted a Convention on the Fight against Terrorism, Separatism and Extrem-

---

ism' (Presidential Bulletin, 8 Sep. 2000), FBIS-SOV-2000-0908, 12 Sep. 2000; and Interfax (Moscow), 20 June 2000, in 'CIS to set up antiterrorist center', FBIS-SOV-2000-0620, 21 June 2000.

[179] Interfax, 28 Mar. 2000, in 'CIS Command-Post operations begin in Tajikistan', URL <http://www.eurasianet.org/resource/kyrgyzstan/hypermail/200003/0056.html>; and Asia-Plus News Agency/BBC Monitoring, 'CIS air defence training held in Tajikistan 5th April', 6 Apr. 2000, URL <http://www.eurasianet.org/resource/tajikistan/hypermail/200004/0007.html>.

[180] ITAR-TASS (Moscow), 24 Mar. 2001, in 'Azerbaijan: Officials welcome foreign military presence' and 'Azerbaijan: Foreign minister sees possible deployment of NATO, Turkish base', FBIS-SOV-2001-0324, 26 Mar. 2001.

[181] Interfax (Moscow), 8 Apr. 2001, in 'Georgia confirms Turkish warplanes will be serviced at Marneuli airfield', FBIS-SOV-2001-408, 9 Apr. 2001.

[182] Lachowski, Z., 'Conventional arms control', *SIPRI Yearbook 1998: Armaments, Disarmament and International Security* (Oxford University Press: Oxford, 1998), pp. 526–27; ITAR-TASS (Moscow), 30 Mar. 2000, in 'Kazakhstan: Five defence ministers sign Astana Communiqué', FBIS-SOV-2000-0330, 4 Apr. 2000; Khovar (Dushanbe)/BBC Monitoring, 'Shanghai Five summit declaration: text', 5 July 2000, URL <http://www.eurasianet.org/resource/tajikistan/hypermail/200007/0001html>; and ITAR-TASS (Moscow), 12 Feb. 2001, in 'Shanghai Five experts to discuss anti-terrorist measures', FBIS-SOV-2001-0214, 15 Feb. 2001.

ism, and decided to change the name of the forum to the Shanghai Cooperation Organization.[183]

The Central Asian Union

The former Soviet republics of Central Asia have also developed security ties among themselves and with non-CIS countries. In 1994 Kazakhstan, Kyrgyzstan and Uzbekistan formed the Central Asian Union (CAU) as a primarily economic entity.[184] Tajikistan joined it in 1999. However, cooperation within this forum extended to defence and security issues with the establishment of a joint Council of Defence Ministers to coordinate 'military exercises, air defence, and defence supplies'.[185] In May 1996 the CAU member countries formed the trilateral peacekeeping battalion, CentrasBat, under the aegis of the UN, to be trained within the PFP programme. CentrasBat has received funding and technical support from the UN and the EU, as well as from the USA. It has also participated in numerous military exercises with armed forces units from Russia, the USA and other Western countries.[186]

In addition to several recent bilateral military cooperation agreements involving regional governments, on 21 April 2000 Kazakhstan, Kyrgyzstan, Tajikistan and Uzbekistan signed a 10-year treaty on the joint fight against terrorism, political and religious extremism, organized crime and other regional security threats. These same countries later signed an agreement aimed at coordinating the activities of their intelligence and security agencies. Under the latter agreement, the participants agree to come to each other's defence in the event of aggression.[187]

GUUAM

In the South Caucasus, Georgia and Azerbaijan have developed security links and military cooperation outside CIS security structures. The GUAM group, founded in October 1997 and at that time made up of Georgia, Ukraine, Azerbaijan and Moldova, was joined in April 1999 by Uzbekistan (thus becoming GUUAM). It is primarily an economic grouping; however, the members also regard cooperation within GUUAM as a viable alternative to the CIS security

---

[183] ITAR-TASS, 14 June 2001, in 'Uzbekistan becomes member of Shanghai Five forum', FBIS-SOV-2001-0614, 14 June 2001.

[184] On the CAU see chapter 1 in this volume.

[185] Allison, R., 'Subregional cooperation and security in the CIS', eds R. Dwan and O. Paviuk, *Building Security in the New States of Eurasia: Subregional Cooperation in the Former Soviet Space* (M. E. Sharpe: London, 2000), pp. 154–55.

[186] Allison (note 185), p. 154; Interfax (Kazakhstan), 'Kazakh leader, US military official discuss Centasian security', 13 Sep. 2000, URL <http://www.eurasianet.org/resource/kazakhstan/hypermail/200009/0033.html>; and Interfax (Kazakhstan), 'Centrasbat peacekeeping exercises end in Kazakhstan', 18 Sep. 2000, URL <http://www.eurasianet.org/resource/tajikistan/hypermail/200009/0034.html>.

[187] 'Uzbek summit participants sign anti-terrorism treaty', *RFE/RL Newsline,* 25 Apr. 2000; and 'Central Asian Pact', *Jane's Intelligence Review,* June 2000, p. 3.

structure and as a way to enhance cooperation with NATO.[188] The new Government of Moldova announced on 29 December 2000 that it would not participate in military cooperation initiatives within the group. Nevertheless, in December 1997 Azerbaijan, Georgia and Ukraine decided to form a tripartite battalion within GUUAM to be tasked with guarding future energy pipeline and regional transport routes, and the three countries have conducted joint military exercises within the GUUAM framework aimed at protecting the Baku–Supsa oil pipeline against terrorist attack.[189] The defence ministers of Azerbaijan and Ukraine reiterated their support for this project during the October 2000 signing of the Azerbaijan–Ukraine Defence Cooperation Program for 2001.[190] The full extent of its responsibilities, the amount of funding it will receive and the sources of that funding are yet to be determined. Reflecting Western interest in the development of GUUAM, in September 2000 the US Government voted $45.5 million in new military aid to its member countries.[191]

VI. Conclusions

Several trends are clear regarding armed forces development in Iran and the newly independent states of the Caspian Sea region.

National trends

First, defence spending is increasing significantly in the region as a whole. Only two countries—Georgia and Kazakhstan—reduced their spending in the six-year period 1995–2000. Georgia is considered a 'failed state' by many, with very few domestic resources to allocate to the armed forces. It therefore relies increasingly on external sources to fund its armed forces. Kazakhstan, on the other hand, although it reduced defence expenditure in the period 1997–2000 (in constant prices), has announced that spending will increase in 2001. The changing security threat assessment that views international terrorism and political and religious extremism as the main threats to Kazakhstan's national security has also resulted in significant attention and resources being devoted to the development of internal security forces.

Second, the countries of the region are importing more and more conventional weapons. These weapons are also becoming more sophisticated and represent a

[188] Valasek, T., *Military Cooperation between Georgia, Ukraine, Uzbekistan, Azerbaijan, and Moldova in the GUUAM Framework*, Caspian Studies Program Policy Brief no. 2 (Harvard University, John F. Kennedy School of Government, Caspian Studies Program: Cambridge, Mass., Dec. 2000).

[189] ITAR-TASS World Service (Moscow), 13 Apr. 1999, in 'Azerbaijan, Georgia, Ukraine begin joint exercises', FBIS-SOV-1999-0414, 15 Apr. 1999; and 'Ukraine: joint military force includes Georgia and Azerbaijan', *RFE/RL Weekday Magazine*, 24 Mar. 2000, URL <http://www.rferl.org/nca/features/2000/03/f.ru.000324145147.html>.

[190] Turan (Baku), 13 Oct. 2000, in 'Visiting Azeri Defence Minister and Ukrainian counterpart sign co-operation deal', FBIS-SOV-2000-1013, 16 Oct. 2000; Turan (Baku), 22 Jan. 1999, in 'Azerbaijan: GUAM members sign communiqué on military co-operation', FBIS-SOV-99-022, 26 Jan. 1999; and 'Ukraine: joint military force includes Georgia and Azerbaijan' (note 189).

[191] Parahonskiy, B., 'The formation of regional cooperation models in GUUAM', *Central Asia and the Caucasus* (Luleå), no. 2 (2000), pp. 73–79; 'Russia and its neighbours: frost and friction', *The Economist*, 30 Sep.–6 Oct. 2000, p. 45; and Allison (note 185), pp. 159–61.

major aspect of national military reform programmes in the region. A major goal of the programmes, which influences the type of weapons transferred to regional countries, is the development of mobile armed forces capable of confronting today's most prominent threats to regional security.

These military reform programmes represent the third major trend in armed forces development in the region. Kazakhstan and Uzbekistan, for example, are creating rapid-reaction units and increasing overall mobility and inter-service coordination and compatibility in order to effectively combat contemporary regional security threats.

Fourth, the countries of the region are developing indigenous defence industrial capabilities. For example, Iran is developing infrastructure for the production of short- and long-range missiles, tanks, fighter aircraft, naval vessels and other weapons. At the same time, certain newly independent states in the region are attempting to re-establish long-standing indigenous military industrial capabilities left over from the Soviet period (in Armenia, Kazakhstan and Uzbekistan).

International trends

US/NATO military aid is admittedly small compared with Russian military assistance to the Caspian region states. However, the amount of US/NATO aid is increasing significantly. For example, there are few recorded US/NATO arms transfers to Caspian region states before 1998. By 2000 the USA/NATO share of arms transfers to the region had increased to 4.1 per cent, with Russia accounting for 90 per cent. There has also been an increase in the role of China in the military affairs of regional states because of its growing political and economic interest in the region, especially in its territories adjacent to Central Asia. It also cooperates extensively with Iran on military issues. By 2000 China's share in arms transfers to the region exceeded 5 per cent.

International military aid from these and other external actors supplements the regional countries' internal efforts to develop their armed forces. The aid comes in numerous forms, including: (*a*) financial assistance in the form of credits and grants, particularly from the West, that supplement national defence budgets; (*b*) increased arms transfers to regional countries; (*c*) training for armed forces personnel from the countries of the Caspian region in the military academies of regional and extra-regional states (e.g., Russia, Turkey and the USA); (*d*) the expansion of various forms of military cooperation between Russia and other Caspian regional states (with the exception of Georgia), particularly since the November 1999 Istanbul Summit Meeting of the OSCE; (*e*) growing military cooperation between the USA/NATO and the new states of the region (excluding Tajikistan)—cooperation which is assuming more sophisticated forms, from training to arms transfers to the organization of military exercises; and (*f*) the involvement of regional states in bilateral and multilateral security arrangements.

The former Soviet republics of the region are still in the early stages of developing their national armed forces, and these internal and external initiatives contribute to this process. These trends are increasing and will most likely continue to do so for several reasons, including: (*a*) the growing and often competing interests of extra-regional countries in regional affairs; (*b*) ongoing conflicts in the region and on its perimeter (Afghanistan, Chechnya and the Ferghana Valley); (*c*) unresolved conflicts where a resumption of violence is highly possible (in Abkhazia, Nagorno-Karabakh and South Ossetia); (*d*) unstable relations between regional states; and (*e*) the many emerging threats to regional stability—international terrorism, religious and political extremism, and drug trafficking. These factors will motivate regional countries to further develop their military capabilities, as domestic resources permit, while at the same time they motivate external actors, most notably Russia, the USA, NATO and China, to extend further assistance for the development of national armed forces in the region.

Part II

National perspectives on security in the Caspian Sea region

6. Russia's national security interests in the Caspian region

Vitaly Naumkin

I. Introduction

The Caspian region has recently assumed increasing significance for the littoral states and for regional and global powers. This has been the result of national and regional security factors as well as purely economic ones. The latter are linked to the prospects of extracting hydrocarbon energy resources to be exported to the world market.

In the works of strategic analysts today several definitions of the Caspian region are to be found, ranging from a purely geographical one, which includes only the Caspian littoral states, to others which notably extend its borders on the basis of economic and geopolitical dimensions. In the latter case the region is regarded as a vast territory from the Pamir in the east to the Black Sea in the west, Kazakhstan's border with Russia in the north and the Persian Gulf in the south. Although this approach—which underlies the SIPRI project on the Security of the Caspian Sea Region—may be questioned, energy resource endowment is the key factor (not denying the importance of others) which is the basis for joining very disparate countries and even subregions—Central Asia, the South Caucasus and part of the Middle East—into a single whole. It is the oil and gas component that makes the extended interpretation meaningful.

In the discussion that follows of Russia's national security interests in this region, both concepts of the Caspian region are used.

II. The southern direction of Russia's national security

An analysis of documents adopted in Russia in recent years suggests that its south is viewed by the Russian leadership as a source of varied threats and challenges of a predominantly non-traditional type. Russia's new national security concept concentrates on the full spectrum of new challenges and threats.[1] Among these terrorism, separatism and internal conflicts are cited. It is in the Caucasus and Central Asia that these threats proliferate.

The national security concept provides for measures which include, in particular, 'contribution to the settlement of conflicts, including peacekeeping activities under the aegis of the UN, the OSCE [Organization for Security and Co-operation in Europe], and the CIS [Commonwealth of Independent States]'. Significantly, Russia's national interests 'require a Russian military presence in

---

[1] The text of Russia's national security concept was published in *Krasnaya Zvezda*, 29 Jan. 2000.

a number of strategically important regions of the world under appropriate circumstances'. Military deterrence is not seen as the only way to meet the challenges discussed above. Nonetheless, the new military strategy bears the mark of these threats.

The national security concept defines the fields in which the armed forces and other military units would be used—in world or regional war, in local wars and international armed conflicts, in internal armed conflicts, and in operations in support of and for the restoration of peace. From this list alone it can be seen that, given the scope and character of the threats coming from the Caspian region, Russia cannot countenance the demilitarization of the Caspian Sea which a number of the littoral states are demanding. Arguing the need for Russia to participate extensively in peacekeeping operations, the head of the Main Directorate for International Military Cooperation, Colonel-General Leonid Ivashov, has noted that they 'must become the most important means of preventing and eliminating crisis situations as they appear and develop'.[2]

III. Russia's interests

In its triple quality as a Caspian state, a regional power and a global power, Russia naturally has vital interests in the Caspian region. This reflects the enhanced role the region has come to play in world politics and the world economy—a salient feature of the new geopolitical reality where geographical factors are closely allied to political interests. The interests of all the actors involved clash to some degree, but this is most evident in the ethno-political conflicts in the Caspian Basin and the belt of states nearest to it, which include the consumers and suppliers of energy and the countries whose territories oil and gas supplies must transit on their way to world markets. The conflicts are those between Georgia and Abkhazia, in Nagorno-Karabakh (between Armenia and Azerbaijan), between Georgia and South Ossetia, between North Ossetia and Ingushetia, in Turkey (with its Kurdish population), in Russia (Chechnya) and Iran (with its Kurdish population), and others.

The situation in the Caspian region and around it has so far been one of conflict and uncertainty. Russia's sensitivity to conflicts there reflects not only its relations with external partners but also the interplay between its geopolitical and its geo-economic interests.

Security threats

Excessive emphasis on the geopolitical aspects of regional problems can impede an accurate assessment of the actual threats and security risks emanating from the area for all the major players, and it is these latter that ultimately shape Russia's interests in the Caspian region, both on the wide and on the narrow definition of the region. A few main arguments illustrate this.

---

[2] Ivashov, L., Briefing at the Russian Defence Ministry, 5 May 2000 (text distributed at the briefing).

First, Kazakhstan lies in the region. It is Russia's key partner among the newly independent states of the former Soviet Union, sharing a 7000 km-long border with it, and ethnic Russians make up more than one-third of the population. Second, the region directly adjoins the North Caucasus, one of the most complex and troubled areas of the Russian Federation where one ethnic zone—Chechnya—has not fully emerged from the acute phase of armed conflict. Third, the most bitter inter-ethnic conflicts in the region have not been settled to this day, to say nothing of the potential, 'slumbering' conflicts. Fourth, some of the states of the region are extremely fragile in terms of their administrative and state polity, ethnic composition, political systems and so on: to give one example, Azerbaijan and Georgia are fragmented in so many ways that keeping them stable and their populations consolidated is a task of enormous complexity. Fifth, the states of the region have become a focus of keen interest on the part of a number of outside powers which are almost openly competing to bring them into their spheres of influence. Sixth, the South Caucasus states border on the biggest regional powers of the Middle East—Iran and Turkey—and the problems of the Caspian hold a conspicuous place in Russia's relations with them. Finally, for Russia the region is the source of such serious threats as international terrorism and religious extremism, drugs and arms smuggling, migration (of refugees and migrant workers), and so on.

In 1999–2000 the states of Central Asia came under attack from Islamic extremists who invaded the territory of Kyrgyzstan, Tajikistan and Uzbekistan from Afghanistan. These events provided a strong impetus towards cooperation between these states and Russia in the security domain. This cooperation has been given a new format in the Shanghai Forum.[3] At a conference in Astana in Kazakhstan in March 2000, representatives of China, Kazakhstan, Kyrgyzstan, Russia and Tajikistan pledged to combat 'international terrorism and religious extremism'.[4] Russia has come to regard the terrorist threat to the Central Asian states as a threat to itself as well. Replying to a question about the ranking of external threats to Russia, Sergey Ivanov, then Secretary of the Security Council of the Russian Federation, assigned second place to international terrorism: 'NATO expansion to the East; international terrorism; and attempts to create a model of the world which would make it possible for one country to act at its own discretion, in disregard of the opinion of the overwhelming majority of countries'.[5]

The fact that the strikes by Islamic extremists in the summer of 1999 in the directions of the Ferghana Valley and of Dagestan took place at the same time was interpreted by Russian strategic analysts as evidence that the extremists wished to entrench themselves in these most vulnerable regions of the CIS, then seize political power there as well as in Chechnya, and thence continue the expansion of Islamic extremism. As things became tough for the extremists in Chechnya and Dagestan, they concentrated their pressure on Kyrgyzstan and

---

[3] On the Shanghai Forum see chapter 5, section V in this volume.
[4] Stern, D., '"Shanghai Five" in big push on international terrorism', *Financial Times*, 31 Mar. 2000.
[5] *Vek* (Moscow), no. 44 (2 Nov. 2000).

Uzbekistan. The military successes of the Taliban in Afghanistan have made these threats, which earlier seemed fantastical, more real.

The perception of a common threat breathed new life into the 1992 Treaty on Collective Security Treaty (the Tashkent Treaty).[6] Within the framework of the treaty, following the setting up of committees of defence and foreign ministers, a new body was created in May 2001—the Committee of Secretaries of the Security Councils of the parties to the treaty, whose tasks include coordination of the struggle against international terrorism, drug and illicit arms trafficking, the joint settlement of regional conflicts and the maintenance of strategic stability. A conference of heads of the parties to the Tashkent Treaty held in October 2000 in Bishkek saw the signing of an Agreement on the Status of Forces and Facilities of the Collective Security System and a plan for measures to set it up in 2001–2005. The aim is to create regional bodies, joint military bodies and a unified command structure.[7] According to Sergey Ivanov,

A question currently under study is the creation of military units, their strength and commanding bodies, joint action, as well as questions of deployment, land use, financial resources, crossing of the border, and so on. That is to say, military forces will effectively be set up in the Central Asian region. In general, military formations across the Tashkent Treaty space (the East European, Caucasian and Central Asian zones) will fall under a single command and act according to the rapid-reaction principle.[8]

Economic interests

Despite the priority attached to security interests, economic interests are also important to Russia. These are: (*a*) the development of mutually advantageous trade and economic relations with the states of the region; (*b*) the use of their transport capacities; and (*c*) participation in the production and shipment of energy resources. The development of a new network of roads and pipelines in the region will create a quite new infrastructure there which will fundamentally alter the geo-strategic situation. However, everything depends on what the true volume of Caspian resources is, whether their development will be profitable, and whether it will be possible to ensure supply to the world oil market. Supply can only be ensured by major international investment.

According to Robert Ebel, the following factors are encouraging investors to tie up capital in Caspian oil:

Oil companies must continually search for new supplies to replace those barrels now being produced and there is nothing as attractive as something which has been denied but which is now available. Second, the Caspian oil potential is world-class. Third, this potential can be developed within an acceptable time-frame only through the involvement of multinational oil companies. And fourth, and possibly most important, the bulk

[6] On the membership of the Tashkent Treaty see the appendix in this volume. The text of the treaty was published in *Izvestiya*, 16 May 1992.

[7] Romanova, L., 'Sozdayutsya sily bystrogo reagirovaniya' [Rapid-deployment force created], *Nezavisimaya Gazeta*, 12 Oct. 2000.

[8] Interview with S. Ivanov, *Vek* (Moscow), no. 44 (2 Nov. 2000).

of the new oil to be developed will be for the oil market; local demand is comparatively small and is likely to stay that way.[9]

IV. Will the Caspian come to rival the Persian Gulf?

The initial estimates of oil reserves in the Caspian seem to have been overstated.[10] The 1995 contract on the Karabakh oilfield in Azerbaijan was considered one of the most promising not only for Western but also for Russian investors. The US company Pennzoil, the project operator, guaranteed 30 per cent of the quota share of the Caspian International Petroleum Company (CIPCO), set up to develop the oilfield on 10 November 1995 in Baku; 45 per cent was guaranteed by the Russian–Italian LukAgip enterprise, 12.5 per cent by Lukoil, 5 per cent by Agip and 7.5 per cent by the State Oil Company of the Azerbaijan Republic (SOCAR). Three years of prospecting yielded no results, and in September 1998, having spent $90 million on prospecting for oil, CIPCO terminated its activities.

A similar fate befell another consortium, the North Apsheron Operating Company (NAOC), whose members were BP (Britain), Unocal and Amoco (the USA), Itochu (Japan), Delta Oil (Saudi Arabia) and SOCAR. As company executives admitted, drilling for oil by the NAOC in three Caspian offshore fields revealed no commercially viable reserves. BP Amoco (as it now is) has decided to leave the consortium. The NAOC cannot be expected to invest $2 billion in the development of the Caspian deposits in the coming years as was planned.

Currently, Azerbaijan itself is suffering a shortage of oil, so that even the new Baku–Supsa pipeline is not working at full capacity. As reported by the Russian press, in order to save the situation, 'the Americans proposed an original project—bringing oil from the Kazakh oilfields in the north of the Caspian by tanker to Baku, to be later transported along the Baku–Tbilisi–Ceyhan pipeline. The economic absurdity of this project is obvious'.[11] Nursultan Nazarbayev, President of Kazakhstan, backed this project, which will become unprofitable anyway after the commissioning of the Tengiz–Novorossiysk oil pipeline in 2001.

Mobil (the USA), Monument Oil (Britain) and Dragon Oil (the Netherlands) have followed the consortia in deciding to reduce the scale of operations on the oilfields of Turkmenistan, a fact explained both by the excessively high costs of oil extraction and transport and by their desire to secure from Turkmenistan a revision of the tax treatment for the development of the Garashsizlik oil deposit.

In contrast to Azerbaijan and Turkmenistan, the chances for Kazakhstan to become a major petroleum extractor look impressive. In the summer of 2000,

---

[9] Ebel, R., 'Introduction', in *Caspian Energy Resources: Implications for the Arab Gulf* (Emirates Center for Strategic Studies and Research: Abu Dhabi, 2000), p. 9.

[10] On the oil and gas reserves of the region see also chapter 3 in this volume.

[11] Pravosudov, S., 'Chislo protivnikov trassy Baku–Dzheikhan uvelichivaetsya' [The number of opponents of the Baku–Ceyhan route is increasing], *Nezavisimaya Gazeta*, 5 Sep. 2000.

the Italian company ENI reported the discovery of the Kashagan oil deposit, the largest in the region, in the Kazakh section of the Caspian shelf. It is at a depth of 4000 metres, and the results of exploratory drilling confirmed that it may yield 600 cubic metres of oil and 200 cubic metres of gas a day.[12]

In the last days of August 2000, Chevron completed the purchase from Kazakhstan of an additional 5 per cent of the quotas of the Tengizchevronoil (TCO) joint venture, thus increasing Chevron's share from 45 to 50 per cent. Since it was founded in 1993, this joint venture has increased output at the Tengiz oilfield from 60 000 to an average of 215 000 barrels a day.[13]

However, this has not changed the overall picture yet. A number of Caspian states had greatly overstated their oil reserves in order to attract investors. For the Western oil companies, some analysts argue, it was not as important to proceed to develop the Caspian reserves as to stake out a claim in the region for the distant future. If this is the case then it will be neither unexpected nor surprising if they gradually freeze work on the Caspian. In this situation it is no longer so important whether the oil reserves in the offshore Caspian fields are 'commercial' today or not. What was unprofitable yesterday may become profitable tomorrow.

Furthermore, it may be presumed that the excitement about the oil reserves of the region is intended as a cover, a justification for penetration into the region for purposes dictated by geopolitical and military–strategic designs.

Thus the reasons why interest in Caspian oil is flagging may include: (*a*) the unexpected mismatch between the real reserves of oil in a number of the Caspian fields and the preliminary estimates, which proved grossly overstated; (*b*) the completion of the initial stage in which the petroleum companies established their positions in the Caspian; (*c*) the completion of the geo-strategic opening-up of the region; (*d*) oil price fluctuations; and (*e*) the desire on the part of the relevant companies to wait for the normalization of relations between Iran and the USA, when it will become possible to negotiate the transport of oil along the Iranian route.

The Iranian route is the most efficient one. In a statement made as early as March 1999, Richard Morningstar, special adviser to the US President and the Secretary of State for Caspian Basin Energy Diplomacy, did not exclude the possibility of a pipeline to Iran being laid if Iranian–US relations warmed up and argued for the Iranian route.[14] As reported by the Russian mass media, during his presidential election campaign in 2000 George W. Bush stated that, since the earlier claims of vast energy reserves at the Caspian shelf were not confirmed, the transport of Caspian oil via the territories of Iran and Russia might be economically appropriate.[15]

[12] Prime-TASS, cited in *Segodnya*, 26 July 2000.

[13] Sidorov, M., 'Dolya Shevrona uvelichilas' [Chevron's share has increased], *Nezavisimaya Gazeta*, 5 Sep. 2000.

[14] Novoprudskiy, S., 'Zlatnik ne tol'ko mal, no i dorog' [Zolotnik is not only small but precious], *Finansovye Izvestiya*, 16 Mar. 1999.

[15] Kolchin, S., 'Kaspiyskaya neft' opazdyvayet' [Caspian oil is late in coming], *Vremya-MN* (Moscow), 9 Nov. 2000.

In any event, the chances for Caspian oil coming on to the world market still remain uncertain. What is going to happen if the fulfilment of all these plans is delayed?

Some factors may call Caspian oil exports into question in the short run. The littoral states—the potential oil exporters—are politically unstable. Transport will be costly along some routes, particularly Baku–Ceyhan; there are political obstacles in the way of others (Iran); and there are threats of instability along third routes—indeed, to a certain degree, along all possible routes. The newly independent states are ill-prepared to handle oil revenues efficiently. Iraqi oil will enter the market; foreign investors may eventually gain access to Saudi Arabia; oil prices may fall again. There is no negotiated legal regime for the Caspian Sea; there are environmental problems; there is keen competition between regional powers; and, finally, there are threats from terrorists, religious extremists and radical nationalists.

Environmental problems may seriously complicate not only the development of the resources of the Caspian but also the maintenance of security and stability in the region. One of these problems is connected with the rise in the level of the Caspian Sea which took place in the last quarter of the 20th century. More than 1400 oil wells drilled shortly before the start of that rise have been flooded. Another problem is the vulnerability of the Caspian's biological resources—the sturgeon, seal and rare bird species. 'Environmental reports caution that an enclosed sea such as the Caspian is particularly vulnerable from an ecological standpoint to oil spills and other related sources of pollution.'[16]

Russia may view the USA's opposition to Russia's advancing its own interests as a risk factor. The USA is undertaking to support the newly independent states in strengthening their sovereignty but understands this mainly as protecting them from Russia. According to one leading US analyst, 'leaders and peoples of Central Asia and the Caucasus see in Russia the main threat to their independence'.[17] Naturally, this understanding of the interests of the Central Asian and Caucasian peoples on the part of US politicians inhibits constructive cooperation between Russia and the USA in the region. At the same time, however, the two powers have common interests, such as combating drugs smuggling, Islamic extremism and international terrorism, the settlement of conflict situations, and the attainment of peace and stability in the region, which chime with the interests of local states. These common interests should foster Russian–US cooperation.

[16] Kemp, G., *Energy Superbowl: Strategic Politics in the Persian Gulf and Caspian Basin* (Center for Peace and Freedom: Washington, DC, 1997), p. 33. On the environmental problems of the Caspian Sea see also chapter 4 in this volume.

[17] Ruseckas, L., in *Caspian Studies Program Experts Conference Report: Succession and Long-Term Stability in the Caspian Region* (Harvard University: Cambridge, Mass., Oct. 1999), p. 109.

V. Is there a conflict of interests between Russia and the USA?

For Russian strategic analysts it is important to understand how significant the Caucasus is for the United States. In the USA itself opinions vary on this point, and the answer is not clear. According to Ambassador Robert Blackwill, one of the main US interests is 'that there be no weapons of mass destruction to attack against the American homeland or American forces abroad'. Where the Caspian is concerned, Blackwill believes, only Iran has a weapons of mass destruction programme, but this has little to do with its being a Caspian state. A second critical US interest, in Blackwill's opinion, is energy security, but today it is the Persian Gulf, not the Caspian, which is vital in this regard. Among other interests he cites 'the absence of hostile hegemons', the opening up of the world trade and financial markets and perhaps the maintenance of the strength of the US alliance system, but the Caspian region does not figure in any of these objectives.[18]

Other opinions suggest much greater US interest in the region. According to Ambassador Thomas Simpson, former coordinator of aid to the newly independent states at the US State Department, speaking at a conference at Stanford in 1999, US policy in the Caspian region has the following objectives: 'strengthening the independence and viability of the new states as market democracies, mitigating regional conflicts and fostering cooperation; bolstering the economic security of the United States, its allies and states of the region by promoting the development and free flow of Caspian energy resources to global markets; and advancing the interests of American companies'.[19]

At the same time the insistent lobbying for the construction of the Baku–Ceyhan pipeline, which may not be worth the money to be spent on it within the foreseeable future, suggests that the USA is ready to sacrifice economic efficiency to political imperatives. The desire to support Turkey as a key US ally in the Middle East undoubtedly played a prominent role in shaping the US position on this question.

Clearly, the most realistic solution to the problem of transport is to construct several pipelines. In any case, the capacity of any one pipeline is limited to 1 million barrels of oil a day. Allowing for the prospect that the region will produce 3–6 million barrels per day in 10–20 years' time, several pipelines will be needed. In addition, irrespective of the cost of laying the pipelines, the petroleum companies do not want all the oil produced to follow the same route—all the more so if the instability in most of the states on whose territory the pipelines will be laid is taken into account. As Kemp notes: 'Ideally, for the world's major energy consumers, the near future will see a harmonious settlement of the legal access disputes and will ensure that sufficient redundancy is built into the pipeline distribution system so that if one transport route is interrupted for any reason, other routes will still keep the energy flowing. In

---

[18] Blackwill, R., in *Caspian Studies Program Experts Conference Report* (note 17), p. 112.
[19] *CISAC Monitor* (Stanford University), summer 1999, p. 2.

theory, the United States should welcome pipelines that run through Georgia, Turkey, Russia and even Iran to ensure this redundancy'.[20]

However, to ensure that the pipelines work at full capacity, it is necessary that sufficient volumes of oil be extracted in the region. This requires not only the availability of reserves and the right technical conditions, but also the devising of a new legal status for the Caspian Sea, insofar as its former status is not recognized by a number of Caspian states and is in need of revision after the breakup of the USSR and the formation of the newly independent states. The development of resources may proceed even without consensus being reached on the status of the Caspian but even so this lack of consensus is a factor of geo-strategic instability.

As is known, Russia has compromised on this issue, having backed down from a position based on the idea of a condominium—that is, joint ownership of the sea and its resources exercised by all the Caspian states—and reached an understanding with Kazakhstan on the partition of the Caspian seabed. An agreement on this was signed on 6 July 1998 by the presidents of Kazakhstan and the Russian Federation.

Iran now has effectively two positions on the legal status for the Caspian—a principal and a 'reserve' one. The principal position, which until recently it shared with Russia, was that of a condominium. Its chances of being implemented began to decline as development of the Caspian oil proceeded, since it was unacceptable to the other Caspian littoral states: for them the condominium principle would have implied that they would have to prevent other Caspian states and foreign oil companies from oil prospecting and production in keeping with contracts already concluded, which would be deemed illegal.

Conscious that this variant was unrealistic after other Caspian states had signed contracts with major oil companies and particularly after Russia had changed its position and negotiated a partition of the Caspian seabed with Kazakhstan, and having expressed opposition to the partition of the seabed, Iran stated in March 2000 that as a 'reserve' variant it will support such a version of legal status as provides for a complete partition of the Caspian into national sectors. Iran believes that it must be divided on the basis of the principle of 'equal division', that is, not along the median line but in a way that would allow each of the Caspian states 20 per cent of the Caspian 'pie'.[21] (Partition along the median, originally proposed by Azerbaijan, would have given Iran a deep-sea sector where either oil resources are entirely lacking or their development will require immeasurably greater effort and, even if technically possible, will be unprofitable.) In addition, there are fears in Iran that, if partition along the median went ahead, its neighbours would not have to contend with such deep water and would moreover simply be able to pump oil from a reservoir which, it is assumed in Tehran, is actually situated under the 'Iranian' sector.

Some experts believe that Iran is not altogether interested in Caspian oil reaching the market, as it already has sufficient oil resources and the ability to

[20] Kemp (note 16), p. 50.
[21] See also chapter 3, section III in this volume.

transport them to the world market. In its hypothetical sector of the Caspian there are few proven reserves, they lie at great depth, and Iran lacks funds of its own to develop them. To transform the sea sectors currently under the jurisdiction of neighbouring states into a sphere of interests of Western oil companies is of no advantage to Iran either. In this connection, it must be noted that the competitiveness of Caspian oil on the world market will be determined both by the market (demand for oil and price levels) and by production costs. Experts consider that: 'New volumes of oil from Azerbaijan or Kazakhstan are expected to involve transportation costs of between $2.50 and $5 per barrel before it has even reached a sea terminal. Given production costs that are not among the world's lowest, the problem of transportation costs calls into question the competitiveness of Caspian oil supplies'.[22]

The Caspian region's great proneness to conflict will be the main barrier to the transformation of the littoral states into petroleum exporters. The opinion is often expressed that the great oil potential (if it is confirmed) will in itself be able to eliminate that conflict-proneness. However, this view is not shared by everybody, the West included. Laurent Ruseckas and Hendrik Spruyt, analysts from Columbia University, believe that:

Economic factors are likely to increase rather than decrease the likelihood of conflict and insecurity in Central Asia and the Caucasus in the years ahead. In conflicts where Western governments are playing a mediating role, they should realize that windows of diplomatic opportunity are closing rather than opening . . . Western policy in the southern republics of the former USSR is based on a liberal perspective, namely, that open markets and energy-induced growth will lead to greater economic expansion and general peace. This view, however, is dubious at best and counterproductive at worst . . . The states of the South Caucasus . . . and Central Asia . . . will handle profits from hydrocarbon exports with great difficulty.[23]

In their opinion, 'hydrocarbon incomes may paradoxically lead to economic stagnation. Worse, income distribution that disproportionately benefits particular patronage networks of ethnic groups could spark civil strife'.[24]

VI. Oil, development and security

Expectations of the oil miracle have already led to negative results in some states of the region. In Kazakhstan, for instance, the economic development strategy geared to giving priority to the extraction of energy resources has been accompanied by neglect of traditional vital economic sectors, animal husbandry and cattle breeding in particular. With fluctuating oil prices, the high cost of hydrocarbon production and transport, and the uncertainty about the size of the

---

[22] Ruseckas, L., 'Caspian oil development, Caspian energy resources', in *Caspian Studies Program Experts Conference Report* (note 17), p. 14; and Jaffe, A. M. and Manning, R., 'The myth of the Caspian "Great Game': the real geopolitics of energy', *Survival*, vol. 40, no. 4 (winter 1999), pp. 112–31.

[23] Briefing on 6 Jan. 1999 by Laurent Ruseckas and Hendrik Spruyt at the East–West Institute on the project 'The 21st-Century Security Environment' (unpublished).

[24] Briefing by Ruseckas and Spruyt (note 23).

reserves, the population's expectations of rapid prosperity may turn into acute discontent at the lack of progress in raising standards of living. Even if all the obstacles are quickly removed it is impossible to be sure that incomes from hydrocarbon exports will quickly and definitively improve the situation. The benefits to be derived 'are the greatest in well-developed countries with functional, multi-sector economies and stable political institutions like Norway'[25] and these conditions are clearly absent in the Caspian littoral states. The political systems dominated by patron–client, clan and tribal networks, authoritarian leaders and widespread corruption, and the long-standing and potential, if so far somnolent, conflicts reduce the possibilities of growth and the appropriate use of oil wealth.

It is true that the oil boom in the Caspian has already brought dividends, both direct and indirect, to Azerbaijan, for instance, which is regarded by the West as a key partner. This has been reflected in the development of infrastructure and oil exploration by foreign investors in Azerbaijan. It would seem that Russia cannot compete with the West in terms of the benefits to Azerbaijan from cooperation. However, about 2 million Azerbaijani citizens, predominantly employed in small and medium-sized businesses, are resident in Russia today. According to the lowest estimates they transfer several billion dollars a year to Azerbaijan, providing the livelihood of several million family members.[26] According to the First Vice-President of SOCAR, Ilham Aliyev, $1.7 billion has been invested in Azerbaijan's oil sector so far, $700 million of it by US companies,[27] but this total is less than the income derived from Azeris working in Russia in the course of a year. (Unfortunately, Russia's lack of a meaningful immigration policy may make it difficult for it to use this factor effectively in its own interest. Its withdrawal from the Bishkek agreements on visa-free movement for citizens of the CIS states within the CIS, announced in August 2000 and dictated by its security interests,[28] may cause additional complications in the development of cooperation around the Caspian.)

The problem of the transit of Caspian oil has also taken on a significance which visibly exceeds the resource and economic potential of the Caspian. The creation of the new pipeline and other infrastructure in the region is, naturally, directly linked to the strategic interests of world and regional powers and the entrenchment of their influence in the region. The struggle for pipeline routes, often lacking in common economic sense, has sometimes taken on a singular intensity—to the point of refusal to observe international treaties in the case of

---

[25] Briefing by Ruseckas and Spruyt (note 23).

[26] At hearings in the Russian Duma in Dec. 2000 it was stated that annual money transfers to Azerbaijan by its citizens working in Russia amount to c. $2 billion. Ayrapetova, N., 'Vizovoy rezhim kak chast' obshchey sistemy bezopasnosti' [Visa regime as part of a general security system], *Nezavisimaya Gazeta*, 12 Dec. 2000.

[27] Gadjizade, A., 'V poiskakh neftyanogo puti' [In search of an oil route], *Nezavisimaya Gazeta*, 11 Jan. 1999, p. 5. According to data cited by Gregory, Azerbaijan received a cumulative foreign direct investment (FDI) of $2 billion over the 9 years 1989–97 and Kazakhstan $4.3 billion. Gregory, P., 'Developing Caspian energy reserves: the legal environment', *Caspian Energy Resources* (note 9), p. 52.

[28] *Diplomaticheskiy Vestnik*, no. 9 (2000).

Turkey's intention to limit tanker movements through the Bosporus[29]—interwoven as it is into the context of the new geopolitical rehashing of the world which has been effectively carried out in the 1990s in place of the Utopian new world order. Unfortunately, the establishment of spheres of influence and double standards have been the decisive elements of this global process. Champions of the Baku–Ceyhan pipeline, for instance, did not conceal that it must be built primarily for political and strategic considerations independently of whether it will be cost-effective. This is a clear indication of the particular importance of Turkey for the United States (it is less important for Europe, which Turkey is striving to join) and of the desire to reduce Russia's influence in the region. These imperatives are so strong that even the argument that the pipeline would help 'pacify' and stabilize conflict territories was used in support of its construction, when in fact it is stability that is the necessary precondition for the construction of the pipeline.[30]

Russian politicians' fears are not explained by primitive mercantile interests of competition with Turkey for the dividends from the transit of oil pipelines, although that competition is quite natural. The concern is rather about geopolitical interests. In the words of Paul Sampson: 'Most potent, however, is the Turks' desire for the political influence that comes from being the transit point for petroleum in the region . . . Ankara fears that if the [Baku–Ceyhan] pipeline is not built, it will lose its foothold in Azerbaijan and its political influence in Central Asia and the Caucasus'.[31] As a Turkish journalist writes: 'Thanks to the projects for the Baku–Ceyhan oil pipeline and the Trans-Caspian Gas Pipeline, Turkey will be able to keep the Straits out of danger, earn money and receive an alternative to the existing pipeline through which it obtains oil from producers in the Middle East. In addition, Turkey will play a significant role in the Eurasian energy corridor via Anatolia'.[32]

It looks as though the United States realizes all the difficulties involved in the implementation of the plan for transit of Caspian oil via Turkey and that the transit of oil by the cheapest, most convenient and efficient route—via Iran—will help lessen the dependence of the newly independent states of the Caspian region on Russia—a goal they seek to attain—but will dash Turkey's hopes of gaining influence in the region. A normalization of Iranian–US relations will mean that the West would switch its attention from the Caspian states to the much more attractive and stable Iran.

The oil companies are also interested in cooperating with Iran on a swap basis. Iranian Foreign Minister Kamal Kharazzi has said repeatedly that Iran was ready to purchase (although he did not specify over what period) up to

[29] On Turkey's policy on tanker movements through the Bosporus and the Dardanelles see chapters 3 and 8 of this volume.

[30] Wirninhaus, R.-F., German Institute of the East, Hamburg, report at the Second International Conference on Oil and Gas Resources of the Caspian: Transportation, Security, Economic Development held on 7–8 Nov. 1998 in Tehran. The text in Russian is published in *Vestnik Kaspiya* (Moscow), no. 1(15) (Jan./Feb. 1999), p. 226.

[31] *Transition*, Feb. 1999, pp. 27–28.

[32] Dikba, K., 'Hazar' da dans' [Dances around the Caspian], *Da (Dyalog Avrasya)* (Istanbul), spring 2000, pp. 16–17.

1.5 million barrels of oil and 200 million cubic metres of natural gas to satisfy its internal needs.

Generally speaking, in Russia specialists already seem to understand that diversification of the transit routes for Caspian oil to suit the strategy of the petroleum companies is inevitable. There is reason to hope that the construction and commissioning of the Tengiz–Novorossiysk oil pipeline by the summer of 2001 will prove to be a model of successful cooperation between Russia, Kazakhstan and the Western oil companies.

Meanwhile, on 17 October 2000, agreements on the implementation of the project for the Baku–Tbilisi–Ceyhan oil pipeline, with an annual capacity of 50 million tonnes, were signed between the government of Azerbaijan and a number of major oil companies—BP Amoco, Unocal (USA), Statoil (Norway), TPAO (Turkey), Itochu (Japan), Ramco and Delta Hess (Saudi Arabia). The estimated cost of the 1730 km-long pipeline is of the order of $2.4 billion. On the part of Azerbaijan, the sponsor group includes the Azerbaijan International Operating Company (AIOC).[33] However, even after the signing of the agreements, debates on the fate of the pipeline continued. ExxonMobil, which is a member of the AIOC, told Azerbaijan that this ambitious project ran counter to the company's interests.[34] The heart of the matter is that Azeri oil alone is not sufficient to fill the oil pipeline to Turkey. Experts therefore did not rule out that its construction would be long-drawn-out.

In order to ensure the profitability of that project, it will also be necessary for Kazakhstan's oil to be pumped along the new pipeline to Turkey. However, an underwater oil pipeline will be needed to deliver it to the western shore of the Caspian, and such a pipeline would entail the risks of blowouts of great quantities of oil if the pipeline were to rupture in conditions of seismic impact, insignificant but chronic oil leaks from crevices in the pipe, and the creation of a vibro-acoustic barrier which could catastrophically alter the migration runs of the Russian sturgeon even when the pipeline was working normally.[35]

The Russian Government also resolutely opposes the construction of the trans-Caspian gas pipeline because in the event of seismic danger it threatens ecological disaster in the Caspian. It seems that by buying Turkmen gas and commissioning the pipeline via the Black Sea to transport Russian gas to Turkey—Blue Stream—Russia will manage to prevent the trans-Caspian pipeline project being realized. The well-known disputes between Azerbaijan and Turkmenistan may also play a role here. 'Having made a bid for the absorption of 50 per cent of the capacity of the Trans-Caspian Pipeline, Azerbaijan has created a new consortium—Shah Deniz—which may simultaneously provide natural gas for Turkey.'[36]

[33] On the membership of the AIOC consortium see chapter 3 in this volume. Oil production began in Nov. 1997.

[34] Kolchin, S., 'Oil market boom missed', *Moscow News*, nos 44–45 (15 Nov. 2000).

[35] Mishin, V., 'Zvukovoy baryer dlya russkogo osetra' [The sound barrier for the Russian sturgeon], *Vremya-MN*, 25 Oct. 2000.

[36] Tesyomnikova, Ye, 'Problema Kaspiya: ostorozhny optimizm Moskvy' [The Caspian problem: Moscow's cautious optimism], *NG-Sodruzhestvo*, no. 5 (31 May 2000), p. 1.

Because the military–strategic importance of the Caspian region is growing both for the West and for the new states on the Caspian, Russia, despite the overall slackening of its military activity, is compelled to pay attention to the military component of its presence in the Caspian. In December 1998 the headquarters of the Joint Grouping of Russia's Defence Ministry forces in Dagestan was set up in Kaspiysk. The grouping includes the 136th Motor Rifle Brigade quartered in Buinaksk, ships of the Caspian flotilla, army aircraft and airborne units. According to press reports, it is envisaged subsequently to set up a naval base there, which would include, apart from coastguard units, a division of hovercraft and marine units.[37]

As mentioned above, calls for the demilitarization of the Caspian which are heard from some of the Caspian littoral states, made as they are at a time when the role of the military factor is clearly enhanced, cannot but be viewed by Russia as an attempt to weaken its already vulnerable southern flank, which is called on to deter the potential threats that abound there. Azerbaijan's President Heidar Aliyev, in particular, has spoken of the need to demilitarize the Caspian. When rifts appeared between Iran and Russia after the signing of the 1998 Kazakh–Russian agreement on the partition of the Caspian seabed, Iranian officials, saying that the agreement was unacceptable to them, argued for demilitarization of the Caspian. The Iranian leadership views the Russian military presence in the Caspian under certain circumstances as a source of possible friction and even challenge to the sovereignty of other states. Moreover, the possibility of Russia's military positions in the Caspian being reinforced as a result of the partition of the seabed is for Iran one of the arguments for not accepting that principle. According to Hosein Kazempur Ardebili, adviser to the Iranian Oil Minister, although the partition of the seabed 'may be of direct economic benefit to the littoral states, it is liable to increase the likelihood of the Russian naval presence in cases where the limits of sovereignty will remain unclear'. Ardebili also stated: 'Russia must withdraw its armed forces from the Caspian in accordance with a definite timetable and then confine its presence to coastguard level'.[38]

VII. Russia's Caspian policy becomes more active

In 2000 Russia's leadership embarked on preparations for the development of the Russian, northern section of the Caspian Sea shelf. A group of Russian companies have pooled their efforts with this aim. On 25 July 2000, Lukoil, Yukos and Gazprom signed the documents creating the Caspian Oil Company. Shortly before drilling of the first exploratory borehole in Astrakhan Oblast had been completed and a deposit discovered with reserves approaching 300 million tonnes of hydrocarbons. The development licence on it belonged to Lukoil.[39]

---

[37] *Nezavisimoye Voyennoye Obozreniye*, no. 8 (1999), p. 2.

[38] Ardebili, H. K., 'The legal regime of the Caspian and its influence on regional energy security', Report to the International Conference in Tehran, 7–8 Nov. 1998.

[39] Ignatova, M., 'Vmeste veselo burit'' [It's fun to drill together], *Izvestiya*, 26 July 2000.

The administration of President Vladimir Putin has stepped up Russia's Caspian policy. The former Minister for Fuel and Energy, Viktor Kalyuzhny, was appointed Deputy Foreign Minister and Special Representative of the Russian President for the Caspian Sea region. Kalyuzhny started with a significant step. As the entire experience of recent years had shown that the elaboration and adoption of a new international status for the Caspian would take time, whereas drilling activity on the Caspian was proceeding anyway, it was worthwhile to start negotiating agreements on individual types of economic activity. The new Russian propositions paid particular attention to the problem of disputed oilfields, which has the potential to aggravate relations between CIS member states neighbouring each other on the Caspian. The significance of this problem goes beyond the economic issues.

At the end of July 2000 Kalyuzhny, starting a visit to the littoral states which dispute the rights of ownership of particular deposits, proposed to them that they should compromise on the basis of the 50 : 50 principle whereby the second claimant compensates half of the costs to the first claimant which started the offshore development and extraction and they then negotiate the partition. This proposal takes into account the real situation—the fact that the Caspian littoral states have already begun tapping the mineral wealth without waiting for the new legal status of the Caspian to be defined.

The centre of gravity in the Russian proposal has been transferred to bilateral agreements between countries directly neighbouring each other in the Caspian. This found expression in the July 1998 agreement between Kazakhstan and Russia on the partition of the seabed. Russian diplomats who championed this approach contend that successive agreements between 'pairs' of neighbours could pave the way for collective agreements. Russia's concern over the problem of disputed fields reflected an understanding of its conflict potential and the possible consequences for peace and security in the region. Offering a solution to this problem, Russia was partly switching the negotiating process on the Caspian onto the track of preventive diplomacy. However, the proposal did not find an echo in such capitals as Ashkhabad and Tehran, whose leaders continued to insist on the need first to elaborate a new status of the sea and only then tackle particular questions on that basis.

Kalyuzhny's visit demonstrated Russia's desire to improve relations with Azerbaijan. This task was facilitated by the fact that he had belonged to the petroleum lobby and was attuned to a pragmatic attitude on Caspian issues, all the more so since it took place against the background of a certain cooling in Azerbaijan's relations with the USA. President Aliyev accepted Kalyuzhny's proposal of the 50 : 50 principle. Kalyuzhny also put forward the idea of creating a centre in Baku for strategic development of the Caspian Sea to monitor the situation and work out proposals.

However, this gesture towards Azerbaijan caused irritation in Iran and Turkmenistan, in spite of the fact that Russia has fewer differences with those states over the Caspian problem. In Yerevan, the steps towards progress in Russian–Azerbaijani relations were also watched attentively. It was not by accident that in the summer of 2000 Russia's mass media published a series of discussion materials on the prospects of relations between Russia and Armenia, and Russia and Azerbaijan. A number of 'hack' articles in the Moscow press, clearly written to order, even warned of the dangerous consequences of a lurch towards Azerbaijan for Russia's interests in the Caucasus. The stepping up of the Caspian negotiating process took place simultaneously with a surge of activity over the costs of the proposed Stability Pact for the Caucasus and with the appearance of new ideas as to how to settle conflict situations in the region.[40] Georgia, which is not a Caspian littoral state, increasingly made itself felt as an important actor in the region because of the role it already plays as one state through whose territory Caspian oil enters the world market.

Thus, despite added activity and fresh ideas, Moscow was unable to smooth out the differences between the five littoral Caspian states on key issues involved in the utilization of the Caspian. To sum up, Russia's greatest partner, Iran, did not change its negative attitude to the two aspects of Russia's policy in the region that are most important for Russia—the principle of partition of the seabed between neighbouring states and continued military activity in the Caspian. For its part Russia failed to give official support (although unofficially some Russian officials did express such support) to Iran's call for the sea, if it is partitioned into sectors, to be divided equally with each littoral state receiving 20 per cent.

In contacts with Kalyuzhny, Turkmenistan voiced doubts about the wisdom of discussing Caspian issues in the framework of the regular CIS summit meeting in Minsk. This, in its view, would have been regarded as discrimination against Iran. Turkmenistan also argued against the proposal, put forward during Kalyuzhny's tour of the littoral states' capitals, that the questions of shipping in the Caspian, the use of its biological resources, its ecology and the creation of a single joint centre to manage the Caspian should be tackled in succession. Russia's argument that the threat of a biological disaster in the Caspian Basin impels the parties to take urgent measures to save the fish resources (to take one example) without waiting until the new status of the Caspian is defined left Turkmenistan unconvinced. Turkmenistan was also anxious about the allegations circulated by the news agencies (although disproved by Kalyuzhny on his arrival in Ashkhabad) that on his visit to Baku he had expressed support for Azerbaijan's position on those oil deposits in the Caspian that are claimed by both Azerbaijan and Turkmenistan.

It must also be stressed that Azerbaijan has reaffirmed its adherence to the principle of partitioning the sea into national sectors, and there was no genuine rapprochement between its position and that of Russia. Russian diplomats say that Russia will never agree to the partition of the Caspian into national sectors. 'Moscow will agree to recognize only the resource jurisdiction of the adjoining countries negotiated among themselves, that is to say, such a division of

[40] Radio Free Europe/Radio Liberty (RFE/RL), *RFE/RL Newsline*, vol. 4, no. 65, Part 1 (30 Mar. 2000); and *RFE/RL Newsline*, vol. 4, no. 99, Part 1 (23 May 2000). On the proposal for a Stability Pact for the Caucasus see chapter 8, section VI in this volume.

resources of the Caspian seabed, on which, say, Azerbaijan, Turkmenistan and Iran may agree among themselves, while keeping the sea and its surface in common ownership.'[41]

Relations among the Caspian littoral 'five' are marked by constant shifts and temporary alliances of states to win support for some demands and block others. The core reason for this situation is the differences in the interests of and the active steps taken by outside actors. However, the course of events in the Caspian region cannot be examined separately from the situation in Central Asia and the Caucasus. The unsettled state of the Chechen problem will continue to have a serious impact on Russia's Caspian policy, while its security interests will hardly be overshadowed by economic ones.

The well-known triad with the help of which Russia had been safeguarding its security interests in this region throughout the 1990s—its military bases, the protection of the CIS external borders and the peacekeepers—had cracked by the end of the 1990s. The evacuation of the Russian military bases in Georgia and the withdrawal of Russian border guards from a section of the CIS external borders[42] are creating additional risks for Russia which aggravate the growing threats from international terrorism, ethnic separatism and Islamic extremism. It is difficult as yet to say how successfully these threats can be countered by means of improved cooperation between Russia and the republics of Central Asia and the South Caucasus in the domain of regional security.

It is hard to predict what turns Russia's policy may take in the turbulent flow of the activities of the numerous actors in the Caspian, but one thing is beyond doubt: in the short run the region will retain a conspicuous place on the scale of Russia's strategic priorities.

<hr />

[41] Dubnov, A., 'Nad sedoy ravninoy morya' [Over the grey expanse of the sea], *Vremya-MN*, 26 July 2000.
[42] See chapter 5 in this volume.

7. US policy towards the Caspian region: can the wish-list be realized?

Amy Jaffe

I. Introduction: the underpinning of US policy towards the Caspian

When the Soviet Union began to collapse in 1991, the US reaction to the possibility that the states of the Caspian Basin would become independent was muted, if not non-existent. US policy makers concerned themselves primarily with the fate of Moscow and its political leadership in a programme that was dubbed 'Russia first' by practitioners.[1] To the extent that the countries of Central Asia and the Caucasus received any notice at all, it was mainly to make sure that nuclear or other major weaponry previously under the control of the Soviet regime was destroyed or returned to Russia. Experts argued that the USA needed to be careful not to give the impression of siding with these new states in their efforts to achieve independence from Russia. The goal of this logic was to avoid the impression that a cordon sanitaire was being created around Russia in order to isolate it from Europe.[2] Some thinkers took it a step farther and argued that universal self-determination was 'not an American constitutional principle' and that, even taking into account the benefits of democratic change, the USA's interest in stability would be threatened by any violent disintegration of the Soviet Union. The breakaway republics and Moscow should find arrangements that were acceptable to both sides and leave the USA out of it.[3]

This lukewarm start in US policy on the Caspian region countries was to give way to growing involvement in the years following the breakup of the Soviet Union. During this process the region attained a surprising salience in the US foreign policy hierarchy of concerns. Although the Caspian region is both geographically remote and of only derivative importance to the USA's key strategic concerns, US diplomatic effort in the region has been extraordinarily active, starting with official visits, first by the leaders of the region to the USA and then by the US Secretary of State to the region.[4] There have also been several

[1] Barnes, J., 'US interests in the Caspian Basin: getting beyond the hype', Baker Institute Working Paper, 1997, available at URL <http://www.bakerinstitute.org>. Barnes served on the US Department of State policy planning staff at the time of the breakup of the former Soviet Union.

[2] Simes, D. K., 'America and the post-Soviet republics', *Foreign Affairs*, vol. 71, no. 2 (1992).

[3] Allison, G. and Blackwell, R., 'America's stake in the Soviet future', *Foreign Affairs*, vol. 70, no. 2 (1991).

[4] Central Asian and Caucasus leaders visited the White House as follows: President Islam Karimov of Uzbekistan in 1996; President Eduard Shevardnadze of Georgia in 1997; President Heidar Aliyev of Azerbaijan in 1997; President Nursultan Nazarbayev of Kazakhstan in 1997; and President Saparmurat

landmark addresses by key officials of the US Administration regarding the 'importance' of Central Asia and the Caucasus to the USA. Perhaps most significant, however, was the appointment of a 'special envoy' to the region.[5] This post, by virtue of its existence, kept Caspian issues on a higher track than might otherwise have been feasible for a remote region which had no significant trade relationship with the USA and which posed no significant threat of major war and no significant immediate threat to regional or international peace and stability.

The region has also received attention from the US military, which has pushed for Western military cooperation with it to be increased under the general umbrella of NATO's Partnership for Peace (PFP) programme. The PFP programme was designed to 'improve practical military cooperation and common capabilities' and 'to enable joint operations with NATO peacekeeping and humanitarian missions', among other functions.[6] On the practical level this has meant US military training programmes in the region under the Cooperative Threat Reduction (CTR) programme and the Foreign Military Financing (FMF) programme, and border security activities. In 1997, as part of a well-publicized joint military exercise in the region, the US Army's elite 82nd Airborne Division sent 500 paratroopers parachuting into the territory, including an Uzbek-born marine. Finally, between 1992 and 1999 the USA provided the region with approximately $1.9 billion under the Freedom Support Act, which promotes democratization and market reforms, improved health care and housing.[7]

The reason why the countries of the Caspian Basin have received such attention from the USA is often described as singularly clear—oil wealth. Secretary of State Madeleine Albright in an address before the Senate Appropriations Committee's Foreign Operations Subcommittee noted that it was 'strongly' in the US national interest to assist these 'strategically located' and 'energy-rich' countries.[8] Other US diplomats speaking on US goals for the region also cite energy security and diversification of supply outside the choke points of the Strait of Hormuz on the Persian Gulf and Turkey's Bosporus and opening up

Niyazov of Turkmenistan in 1998. US Secretary of State Madeleine Albright toured the region in early 2000, holding press conferences and meeting leaders there. The texts of relevant press conferences are available at URL <http://www.state.gov>.

[5] The Clinton Administration in 1994 established a special inter-agency working group to focus on Caspian policy. In May 1998, the US Trade and Development Agency, the US Export–Import Bank and the Overseas Private Investment Corp. announced the formation of the Caspian Finance Center in Ankara to facilitate the development of energy and other infrastructure projects in the Caspian region. Then in July 1998 President Clinton appointed Ambassador Richard Morningstar to the new position of Special Advisor to the President and Secretary of State for Caspian Basin Energy Diplomacy. For further detail see White House Fact Sheet, URL <http://www.usis.it/file9911/alia/99111705.htm>.

[6] Strobe Talbott, Richard Morningstar and John Wolfe have made several addresses on this subject at various conferences and universities. The most notable was Talbott's speech 'A farewell to Flashman: American policy in the Caucasus and Central Asia' delivered at Johns Hopkins University on 21 July 1997. The texts of these speeches are available at URL <http://www.state.gov>.

[7] For a detailed discussion of this involvement see Sokolsky, R. and Charlick-Paley, T., *NATO and Caspian Security: A Mission Too Far*, Report MR-1074-AF (RAND Corporation: Santa Monica, Calif., 1999).

[8] Bhatty, R. and Bronson, R., 'NATO's mixed signals in the Caucasus and Central Asia', *Survival*, vol. 42, no. 3 (autumn 2000), pp. 129–45.

access to promising investment opportunities for US companies on a list that includes vaguer references to conflict resolution and state-building.[9]

There is evidence for this perception that the Caspian region is the focus of US diplomats seeking to help US companies lock up oil and gas assets. More than 30 US companies have invested billions of dollars in the region in hopes of 'striking it big'. Those same companies over the years have hired expensive lobbyists and specialists to enhance attention to issues relating to this business.[10] The oil companies have had an easy time finding allies among the US foreign policy establishment, and the reason for this underscores the fact that other factors besides oil are at play. Oil men looking for a willing ear needed to look no farther than to former 'cold warriors' who still believed in the early 1990s that US foreign policy must focus first and foremost on countering any resurgence of Russian power. Part and parcel of this preventive attitude was to weaken Russia's influence on its southern flank by propping up the sovereignty and strength of Central Asian and Caucasus countries.[11]

However, besides those who remained nervous about Russia's long-term intentions, there was also a plethora of policy advocates who feared the rising influence of China and Iran. Hence, planting the US flag in the Caspian Basin was viewed as a strategic countermeasure to contain the regional power of these two countries as well. In the case of Iran, US policy has been more explicit. US sanctions against Iran are designed to prevent energy companies from investing in pipelines that would carry Caspian oil or gas to international markets.[12] The US Government has worked behind the scenes with mixed success to thwart foreign companies from joining with the National Iranian Oil Company (NIOC) to construct energy export outlets via Iran.

Were US sanctions against Iran to be eased in the event of a rapprochement between Iran and the USA, the attractions of various Iranian export routes from the Caspian could be compelling.[13] Ironically, the domestic political barriers to the US Government getting out quickly from under its slowly evolving Iran policy may be inadvertently fostering tension between the USA on the one hand and Kazakhstan and Turkmenistan on the other. These states, faced with the imperative to export oil as soon as possible, are already looking to Iran regard-

---

[9] Federal News Service, 22 May 1997.

[10] Speeches by Ambassador John Wolfe and his staff at various meetings attended by the author. See also texts available at URL <http://www.state.gov>.

[11] Morgan, D. and Ottoway, D., *Washington Post*, 6 July 1997. For a closer look at the intellectual underpinnings of this realist-school thinking see Brzezinski, Z., *The Grand Chessboard* (Basic Books: New York, 1997). A good critique of this school is provided by Harries, O., 'The dangers of expansive realism', *National Interest*, winter 1997/1998, pp. 3–7.

[12] The US Congress passed legislation, the Iran–Libya Sanctions Act (ILSA) of 1996, that would allow it to impose sanctions on third parties which invested in Iran's oil and gas industry. Other US laws restrict such investments by US companies to $40 million. This policy is nicely described by Washington analyst Robert Ebel as 'ABI: anywhere but Iran'. See Ebel, R. E., Center for Strategic and International Studies, *Energy Choices in the Near Abroad: The Haves and Have-Nots Face the Future* (CSIS: Washington, DC, 1997); and Kemp, G., 'The Persian Gulf remains the strategic prize', *Survival*, vol 40, no. 4 (winter 1998), pp. 132–49.

[13] For economic comparisons and options see Soligo, R. and Jaffe, A. M., 'The economics of pipeline routes: the conundrum of oil exports from the Caspian Basin', Baker Institute Working Paper, Apr. 1998, available at URL <http://www.bakerinstitute.org>.

less of the US position, creating an embarrassing backdrop to their bilateral relations with Washington.

In the case of China US policy is more ambiguous. The USA has not opposed oil or gas pipeline routes from Kazakhstan to China and has even given consideration to providing credits to a US firm to participate. However, China is still viewed as a strategic competitor whose activities in the region can be cited as another reason why the USA should also have a presence.[14]

The vital interest of maintaining good relations with NATO ally Turkey also dictates that US policy makers give Caspian energy issues high priority. Turkey has actively lobbied the USA and its oil companies to help it find a solution to what it terms unacceptable shipping congestion through its environmentally sensitive Bosporus, through which 1.2 million barrels a day (b/d) of oil are currently transported. A large rise in Caspian and Russian oil exports could potentially bring tanker traffic through the Bosporus to dangerous levels, Turkey argues, endangering the population of Istanbul, which lies on the waterway.[15] The matter is being investigated by several world bodies, including the International Maritime Organization (IMO), and Turkey has already sparred with Russia over the issue of accident insurance for tankers passing the Turkish Straits (the Bosporus and Dardanelles). Russia argues that improved management and traffic control equipment would permit safe passage of projected oil exports through the Straits. Free passage through the waterway is guaranteed by the Convention Regarding the Regime of the Straits (the Montreux Convention) of 1936.[16]

Turkey's concern for the future of the Bosporus Straits has led it to lobby for the construction of an oil pipeline that would extend from Baku in Azerbaijan to the Turkish Mediterranean port of Ceyhan. Since 1995, the US Government has assertively backed this route, not only to show support for Turkey but also because it believes that such a pipeline will enhance economic and political ties in the region and cement its independence from the undue influences of Russia and Iran.[17] In October 1998 the US Administration helped choreograph the Ankara Declaration of support for the Baku–Ceyhan pipeline project by the Turkish President and other regional leaders, including the presidents of Georgia and Azerbaijan.[18] This was followed by a high-profile signing ceremony of the pipeline initiative by the presidents of Turkey, the USA and certain Caspian Basin countries during the Summit Meeting of the Organization for

[14] Most US authors discussing geopolitical competition in the Caspian region mention China on the list, among them Starr, S. F., 'Power failure: American policy in the Caspian', *National Interest*, spring 1997. For a good survey of China's moves see Xiaojie Xu, 'The oil and gas links between Central Asia and China: a geopolitical perspective', *OPEC Review*, Mar. 1999; and Christoffersen, G., 'China's intentions for Russian and Central Asian oil and gas', *NBR Analysis Series* (National Bureau of Asian Research), vol. 9, no. 2 (Mar. 1998).

[15] Author's interviews with US State Department officials show this latter concern to be cited as more important than the others, although public pronouncements do not emphasize it. For a more detailed discussion of the problem of the Bosporus see Soligo and Jaffe (note 13).

[16] See also chapter 3, section IV and chapter 8, section III in this volume.

[17] See note 10.

[18] Signed on 29 Oct. 1998. The complete text is available on the US Department of Energy Internet site at URL <http://energy.gov/HQPress/releases98/octpr/pr98161a.htm>.

Security and Co-operation in Europe (OSCE) in Istanbul in November 1999, which US President Bill Clinton attended. However, commercial and political barriers have so far blocked the development of the Baku–Ceyhan line, and this has raised questions about the effectiveness of US diplomacy in the region.[19]

II. Oil as a driving factor: myths and realities

Ironically, a key problem for the success of the Baku–Ceyhan line, and US policy towards the region with it, is the fact that not enough oil has been discovered yet to justify its construction.[20] Indeed, the scale of the oil potential of the region as a whole and the monumentally difficult logistics of developing it may argue against the deepening of US involvement in the region.

A new oil find in Kazakhstan at Kashagan was touted in mid-2000 as confirming that sceptics might be wrong about the potential of Caspian resources, but even if Kashagan's reserves are confirmed to be as large as an average field in Saudi Arabia the story does not end there. The Caspian will still not be the next Middle East.

There is no question that the oil reserves of the Caspian Basin are significant, but they do not come near to matching those of the Persian Gulf. The proven reserves of the Persian Gulf top 600 billion barrels (bbl), spread across eight different countries. Saudi Arabia's proven oil reserves alone are 269 bbl. There are also vast areas of the Persian Gulf that have still not been fully explored, such as Iraq's western desert and Kuwait's deeper strata.

By contrast, in Central Asia and the Caucasus, only three countries are thought to have major hydrocarbon deposits—Azerbaijan, Kazakhstan and Turkmenistan. Of the three, only Kazakhstan is expected to have Saudi-size billion-barrel oilfields. In fact, geologists predict that Kazakhstan is likely to hold up to 80 per cent of the region's future oil potential. Exploration in Azerbaijan and Turkmenistan so far has found proven riches in natural gas and condensate, but some geologists are doubtful that these two countries will turn out to be major players.[21] According to geologists, future exploration may confirm that the Caspian region holds potentially 140 bbl of oil, but this figure remains speculative. The proven oil reserves of Central Asia and the Caucasus currently represent less than 3 per cent of world proven oil reserves. By comparison, the Middle East accounts for 55 per cent of the world's proven reserves.

Moreover, even if it turns out that geologists are too pessimistic about the promise of Kazakhstan's geology, the Caspian Basin still remains one of the most difficult oil prospecting terrains in the world. This will limit its geopolitical and commercial importance as a vital oil supply centre on the scale of

[19] Fitchett, J., 'A resurgent Russian influence grips former Soviet Central Asia', *International Herald Tribune*, 9 July 2000.

[20] Aliriza, B., 'US Caspian pipeline policy: substance or spin?', Center for Strategic and International Studies, Washington, DC, Aug. 2000, available at URL <http://www.csis.org/turkey/CEU000117.html>. See also chapter 3, section I in this volume.

[21] Talwani, M. and Belopolsky, A., 'Geology and petroleum potential of the Caspian Basin Sea Region', Baker Institute Working Paper, 1998, available at URL <http://www.bakerinstitute.org>.

Africa or Latin America. No solution is in sight to the crippling dearth of drilling rigs and other necessary equipment. Eight years of effort have not eased this shortage. Currently only two semi-submersible rigs operate in the Caspian Sea, in contrast to 90 or so in Britain's North Sea. Without more drilling rigs and production platforms, the oilfields of the Caspian cannot hope to reach their optimum production potential in the coming years. Already, analysts are saying that the Kashagan find, regardless of its size, may not be able to reach optimum production rates until 2015.[22]

The Caspian region is far from major supply centres for exploratory equipment, and the shortage of modern drilling platforms and other related supplies is worse than almost anywhere else in the world because the region is landlocked and has to rely on extremely limited supply routes, such as the Volga River, for bringing in necessary equipment. Despite huge demand for equipment, there are only two assembly yards equipped for manufacturing or refurbishing offshore drilling rigs for the region: one at Astrakhan in Russia along the northern Caspian and one in Primorsk, near Baku. Such constraints severely limit the amount of drilling that can take place in the region at any one time. They also mean that oil well completions take considerably longer—in some cases up to two years as compared with two or three months in many other oil provinces in other parts of the world. Kashagan's first well, for example, took a year longer to drill than planned.

Obstacles to drilling mean that, while Kazakhstan's resources may be geologically exciting, the region's output could remain constrained for years to come just because several wells cannot be drilled simultaneously. Exploration and production consultants Wood Mackenzie project that oil production could rise to 3.4 million b/d by 2010, up from 900 000 in the late 1990s, with the increases coming primarily from Kazakhstan and to a lesser extent Azerbaijan, but even this assumes that obstacles to drilling and export routing will be eased over time. This rate of production may not justify several large export pipelines to the West. Increased exports to the Black Sea littoral states such as Bulgaria, Romania, Turkey and Ukraine could be expected to handle at least one-third to half of the expected volume, for example, allowing producers to maximize profits by cutting transport costs to more distant buyers.[23]

The problem of the transport of oil from the Caspian region to consumers beyond the Black Sea remains to be tackled. Since Caspian hydrocarbon resources are both landlocked and located at a great distance from the world's major energy-consuming regions, the region's producers cannot simply ship oil by tanker from domestic ports to international sea-lanes as is done from the Persian Gulf. Instead, the Central Asian and Caucasus states must rely on expensive pipelines built through neighbouring countries as the chief means of transport.

[22] Author's inteviews with shareholders of the Kashagan field, 19 Sep. and 3 Oct. 2000.
[23] For more detailed discussion see Soligo and Jaffe (note 13); and Jaffe, A. M. and Manning, R., 'The myth of the Caspian "Great Game": the real geopolitics of energy', *Survival*, vol. 40, no. 4 (winter 1998/99), pp. 112–29.

So far, Caspian oil producers have dabbled with a variety of export routes, mostly unsatisfactorily. BP is transporting some limited volumes of oil from the Chirag field in Azerbaijan through a refurbished pipeline from Baku to the Georgian port of Supsa on the Black Sea. BP would like to enhance the size of this line eventually but is being pressed by the US and Turkish governments to favour the longer, more expensive Baku–Ceyhan route. As mentioned above, the US efforts in favour of Baku–Ceyhan are designed to enhance energy security by moving oil supplies away from critical choke points and to re-establish economic cooperation in the region. The USA would also like to eliminate any risk of conflict between Russia and Turkey over congestion on the Bosporus.

For its part, Russia claims that it is aware of Turkey's concerns and is working diligently to open new export routes for its own oil from its own northernmost ports.[24] Routing from Russia's oilfields to the Adriatic is still an economically viable possibility. Neither the US Government nor Turkey has adequately explained why international oil company proposals for shorter, more economic bypasses of the Bosporus across Turkish territory are unacceptable. Land rights might be one issue, but ultimately the focus on the Baku–Ceyhan route, which is the most expensive of all proposed, has sidetracked pursuit of other Turkish alternatives that might be favoured by oil company investors.

The potential of alternative routes through Russia remains a huge 'wild card' in the debate over Caspian oil exports. A resurgence of Russian concern with and influence in Central Asia and the Caucasus under the new government of President Vladimir Putin has raised the prospects that increased exports may soon flow as Moscow steps out of the way and removes the kind of obstacles it imposed on transport out of the region in the early 1990s.[25] However, BP's experience with one Russian oil export route, called the Northern Route, provides an instructive glimpse of potential problems. The line, which extended from Baku through Grozny and Tikhoretsk to the Russian Black Sea port of Novorossiysk, was supposed to carry 120 000 b/d of newly produced oil from Azerbaijan. Ultimately, however, the safety of the line could not be secured. It was not just that security at Grozny could not be ensured because of Russia's armed conflict with Chechnya: routine pilfering from the line by local residents along its extended route meant that BP was unable to maintain the pumping pressure needed to keep commercial flows going, regardless of the state of war or peace along with route.[26]

In his early days as Russian President, Putin referred to the need for international cooperation in the development of the Caspian resources, thus encouraging optimism in the West. Russia also recently increased Kazakhstan's oil export quota to 15 million tonnes for 2000, up from a previously specified annual volume of 9.5 million tonnes. Transneft is also reportedly inviting Caspian neighbours to use a new line to Makhachkala on the western shore of

---

[24] Fitchett (note 19).
[25] Fitchett (note 19).
[26] Author's interviews with oil company executives involved in the BP consortium, 19 Sep., 3 Oct. and 12 Nov. 2000.

the Caspian in Dagestan.[27] Given its geographical position, exporting through Russia is the most viable option for Kazakhstan because it obviates the need to cross the Caspian Sea or follow a wide span of its coastline before connecting to existing or proposed pipeline export facilities in third countries.

It is hoped that Russia will be able to deliver on its promise to support a new export system from Kazakhstan that will extend from the large Western-run Tengiz oil field through Russia to Novorossiysk. Initially that pipeline, run by the Caspian Pipeline Consortium (CPC), which involves Kazakh, Russian and US oil company shareholders, will carry 28 million tonnes of oil per year from Kazakhstan and Russia. It is expected to be in operation by late 2001.[28]

However, the limited ability of the Russian military to protect and operate such lines is highlighted by Moscow's less than successful military operations in Chechnya and its inability to protect public facilities inside Russia.[29] Serious questions remain as to whether Russia has the capability to fill the vacuum of power that has prompted the rise of non-state actors and the slide into instability that now plagues parts of the region. Moscow's troubles raise important strategic questions for all those involved in the Caspian region. Increasingly, Central Asian leaders like President Islam Karimov of Uzbekistan are looking to Russia for help in controlling an upsurge in Islamic militancy and illegal running of drugs and arms across the region.[30] Neither the USA nor any of its fellow NATO members, including Turkey, can put ground forces into the region even approaching the size and capability of Russia's army. NATO's will to do so is also increasingly questioned inside the Caspian region. Russia's willingness to take on religious groups in Tajikistan and Chechnya adds credibility to any security arrangements that it might offer. In the spring of 2000, news reports surfaced that the Central Asian republics were discussing the possibility of opening a joint anti-terrorism centre in Moscow.[31] The discussions came at the same time as Secretary of State Albright was touring Central Asia and expressing her dissatisfaction with human rights abuses and political repression in the region.[32] The US emphasis on these themes and on economic transparency was not well received by local regimes, who prefer Russia's more 'practical' military approach to the region's social problems.[33]

According to diplomatic sources, the USA has begun trying to establish a regional body—to include Georgia and Turkey—to maintain security for oil

---

[27] Fitchett (note 19); and 'In the Caspian, it's all pipelines and no oil', *Petroleum Intelligence Weekly*, 11 Sep. 2000, p. 3.

[28] 'In the Caspian, it's all pipelines and no oil' (note 27); 'PIW Kazakh discovery eclipses Azeri pipeline progress', 9 Oct. 2000, p. 3, also in *Petroleum Intelligence Weekly* (Energy Intelligence Group, New York, various issues); and author's interviews with shareholders for the various pipelines between Aug. and Nov. 2000. On the membership of the CPC see chapter 3, section I in this volume.

[29] On the decline of the Russian military see Pipes, R., 'Is Russia still an enemy?', *Foreign Affairs*, vol. 76, no. 5 (Sep./Oct. 1997).

[30] Fitchett (note 19).

[31] Fitchett (note 19).

[32] The texts of Secretary of State Albright's speeches and press conferences are available at URL <http://www.state.gov>.

[33] Author's interviews with regional diplomats on 3 Aug. and 15 Nov. 2000.

pipeline routes, presumably bypassing Russia and Iran.[34] Among US strategic specialists, however, the extension of the PFP programme into Central Asia has raised new concerns. It has been argued in US policy circles that local conflicts could easily draw Russia and any Western-sponsored or Turkish-led body into an unwanted confrontation if these larger patrons were to support different sides.[35] Russia's military support to and presence in Abkhazia in Georgia is one case in point.[36] Turkey's previous support of the Azeri war effort in Karabakh and Russia's support of Armenia is another. Thus, it seems advisable for all concerned to re-evaluate strategic priorities and see where common ground exists. There is no point in routing oil expensively all the way to Ceyhan in order to prevent a conflict between Russia and Turkey while at the same time creating the underpinnings for such conflict in protecting that same pipeline.

III. Natural gas: equal export troubles for US policy

The export of natural gas from the Caspian Basin is facing no less complex and difficult problems than the oil pipeline routes. In 1999 the US Government backed efforts to establish the Trans-Caspian Gas Pipeline (TCGP). This $2 billion line would carry up to 30 billion cubic metres (bcm) of natural gas per year from Turkmenistan to Azerbaijan under the Caspian Sea to Georgia and Turkey. Several private energy companies have looked at the feasibility of the project, including a grouping of Bechtel, General Electric and the Royal Dutch/Shell Group. While technically feasible, the project still faces stiff competition from other, better-organized, cost-effective competitors, including BP's Shah Deniz gas field in Azerbaijan and a $3.2 billion Russian–Italian–Turkish project called Blue Stream which would bring Russian gas to Turkey via a 750 mile-long pipeline beneath the Black Sea. Moreover, political tensions between Azerbaijan and Turkmenistan make negotiation of the final plans for the TCGP extremely difficult. Iran and Russia also have pre-existing 'take or pay' gas agreements with Turkey that take precedence over proposed projects and involve pipeline infrastructure that already exists.[37]

US rhetoric continues to support the TCGP project but its competitors were gaining momentum in late 2000. Blue Stream, which partners Russia's state gas monopoly Gazprom with Italy's ENI, has announced that it has arranged $1.7 billion in credits and expects an additional $660 million from the Japan Bank for International Cooperation and Japan's Ministry of International Trade and Industry (MITI).[38]

[34] Author's interviews at the US Department of State on 3 Aug. 2000.

[35] Sokolsky and Charlick-Paley (note 7); Bhatty and Bronson (note 8); and Jaffe, A. M. and Manning, R., 'The shocks of a world of cheap oil', Foreign Affairs, vol. 79, no. 1 (Jan./Feb. 2000), p. 16.

[36] Pipes (note 29).

[37] Joseph, I., 'Caspian gas exports: stranded reserves in a unique position', Baker Institute Working Paper 1998, available at URL <http://www.bakerinstitute.org>.

[38] Aliriza (note 20).

IV. US strategic interests: what is at stake?

All this begs the strategic question: What is truly at stake for the USA? If the answer is oil and natural gas, this resource prize hardly seems worth the risks and costs of intervention in a messy, tangled patchwork of ethnic conflict. Even in the event of greater flows than expected from Kazakhstan's Kashagan field, the region's output is still likely to be less than 5 per cent of world oil demand by 2010.[39] The region is also very distant from the heart of Europe (unlike the Balkans), and this raises questions about the costs to NATO of instability there. Other types of trade with the Caspian region are also relatively limited in comparison with other regions, again raising questions about the Caspian region's strategic economic importance, especially when viewed against the promising and less difficult markets of Asia and the Indian subcontinent, for example. In this regard NATO's economic interests might diverge somewhat from those of Turkey, which is a more prominent trading partner with the Caspian region.[40] For Turkey, which has strong cultural links to the Caspian Basin countries, the region remains an important nearby source of energy supplies as well as a major market for its goods and services.

For Russia, the experience of the breakup of the Soviet Union has demonstrated to some extent that the region and its poverty were more of a drain on its resources than an asset.[41] Russia itself also has vastly superior energy resources but cannot muster the finance, technology and logistics to exploit them.[42] It hardly needs the extra barrels in Kazakhstan. That leaves only the prize of preventing Central Asia from competing with it for international markets, and the responsibilities that would go with blocking Central Asia from earning revenues to sustain itself seem far more costly than letting the region have a minute share of international markets.

The Caspian Basin region's problems of arms proliferation, Islamic militancy and drug trafficking may be more pressing for NATO ally Turkey and for Russia itself, and this is a serious, if corollary, interest for the West. Turkey in particular has suffered from instability and terrorist groups operating along its border areas and must consider the fate of this region in its strategic calculus. However, the question must be asked whether such concerns and the humanitarian considerations that accompany them would not be better handled through multilateral cooperation than through strategic competition.

Given its experience in Chechnya, Russia should have serious reservations about whether it can police the region by itself. There is no question that many influential politicians and military leaders would like to regain not only the full mantle of superpower status but also Russia's historical empire. However,

[39] For further detail see Soligo and Jaffe (note 13).

[40] Bhatty and Bronson (note 8).

[41] Kortunov, A., 'Russia and Central Asia: evolution of mutual perceptions, policies and interdependence', Baker Institute Working Paper, 1998, available at URL <http://www.bakerinstitute.org>. See also Olcott, M., 'The Caspian's false promise', *Foreign Policy*, no. 111 (summer 1998), pp. 95–113.

[42] Rutland, P., *Lost Opportunities: Energy and Politics in Russia*, NBR Policy Analysis Series (National Bureau of Asian Research: Seattle, Wash., 1997).

Russia's world-power status derived in large measure from its military prowess and its nuclear arsenal.[43] At present, its generals must face the reality that the country's armed forces are destitute and their morale low. The Russian Army can no longer brandish unlimited manpower, nor is there money to rebuild or maintain large, well-equipped forces.[44] Similarly, funds to finance a modernized arsenal of new-generation military technologies are lacking. This raises questions about whether there is a gap between any Russian ambitions in the Caspian and Russian capabilities.[45]

For the USA, notwithstanding the 1997 Central Asian Battalion (CentrasBat) exercise which brought US paratroopers parachuting into Uzbekistan, it remains to be seen if policy makers could realistically rally public support for a major operation in a region that most Americans cannot point out on a map and where the vital interests at stake, apart from a small volume of oil, will be hard to articulate convincingly. It took years for US policy makers to clear the idea of intervening in conflicts in the Balkans, which are distinctly closer to the heart of Europe and NATO—literally and figuratively—than the Caucasus, let alone Central Asia. A large and effective US military presence in Central Asia would be not only costly but also politically difficult to 'sell' at home. US civilian and military assistance to the region remains notably minimal. Without the expenditure of vast resources and extensive guarantees, talk of containing Russia in Central Asia and the Caucasus will be counterproductive.

Recommendations that the USA should proactively counter Russia in the Caspian Basin now while Russia is weak may, ironically, only serve to increase the likelihood of a Russian effort to re-assert itself there by fuelling popular support that might otherwise have been missing.[46] Suggestions that Uzbekistan could serve as the USA's regional military surrogate are even more unwise.[47] Religious, ethnic and other cultural factors still influence the stability of Central Asia and the Caucasus and threaten relations between neighbours. Increasing arms shipments to indigenous players in the region would risk escalating stubborn and simmering tensions. Moreover, history shows that US efforts to develop such surrogates in other countries can produce questionable results. Surrogates tend to have their own, rather than their masters', interests in mind as they gain military strength. The horrendous blow-back from US covert support to Afghan rebels against the USSR in the 1980s is a dramatic case in point.

---

[43] Pipes (note 29). Richard Starr of the Hoover Institute has estimated that high-technology investment represents 40% of Russia's military budget. He argues that US cooperation with Russia is necessary to prevent Russia from coping with economic failure by resorting to military force as a means to assert itself because he claims that the 'emotional demands' of the elite and older generations inside Russia are pulling away from a pro-Western alignment and integration into the world economy and back towards a military posture and alignment with countries isolated from the West.

[44] Dick, C. J., *Russian Military Reform: Status and Prospects* (Conflict Studies Research Centre: Canberra, June 1998).

[45] Pipes (note 29).

[46] Chufrin, G. and Saunders, H., 'The politics of conflict prevention in Russia and the near abroad', *Washington Quarterly*, vol. 20, no. 4 (1997).

[47] Starr, S. F., 'Making Eurasia stable', *Foreign Affairs*, vol. 75, no. 1 (Jan./Feb. 1996), pp. 80–92.

V. Russia and the USA: a cooperative framework?

The choices left open to both Russia and the USA suggest that the USA should put Moscow's relationship with the region on its broader bilateral agenda. Neither country is likely to succeed in excluding the other from the region. A more realistic stance is therefore needed by both.

The US agenda should be to shape Russia's role on its southern flank in such a way as to enhance those interests which Russia, Turkey and the USA share. They are surprisingly numerous—to name a few, regional stability, economic development, trade, and a reduction of human suffering and ethnic warfare.[48]

Its experience in Chechnya and Tajikistan should have demonstrated the costs to Russia of simmering discontent and instability on its borders. The USA's experience in the Balkans should make it similarly cautious about single-handedly tackling similar problems in a more remote and difficult terrain. Neither country benefits from having powerful non-state actors launching terrorist attacks inside its territory. For both, the lessons of the former Yugoslavia underscore the dangers of allowing rampant ethnic separatism in the Caucasus and Central Asia to stimulate political devolution in neighbouring states such as Russia and China or on the Indian subcontinent.[49]

Options for cooperation between the USA and Russia do exist. The 1990 Treaty on Conventional Armed Forces in Europe (the CFE Treaty) is an excellent starting point. Joint peacekeeping operations in Bosnia and Herzegovina and Kosovo have created other positive precedents. Old habits may die hard but ultimately the presence of hard-to-control armed factions in the fractious Caspian region is in no one's long-term interests. Cooperation in apprehending and limiting the reach of operational cells of the Taliban is of paramount importance to Russia, Turkey and the USA. If competition among major powers can be reduced, precedents exist for cooperation on conflict resolution in the region, especially between Armenia and Azerbaijan, supported either by the UN or by the OSCE. Finally, multinational humanitarian programmes which provide educational opportunities, jobs and medical assistance can lessen the appeal of radical leaders by providing an alternative window of hope for the populations of the region.

VI. US policy change expected

The change of leadership in the USA is bringing a review of US policies towards the Caspian region. Such a review is likely to focus its conclusions on several key points.

1. Both Central Asia and the Caucasus have unique problems and concerns and should not be an adjunct to US policy towards Russia.

---

[48] Chufrin and Saunders (note 46).
[49] Jaffe, A. M. and Olcott, M. B., 'The geopolitics of Caspian energy', eds E. Kalyuzhnova and D. Lynch, *The Euro-Asian World: A Period of Transition* (St Martin's Press: New York, 2000).

2. Conflict resolution is an important element in drafting a successful US policy towards the region.

3. Energy assets are not large enough on their own to justify giving the region a vital status in the analysis of the USA's broad strategic interests.

These conclusions will have several different effects on US policy. US attention to the region is likely to be downgraded in the coming years. A Pentagon review of US interests in the region has not supported contentions that these interests merit top priority comparable, for example, to interests in the Persian Gulf.[50] Under the new presidency of George W. Bush a reorganization of the offices responsible for the Caspian region may in fact strip away much of the separate bureaucratic attention it has been receiving and reduce the number of official visits and diplomatic tours the region enjoys.

Problems of human rights and corruption in Central Asia are being given a higher profile in US policy circles and could begin to weaken public support for the region's leaders, such as Turkmenistan's President Saparmurat Niyazov, in the USA. US National Security Adviser Condoleezza Rice believes that domestic reform is needed in the region before its countries can be strong enough to resist Russia's unwanted meddling.[51]

Western oil companies can be expected to continue to lobby the new US Administration to take a lower profile on questions of export routes and regional geo-politics in the coming years and to reverse the four-year-old plan to move 'early oil' through Iran by means of swap arrangements or by pipeline. The companies would like to see US diplomatic activity on the Eurasia energy corridor move closer in line to commercial realities and the economic and logistical practicalities of exporting oil profitably from the landlocked, distant area. The new presidency with its strong ties to the US petroleum industry will be more inclined to do this. The attraction of the Baku–Ceyhan route may also wane as the administration listens to the concerns of the US Armenian community, which backed the Republican election campaign. Such policies will, however, be tempered by Republican conservatives who concern themselves with big-power relations. A Republican administration will be less likely to indulge diplomatically any Russian military adventurism in its 'near abroad' and to deal more 'resolutely and decisively' with 'rogue elements'.[52] Thus, if Iran's support for international terrorism becomes a policy problem for the new

[50] Author's conversations with Pentagon officials, 16 Nov. 2000.

[51] Rice, C., 'Promoting the national interest', *Foreign Affairs*, vol. 79, no. 1 (Jan./Feb. 2000), pp. 45–62. She writes: 'The war [in Chechyna] is a reminder of the vulnerability of the small, new states around Russia and of America's interest in their independence. If they can become stronger, they will be less tempting to Russia. But much depends on the ability of these states to reform their economies and political systems—a process, to date, whose success is mixed at best'.

[52] Rice (note 51) outlines a stronger initiative against 'rogue regimes' and international terrorism. While she does not mention the Taliban explicitly, the principles she espouses could clearly apply to Taliban-sponsored terrorism in Eurasia. The new US Trade Representative, Robert Zoellick, also refers to the benefits of coalitions in dealing more forcefully with such problems as 'dangerous powers' that threaten US interests in Eurasia. Zoellick, R., 'A Republican foreign policy', *Foreign Affairs*, vol. 79, no. 1 (Jan./Feb. 2000).

US leadership, any hopes of activating Iranian routes for oil produced by US companies will be dashed.[53]

Any evolution of Iran's domestic politics in favour of the rule of law and the democratic principle is bound to create a better atmosphere for improved relations with the USA. However, the current deterioration of the Arab–Israeli dialogue and the negative public relations impact of the military activities of Iranian-supported groups like Hamas and Hizbollah can be expected to slow the process of normalization for the foreseeable future.

The big Western oil companies remain optimistic about the size of the assets that may be discovered in the region but are now more sanguine about the long-term, thorny bureaucratic issues and severe technical difficulties that will be entailed in bringing them to market. Economically viable line fill for a major oil pipeline out of the region is not expected until 2007 at the earliest and maybe even as late as 2015. Privately, ExxonMobil has made clear its lack of interest in committing export volumes to the uneconomic Baku–Ceyhan route and few, if any, other oil companies have substantial discoveries to offer it at the present juncture. BP Amoco's objections to the costly pipeline have been muted by its interest in exporting Shah Deniz gas to Turkey, which is trying to force the British oil giant to offer a small 500 000 b/d oil pipeline as a loss leader to any gas sales.

Few Western companies, if any, believe that it will be possible to exclude or bypass Russia in the process of identifying secure export routes. Rather, many of them are trying to improve their relations with Russia's Gazprom and other Russian parties that may help enhance their chances of monetizing assets. Several companies kindle hopes that Iranian–US relations will improve in the coming years, thus opening up the possibility of more economic export routes through Iran. Other companies would like to see a shorter and cheaper bypass of Turkey's Bosporus Strait constructed only once it is seen definitively that the waterway cannot handle increasing oil tanker traffic.[54] It remains to be seen whether the change of administration will be enough to rein in quickly a massive US bureaucracy that has been committed to the Baku–Ceyhan line and accompanying anti-Russia, anti-Iran export policies for almost a decade.

VII. Conclusions

The states neighbouring the Caspian Basin—China, Iran, Russia and Turkey—all perceive a degree of interdependence with the fate of Central Asia and the Caucasus countries. This will be true even if the region's oil and gas bounty does not turn out to be as great as some now expect. While the greatly antici-pated wealth of Caspian oil might prove a chimera, geopolitical interest in the region is likely to be sustained.

---

[53] This is the stated policy of the Bush foreign policy team. 'Changes in US policy toward Iran would require changes in Iranian behavior.' Rice (note 51).

[54] Author's conversations with Western oil company executives over the last 6 months of 2000.

For the USA, then, its national interests in the Caspian Basin are more deriv-ative than fundamental. The region will be strategically tangential as long as its resources are accessible to competing interests. Apart from oil and gas which may not be plentiful enough to justify a major US commitment to the region, US interests should be viewed as case-specific and part of a wider focus on stability in China, Russia, Turkey and the Persian Gulf. On an international level, they are oriented towards ensuring that the region does not become a breeding ground for illicit trafficking in arms, controlled technologies and drugs or a centre of ethnic and religious separatism that could spread political devolu-tion to China, Russia, Turkey or South Asia. Finally, US policy towards the region must take into account humanitarian concern about the basic human suffering that has come about with the collapse of the former Soviet Union and the breakdown in basic economic activity and delivery of social services previously provided by the Soviet system.

8. Turkey's objectives in the Caspian region

Ali Karaosmanoglu

I. Introduction

The emergence of the trans-Caucasian and Central Asian states as independent actors has significantly changed the geopolitics of Eurasia. The new republics are facing the problems of transition to a market economy and making efforts to open up to the international economic system. They are seeking ways to be the masters of their own resources and to change the terms of their relationship with Moscow. Their major concern is the consolidation of their independent status. Moreover, after the cold war, the Caspian region has grown in import-ance as a source of energy. In the words of Geoffrey Kemp and Robert E. Harkavy, the resources of the Caspian Sea Basin should be considered together with those of the Persian Gulf and the 'Gulf–Caspian energy ellipse' has become 'one of the most significant geostrategic realities of our time'.[1] The Caspian region is also an essential link between Central Asia, the Black Sea and Turkey. The issue of energy and possible oil transport routes has come to be regarded by regional and extra-regional states as a significant 'determinant for the long-term geopolitical orientation of the region'.[2] This has in turn has exacerbated rivalries among the regional states as well as between Russia and the United States.

Since the breakup of the USSR Turkey has become increasingly involved in this new and dynamic geopolitical environment, which presents it with oppor-tunities as well as challenges. The Turkic world which was previously closed to Turkey has opened up to it. Turkey's foreign relations have acquired new political and economic dimensions with a new Russia and with the emergence of independent Azerbaijan, Georgia and Ukraine. For various reasons, however, Turkey's initial high expectations about the expansion of its influence in the newly independent states have not fully materialized. This is particularly true of Central Asia; in the South Caucasus, by contrast, Turkey has gradually con-solidated its position since the early 1990s.

The South Caucasus is of particular geopolitical interest for three reasons. First, the region is a gateway to Central Asia. Second, it provides direct access to the markets of the West for the Caspian oil and gas. Here Iran's anti-Western policies and US 'containment' of Iran have made the region even more sig-nificant. Third, Azerbaijan and Georgia are of the utmost strategic importance

---

[1] Kemp, G. and Harkavy, R. E., *Strategic Geography and the Changing Middle East* (Brookings Institution: Washington, DC, 1997), p. 111.

[2] Ruseckas, L., 'Turkey and Eurasia: opportunities and risks in the Caspian pipeline derby', *Journal of International Affairs*, vol. 54, no. 1 (fall 2000), p. 223.

to Turkey. Their independence and territorial integrity are regarded as indispensable for the security and stability not only of the Caucasus but also of Central Asia.

This chapter examines Turkey's objectives and strategies in the Caspian region in general and in the South Caucasus in particular. It focuses on Turkey's priorities not only from a regional perspective but also in terms of trans-regional linkages which usually exert considerable influence on Turkey's decisions and actions.

Turkish policy is widely viewed as being motivated almost solely by economic considerations, particularly by the energy (oil and gas) issue. Turkey's political and other non-economic interests are often neglected or, at best, only touched on briefly. In fact, Turkey's primary long-term objective is political—the creation and maintenance of a pluralistic Eurasia which is open to the West in general and to Turkey in particular. It also has other serious concerns—environmental concerns about the transport of oil by tanker through the narrow straits of the Bosporus and the Dardanelles (the Turkish Straits) and the maintenance of good, cooperative relations with Russia in the interests of regional stability and economic benefit. This, however, is not to overlook the energy issue, which is undoubtedly important both in itself and because of Turkey's rapidly growing energy needs. It is also regarded as an instrument for the realization of the long-term political objective of building a pluralistic Eurasia. In this sense, the exploitation of energy resources and the transport of oil and gas are often seen as promoting stability, nation-building and independent statehood rather than the causes of rivalry and conflict. The energy issue is in one way or another related to other objectives.

This raises the question of the compatibility of different objectives. To what extent does Turkey's policy in the region contribute to minimizing conflictual tendencies and promoting stability?

Finally, trans-regional linkages should be taken into account in dealing with Turkey's objectives in the Caspian region. Turkey's regional policies cannot be adequately understood separately from its Western vocation and its relations with the United States and the European Union (EU).

II. Energy and the economy

Since the breakup of the Soviet Union there has been growing Western interest in the Caspian region's oil and gas resources. It is expected that sustained economic growth in North America, Europe and Asia during the first decade of the 21st century will bring about a considerable increase in demand for energy. Although the significance of the Caspian energy reserves is modest, they have the potential to supplement the Persian Gulf production on which most countries are expected to be increasingly dependent. Consequently there is a growing need to exploit the energy resources of Central Asia and the Caucasus by opening up these regions to foreign investment and international cooperation.

Turkey is one of the most important potential markets for the oil and gas production of the Caspian region and Russia. Its need for energy has been increasing rapidly and will continue to do so if the present rate of economic growth is to be sustained. Energy security is also extremely important for sustained economic growth.

Turkey is estimated to import around 28 million tonnes of crude oil in the year 2000 and over 40 million tonnes by 2010. The increase in the demand for natural gas is even more striking. On one very conservative estimate it is expected to rise from 10 billion cubic metres (bcm) in 2000 to over 30–40 bcm in 2010. Turkey currently depends on imports for approximately 62.6 per cent of its energy consumption and for more than 95 per cent of the oil and gas it consumes. The major suppliers of crude oil are the Persian Gulf countries and Libya; the major supplier of natural gas is Russia.[3] This trend has prompted Turkey to diversify its energy suppliers and to regard the Central Asian and trans-Caucasian states as important energy partners.

Turkey is already beginning to suffer a shortage of gas supply. It plans to build new gas-fired power stations in order to meet the growing demand for electricity and a shortage of natural gas to supply them could cause economic crisis. All this makes it a very important market for the Caspian region's gas and gives additional economic significance to Turkey's relations with the region, which has the potential to become its main gas supplier in the very near future.[4] Its growing demand for natural gas has led to Turkey concluding agreements to buy additional gas from Azerbaijan, Iran, Russia and Turkmenistan.

All these new supplies require new pipelines connecting the suppliers to the Turkish market. However, the construction of infrastructure may take years, while the country's gas shortage worsens in the meantime. Gas is therefore an urgent issue for Ankara which requires a short-term solution. This also makes the gas issue primarily an economic one, which hardly lends itself to longer-term political considerations. Russia currently supplies more than 11 bcm of natural gas to Turkey per year through a pipeline across Ukraine, Moldova, Romania and Bulgaria. The parties are planning to upgrade the capacity of this pipeline. Moreover, Turkey and Russia have concluded an agreement providing for the transport of 16 bcm per year of Russian gas to Turkey by an underwater pipeline across the Black Sea shelf. The project, which is called Blue Stream, has already received the support of Russia's Gazprom, Italy's ENI, three Japanese companies and a French company. The Blue Stream pipeline is to be built by ENI.[5] In contrast to the politics of oil, Russia is thus becoming 'an important partner for Turkey rather than a rival in the field of gas'.[6]

[3] On Turkey's energy needs and policies see Söylemez, Y., 'Turkey as an energy terminal in the 21st century', *Turkish Daily News* (15 Feb. 2000), p. 16. The figures concerning Turkey's energy needs that appear here are taken from this article.

[4] Kramer, H., *A Changing Turkey: The Challenge to Europe and the United States* (Brookings Institution: Washington, DC, 2000), p. 101.

[5] Pamir, A. N., 'Is there a future for the Eurasian corridor?', *Insight Turkey*, vol. 2, no. 3 (July/Sep. 2000), pp. 35–38. On this and other pipeline projects see also chapter 3 in this volume.

[6] Winrow, G. M., 'Turkey and Caspian energy: the importance of geopolitics', *Insight Turkey*, vol. 2, no. 2 (Apr./June 2000), p. 64.

There are two more gas pipeline projects at issue.

The second project is the US-backed Trans-Caspian Gas Pipeline (TCGP) project, which Turkey is pursuing simultaneously with Blue Stream. The TCGP is envisaged to transport Turkmen gas to Turkey via the Caspian, Azerbaijan and Georgia. Although the Turkish Government believes otherwise, most experts in the United States and Turkey argue that demand for natural gas in Turkey means that only one of the pipelines is economically feasible and that it should choose between Blue Stream and the TCGP. Furthermore, they contend that the TCGP is politically more appropriate than Blue Stream, which will inevitably increase Turkey's energy dependence on Russia.[7]

Turkish officials believe that Blue Stream is less costly because it is geographically more direct. It is also politically simpler to realize because Russia is Turkey's only partner. As a US analyst has pointed out, 'Blue Stream also tracks with traditional Turkish strategic thinking regarding Russia . . . Turkey has always been loath to antagonize Moscow.'[8] Thus, one of the political reasons why Turkey prefers Blue Stream is probably that it will help to moderate Turkish–Russian rivalry in the Caucasus and the Black Sea.

The third project is for a pipeline across Iran. Given its huge oil and gas reserves, Turkey has always regarded Iran as a potential economic partner. Cooperation with Iran is also seen as important in order to diversify sources and avoid excessive dependence on Russia. Hence, Turkish policy makers have not been comfortable with the US-led policy of 'dual containment'. Turkey signed gas agreements with Iran in 1996 and 1997 which provide for the transport of Turkmen and Iranian gas to Turkey. Iran has already finished constructing the pipeline on its own territory while Turkey has failed to fulfil its obligations. This has brought about a dispute between the two countries. Nevertheless, the parties have agreed to postpone the fulfilment of Turkey's obligations.

It should be noted that the gas deal with Iran has not been welcomed unanimously in Turkey. At times it has been criticized because of Iran's support for terrorist groups such as the separatist Kurdish Workers' Party (PKK) and Turkish Hizbollah.[9]

III. The environmental risks of oil transport

While Turkey has adopted a mainly economic approach to the natural gas issue, its policy towards the oil transport issue is dominated by environmental concerns and political considerations.

The present low-level Caspian production ('early oil') is being carried by the existing pipelines. One connects Baku to the Russian Black Sea terminal at Novorossiysk; a second links Baku to the Georgian port of Supsa; a third goes through Russia to the Black Sea coast from Kazakhstan. The total capacity of

---

[7] Makovsky, A., 'US policy toward Turkey: progress and problems', ed. M. Abramowitz, *Turkey's Transformation and American Policy* (Century Foundation Press: New York, 2000), p. 242; and Pamir (note 5), p. 37.

[8] Makovsky (note 7), p. 243.

[9] Pamir (note 5), p. 40.

all three is limited to about 150 000 barrels a day (b/d). This will not be sufficient when the exploitation of the bulk of the Caspian reserves ('main oil') begins. Setting aside the Russia–Balkan route, which is under consideration, and the Iranian–Persian Gulf route, which is vehemently opposed by the USA, there are today three more or less equally viable options for transporting the 'main oil' from the region to consumers in the West. One is to expand and refurbish the northern route from Baku to Novorossiysk; the second is to build a new pipeline from Baku to Georgia's Black Sea coast; and the third is to build a pipeline from Azerbaijan through Georgia to Turkey's Mediterranean port of Ceyhan. This is called the Baku–Tbilisi–Ceyhan (BTC) pipeline.

Turkey is energetically promoting the BTC project, which will avoid all transport by sea through the Black Sea and the Turkish Straits. One of its major objectives in doing this is to restrict tanker traffic through the straits because of the growing risk of accidents that would particularly affect Istanbul, Turkey's largest city and business metropolis. The passage from the Black Sea into the Aegean and the Mediterranean is through two narrow straits, the Bosporus and the Dardanelles, as well as the semi-enclosed Sea of Marmara. The 1936 Convention Regarding the Regime of the Straits (the Montreux Convention) provides for the free passage of commercial vessels through the Turkish Straits and makes no environmental protection provisions. The size and speed of vessels have increased since 1936 and the volume of traffic has grown considerably: the number of vessels passing through the straits annually increased from 4500 in 1934 to 47 000 in 1995 and 49 304 in 1998.[10] Occasional accidents have brought the environmental risks to the forefront and each successive shipping accident has hardened Turkey's position on the limitation of tanker traffic through the straits.

The adaptability of the Montreux Convention to changing circumstances has recently been a matter of debate in Turkey. Some experts emphasize the need for revision, arguing that as it applies today the convention considerably limits the powers of the Turkish Government. The Turkish authorities should be given the necessary powers to take measures of environmental protection and to stop and search vessels for security reasons. They also insist that pilotage must be obligatory for merchant vessels.

Turkey, however, has always been unfavourable to any modification of the Montreux Convention. Turkish officials believe that its main provisions are still quite satisfactory with respect its interests and that even further discussion of its detailed provisions might open a Pandora's box. Thus, while acknowledging the need for a certain degree of adaptation, they argue that this could be done through an evolutionary process of interpretation.[11] Accordingly, in January 1994, the Turkish Government adopted new Maritime Traffic Regulations for

---

[10] Turkish Ministry of Foreign Affairs, *Rapport Annuel sur le Mouvement des Navires à Travers les Détroits Turcs* [Annual report on the movement of shipping through the Turkish Straits], (Ministry of Foreign Affairs: Ankara, 1999).

[11] Karaosmanoglu, A. L., 'Naval security in the Black Sea and the Mediterranean', *International Spectator*, vol. 28, no. 4 (Oct./Dec. 1993), pp. 139–44. For recent developments see Yuksel, I., 'The current regime of the Turkish Straits', *Perceptions*, vol. 6, no. 1 (Mar./May 2001).

the Turkish Straits and the Marmara Region. These introduced a rigorous regulatory regime for passage through the straits without violating the Montreux Convention principle of free passage. The purpose of the regulations was 'to regulate the maritime traffic scheme in order to ensure the safety of navigation, life and property and to protect the environment in the region'.

Turkey implemented the regulations, with the approval of the International Maritime Organization (IMO), but in November 1998, in response to Russia's objections to the new regime, replaced the 1994 regulations by new Maritime Traffic Regulations for the Turkish Straits.[12] The 1998 regulations are simpler than those of 1994 and strengthen the principle of freedom of passage. At the same time, however, they maintain a rigorous regulatory regime not only in the interests of the security of passage and navigation but also for the security of the lives and property of the people living in the Istanbul area and that of the environment. Turkish officials believe that because of the new regulations and the approval by the IMO Russia is now tending to moderate its position and limit its objections to technical issues, demanding only certain exceptions for its vessels on the traffic separation schemes provided for by the 1998 regulations. Moreover, in April 2000 Turkey signed a contract with Lockheed Maritime Overseas for the construction of a high-technology Turkish Straits Vessel Traffic Management and Information System.

Turkey's environmental concerns are to some extent shared by the South Caucasian states. They also believe that a substantial increase in tanker traffic would do great harm to the Black Sea, which is already dangerously polluted. As a result of a Turkish initiative, the Ankara Declaration of 29 October 1998, signed by the presidents of Azerbaijan, Georgia, Kazakhstan and Turkey, pointed out 'the importance of protection of the natural environment of the Turkish Straits, the Black Sea and the Mediterranean coast'. It also emphasized that 'the transportation of oil through pipelines is a vital matter for reducing the threat caused by tanker traffic'.[13]

IV. The geopolitics of pipelines

From the beginning, with the exception of the State Oil Company of the Azerbaijan Republic (SOCAR) and the Turkish Petroleum Corporation (TPAO), almost all the major oil companies have opposed the BTC as the main export pipeline, for two reasons: (*a*) the inadequacy of reserves; and (*b*) its high cost compared to the other possible routes such as Baku–Supsa, Baku–Novorossiysk and the Iran–Persian Gulf route.

These economic impediments seem to have lost some of their significance recently as a result of a number of developments.[14] The objection of high cost

---

[12] The new regulations were approved by IMO document MSC 71/ WP.14/Add.2 of 27 May 1999, which continues the IMO rules and recommendations adopted in 1994 (Res. A7857).

[13] For the Ankara Declaration see *Turkish Probe*, no. 304 (8 Nov. 1998), p. 15.

[14] Demirmen, F., 'Baku–Tbilisi–Ceyhan: the project enters a new phase, Part 1', *Turkish Daily News*, 20 Oct. 2000, p. 5.

was mitigated when Turkey granted tariff reductions and guaranteed to cover construction costs above $1.4 billion for the section of the pipeline that passes through Turkish territory. Objections based on the insufficiency of reserves were mitigated by the recent discovery of oil on the Kashagan East-1 field in Kazakhstan and by the recent announcement of new reserves on the Azerbaijani fields of Muradhanli, Gobustan, Mishovdag, Kemaleddin and Dan-Ulduzu-Ashrafi (offshore condensate). During a visit by the Turkish President, Ahmet Necdet Sezer, to Kazakhstan in October 2000, President Nursultan Nazarbayev declared that he would support the BTC project by supplying 15 million tonnes of crude oil from Kazakhstan's newly opened reserves.[15] Another development was the increase in the price of crude in the second half of 2000 to $30 per barrel. It is expected that the price will stabilize at around $20 per barrel, and this will positively affect the economic viability of the project.[16] These new developments are expected to change the negative attitude of the oil companies towards the BTC project.[17]

Despite these economic factors, political considerations dominate the entire issue of oil pipelines. Regional states and other interested governments such as the USA's view the question of oil pipeline routes as a crucial factor which will directly influence the long-term geopolitical orientation of the Caucasus. The Baku–Novorossiysk route would increase Russia's control of the region. The Iranian route would violate the USA's policy of containment and increase Iranian and other Middle Eastern influence in the Caspian region. The BTC route would make regional states such as Azerbaijan and Georgia more inclined towards the West and Turkey, and it is believed that this is precisely why Iran and Russia are against it.[18]

Turkey is willing to buy a considerable share of the oil flowing through the BTC pipeline. Moreover, it expects some financial benefit from the pipeline. Its main interest, however, is political. Turkey regards a main export pipeline (MEP) crossing its territory as an instrument for extending its influence in the region and, and more significantly, as an opportunity to consolidate its role as a crucial link between Central Asia, the Caspian region and Europe.[19] Turkish policy makers believe that their country's importance for the West in general, and for the EU in particular, will increase to the extent that its role and influence are solidified in the Caspian region and Central Asia.

Energy resources and pipeline routes in the Caspian region are also considered a convenient instrument to create a web of interdependence which, in turn, will promote welfare, stability and independent statehood in the region.

[15] *Turkish Daily News*, 21 Oct. 2000, p. 9.

[16] Demirmen, F., 'Baku–Tbilisi–Ceyhan: the project enters a new phase, Part 2', *Turkish Daily News*, 21 Oct. 2000, p. 5.

[17] In Oct. 2000 Azerbaijan, Georgia and Turkey signed the Full Handover Agreement, the Transit Country Agreement, the Guarantee Documents Agreement and the Host Country Agreement, which are regarded as a major step towards implementation of the BTC project. *Turkish Daily News*, 20 Oct. 2000, p. 5.

[18] Ruseckas (note 2), pp. 223–24.

[19] Rubin, V., *The Geopolitics of Energy Development in the Caspian Region*, Conference Report (Stanford University, Center for International Security and Cooperation: Stanford, Calif., 1999), p. 15.

The consolidation of the independence of regional states, especially Azerbaijan and Georgia, is Turkey's highest stake in the region.[20] In the Ankara Declaration of October 1998 this is clearly stated as the major political objective: 'The Presidents affirm that it is necessary to carry the oil and gas resources of the region through multiple pipelines, which is also optimal economically and commercially for strengthening the independence and security of the Caspian states and their neighbors'. In the same declaration the presidents also agreed on 'giving directives to the relevant authorities in their countries for the realization of the East–West energy corridor and Baku–Tbilisi–Ceyhan pipeline'.[21]

This approach to the pipeline issue, including the BTC project, is being actively promoted by the USA. Ambassador Richard Morningstar, Special Advisor to the President of the United States, described his government's position quite clearly in a conference on December 1998. After emphasizing the BTC project as the best solution for transporting oil from the Caspian to foreign markets, he listed the USA's main policy objectives regarding the Caspian energy resources as: (*a*) strengthening the independence and prosperity of the new states; (*b*) encouraging political and economic reform; (*c*) mitigating regional conflicts by building economic linkages between regional states; (*d*) bolstering the energy security of the USA and its allies and regional states by ensuring the free flow of oil and gas to the world market; and (*e*) enhancing commercial opportunities for US and other companies.[22]

With a few exceptions, Turkey shares the US approach to the South Caucasus. Turkish officials, like their US counterparts, view the pipelines as a useful tool to consolidate the independence and territorial integrity of the new states and reduce regional tensions through regional and inter-regional cooperation. The region's energy resources should be exploited to the benefit of all the states of the region. To this effect it is essential to create a web of multiple pipelines in the region, involving all the states of the South Caucasus and Russia.

Although there is a striking parallel between Turkish and US policies on the MEP issue, Turkey differs from its ally and supporter where Iran and Russia are concerned. First, it puts stronger emphasis on economic and political cooperation with Russia. Second, it is uncomfortable with the policy of containment of Iran. Turkey wants to transfer Turkmenistan's natural gas through a pipeline across Iranian territory. It would also like to develop closer trade relations with Iran. Third, Turkey believes that the present US approach to the Nagorno-Karabakh conflict is biased in favour of Armenia. This is especially observable in US assistance to the region: while Armenia receives US economic aid, sanctions passed by the US Congress in 1992 impede all US assistance, including aid for privatization, to Azerbaijan. The restrictions imposed by the Congress are not consistent with US policy objectives in the Caucasus, prevent the USA

[20] Karaosmanoglu, A. L., 'Turkey and the new geoeconomics in the Black Sea region', eds H. Bagci, J. Janes and L. Kuhnhardt, *Parameters of Partnership: The US, Turkey, Europe* (Nomos: Baden-Baden, 1999), pp. 187–89.

[21] See note 13.

[22] *Turkish Daily News*, 10 Dec. 1998, p. A3. See also Rubin (note 19), p. 9.

from acting as an effective mediator and constrain its ability to become fully involved in the development of Azerbaijan's oil sector.[23]

V. Cooperation with Russia

Turkey values its cooperation with Russia highly. Despite acute rivalry over issues such as the oil pipeline, the status of the Turkish Straits, and Turkey's and NATO's increased naval presence in the Black Sea, economic relations have grown rapidly since the end of the cold war, to the benefit of both countries.[24] Turkey's growing activism, on the one hand, and Russia's considerable loss of power after the end of the cold war, on the other, have made the two states more cooperative in dealing with each other more or less on the footing of equality.[25] Each today has a strong economic interest in business with the other. Russia has become one of Turkey's leading trading partners and will soon become its major energy supplier. Both governments are increasingly careful in their rhetoric. They play down their differences but emphasize the mutual benefits to be derived from cooperation. As a result of growing business interests, a significant pro-Russian lobby is becoming increasingly influential in Turkish business and political circles.

From the end of the cold war to Russia's economic crisis in 1998, the value of trade between Turkey and Russia increased to $8–10 billion annually. Official trade represented only $3.5 billion in 1998, the remainder being accounted for by the unregistered 'suitcase trade' which largely worked in favour of Turkey's balance of trade.[26] Russia's economic crisis mainly affected Turkish exports. The 'suitcase trade' almost stopped. Turkey's foreign trade deficit, according to the official statistics, soared to $807 million following Russia's cutting down its imports in the 1998 financial crash. The deficit grew even further in 1999, to the detriment of Turkey. In 1999 Russian imports from and exports to Turkey were $588 million and $2.37 billion, respectively.[27]

Another cause of Turkey's trade deficit is the steady increase of its gas purchases from Russia. These rose from 6.5 bcm in 1997 to 11 bcm in 2000 and are expected to increase to 30 bcm in 2012 when Blue Stream is completed. If natural gas prices remain the same, Russian gas will then cost Turkey $2.5 billion each year. In order to solve the trade deficit problem, Turkey proposed to reactivate the barter trade system which functioned from 1984 until 1994, when Russia started liberalizing its foreign trade policy. Russian officials

[23] On sanctions against Azerbaijan see Cohen, A., 'US policy in the Caucasus and Central Asia: building a New Silk Road to economic prosperity', *Heritage Foundation Backgrounder*, no. 1132 (24 July 1997), pp. 3, 13; and Larrabee, F. S., 'US and European policy toward Turkey and the Caspian Basin', eds R. D. Blackwill and M. Sturmer, *Allies Divided* (MIT Press: Cambridge, Mass., 1997), p. 173.

[24] On the contradictions in Turkish–Russian relations see Sezer, D. B., 'Turkey–Russian relations: the challenges of reconciling geopolitical competition with economic partnership', *Turkish Studies*, vol. 1, no. 1 (spring 2000), pp. 59–82.

[25] Markuskin, V., 'Russia–Turkey: doomed to be eternal neighbors', *Perceptions*, vol. 2, no. 1 (Mar./May 1997), p. 98.

[26] Sezer (note 24), p. 73.

[27] *Turkish Daily News*, 26 Oct. 2000, p. 6.

argue that there is no imbalance in the trade between the two countries when the 'suitcase trade' is taken into account. Nevertheless, when Russian Prime Minister Mikhail Kasyanov visited Ankara in October 2000, both governments agreed to hold talks on reactivating the old system of payment by adapting it to the requirements of liberal economies.[28]

The activities of Turkish construction firms in Russia are another aspect of economic relations. The total value of this work exceeded $6 billion by 1996 and Turkish officials hope that reactivation of the barter system will encourage this as well. Tourism is growing between the two countries. Finally, arms deals are another item on the economic agenda. Russian companies seem to be eager not only to sell arms to Turkey but also to start co-production projects.

Turkish businessmen, referring to Russia's vast resources and industrial infrastructure, believe that in the long term a collapse of the Russian economy is out of the question. This sanguine view is shared by many Turkish officials. A recent exchange of visits between the two countries highlighted the significance of economic links and made clear that the effects of the 1998 financial crisis in Russia had to a considerable extent been overcome. Economic cooperation even encouraged speculation on the possibility of a strategic relationship between Russia and Turkey. When Alexander Lebedev, Russia's Ambassador to Turkey, was asked in an interview if cooperation between Russia and Turkey could grow into a strategic partnership, he said: 'After all, Russia and Turkey are two major Eurasian countries. In fact, because of the coexistence of national interests in many ways, I do believe that Russia and Turkey can cooperate very closely in the former Soviet republics of Central Asia and in the Caucasus. The two countries' positions towards the region are very close if not identical'.[29]

The growth of economic relations has yet to lead to political cooperation. Turkey's relations with Russia seem likely to involve serious misunderstandings, if not tension, for several decades to come. Nevertheless, in spite of the presence of influential Caucasian groups in Turkey and Moscow's complaints that they were sending military assistance to Chechnya, Turkey has supported Russia's territorial integrity and Turkish officials consider the Chechen war as a matter of Russia's domestic jurisdiction (although they also believe that the use of excessive and disproportionate force by Moscow is an international human rights issue). Russia has responded accordingly. Despite the Duma's anti-Turkish attitude, the Russian Government in October 1998 refused to give asylum to Abdullah Öcalan, leader of the PKK, and expelled him from the country. Russia's attitude was welcomed by public opinion in Turkey.

Turkey's major concern is in fact the possibility of a Russian military intervention in Georgia under the pretext of stopping incursions from Georgia into Chechnya. It does not want to see any curtailment whatsoever of the political independence or territorial integrity of Georgia.

---

[28] *Turkish Daily News*, 26 Oct. 2000, p. 6.
[29] *Turkish Daily News*, 4 Dec. 1988, p. A4.

VI. Multilateralism and Western orientation

Multilateralism and cooperation with the West are the principal characteristics of Turkey's diplomatic and strategic approach to the Caspian region. Its policy is far from being unilateralist and adventurist. Its activism in the region is a 'measured activism'. Most manifestations of Turkey's assertiveness 'are in the realm of diplomatic relations, not the use of force'.[30] Moreover, it prefers to act together with its Western allies. Its multilateralism extends from participation in peace operations, such as the Organization for Security and Co-operation in Europe (OSCE) Minsk Group in Nagorno-Karabakh and the UN Observer Mission in Georgia, to the initiation of regional arrangements such as the Black Sea Economic Cooperation (BSEC) scheme. Turkey's starting point is often its own Western vocation and Western values. Statements by Turkish officials clearly reflect the way Turkey views its mission in the region. A recent example is an article by Ismail Cem, Turkey's Minister of Foreign Affairs: 'As the only country with a predominantly Muslim population and that has the ideals and practices of a pluralist democracy, secularism, the rule of law, human rights and gender equality, Turkey enjoys the privilege of being a paradigm of moderniza-tion . . . Turkey thus becomes a center for the emerging Eurasian reality and constitutes Western Europe's major historical, cultural and economic opening to Eastern horizons'.[31]

In this ideological context, Turkey views NATO and the EU as the linchpins of stability not only in Europe but also in the new transatlantic area extending to the Black Sea region and to the Caucasus and Central Asia. Turkey contributes enthusiastically to NATO's Partnership for Peace (PFP) programme, including military and naval exercises in the Black Sea in which Azerbaijan, Georgia and Ukraine participate. Units from Azerbaijan and Georgia are also participating in the Kosovo Force (KFOR) as part of a Turkish battalion. In 1998 Turkey set up a PFP Training Center in Ankara whose function is to provide training and edu-cation to military and civilian personnel of partners, including Azerbaijanis and Georgians, to prepare them for NATO standards. Turkey also proposed a project for a multinational Black Sea Naval Cooperation Task Force which is at present being discussed among the regional states.[32] Furthermore, in pursuance of PFP objectives, Turkey has carried out special military training and educa-tional programmes in Azerbaijan and Georgia.

The purpose of the PFP programme is not only to encourage military coopera-tion or promote interoperability and transparency among NATO members and partner countries. Its final objective is to project stability eastwards by sub-stituting cooperative security for balance-of-power policies.[33] Institutions such

[30] Makovsky, A., 'The new activism in Turkish foreign policy', *SAIS Review*, vol. 19, no. 1 (winter–spring 1999), p. 94.

[31] Cem, I., 'Turkey and Europe: looking to the future from a historical perspective', *Perceptions* (Turkish Ministry of Foreign Affairs), vol. 5, no. 2 (June/Aug. 2000), p. 9.

[32] See the interview with Gen. Hüseyin Kivrikoglu, Chief of the General Staff, 'Turkish armed forces: peace in the nation, peace in the world', *Military Technology*, vol. 23, no. 9 (1999), pp. 9–20.

[33] Ruggie, J. G., *Winning the Peace: America and World Order in the New Era* (Columbia University Press: New York, 1996), p. 88.

as the PFP 'help mobilize material and normative resources for the development of a transnational liberal collective identity'.[34] In this way a 'we feeling' is
expected to develop, replacing fragmentation, balance of power and unilateral-
ism.[35] Thus, the Turkish foreign policy elite, by actively supporting the PFP,
expect their multilateralist activism to consolidate Turkey's 'unique position' to
project Western values to the newly independent states in the Caucasus and
Central Asia; this, in turn, will strengthen Turkey's Western identity.

Both Azerbaijan and Georgia have further expectations of NATO. They look
forward to becoming full members of the alliance and seek solid security guarantees. NATO members, however, will not be able to respond to these expectations for some time to come, for several reasons. The USA has other commitments in other parts of the world. The European allies have priorities in their
own vicinity. NATO is careful about Russia's sensitivities. In the long run, the
interest of the West will most probably increase in the South Caucasus. In the
medium term, however, NATO engagement in the Caspian region will be confined to advisory assistance, training, joint military exercises, and restructuring
the military establishments of the Caspian states along Western lines.[36]

The same vision of integration with the Western community of nations was
part of the BSEC scheme, which was a Turkish initiative. The BSEC's Charter
of 25 June 1992 confirmed the participants' intention to develop economic
cooperation as a contribution to the Conference on Security and Co-operation in
Europe (CSCE) process,[37] to the establishment of a Europe-wide economic
area, and to greater integration into the world economy, and stated that economic cooperation would be developed in such a way as not to prevent the
promotion of the participating states' relations with the European Community.[38]
These provisions in its founding document show that the BSEC initiative is
viewed by all the participants as complementary to the broader scheme of
European integration.[39]

Another example of multilateralism is the Turkish initiative for the creation
of a Stability Pact for the Caucasus. On the occasion of President Suleyman
Demirel's visit to Tbilisi in January 2000, Georgia and Turkey proposed that a
Stability Pact for the Caucasus should be concluded which would include
Azerbaijan, Armenia, Georgia, Turkey, Russia, the United States, the EU, the
OSCE and possibly Iran. The purpose of the pact would be the promotion of
cooperative security and conflict resolution. It has already received support

[34] Adler, E., 'Seeds of peaceful change: the OSCE's security community-building model', eds E. Adler
and M. Barnett, *Security Communities* (Cambridge University Press: Cambridge, 1998), p. 152.

[35] Waever, O., 'Insecurity, security and asecurity in the West European non-war community', eds Adler
and Barnett (note 34), pp. 98–101.

[36] On NATO's limitations see Sokolsky, R. and Charlick-Paley, T., *NATO and Caspian Security: A
Mission Too Far?*, Report MR-1074-AF (RAND: Santa Monica, Calif., 1999); and Bhatty, R. and
Bronson, R., 'NATO's mixed signals in the Caucasus and Central Asia', *Survival*, vol. 42, no. 3 (autumn
2000), pp. 129–46.

[37] The CSCE became the OSCE in Jan. 1995.

[38] Charter of the Organization of the Black Sea Economic Cooperation (BSEC), 25 June 1992, URL
<http://www.bsec.gov.tr/Charter.htm>.

[39] Çeviköz, Ü., 'Sub-regional cooperation and pan-European integration', Thesis for the Master's
degree presented at the Université Libre de Bruxelles, July 1993, pp. 42–44 (unpublished).

from Azerbaijan and Western governments and attracted positive attention from the EU. The Centre for European Policy Studies, a research institute in Brussels which works mostly for the EU, published in May 2000 a working document on the initiative for a Caucasus Stability Pact.[40]

The EU has strongly supported the idea of the Transport Corridor Europe Caucasus Asia (TRACECA)[41] and, to that affect, signed a series of Partnership and Cooperation Agreements with the South Caucasus and Central Asian states. The EU engagement, however, has also its limitations. The EU does not seem comfortable with its present aid policy, which mainly consists of grants. It is beginning to adopt a more political approach, putting emphasis on condition- ality, trade and investment.[42]

Turkey would like to see the EU make further efforts to contribute to the stability and development of the South Caucasus, but West Europeans are ambivalent as regards the region and Turkey's role there. Although Turkey's role is generally viewed positively, there is at the same time a certain suspicion about its new activism. Many Europeans think that its activist policies could indirectly and inadvertently embroil the NATO allies in regional conflicts.

VII. Turkey's internal and external constraints

Turkey's ability to achieve its objectives in the Caspian region faces important internal and external constraints. First, Turkey has been unable to supply large amounts of aid because its own resources are limited. The Turkish public sector could not undertake large-scale investment in the South Caucasus while its own state enterprises were facing a dwindling budget for domestic investment. Many private companies in Turkey regarded the region as a high-risk area and refrained from investing, preferring Russia for trade and investment. Second, Turkey's own internal political problems, such as terrorism, separatism and Islamic extremism, and its human rights problems have preoccupied politicians and the civil and military bureaucracy and diverted their attention away from the South Caucasus. Third, Turkey has had to deal with other foreign and security policy issues in Western Europe, Cyprus, the Aegean, the Balkans and the Middle East. Most of these problems touched on its vital or major interests and required urgent treatment. Turkey has had to deal with all these issues with an understaffed foreign ministry which was overwhelmed by routine work and lacked a tradition of policy planning.

Turkey also faces even more formidable external constraints and policy dilemmas in the Caspian region. First, Russia's political objectives and military presence (bases in Armenia and Georgia)[43] often clash with Turkey's interests

[40] For the Executive Summary of Working Document no. 145 of May 2000 see Emerson, M., 'A Stability Pact for the Caucasus', *Insight Turkey*, vol. 2, no. 3 (July/Sep. 2000), pp. 23–30 and 199–204.

[41] See, e.g., the TRACECA Internet site, URL <http://www.traceca.org>.

[42] Wittebrood, C. F., 'Towards a partnership with the countries of the Eurasian Corridor', *Insight Turkey*, vol. 2, no. 3 (July/Sep. 2000), pp. 11–21.

[43] In Nov. 1999 at the OSCE Summit Meeting in Istanbul Russia agreed to evacuate its 4 bases in Georgia. It has begun to withdraw from the bases at Gudauta and Vaziani, and withdrawal is expected to

in the region. Russia is Turkey's major economic partner and its most important energy supplier. Moreover, despite its deficiencies in conventional weapons, it is still a significant nuclear power. These factors lead Ankara to act cautiously so as not to antagonize Moscow.

The Nagorno-Karabakh conflict and Turkey's poor relations with Armenia are also obstacles to the realization of Turkey's objectives. If the events of 1915 can be put aside, a Turkish–Armenian rapprochement will primarily depend on the resolution of the Karabakh conflict and the evacuation of the occupied Azeri territories by Armenian forces. Although Turkey strongly supports Azerbaijan's (as well as Georgia's) territorial integrity, it also favours a considerable degree of autonomy for Nagorno-Karabakh on the condition that the Armenian and Azerbaijani peoples accept this solution. Such a settlement would greatly contribute to regional stability, open the region and Armenia itself to the West even further, and lead very soon to cooperation between Armenia and Turkey, to the benefit of both as well as the region as a whole.

VIII. Conclusions: future trends

In the Caspian region Turkey has political, economic and environmental interests. Its first priorities are political and its main political objective is to contribute to the creation of a favourable milieu in the region for cooperation in every field. To this effect, the development of a web of multiple pipelines is instrumental. Moreover, for the security and stability of the region, the maintenance of the independence and territorial integrity of regional states is of the utmost importance.

Western involvement, together with Turkey's activism, has so far contributed particularly to the consolidation of the independence of Azerbaijan and Georgia and promoted cooperation especially between these two states and the West. Turkey's economic cooperation with Russia has also been successful. Turkish and Western involvement has not caused new instabilities in the region, but it has not been able to minimize power politics. Today the trends of power politics and cooperation are juxtaposed. To change the balance in favour of cooperation, Turkish, US and European policy makers should work to fill a number of gaps.

The most formidable problem arises from the uncertain future of Russia. The prospects for sustained cooperation depend on the future of Russia more than anything else. Russia's future will be determined primarily by internal developments. However, the policies of the West will definitely affect Russia's orientation in both the domestic and the international arenas. More than any other country in the region, Russia reflects contradictory tendencies. On the one hand,

be completed in July 2001. However, it is seeking a 15-year lease on the 2 largest bases at Akhalkalaki and Batumi. Although several rounds of negotiations have been held, the parties have not yet reached agreement on these 2 bases or on the issue of the Vaziani military airfield, over which Russia insists on retaining control. 'Russian withdrawal from Georgia bases in doubt', *Jane's Intelligence Review*, Sep. 2000, p. 4.

influential foreign and security policy circles view the Caspian region in terms of power politics and wish to see Russia as the dominant power in the region. On the other hand, the new business circles promote a more liberal policy towards the region, advocating cooperative approaches and the benefits of integrating Russia and the region in the world economic system.

Russia will certainly remain a very important actor in the region. Its role and influence will grow to the extent that its economic and financial possibilities increase. A powerful Russia will be a stabilizing factor if it can get away from its imperialistic tendencies and heavy-handed tactics, and if it agrees to play its role in a truly competitive economic environment. Should Russia return to its anti-Western and anti-liberal traditions, the Caspian region is very likely to become an area of incessant tension and power politics. Russia can never be a fully credible partner for the West and regional states if it persists in its present ambivalent position. As a NATO member on the front line, Turkey will be most vulnerable to the risks of such an eventuality. Turkey, therefore, has a vital security and economic interest in Russia's future.

The best way to influence Russian behaviour in a constructive direction is to induce Russia to enter into cooperative relationships as an equal partner. If it is crucial to include Russia in regional cooperative arrangements, it is equally important to take the necessary measures to prevent it from dominating these arrangements.

9. The evolving security role of Iran in the Caspian region

Mehrdad M. Mohsenin

I. Introduction

The Caucasus Mountains were the birthplace of some of humankind's earliest legends. It was from here that Prometheus stole fire from the gods and gave it to Man. The Svanetia region of western Georgia was the land Jason and the Argonauts searched to find the Golden Fleece, and in Azerbaijan Zoroastrian mystics discovered the thick, black water that fuelled the smelly flames of torches and cooking fires and was believed to be magic. Marco Polo wrote of the mysterious liquid on his way to China in the 13th century. By the late 1600s, Azeri locals constructed the first hand-dug wells and were using oil in their lamps.

Two hundred years later, tsarist Russia permitted the first commercial enterprises to operate in Azerbaijan. In 1920, things had changed when the Bolsheviks subjugated all their neighbours. In the subsequent 70 years, the Soviets tapped the potential of the Caspian Sea Basin.

The collapse of the Soviet Union—the most important event of the second half of the 20th century—opened up new dimensions for the security and national interests of the Islamic Republic of Iran. The vast region which surrounds the Caspian has been influenced by great civilizations on its periphery. The region has been at the crossroads of Confucianism, Buddhism, Islam and Christianity and the crossing of the Silk Road, the ancient route that transferred science, skills and knowledge as well as merchandise between the civilizations of China, India, Iran and Europe. 'The influence of Iran—although the core of its civilization lies in south-west Asia—was particularly strong, to the extent that it is sometimes difficult to establish a clear boundary between the civilization of the Iranian motherland and that of the outlying lands of Central Asia.'[1]

Iran could therefore not remain a passive spectator of the immediate consequences of the collapse of the Soviet system and the subsequent changes which have created a sort of vacuum beyond its northern borders. A response to the desire of the people of the region to expand a relationship that was rooted in history and a new definition of Iran's national interests were among the top priorities of Iranian foreign policy in Central Asia and the Caucasus.

In fact, after the breakup of the Soviet Union, Iran's geopolitics underwent a change. In addition to its security interests in the south and the Persian Gulf, a new dimension of national interests emerged on its northern borders. Reflecting

---

[1] Preface by Federico Mayor, former Director General of UNESCO, to UNESCO, *History of the Civilizations of Central Asia*, vol. I (UNESCO: Paris, 1992).

its new national concern, Iran's approach to peace and stability regarding the newly independent neighbouring countries is a sensitive one. These new considerations called for greater vigilance on the part of Iran as regards the security concerns of Central Asia and the Caucasus. One thing remains certain—the security posture of these states is fragile. Should any one of them attempt to preserve its unity through coercive measures, then the stability of the whole region will be at risk.

The Central Asian states are determined to preserve their national independence and not to let their gas- and oil-rich region be treated as a plaything of the superpowers. They do not want to exclude Russia, but they are very interested in attracting Western investment. In the meantime they are encouraging the increased presence of East Asian countries, Turkey and Iran.[2] At present a number of regional and international actors, such as NATO and the Organization for Security and Co-operation in Europe (OSCE), are in the process of consolidating their security roles in the region. In fact, both these organizations are reaching way beyond their traditional sphere of influence, that is, Europe. While they are assisting the West in expanding its sphere of security influence, there is no doubt that they are also helping the countries of Central Asia and the Caucasus to establish themselves on the international scene and reduce their dependence on Russia. However, the cooperation of these countries with NATO is not risk-free, especially given Russia's vehement opposition. Another problem is that NATO will not be able to admit new members until structural changes are made, and these changes can cause numerous problems for the organization. The admission of the Central Asian and Caucasian countries will not be a smooth process, for it calls for a process of democratization in their political systems and civilian control over their military institutions.[3]

The definition of Central Asia and the Caucasus has always been a matter of debate among scholars. Some geographers consider it the continuation of the Middle East; others prefer to include Afghanistan and parts of China in the region; and, as it was once annexed to the Soviet Union, some consider it as the furthest frontier of Europe. Perhaps the closest definition is the classic, 1904 concept of the 'Heartland' associated with the name of Sir Halford Mackinder, which has somehow been revived: a major part of the 'Heart of the Earth' encompasses present-day Central Asia. Although today in the age of missiles the military part of Mackinder's theory has apparently lost its former importance, the fact that the Central Asian countries are landlocked is still considered to be the most important economic factor in the regional and international relations of the Central Asian states. Meanwhile, a newer theory, which has recently been propounded as 'geo-culture', may be better able to explain the post-cold war trend because it pays more attention than Mackinder's theory to

---

[2] Brzezinski, Z., 'Russia's new battleground', *Washington Post*, 8 Sep. 1995.

[3] Rahmani, M., 'NATO and OSCE: new security roles in Central Asia and the Caucasus', *Amu Darya: the Iranian Journal of Central Asian Studies* (Center for the Study of Central Asia and the Caucasus, Tehran), vol. 4, no. 1 (spring 1999), p. 89 (in English).

factors such as culture, language, ethnicity and religion and the role they play as political parameters.

One of the most important consequences of the demise of the Soviet Union was the rise of intense political and commercial competition—competition for control of the vast energy resources of the newly independent and vulnerable states of the Caucasus and Central Asia in the Caspian Sea Basin. These energy resources, and in particular the oil and natural gas deposits, have become the point of discord in Central Asia and the Caucasus, introducing, according to analysts, a new chapter in the 'Great Game' for control over Eurasia. The Great Game was the rivalry between tsarist Russia, Great Britain and the Ottoman Empire in Central Asia for control of the trade routes to India in the 19th century. However, the number of players has increased dramatically compared to the 19th century: China, Iran, Pakistan, Russia, Turkey, Saudi Arabia, the USA, the European Union (EU) and even Afghanistan are now involved. It could therefore be said that energy resources are now shaping the geopolitics of Central Asia. Eventual control of the development of oil and gas deposits and the routing of the pipelines that will take the oil and gas to international markets will determine the political and economic future of Russia, Turkey, the Caucasus and the Central Asian states; it will determine Iran's position in the region and its relations with the West; it will determine the realignment of the strategic triangle of China, Russia and the USA; and it will have strategic consequences by reducing dependence on Persian Gulf oil.[4]

Studies show that there is considerable oil and gas potential in Central Asia and the Caucasus but any attempt to quantify that potential is fraught with uncertainty, since (a) there are areas which have not been seriously explored, and (b) the accuracy of the available data for those which have been explored is particularly doubtful. Initial estimates by Western sources after the breakup of the Soviet Union projected the quantity of energy reserves at 200 billion barrels (bbl) of oil and 279 trillion cubic feet of gas. The region would thus rank second after Saudi Arabia in terms of hydrocarbon reserves.[5]

The numbers put forward initially were exaggerated, but recent studies still estimate the oil reserves at somewhere between 15 and 29 bbl,[6] in which case the Caspian Basin would be comparable to the North Sea, which has 17 bbl of proven reserves, and the USA, which has 29.8 bbl. Proven gas reserves in the Caspian region range between 5.58 and 8.3 trillion cubic metres. With the addition of the Shah Deniz gas field, with deposits of approximately 700 billion cubic metres (bcm), the estimated quantity has increased.[7] Another estimate puts oil deposits at 57.1–59.2 bbl.[8]

---

[4] Arvanitopoulos, C., 'The geopolitics of oil in Central Asia', *Thesis* (Athens), vol. 1, no. 4 (winter 1998).

[5] Saghafi-Ameri, N. and Naqi-Zadeh, S., 'Pipeline policy: symbol of strategic challenges in the Caspian Sea region', *Amu Darya* (Tehran), vol. 4, no. 3 (autumn 1999), p. 290.

[6] See note 5.

[7] Islamic Republic News Agency (IRNA), 12 July 1999.

[8] Mojtahed-zadeh, P., [Iran's views on the Caspian Sea, Central Asia, the Persian Gulf and the Middle East], *Etelaat Siasi va Eghtesadi Journal* (Tehran), no. 95–96 (Sep. 1995), p. 9.

II. The legal status of the Caspian Sea

Regarding the legal status of the Caspian Sea there is general recognition: the understanding that always existed in the past is reflected in the treaties of 1921 and 1940 between Iran and the USSR.[9] Both countries referred to the Caspian as the 'Iranian–Soviet Sea' and underlined its 'special importance'. In these documents both sides reaffirmed two important principles: the two countries have equal access to the sea and its use; and the sea is closed to all countries not located on its shores. Under international law, these treaties remain valid, despite the breakup of the Soviet Union. Moreover, in the Alma Ata Declaration of 21 December 1991, Azerbaijan, Kazakhstan and Turkmenistan (with other countries) stated their binding commitments to the provisions of the treaties signed by the former Soviet Union.[10]

The only issue of relevance not covered by the 1921 and 1940 treaties is the exploitation of mineral resources under the seabed. Iran believes that the agreement of 1940 refers neither to the exploitation of seabed resources nor to the benefits accruing from these resources. Rather, the common property clause indicates that two countries cannot claim sovereignty over the same part of the Caspian seabed. Iran also considers that countries such as Azerbaijan, Kazakhstan and Turkmenistan are acting in contravention of this principle in signing agreements with oil consortia.[11]

The dispute over the status of the Caspian Sea has been going on throughout the 1990s. The positions of the littoral states have been shifting with the evolution of their domestic politics, their economic situation, their foreign policies and the international environment. Analysis of the national interests of the littoral states and of the activities of outside powers shows that there is potential for further friction in the Caspian Sea Basin. At the same time, possibilities do exist of the region becoming a zone of stability and cooperation. To see both the negative and the positive aspects of the situation, it is necessary to analyse the strategies of the principal actors in the Caspian Sea region.

Russia has been consistently against the division of the Caspian Sea. Only recently, under pressure of circumstances, did the Russian Government agree to the division of the seabed but not the surface or the water. Its unwillingness to divide these stems from its fear of losing control over an area which used to be almost virtually its own; of being denied rich mineral and other resources; of giving further grounds for much more independent postures on the part of the former Soviet republics of Azerbaijan, Kazakhstan and Turkmenistan; and of allowing Turkey and the West to fill the vacuum and threaten Russia's interests in the South Caucasus and Central Asian regions.

Azerbaijan sees division as the only logical and fair solution of the problems. Division of the sea should bring Azerbaijan the necessary funds for economic

[9] Treaty of Friendship between the Russian Soviet Federal Socialist Republic and Iran (Persia), 1920, and the Soviet–Iranian Trade and Navigation Agreement, 1940.

[10] Ardebili, H. K. (Senior Adviser to the Iranian Minister of Oil and Foreign Affairs), 'The Caspian Sea, its resources, legal status and its future', *Forum* (OPEC), Nov./Dec. 1996.

[11] Momtaz, J., 'Iran's views on the Caspian administration', *Iran Today* (Tehran), May/June 1998.

development, greater independence from Russia and an increased presence in the region of 'friendly' powers (the West and Turkey).

Turkmenistan has shifted from an anti-division position to one identical to that of Azerbaijan. The main reasons for the change are economic, plus the growing political aloofness of Turkmenistan from Russia.

Kazakhstan on the contrary has been increasingly willing to cooperate with Russia in the Caspian Sea region and has shifted to a pro-Russian stance on the status of the sea.

Turkey, in supporting the division of the sea, hopes to weaken the positions of Iran and Russia, to enhance its own presence in the newly independent states and to secure for itself the main transport routes for Caspian oil and gas.

The West is behind the movement for a division of the Caspian Sea. It wants to turn the region into an alternative source of energy resources, to build up its political influence in this important part of the world, to prevent Russia from dominating it, and to be able to put pressure on Moscow from this direction if needed in the future.

Iran views the Caspian Sea as the gem of the region, and the completion of its legal regime at the earliest possible time would be a symbol of a balance of power and economic convergence in the region in the new century. It may provide the proper and legal access to the Caspian Sea and its hidden resources. To this end Iran maintains that the Caspian Sea legal regime should be completed as part of a 'win–win' strategy for all littoral countries on the basis of the following principles: (*a*) the 1921 and 1940 treaties must be the basic instruments for completion of the future legal regime; (*b*) the principle of unanimity in all decisions made in relation to Caspian Sea affairs must be established; (*c*) the demilitarized status of the sea must be established; (*d*) the Caspian must be a centre for trade, cooperation and economic convergence among the littoral states; (*e*) environmental principles must be observed and any measure that would be harmful to the environment, such as the laying of gas and oil pipelines on the seabed, prevented; and (*f*) the eventual regime must be defensible at the national level.[12]

At his meeting with the Russian President's special envoy, Viktor Kalyuzhny, on 1 August 2000 the Iranian Foreign Minister, Kamal Kharazzi, repeated that Iran prefers joint ownership of the Caspian Sea, as built in to the 1921 and 1940 treaties, but in order to speed up the resolution of the issue is ready to accept complete division, with Iran having a 20 per cent share. He further stated that as early as February 1992 Iran had introduced a proposal to set up a Caspian Sea Cooperation Organization (CASCO) comprising the five littoral states that would be mandated to deal with economic, fisheries, shipping, environment, energy and security issues, and that it still supports that proposal today.[13]

---

[12] Quoted from a speech delivered by Morteza Sarmadi, Iranian Deputy Foreign Minister, at the Eighth International Conference on Central Asia and the Caucasus, at the Institute for Political and International Studies (IPIS), Tehran, 12 June 2000.

[13] *Iran News* (Tehran), 2 Aug. 2000, p. 1.

III. Oil and gas transport routes

With deals already signed, the biggest problem still facing the investing countries is how to transport their oil to the international markets. The problem involved in tapping the Caspian oil and gas resources, and one which makes the region completely different from the Persian Gulf, is that the oil and gas produced in or in the vicinity of the Caspian Sea must be transported through a third country or countries in order to reach deep-sea ports and major markets. The issue of pipeline selection has therefore acquired enormous geopolitical significance for the future of the region.

In theory, new pipelines could go in almost any direction, but the main options are as follows.

1. *The northern route*, preferred by Russia. The existing oil pipelines from Azerbaijan and Kazakhstan run through Russia to the port of Novorossiysk on the Black Sea. The shortcomings of this option have to do with (*a*) fears of excessive Russian control over the pipelines and (*b*) security, since the pipeline that goes through Dagestan is threatened by the conflict in Chechnya.

2. *The western routes*, favoured by Turkey, Azerbaijan, Georgia and the United States. There are three.

The first is a pipeline to bring oil from Baku to the port of Supsa on the Georgian Black Sea coast and then ship it through the Bosporus to Europe. It would cost about $1.5 billion to upgrade the pipeline to Supsa (near the troubled area of Abkhazia in north-eastern Georgia), but the main problem with this option is Turkey's claim that the Bosporus cannot cope with any more tanker traffic. The Turkish Foreign Minister has already announced that the Straits will no longer be able to handle 4500 tankers passing through them annually, and, because of ecological problems, there will be no priorities for oil tankers.[14]

The second is a pipeline from Baku to the port of Ceyhan on the Turkish Mediterranean coast. This is favoured by Turkey and the USA. However, many sources in the oil industry have objected to the cost of this option, which is estimated at $2–4 billion, and there are doubts about its economic viability given the fluctuations in the price of oil and disappointing levels of production in Central Asia. This route also involves serious security concerns as it would pass through unstable Kurdish territory in the eastern parts of Turkey.

The third option is a pipeline bypassing the Bosporus and linking the Bulgarian port of Burgas with the Greek port of Alexandroupolis.

3. *The eastern route*, highly favoured by China, which in September 1997 signed a memorandum of understanding to build an eastward pipeline to China as part of a deal to buy two oilfields in Kazakhstan. About 2000 km long in Kazakhstan alone, this pipeline will almost certainly cost considerably more than the $3.5 billion China has estimated.

[14] *International Herald Tribune*, 26 Oct. 1998, p. 1.

4. *The south-eastern route.* The US oil company Unocal wants to build gas and oil pipelines from Turkmenistan through Afghanistan to Pakistan (and perhaps to India later) at an estimated cost of $1.9 billion each. Geographically the route makes sense, but it passes through Afghanistan. Bankers might jib at funding a deal with the Taliban.[15] However, this option was abandoned in August 1998 as it made no sense politically.

5. *The southern route.* This would go through Iran and is economically the most viable option for two reasons. First, most of the infrastructure is already in place and the Caspian oil can be moved quickly and cheaply across Iran by 'displacement', that is, by Iran's northern and central refineries absorbing early volumes of that oil and reversing the flow of certain existing pipelines. Iran has four refineries in the north of the country which with less than $150 million of investment could refine 300 000 barrels per day of Azeri, Kazakh and Turkmen oil. Second, the Persian Gulf is an good exit point from which most Asian markets can be served. The volume of crude oil from the Caspian Basin could be exported from Iran's southern export terminal at Kharg Island, which currently handles 2–2.5 million barrels per day but could accommodate up to 8 million barrels per day.

Swap arrangements with Iran, another alternative, would give maximum security to the producers and operating companies as the deal would be based on the direct purchase of oil at Caspian Sea ports and would not involve transit through other countries. Northern Iran is the most logical market for the crude oil and gas from Azerbaijan, Kazakhstan and Turkmenistan. Crude oil could be shipped from the Caspian Basin to the ports of Anzali and Neka and transported to refineries in Tabriz and Tehran. The cost of building the necessary infrastructure in these ports and additional pipelines to link them to the existing Iranian pipeline network (1500 km of pipeline already exist) is much less than the cost of any of the alternatives. The initial capital investment for port facilities, storage tanks, pipelines, new pumping stations and so on will be around $60 million, with a similar amount needed to add new units to the existing refineries.

So what prevents economics from prevailing? The answer is the USA's sanctions on Iran. Two Executive Orders of 1995 issued by the Clinton Administration bar US companies from trading with or investing in Iran, and the 1996 Iran and Libya Sanctions Act imposes sanctions on foreign companies which invest more than $20 million a year in oil and gas development in Iran. Since then the USA has spent enormous financial and political capital to prevent Iran from benefiting from the development of the Caspian Basin oil resources. There are, however, forces within the United States, including oil interests, which question the wisdom of continuing this policy, while some European and Turkish firms have already ignored the sanctions.[16]

[15] 'Central Asia: a Caspian gamble', *The Economist*, 7 Feb. 1998, p. 11.
[16] For further information see Mohsenin, M. M., 'Pipeline options for exporting oil and gas from the Caspian Basin', *Relazioni Internazionali* (Milan), no. 47 (Dec. 1998) (article in English).

IV. Iran's policy in the Caspian region

Iran's foreign policy towards the Central Asian and Caucasian countries since 1992 has been more to do with national interests than with ideological commitments. Its main lines can be described as follows. First, Iran has seen the instability in the region as a serious threat to its national security and has looked for ways to counter or contain that instability. Second, in the economic sphere, the way is open for a general intensification of relations with the neighbouring countries, whose economies used to be oriented towards Moscow and the inter-republican trade of the Soviet Union. Iran sees potential new markets for its non-oil exports, potential supplies of raw materials for its industries, and potential partners in economic cooperation of all kinds, particularly the energy sector. The development of economic links offers special benefits to Iran's northern frontier provinces.

Iran's policy in facing the security risks and the possibilities of instability in the region emerged in stages. This policy was firmly based on enhancing areas of cooperation with the newly independent states and assisting them in their socio-economic development. Iran's help involved providing access to international markets and improving trade relations with these republics.

Perhaps the most important steps in this direction were the construction of the Mashhad–Sarakhs–Tedzhen railway and the revival of the Silk Road, inaugurated in May 1996. This project started in 1993. A single-track railway branches away from the Fariman station on the existing Tehran–Mashhad railway and runs 168 km to the border town of Sarakhs. It then penetrates 130 km deep into Turkmenistan to join the Merv–Ashkhabad axis at Niyazov station. This project has been compared to the trans-Siberian railway: it shortens the distance between Central Asia and Europe by 3000 km. This factor in itself will be instrumental in revitalizing trade and tourism in the region. In the first phase 2 million tons of cargo and 500 000 passengers per year can be moved along this railway. In the second phase, these numbers will increase to 8 million tons of goods and 1 million passengers.[17]

The Kerman–Zahedan railway is also under construction. It will connect Central Asia to Pakistan, India and South-East Asia through Mashhad, Tehran, Kerman and Zahedan. Once completed the Bafgh–Mashhad railway will reduce this distance by 900 km. Studies are under way for a connection between the port of Chah-Bahar on the Gulf of Oman and the Kerman–Zahedan railway, which would link the Central Asian countries with the ports of Imam Khomeini, Bandar Abbas and Chah-Bahar.[18]

In addition to these plans, Iran is cooperating with the Central Asian countries in other areas. The first is the expansion and strengthening of the Economic Cooperation Organization (ECO).[19] The ECO covers an area of 7 million km²,

---

[17] *Eghtesad-e-Khorasan* (Mashhad), special issue, May 1996, p. 30.

[18] *Eghtesad-e-Khorasan* (Mashhad), 20 Apr. 1996, p. 8.

[19] The ECO was established in 1985 by Iran, Pakistan and Turkey. Its membership is now Afghanistan, Azerbaijan, Iran, Kazakhstan, Kyrgyzstan, Pakistan, Tajikistan, Turkey, Turkmenistan and Uzbekistan. Its main objectives are to increase mutual trade and to promote conditions for sustained economic growth in

has a population of 300 million and is one of the world's larger regional organizations. It emphasizes regional cooperation, particularly in trade, transport and communications, and energy, and its cooperation strategy attaches great importance to the active participation of the private sector and the attraction of foreign investment to the region. The development of the transport sector is vital for the promotion of intra-regional trade.

Second, Iran's diplomacy is directed at the encouragement of both bi- and trilateral relations. For instance, Turkmenistan is viewed as a prospective partner in trilateral schemes because of its positive and independent foreign policy. At a tripartite meeting of the foreign ministers of India, Iran and Turkmenistan in Tehran on 22 February 1997, a memorandum of understanding was signed on the future of cooperation between the three in the fields of trade and industry and an agreement on the international transit of goods was signed which will reduce cargo transport costs between India and Central Asia by two-thirds.[20]

In the area of culture there is the inviting prospect of resuming cultural relations with countries that were for centuries part of the same Persian Islamic cultural world. A cursory survey of the art, architecture, painting, literature and history of the region, both in ancient times and during the Islamic civilization, reveals the affinity and unity of Iranian culture and civilization with this region. The grandeur and cultural spread of Central Asia and its strong links with Iranian culture have gradually weakened since the tsarist period, and particularly with the suppression during the communist era. Iran therefore sees a special role for itself in helping these countries to rediscover their cultural roots and in assisting them to rejoin the mainstream of world culture and civilization.

Iran stresses the need for timely consultation on issues of vital interest with the countries of Central Asia and the Caucasus. Thus it can hope to contain and possibly exclude the influence of extra-regional powers. Iran is convinced that the only way to ensure peace and regional stability is through regional cooperation.

In order to promote security in the region, Iran has focused on confidence building while eliminating causes of tension and working towards lasting peace. Its efforts in Tajikistan are a case in point. The conflict there came to a swift resolution because the realities of Tajik culture were factored into the solution. Nonetheless, the situation in that country remains fragile and the contenders need to exercise care and patience, while taking note of the fact that any unilateral action can easily backfire. The reconstruction of Tajikistan is an essential prerequisite for the maintenance of a just and lasting peace.

On the economic front, it is through regional cooperation that the potentials of these countries can be synthesized. The ECO has contributed to the consolidation of amicable and promising relationships among its members. It was in this spirit that Iran hosted the eighth summit meeting of the Organization of the Islamic Conference (OIC) in Tehran in December 1997, fully convinced that the

the region. The revised 1997 Treaty of Izmir is its charter. Protocols amending the Treaty of Izmir were adopted on 18 June 1990 and 28 Nov. 1992.
[20] *Kayhan* (Tehran), 23 Feb. 1997, p. 3.

prospect of mutual confidence and trust among Islamic countries can sustain cooperation and harmony in all areas of human activity.

Iran has declared its readiness to facilitate development in these countries by providing access to its refineries, pipelines and terminals. Given the sensitivity of the situation in the Caspian region, it is of the utmost importance that the littoral states resolve all areas of misunderstanding as soon as possible and devise a suitable legal regime that provides for the ownership of the oilfields, shipping and environmental preservation. Iran categorically opposes any attempt at the unilateral exploitation of the Caspian Sea's resources. Any kind of agreement should rest upon cooperation and participation of all the littoral states, guaranteeing their interests.[21]

Iran's national interests and concerns on Caspian Sea issues can be outlined as follows.

1. Only one legal regime will govern activities in the Caspian Sea, on the seabed and under the seabed. Iran prefers a condominium arrangement. In other words, all of the sea, its water, the seabed and the region beneath it should be used on a condominium basis. However, should other littoral states prefer the 'division' option, that alternative can also be taken into consideration. The only unacceptable situation would be a 'dual regime'.

2. The legal regime can only be developed on the basis of the agreement of all the littoral states. No country is allowed to exercise its will unilaterally or without the consent of the others.

3. In devising the legal regime for the Caspian Sea, national security considerations, the exercise of national sovereignty and the imperatives of national interests will have to be categorically factored in. Iran's neighbours in the Caspian region should not doubt its resolve to preserve and enhance amicable relations with them. At the same time this willingness in no way diminishes Iran's intention to safeguard its territorial integrity, sovereignty and national interests. It must be added that, should the 'division' option be chosen, Iran would be more insistent on obtaining its fair share of the sea and its resources than on establishing friendly relations with its neighbours.

4. The demilitarization of the Caspian Sea will indubitably guarantee the security imperatives of all littoral states. The absence of extra-regional powers would be the first step in this direction.

5. Within the framework of its national interests Iran will greatly value the principle of full cooperation with the Caspian Sea littoral states on all sea-related matters and will act on this conviction.[22] It seems logical to concentrate all security-related issues within the context of a single and common organization supported by all the littoral states. CASCO would provide the most suitable framework. It could be mandated to safeguard the common interests of the

---

[21] Speech by H. E. Kamal Kharazzi, Foreign Minister of Iran, at the seminar on Central Asia and the Caucasus: Role of the Regional Powers in Conflict Resolution and Economic Development, Institute for Political and International Studies, Tehran, 27–28 Apr. 1998.

[22] Ardebili, H. K., 'The legal regime of the Caspian Sea: development of resources and energy pipelines', *Amu Darya* (Tehran), vol. 4, no. 1 (spring 1999), p. 16 (in English).

regional states, promote the idea of demilitarization of the sea, help to contain the arms race, bring drug trafficking under the control of multinational forces and eliminate redundant spending, since parallel budgets will not be channelled towards the same tasks and hence national savings will increase.

The Caspian Sea must be a demilitarized zone. Even at the peak of the rivalry between NATO and the Warsaw Pact the Caspian was spared military involvement. The presence of the Soviet Union was kept to a minimum. This should be sustained at any price. Relations among the regional states must develop to preserve the demilitarized status of the sea. This requires the adoption of long-term and common strategies. The Caspian must not be regarded from a military angle. Cooperation and collaboration can be far more productive than rivalry and militarism.[23]

On balance, the Iranian Government's record of achievement in this area is fairly satisfactory, if not wholly positive. The development of political and economic relations has proceeded relatively smoothly: despite some significant obstacles, such as active US opposition to and prevention of any Iranian role in the region, Iran has managed to overcome much of the suspicion and develop normal political relations with all the Central Asian and Caucasian states.

The USA is sensitive to Iran's relations with the countries of Central Asia and the Caucasus. This sensitivity lingers from past years and is of immense consequence for regional peace and security. The US reaction to Iran's relations with these countries has had several repercussions: in particular, the economic development of the region has been delayed. Oil and energy are the engine of development in this region, and in the absence of oil income the progress of these countries will be delayed. By preventing the passage of oil pipelines through Iran, this is exactly what the USA has been doing.[24]

The 1997 Caspian Region Energy Development Report to the US Congress, which addressed 'the request of the FY [Fiscal Year] 97 statement of managers accompanying the FY 97 Foreign Operations bill as incorporated in Public Law 104-208', clearly defined US policy as support for the development and diversification of regional infrastructure networks and transport corridors to tie the region securely to the West and providing alternatives to Iran.[25] Given its lack of investment capacity, however, Iran in developing its foreign policy in Central Asia, the Caucasus and the Caspian Basin has to count more on its geo-strategic advantages and to promote such objectives as participation, dialogue, security, confidence building and development for the common prosperity of the whole region. Recent changes and political developments in Iran have paved the way for the smooth, indigenous development of relations with the region. Moreover, moderation in political culture invigorates the momentum for

[23] Hajihosseini, A., 'The prospects of the Caspian region in the 21st century', *Amu Darya* (Tehran), vol. 1, no. 2 (summer/fall 1996), p. 211 (in English).

[24] Sajjadpour, S. K., 'Iran's relations with the Caspian Sea littoral states: US reactions', *Amu Darya* (Tehran), vol. 4, no. 1 (spring 1999), pp. 40–45 (in English).

[25] Ardebili, H. K., 'Caspian region energy development', *Amu Darya* (Tehran), vol. 4, no. 1 (spring 1999), p. 34 (in English).

increasing regional cooperation. Here it is necessary to quote from a statement by President Mohammad Khatami of Iran at the eighth session of the Islamic Summit Conference in Tehran on 9 December 1997: 'Our civil society neither seeks to dominate others nor submits to domination. It recognises the right of other nations to self-determination and access to the necessary means for an honourable living. We welcome the active and self-assertive presence of the states of Central Asia and the Caucasus in the process of independence and development towards the honour and dignity of the Islamic world'.[26]

---

[26] *Iranian Journal of International Affairs*, vol. 9, no. 4 (winter 1997/98), pp. 599–600.

10. Azerbaijan's strategic choice in the Caspian region

Sabit Bagirov

I. Introduction

Azerbaijan became independent on 18 October 1991, when its parliament adopted the constitutional act on state independence. Since then it has managed to determine and re-determine its objectives and priorities in the foreign and domestic spheres. These years have been years of search, doubt and disappointment, but also of hope and a certain success. The strategic goal of its governments has been to strengthen the country's independence and national security, and Azerbaijan has achieved palpable success on this road. Today it is recognized by the world community, is a member of many authoritative international organizations and financial institutions, maintains diplomatic relations with many countries, has attained considerable results in attracting foreign investments and is successfully integrating with the world economy.

Important elements in Azerbaijan's strategic choice in the Caspian region are: (*a*) the strengthening of political and economic relations with Western countries, particularly the USA; (*b*) the maintenance of stable political relations with Russia, Turkey and Iran; (*c*) the development of free trade with all countries; (*d*) the development of strategic partnership with the other members of GUUAM,[1] especially Georgia; (*e*) the delimitation of frontiers on the Caspian Sea; (*e*) assistance in the development of the Transport Corridor Europe Caucasus Asia (TRACECA);[2] and (*f*) the establishment of a diversified system of oil and gas pipelines.

This set of policy elements developed over several years. Under the first two presidents after independence, Ayaz Mutalibov and the late Ebulfez Elcibey—quite a brief period: the former led Azerbaijan for less than five months and the latter for only one year—work only began on the first three of them, although Elcibey, for instance, attached particular importance to the development of strategic relations with Ukraine. Mutalibov, unlike both Elcibey and the incumbent president, Heidar Aliyev, paid great attention to strategic cooperation with Iran and Russia. Elcibey gave primary attention to the development of strategic partnership with Turkey and regarded this, as well as expanding contacts with the West, as a key factor in strengthening national independence.

After Heidar Aliyev came to power in July 1993, Azerbaijan reconsidered its foreign political priorities. The first 8–10 months of his rule were characterized

---

[1] Georgia, Ukraine, Uzbekistan, Azerbaijan and Moldova. The grouping was originally created in 1997. Uzbekistan joined in 1999. See chapter 1 in this volume.

[2] See, e.g., the TRACECA Internet site, URL <http://www.traceca.org>.

by a predilection for Iran and Russia. Particular importance was attached to the relationship with Russia. Azerbaijan joined the Commonwealth of Independent States (CIS) in September 1993, presented the Russian company Lukoil with a 10 per cent interest stake (valued at some $1 billion) in the 'Contract of the Century'[3]—the first oil contract between the Azerbaijan Government and foreign oil companies, signed on 20 September 1994—and demonstrated the opening of a new 'cold era' in relations with the West and even with Turkey. These swings in foreign policy over a short period are explained by the government's continuing search for a resolution to the Nagorno-Karabakh conflict.

Of the former republics of the USSR, except for Georgia, Azerbaijan has been the least lucky. After gaining independence it inherited the problem of ethnic confrontation between the Armenian population of Nagorno-Karabakh and the rest of Azerbaijan. The consequences are still palpable in many foreign policy actions. While developing relations with other countries, Azerbaijan has often had to view them through the prism of the Karabakh problem.

In July–December 1993, therefore, Azerbaijan's foreign policy priorities changed. It considerably improved its relations with Iran and Russia, generating hope that those two countries would be neutral on the issue of liberating the 20 per cent of Azerbaijan's territory that was occupied by Armenia. In early 1994 Azerbaijan started military operations aimed at liberating these territories, but it was soon halted and there were heavy casualties. It became evident that Russia, despite the concessions on the part of Azerbaijan mentioned above, considered Armenia as its strategic partner and would not accept Armenia being defeated in the war with Azerbaijan. Other factors also became obvious which made the choice of strategic partnership with Azerbaijan's southern neighbour, Iran, undesirable. These factors are analysed below.

Having discarded the idea of a northern or southern orientation, Azerbaijan therefore made its strategic political choice in favour of the West.[4] It is by these priorities that its foreign policy is still governed.

II. Strengthening political and economic relations with the West

Having realized that in order to resolve the Nagorno-Karabakh problem it was necessary to oppose the Armenian–Russian alliance with a unity that was at least as strong, Azerbaijan set itself the goal of improving its economic and political relations with the West, especially with the USA. The only way to accomplish these goals was to resort to the 'oil card' and to offer the territory of

---

[3] This first oil contract was given this name because of its immense value ($7.4 billion) and the participation in it of many international oil companies from major countries.

[4] There are no official documents of the government or parliament to corroborate this conclusion. These priorities are, however, unequivocally stated in Hasanov, A., [Azerbaijan's foreign policy: countries of Europe and USA, 1991–96], Baku, 1998 (in Azeri). Ali Hasanov heads one of the departments in the Azerbaijani Administration and is considered to be one of the people closest to Heidar Aliyev. Although his research is somewhat subjective where the assessment of previous administrations is concerned, which makes it difficult to agree with some of the his conclusions, it nevertheless contains valuable factual material related to the foreign policy of the country and substantiates its foreign policy decisions.

Azerbaijan for the West's new strategic routes to Central Asia—in other words, it was necessary to return to the pro-Western course of the foreign policy launched under President Elcibey.

Elcibey understood clearly how important the possession of hydrocarbon resources was for the rapid development of relations with the West. Negotiations with foreign oil companies on the exploration and development of Azerbaijan's oil and gas fields, which had been started in 1990 by the USSR, were therefore accelerated after 1992, especially after Elcibey was elected president. He held meetings with executives of a number of international oil companies, first of all with Amoco which, following a 1991 tender, was working in cooperation with some other oil companies on a feasibility study for the development of the Azeri oilfields. All representatives of the international oil companies were informed by Azerbaijan's new government of its readiness to sign mutually beneficial oil contracts.[5]

As early as three months after Elcibey was elected, on 7 September 1992, an agreement was signed with the BP–Statoil consortium on the Chirag field and the Shah Deniz prospect area. The agreement gave BP–Statoil the exclusive right to prepare feasibility studies and draft contracts. Under the agreement, the consortium paid the Government of Azerbaijan a bonus of $30 million. On 1 October the government also signed an agreement with the Pennzoil–Ramco consortium, whereby the latter agreed to implement a $50 million gas recovery project on the Oil Rocks and Guneshli fields, where 1.5 billion cubic metres (bcm) of gas a year had been discharged into the atmosphere for many years, in exchange for the exclusive right to prepare a feasibility study for the Guneshli field.[6] These agreements, which promised obvious economic benefits, also pursued political objectives. They demonstrated to the world the readiness of the new government of a newly independent country to cooperate in such a crucial sphere as the development of natural wealth and its preparedness for integration into the world economic system. An important political backdrop for the signing of the first of these agreements was a visit to Azerbaijan in September 1992 by former British Prime Minister Margaret Thatcher. Government ministers, congressmen and senators from different countries became frequent guests in Azerbaijan.

The Azerbaijan Government was fully aware of the importance of oil contracts for the economic and political independence of the country, and by signing various interim memoranda and agreements was moving in this direction. Thus, on 4 June 1993, on the very day when an anti-government insurgency in

---

[5] The author, who held the positions of state adviser on strategic programmes and President of the State Oil Company of the Azerbaijan Republic (SOCAR), took part personally in almost all these meetings and witnessed these statements by President Elcibey.

[6] The document signed with BP–Statoil was the Agreement between the Government of the Azerbaijan Republic and BP Exploration Operating Company Limited and Den Norske Stats Oljeselskap concerning the Appraisal and Development of the Chirag Field and the Shah Deniz Prospect Area. The document signed with Pennzoil–Ramco was the General Agreement on Terms and Principles for Concluding the Guneshli Field Development Contract. They were signed on behalf of Azerbaijan, on the instructions of President Elcibey, by the author of this chapter. The second was also signed by the first Vice-Premier of the Azerbaijan Government, Vahid Ahmadov.

Azerbaijan began which in two weeks led to the collapse of the Elcibey Administration, the Board of Directors of the State Oil Company of the Azerbaijan Republic (SOCAR) adopted a declaration on the unified development of the Chirag and Guneshli fields.[7] This six-page document determined a number of key items in the contract prepared for signing—the shares of the foreign companies and SOCAR in the project, the volume of bonuses and schedule of their payment to the Azerbaijan Government, SOCAR's requirements for the establishment of special funds to finance primary operations, and so on. All the oil companies confirmed their agreement with the document within one week, and preparation and coordination of the main commercial terms of the future contract began. However, the anti-government insurgency, led by Colonel Surat Husseinov, was unfolding very rapidly and the government fell. Husseinov became prime minister and Heidar Aliyev, who had been elected speaker of the Azerbaijan Parliament on 14 June 1993, became acting president in July. In this complicated domestic political situation, work with foreign oil companies was suspended for a while.

Finally, on 20 September 1994 Azerbaijan signed its first oil contract on the Azeri, Chirag and Guneshli fields with BP Amoco, Statoil, the Turkish Petroleum Corporation (TPAO), Pennzoil, Ramco, Delta, Macdermott, Unocal and Lukoil.[8] By November 2000 it had concluded 19 more agreements on the development of its on- and offshore fields. The total combined investment is expected to be worth around $50 billion, while expected production is expected to be around 10 billion barrels (bbl) of oil and some 2 trillion cubic metres (tcm) of gas. On a world scale these figures are not very significant, especially since the contracts will run for 30–35 years. Azerbaijan cannot be compared with Kuwait or any other major oil producers. If the oil contracts are successfully implemented, Azerbaijan's annual production by volume will barely exceed 1.5 per cent of world output. Even so, for such a small country as Azerbaijan the production of hydrocarbons may play a great role in its economic development.

Oil companies from 14 countries (Belgium, Canada, France, Germany, Iran, Italy, Japan, Norway, Russia, Saudi Arabia, Spain, Turkey, the UK and the USA) are participating in oil contracts with Azerbaijan. These contracts have enabled Azerbaijan to establish close political contacts at the level of heads of state, to embark on the development of trade relations, and to win the trust of international organizations and financial institutions. In terms of foreign investment per capita, by 1998 Azerbaijan was ahead of all the other CIS countries.[9]

---

[7] The document, called Declaration on Unitized Development of the Guneshli, Chirag and Azeri Fields, was approved by the SOCAR Board of Directors and signed by the author as President of SOCAR.

[8] Later some of these companies sold their equity to other companies partially or fully.

[9] According to a report from the Azerbaijani Ministry of Economics in *Mulkiyet,* 10–17 Nov. 1998, investment per capita in 1998 was worth in Azerbaijan $172, in Russia $90, in Kazakhstan $72, in Uzbekistan $75, in Georgia $40 and in Armenia $15. According to official data, foreign investment in Azerbaijan over the 5 years 1995–99 totalled $4866 million. *Statistical Yearbook of Azerbaijan 2000* (Statistical Committee of the Azerbaijan Republic: Baku, 2000), p. 274 (in English).

It should also be mentioned that by signing oil contracts Azerbaijan immediately encountered opposition, first from Russia, then from Iran and more recently from Turkmenistan. Nevertheless, its example stimulated other littoral countries—Iran, Kazakhstan, Russia and Turkmenistan—to step up their operations in the Caspian Sea.

III. The policy of balanced relations with Russia, Turkey and Iran

Having become independent, Azerbaijan found itself in the centre of a geopolitical triangle dominated by Russia, Iran and Turkey, whose goals and interests in the comparatively small Azerbaijan differ. Each of these countries is, to a certain extent, a centre of power for Azerbaijan, but their powers are unequal. Iran today looks a little weaker than the other two, and Russia and Turkey are roughly balanced. Can Azerbaijan draw closer to one of the three by its own will? In principle, this is possible. However, the competing interests of the three countries may mean considerable losses for Azerbaijan, as has been proved by its brief historical experience: Azerbaijan is connected to each of the three by a multitude of historical, cultural, economic, ethnic and religious links, and the interest of these big neighbours in Azerbaijan is enhanced because this small country attracts other, more distant, countries by virtue of its mineral wealth and its geographical location—on the crossroads between the Western and Central Asian countries and in the vicinity of traditional rivals of these countries. All these circumstances require of Azerbaijan a rather careful and balanced foreign policy in the geopolitical triangle.

Azerbaijan and Russia

In 1992 Azerbaijan and Russia concluded a Treaty of Friendship, Cooperation and Mutual Security[10] which was prolonged in 1997 by President Aliyev. It was supplemented by several dozen bilateral and multilateral agreements regulating military, political, economic and cultural cooperation between the two countries. However, relations between Azerbaijan and Russia are characterized by great mutual distrust, which is explained by Russia's strategic partnership with Armenia, to which Azerbaijan responded by strategic partnership with the West and the USA in particular.

There is sufficient reason today—numerous chauvinist statements by some Russian politicians, Russia's attempts to set up closer alliances with several post-Soviet states under its leadership, and its attempts to create supranational administrative organs in the CIS—to believe that Russia still aspires to pursue the model of the Soviet Union's relations with the 'socialist camp' countries, which ruled out any independent foreign policy decision making by them that did not agree with Soviet policy. This model has so far been effective with only

[10] The treaty was signed in Moscow during an official visit of President Elcibey on 12–13 Oct. 1992.

some of the post-Soviet states, and obviously not with Azerbaijan. Russia is currently pursuing another, more realistic approach in its relations with Azerbaijan which is focused on economic aspects. In this respect, Lukoil, chaired by an ethnic Azeri, Vagit Alikperov, has achieved considerable success. It is in fact operating not only in the oil but also in other economic sectors in Azerbaijan. Nonetheless, Russia continues to apply considerable pressure both on the domestic political situation in Azerbaijan and on its foreign policy.

Several aspects compel Azerbaijan to reckon with the Russian factor.

The problem of Nagorno-Karabakh

Russia is trying to take advantage of the Nagorno-Karabakh conflict to the maximum extent possible by influencing Azerbaijan and trying to make it submissive. Having received the baton from the USSR, Russia quickly understood how important it was to preserve this means of putting pressure on Armenia and Azerbaijan and not to let the conflict fade away in order to complicate the strengthening of these countries' independence.

Russia has done a great deal in this regard. It is intensifying its military and strategic cooperation with Armenia, building up Armenia's military power, influencing domestic political developments in Armenia and impeding their development in the direction of independence. Paradoxical as it may seem, Russia, with the consent of Azerbaijan, is managing to remain co-chair of the Organization for Security and Co-operation in Europe (OSCE) Minsk Group[11] even though Azerbaijan clearly understands that Russia is interested in preserving the situation as it is now—neither peace nor war.

The land frontier between Azerbaijan and Russia is 285 km long, while their sea frontier on the Caspian is undefined. Both on- and offshore, the present territory of Azerbaijan was for centuries subject to Russian incursions, and after the Russian–Iranian wars of the early 19th century it was annexed to Russia. Today the likelihood of such attacks is rather hypothetical, but history compels Azerbaijan to exercise caution with regard to its great northern neighbour because of the war in Chechnya, in the vicinity of Azerbaijan's borders, and because there are two Russian military bases in Armenia.

The Russian population in Azerbaijan

The Russian population in Azerbaijan has been reduced by half in the past 10 years, to 150 000 or 2 per cent of the total population. The main reasons for the reduction are better living conditions in Russia than in Azerbaijan, the growing importance of Azeri as a state language and the need for the local Russian population to learn it because no attention was paid to it in Soviet

---

[11] The Minsk Group was set up by the Conference on Security and Co-operation in Europe (CSCE), the predecessor of the OSCE, in Mar. 1992 to monitor the situation in Nagorno-Karabakh. The members at the time of writing (2000) were Armenia, Austria, Azerbaijan, Belarus, Finland, France, Germany, Italy, Norway, Russia, Sweden, Turkey and the USA. See, e.g,. Organization for Security and Co-operation in Europe, *OSCE Handbook* [2000], URL<http://www.osce.org/publications/handbook/index.htm>.

times. Even so, the presence of this insignificant Russian population seems to be excuse enough for Russia to remind Azerbaijan at the slightest opportunity of its concern for the fate of Russians living in Azerbaijan.

Azerbaijanis in Russia

The number of Azerbaijanis living in Russia is increasing by the day, not so much because of natural growth—there has long been an Azerbaijani population in Russia—but because Azerbaijanis are constantly arriving in Russia in search of work and a better life. According to the last Soviet census (1989) there were only 336 000 Azerbaijanis in Russia; currently, according to expert assessments made both in Russia and in Azerbaijan, they number 1.5–2 million. Again, Russia takes every opportunity to remind Azerbaijan of its ability to create unbearable conditions for the those who have found refuge in Russia and eventually to drive them out. Although this is not an official Russian policy reflected in any government documents, in the past several years cases of persecution, including in Moscow, have become frequent. This has been extensively reported in the media, including the Russian media.[12]

Russian cultural influence in Azerbaijan

More than 100 years of the colonial past, when the territory of Azerbaijan was part of the Russian Empire from 1812 to 1918, as well as 71 years of Russian domination during Soviet times could not but leave an indelible trace on the contemporary culture of the Azerbaijanis. The overwhelming majority are fluent in Russian, were influenced by Russian culture through literature, music and art, and hold these cultural values dear. There is also quite a large category of Russian-speaking Azeris who have been brought up in the spirit not of the Azerbaijani but of the Russian culture because they studied in secondary schools and universities in the Russian language. These Russian-speaking Azeris currently account for a considerable part of the local elite. Another manifestation of the Russian cultural presence is the popularity of Russian television channels, such as ORT, NTV and RTR, in Azerbaijan. There are as many of them as of Turkish channels and according to various surveys they are no less popular.

The network of Russian-language schools has not shrunk much, nor have Russian-language departments at universities. Russian theatre still functions and a number of Russian-language newspapers are published. An obvious information vacuum and an interruption in the supply of books and journals on many scientific, educational, cultural, sport and other issues (carrying not only Russian but also foreign information through the translation of foreign literature into Russian) followed independence but were only short-lived, and Azerbaijan's publishing market is once again filled with Russian-language editions.

---

[12] See, e.g., [Compatriot murdered in Russia], *Yeni Musavat*, 30 Nov. 2000 (in Azeri); [Crackdown in Moscow markets], *Azadlyg*, 24 Oct. 2000 (in Azeri); and Irzabekov, F., 'Azerbaijantsy v Rossii' [Azerbaijanis in Russia], *Sodruzhestvo NG* (supplement to *Nezavisimaya Gazeta*) no. 6 (28 June 2000).

Thus, although since 1992 cultural contacts between Azerbaijan and Russia have become less frequent, they are far from absent and there is no reason to speak of any cultural intolerance towards Russians.

Ethnic minorities residing in border areas

There are several ethnic minorities living in border areas. The largest of them is the Lezgins who live in the north-eastern Azerbaijan and south-eastern Russia. The total number of Lezgins in Azerbaijan according to the 1989 census is 170 000, or 2.4 per cent of the total population. Only an insignificant number live in the rural provinces bordering on Russia; the overwhelming majority live in Baku, the capital. There has been significant suspicion in Azeri society concerning support by the Russian secret services to nationalist Lezgin organizations which tried to instigate a separatist movement in northern Azerbaijan.[13]

The Russian military presence

After the collapse of the USSR, Azerbaijan was the first of the former Soviet republics to achieve the withdrawal of Russian troops from its soil. This happened in the spring of 1993. However, it did not result in a complete end to Russia's military influence. Most of Azerbaijan's arms and ammunition are of Russian origin. The majority of Azerbaijani officers were trained in the former Soviet Union and there is little reason to consider them independent of Russian influence. In the opinion of some experts the failures of the Azerbaijani Army in the military conflict with Armenia are explained by this very fact.

There is also direct military cooperation between Azerbaijan and Russia. Azerbaijan inherited one of the three largest Soviet radio location stations (RLSs), located in Gabala. While Latvia and Ukraine managed to close similar RLSs on their territories, the Gabala station remained under the Russian Army's control, although it is officially said to be leased. Paradoxically, while Azerbaijan has not joined the CIS air defence system, that system's largest military facility is located on its territory and is outside its control. The station enables electronic surveillance of the Indian Ocean and the Middle East—the regions with which Azerbaijan has been building new relations. The environmental impact of the Gabala RLS is extremely negative and the Azerbaijani public has been voicing its outrage and demanding its immediate closure. Trying to avoid damaging its relations with Russia, and especially with the Russian military, the Azerbaijani Government has not yet raised the issue of the immediate dismantling of the RLS. At the same time, no formal agreements have been concluded between Azerbaijan and Russia whereby the Gabala RLS could function on a long-term basis as a foreign military base, thus enabling Azerbaijan to earn money from the lease. An attempt to agree on leasing terms was made on the eve of and during Russian President Putin's visit to Azerbaijan in

---

[13] One such organization is Sadval, which operates in Russia.

January 2001, but the negotiations foundered on the issue of the lease period and no agreement was signed.[14]

Participation in Azerbaijan's oil projects

Azerbaijan allowed Lukoil to take part in the first consortium implementing the Contract of the Century. This gives Russia the possibility to influence the speed of implementation of the project and decisions on the selection of transport routes both for the 'early' and for 'main' oil.

Russia is unlikely to be interested in early implementation of Azerbaijan's oil projects, (a) because these projects accelerate the process whereby Western companies, and thus, naturally, the countries where they are based, 'tap' the Caspian region to which they were denied access for many years by the Soviet Union, and (b) because their implementation means the building up of Azerbaijan's economic potential and thus the strengthening of its political and economic independence.

Economic relations

Azerbaijan's economy was closely integrated into the economy of the USSR. After the breakup of the Soviet Union economic relations among its former constituent republics started to collapse. Nevertheless, Russia remained Azerbaijan's major foreign trade partner in 1999, being the largest in both imports (with 52.3 per cent of the total) and exports (with 30.7 per cent of the total).[15]

Azerbaijan and Iran

The territory of present-day Azerbaijan was taken over by Russia from Iran in the early 19th century. Logically, Iran should have been the first country to welcome Azerbaijan's independence. However, shortly after Azerbaijan adopted the Independence Act, Iranian Foreign Minister Ali Akbar Velayati stated that Iran intended to continue to deal with the Soviet Administration in Moscow.[16] This could not but cause public outrage in Azerbaijan. Eventually Iran recognized Azerbaijan's independence, but its first reaction showed that there were reservations in its attitude towards Azerbaijan's independence. In other words, in addition to the mutual affinity between Azerbaijan and Iran, there was also distrust and caution in their relationship.

Three key factors draw the two countries together. The first is their centuries-long common history. Neither Azeris nor Iranians are indifferent to their history; they cannot forget or neglect their similar historical backgrounds. The second is ethnic similarity. Most Azeri Turks live in Iran, not in Azerbaijan;

---

[14] Radio Free Europe/Radio Liberty (hereafter RFE/RL), *RFE/RL Newsline*, vol. 5, no. 6, Part 1 (10 Jan. 2001).
[15] *Azerbaijan Economic Trends: Quarterly Issue, Apr./June 2000* (European Commission, Brussels), Sep. 2000.
[16] Personal communications of the author with senior Azeri politicians and experts.

according to different experts, they number between 20 and 30 million,[17] 150–280 per cent more than the number in independent Azerbaijan. In fact, the number of Azeri Turks in Iran is comparable to the number of Persians, Iran's dominant ethnic group. The third is religious similarity: at least two-thirds of Azerbaijan's Muslim population are Shi'ite, like most Iranian Muslims.

Three main factors cause Iran concern or annoyance—Azerbaijan's strategic cooperation with the USA, its cooperation with NATO and the fact that it is a secular state oriented towards Western liberal values, which could be a dangerous example for the Iranian population. (The successful development of the economy and improving living standards in Azerbaijan are important pre-conditions for Azerbaijan's becoming a dangerous example for Iran. Azerbaijan has not yet reached this goal but the chances that it will succeed in doing this are very high taking into account its potential oil revenues, as long as they are efficiently utilized.)

A fourth factor is the nationalism of Azeri Turks living in Azerbaijan: if this nationalism were to spill over to the Azeri Turks living north-western in Iran it could encourage separatist sentiment there: this has already happened three times in the 20th century. Significant numbers of people in Azerbaijan, espe-cially among intellectuals, consider the division of Azerbaijan into two parts a historical injustice. There is a non-government organization in Azerbaijan, the Integral Azerbaijan Union, the objective of which is to achieve the unification of Azerbaijan. It was founded in November 1997 and led by former President Elcibey. Its activity focuses on discussion of the problem of unification of northern and southern (Iranian) 'Azerbaijan'. The organization has not been registered by the Ministry of Justice for two years, but the government has not banned it either.

A fifth factor is Azerbaijan's affinity with Turkey. Iran and Turkey have historically been rivals in the region. Azerbaijan's proximity to Turkey cannot but perturb Iran, for two reasons: Iran does not forget that it once owned this territory; and Azerbaijan can supply Turkey with the hydrocarbon resources the latter badly needs, thus depriving Iran of a large market for its oil and gas. This might also mean that Turkey becomes more energy-independent.

Finally, the oil export route has caused Iran concern. The Azerbaijan Government has chosen the territories of Georgia and Turkey for the main export pipeline (MEP) despite Iran's effort to coerce Azerbaijan to lay the pipeline in its direction. Iran is not only losing potential economic dividends; it is also unable to control the export of hydrocarbons from the Caspian Basin.

Five main factors perturb Azerbaijan.

The first is Iran's cooperation with Armenia. Armenia has stated on many occasions that without its cooperation with Iran it would have been in a much

---

[17] There are no official statistics of the number of Azeri Turks in Iran because no census in Iran has recorded the ethnic composition of the population. Specialists on Iran use different methods in evaluating the strength of different ethnic groups in its population, which leads to a diversity of opinion. E.g, Nasibli, N. (Azeri Ambassador to Iran 1992–93), [Unified Azerbaijan] (Ay-Ulduz, Baku, 1977) puts the number of Azeri Turks in Iran at 25 million, while Taghiyeva, S., [South Azerbaijan] (Orxan Publishers: Baku, 2000) puts it at 30–35 million.

more difficult situation. Numerous facts illustrate the negative effect this has on Azerbaijani–Iranian relations. Iran is aware of this but continues the policy of cooperation nonetheless. It should be admitted, however, that Iran has condemned Armenian separatism and has repeatedly supported Azerbaijan in the United Nations and at conferences organized by the Organization of the Islamic Conference (OIC). Iran is therefore pursuing a policy of double standards.

The second factor is Iran's support for the forces openly opposed to the Azerbaijan Government which are led by Mahir Javadov, brother of the late Rovshan Javadov who led the anti-government uprising in 1992. Mahir Javadov was also an active participant in the 1992 mutiny. After it was suppressed he fled to Austria. Since 1992 he has lived in Iran and has been castigating the present authorities and even threatening them.

Third, Iran's religious activities in Azerbaijan could be the basis for a political and ideological expansion of Iran in Azerbaijan, although this is most probably an illusion because the influence of Soviet atheist propaganda on the people of Azerbaijan remains too strong. A fourth issue is the national rights of Azeris living in Iran. Many politicians and intellectuals in Azerbaijan believe that the language of the Azeri Turks living in Iran and their culture must be recognized on an equal footing with Persian and enjoy official status and state support. Finally, there is Iran's position on the problem of the legal status of the Caspian Sea and its negative attitude to Azerbaijan's developing its oil and gas resources in the Caspian Sea, despite the fact that an Iranian oil company is participating in one of three projects there.

IV. The delimitation of sea frontiers on the Caspian Sea[18]

The issue of the status of the Caspian Sea was raised for the first time since the breakup of the Soviet Union in 1993. The discussion among the governments of the littoral countries was probably triggered by Azerbaijan's intensive negotiations with transnational oil companies concerning their involvement in the development of hydrocarbon resources in the previously closed Caspian. It should be remembered also that it was necessary to come to terms not only on the issue of the development of offshore fields but also on such issues as navigation, the utilization of fish stocks and the observance of environmental standards. From the very beginning of discussions on this issue it emerged that the countries involved had differing views on how to divide the sea. Over the years that followed the positions of almost all the littoral states were revised more than once.

Russia insists that until a new multilateral agreement on the Caspian Sea is signed the Soviet–Iranian agreements of 1921 and 1940 remain in effect. As far as a new agreement among all the littoral countries is concerned, Russia wants to divide not the Caspian Sea itself but its mineral resources. It proposes that

---

[18] See also chapter 3, section III in this chapter.

the line of division be drawn not over the surface of the water but on the seabed. In accordance with this principle Kazakhstan and Russia signed an agreement in July 1998 On the Delineation of the Northern Part of the Caspian Sea Bed.[19] Subsequently, in 2000 the Russian formula of 'dividing the seabed but keeping the water in common use' was supplemented with a proposal for joint development of borderline hydrocarbon resources on the principle of equal participation in corresponding projects.[20]

Azerbaijan retained its initial position on the delimitation of the Caspian Sea until Putin's visit to Baku in January 2001. One of the results of this visit was an agreement between Azerbaijan and Russia on principles of cooperation in the Caspian Sea. They decided to resolve the issue of the legal status of the sea on a stage-by-stage basis and that the neighbouring and opposite states should divide the seabed into sectors or zones on the basis of a median line drawn in accordance with the principle of equal distance from the coastline, as well as on the basis of principles of international law and existing practice in the Caspian. The parties agreed that each of the littoral countries would have exclusive rights for the exploitation of mineral resources and other legal economic activities on the seabed in the sectors or zones formed as a result of this division.[21]

Thus Azerbaijan, following Kazakhstan and Russia, has backed down from its initial position in the interests of consensus among all the littoral states over the legal status of the Sea.

Turkmenistan supports Azerbaijan's position of division on the basis of the median line. However, it takes a different view of the methodology to be used: it wants the line to be drawn in the middle of geographical latitudes, while Azerbaijan wants it to run through points equally distant from opposite coasts. This would result in a number of oil and gas fields being disputed, including some of those already being developed. (Turkmenistan has claims on part of the Chirag field and the Azeri field, which are already being developed.)

Iran's position has shifted from the initial 'condominium' idea to the division of the Caspian into equal sectors, which it currently advocates. Such a division would be to the advantage of Iran because its coastline is the shortest of all the littoral countries.

Azerbaijan's support for the Kazakh–Russian approach may seriously influence the positions of Iran and Turkmenistan. If Turkmenistan also supports the formula proposed by Russia, which for a number of reasons is likely to happen, then Iran will find itself alone in opposition to the CIS group and it will be difficult and probably even counterproductive for it to stick to this position, because it would mean that nothing changes for Iran in the Caspian and it will continue to face the constraints on navigation that arise from the 1921 and 1940 agreements.

[19] *Diplomaticheskiy Vestnik*, no. 8 (1998), pp. 35–35.
[20] *Diplomaticheskiy Vestnik*, no. 8 (2000), pp. 79–80.
[21] ITAR-TASS, 9 Jan. 2001, in 'Russia, Azerbaijan issue statement on need for consensus on carving up Caspian', Foreign Broadcast Information Service, *Daily Report–Central Eurasia (FBIS-SOV)*, FBIS-SOV-2001-0109, 9 Jan. 2001.

V. A diversified system of oil and gas pipelines

The first research on possible routes for the transport of Azerbaijan's oil from the Guneshli and Azeri fields started in 1991, when Amoco, BP, Pennzoil, Unocal, J. P. Kenny and the Oman Oil Company were involved in in-depth investigations. A more thorough analysis of the technical and economic aspects of various routes for an export pipeline began in November 1992 after SOCAR, Amoco, BP and Pennzoil signed a memorandum of understanding on a common oil export pipeline. A working group of specialists from these companies started investigating seven principal directions for an export pipeline. Three of them ended in Black Sea ports (Novorossiysk, Poti/Supsa and Khopa), three at Turkey's Mediterranean terminal of Ceyhan, and one at Iran's Kharg terminal on the Persian Gulf.

Although calculations proved the Baku–Tbilisi–Poti/Supsa route to be the cheapest, this line, like any other with access to the Black Sea, had the considerable drawback that it involved subsequent transport through the Bosporus and Dardanelles. The results of the research completed by late February 1993 and certain political factors laid the groundwork for the negotiations to be started with the governments of the neighbouring countries on the construction of an export pipeline through their territories. The Azerbaijan Government, however, considered the route to the Ceyhan terminal to be of higher priority. In early March 1993 an agreement was signed with the Turkish Government whereby the parties agreed on the main terms and tariffs of the construction of the Baku–Ceyhan pipeline through Turkey.[22] Preliminary agreement was also reached with Iran and Georgia on corresponding alternatives to the route.[23]

Interest in participating in the Baku–Ceyhan pipeline project as members of the future pipeline consortium, the Azerbaijan International Operating Company (AIOC),[24] was also voiced in the spring of 1993 by the ministries of fuel and energy of Kazakhstan and Russia.[25] Then, owing to the political situation in Azerbaijan, the negotiations on selection of the pipeline route came to a halt.

After the first oil contract was signed in September 1994, the decision on an export route for 'early oil' (32 million tonnes) became a priority. Azerbaijan needed to begin oil production in order to tackle its growing energy problems. It may also have believed that decision making on the MEP would be slow considering the conflicting interests of its powerful neighbours. Azerbaijan there-

[22] Agreement between the governments of the Azerbaijan Republic and the Turkish Republic on Construction of the Pipeline, 9 Mar. 1993. The document was signed by the author of this chapter, at that time President of SOCAR, on behalf of Azerbaijan.

[23] The author of this chapter paid a special visit to Iran in Apr. 1993 to hold talks with the President of the National Iranian Oil Company (NIOC) concerning construction of a section of the Baku–Ceyhan pipeline through the territory of Iran. It was agreed then that negotiations should be continued and an agreement prepared on key conditions for the construction of the pipeline via Iran. A SOCAR delegation visited Georgia in Dec. 1992 and was received by President Eduard Shevardnadze.

[24] For the membership of the AIOC see chapter 3, section I in this volume.

[25] A letter of the Russian Ministry of Fuel and Energy to that effect, no. MT-3318, dated 24 May 1993, was signed by Minister Yuriy K. Shafrannik and addressed to the President of SOCAR. A similar letter from the Ministry of Energy and Fuel Resources of Kazakhstan dated 14 May 1993, no. 7-03-1450, was signed by the First Deputy Minister N. U. Bekbosinov and addressed to the President of SOCAR.

fore chose the early oil export route by June 1995 so that the AIOC could start production in accordance with the work schedule. In other words, the Azerbaijan Government and the AIOC decided where to export early oil before the decision on the MEP was made. The route for the MEP, according to the contract, was to be determined as part of the Minimum Required Work Program within 30 months.

However, the Azerbaijan Government failed to agree on the route for early oil by the deadline originally set (June 1995), hesitating between the Russian and Georgian alternatives. Financially the viability of the Georgian route was beyond doubt, but pressure from Russia was so strong that Azerbaijan eventually opted for the northern route as well. The decision on the Georgian route was arrived at during a telephone conversation between the Azerbaijan and US presidents on 2 October 1995. Not until 9 October 1995, on the basis of the earlier agreement with the Azerbaijan Government, did the AIOC decide on two routes for the export of early oil — northern, to the Russian port of Novorossiysk (with a capacity of up to 5 million tonnes of oil a year—mt/y); and Western, to Supsa in Georgia (with a capacity of up to 7 mt/y of oil).

Russia has thus managed not only to coerce Azerbaijan into choosing the northern route but also to obtain quite beneficial terms in exploiting this route. However, it seems to have over-exerted itself, because the AIOC has hardly used the route since the Baku–Supsa line was commissioned in 1999: calculations show that losses per tonne of exported oil amount to $50–60 as a result of high transit fees and the mixing of high-quality Azeri oil with heavy West Siberian oil, while the Azerbaijan Government, having taken on the commitment to fill the pipe, is unable to do so.

After completing the development of the early oil export schedule in April 1996, the AIOC launched extensive work on the MEP project. In August 1996 SOCAR and the AIOC agreed on the official start of operations on the MEP and established the Strategic Management Committee (SMC).[26] The work programme, coordinated with the SMC, envisaged such operations as analysis of MEP options, market and risk evaluation, investigating financing prospects, talks with the governments of transit countries and so on.

In the initial stage of the research, the following routes for the pipeline were under consideration: (*a*) from Baku to Supsa (in Georgia); (*b*) from Baku to Tbilisi (Georgia) and thence Ceyhan (Turkey); (*c*) from Baku to Novorossiysk (Russia); (*d*) from Baku to Astara (Azerbaijan) and thence to Tabriz (Iran) or Kharg Island (Iran); (*e*) from Samsun (Turkey) to Kyryk kala (Turkey) and then Ceyhan (Turkey); (*f*) the AMB (Albania–Macedonia–Bulgaria) route; (*g*) a route through Ismit (Turkey); (*h*) a Bulgaria–Greece route; (*i*) increasing the capacities of the northern and western routes for early oil; and (*j*) transport by sea from Baku to Bandar Anzali (Iran) and by pipeline to Aliabad (Iran), joining the pipeline to the Tabriz refinery. Then the options that involved transit through Iran were withdrawn because of political factors: the participation of

---

[26] The agreement on establishing the committee is available in the SOCAR and AIOC archives.

US companies in projects that would promote the economic development of Iran is prohibited by US legislation. Option (*e*) was withdrawn after being analysed by SOCAR and Botas. Option (*f*) was also withdrawn as it was considerably less cost-effective than option (*h*). Option (*g*) was withdrawn because the capacity of the Izmit refinery was insufficient.

Thus, the research focused on routes (*a*), (*b*) and (*c*). Since two of these ended on the Black Sea and because of the problem of oil transport through the Bosporus and Dardanelles, the route bypassing the straits through Bulgaria and Greece was also reassessed.

The research produced the following conclusions. First, all three alternatives were technically viable. Second, all were within the definition of cost-effectiveness of the Azeri–Chirag–Guneshli contract, even with the volumes of oil specified in the contract. Third, the economic parameters of the two routes with their destination on the Black Sea were competitive compared to the Mediterranean alternative, even if they had to bypass the Bosporus and Dardanelles. Fourth, it would be better to implement the MEP project on the basis of the Azeri–Chirag–Guneshli contract, so long as additional volumes were eventually assured, than to delay it in anticipation of the guaranteed oil export volumes from other projects. Fifth, the alternative of expanding the northern pipeline for early oil seemed competitive as an interim measure so long as the transition to full-field development (i.e., development of the contract area after the early oil production project) started before construction of the MEP was complete. Finally, the MEP could be constructed and put into service within 7–8 years, of which 1–2 years would be needed for the coordination and signing of agreements involving different parties such as transit countries, financing organizations, contractors and so on.

On the basis of these results, Azerbaijan chose the Baku–Tbilisi–Ceyhan (BTC) route as the one which met the interests of Azerbaijan best. This route was also supported by the governments of Georgia, Kazakhstan, Turkey, the USA and Uzbekistan. On 29 October 1998, all these countries signed the Ankara Declaration supporting the BTC route.[27] On 18 November 1999, at the OSCE Istanbul Summit Meeting, the presidents of Azerbaijan, Georgia, Kazakhstan and the USA signed the Istanbul Declaration in support of the BTC pipeline.[28]

Then, in the first six months of 2000, a number of agreements were prepared and signed with the governments of host countries, as well as an agreement on Turkish Government guarantees to cover expenditure in excess of $2.4 billion.[29]

---

[27] The text of the Ankara Declaration was published in the Azerbaijani government gazette, *Khalg Gazeti*, on 5 Nov. 1998. After the signing it was also disseminated by leading news agencies worldwide.

[28] Interfax, 18 Nov. 1999, in 'Baku–Ceyhan oil agreements signed in Istanbul', FBIS-SOV-1999-1118, 18 Nov. 1999.

[29] These agreements were ratified by the parliaments of Azerbaijan on 25 May 2000, of Georgia on 31 May 2000, and of Turkey on 21 June 2000. The package of ratified documents includes the agreement between Azerbaijan, Turkey and Georgia on the transport of crude oil through the territories of these countries by means of the BTC MEP; agreements between the Azerbaijani, Georgian and Turkish governments and MEP investors; a turnkey agreement between MEP participants and conractors commissioning the facility on a turnkey basis; a letter of guarantee by the Turkish Treasurer which guarantees con-

Finally, in October 2000, a group of project sponsors was set up to finance engineering operations and agreements were signed with the governments of Azerbaijan, Georgia and Turkey. Eight companies—SOCAR (50 per cent interest in the group of sponsors), BP (25.41 per cent), Unocal (7.48 per cent), Statoil (6.37 per cent), TPAO (5.02 per cent), Itochu (2.92 per cent), Ramco (1.55 per cent) and Delta Hess (1.25 per cent)—joined the group of project sponsors. All except Ramco are partners in the AIOC. Sponsors will automatically become members of the Main Export Pipeline Company (MEPCO), a new consortium, which will finance, build and operate the pipeline.

Construction of the BTC pipeline is expected to take 36 months and the filling of the pipe another 5–6 months, while the project is expected to cost $2.4 billion.[30] The 1022-mm pipeline, with a capacity of 50 mt/y, will be 1730–1830 km long, with stretches of 1037 km running through Turkey, 250–350 km through Georgia and 468 km through Azerbaijan.

Three risks remain. They relate to the availability of oil to fill the pipe, the price of crude and the mobilization of financial resources. Azerbaijan's proven oil and condensate reserves already exceed 7 bbl, of which some 2 bbl will be needed for domestic needs within 30 years.[31] The rest will be exported. Some 1 bbl of this can be expected to be transported through Novorossiysk and Supsa because Exxon/Mobil, Lukoil, Devon and Amerada Hess have so far refused to take part in the BTC project, even though they are part of the production contract. Four bbl remain, which may not be sufficient to ensure profitability of the pipeline with a base price of $15 per barrel. However, so far exploration operations have been carried out on only one-quarter of the licence area on the 20 oil contracts which Azerbaijan has signed. Experts believe that the discovery of new oilfields can be confidently expected. It is also believed that part of the oil from Kazakhstan's gigantic new oilfields will also be transported through the BTC pipeline. Kazakh oil—15 million barrels a year—is already being transported through Azerbaijan and the volume has been increasing. Construction in future of a trans-Caspian pipeline, which would connect Aktau in Kazakhstan with the BTC pipeline, is not ruled out either.

Lukoil has not yet joined the BTC project for two reasons: (a) Russia's negative attitude to the project; (b) and the fact that Lukarco holds a 12.5 per cent share in the Caspian Pipeline Consortium (CPC)[32] and is interested in using that pipeline. However, Lukoil may join the project at the construction stage or during exploitation. It can be confidently expected that after the BTC pipeline is built Lukoil will want to export a part of its oil to the Mediterranean, particularly as it is going to have such oil in the wake of the discovery of major

struction and commissioning, within the previously established period and in accordance with the previously established prices, of the Turkish section of the MEP project; the Istanbul Declaration; and the protocol on the introduction of changes to the agreement between Azerbaijan, Georgia and Turkey on the transport of crude oil through these countries by means of the BTC MEP, signed on 9 May 2000.

[30] Caspian News Agency, 21 June 2000.

[31] During 1995–99 Azerbaijan's average domestic consumption was 45–50 million barrels of oil per annum. It is expected to reach 65–70 million barrels per year over the next 30 years. Thus, over 30 years Azerbaijan will consume a total of 2 billion barrels of oil.

[32] For the shareholders in the CPC see chapter 3, section I in this volume.

oilfields in the Caspian Sea. After construction of the BTC line starts it is not ruled out that Russia, having acknowledged its defeat in the struggle for construction of the MEP through its territory, will stop boycotting the route and try to gain something from it. After all, Russia is selling gas to Turkey and is building a new gas pipeline to Turkey in implementing the Blue Stream project.

As far as world oil prices are concerned, there are reasons to believe that they are unlikely to fall to less than $15 per barrel, which has been accepted by the AIOC as the base price. Prices are more likely to rise a little in the future, which will, of course, contribute to the profitability of the project.

The risks related to mobilization of financial resources for the project remain, but there have been reassuring statements by senior US officials that the project will be supported by a number of US financial institutions. There are also similar statements by other international financial institutions.[33]

VI. Conclusions

This chapter does not aim to be a comprehensive and detailed analysis of Azerbaijan's strategic choice of its foreign policy priorities since independence. These priorities were formed gradually under the influence of both external and internal factors and on the basis of the country's national interests in the present stage of its development. In these nine years, Azerbaijan has aspired to strengthen its independence through integration with the world's political organizations and to form stable and normal relations with many countries, and first of all with its neighbours, thus laying the groundwork for sustainable economic development in the future. It has done much towards achieving these goals in the years of independence. Much remains to be done to promote sustainable development, but there appears to be sufficient reason to believe that this course is the one that has been irrevocably chosen.

[33] E.g., in an interview given in July 2000 in Tbilisi, Deputy Executive Director of the International Financial Corporation (IFC) and Managing Director of the World Bank Group Peter Voyk expressed the IFC's readiness to take part in financing the BTC project 'if necessary'. Caspian News Agency, 17 July 2000.

11. The choice of independent Georgia

*Alexander Rondeli**

I. Introduction

The collapse of the Soviet Union in 1991 gave birth to 14 independent republics with little or no experience of modern independent statehood and a post-imperial Russia as a struggling but still powerful neighbour. Georgia was one of those republics, and was confronted first with the issue of survival and security and later with the choice of strategic orientation. This chapter describes how a small and weak independent Georgia, almost a quasi-state torn apart by internal contradictions and economic problems, has struggled to define its strategic orientation and main national security and foreign policy priorities. The objective is to identify alternatives that Georgia may consider in the process of strategic decision making and to pinpoint the factors that determine its strategic and security choices. Has Georgia chosen its political orientation? If it has, is its choice realistic and sustainable or is it based on political idealism and lack of sufficient strategic experience? The question of political realism is particularly important for a country like Georgia, which has found itself part not of the globalized and pluralistic world, but instead of the post-Soviet space still dominated by principles of nationalism and even aggressive militarism.

After the short period of so-called strategic idealism that characterized the early days of independence, Georgia began to develop an increasingly realistic foreign policy, which has been less motivated by the fear of Russia and not solely driven by the short-term survival agenda.

The strategic idealism of the young Georgian state was characterized by the dominance of what Stephen Jones calls cultural paradigms.[1] These are traditional Georgian values, perceptions and attitudes towards foreign peoples and states and the outside world in general. These values often coloured the judgement of the Georgian authorities which, together with their lack of political experience and populism, led the country in the early 1990s into strategic wish-

---

[1] Stephen Jones offers a new and stimulating argument about the possible connection of Georgia's political culture with its foreign policy. Jones' interpretation of political culture, as he admits, is rather narrow and focused on traditional values, which he calls Georgian cultural paradigms or global paradigms. They explain the role of national identity in foreign policy and will be the reference points for any foreign policy 'ideology' that may emerge in the future. These global paradigms, according to Jones, are the religious identity of a Christian nation; the Western identity of Europeanness; pan-Caucasianism as a vague regional identity; and rejection of Russia. Jones, S., 'The role of cultural paradigms in Georgian foreign policy' (manuscript), Mount Holyoke College, Mass., 1999. For the last paradigm the term 'fear of Russia' is perhaps more appropriate than 'rejection'.

* The author wishes to thank Natalie Sabanadze, Wendell Steavenson and Professor Stephen Jones for their valuable comments.

ful thinking or strategic idealism. Since the return of President Eduard Shevardnadze in 1992 and the relative stabilization of the country by the mid-1990s, the Georgian elite has shown a better understanding of the surrounding geopolitical environment and begun to promote a cautious but nevertheless consistently Western-oriented foreign policy.

By the late 1990s it became clear that Georgia's foreign policy was largely determined by two main circumstances. One is its regional context and its especially strong dependence on a volatile neighbouring Russia, and the second is its internal weakness and disunity, which limits its ability to make independent and confident foreign policy choices. Under these circumstances the achievement of Georgia's strategic goals, such as integration with Europe and increased regional cooperation, seems extremely complicated. The authorities, however, consider participation in large international economic projects, such as Caspian Sea energy projects and transport corridors, to be decisive in the achievement of these goals. The following main foreign policy orientations can therefore be outlined: (a) the re-establishment of the territorial integrity of the country; (b) friendly, balanced relations with all neighbouring countries; (c) the reduction of the Russian military presence on Georgian territory; (d) integration with European and Euro-Atlantic structures; (e) the development of regional cooperation within the region; (f) the internationalization of local conflicts in the region; (g) attracting foreign economic interests to Georgia and the region; and (h) participation in regional economic projects.

Until 2000 the Georgian authorities refrained from officially publishing their concept of the country's security and political orientation. There was no official document arguing the government's vision of Georgia's future development, strategy and political orientation. The work of devising a concept of national security started in 1996 but has yet to be completed. One factor explaining the delay has been a lack of internal consensus on many important issues, both among the public and among the ruling elite. Another factor was the unwillingness of the authorities to annoy neighbouring Russia with loud pro-Western statements.

At last, in October 2000 a document prepared by the Ministry of Foreign Affairs of Georgia entitled 'Georgia and the world: a vision and strategy for the future' was presented by the government at the international conference on Georgia and its Partners: Directions for the New Millennium, held in Tbilisi.[2] It is an attempt to clearly define Georgia's strategic goals and objectives. It had been approved by the National Security Council.

The document states that an independent, prosperous, stable and unified Georgia is clearly in the best interests of its neighbours and that 'this applies especially to Georgia's relations with the Russian Federation, with which Georgia seeks the same stable and harmonious relationship that it enjoys with other countries. Georgia poses no threat to its neighbours and intends to play a positive role in the region's economic growth and political development'. It

---

[2] Georgian Ministry of Foreign Affairs, 'Georgia and the world: a vision and strategy for the future', Tbilisi, Oct. 2000, pp. 3–4 (in English).

also declares that 'the highest priority of Georgian foreign policy is to achieve full integration in the European political, economic and security structures, thus fulfilling the historical aspiration of the Georgian nation to participate fully in the European Community' and that 'deepening cooperation with the [European Union] represents a paramount aim of Georgian foreign policy'. The following statement in the document stresses Georgia's pro-Western orientation: 'Georgia considers cooperation with the United States of America and European countries as a main segment of the strategy of integration into European and Euro-Atlantic structures'.[3]

The following sections briefly describe the main political events that illustrate Georgia's recent strategic choices and analyse Georgia's behaviour as a small state, its relations with its powerful neighbour, Russia, and the impact of regional oil politics.

II. Recent political developments

An account of Georgia's most recent history and important political decisions illustrates the development of its strategic orientation better than any analysis of official documents or the limited scholarly work available. This section describes briefly the events that determined and shaped Georgia's national security interests and the character of its foreign policy.

In April 1991 Georgia declared independence without being recognized by the international community. In December of the same year the dissolution of the Soviet Union was officially announced, while in Georgia the first president, Zviad Gamsakhurdia, was ousted as a result of a military revolt. For a short period Georgia was ruled by a Military Council, which in March 1992 decided to invite Eduard Shevardnadze, former Foreign Minister of the Soviet Union, back to Georgia. After Shevardnadze's return the process of Georgia's achieving international recognition was begun. In 1992 Georgia joined the United Nations, the Conference on Security and Co-operation in Europe (CSCE, which in 1995 became the Organization for Security and Co-operation in Europe, the OSCE) and several other international organizations.

At the same time, separatist movements in Abkhazia and South Ossetia began to gain momentum as a result of multiple factors, the main one being Russian military and political support to these movements, and another the clumsy nationalism developed under President Gamsakhurdia. The result was the defeat of the Georgian forces in Abkhazia in 1993. Russia demanded that Georgia join the Commonwealth of Independent States (CIS) and Shevardnadze was forced to sign an agreement allowing Russian military bases to remain on Georgian territory for 25 years. In 1992–93 Georgia had been against joining the CIS, but by the end of 1993 Russian coercive diplomacy had resulted in its eventually joining.[4] In 1994 Georgia and Russia signed a bilateral agreement on friendship

---

[3] 'Georgia and the world: a vision and strategy for the future' (note 2), p. 12.
[4] Kortunov, A., 'Russia, the near abroad and the West', ed. G. Lapidus, *The New Russia: Troubled Transformation* (Westview Press: Boulder, Colo., 1995), pp. 172–73.

and cooperation, which was ratified only by the Georgian Parliament: the Russian Duma has yet to ratify this already outdated document.[5]

In 1994 Georgia also joined the NATO Partnership for Peace (PFP) programme, which marked the beginning of its relations with NATO. In the same year President Shevardnadze paid an official visit to the USA and established initial contacts with the International Monetary Fund (IMF) and the World Bank, the two biggest donors which now define the main orientation of Georgia's economic development.

In 1995 Georgia and Russia signed another treaty on Russia's military presence in Georgia, which was agreed for 25 years.[6] Ratification of this agreement by Georgia was conditional on Russia's support for Georgia's territorial integrity and the build-up of its military power. Since 1995 Russia has failed to meet any of these conditions, and the agreement has lost its legal as well as moral force.

In 1996, under the umbrella of the 1990 Treaty on Conventional Forces in Europe (the CFE Treaty), it was possible to resume talks about the Russian military presence in Georgia. During the same year in Vienna a special inter-state consultative body, GUAM, was created, which included Georgia, Ukraine, Azerbaijan and Moldova. These countries had similar problems with Russia and decided to hold consultations on a regular basis in order to coordinate their policies under a common OSCE umbrella. (Officially, GUAM was founded at the Council of Europe meeting in October 1997 in Strasbourg.) Economically the GUAM countries are unified by the TRACECA (Transport Corridor Europe Caucasus Asia) project, which envisages the restoration of the historical Silk Road. Uzbekistan joined GUAM in April 1999 at the NATO 50th anniversary summit meeting in Washington, DC, and it now became GUUAM. It is still a consultative body, since its institutional structure has yet to be developed. In the future, however, it may play an important role in fostering political cooperation among its member states. Russia's attitude towards GUUAM has been extremely negative.

In 1999 Georgia joined the Program Analysis and Review Process (PARP), which envisages the upgrading of its military forces to NATO standards and the participation of Georgian forces in peacekeeping operations. For the first time a Georgian unit joined the NATO peacekeepers in Kosovo.

The year 1999 was marked by many important political developments and critical foreign policy decisions. Georgia joined the Council of Europe and the World Trade Organization and withdrew from the 1992 Treaty on Collective Security (the Tashkent Treaty).[7] The Helsinki European Council meeting in December 1999 began talks about the possible inclusion of Bulgaria, Romania and Turkey in the European Union (EU), which seemed to signify that the

[5] *Izvestiya*, 2 Feb. 1994, p. 1.

[6] Shermatova, S. and Mikadze, A., 'Russia strikes deep roots in the Caucasus', *Moscow News*, 31 Mar.–6 Apr. 1995.

[7] The original members were Armenia, Kazakhstan, Kyrgyzstan, Russia, Tajikistan and Uzbekistan. Azerbaijan, Belarus and Georgia also joined later. Azerbaijan, Georgia and Uzbekistan left in 1999. On the Tashkent Treaty see chapter 5 in this volume. For the text see *Izvestiya*, 16 May 1992, p. 3.

Black Sea region was slowly coming to be considered EU territory. At the OSCE summit meeting in Istanbul in November 1999 an agreement on the Baku–Tbilisi–Ceyhan pipeline route for the export of oil from the Caspian region was signed by Georgia, Azerbaijan and Turkey.[8] At the same meeting Russia agreed to start its withdrawal from its military bases in Georgia in 2000. By the end of 1999 all Russian border guards had left Georgia and were being replaced by Georgian forces.

For a small and newly independent state such as Georgia, it is particularly important to achieve economic and political stability, as well as internal social cohesion. These are necessary preconditions for any country's foreign policy to be effective and forward-looking. Internal weaknesses and contradictions also make other members of the international community cautious and tense. In this respect the relative success or failure of Georgia's foreign policy largely depends on its internal problems and difficulties. The international community watched with a certain fear and alarm the chaos of 1991–95. In 1996–98, however, the situation improved when Shevardnadze managed to stabilize the country and embark on the process of reform and economic development.[9] During this period, the foreign policy of Georgia was refined and included long-term strategy aimed at fostering regional cooperation and reducing Georgia's dependence on Russia, which itself was going through a painful transition period.

The oil and gas reserves in the region could become a catalyst for further development and an important tool in helping the region out of the current economic crisis. The development of the oil and gas sector, along with the increasing presence of foreign economic interests, could contribute not only to regional cooperation and economic development but also to regional security.

However, despite Georgia's improved internal and external position, 1999 was also characterized by a severe economic downturn resulting from the failure of reform, corruption and increasing social tensions. According to a United Nations Development Programme (UNDP) report, about 40 per cent of Georgia's population were living below the poverty line.[10] Salaries in the public sector and pensions were not paid for months and even years. Unemployment was officially as high as 16.8 per cent—according to unofficial estimates 25.6 per cent.[11] Public expenditure on health, already very low in 1993–98 (at 0.7 per cent of gross domestic product, GDP), dropped further to 0.6 per cent of GDP in 1999.[12] The conflicts in Abkhazia and South Ossetia remained unresolved, and Georgia's international positions had begun to weaken. Increasing internal problems raised doubts about the viability of the state and its elite, which had failed to maintain the success of 1996–98. Georgia's foreign

[8] 'Baku–Ceyhan oil agreements signed in Istanbul', Foreign Broadcast Information Service, *Daily Report–Central Eurasia (FBIS-SOV)*, FBIS-SOV-1999-1118, 18 Nov. 1999.

[9] Jones, S., 'Georgia's return from chaos', *Current History*, vol. 95, no. 603 (Oct. 1996), pp. 340–45.

[10] United Nations Development Programme (UNDP), *Human Development Report, Georgia 2000* (UNDP Country Office: Tbilisi, 2000), p. 27.

[11] *Human Development Report, Georgia 2000* (note 10), p. 31.

[12] *Human Development Report, Georgia 2000* (note 10), p. 76.

standing and reputation now greatly depend on the resolution of its internal socio-economic problems and on the government's determination to fight corruption. By the middle of 2000 it was clear that the pro-Western orientation would be severely tested domestically.

III. Georgian foreign policy

According to Article 48 of the Georgian Constitution, the Georgian Parliament is responsible for developing and defining the country's foreign policy.[13] The Ministry of Foreign Affairs and the State Chancellery are responsible for carrying out the policy. At the same time, however, President Shevardnadze plays a special and decisive role in defining foreign policy. When Georgia became an independent state, few Georgian diplomats enjoyed international recognition and respect. Among them Shevardnadze stood out not only as an experienced diplomat but also as a well-known public figure. For a newly independent state like Georgia, which found itself in complete chaos and internationally isolated, the return of the experienced Shevardnadze with his extensive political connections and international recognition was a boon. It is therefore only natural that Shevardnadze still uses his extensive diplomatic experience and plays a critical role in defining his country's foreign policy.

One of the other agencies working on foreign policy issues is the National Security Council, set up in 1996 and headed by the president. The Ministry of Foreign Affairs coordinates inter-agency efforts. To foster better coordination the ministry holds regular consultations with other relevant agencies and involves them in the decision-making process, later presenting final draft documents to the president.[14] This has been very successful in reducing inter-agency conflicts and disagreements. However, there have also been clear cases of failure in coordination. One example is the resolution on 'Basic principles of the sustainability of social life, the strengthening of state sovereignty and security, and restoration of the territorial integrity of Georgia', passed by the parliament in April 1997.[15] This document was an incomplete draft of Georgia's foreign policy strategy and was overloaded with anti-Russian rhetoric and emotional statements. Its tone was not consistent with the actual foreign policy conducted by Georgia's executive elite.

After the declaration of independence in April 1991 and the election of Gamsakhurdia as president, the Georgian authorities began to seek recognition and legitimacy for Georgia and tried to establish links with the outside world. There were numerous unofficial visits and consultations during the early period of independence.

Some observers divide the development of Georgia's independent foreign policy into two main periods—the presidency of Gamsakhurdia, from the

[13] 'The Constitution of Georgia', Tbilisi, 1998, p. 224 (in English).
[14] Personal interview with the Georgian Minister of Foreign Affairs, Irakli Menagarishvili, 28 June 2000.
[15] Resolution of the Parliament of Georgia, 3 Apr. 1997.

announcement of independence until December 1992, and the presidency of Eduard Shevardnadze from December 1992 to the present.[16] This chapter focuses on the latter period, which marks the turning point in the development of Georgian strategic thinking and foreign policy analysis. There were attempts to think through foreign policy priorities during the Gamsakhurdia period, especially with regard to neighbouring countries, and many Georgians publicly debated the role of Georgia in the Caucasus and the choice of foreign policy orientation. However, Gamsakhurdia's presidency is not discussed here as a separate period in the development of Georgia's foreign policy because the country was not a completely sovereign state. Georgia at the time was trying to separate itself from Russia and establish contacts with other powers, but this was only an attempt to develop a foreign policy rather than an already established and well-thought-through strategy. Attempts to conduct foreign policy were mostly characterized by an idealistic understanding of the international environment and were full of slogans and what could be called strategic wishful thinking.

The return of Shevardnadze in 1992 marked the beginning of the development of a sovereign foreign policy. For almost 10 years Georgia has been trying to find its place in the international community, ensure its national security and carry out its foreign policy in accordance with the national security priorities. Over this period the political elite has tried to define the country's main strategic orientation and come up with ways of achieving its political goals.

It can be argued that 10 years is not long enough for a country with no experience of modern independent statehood to define its goals and long-term political perspective; that for the past decade Georgia has only been able to focus on its survival and immediate concerns rather than on concepts of 'strategic choice', foreign policy orientation, long-term perspective and so on. These are big concepts that a weak and small state like Georgia cannot yet grapple with. This chapter argues, however, that since 1995, after a period of strategic uncertainty caused by the conflict in Abkhazia and internal instability, Georgia has managed to embark on an active foreign policy. Despite the unresolved conflicts in Abkhazia and South Ossetia and the pending issue of the Russian military bases, Georgia's foreign policy has become consistently Western-oriented, with the goal of final integration into the European community. This tendency has become more and more obvious.

In this author's view there are two stages in the development of Georgia's foreign policy—1992–94 and 1995 to the present. In the first period, as a result

[16] Hunter, S. T., 'The evolution of the foreign policy of the Transcaucasian states', eds G. K. Bertsch *et al.*, *Crossroads and Conflict: Security and Foreign Policy in the Caucasus and Central Asia* (Routledge: New York, 2000), pp. 98–99. See also Darchiashvili, D., *Georgia: The Search for State Security*, Caucasus Working Papers (Center for International Security and Cooperation (CISAC), Stanford University: Stanford, Calif., 1997), pp. 2–3. Edmund Herzig writes about the Gamsakhurdia period as the 1st stage of Georgia's foreign policy development. Herzig, E., *The New Caucasus* (Royal Institute of International Affairs: London, 1999), pp. 98–99. Helena Frazer discusses Georgia's foreign policy since 1992. Before then, according to Frazer, Georgia, not being a sovereign state, was not able to conduct an independent foreign policy. Frazer, H., 'Managing independence: Georgian foreign policy 1992–1996', thesis for the M.Phil. in International Relations, University of Oxford, Apr. 1997 (manuscript), p. 2.

of severe domestic problems and external pressures, Georgia's foreign policy was reactive and short-term oriented. In the second period, Georgia managed to achieve political stability and gain enough political experience to enable it to become more active in foreign affairs and more determined in carrying out a pro-Western foreign policy.

During 1992–94 Georgia's foreign policy was largely determined by the domestic political situation. It is not surprising that a small and newly independent state like Georgia, which found itself in total economic and political crisis, ethnic conflicts and paramilitary struggles, failed to conduct a fruitful and constructive foreign policy driven by long-term strategic thinking. This was particularly difficult under constant pressure from its former master, Russia. Some observers note that Georgia represented the clearest and perhaps the worst case of Russian involvement in the 'near abroad'.[17] There was also a politically inexperienced and to a certain extent destructive opposition which often obstructed rational and realistic foreign policy choices. Aves argues that, of the three South Caucasian states, Georgia adopted the most radical stance in asserting its independence from Moscow.[18]

Although Shevardnadze was trying to make Georgia's foreign policy more realistic, balanced and pragmatic, his ideas were often disapproved of by a large part of the Georgian public and by the political elite. People were still going through the post-independence euphoria characterized by high expectations largely generated by irresponsible nationalist and populist figures, the most prominent example being the former president, Gamsakhurdia. During this period Georgia lost the war in Abkhazia, joined the CIS and signed the agreement with Russia on the Russian military bases.

This period was also marked by the spread of anti-Russian feeling among the Georgian public. In March 1993 President Shevardnadze openly called the war in Abkhazia a Russian–Georgian conflict.[19] The decision on CIS membership was a direct result of Russian pressure in the form of an ultimatum from Russia's defence minister.[20] Frazer in her study of Georgia's foreign policy characterizes this decision as 'omnibalancing' as opposed to the traditional 'bandwagoning'. She argues that the Georgian authorities were trying to appease the secondary adversary—Russia—in order to allay the primary threat of internal disintegration and to ensure the regime's survival.[21] However, most Georgian observers believe that joining the CIS was a clear case of capitulation and not 'bandwagoning'.

The connection between domestic and foreign policies is widely known. However, the type and the character of this connection are often determined by

[17] Lepingwell, J. W. R., 'The Russian military and security policy in the near abroad', *Survival*, vol. 36, no. 3 (fall 1994), p. 75.

[18] Aves, J., 'The Caucasus states: the regional security complex', eds R. Allison and C. Bluth, *Security Dilemmas in Russia and Eurasia* (Royal Institute of International Affairs: London, 1998), p. 176.

[19] Litovkin, V., 'Rossiyskiye voyennye otritsayut svoyo uchastiye v boyakh' [Russian military deny taking part in hostilities], *Izvestiya*, 17 Mar. 1993.

[20] Odom, W. and Dujarric, R., *Commonwealth or Empire? Russia, Central Asia and the Transcucasus* (Hudson Institute: Indianapolis, Ind., 1995), pp. 85–86.

[21] Frazer (note 16), p. 23.

the specifics of each country and its surrounding regional security environment. In the newly independent Georgia, internal factors significantly influenced not only foreign policy and strategic thinking, but also the country's positions on the international and regional levels. Frazer was right to argue that internal factors have been at least as important as external ones in influencing the foreign policy of Georgia since 1992.[22]

If initially internal factors such as ethnic tensions, rising ethnic nationalism and a severe energy crisis were the government's main concerns, by 1998 poor governance and rapidly spreading corruption had become the two main factors threatening the viability of Georgia's statehood.[23] The government, however, only admitted the existence and overwhelming importance of these problems in 1999–2000, when the IMF and the World Bank refused to provide further assistance and it became obvious that the country's international reputation had been severely damaged by domestic mismanagement.

Generally, the national interests and security concerns of small states have a relatively local character, and only in a few cases reach the regional level. The main, and often the only, priority of a small country is ensuring its independent and sovereign existence. Among the critical external factors one is the neighbouring presence of a great power which plays an important role in the international system. However, an increasingly important factor for small states in the modern world is the ongoing process of globalization and the role of international organizations and institutions. The foreign policy of a small country typically has to provide for quick adjustment to a changing environment, since it is unable to influence the international system.

From the very first days of its sovereign existence any country should try to ensure its security and economic development, and establish itself as a competitive partner and a responsible member of the international community. It should aim to achieve the trust and recognition of its neighbours and create the proper external conditions for a well-functioning economy. Georgia in early 1992 was in severe political and economic crisis. The state authorities began to look for options that would bring recognition of and support to Georgia by the international community. Tense relations with the new Russia, which was itself torn apart by internal problems, promised very little.

IV. Georgia, Russia and the West

Georgia's relations with Russia cannot be described as simple and straightforward. The two countries have a history of close bilateral relations reinforced by Georgia's existence first as part of the Russian Empire and later as part of the USSR. The Russian and Georgian peoples have shared their culture and history for almost two centuries. On the one hand, Georgia in the 19th and 20th centuries considered Russia as a door to Europe and a link to European culture,

[22] Frazer (note 16), pp. 14–24.

[23] United Nations Development Programme (UNDP), *Human Development Report, Georgia 1999* (UNDP Country Office: Tbilisi, 1999).

as well as a powerful neighbour sharing the same faith and ready to protect Georgia at critical moments. On the other hand, Russia appeared to Georgians as an imperial power, shamelessly violating all the agreements and promises it had made to Georgia as its regional supporter.

It would be an oversimplification to say that Georgia now considers Russia as the devil incarnate, an enemy. As Stephen Jones notes: 'Until the Bolshevik Revolution of 1917, liberal Russia was for Georgians, despite its autocratic tradition, a channel to the west and Georgia's incorporation into the Russian Empire in the first decade of the 19th century reinforced the Georgian sense of Europeanness'.[24] After 1917 Bolshevik Russia, no longer looking West, was not regarded by independent Georgia (1918–21) as a part of modern Europe. According to Jones, the Soviet attempt to 'isolate Georgia from Europe made the latter a pristine and symbolic antithesis to communism's Oriental backwardness'.[25] Georgians are extremely resentful of Russia's imperial policies in the Caucasus and towards Georgia in particular. However, according to a 1997 opinion poll 24 per cent of them still considered Russia important for Georgia's future.[26] In 1999 the figure was reduced to 13 per cent but, despite disillusionment with Russia and the failure of the CIS, 24 per cent of those polled then still believed that Georgia should define clearly its security relations with Russia and the CIS (40 per cent named the USA and other Western countries).[27]

Georgia's attitude towards Russia has never been simple, partly because 30 per cent of Georgia's population is non-Georgian. In addition, the persistent socio-economic crisis and resulting disillusionment with the Western orientation encourage a certain feeling of nostalgia about the former association with Russia. It is important to note that the Georgian view of Russia is characterized not only by fear but also by long-standing cultural connections and respect for Russian power. The argument that there are two Russias—the democratic and the imperial—is very popular among the Georgian officials and well explains the often contradictory and complex legacy of Georgian–Russian relations. However, Georgia takes the Russian military's support for the Abkhaz and South Ossetian secessionists and an ongoing anti-Georgian campaign in the Russian media as signs of clear hostility. In 1999 Georgia withdrew from the Tashkent Treaty, mainly because it had failed as a tool for restoring Georgia's territorial integrity. That was one of the main responsibilities of the treaty and it was not fulfilled either in Georgia or in Nagorno-Karabakh (Azerbaijan).

In December 2000 Russia imposed visa regulations on Georgians for the first time since Georgia regained independence. The Russian authorities explained that the visa policy would make Russia's borders more secure against alleged

[24] Jones (note 1), p. 6.

[25] Jones (note 1).

[26] US Information Agency, Office of Research and Media Reaction, 'Opinion analysis: Georgians trust US more than Russia to act responsibly in the Caucasus', 28 Jan. 1997, p. 20, table 14.

[27] US State Department, Office of Research, 'Opinion analysis: Georgians increasingly view the US as their country's main ally', Washington, DC, 29 Nov. 1999, p. 6, table 1.

infiltration by Chechen terrorists.[28] In reality Russia's visa policy toward Georgia will do little if anything to stop Chechen terrorists from trying to cross the Russian–Georgian border. At the same time new visa requirements do not include the inhabitants of secessionist Abkhazia and South Ossetia, which border Russia. This goes against international law and can be considered as an attempt by Russia to annex Georgian territory. In fact the new visa regulations were planned to apply economic pressure on Georgia. They created severe problems for hundreds of thousands of Georgians living and earning money in Russia. Their remittances to Georgia are estimated to be equivalent to almost one-quarter of Georgia's GDP.[29] Any serious reduction of these remittances will be a severe blow to a weak Georgian economy and will add to social discontent.

Russia's policy in the Caucasus continues, unfortunately, to be driven by fear of the Western powers, and of the USA in particular. This is expressed in Russia's treatment of Georgia and the rest of Caucasus as either satellites or adversaries. For some reason Russia has not considered the option of partnership with the South Caucasian states, in which it could guarantee its influence through economic participation and serve as a security guarantor. Currently Russia is undergoing serious difficulties, but in the future it may regain its economic power and its participation in the economic life of the region could become quite substantial. Such a turn of events could be mutually beneficial for Russia and the South Caucasian states. Ultimately it is not feasible to expect that Western interest in the region will be so strong that it will exclude Russia. Russia's geographical proximity, its resources, the size of the market and cultural ties are all important for the future of the South Caucasus. The Georgian elite therefore considers the constructive participation of Russia in the development of the regional economy as a positive and highly desirable step. So far, however, Russia has not sent positive signals to Georgia, thus giving the impression that it sees the political processes in the South Caucasus only as a 'zero-sum' game.

Georgia has clearly tried to reduce its uneven dependence on Russia and slowly move out of the Russian sphere of influence. For many Russian commentators this is a clear sign of an ungrateful and treacherous attitude towards Russia. This kind of emotional judgement is easy to understand, as Georgia has been trying to conduct an independent foreign policy and define its national security priorities. Its attempts to reduce its dependence on Russia and establish close relations with other neighbouring and Western countries are taken by the Russian authorities not only as anti-Russian moves but also as strategically incorrect ones for Georgia, given its proximity to Russian power. The Georgian authorities' efforts to integrate their country into European structures is often seen as strategic idealism which goes against all geopolitical arguments and even common sense.

---

[28] Interview with Sergey Yastrzhembsky, assistant to the Russian President, *Krasnaya Zvezda*, 21 Dec. 2000.
[29] *Financial Times*, 4 Jan. 2001.

Certain political forces in Georgia, especially the communists and others on the left wing, consider the current pro-Western stand to be a fatal mistake. This view is shared by certain segments of the Georgian public, especially the Russian-speakers, who still believe that Georgia's future lies with Russia. In the view of this author, Russia, because of a skewed perception of its interests in the South Caucasus, has in fact been forcing Georgia to become even more politically detached from Russia.

Russia fears the increase of Western interests in the Caspian region, and Western involvement in the exploration and exploitation of Caspian oil has triggered a Russian confrontation with the West, and in particular the USA. Russian–US rivalry is affecting the security environment and economic situation in the South Caucasus in a major way and contributing to the further deterioration of relations between Georgia and Russia.

Foreign policy alternatives

The Georgian political elite has traditionally considered several alternatives for the future development of Georgia.

The first alternative can be called pro-Russian. It calls for close connection with and dependence on Russia—becoming a Russian 'satellite'. Given Russia's current difficulties and the continuing legacy of 'imperial' thinking, such unilateral dependence on Russia would not allow Georgia to develop as an independent state fully integrated into the world economic system.

The second choice is pro-Western. This can be interpreted in many different ways but in general is defined as full-scale integration in the European political, economic and security system. The main way of achieving this goal is through increased cooperation with the EU. As illustrated by the historical overview in this chapter, the Georgian authorities have so far opted for a European or Western orientation as the best way to ensure Georgia's security and economic development (although it is worth mentioning that the majority of the population have no illusions as to how easy it will be to reach this goal).

It must be stressed that the desire to be European and part of Europe is rooted in the Georgian national consciousness. Georgians associate Christianity with Europe and, perhaps naively, count themselves as Europeans. According to Jones, 'Georgians' Europeanness is bound up with the church, which since the 4th century has been an outpost of Western Christendom in a Muslim region'.[30] Later many Georgians associated their connection to the Russian Empire with the increased Westernization of their country. Jones also argues that:

Incorporation into the Russian Empire in the first decades of the 19th century reinforced the Georgian sense of Europeanness. The Georgian intelligentsia rapidly adapted to the ideas, imbibed through Russian universities, of progress, individualism and liberty. The liberation movements of Greece and Young Italy became the model

[30] Jones (note 1), p. 9.

for Georgian progressives. At the turn of the century, another Western ideology—socialism—usurped liberalism's place among the educated.[31]

However, after 1917, Georgia tried to establish relations with Europe independently, considering Bolshevik Russia as a non-European state. Even former President Gamsakhurdia elaborated this connection of Georgia with Europe.[32] In the early 1990s Russia was sometimes associated with Europe and sometimes not. This association was mostly political as opposed to cultural, but the public in the Caucasus and Central Asia has a rather vague understanding of the West and Western traditions.[33]

In the late 1980s, when the Soviet Union was already entering its death throes and national liberation movements were gaining strength, some thought that Georgia, along with its neighbours Armenia and Azerbaijan, would become a buffer state balancing the interests of the regional great powers—Russia, Iran and Turkey.

Wight defines a buffer zone as 'a region occupied by one or more weaker powers between two or more stronger powers; it is sometimes described as a power vacuum'. He also notes that 'a buffer state is a weak power between two or more stronger ones, maintained or even created with the purpose of reducing conflict between them'.[34] Given the current geopolitical situation in the region, as well as the increasing interdependence and economic integration of the world as a whole, the buffer zone alternative could be an ideal strategic choice, a third alternative for Georgia. The concept of a buffer implies the presence of strong and often hostile neighbours. In today's changing world, however, the geopolitical function of a buffer may be more connective than divisive.

In 1991–92 part of the Georgian elite seriously considered the 'bufferization' of Georgia as an ideal strategic move which would bring Western support. Later, however, Russia's involvement in South Ossetia and Abkhazia, the imposition of economic sanctions and forcible integration into the CIS shook the inexperienced Georgian elite and dashed their hopes. It turned out that Russia sees its presence in Georgia as vital for its own national security and does not perceive the Caucasus as anything but a completely subordinated zone of influence. Russia is afraid that a power vacuum in the Caucasus would be filled by other, rival powers.[35] At the same time, Russia's increasing political and economic weakness does not allow it to maintain such a dominant position in the region.

---

[31] Jones (note 1), p. 6.

[32] Gamsakhurdia, Z., *Sakartvelos Sulieri Missia* [Georgia's spiritual mission] (Ganatleba: Tbilisi, 1990).

[33] MacFarlane, N., *Western Engagement in the Caucasus and Central Asia* (Royal Institute of International Affairs: London, 1999), pp. 2–5.

[34] Wight, M., 'The pattern of power', eds H. Bull and C. Holbraa, *Power Politics* (Leicester University Press and Royal Institute of International Affairs: London, 1995), p. 160.

[35] Rotar, I., 'Stat' nashimi satellitami ili umeret'' [Become our satellites or die], *Nezavisimaya Gazeta*, 5 May 1994; and Nikitin, V., 'Vneshnyaya politika Gruzii: idealy i interesy' [Georgia's foreign policy: ideals and interests], *Nezavisimaya Gazeta*, 4 Jan. 1996.

The buffer zone idea looks increasingly unrealistic for Georgia now, but it should not be dismissed completely given the volatile and changing political environment in the region. Under certain circumstances a move towards becoming a buffer state guided by the 'responsible supervision' of interested parties would be a positive step for Georgia and might lead to greater internal and regional stability.

V. Georgia's choice

It is 10 years since Georgia became a sovereign state conducting its own independent foreign policy. The national security and foreign policy priorities have been widely debated over the past few years, but the official concept of that foreign policy has yet to be fully developed.[36]

In the early days of independence, the Georgian elite tended to rely on intuition and President Shevardnadze's personal insight in determining foreign policy and national security priorities. In the late 1990s, however, analytical work by different think tanks and non-governmental organizations (NGOs) has became more important and valuable for the state elite. Enriched by some practical experience, that elite has also begun to take into consideration scholarly and analytical work. According to David Darchiashvili, however, Georgia's national security and foreign policies are more 'practical' than conceptual and lack a serious theoretical basis.[37]

President Shevardnadze declared in his state of the union address in 1997 that joining Europe 'was for centuries the dream of our ancestors'.[38] In a speech of January 1999, Foreign Minister Irakli Menagarishvili emphasized that the first priority of Georgia's foreign policy was European integration, and as a first step the harmonization of Georgian and European legislation.[39] In 1999 Shevardnadze seemed overly optimistic about the future prospects for Georgia, stating in one speech that 'if processes underway in today's world continue at the current pace, membership in all major Euro-Atlantic and European structures of Georgia and other newly independent states would be inevitable'.[40] The Chairman of the Georgian Parliament, Zurab Zhvania, declared in his speech of accession to the Council of Europe in February 1999, 'I am Georgian, therefore I am European'.[41]

It is becoming clear that the Georgian elite has chosen a pro-Western orientation. At the same time the Georgian authorities try to be cautious and refrain from frequent declarations of their Western aspirations in order not to irritate

[36] Darchiashvili, D., 'Trends in strategic thinking in Georgia', eds Bertsch et al. (note 16), pp. 66–74.
[37] Darchiashvili (note 16), p. 14.
[38] Speech at the parliamentary session of 27 May 1997, Parlamentis Utskebani [Parliamentary gazette], 31 May 1997, p. 30.
[39] Recent Political Developments in Georgia, no. 1 (31 Jan. 1999), document held by the US Embassy in Georgia.
[40] Address of H. E. Eduard Shevardnadze at the Inauguration of the Partnership and Co-operation Agreement in Luxembourg, June 1999, Georgia's State Chancellery Archive (in English).
[41] Parliament of Georgia Newsletter, no. 2 (Feb. 1999), p. 1 (in English).

neighbouring Russia. Recently pro-Western rhetoric has become even weaker because of increasing public discontent with the much-vaunted Westernization, which has failed to benefit the average citizen. An ineffective socio-economic policy, pervasive corruption, increasing social polarization and poverty are associated among certain segments of the Georgian public with the pro-Western policies of the current government.

Paradoxically, Russia has contributed to the popularization of Western ideas in Georgia as a result of its open support of separatist forces in Abkhazia and South Ossetia.[42] The Georgian public in general hoped that Western help would improve their dire living conditions, while the so-called elite, largely made up of the old Soviet *nomenklatura*, hoped to benefit personally from foreign grants and assistance. This latter hope was realized.

The Georgian authorities soon realized that Western interest in the Caucasus was triggered by its substantial natural resources. The South Caucasus, luckily, is rich in oil and gas resources, which has brought serious Western economic interests into the region and is expected to contribute to the economic development of the region as a whole and Georgia in particular. Without the development of the region as a whole, Georgia's chances of economic revival look slim. However, together with the rest of the Caucasus and Central Asia, Georgia has good prospects for the future. It should also be noted that, since regional economic development largely depends on regional stability and security, the Georgian Government is trying to promote regional cooperation through the transport corridor and pipeline projects. Georgia's calculations are simple and obvious: large-scale international projects will attract significant Western investment, stimulate the economy and create a vested Western interest in preserving political stability and security in the region.

The Georgian authorities now clearly link the country's prospects to increased regional cooperation and use every opportunity to underline the importance of rational economic and security cooperation. In order to further promote the idea of mutually beneficial cooperation in the Caucasus, President Shevardnadze in February 1996 came up with six main principles to govern interstate relations among Armenia, Azerbaijan, Georgia and Russia.[43] Later these principles became known as the Peaceful Caucasus Initiative. They include: (*a*) renunciation of territorial claims and recognition of existing borders; (*b*) commitment to the protection of human rights; (*c*) protection of transport and communication assets; (*d*) joint efforts to preserve the natural environment and deal with natural disasters; (*e*) promotion of ethnic and religious tolerance and the renunciation of extreme forms of nationalism; and (*f*) support for and comprehensive protection of international projects and investments in the Caucasus region.

---

[42] On Russia's policy towards Georgia see Arbatov, A., *Bezopasnost': Rossiyskiy Vybor* [Security: Russia's choice] (EPI Tsentr: Moscow, 1999), pp. 163–70; and Trenin, D., 'Russia's security interests and policies in the Caucasus region', ed. B. Coppieters, *Contested Borders in the Caucasus* (VUB University Press: Brussels, 1995), pp. 115–30.

[43] *Sakartvelos Respublika* [Republic of Georgia], 1 Mar. 1996, p. 1.

Unfortunately, the current political and economic situation in the Caucasus does not allow the countries of the region to engage in extensive and effective cooperation. However, it remains one of the top foreign policy priorities for Georgia.[44]

To a certain extent, Georgia's future plans and hopes were connected to the Black Sea Economic Cooperation scheme (BSEC) which was set up in 1992. Under Georgian chairmanship in 1999 the BSEC received the legal status of an international organization[45] and opened up a new way for the member states to get closer to the EU. BSEC membership not only provides advantages stemming from regional cooperation; it also protects Georgia from the side effects of ongoing globalization.

Georgia also has hopes for GUUAM. However, this organization is still very young and has been slow to develop, so that many commentators are sceptical about it. Currently the main binding interest of the GUUAM countries is economic, and the organization may develop into a free trade zone.[46] The chances of improving economic cooperation among the member countries look good, especially since GUUAM is open to other, non-CIS members as well. It is too early to discuss possible security and military functions for GUUAM. However, recent discussions regarding the creation of a GUUAM battalion indicate that such developments are possible.

Georgia also remains part of the CIS, although the organization has proved rather ineffective, both politically and economically, and increasingly seems to have been stillborn. The reason for its failure may lie in the inability of Russia to play the locomotive role in the organization, as well as its clumsy attempts to use the CIS to restore a quasi-Soviet Union under clear Russian hegemony. Georgia's disappointment with the CIS has been growing irreversibly.

Given these circumstances it is not surprising that Georgia considers Russia's attempts to dominate the region through destabilization and ethnic confrontation as extremely destructive. At the same time, Russia's more constructive policies aimed at strengthening regional security and promoting regional cooperation can only be welcomed by the Georgian authorities.[47] Unfortunately, as mentioned above, the Russian political elite considers political processes in the Caucasus only as a 'zero-sum game'.

Integration with Europe is clearly becoming the main objective of the current Georgian Government, which often considers Russia also as part of Europe. At the same time, neither the Georgian people nor the authorities believe that this goal will be easy to achieve in the near future. On the contrary, despite increasing cooperation with European structures and states, the Georgian elites are

---

[44] Rondeli, A., *Georgia: Foreign Policy and National Security Priorities*, Discussion Paper Series 3 (UNDP Country Office: Tbilisi, 1999), pp. 19–29.

[45] The BSEC became a regional economic organization on 1 May 1999 after its charter was ratified by 11 member states. On 8 Oct. 1999 it was granted observer status by UN General Assembly Resolution 54/5. For the charter see, e.g., the BSEC Internet site, URL <http://www.bsec.gov>.

[46] 'Na osnove obshchikh tseley i podkhodov' [On the basis of common goals and approaches], *Svobodnaya Gruziya*, 28 Sep. 2000.

[47] Shevardnadze has emphasized this on different occasions. See, e.g., Shevardnadze's speech in the Parliament of Azerbaijan on 19 Feb. 1997, Archives of the State Chancellery.

now more realistic in assessing their chances and the prospects for what they call the 'return to Europe'. Even though concrete steps have been taken towards integration into European structures and the harmonization of Georgian legislation with that of Europe, the population as a whole has a very vague understanding of these measures. Popular scepticism is understandable: the general public is tired of promises and deteriorating living conditions. The widely-hailed Western orientation has brought no tangible results, and this feeds into public disappointment and frustration.

VI. Conclusions

In the current transitional stage, Georgia has clearly made its choice in favour of the West. The question remains, however, whether this choice is final and irreversible. To a great extent the answer depends on the ability of the local elite to deal with the complex issues of state-building and economic development, and to settle the conflicts in Abkhazia and South Ossetia. Successful resolution of these problems may not only improve Georgia's international image and make it more attractive to foreign investors, but also increase social and political cohesion.

The sustainability of Georgia's pro-Western policies will also depend on the succession to Shevardnadze. Personalities continue to play a decisive role in Georgian politics because its state institutions are not fully developed and are still unable to ensure an automatic and uninterrupted transfer of power through democratic mechanisms. The successor to Shevardnadze will therefore largely determine Georgia's future strategic choices.

External factors and conditions that may influence Georgia's foreign policy behaviour and strategic orientation (including Caspian energy policy, the situation in Russia, relations with the West, regional problems and so on) are uncertain and volatile, and thus difficult to predict.

12. Kazakhstan's security policy in the Caspian Sea region

Konstantin Syroezhkin

The analysis of Kazakhstan's role in the Caspian Sea region requires an exploration of the specific geopolitical processes that are taking place in the region as well as of the various aspects of the social, economic and political situation in the republic. This chapter deals with both.

I. The concept of national security

The shaping of the security doctrine of Kazakhstan has been influenced by a number of internal and especially external factors. The country's leadership has had to take into account (*a*) the ethnic and social composition of the population of the republic; (*b*) the need at least partly to retain economic relations within the framework of the once unified economic complex of the former USSR; (*c*) the activation of the idea of Turkic unity at the beginning of the 1990s; (*d*) the acute need for foreign investment in the economy of Kazakhstan; (*e*) the unfolding geopolitical 'game' around the Central Asian region; and (*f*) the inadequacy of Kazakhstan's own economic and military potential and the need to establish a collective security system.

In its first security doctrine worked out at the end of 1991 and early 1992, Kazakhstan formulated the goal of carrying on bilateral negotiations outside the Commonwealth of Independent States (CIS) mechanism, but at the same time continuing to support the development of the institutions of the CIS. To achieve this goal the country's leadership set three objectives: (*a*) to retain special relations with the Russian Federation; (*b*) to establish a Central Asian Union (CAU); and (*c*) to support the conclusion of a wide-ranging security treaty within the framework of the CIS.[1]

The signing on 15 May 1992 of the Treaty on Collective Security (the Tashkent Treaty)[2] was the first step in attaining one of those objectives. The treaty prohibited its member states from forming other alliances or groups among themselves or with third countries that would be directed against any other signatory. It also specified principles of common security whereby all its

---

[1] Laumulin, M., *Kazakhstan v Sovremennykh Mezhdunarodnykh Otnosheniyakh: Bezopasnost', Geopolitika, Politologiya* [Kazakhstan in present international relations: security, geopolitics, politology] (Almaty, 2000), pp. 130–31.

[2] The original members were Armenia, Kazakhstan, Kyrgyzstan, Russia, Tajikistan and Uzbekistan. Azerbaijan, Belarus and Georgia also joined later. Azerbaijan, Georgia and Uzbekistan left in 1999. On the Tashkent Treaty see chapter 5 in this volume. For the text see *Izvestiya*, 16 May 1992, p. 3.

members would recognize aggression against one as aggression against all.[3] However, the conclusion of the treaty did not solve the problem of creating an integrated collective security system. It began to gain strength only in 1994 when the Taliban movement became active in Afghanistan, and by 1998 the treaty had started to fall apart.

It was not mutual consent of the member states but rather the external threat from the Taliban movement that prolonged the life of the Tashkent Treaty. The seizure of Kabul by the Taliban militia in late 1996 led to the interests of the new independent states of Central Asia and Russia consolidating around the idea of maintaining regional stability and security. Their meeting in Almaty on 4 October 1996 provided a new impulse for the creation of a united anti-Taliban coalition in northern Afghanistan, the Northern Alliance, which was viewed as a buffer screening the Central Asian states from an undesirable influence from outside and a key factor of a stable regional security system.[4] When the anti-Taliban coalition split in 1997–98 and ceased to play the role of a buffer securing the southern frontiers of the CIS, attitudes among the Tashkent Treaty states changed radically. Kyrgyzstan in fact blocked supplies of arms to the Northern Alliance,[5] and Uzbekistan in February 1999 decided to withdraw from the Tashkent Treaty.

In May 1992 President Nursultan Nazarbayev took the first step towards a military doctrine.[6] He formulated its general principles, to be based on peaceful coexistence, non-interference in the internal affairs of other states, the preservation of existing state borders and refusal to use weapons of mass destruction. Practical steps were taken to stabilize the situation in the military sphere, especially in respect of the armed forces. On the political level Nazarbayev was working to obtain security guarantees for Kazakhstan from the USA, China and Russia prior to the removal of nuclear weapons from its territory. The country's leadership succeeded to a certain degree in attaining those objectives. In 1994 Kazakhstan received security guarantees from the USA, China and Russia, and managed to stabilize the situation in the military sphere by concluding a number of bilateral agreements with the Russian Federation.[7]

Kazakhstan's second objective was achieved after Nazarbayev's proposal of March 1994 for a Eurasian Union to be established failed to find support, and the integration processes in the post-Soviet space began to move towards the formation of alternative alliances. The CAU was set up in April 1994. It

[3] 'Dogovor o kollektivnoy bezopasnosti' [Collective security treaty], in *Sbornik Dokumentov po Mezhdunarodnomu Pravu* [Collection of documents on international law] (Almaty, 1998), pp. 260–63. The text was also published in *Izvestiya*, 16 May 1992, p. 3.

[4] Akimbekov, S., *Afganskiy Uzel i Problemy Bezopasnosti v Tsentral'noy Azii* [The Afghan knot and problems of security in Central Asia] (Almaty, 1998), p. 196.

[5] On 9 Sep. 1998 in the town of Osh the Kyrgyz authorities stopped a train carrying arms and ammunitions addressed to Ahmad Shah Massoud. The freight must then have been directed by the Pamir highway to Badakhshan in Afghanistan. This channel of arms supply had probably existed for some time. The Kyrgyz secret services exposed it to the world community and in this way established an actual blockade of the anti-Taliban Northern Alliance. *Izvestiya*, 15 Oct. 1998.

[6] The text of the military doctrine was published in *Kazakhstanskaya Pravda*, 12 Feb. 2000, p. 2.

[7] On these agreements see chapter 5 in this volume.

included Kazakhstan, Kyrgyzstan and Uzbekistan.[8] Although the economic and political problems between its member states continued to be stronger than the forces for unity, the Union did make possible the resolution of certain issues related to their collective security. The formation of another alliance must also be mentioned. This was the 'Shanghai Five', consisting of China, Kazakhstan, Kyrgyzstan, Russia and Tajikistan, which first met in April 1996. Uzbekistan joined in June 2001 and today the organization, originally created to provide a forum for consultation on frontier disputes, build up trust in the military sphere and encourage mutual reductions of armed forces in the frontier areas, has become the Shanghai Cooperation Organization and extended its remit to addressing urgent problems of regional security.[9]

In November 1997 the concept of Kazakhstan's national development until the year 2030 was adopted. National security was the first priority. This strategy was based on the strong belief of the Kazakhstan leadership that neither Russia nor China, nor the Western or Muslim countries had any motive for aggression against Kazakhstan. That presented Kazakhstan with an opportunity to strengthen its economic potential and to build up on this basis a reliable system of national security. Considering this, the following priorities were singled out by the concept of national development: (a) the strengthening of reliable and equitable relations with Russia, the nearest and historically friendly neighbour; (b) the development of trust and good-neighbourly relations with China; (c) the strengthening of relations with leading democratic industrialized countries, including the United States, which were beginning to realize that an independent and prosperous Kazakhstan would suit their national interests; (d) the optimal use of aid and assistance from international institutions and forums (the United Nations, the International Monetary Fund (IMF), the World Bank, and the Asian, European and Islamic development banks); (e) the development of the country's natural resources into a reliable basis for the protection of national sovereignty and territorial integrity; (f) the promotion of patriotism and love of their country among all citizens of Kazakhstan; and (g) a strong demographic and migration policy.[10]

Basically, none of these points is controversial. All are more or less consistent with the geopolitical realities that have developed; but to what extent have these objectives been realized? Has an appropriate economic, political and military potential been built up in Kazakhstan to ensure adequate national security and help Kazakhstan to influence the geopolitical processes under way in Central Asia in general and in the Caspian region in particular? To answer these questions it is necessary to analyse, at least briefly, (a) the way the new balance of forces has developed in the region, (b) the social, economic, political and military reforms in Kazakhstan, and (c) the nature of the new geopolitical

---

[8] On the Central Asian Union see chapter 1 in this volume.

[9] On the Shanghai Cooperation organization see chapter 5, section V in this volume.

[10] Nazarbayev, N., 'Kazakhstan 2030: poslaniye Prezidenta narodu' [Kazakhstan 2030: the message of the president to the people], Almaty, 1997, pp. 119–24.

realities and of the internal and external threats to the national security of Kazakhstan.

II. The development of a new balance of forces

The collapse of the USSR not only meant the disappearance of a superpower but also produced a geopolitical vacuum in Central Asia. Initially, in 1990–96, the existence of this vacuum seemed to be acceptable for all or nearly all the countries that had interests in the region. It was on the whole acceptable for the United States and the West because it guaranteed them against the formation of an anti-US or anti-Western alliance there, meant a further weakening of Russian influence in the region and created opportunities for them to strengthen their own positions. It was acceptable for China because the rivalry between Russia and the USA in the region and the economic and political chaos in the regional states created favourable opportunities for it to build up its own positions there and attain its objective of restoring Great China. It was acceptable for the Islamic countries, mainly because the emergence of new independent states in Central Asia significantly expanded the area for Islam and for Turkic and Muslim solidarity. It suited Russia as well, if not completely. Lacking the material, financial and military resources for unconditional dominance in the region, and being busy establishing links with the USA and West, Russia reduced its presence and influence in Central Asia to control over existing transport routes, predominance in foreign trade, participation in the Tashkent Treaty, and maintaining its military presence in Kyrgyzstan, Tajikistan and Turkmenistan.[11] Finally, it was acceptable for the Central Asian states as well since it provided them with conditions not only for their independent development but also, especially significantly, for the financial prosperity of the local political elites.

However, this did not mean that the geopolitical vacuum and the particular consensus about it would remain for long. The geopolitical importance of the region was much too great.

A most significant change has taken place in recent years in Central Asia. A new balance of geopolitical forces has been formed, and a fundamental revision of political and ideological values and realignment of strategic partners have taken place. Largely this was caused by the policies of Russia towards the states of the region.[12] Russia, having made active efforts for rapprochement with the

[11] E.g., in July 1992 Russia and Turkmenistan signed an agreement on joint command over the former Soviet Armed Forces on the territory of Turkmenistan. Under the agreement, 15 000 (air defence and aviation) of the 60 000 troops were placed under direct Russian control, and others under joint command. In Aug. of the same year another agreement was signed that provided for the presence in Turkmenistan of Russian frontier guards for 5 years, during which they were to provide assistance in the formation of the Turkmen frontier troops. Clark, S., 'Central Asian states: defining security priorities and developing military forces', ed. M. Mandelbaum, *Central Asia and the World: Kazakhstan, Uzbekistan, Tajikistan, Kyrgyzstan, and Turkmenistan* (Council on Foreign Relations Press: New York, 1994), pp. 193–94.

[12] For further detail see Syroezhkin, K., 'The policy of Russia in Central Asia: a perspective from Kazakhstan', ed. G. Chufrin, SIPRI, *Russia and Asia: The Emerging Security Agenda* (Oxford University Press: Oxford, 1999), pp. 100–109.

USA and Western countries, almost lost the opportunity that existed in the 1990s to keep its influence in Central Asia. Moreover, it saw the Central Asian countries as the 'soft underbelly' from which it was prepared to cut itself off at any cost in order to become a part of Europe quickly. Russia in fact still retained its positions in the region. This was not the result of the official policy of Moscow but happened in spite of it. The key role here was played by the weakness of the Tajik political elite. The civil conflict which started in Tajikistan in 1992 left Russia no choice. Its return to the region was conditioned by its involvement in the Tajik conflict and by the need to counter the external threat coming from Afghanistan. From then on Russia's relations with the Central Asian states developed under the influence of this factor.

The openness of the Central Asian states to the outside world created the conditions for them to be increasingly influenced by extra-regional countries, and the geopolitical vacuum in the region began to fill quite rapidly. The countries on the perimeter of Central Asia and the main world powers were tempted to undertake a redistribution of spheres of influence in the post-Soviet space. The strengthening of the USA's role and of the international political and financial institutions controlled by it in the region, attempts by Turkey and Iran to dominate in post-Soviet Central Asia, the strengthening of China's position there, the rearmament and consolidation of Islamic countries—all those factors helped to change the balance of geopolitical forces in the region.

Another factor to be taken into account was that by the end of the 1990s the redistribution of property in Kazakhstan was in the main completed. A new and quite significant player emerged in interstate relations—major domestic and foreign owners of property whose business interests frequently prevailed over the political will of the leaders of their states and determined the dynamics of most of the political processes in the region.

By the end of the 1990s the USA had become one of the main geopolitical players in Central Asia. This was quite logical considering its economic, military and political potentials and the policies of Russia at that period. In the opinion of US analysts, the interests of the USA at that period lay in three areas: (a) the support of democracy and free enterprise; (b) the development of the rich natural resources of the region, first of all in Kazakhstan; and (c) the elimination of a potential threat coming from the strategic nuclear weapons in Kazakhstan.[13] More specifically these objectives were elaborated by Martha Brill Olcott, then adviser to US President George Bush: the United States must work closely with the Central Asian elites, prevent an emergence of anti-US sentiments among them, and have a detailed plan to provide access for young people, scholars and the cultural elite of those republics to 'American' values. Furthermore, the USA must help the Central Asian countries to become independent states—independent first of all from Russia, since only then will

---

[13] Undeland, C. and Platt, N., *The Central Asian Republics: Fragments of Empire, Magnets of Wealth* (Asia Society: New York, 1994), pp. 117–18.

Central Asia, *de jure* independent, become independent de facto; this would help the USA promote its own interests in the region.[14]

In other words, it was important for the USA to resolve several strategic problems in the region: (*a*) preserving strategic stability in Central Asia, since otherwise it would be impossible to maintain US influence there; (*b*) ensuring the elimination of nuclear arms, of the means of their delivery and of nuclear materials deployed there; (*c*) creating conditions that would limit the opportunities for Russia to restore its position as a serious geopolitical force: without Central Asia, or at least without Kazakhstan, this would be impossible; (*d*) taking steps to contain China, which many US analysts saw as about to take its place among the world leaders of the 21st century—control over Central Asia would allow the USA to establish a presence on the western borders of China, where the Xinjiang Uighur Autonomous Region of China, a region of critical importance for China, is located; (*e*) containing Iran; and (*f*) creating conditions that would help strengthen the USA's economic and political influence in Central Asia.

By the mid-1990s the USA had succeeded in attaining most of those objectives. By May 1995 nuclear weapons were withdrawn from the territory of Kazakhstan and launching facilities were dismantled.[15] The TRACECA (Transport Corridor Europe Caucasus Asia) and GUUAM projects were started with a view to preventing the re-emergence of the Russian empire[16] and limiting the influence of Russia in the Caucasus and Central Asia. In 1993–99 US direct investment in Kazakhstan reached approximately $4 billion,[17] making the USA its largest foreign investor. Most US investment went into exploration and production of hydrocarbons and the development of energy and communications facilities—that is, into the spheres whose normal functioning has a direct influence on the country's capabilities and national security. In November 1997 a major production-sharing agreement was signed between Kazakhstan and the USA concerning the Kazakh part of the Caspian Sea shelf, as well as an agreement on economic and strategic partnership. US President Bill Clinton stated that the USA saw Kazakhstan as a key state in Central Asia.[18] In October 1999 Kazakhstan and other states of Central Asia were placed under the responsibility of the US Central Command (CENTCOM).[19]

However, these developments were not without complications. They led to tension between Kazakhstan and the USA, in particular in connection with the

[14] 'United States policy toward Central Asia: statements by F. Kazemzadeh, M. Olcott and G. Mirsky', *Central Asia Monitor*, no. 5 (1992), pp. 24, 28.

[15] For further detail see Laumulin (note 1), pp. 143–59; and Ivatova, L., *SSha vo Vneshney Politike Respubliki Kazakhstan* [The USA in the foreign policy of the Republic of Kazakhstan] (Almaty, 1999), pp. 142–44.

[16] On the TRACECA project see the Internet site, URL <http://www.traceca.org>. GUUAM consists of Azerbaijan, Georgia, Moldova, Ukraine and Uzbekistan, which also participate in the TRACECA project. Their relations with Russia are complex, and to a great extent they depend economically and politically on the West.

[17] Kaufman, W., 'Where investments go', *All Over the Globe*, 7 Dec. 1999, p. 16.

[18] *Kazakhstanskaya Pravda*, 19 Nov. 1997, p. 1.

[19] Burk, A. U., 'The strategy of the USA in the Caspian Sea region', *Strategic Review*, vol. 27, no. 4 (1999), pp. 18–29.

USA's evaluation of the level of democracy of the regime as it has developed in Kazakhstan. The first crisis in relations occurred in 1995 when the Supreme Soviet of Kazakhstan was dissolved and a referendum was held on the extension of the president's powers until 2000. On 29 March 1995 the then US Secretary of State, Warren Christopher, in a speech at the University of Indiana in Bloomington described what had happened in Kazakhstan as a step backwards, and called on Nazarbayev to cancel the referendum and hold parliamentary elections immediately and presidential elections in 1996.[20]

Kazakhstan's leaders did not respond. The crisis was contained, for several reasons. First, the USA wanted to continue to keep under observation the incomplete process of defence industry conversion in Kazakhstan. Second, a break in relations between Kazakhstan and the USA would have substantially reduced the opportunities for the USA to realize its geopolitical strategy in Central Asia. Third, it would entirely destroy the USA's strategy of diversification of Caspian energy strategy. Finally, it was not consistent with the interests of private US business.

Although it was contained, the crisis did not pass unnoticed for Kazakhstan. The USA made it clear that the future status of Kazakh–US relations would be in direct relation to the development of democratic processes in Kazakhstan.[21] As the events of 1998–2000 showed, that was not a mere warning. Whenever the USA needed to put political pressure on the Kazakhstan leadership, the issues of democracy or human rights in Kazakhstan were always brought up, and there was ample occasion for that.[22]

China in its turn clearly understood that internal instability in Central Asia and unresolved problems between the newly independent states there were aggravated by the struggle for spheres of influence in the region between Iran, Russia, Turkey and the USA, while open confrontation with any of them was not in China's interests. Using its potential for expanding trade and economic relations with Central Asia and limiting the negative influence of the political processes going on there on its own predominantly Muslim regions, China encouraged the Central Asian states to define their foreign economic and political priorities for themselves. The political role of the USA in the region was fairly acceptable for the Chinese leadership as it restricted Iran's influence, ensured at least the semblance of market reforms in the region, and reduced the influence of nationalist political forces there.

The presence in the region of Russia, which performed a similar function in relation to the growing Turkish influence, was also acceptable for China.[23] The evaluation of the social and political situation in the new states, which with the

[20] For further detail see Laumulin (note 1), pp. 213–14.

[21] Interview of W. Courtney, US Ambassador to Kazakhstan, in *Panorama* (Almaty), 26 June 1995 (in Russian).

[22] On the controversial character of the US policy towards Kazakhstan see Markin, S., 'Kazahstanskaya politika vashingtonskoy administratsii' [The Kazakhstan policy of the Washington Administration], *Central Asia and the Caucasus* (Luleå), no. 2 (8) (2000), pp. 79–87.

[23] *ZhongYa Yanjiu*, nos 1–2 (1992), pp. 14–15; and Harris, L. C., 'Xinjian, Central Asia and the implications for China's policy in the Islamic world', *China Quarterly*, no. 133 (Mar. 1993), p. 125.

exception of Tajikistan was viewed as relatively stable, was also of substantial importance for Chinese policy in post-Soviet Central Asia. In China's opinion, in spite of the significant political changes that had taken place in these states and the renaming or dissolution of former communist parties, real power still remained in the hands of reformers from the leadership of those parties.[24] The Chinese leadership therefore set itself the goal of supporting the existing political regimes in the Central Asian states. It also aimed among other things to help to resolve the problem of the growing influence of Islamic fundamentalists and Pan-Turkists in the Muslim regions of China itself, since, in the opinion of Chinese analysts, the Central Asian regimes were also apprehensive of the threats of Pan-Turkism and Islamic fundamentalism (especially the latter) and wanted to keep them in check.[25] This formulation of the issue was explained by the need to preserve stability in those regions of China that are predominantly Muslim. Both the central and the local Chinese authorities believed that their stability was directly related to the situation in the neighbouring Muslim republics that had gained independence.[26]

By following this course over the past decade China has succeeded in solving four important problems. First, the territorial disputes with Central Asian states were settled in its favour, and the latter lost their major negotiating chip in any further dealings with China. Second, China strengthened its positions in all the states of the region both by building up its economic presence there and by becoming one of the main participants of the regional security system being formed. Third, in signing treaties with the states of Central Asia, China succeeded in gaining their support regarding the need to resist ethnic separatism and thus in splitting the Muslim population of Xinjiang from related ethnic groups in Central Asian states. Finally, as Russia and the new Central Asian states remained engulfed in political and economic crisis, a security threat from the north disappeared, thus leaving China with an opportunity to focus its attention on resolving other problems, such as developing its national economy and restoring Great China.

Iran, Pakistan and Turkey can hardly be considered important independent geopolitical players, despite the recent strengthening of their positions in Central Asia. However, having strong interests in the region and having established relations with various political factions there, those countries were playing an important role in the geopolitical game in Central Asia. Their policies were taken into account not only by the main geopolitical players—China, Russia and the USA—but also by the regional states, as the latter were striving to gain the maximum dividends from the conflict of interests between Russia and the USA in the Caspian region. Clear confirmation of that was provided by the positions taken by the Central Asian states, and by Kazakhstan in particular, in the debates regarding (a) the routes for the transport of hydrocarbon raw materials from the Caspian region, and (b) ways to resolve the Afghan problem.

[24] *ZhongYa Yanjiu* (consolidated issue), 1993, p. 24.
[25] *ZhongYa Yanjiu* (consolidated issue), 1993, p. 29.
[26] Harris (note 23), p. 125.

To conclude this analysis of the present geopolitical situation in the region, Kazakhstan has succeeded in solving its main national security problem, the preservation of its sovereignty and territorial integrity. This is partly thanks to its declared multi-directional foreign policy, but mainly because of Russia's lack of a clear Central Asian policy and the interest of China and the USA in maintaining the current political regime. Kazakhstan also succeeded in another foreign policy task—maintaining equitable relations with all interested states and keeping away from anti-Russian or anti-US blocs.

III. Social and economic reforms in Kazakhstan as a precondition of its national security

The concept of national security in relation to the nature of a political regime and the objectives proclaimed for the development of the state and society can be viewed in two ways. In a broad sense they can be seen as a set of measures ensuring favourable conditions for a normal life for the citizens of the country, who provide the basis for the free development of future generations. The role of the state as an institutional and ideologically organized form of power in this case is in making those conditions secure. In a narrow sense they can be seen as a set of measures to ensure the security of a state as an instrument of power for the ruling elite, that is, a group of individuals brought together by their corporate interests who are interested in creating the conditions to ensure their personal security and the security of their closest entourage. In this case the role of the state is to protect the corporate interests of this group from a negative reaction from the society and from external factors.

It is in this narrow sense that the national security strategy of Kazakhstan and the consequences of the social, economic and political reforms there are to be understood. A detailed description of the process of those reforms will not be attempted here: this chapter instead presents a few of their consequences in the context of the future development of the security of the state and of the society as a whole.

After national statehood was achieved, the development of society in Kazakhstan went in three directions. First, a bureaucratic ('comprador') bourgeoisie, wrongly identified as a national bourgeoisie, was formed. Second, different social groups were struggling to adapt more or less to the new economic realities. Among them were a few national entrepreneurs; workers and employees of industrial enterprises mainly operated by foreign managers; farmers who had changed over to traditional forms of labour; and those engaged in different services, such as 'shuttle traders', small and medium-size traders and craftsmen, and certain categories of technocrats and intellectuals. Third, an integral and constantly growing part of the society was the huge mass of marginalized individuals formally rejected by the society.

According to Arystan Esentugelov, Director of the Institute for Economic Research, the share of the most affluent in the population of Kazakhstan is only

3.3 per cent, while that of the poorest is 61 per cent.[27] According to Alikhan Baimenov, Minister of Labour and Social Welfare, around 66 per cent of the working population of the republic earn less than 13 000 tenge per month and 90 000 employees earn less than the minimum wage (2680 tenge).[28] The dangerous dynamic of the spread of poverty in Kazakhstan since 1996 has been reflected in official statistical publications. According to them the proportion of the population that is living on an income below subsistence level is now around 33 per cent.[29] In the opinion of this author this figure is substantially understated: after the major devaluation of the tenge in April 1999,[30] even judging by official publications, it was rapidly approaching 50 per cent.[31]

Thus, the transformation of the socialist property system has not led to the expected emergence of free property-owners and a free market, the establishment of a fair economic and legal environment, or the formation of a middle class. On the contrary, the society has found itself split into a minority of owners and a majority of non-owners. Instead of the emergence of free entrepreneurs it saw the development of the comprador bourgeoisie with all the attendant consequences associated with the growth of the 'shadow' economy and the collapse of the 'real' sector of the economy, the spread of corruption, the coalescence of power and mafia structures, and insufficient development of national industry. Kazakhstan was becoming a 'banana republic'.

First and foremost, this was the result of lack of vision in the economic development strategy of Kazakhstan. Second, as there has been extensive destruction of the country's productive forces the normal production process has become increasingly threatened. There are certain limits to the destruction of industrial infrastructure after which a nation loses its capacity to have an independent economy. In Kazakhstan those limits have not been reached yet, but if the existing trends continue the probability of them being reached will greatly increase. Third, the practice of transferring (in fact, selling) national enterprises to foreign owners has reached a scale which is disastrous for the country's economy. Foreigners already control entire sectors of the economy—the greater part of the oil and gas sector, the chemical industry, and ferrous and non-ferrous metals. In a situation when more than 70 per cent of industrial output and 90 per cent of industrial capacity are owned or controlled by foreign firms and companies it is difficult not to agree with Umirserik Kasenov, who claimed that it

---

[27] Esengulov, A., 'Novoye pravitelstvo Kazakhstana: naslediye i perspektivy' [The new government of Kazakhstan: heritage and prospects], *Asia: Ekonomika i Zhizn'*, no. 51 (Dec. 1997).

[28] Interfax (Kazakhstan), 25 Sep. 2000.

[29] *Kratkiy Statisticheskiy Ezhegodnik Kazakhstana, 2000* [Short statistical yearbook of Kazakhstan, 2000], Almaty, 2000, p. 25.

[30] The tenge fell against the US dollar by almost 50%. *Kazakhstan Economic Trends: Quarterly Issue Apr.–June 1999* (European Commission, Brussels), Sep. 1999, p. 115.

[31] Nusupova, A. and Nusupov, A., 'Za chertoy bednosti' [Below the poverty line], *Delovaya Nedelya*, 9 June 2000.

was no longer a threat, but that Kazakhstan had actually lost its economic independence[32]—incidentally paid for at the expense of Kazakhstan itself.[33]

These processes resulted in comprador businesses dominating those business groups in the 'real' economy which work (or are trying to work) for the local market and for the development of genuine productive industry. This phenomenon is known to all countries that have been undergoing transformation and is quite understandable: the market immediately finds the fastest and easiest methods of making money. The experience of the countries that were most successful in the transformation proves that the main part in fighting the compradors has to be played by the state. Unfortunately productive business has not yet begun to overtake comprador business in Kazakhstan. As of today, the argument between the comprador bourgeoisie and the nascent national bourgeoisie has been won by the former, supported by foreign owners.

The main reason for this was political. The government openly changed its attitude towards the nascent national bourgeoisie when it saw in it a serious force. However, the government's hope that dealing with foreign capital would be easier and simpler than dealing with the national entrepreneurial bourgeoisie proved to be a myth.

This problem was one of the main issues of national economic security discussed in the National Security Council (NSC) in 2000. President Nazarbayev unequivocally emphasized that on the agenda was the defence of Kazakhstan's national interests, while Kairat Kelimbetov, Chairman of the Agency for Strategic Planning, specified that this problem was related to the activities of foreign companies in the republic and their failure to comply with national legislation.[34] The intention of the leadership to rely on oil and gas resources in national development is therefore untenable. Today foreign companies in Kazakhstan already control more than 80 per cent of crude oil production, own the most advanced refinery, and control 95 per cent of shares in the Offshore Kazakhstan International Operating Company (OKIOC),[35] and when oil and oil products account for over 40 per cent of export revenues[36] the question arises what will happen if foreign companies reduce or stop production, even for the most justifiable reason (such as a fall in oil prices, as has already happened more than once).

As 'reforms' went on, the motivation for conscientious creative work was destroyed. Standstills, a high turnover of personnel and rising unemployment drastically facilitated the process of deprofessionalization of personnel, and this resulted in significant losses of the intellectual and organizational potential of the country. According to Alikhan Baimenov, out of an economically active

[32] Kasenov, U., 'Natsional'naya bezopasnost' Respubliki Kazakhstan: "okna uyazvimosti"' [National security of the Republic of Kazakhstan: 'windows of vulnerability'], *Delovaya Nedelya*, 11 Sep. 1998.

[33] According to the latest available data capital flight from Kazakhstan has been on the increase, reaching 3% of GDP in 1996, 5.2% in 1997 and 7.7% in 1999. Diugai, N., 'On capital flight from Kazakhstan', *Kazakhstan Economic Trends: Quarterly Issue, Apr.–June 2000* (European Commission, Brussels), p. 21.

[34] *Panorama* (Almaty), no. 47 (1 Dec. 2000).

[35] *Delovoye Obozreniye Respublika*, no. 25 (16 Nov. 2000), p. 2.

[36] *Kazakhstan Economic Trends: Quarterly Issue, Apr.–June 2000* (note 33), p. 182.

Table 12.1. Immigration to and emigration from Kazakhstan
Figures are in thousand persons.

Year	No. of immigrants	No. of emigrants	Balance
1990	155.1	300.2	− 145.1
1991	206.1	255.0	− 48.9
1992	190.3	369.2	− 178.9
1993	111.3	333.4	− 222.1
1994	70.4	480.8	− 410.4
1995	71.1	309.6	− 238.5
1996	53.9	229.4	− 175.5
1997	38.1	299.5	− 261.4
1998	40.6	243.7	− 203.1
Total	**936.9**	**2 820.8**	**− 1 883.9**

Source. Statistical Agency of the Republic of Kazakhstan.

population of 7 million, only 2.68 million people or 38.3 per cent are employed by large legal enterprises. The other 61.7 per cent are either self-employed or unemployed.[37] The number of the officially registered unemployed increased from 4000 in 1991 to 287 900 in April 2000.[38] Not only are those figures depressing; they also mean either that the state is not interested in the development of domestic production or that it is not interested in helping local manufacturers. Neither of these possibilities promises anything good for the ordinary citizens of Kazakhstan.

The narcotics trade and drug addiction are another major threat to the social and political stability of the country. The number of drug addicts increased by 400–13 000 per cent in different regions of the country over the 10 years 1991–2000. In 1997 there were 26 584 addicts officially registered in Kazakhstan, but according to the UN Office for Drugs Control and Crime Prevention (UNODCCP), their number is actually around 200 000.[39] Addicts have become much younger—the average age is down to 25 years and the majority are juveniles between 13 and 16 years of age. According to Rahat Aliyev, Deputy Chairman of the NSC and Director of the NSC division for the city of Almaty and Almaty Province, the number of children and juveniles who use drugs has grown 10-fold within the past five years.[40] The volume of traffic in narcotics has also increased significantly. Not very long ago people spoke in terms of grams and kilograms; now it is tonnes of drugs, not only of the cannabis group but also of opiates, psycho-stimulants and hallucinogens. Heroin and its derivatives have an increasing share in the traffic. According to the NSC division for

[37] Interfax (Kazakhstan), 25 Sep. 2000.
[38] *Statisticheskiy Press-Bulleten* [Statistical press bulletin] (Almaty), no. 1 (2000), p. 63.
[39] UN Office for Drug Control and Crime Prevention, *Central Asia Review 2000* (Tashkent), p. 7.
[40] *Panorama* (Almaty), no. 47 (1 Dec. 2000), p. 1.

the city of Almaty and Almaty Province, in 2000 alone the authorities there seized 2 tonnes of drugs, of which 1150 kg were strong narcotics.[41]

The states of Central Asia have become involved in international drug transit and turned into an entrepôt for drugs of Afghan origin. Stable criminal groups have formed which are oriented exclusively to the drugs business. There is a high probability (in some cases it is already a reality) of their merging with the government and law enforcement structures. The seizure of 86 kg of heroin in cars owned by the Embassy of Tajikistan in Kazakhstan and the liquidation of 31 drug transit channels by the NSC division for the city of Almaty and Almaty Province are examples of that.[42] For a large part of the population in some Central Asian states the drugs business has become the principal source of their livelihood, and this is understandable. It is tempting to receive $100–200 for taking drugs over the border in a country where the minimum living wage is $5–10 per month. The activities of criminal gangs and terrorist groups operating in Afghanistan, Russia and a number of areas in Central Asia are directly connected to the drugs business. They use drugs not only for the purchase of arms but also to apply pressure on their political opponents.

Aside from that the drugs trade is creating permanent tensions at the Afghan border and indirectly helps to expand the social base of ethnic separatism and Islamic extremism in the region, whose followers' activities look increasingly like terrorist acts.[43]

Evaluating Kazakhstan's potential to ensure its national security, the government's demographic policy should be mentioned. As was mentioned above, it is seen as a national security priority. Around 3 million people have left Kazakhstan in the 10 years since it became independent (see table 12.1). It is active and educated people who emigrate. Of those 3 million who emigrated, 65 per cent were people of working age, 25 per cent were young people, and 45 per cent had higher and secondary vocational education.[44] Also, as surveys show, it is not so much the economic situation that drives people from Kazakhstan as uncertainty as to their own future, moral and psychological dissatisfaction with their status, and concern about the future of their children.[45]

In the opinion of many experts, the main domestic threats to national security are the criminalization of society and official corruption.[46] The two are related.

[41] Nazarbayev, N., 'Bezopasnost' v regione mozhno obespechit' tolko sovmestnymi usiliyami' [Security in the region can be ensured only with joint efforts], *Analiticheskoye Obozreniye*, no. 1 (Oct. 2000), p. 4; and *Panorama* (Almaty), no. 47 (1 Dec. 2000).

[42] Aliyev, R., 'S narkomaniyey nuzhno borotsya vsem obshchestvom' [Drug addiction must be fought by the entire society], *Kontinent* (Almaty), no. 15 (2000), p. 17; and *Panorama* (Almaty), no. 47 (1 Dec. 2000), p. 1.

[43] For more detail on the problem of drug addiction and narcotics transit in Central Asia see *Kontinent* (Almaty), no. 15 (2000).

[44] Shaimerdenov, I., 'Po nekotorym otsenkam za posledniye 10 let Kazakhstan pokinulo okolo 3 millionov chelovek' [According to some estimates 3 million people left Kazakhstan in the past 10 years], *Panorama*, no. 3 (Jan. 2000).

[45] Brusilovskaya, Ye., 'Chego my boimsya bol'she vsego' [What we fear more than anything], *Argumenty i Fakty*, Mar. 1999; and Sergienko, V., 'Migratsiya v Kazakhstane: poteri i priobreteniya' [Migration in Kazakhstan: losses and acquisitions], *Kontinent* (Almaty), no. 9 (1999), pp. 16–18.

[46] *Natsional'naya Bezopasnost' Kazakhstana: Ierarkhiya Ugroz* [National security of Kazakhstan: hierarchy of threats] (Almaty, 2000), pp. 81–83.

Many officials feel that they are above the law and indulge in arbitrary and permissive behaviour. This is accompanied by a complete loss of control by the state, and democratic institutions are weak. It is therefore quite natural that corruption in Kazakhstan has penetrated practically all the branches of power. Under conditions when the share of the 'shadow' economy is estimated at 40–50 per cent of gross domestic product (GDP),[47] this permissiveness and arbitrariness on the part of officials leads to them merging with the criminal world and to the state being transformed into a mafia state.

There is no doubt that a reduction of the role of the state in the society, especially in the economic sphere, is necessary in the future. However, there is a real question mark over how far the society is ready to accept a reduced regulatory role for the state. Under existing conditions in Kazakhstan, such a reduction looks like a departure by the state from its responsibilities, in particular its responsibility for social and political stability. The more the state promotes ideas of free economy, the more difficult it is for it to control the social and political processes which are under way, especially in conditions where there is no self-regulation of social processes at all.

It is quite logical that the majority of the population of Kazakhstan view the situation in the country as a crisis, close to disaster or even already a disaster.[48] Hence the growth of social tensions in Kazakhstan. According to information provided by the office of the Procurator General, in January–September 1999 alone 808 protest actions took place in Kazakhstan, of which 284 were unauthorized. According to an opinion poll conducted in January 2000 by the Almaty Association of Sociologists and Politologists, 30.1 per cent of those polled answered 'yes' and another 16.8 per cent 'perhaps' when asked if they were ready to participate in actions of mass protest to defend their constitutional rights and freedoms.[49]

To summarize, the political situation in Kazakhstan is approaching a critical stage characterized by: (a) a general popular distrust of politicians; (b) the incompetence of the authorities and their inability to resolve the accumulated social and economic problems, while social polarization continues to grow and contradictions between the managed and the managers become more and more obvious; (c) a personnel crisis, which is becoming all the more evident because of the widespread corruption of officials and the authorities' inability to take adequate measures to eradicate this corruption; (d) the criminalization of society, the coalescence of government officials with the underworld and the growth of organized crime; and (e) an increase in inter-ethnic tensions and irredentist movements.

---

[47] 'V Kazakhstane s korruptsiyey borotsya ne tolko ne umeyut, no i ne hotyat' [In Kazakhstan they not only cannot, they do not want to fight corruption], *Nachnem s Ponedel'nitsa*, 17 Nov. 1999.
[48] 'Aktsii massovogo protesta: eto nashe zavtra, a segodnya?' [Actions of mass protest: this is our tomorrow, but today? Poll by the Almaty Association of Sociologists and Politologists in Jan. 2000], *All Over the Globe*, 11 Feb. 2000.
[49] 'Aktsii massovogo protesta: eto nashe zavtra, a segodnya?' (note 48).

IV. New challenges and new approaches

At the end of the 1990s several significant events took place which in one way or another influenced the geopolitical situation in Central Asia and the balance of forces there.

Above all the foreign policy of Russia changed. In contrast to the period of orientation towards the USA when Andrey Kozyrev was foreign minister, the foreign policy of Russia, without denying the need to expand and strengthen relations with the West, is now focused on the East as well, in particular on Central Asia. It has become, if not tougher, certainly more pragmatic, and the national interest, in particular economic interests, predominates. These aspects of the Russian foreign policy became especially clear after the election of Vladimir Putin as president. Although it would be premature to speak of an integrated Russian foreign policy concept with regard to Central Asia today, it is impossible to deny that Russia is returning to this region, and not only in the political but also in the economic sense.

Notwithstanding the Central Asian states' participation in the NATO Partnership for Peace (PFP) programme, the USA's financing of certain programmes for ensuring security in the region, and uncertainty as to the positions of several Central Asian states on some key security issues, it is Russia (albeit jointly with China) that has become the main guarantor of security in Central Asia. Moreover it can be safely predicted that Russia's significance as protector of the security of the region will only increase because: (*a*) a repetition of the events of 1999 and 2000 in Kyrgyzstan and Uzbekistan is inevitable;[50] (*b*) new security challenges are emerging in the region; (*c*) there will inevitably be changes in the US foreign policy priorities following the change of administration in Washington; and (*d*) Russia will become economically stronger.

This became particularly evident between the spring and autumn of 2000, when the incursion of Islamic militants into Kyrgyzstan and Uzbekistan took place and theoretical talks on the need to coordinate interstate positions on ensuring security moved onto a practical plane. In March 2000 in Astana at a session of the ministers of defence of the Shanghai Forum, Kazakhstan, Kyrgyzstan, Russia and Tajikistan announced the formation of a CIS anti-terrorist centre.[51] In May 2000 the Collective Security Council (CSC) of the six Tashkent Treaty member states[52] met in Minsk. A number of important documents and decisions aimed at reanimating the Tashkent Treaty and transforming it into a functioning tool for ensuring the security of the member states were considered and adopted at this session.[53] In September 2000 Sergey

---

[50] These fears are expressed by the leadership of Kazakhstan. The Secretary of the NSC, Marat Tazhin, stated that there was every reason to expect an aggravation of the situation on the southern frontiers of the Central Asian region in the spring and summer of 2001 (although there is no direct threat to Kazakhstan yet). *Panorama* (Almaty), no. 47 (1 Dec. 2000), p. 2.

[51] See also chapter 5 in this volume.

[52] Now Armenia, Belarus, Kazakhstan, Kyrgyzstan, Russia and Tajikistan.

[53] Nikolayenko, V., 'Netraditsionnye otvety novym ugrozam' [Non-traditional responses to new threats], *Sodruzhestvo NG* [supplement to *Nezavisimaya Gazeta*], 27 Sep. 2000.

Ivanov, Secretary of the Russian Security Council, called on the heads of security councils of the Tashkent Treaty countries to stand up jointly to international terrorism. Finally, in October at the session of the CSC in Bishkek, the six heads of state signed an agreement on the Status of Forces and Facilities of the Collective Security System in the region, and approved a plan for the formation of a regional system of collective security. Under the agreements reached the parties may send military formations to the territories of Tashkent Treaty member states at their request and in coordination with them for joint deterrence of external military aggression, joint counter-terrorist operations, or command-and-staff and military exercises.[54] In December 2000 the Kazakhstan Majlis adopted a decision that allowed for Kazakh military contingents to participate in military operations beyond the national borders. No less significantly, the Tashkent Treaty countries were given the opportunity to buy Russian arms at reduced prices, which was important not only for the modernization of their armed forces but also for enhancing their combat readiness.[55]

Russia is also winning the battle for transport of hydrocarbons from the Caspian region. Today the Russian routes and the Caspian Pipeline Consortium (CPC) are the only real option. The last joint of the CPC Tengiz–Novorossiysk pipeline system which provides a link between the new pipeline and the sea terminal has been welded. On 30 June 2001 the first tanker loaded with Caspian oil was expected to depart from the terminal in Novorossiysk, and this means that the route for the transport of Caspian oil has been finalized. This does not, of course, preclude the possibility of alternative routes being built, but at least two prerequisites are necessary for that—confirmation that commercially viable hydrocarbon reserves in the Caspian are available, and confirmation that those alternative routes are cost-effective. For the immediate future, neither of these conditions is met.

Some progress, at least within the framework of the Tashkent Treaty, was also made with regard to the threat from the Taliban in Afghanistan. The USA takes a similar view of the Taliban. Thomas Pickering, former US Under Secretary of State, has stated that Russia and the USA share the profound sense of threat from the Taliban and have agreed to strengthen sanctions against their regime because of its support for international terrorism and drugs dealing.[56] Unfortunately, so far this threat has been underestimated by Turkmenistan and Uzbekistan, which are ready to collaborate with the Taliban,[57] and by certain officials in Astana who are not hostile to such groups in Afghanistan.[58] Time will show how Russia and the USA will act, but it is already clear that Kazakhstan's multi-directional policy has nothing further to offer and that in the

[54] Odnokolenko, O., 'Kontingent vyzyvali?' [Called a contingent?], *Segodnya*, 12 Oct. 2000.

[55] Mohov, V., 'Dogovor o kollektivnoy bezopasnosti napolnyaetsya konkretnym soderzhaniem' [The Collective Security Treaty is given concrete substance], *Krasnaya Zvezda*, 13 Oct. 2000.

[56] 'Pickering on talks with Russians about Taliban', URL <http://www.usembassy.ro/USIS/Washington-File/300/00-10-18/eur311.htm>.

[57] Chernogayev, Yu., 'Podal'she ot Talibov' [Keep away from the Taliban], *Kommersant*, 5 Oct. 2000.

[58] 'K vizitu glavy Islamskoy Respubliki Pakistan generala Perveza Musharafa' [On the visit of General Pervez Musharaf, Head of the Islamic Republic of Pakistan], *Kazakhstanskaya Pravda*, 7 Nov. 2000.

immediate future all the states of Central Asia will have finally to determine their strategic priorities.

What has happened in Central Asia, and why did the return of Russia to the region happen so quickly? Doubtless the main factor in this, as mentioned above, was the change in Russia's foreign policy. The states of the region ceased to be seen as the Asian 'soft underbelly' and were placed in the category of strategic partners who are able to help in building not only their own security but also the security of Russia on its southern frontiers.

There were also other factors.

First and foremost, threats that had previously been discussed on an academic level suddenly became a reality. The spread of drugs and drugs trafficking through the territory of the Central Asian states, terrorism and extremism in their various manifestations, the prospect of another military intrusion, frontier problems, latent ethnic conflicts, confrontation over water and natural resources—all have priority in national security. Those problems are real not only for the states of Central Asia but for Russia itself, which encountered them before they did. Today, when those problems are becoming more acute in the region, the Russian experience of dealing with them is more useful than ever. Because of their economic situation and limited military potential, the states of Central Asia are not in a position to deal with these problems on their own. Finally, it is understood in Russia that if it does not localize these threats in the Central Asian region then it runs the risk of expanding the instability on its own southern frontiers.

Second, Russia's return to the region was also just as much influenced by the change in the attitude of the regional states—particularly Kazakhstan—towards the USA and by US policy in the region. By the end of the 1990s relations between the USA and the states of Central Asia had gradually moved from the economic to the political sphere. The logic of these changes is quite under-standable. The USA has gained such a degree of influence in the region that it can use a wide range of methods of economic and political leverage in the event of a threat to its national interests. The strengthening of Russia's position in Central Asia was regarded as such a threat. As soon as the administration of President Bill Clinton realized that years of effort to draw the Central Asian states into the sphere of US foreign policy might be lost, massive political coercion began. The political regimes of Central Asian states began to be described as authoritarian. Scandalous material on corruption in the highest echelons of the Central Asian governments appeared in the US press.[59] In the spring of 2000, Uzbekistan, Kyrgyzstan and Kazakhstan were visited, literally one after another, by the Director of the US Central Intelligence Agency (CIA), George Tenet, the Director of the Federal Bureau of Intelligence (FBI), Louis Freeh, and finally then Secretary of State Madeleine Albright. Aside from the

[59] Minutes of the US Congress Sessions, 2nd session of the 106th Convocation: Resolution 397 of the House of Representatives, *Congressional Record*, 1 Nov. 2000, URL <http://frwebgate.access.gpo.gov/cgi-bin/multidb.cgi>; Tagliabu, J., 'Kazakhstan is suspected of oil bribes worth USD100 million', *New York Times*, 28 July 2000; and Perlmutter, A., 'Kazakhstan: more words than deeds', *Washington Times*, 4 Oct. 2000.

declared objectives (clarifying the prospects for US business in the region and the human rights situation), all these visitors explored the attitudes of the Central Asian presidents to strengthening ties with Moscow. Nor was it by chance that these visits were made by very senior representatives of the US Administration: they were to demonstrate the USA's potential to influence the political situation in Central Asian states in the event of any of them being inclined to take decisions which were not in the strategic interests of the USA in the region. (The results of this strategy proved, in fact, quite discouraging, because the real threats to the region's security were more significant than those that can be dealt with by injections of cash or troop landings in the framework of PFP exercises.) The USA's persistent attempts to put political pressure on the states of the region were not only negatively received in those states, but were criticized in the USA, too.

A third factor that helped the states of Central Asia and Russia to draw closer was their liberation from the illusions of the first years of independence. While their own resources turned out not to be a sufficient basis for ensuring economic growth, the financial aid and investment promised by the West remained mainly good intentions. Furthermore, as became apparent, at least to the Kazakhstan leadership, foreign investors were no less a threat to the economic security of the country than dishonest domestic businessmen. In conformity with the new realities certain changes appeared in Kazakhstan in approaches to the issues of national security.

In a message to the people of the country on 24 October 2000, President Nazarbayev set out four principal priorities for the medium term.[60] The first was building an efficient system of regional security in Central Asia with the Tashkent Treaty and the Shanghai Forum as its basis. The second was military reform aimed at building a strong modern army. The objectives of implementing the military doctrine and military reform concept that had already been adopted were highlighted within the framework of this priority. The government was instructed to allocate annually not less than 1 per cent of GDP for the needs of the Ministry of Defence, to build an advanced system of territorial defence and to restore a comprehensive system of mobilization training. Third was the fight against drugs and drugs trafficking. Concrete objectives were set to introduce programmes to fight drugs and drugs trafficking in every province and to earmark funds in the budget of every district for such programmes. Finally, the fourth priority was the implementation of an economic security strategy. In accordance with presidential instructions, the Agency for Strategic Planning and the NSC prepared a draft Strategy of National Economic Security in which the experience of other countries that had undergone similar economic transformation was examined exhaustively. This allowed four main elements of the economic security of Kazakhstan to be identified—structural, technological, institutional and financial—as well as specific measures to implement them.[61]

[60] *Kazakhstanskaya Pravda*, 25 Oct. 2000, p. 1.
[61] Tazhin, M., 'Vyzovam vremeni—pravil'nye otvety' [Right response to the challenges of the time], *Kazakhstanskaya Pravda*, 24 Nov. 2000.

Some work is being done today on the practical implementation of those priorities. The strengthening of the Tashkent Treaty system and the creation of the CIS anti-terrorist centre have been mentioned above. In April 2000 a treaty on 'joint efforts to fight terrorism, political and religious extremism, transnational organized crime and other threats to the stability and security of the parties' was signed by all the Central Asian states with the exception of Turkmenistan. Work continued on ways of enhancing the potential of the Shanghai Forum in fighting security threats in the region. Along with this Kazakhstan is continuing the speedy reinforcement of its borders. This includes the creation of four military districts, additional military units and formations along the border, new clearance points in the southern part of the border, mobile military units, and an air force formation to secure efficient control of the entire airspace of Kazakhstan. In order to fight extremism and terrorism Kazakhstan is taking a range of legal and operative measures to prevent illegal activities of unregistered religious communities, sects and spiritual educational organizations. Finally, measures are being undertaken to strengthen passport and visa controls as well as control of international transport communications.[62]

[62] Tazhin, M., 'Natsional'naya bezopasnost' Kazakhstana: novoye ponimaniye, novye podkhody' [The national security of Kazakhstan: new understanding, new approaches], *Analiticheskoye Obozreniye*, Oct. 2000, pp. 9–10.

13. Turkmenistan's quest for economic security

Najia Badykova

I. Introduction

Today Turkmenistan is one of the largest gas-producing countries in the Caspian Sea region. However, at present it cannot fully use its vast potential. The major problems it faces are a lack of alternative gas export routes—it is still very dependent on the existing Central Asia–Centre pipeline, which runs from Ashkhabad to Aleksandrov-Gay; the need for foreign investment and technologies to fully develop the energy industry; and competition among gas-producing countries in the region.

The energy sector is central to Turkmenistan's economic security. However, the availability of vast resources does not by itself guarantee political or economic security. These resources, being strategic by their nature, have attracted the attention of large countries which already control or are trying to maintain control over energy markets. A paradoxical situation exists in another sense as well: hydrocarbon resources can both ensure economic security and destabilize the economy at the same time. Algeria, Gabon and Nigeria, for example, have considerable hydrocarbon resources but have failed to use them in a such way as to benefit their economies because economic programmes, the development of infrastructure and the distribution of revenue also play a significant role in overall economic success.

The current situation regarding the energy resources of the Caspian Sea region is volatile and almost impossible to predict, but the issue of gas exports has become crucial for its future as well as for the future of Turkmenistan, as gas is Turkmenistan's major export commodity.

II. The role of energy resources in the political and economic security of Turkmenistan

The present state of the fuel and energy sector[1]

The energy sector is the core of the Turkmen economy. It generates 80 per cent of all foreign currency revenues and accounts for 50 per cent of budget revenues. The share of the oil and gas industry in gross domestic product (GDP) hovers around 30–50 per cent. The degree of export specialization of the energy

---

[1] All data presented in this section are calculated by the author from official data published by the Statistical Office, Ashkhabad, in *Social–Economic Situation in Turkmenistan 1998–99* and *Jan.–Oct. 2000* (2000); *Foreign Economic Activity of Turkmenistan 1994–97* and *1997–99* (2000); and *Turkmenistan's Industry in 1999* (2000) (in English).

industry is very high. Up to 92 per cent of total gas production and approximately 65–70 per cent of the oil produced are currently exported.[2]

Turkmenistan supplies all its needs for oil and gas products. Its economic policy is focused on minimizing dependence on exports of gas and the import of food products. For example, in 1999 grain imports fell by volume to 0.15 per cent of what they had been in 1990, while domestic grain production increased from 450 000 to 1 510 000 tons. At present Turkmenistan meets its own needs for grain for food and animal feed. There was also a significant increase in the role of oil production and oil-processing industries in the national economy during the 1990s. Oil production in 1999 was twice that of 1990, which, along with increased oil prices, boosted export revenues from oil production.[3]

Significant progress has been made in cotton processing. In recent years over 30 factories have been built and the proportion of locally-produced cotton that is processed has increased from 3 per cent in 1990 to 35 per cent in 1999.

It is difficult to overestimate the role of the energy sector in the economy of Turkmenistan. Despite numerous programmes targeting the development of other sectors, high priority is given to the oil and gas industry and the maximization of revenues from the export of hydrocarbons. The economy is organized in a such way as to allow the government to control all hard-currency transactions, especially revenues from gas exports. More than 50 per cent of foreign credits are allocated for the development of the gas industry while 60 per cent of total investments are directed to the energy sector.

Fluctuations in the balance of trade are directly correlated with the volume of gas exports. For example, a sharp decline in exports in 1997 along with a boom in construction radically affected the balance of trade. During the four years 1997–2000 the national balance of trade went into deficit, which caused a growth of external financing and difficulties in debt servicing, but a further crisis was prevented by an increase in gas exports. During the first nine months of 2000, the balance of trade was over $400 million in surplus.

The export potential

Turkmenistan has strong export potential. According to the programme on Social–Economic Development of Turkmenistan to the year 2010,[4] as of now more than 1000 prospective oil and gas fields have been discovered. Within the national boundaries of Turkmenistan in the Caspian Sea over 70 potential oil reservoirs have been located. Major deposits of hydrocarbon resources are concentrated in two regions—the south Caspian and the Amu Darya river.

There are 127 gas fields listed on government accounts as assets, 39 of which are being actively explored. Total gas reserves, including those in production,

---

[2] Turkmenistan Ministry of Economy and Finance and Turkmenistan National Institute of Statistics and Forecasting, 'National programme of President Saparmurat Turkmenbashi: Social–economic development to the year 2010', Ashkhabad, 1999, p. 204 (in English).

[3] 'Gazprom: po materialam godovogo otchota' [Gazprom: from the annual report materials], *Neftegazovaya Vertikal* (Moscow), nos 7–8 (2000), pp. 63, 66.

[4] 'National programme of President Saparmurat Turkmenbashi' (note 2).

prospective reserves and others, amount to around 23 trillion cubic metres. In oil equivalent, total hydrocarbon reserves amount to 35.5 billion tons.[5]

Strategic trends in the oil and gas industry of Turkmenistan

The Program of Development of the Oil and Gas Industry outlines a large-scale development of the energy sector up to the year 2010.[6] Priority is given to increasing gas production: total production in the period 2001–2010 is planned to be 450.9 billion cubic metres (bcm). Plans are to produce 8 bcm of gas in 2005 and 120 bcm in 2010.

It is estimated that total production of oil and gas condensate over the 10 years 2001–2010 will reach 144 million tons. In 2005 annual production of oil is planned to reach 28 million tons, and in 2010, 48 million tons.[7] Achievement of these targets will depend on the availability of material and financial resources and investments, and the latter will depend on the level of oil prices and investment policy in Turkmenistan.

Along with forecast increases in the production of oil, natural gas and gas condensate, it is planned to increase the output and improve the quality of oil refining in order to satisfy domestic demand in fuel and lubricants and increase exports. After completion of the first phase of retrofitting of the Turkmenbashi refinery, processing of oil will increase to 6 million tons per year. This will significantly increase output of all refined products, and then production of polymers will begin. After the second phase is complete by 2010 the refinery will be capable of processing 9 million tons of products annually.

To increase exports of liquid gas it is planned to construct additional storage and distribution facilities in the Turkmenbashi port and at the Serhetabat (Kushka) and Atamurat (Kerki) rail stations. It is also planned to build a gas processing facility with the capacity to produce 200 000 tons of polyethylene annually. The volume of oil processing (including gas condensate) is expected to reach 12 million tons in 2005 and 15 million tons in 2010. Priority tasks include the reconstruction of the existing pipeline system and the construction of additional pipelines for domestic distribution as well as for export.

The development of the gas distribution infrastructure will include providing an adequate gas supply to consumers and industrial users and new routes for the export of gas. In western Turkmenistan the development of the transport infrastructure implies the construction of pipelines for newly discovered gas fields in order to connect them subsequently to the Turkmenistan–Iran trunk route, thus creating a unified gas distribution network within the south-western region. There are already plans to construct an identical system to produce and transport liquid gas.

In the interests of its economic security, Turkmenistan is pursuing a programme of multi-directional pipeline routes for its exports of oil and gas. This

[5] *Neftegazovaya Vertikal*, nos 7–8 (2000), p. 67.
[6] 'National programme of President Saparmurat Turkmenbashi' (note 2), p. 209.
[7] 'National programme of President Saparmurat Turkmenbashi' (note 2).

involves study of: (*a*) the trans-Caspian route (Turkmenistan–Azerbaijan–Turkey–Europe); (*b*) Turkmenistan–Iran–Turkey–Europe; (*c*) Turkmenistan–Afghanistan–Pakistan; and (*d*) Turkmenistan–China. The trans-Caspian route is discussed in section IV below, and other routes for the export of gas and oil in section V.[8]

III. The major competitors and partners of Turkmenistan

Russia has the largest gas deposits in the world. As Turkmenistan's current gas export routes pass through Russian territory, Russia intends to continue to control the transport of Turkmen gas. Russia is also the largest exporter of gas in the world. In 1999 the Russian utility Gazprom exported record amounts of gas (126.8 bcm) to European markets, Turkey and the Commonwealth of Independent States (CIS) countries.[9] Under the Blue Stream programme (the Russian alternative to a trans-Caspian pipeline project) Russia intends to supply an additional 16 bcm of gas per year to Turkey.[10] Russia is also actively discussing options to supply gas from eastern Siberia and Sakhalin to the Japanese and Chinese markets. All this means that Russia is currently a major competitor of Turkmenistan in the European, Chinese and Turkish markets.

Its control over access to the Central Asia–Centre pipeline gives Russia an advantage over other CIS countries. Moreover, recently Russia (Gazprom and its pipeline operator, Itera) has been actively seeking to further tighten its control over the gas distribution network that starts in Aleksandrov-Gay. In May 2000 Gazprom, Itera and the Government of Kazakhstan agreed to establish a joint company which would provide maintenance and supervision for this network.[11] A similar agreement was reached with Armenia in August 1997 and a similar deal with Georgia is expected to be reached soon.[12] In essence Russia, by gaining control over the gas distribution system, gains leverage over Turkmenistan. However, Russia is encountering major problems in providing substantial capital investments to the gas industry in order to maintain existing production levels. From that point of view Russia needs Turkmenistan as a partner.

Iran has the second-largest gas deposits in the world. At present it is unable to meet domestic demand and imports gas to supply its northern regions, which are densely populated and whose own gas production capacities are insignificant. It should not be overlooked that if Iran decides to develop its own gas

---

[8] On the existing and planned pipeline routes see chapter 3, figure 3.1 in this volume.

[9] Serjantov, S., 'Gazprom s Iteroy vernulis na gazovy rynok Sredney Azii' [Gasprom and Itera come back to the gas market of Central Asia], *Neft' i Kapital* (Moscow), no. 5 (2000), p. 28.

[10] The Blue Stream pipeline, with a total length of 1263 km, would run over 370 km across Russia (from Izobil'noye to Dzhubga) then for 392 km via the Black Sea bed to Turkey (Samsun) and from there for another 501 km across Turkey to Ankara. Novopashin, A., 'Gaz—toplivo rossiyskikh reform' [Gas: the fuel of Russian reforms], *Nezavisimaya Gazeta*, 26 Oct. 2000. See chapter 3, figure 3.1 in this volume.

[11] Berezovsky, V., 'Ashkhabad brosaet perchatku Gazpromu i Baku' [Ashkhabad throws down the gauntlet to Gazprom and Baku], *Rossiyskaya Gazeta*, 21 Aug. 1999.

[12] Verezemsky, S., 'Dobro pozhalovat' v kavkazskiy gazovym koridor' [Welcome to the Caucasus gas corridor], *Neft' i Kapital* (Moscow), no. 10 (1997), p. 52.

fields it could become a serious competitor to Russia and Turkmenistan. Iran also plans to expand on the European, Pakistani and Turkish energy markets, but hitherto US sanctions have restricted the development of its energy complex. In order to jump-start its gas industry Iran plans to commission the South Pars gas field. Until recently Iran has maintained a partnership relationship with Turkmenistan.

Kazakhstan and *Uzbekistan* lack substantial gas deposits and thus cannot present real competition to Turkmenistan, although they are better strategically positioned. In 2001–05 Gazprom intends to buy up to 5 bcm of Uzbek gas. Such amounts could have a significant impact on regional dynamics. Turkmenistan joined Uzbekistan in development of its Kokdulamak oilfield, which is on their common border. The Uzbek side operates the site and according to the existing agreement has to deliver to Turkmenistan around 574 000 tons of oil annually: the total amount to be delivered between 1995 and 2015 will be 6 million tons of oil and 16 bcm of gas condensate. Turkmenistan has thus developed a positive partnership with Uzbekistan. Kazakhstan is the largest transit country in the region and is also Turkmenistan's strategic partner. The two countries share many interests, such as the transport of oil through Iran to the Persian Gulf and across Afghanistan and Pakistan, and the transport of gas through Kazakhstan to China.

Azerbaijan until recently hardly qualified for the role of a competitor, but since the Shah Deniz field was discovered offshore south-east of Baku it has been actively seeking new positions on energy markets and trying to upgrade its status from that of just a transit country to that of a potential competitor. Initial drilling confirmed Shah Deniz's commercial viability and the existence of 700 bcm of gas.[13] According to existing estimates the volume of exports from this field could reach 5 bcm annually. Even without having complete data on its potential, Azerbaijan began serious discussion on the possibilities of gas exports either through participation in the trans-Caspian pipeline project or by using the already available pipeline to Georgia (which would require renovation if it were to handle 10–15 bcm of gas per year). Natiq Aliyev, President of the State Oil Company of the Azerbaijan Republic (SOCAR), was quick to state that the results of tests on Shah Deniz would drastically change SOCAR's position on the trans-Caspian pipeline and that Azerbaijan was no longer willing to be just a transit country, but wanted a place in the Turkish market as well.[14] The discovery of Shah Deniz is also important for any future deliveries of Azerbaijani gas to Turkey and the northern regions of Iran.

---

[13] Serjantov, S., 'A u nas pod morem gaz' [And we have gas under the sea], *Neft' i Kapital* (Moscow), no. 5 (2000), p. 29.

[14] Badykova, N., *Iran i Perspektivy Eksporta Gaza iz Kaspiyskogo Regiona* [Iran and the prospects of gas export from the Caspian Region], Occasional Papers (Slavic Research Center: Sapporo, 1998).

IV. The trans-Caspian gas pipeline

The idea of a trans-Caspian pipeline was born in 1997 at a time when Russia and Turkmenistan had differences of opinion on gas issues and Russia was using old-style 'Soviet' methods in an attempt to pressure Turkmenistan to accept inherently disadvantageous terms. This was also the time when it was realized that the Turkmenistan–Afghanistan–Pakistan pipeline project was not feasible and the Turkmenistan–Iran project was torpedoed by the USA. This was the right time for the USA to bring up the idea of a trans-Caspian pipeline, which was in complete accord with US policy goals in the region—weakening Russia and isolating Iran. In April 1998 an agreement was signed between Turkmenistan and the USA on a feasibility study for the proposed project. The US Trade and Development Agency granted funds to conduct the study and the US Eximbank agreed to provide credit to the amount of $3 billion.[15] The major obstacles to realization of the project were legal controversies between Turkmenistan and Azerbaijan over sovereign rights to the oilfields in the Caspian Sea and the unresolved legal status of the Caspian Sea.

The major and obvious opponents to the trans-Caspian pipeline were Iran and Russia. In August 1998 the Minister of Foreign Affairs of Iran, at a meeting with Turkmen President Saparmurat Niyazov in Ashkhabad, emphasized that until all issues regarding the legal status of the Caspian Sea were resolved the littoral countries should not consider building a pipeline across the seabed. Even if the sea is divided into national sectors, the use of the seabed must be regulated.[16]

Americans became actively involved in the settlement of the disputed issues between Azerbaijan and Turkmenistan, hoping to lead them to an agreement. In response to US efforts, Azerbaijan and Turkmenistan established a committee to determine the median line of the Caspian Sea so as to determine ownership of the disputed oilfields. Azerbaijan realized that Turkmenistan was in the process of seeking an alternative route to energy markets, and that this route could go through its territory. Azerbaijan assumed that since Turkmenistan was very interested in this project and had no choice it would eventually compromise. In March 1999 President Niyazov stated that the disputed fields in the Caspian Sea and the trans-Caspian pipeline were two separate issues and should be treated separately.[17]

At the Istanbul Summit Meeting in November 1999 of the Organization for Security and Co-operation in Europe (OCSE), numerous papers were signed concerning the development of the trans-Caspian pipeline. The key document was a multilateral agreement on the construction of the pipeline between Azerbaijan, Georgia, Turkey and Turkmenistan. This document was a follow-up to

---

[15] Turkmenpress, official news column, 6 July 1998.
[16] *Vestnik Ministerstva Inostrannykh Del Turkmenistana* (Bulletin of the Turkmenistan Ministry of Foreign Affairs), no. 3 (1999).
[17] 'V Ashkhabade podpisan istoricheskiy dokument' [A historic document signed in Ashkhabad], *Neytral'ny Turkmenistan* (Ashkhabad), 20 Feb. 1999.

one already signed on 29 October 1998 between Turkmenistan and Turkey on the export of Turkmen gas to Turkey. The two countries agreed on 30 bcm per year. Turkey would consume 16 bcm and the rest would be re-exported to European markets. President Niyazov also signed an agreement with the Minister of Energy of Turkey, which stipulated that two companies, Botas and XXI Asyr Turkmenin Altyn Asyry, would sell the Turkmen gas on the Turkish and European markets.[18]

In early 2000, at a conference between the four countries on the question of the trans-Caspian pipeline, Azerbaijan disagreed on its quota in the trans-Caspian project and demanded a 50 per cent share of the pipeline capacity.[19] This meant that the project would not start at all. In March 2000 President Niyazov in an interview with the magazine *Caspian* said:

Our initiatives and actions stem from our national interest to strengthen the political and economic independence of our country. Having said that I have again to clarify our position on the issue of the trans-Caspian pipeline during the meeting with the Special Adviser to the US President and Secretary of State. Turkmenistan intends to act on the basis of its national interests and concerns about its economic security. In this context I had to say that offering a 50 per cent quota of the trans-Caspian pipeline with 30 bcm/year capacity to Azerbaijan is against the economic interests of Turkmenistan, and previously signed agreements make this impossible to agree. Azerbaijan's intentions to use half of the pipeline's capacity to transport its gas makes this project unprofitable for Turkmenistan. If the project is commercially non-viable, we reserve the right to choose alternative routes to transport gas.[20]

In March 2000 the US firm PSG was refused renewal of its sponsor mandate of the trans-Caspian pipeline.[21] This coincided with the period when Russia and Turkmenistan were actively discussing a long-term gas export contract. On 23 March 2000 President Niyazov met representatives of Shell International and the parties discussed the prospects of the trans-Caspian project, of which Shell was a sponsor. Niyazov raised concerns about the unsatisfactory progress of the project, mentioned that this was not Turkmenistan's fault, asked to continue to work in this direction, and emphasized that Turkmenistan intended to increase exports to Iran and Russia.[22]

The situation of the trans-Caspian pipeline can best be described as hopeless for the foreseeable future. Sporadic articles appear in the media on developments concerning the pipeline but it is doubtful that the problem can be resolved at all. The Russian side will try not to lose its edge over the USA; Iran is involved and is determined to increase the capacity of its own existing pipe-

[18] *Neytral'ny Turkmenistan*, no. 297 (20 Nov. 1999).

[19] Vinogradov, B., '"Gazovy kvartet" ukhodit na dno Kaspiya' ['Gas quartet' goes to the bottom of the Caspian], *Izvestiya*, 20 Jan. 2000.

[20] *Arkhiv Vneshney Politiki* [Archive of foreign policy] (Ministry of Foreign Affairs, Ashkhabad), no. 1 (Jan./Mar. 2000), p. 30.

[21] Vladimirov, Ye., 'Niyazov otodvinul Ameriku' [Niyazov put off the US], *Finansovaya Rossiya* (Moscow), no. 13 (Apr. 2000).

[22] 'Saparmurat Turkmenbashi vstretilsya s Shell International' [Saparmurat Turkmenbashi meets Shell International], *Neytral'ny Turkmenistan*, no. 74 (23 Mar. 2000).

lines; and it is doubtful that the USA will ever persuade Turkmenistan to accept Azerbaijan's conditions. Turkmenistan has already compromised once when the USA failed to find an acceptable solution to the issue of the disputed oilfields in the Caspian Sea: Turkmenistan agreed then not to link those issues with the trans-Caspian pipeline. It cannot be expected to compromise again, even if the situation with gas exports worsens. Efforts to give impetus to the trans-Caspian project continued at a meeting of the presidents of Turkey and Turkmenistan in October 2000 but Turkmenistan made no further statements on the issue.

V. Existing pipelines

At present the Turkmen gas is exported via two routes: directly to Iran and through the Central Asia–Centre pipeline.

Iran

The Korpedje–Kurt-Kui (KKK) gas pipeline was commissioned in 1998 as an alternative to the Central Asia–Centre pipeline, which is controlled by Russia. During the two years 1998–99, 3.5 bcm of gas were transported via the KKK pipeline and during the first eight months of 2000, 1.4 bcm. According to the Programme of Development of Oil and Gas Industry it is planned to transport up to 5 bcm annually, although this is unlikely to be achieved yet because of technical constraints on the capacity of the pipeline. In March 2000 President Niyazov and the Iranian Minister of the Oil Industry agreed to increase the capacity of the pipeline to 8 bcm annually by the year 2002, with a subsequent increase in its capacity to 13 bcm/year.[23] Niyazov emphasized that Turkmenistan has several options for the export of gas. It was agreed to continue to explore further possibilities of increasing exports by upgrading the pipeline system to Iran and to consider the possibility of building a pipeline to the Iranian port of Neka. Iran, like Russia, is interested in strengthening its positions in the region and is working hard to be Turkmenistan's partner.

Russia

Difficulties with the trans-Caspian pipeline, differences between Azerbaijan and Turkmenistan on the issue of export quotas in particular, the continuing lack of financial resources to carry out this project and the fall in gas production in Russia led to Russia and Turkmenistan renewing their dialogue. For Turkmenistan these factors meant that it needed to use the Central Asia–Centre pipeline for gas exports and to receive hard currency immediately. For Russia it was a good opportunity to get control over part of the Turkmen gas and use it to offset apparent shortages in its own domestic gas supply at no financial cost.

While Turkmenistan has no ambitious plans in the region, except to keep good relations with its neighbours on the basis of the principle of neutrality, and

---

[23] *Arkhiv Vneshney Politiki*, no. 1 (Jan./Mar. 2000), p. 38.

is pursuing the goal of diversification of gas routes in order to protect its economic interests, Russia intends to reinforce its position in Central Asia as an important player with far-reaching geopolitical interests.

Russia's positions in Central Asia had weakened during the 1990s as a result of its clumsy and rigid foreign policy: as recently as 1998 the chances that it would participate in the development of the energy sector in the region were slim. This situation changed drastically in 1999 when the discovery of the Shah Deniz field called into question the feasibility of the trans-Caspian pipeline. The political climate in Russia also changed when the new government of President Vladimir Putin faced the task of regaining Russia's lost positions in the region. This was the right time to gain an advantage over the USA. Moreover, the financial situation in Russia also played a major role in transforming Russian policy in Central Asia. Russia was keen to hold on to its old positions and gain new positions in energy markets, but as a result of the financial crisis of August 1998 Gazprom was underfunded. This was causing delays in the realization of Gazprom's projects—for instance, the Blue Stream project, even though it was supposed to be a high priority. The financial crisis also caused delays in financing the gas and oil sector in order to keep existing production levels.

To reduce the risk of gas deliveries to both external and domestic consumers being cut, Gazprom had the choice of either spending substantial amounts of money to expand domestic gas production or seeking an alternative way to import gas from abroad to cover the existing gas shortages. At this point Turkmenistan became a relief gas supplier. Moreover, Turkmen gas became an acceptable alternative for Russia to increase its domestic gas production and offered Russia an opportunity to influence the balance of forces in the region. In December 1999 an agreement was signed between President Niyazov and the Chairman of Gazprom, Rem Vyakhirev, on the sale of 20 bcm of gas in 2000.[24] Gas deliveries to Russia were renewed on 28 December 1999.

In February 2000 at another meeting of Niyazov and Vyakhirev it was agreed to increase gas exports to Russia by 10 bcm to a total of 30 bcm (at the price of $36 per thousand cubic metres, tcm, 40 per cent to be paid in cash and 60 per cent in kind). Niyazov also offered the Russian side participation in any prospective pipeline projects, including the trans-Caspian project.[25] This was a major breakthrough in the economic relationship between the two countries.

For the USA this meant the beginning of the struggle to maintain its positions in the region. It reacted by sending its Special Adviser to the President on issues of the Caspian region, John Wolf, to Turkmenistan in February 2000. In the same month Turkey also sent a special envoy and the Chairman of the Botaj Company, which had earlier signed a sale contract with the Government of Turkmenistan. The USA assured Turkmenistan of its seriousness in supporting the trans-Caspian project. It was also mentioned that Eximbank and the

---

[24] 'V 2000 godu Turkmenistan vozobnovit postavki gaza v Rossiyu' [Turkmenistan will resume gas deliveries to Russia in 2000], *Neytral'ny Turkmenistan*, 18 Dec. 1999.

[25] 'Prezident Turkmenistana vstretilsya s Predsedatelem Gazproma Remom Vyakhirevym' [President of Turkmenistan meets Gazprom Chairman Rem Vyakhirev], *Arkhiv Vneshney Politiki*, no. 1 (Jan./Mar. 2000), p. 44.

Overseas Private Investments Corporation would underwrite the project and provide necessary financial support.[26]

However, despite all the efforts of the US and Turkish parties, Turkmenistan did not change its plans. President Niyazov, citing the importance of economic security, stated that Turkmenistan would continue to support the idea of a multi-directional pipeline system and emphasized its right to seek additional routes to export its energy resources. He also stated that Turkmenistan was working on finding new ways to sell its gas on other markets and to increase exports through the existing Russian pipelines.

The visit of President Putin to Ashkhabad in May 2000 was a turning point in relations between Russia and Turkmenistan. After a period of souring relations, the two countries united again in gas affairs. Moreover, they entered a long-term strategic agreement by to which Turkmenistan would export 50 bcm of gas annually over the next 30 years.[27]

However, this did not mean that the problem with gas exports to Russia was completely resolved. As mentioned above, Russia is experiencing problems with its falling gas production, and this may threaten its contractual obligations to other countries. That is why Gazprom is considering the possibility of cur-tailing Russia's domestic consumption. In order to meet its contractual obli-gations Russia has either to cut back domestic consumption to 55 bcm per year or to find other ways to buy Turkmen gas, but that will be difficult.[28] Russia already has the contract with Turkmenistan to import 30 bcm in 2000, and under another agreement signed in October 2000 Turkmenistan is obliged to export another 30 bcm to Ukraine in 2001. This limits the possibility of using Turkmen gas to meet Russian requirements. Moreover, the Central Asia–Centre pipeline system has been in use for more than 20 years and requires a major overhaul in order to achieve the capacity it had in 1991—over 80 bcm annually—a task which will not be easily accomplished.

Ukraine

Exports of gas to Ukraine were cut off in May 1999 when payments for delivered were long overdue. A contract for the export of 20 bcm was fulfilled only up to 45 per cent. New negotiations began in October 2000, when Ukraine agreed to pay its current debt in cash and goods by the end of the year. On 4 October 2000 when President Leonid Kuchma of Ukraine visited Turkmen-istan he and President Niyazov reached an agreement stipulating the delivery of gas for the period of 2000–2001: Turkmenistan was to sell Ukraine 5 bcm of

---

[26] 'Prezident Turkmenistana vstretilsya so spetsial'nym sovetnikom Prezidenta Turtsii i so spetsial'nym sovetnikom Prezidenta Ameriki' [The President of Turkmenistan meets the Special Adviser to the President of Turkey and the Special Adviser to the US President], *Arkhiv Vneshney Politiki*, no. 1 (2000), p. 41.

[27] 'Prezident Turkmenistana vstretilsya s Prezidentom Rossii Putinym' [The President of Turkmenistan meets Russian President Putin], *Neytral'ny Turkmenistan*, 20 May 2000.

[28] Reznik, I., 'Rem Vyakhirev vybiraet gazodollary' [Rem Vyakhirev chooses gas dollars], *Kommersant* (Moscow), no. 187 (6 Oct. 2000).

gas in 2000 and 30 bcm in 2001 at a price of $40/tcm. Gas would be transported to the Uzbekistan border and Ukraine would make weekly payments for equivalent to $7 million in cash and $9 million in goods and construction services. In other words, Ukraine will pay for 60 per cent of its gas imports by delivering goods and by carrying out construction of industrial projects in Turkmenistan. The two sides also agreed to consider a longer-term contract for the delivery of gas to Ukraine for the five-year period 2002–2006.[29] On 16 October 2000 Kuchma and Putin agreed on the payment for transit of gas across Russian territory. If payments fall overdue, Russia has the right to convert the debt into securities with the right to participate in the privatization of the Ukrainian gas distribution network. Thus Russia can tighten its control over the Ukrainian and CIS pipeline systems.

It seems that the export of Turkmen gas is going well and there are several customers, but this does not mean that Turkmenistan should stop its search for alternative routes. Many contracts in the past were breached because of failure to pay for gas. Moreover, substantial amounts of gas will be transported through pipelines that are controlled by Russia. For this reason, the Turkmenistan–China route is being actively studied at the present time.

VI. The legal status of the Caspian Sea

Determining the legal status of the Caspian Sea is currently one of the most difficult issues. Although in recent years some countries have been revising their positions on the issue, it is not completely settled. Moreover it seems that the problem is being used when needed by certain countries to gain leverage over others. For example, Iran and Russia used this tactic to thwart the building of the trans-Caspian pipeline. During their last meeting in Astana in October 2000, the Russian and Kazakh presidents again tried to settle the issue of the legal status of the sea, but a resolution of the problem is hardly possible without the participation of all interested parties.

Turkmenistan's position on the issue can be illustrated by official statements and numerous comments on them. On 12 August 1999 President Niyazov signed a decree on the National Service for Developing the Turkmen Sector of the Caspian Sea.[30] It emphasized that the 'development of the Turkmen sector of the Caspian Sea is becoming an ever more important task and is essential for the economy of Turkmenistan. The end result of these efforts should be that the Turkmen sector of the Caspian Sea is completely integrated into the national economy of Turkmenistan and Turkmenistan becomes a leader in the region'. In the decree the following tasks were set: (*a*) to develop a national programme on

---

[29] *Neytral'ny Turkmenistan*, 5 Oct. 2000.
[30] 'Ukaz Prezidenta ob obrazovanii Natsional'noy Sluzhby osvoyeniya turkmenskogo sektora Kaspiyskogo morya pri Prezidente Turkmenistana' [Presidential Decree on establishment of the National Service under the President of Turkmenistan for developing the Turkmen sector of the Caspian Sea], *Sobraniye Aktov Prezidenta Turkmenistana i Reshenii Pravitel'stva Turkmenistana* [Collection of presidential decrees and government resolutions of Turkmenistan] (Office of the President of Turkmenistan, Ashkhabad), no. 8 (1999), p. 64.

the rational utilization of the natural resources of the Caspian; (*b*) to develop a legal framework for the prompt exploration of the sea; (*c*) to ensure inter-departmental coordination in the development of the Turkmen sector of the sea; and (*d*) to provide control over the rational utilization of hydrocarbon, mineral and fish resources of the sea and the facilitation of navigation. The National Service was given rights to license and control mineral resources, fisheries and the merchant fleet.

However, the legal definition of the Turkmen sector of the Caspian Sea is nowhere to be found in these papers. The Russian Ministry of Foreign Affairs reacted to this by issuing a statement claiming that the actions taken by Turk-menistan contravened the current legal status of the Caspian Sea. Explaining its position, Russia confirmed that it would not accept actions of other countries to divide the sea surface into national sectors as legal until all controversial issues were resolved; furthermore, such actions are in clear violation of the Soviet–Iranian agreements of 1921 and 1940.[31] In a 1999 interview with *Neytralny Turkmenistan* President Niyazov commented on the issue of the legal status of the Sea: 'As for Turkmenistan, during the talks we stated repeatedly that we are satisfied with any outcome, even a sectional division or a joint use of the sea; the most important thing is that all countries should reach consensus on this issue'.[32] A similar statement was made in *Central Asian News*: 'Many countries now support the idea of a sectional division of the Caspian Sea. As already mentioned, Turkmenistan agrees with this as well as with the earlier concept of condominium'.[33]

VII. Conclusions

1. The development of the economy of Turkmenistan is determined by a number of internal and external factors. The influences of these factors vary at different stages of development, so that the programme on Social–Economic Development of Turkmenistan to the year 2010 can only be considered a rough yardstick. As the programme is carried out it will be adjusted according to realities, and although several major pipeline projects are listed in the pro-gramme this does not mean that all of them will be implemented.

The development of the economy will be heavily influenced by trends in the oil and gas complex. Without doubt the development of this complex will be a national priority in the coming decades. However, the government should con-tinue to give attention to developing the processing industry, which would help reduce the country's dependence on gas exports. In other words, economic policy should pursue the goal of strengthening economic security by increased spending not only on the oil and gas complex but on other industries as well.

[31] [Statement by the Russian Ministry of Foreign Affairs on the establishment by Turkmenistan of the National Service for developing the Turkmen sector of the Caspian Sea made on 20 Sep. 1999], *Diplomaticheskiy Vestnik*, no. 10 (Oct. 1999), p. 32.

[32] [Interview with the President of Turkmenistan on 27 Oct.], *Arkhiv Vneshney Politiki*, no. 4 (Oct./Dec. 1999), p. 10.

[33] [Interview with the President of Turkmenistan] (note 32), p. 13.

This will guarantee against syndromes such as 'Dutch disease', and avoid the fate of countries such as Algeria, Ecuador, Gabon and Nigeria, whose very negative experiences should serve as a reminder to the Caspian countries and to Turkmenistan in particular. Major threats may emerge if Turkmenistan repeats mistakes that have been made elsewhere—of government accumulating hard-currency revenues and taking these monies for granted (free money); of the development of inefficient industries; of excessive spending of hard currency on infrastructure development; and of the uncontrolled import of consumer goods.

Turkmenistan is already working on changing the structure of its economy, although the efficiency of its new industries will be seen only when all the conditions for fair internal and external competition are in place. Otherwise, in order to provide for the survival of these new industries, the government will be required to subsidize them or to protect them by customs regulations or similar measures.

2. For the time being expectations of miraculous windfalls for Turkmenistan from the export of gas are premature. National policy for the development of the oil and gas industry is quite ambitious and can only be accomplished if all contracts are fulfilled and all payments are received. Without doubt Turkmenistan will continue to seek alternative routes to energy markets in order to reduce its dependence on the Central Asia–Centre pipeline.

3. It is also important that Turkmenistan creates a favourable investment climate in order to attract foreign capital. Iran is a potential source of capital, but only if the USA either lifts or eases sanctions against Iran.

4. It is hard to say how competitive Azerbaijan can be with Turkmenistan, even though Azerbaijan is better located in terms of ability to export hydrocarbons to Turkey and Europe. The situation with the 'proven reserves' Azerbaijan claims to have is still unclear. According to some experts, members of Azerbaijan's consortium (the Azerbaijan International Operating Company, AIOC) are rather liberal in their estimates.[34]

5. Russia can continue to be Turkmenistan's partner if financial or other problems do not intervene. In the competition between Russia and Turkmenistan for a more attractive investment climate Russia will probably have the advantage as it has a more developed economy, but when their gas and oil production costs are compared Russia without doubt loses out to Turkmenistan.

Russia has ambitious plans to extend its influence in Central Asia and to emerge on the Chinese and Japanese markets, but it has to take gas-rich Turkmenistan into account.

---

[34] Mishin, V., 'Tayny Kaspiyskogo geofizicheskogo dvora ili kto i kak opredelyaeyt zapasy uglevodorodov Azerbaijana' [Mysteries of the Caspian geophysical court, or who determines the hydrocarbon resources of Azerbaijan and how], *Neft' i Kapital*, nos 7–8 (2000).

14. Turkmenistan and Central Asian regional security

Murad Esenov

I. Introduction

The emergence of new states in Central Asia drastically changed the political landscape not only within the region itself but also outside. Whereas Central Asia as part of the Soviet Union was basically on the periphery of a unified geopolitical area, after the breakup of the USSR it took centre stage in the political processes across the vast Eurasian area, becoming an object of geopolitical confrontation between world and regional centres of power.

Under the new set-up the states in the region began, virtually from nothing, to search for a new identity, a form of internal political order reflecting the interests of society; to set foreign policy priorities designed above all to put in place a credible state and regional security system; and to define their places and roles within the system of international relations.

The past decade has shaped in general outline an internal political order and development model for states in the region, which have already made their choices, but the main task—establishing foreign policy priorities and putting in place a credible regional security system—has yet to be addressed. None of the attempts made within the framework of the Commonwealth of Independent States (CIS), the Central Asian Union, the Shanghai Cooperation Organization[1] and other vehicles of integration to put in place a regional security system that would guarantee the military–political and socio-economic stability of the region has yet produced a result.

It is fairly unlikely that a result will be achieved in the foreseeable future. The main reasons for this are the competing economic potentials of states in the region and their mutually exclusive tactics and strategies for achieving economic prosperity. This to a great extent is propelling the states in the region towards an independent search for foreign economic and political partners. They are ignoring the interests of regional geopolitical unification and the importance of concerted efforts on such matters as regional security. Furthermore, there are differences between them in their assessments of security threats, with all the ensuing consequences.

A case in point is Turkmenistan with its policy of 'positive neutrality', as manifested in its distancing or sometimes even completely isolating itself from other countries of Central Asia.

[1] On the Central Asian Union (CAU) see chapter 1 in this volume; on the Shanghai Cooperation Organization (previously the Shanghai Forum) see chapter 5, section V.

II. The neutrality concept

Turkmenistan's foreign policy raises a number of questions. Why does it aspire to political neutrality? Just how neutral in fact is the policy line followed by the country's leadership? How does Turkmenistan's stance reflect on the overall situation in the region, above all in the sphere of regional security in Central Asia and in Turkmenistan itself?

Turkmenistan became an independent state quite unexpectedly. Neither its leadership nor its population was prepared for such a development. The results of the all-union referendum of 1989 are very indicative in this respect: at the time more than 90 per cent of the population favoured the preservation of the Soviet Union and of Turkmenistan remaining a union republic. When the Soviet Union broke up, the only characteristics of a state that Turkmenistan had were a distinct territory and a rather feeble administrative structure. None of the other important characteristics that constitute a state, such as a unified socio-cultural area, a national identity, an awareness of the law on the part of the general public and a self-sufficient economic and institutional infrastructure, existed. They are still evolving.

The country's territorial integrity is not as yet recognized by neighbouring states on the official level, and to judge from some unofficial statements (for instance, in the press), its neighbours even have some territorial claims on Turkmenistan. Uzbekistan has made no particular secret of its claims to border areas in the Tashauz and Chardzhou regions, which are populated mainly by ethnic Uzbeks. The leadership of Turkmenistan is also concerned about the political instability in some CIS member states, which could under certain circumstances have spilled over to Turkmenistan's territory.

In addition, according to some estimates, Turkmenistan is among the richest countries in the world in terms of hydrocarbon resources, while its population is just 4.5 million.

In that context, any ill-considered move on the part of the political leadership in building an independent state could have led to its becoming an object of discord between regional centres of power or a raw materials appendage to any of those power centres, which would have been entirely unacceptable to Turkmenistan.

All these factors prompted the country's leadership to search for some unorthodox ways to help achieve the following objectives: (a) preserving the country's territorial integrity; (b) guaranteeing its security; (c) establishing favourable conditions for vital political and economic reforms in the country; and (d) realizing its raw materials potential without becoming politically dependent on countries via whose territory export routes would pass.

The leadership thought that all this could be ensured by adopting neutral status recognized by the world community, whereby Turkmenistan would not be affiliated with any political or military blocs but would develop equal-to-equal relations with all the states of the world.

President Saparmurat Niyazov first proposed that Turkmenistan should adopt neutral status in March 1995 at a conference of the Economic Cooperation Organization (ECO).[2] The proposal received full support from the participants. In October 1995, a meeting of the heads of state of the Non-Aligned Movement also backed the initiative. On 12 December 1995 the UN General Assembly adopted a special resolution calling on UN member states to recognize Turkmenistan's status as a neutral state.[3]

The newly acquired neutral status considerably facilitated the process of nation-building. It also enabled Turkmenistan to revise its military doctrine and by doing so restrict defence spending, funnelling the resources thus saved to the national economy.[4] However, it would probably not be correct to say that neutral status has freed the country from the influence of external forces or that Turkmenistan has been pursuing a policy of 'pure neutrality', adhering to the principle of 'equal distance and equal rapprochement' with respect to all countries in the region and in the world alike. Considering its economic situation and its geographic location, the adoption of neutrality was rather unexpected. Turkmenistan has an economic potential that has yet to be tapped, which in its turn requires large-scale investment, the choice of convenient export and import routes, and so on. It is no secret that behind any large investment, especially in building large oil and gas pipelines, lie the political interests of particular countries or groups of countries.

III. The Taliban connection

When it became independent, Turkmenistan placed its bets on the export of raw materials by building new oil and gas pipelines, roads and railways. Several alternative routes for the transport of raw materials and the export of natural gas were developed, the country's leadership favouring the idea of a gas pipeline to Pakistan via Afghanistan.[5]

Geographic factors, low costs and good market prospects do indeed make the Afghan route for the transport of natural gas an attractive option. The only shortcoming of this route is its political inexpediency in the light of the sanctions imposed on Afghanistan by the world community and the lack of security guarantees for the construction and subsequent operation of the pipeline. The attractions of the route rather misled the Turkmen political leadership, not only resulting in deviation from the proclaimed political neutrality but also disturbing the emerging regional security system in Central Asia.

The idea of using the Afghan route to carry Turkmen raw materials to Pakistan and further on to world markets was born in May 1992, in the course of business consultations between President Niyazov and Pakistani Prime Minister

[2] The ECO was established in 1985. The current members are Afghanistan, Azerbaijan, Iran, Kazakhstan, Kyrgyzstan, Pakistan, Tajikistan, Turkey, Turkmenistan and Uzbekistan.
[3] UN General Assembly Resolution no. 50/80, 12 December 1995.
[4] See also chapter 5, section IV in this volume.
[5] See also chapter 13 in this volume.

Nawaz Sharif at a working meeting of ECO heads of state in Ashkhabad. The outcome of the meeting was an agreement to build a gas pipeline and a highway connecting the two countries, via Afghan territory. Subsequently, similar meetings were held on 6–7 February 1993 in Quetta and on 28 November 1993 in Islamabad.

In April 1994, in the course of a visit to Ashkhabad by a delegation of the Pakistani Air Force led by Vice-Marshal Farug Usman Haider, a bilateral agreement on military cooperation between the two countries was signed. Under the agreement Pakistan is to help organize an Air Force Academy in Turkmenistan and to train military specialists for Turkmenistan's armed forces at its military training establishments.[6] In March 1995 in Islamabad Pakistani Prime Minister Benazir Bhutto and Turkmen President Niyazov signed a memorandum on building a gas pipeline from Turkmenistan through Afghanistan to Pakistan and on reopening a road between the town of Haman in Pakistan and the town of Turgundi on the Afghan–Turkmen border.

Such intensive meetings and the resulting accords showed the two sides' determination to achieve their objectives.

All the agreements reached between Turkmenistan and Pakistan relied on the use of Afghan territory to promote bilateral cooperation. However, representatives of Afghanistan itself were not parties to these accords. Moreover, on 5 March 1995, the then President of Afghanistan, Burhanuddin Rabbani, speaking on Kabul Radio, sharply criticized the agreements that had been reached between Pakistan and Turkmenistan and the intentions behind them. In particular, he described these plans as 'attempts by the Pakistani leadership to help the opposition Taliban movement'.[7]

Practical implementation of the Pakistani–Turkmen accords began in the autumn of 1994, when cargo convoys started shuttling between Turkmenistan and Pakistan across Afghan territory and preparations got under way to set up an international consortium on a gas pipeline construction project. It is noteworthy that the emergence of the Taliban movement on the Afghan military–political scene was directly related to an active phase in this Pakistani–Turkmen cooperation. In the late autumn of 1994 a group of Afghan Mujahideen seized a caravan moving from Pakistan to Turkmenistan. To secure its release, the Pakistani Interior Ministry tapped a small and little-known religious sect, led by Mullah Muhammad Omar, based in the south of Afghanistan. Before long that sect had evolved into the Taliban movement, which subsequently began its triumphant march across Afghan territory, turning round the entire military–political situation in the country.[8]

The Turkmen leadership immediately established contacts with the leadership of the Taliban, an obscure movement at the time—in fact, Pakistan and Turk-

[6] During President Niyazov's official visit to Pakistan in Aug. 1995 this accord evolved into an official bilateral agreement on military cooperation between Turkmenistan and Pakistan. Hussein, R., 'Pakistan and Central Asia', *Central Asia and the Caucasus* (Luleå), no. 7 (1997), pp. 72–73.

[7] Open Media Research Institute (OMRI), *OMRI Daily Digest*, 7 Mar. 1995.

[8] For further detail see Dubnov, A., 'Stolknoveniye tsivilizatsii? Net, interesov' [A clash of civilizations? No, of interests], *Tsentral'naya Aziya i Kavkaz* (Luleå), no. 7 (1997), pp. 73–75.

menistan were the Taliban's only foreign partners at the time the movement was formed. In the winter of 1994, after advance groups of Taliban appeared on a section of the Afghan–Turkmen border, a railway link was opened from Kushka in Turkmenistan to Turgundi in Afghanistan with intensive trade exchange. It is still not known what sort of cargo the freight trains were carrying at the time, but Turkmen officials maintained that the Turkmen side was 'providing humanitarian assistance to the fraternal Afghan people'.[9] At the time the population of Turkmenistan itself was in acute need of economic, including humanitarian, assistance. The country was going through an unprecedented crisis. There are therefore serious doubts about the humanitarian character of the shipments.

Prior to September 1996, when Taliban units began rapidly to take control of the eastern provinces of Afghanistan and then the capital, Kabul, few paid attention to developments there or to the role of Turkmenistan's political leadership in Afghanistan's internal affairs. It was not until the Taliban seized Kabul and the forces of Ahmad Shah Massoud and General Abdul Rashid Dostum had to retreat to the north of the country that the leaders of the Central Asian states began to take steps to strengthen and consolidate the regional security system.

On 4 October 1996 an emergency consultative meeting of the Central Asian and Russian heads of state was held in Almaty to consider the situation in the region following the seizure of Kabul by the Taliban. Taking part were the presidents of Kazakhstan, Kyrgyzstan, Tajikistan and Uzbekistan, and the Russian Prime Minister, Viktor Chernomyrdin. President Niyazov ignored an invitation from the President of Kazakhstan, Nursultan Nazarbayev, and did not take part in the meeting, citing his country's neutral status. The meeting adopted a joint statement expressing concern at the ongoing events in Afghanistan. It was stated that any actions that undermined stability on the borders between Afghanistan and any of the CIS states would be dealt with accordingly. The CIS Collective Security Council was directed to set up an ad hoc group to study the situation and prepare proposals on measures to stabilize the situation near the border with Afghanistan, and the CIS Council of Defence Ministers was instructed to work out proposals to ensure the security of the CIS southern borders. In addition, participants in the Almaty meeting recommended the UN Security Council to hold an emergency session on the Afghan problem.

Commenting on the results of the Almaty meeting and explaining the reason for his non-participation, Niyazov said: 'Being a neutral state, Turkmenistan does not intend to take part in such meetings. All that is happening in Afghanistan is the internal affair of the Afghan people while we do not see the Taliban movement as a threat to our security. For more than a year now, a part of the Turkmen–Afghan border has been controlled by representatives of this movement and this section of the border is by far the quietest today'.[10]

[9] *Turkmenskaya Iskra*, 25 Nov. 1994.
[10] From Niyazov's statement on Turkmenistan television, 6 Oct. 1996.

While President Niyazov's position on the matter is open to interpretation, it could hardly be attributed to the country's neutral status. The meeting was of a consultative character, devoted to a problem affecting the interests of all states in the region not only in the military but also in the humanitarian sphere. Further Taliban advances to the north of Afghanistan, populated by ethnic minorities related to ethnic groups living in Central Asia countries, could have led to mass migration to bordering countries, including Turkmenistan. Discussion of those matters and the elaboration of measures to avert a humanitarian catastrophe not only would not conflict, but would in fact be in conformity, with Turkmenistan's declared neutrality.

Soon after the Taliban increased their presence in the north of Afghanistan, Turkmenistan was indeed confronted with such problems, although the leadership tried hard to hide the fact. In the summer of 1997, ethnic cleansing began in two villages on Afghan territory, populated by Taliban 'friendly to Turkmenistan'. As a result, on 20 June about 1500 refugees crossed the border into Turkmenistan, and in the subsequent week the number increased to 8000.[11] Turkmenistan refused to accept these refugees, using its border guards to push them back into Afghanistan.

The facts also belie statements by Turkmen officials concerning 'stability on its borders following the advent of the Taliban'. In 1995, there were more than 50 armed clashes on the Afghan–Turkmen border, 1800 Afghan citizens were detained as a result and about 2 tonnes of drugs were seized.[12]

The situation did not change even after the Afghan–Turkmen border on the Afghan side came under the control of Taliban units: in fact it became even worse, aggravated by the fact that drug trafficking across the border was on the rise. For example, in 1996 more than 14 tonnes of drugs were confiscated from smugglers, and in 1997 approximately 42 tonnes. In 1999 alone, 50 tonnes of hashish, 2.3 tonnes of heroin and 7.7 tonnes of opium were confiscated and destroyed. Taking into account that according to the statistics of the UN STOP Program only 10 per cent of the total volume of 'commodities' shipped is usually detained, it is not difficult to imagine the real situation. According to Western experts, Turkmenistan was turning into one of the main transit routes for transporting drugs from Afghanistan and Pakistan to the CIS counties and via Russia to Europe. Some of the 'poison' also remained in Turkmenistan, aggravating the drug situation in the country.[13]

In the light of this, Niyazov's refusal to take part in the Almaty meeting could have been due to an entirely different reason. In this context, few would disagree with the following comment: 'The fact that the Taliban movement controls the southern part of Afghanistan could be advantageous for Turkmenistan. It could finally enable President Niyazov to see his dream come true: build an oil and gas pipeline to Pakistan and India for Turkmenistan to export its mineral

---

[11] NEGA (Moscow), citing sources in Abu Dhabi, 27 June 1997.

[12] Interfax, 23 Nov. 1995, citing the press service of the Russian border forces in Turkmenistan.

[13] Komissina, I. and Kurtov, A., 'Narcotic "glow" over Central Asia—a new threat to civilization', *Central Asia and the Caucasus* (Luleå), no. 5 (2000), p. 122.

resources'.[14] On 7 October 1996, two days after the Almaty meeting, Iglal Haider Zaidi, a special envoy of the Pakistani Prime Minister, met President Niyazov. After the meeting the sides noted that 'the views of Turkmenistan and Pakistan on the situation in Afghanistan fully coincide'.[15]

The subsequent course of events showed exactly why Pakistan and Turkmenistan were so interested in the Taliban expanding their presence on Afghan territory. On 27 October 1997 President Niyazov signed a protocol with the head of the US oil company Unocal granting the latter exclusive rights to set up a consortium to build a Turkmenistan–Afghanistan–Pakistan oil pipeline. Tellingly, when commenting on the security of the Afghan section of the gas pipeline, President Niyazov said: 'There is no reason to worry. We have reached accords with representatives of all groups based along the route of the future gas pipeline'.[16] All the Afghan territory through which the pipeline was to pass (via the towns of Turgundi, Great, Kandahar and Spin Buldak to the Pakistani town of Quetta) was at the time already controlled by the Taliban.

A year later, Unocal suspended its participation in the project. It made that decision following growing hostilities between Taliban and the opposition Northern Alliance forces and in the context of a serious aggravation of relations between the Taliban and the USA following US missile strikes on terrorist training bases in Afghanistan.[17] In addition to Unocal, Russia's Gazprom stated that it would not be involved in the project.

The withdrawal of the main participants in the project did not in any way affect Turkmenistan's plans. Commenting on Unocal's decision, President Niyazov observed that his country would not seek to hold anyone against their will, would continue to look for partners and believed that the project would in the end be successfully implemented. Significantly, he chose not to mention the reason for Unocal's refusal—the presence of international terrorist training camps on Afghan territory.

The Taliban leadership came out with a similar statement. Speaking at a news conference in Kabul, Amir Han Muttaki, Taliban Information Minister, said that 'several other large foreign companies were interested to get a contract to build the gas pipeline while all countries concerned—Afghanistan, Turkmenistan and Pakistan—will likely make their final choice in the foreseeable future'.[18]

Subsequently, Turkmenistan stepped up its diplomatic efforts to expedite the project and to ensure its security. In late February 1999, Boris Shikhmuradov, Foreign Minister of Turkmenistan, visited Kandahar where he met Mullah Muhammad Omar, the Taliban spiritual leader, to discuss only one problem— starting construction of the Turkmenistan–Afghanistan–Pakistan gas pipeline. On 29 April of the same year, energy ministers from the three countries met in

---

[14] Interview with Shirin Akiner of the Royal Institute of International Affairs, London, BBC Russian Service, 6 Oct. 1996.
[15] Interfax, 7 Oct. 1996.
[16] ANI, 30 Oct. 1997.
[17] ITAR-TASS, 2 Sep. 1998.
[18] RIA-Novosti, 20 Sep. 1998.

Islamabad and adopted a joint declaration reaffirming their intention to take part in preparation and implementation of the gas pipeline project. They also agreed to hold government-level negotiations every three months on setting up a joint working group of senior officials to maintain regular contacts between the sides.[19] On 10–12 May 1999, Abdur Rahmad Zahid, Deputy Foreign Minister in the Taliban administration, visited Ashkhabad. During the course of the meeting, the Taliban administration signed official economic agreements— for the first time since it emerged on the political scene—with a foreign state, and that state was Turkmenistan. Accords were also reached on opening an air corridor to flights by an Afghan airline to Turkmenistan, shipments of natural gas to Afghanistan and participation by Turkmen specialists in rebuilding two electric power stations in Afghanistan.[20]

In November 1999, a Turkmen military delegation, led by Deputy Prime Minister Sardzhayev, made a five-day visit to Pakistan. The main objectives of the visit were to discuss the security of a future gas pipeline from Pakistan to Turkmenistan and to expand military cooperation between them. The delegation was received by General Pervez Musharraf, head of Pakistan's military/civilian administration, and by its air force and navy chiefs of staff.[21]

It is noteworthy that this diplomatic activity on the part of Pakistan and Turkmenistan, aimed at using Afghan territory for commercial purposes, basically coincided with the military and terrorist activity of the Taliban movement. Before long, Taliban armed groups took control of large cities in northern Afghanistan. The foreign media produced incontrovertible evidence of the Taliban's involvement in acts of terrorism, the operation of international terrorist training bases on Taliban-controlled territory, drug trafficking and so on. Meanwhile, activism by various terrorist groups in Central Asian countries was growing. Those groups were based in Taliban-controlled areas of Afghanistan while their actions were coordinated by the Taliban leadership. Charges of sponsoring international terrorism were made against the Taliban not only by the leaders of Central Asian states, whose statements could often be seen as rather subjective, but also by the world community at large.

In July 1999 the USA imposed economic sanctions against the Taliban movement following its granting of asylum to Usama bin Laden, the 'number one international terrorist'. A written statement by President Bill Clinton released in this connection stressed that the sanctions would deepen the international isolation of the Taliban movement, thus limiting its potential for maintaining a network of terrorist groups, and highlighted the need to observe the generally accepted norms of conduct on the international arena.[22] In October of the same year sanctions against the Taliban were introduced for the same reason—the sponsoring of international terrorism—by the UN Security Council in a special resolution.[23]

[19] ITAR-TASS, 30 Apr. 1999.
[20] ITAR-TASS, 13 May 1999.
[21] ITAR-TASS, 29 Nov. 1999.
[22] ITAR-TASS, 6 July 1999.
[23] UN Security Council Resolution 1267, 15 Oct. 1999.

IV. The reality of Turkmenistan's neutrality

These facts and their dynamics show that Turkmenistan's political leadership to a certain extent remains hostage to its idea of using Afghan territory to create alternative routes for the export of its mineral resources, thus ending up involved in dubious political games. Moreover, the leadership has been acting in defiance of the emerging political situation in the region and ignoring the position of the world community with respect to the Taliban movement.

The country's foreign policy has in fact turned out to be rather remote from the declared policy of neutrality. In reality that 'neutrality' added up to uni-lateral, one-sided activity aimed at isolating Turkmenistan from the other Central Asian states and at rapprochement with dubious forces pursuing objectives that are far from peaceful. There is no doubt that this policy conflicts with the security interests of other states in Central Asia and carries the risk of a confrontation with them.

It is also important to remember that the Taliban movement is seen by the world community as a sponsor of international terrorism and is a main producer of and trafficker in drugs. At the present stage, when the policy followed by the Turkmen leadership in effect corresponds to Taliban interests, Turkmenistan may be harbouring the illusion that its security will not be jeopardized by a future Islamic Emirates of Afghanistan. Yet can there be any guarantee that this situation will last and that the Taliban will not want to impose their ways in Turkmenistan? Given Turkmenistan's military and political weakness, it is unlikely that it would be able to safeguard its security under such a scenario. Furthermore, its security has in fact already been violated, as is evidenced by the growing volume of drug trafficking from Afghanistan across Turkmenistan.

Assertions by the Turkmen leadership to the effect that neutral status auto-matically ensures the country's security since it is guaranteed by the world community appear to be rather misguided. First, the structures that pose a threat to the security of the country and the region as a whole—the drug mafia, religious extremists, international terrorists and so on—have never observed the norms of international law and will never do so. Second, the international community—if by this is meant the West as a whole and NATO in particular—will never get involved in conflicts in this part of the world. Its official representatives have long been making open statements to that effect. S. Neil MacFarlane, for example, does not believe that NATO forces are likely to be used to settle conflicts in the Caspian region. He quotes from an article by Anatol Lieven to back up his assessment: 'If you go to a senior Pentagon official, or the great majority of congressmen, and suggest the deployment of US troops to the Caspian region—to bases or as peacekeepers, let alone in conflict—they look at you as if you had sprouted a very large pair of hairy ears'.[24] Further comment would be superfluous.

[24] Quoted from MacFarlane, S. N. (Professor at the Centre for International Studies, Oxford University), 'What the international community can do to settle the conflict', *Central Asia and the Caucasus* (Luleå), no. 4 (2000), p. 155.

The character of threats in the world has changed. Whereas in the past the main threat was direct aggression and violation of the territorial integrity of sovereign states, now the main security threats are the various forms and manifestations of terrorism, extremism and drug trafficking. The countries of Central Asia are no exception in this respect. The main threat to their security is not Russia's 'imperial ambitions', as is assumed by many politicians in the region itself and beyond. The events of recent years in the region show beyond any doubt that the main threats are religious extremism, the spread of drugs and terrorism. It is also clear that all these negative developments gained ground just as the Taliban movement emerged as a major force on the political arena.

The intrusions of Islamic radicals into the Batken region of Kyrgyzstan in the summer of 1999 and 2000, the bomb attacks in Tashkent in February 1999, the penetration by religious fanatics of Uzbekistan's Syr Darya Region in the summer of the same year, the highly explosive situation in Tajikistan and the endless armed skirmishes on the region's southern borders were the direct result of religious extremist activity, coordinated by the Taliban movement and other terrorist organizations standing behind it.

The policy of the Turkmen leadership—whatever the good intentions behind it—was ultimately the main factor in the rise of Taliban activism. No one questions Turkmenistan's sovereign right to follow a policy that it deems fit— one that corresponds to its own national interests. No one is urging it to go to war with Afghanistan—a country with which it has an 840-km border. At the same time, however, the country's political leadership should be aware of its responsibility for the policy it pursues and anticipate its possible negative fallout, also taking into account the interests of other countries in the region.

Turkmenistan should also realize that it is an inalienable part of Central Asia which constitutes a unified geopolitical area. The peoples living on its territory have historically related connections and a common history and culture, and are at the same level of development. Moreover, the countries in the region are faced with the same security threats. In this context it is important to stress that Turkmenistan's withdrawal from the unified geopolitical area in itself jeopardizes regional security.

Turkmenistan should aim to work out, jointly with other countries in Central Asia, a well-defined line of conduct in adjusting conflict situations and protecting its own borders. This does not involve the creation of new military blocs or bloc-related confrontation with its southern neighbours. It is basically a question of the country's civilized choice. It is vital to decide in which direction the people of Turkmenistan will look in the future—towards the related ethnic groups and peoples of Central Asia or towards the Taliban, who are imposing medieval ways across Afghan territory. The course currently taken by the Turkmen leadership under the cover of neutrality provides no guarantee that the first scenario will in fact be chosen. This prospect would hardly be in the interests of the Turkmen people.

Part III

The changing conflict dynamics in the Caspian Sea region

15. The conflict in Nagorno-Karabakh: its impact on security in the Caspian region

Dina Malysheva

I. Introduction

The Caspian region is a crossroads where the interests of many states meet to form a complex pattern. First and foremost are the states bordering the Caspian Sea itself—Azerbaijan, Iran, Kazakhstan, Russia and Turkmenistan. However, the full set of problems related to the region is so important that it also affects the interests of many other countries—of every Central Asian state, as well as Armenia, Georgia, Turkey, and even Moldova and Ukraine, for which the oil and gas of the Caspian region are of vital concern. The Caspian region is not merely a hub of entrepreneurial interests. It is also fraught with the danger of political and military conflicts, long-running and new, both in the areas of oil and gas extraction and in the zones providing outlets for this mineral wealth.

The conflict in Nagorno-Karabakh, a mainly Armenian-populated enclave of Azerbaijan, began in the late 1980s following a sharp escalation of ethnic tensions between Armenians and Azeris, and remains basically an inter-ethnic conflict.[1] It has, however, been strongly influenced over the past decade by a geopolitical struggle developing in the South Caucasus over its energy resources and energy transport routes. The conflict has become a local manifestation of the worldwide battle for another redivision of the world market and for political and economic control over the Caucasus and the Caspian region. There is a direct link between the settlement of regional security, on the one hand, and the geopolitical, economic and strategic interests of the conflicting sides, the mediators ('third parties') and the international community as a whole, on the other. The Karabakh issue would lend itself to a resolution much more easily were it not for the involvement of the strategic interests of other states and of major international companies taking part in prospecting for or mining the natural resources of the successor states of the USSR in the Caspian region. This simple truth has long been recognized by both Armenia and Azerbaijan.

The matter in dispute is the Nagorno-Karabakh Autonomous Region of Azerbaijan (NKAR). On 20 February 1988 the NKAR's Deputies asked the Supreme Soviet of the USSR and Armenia and Azerbaijan to endorse the withdrawal of the NKAR from Azerbaijan and reunite it with Armenia. This was the starting point of the conflict. It was followed by the adoption of legislative acts

[1] On the history of the conflict see, e.g., successive editions of the SIPRI Yearbook.

to legalize the formation of the Nagorno-Karabakh Republic (NKR)—a resolution on Nagorno-Karabakh's Reunification with the Armenian Soviet Socialist Republic, passed by both Armenia's Supreme Soviet and the NKAR's Regional Soviet on 1 December 1989; and the decree of the NKAR Deputies on the Formation of the Nagorno-Karabakh Republic, 2 September 1991. Previously, on 30 August 1991, Azerbaijan's Supreme Soviet had approved Azerbaijan's declaration of independence.[2] After a referendum in December 1991 on the official status of Nagorno-Karabakh (which took no account of the opinion of its non-Armenian population, which by then had suffered ethnic cleansing),[3] the NKR proclaimed independence in 1992, its territory including not only the proper territory of the NKAR, but also the Shaumyan District of Azerbaijan. In the course of fighting which took place in 1993 the NKR Army (with the support of Armenia) gained control of seven contiguous districts of Azerbaijan, declaring them to be a security belt. The ceasefire agreement signed by Armenia and Azerbaijan in Bishkek on 16 May 1994 is on the whole in force, but there are still shoot-outs on the line of contact between the two sides.

It is an open secret that the Nagorno-Karabakh conflict is in many respects determined by the struggle for Caspian oil and the future pipeline routes for the export of this oil. At the beginning of the 1990s the West initiated 'pipeline diplomacy' aimed at finding new routes for Caspian oil exports that would be alternatives to routes across Russia. The USA's strategic interests and conflict with Iran were behind the promotion of the Baku–Ceyhan pipeline project.[4] However, in order to implement the project several obstacles had to be overcome, the foremost of which was the Nagorno-Karabakh conflict.

The 'oil slick' of the Nagorno-Karabakh conflict came to the surface in 1993, and the debates over the routes that will carry Caspian oil to the world markets are still lively. The debating sides—the Caspian states and their neighbours—are trying to estimate not only the future revenues from the transit of oil over their territories but also the political dividends accruing from control over the energy transmission systems of the Caspian region.[5] It is clear that the countries of the region are highly dependent on whoever is to provide the outlet for their oil. Yet the security of the oil pipeline routes cannot be guaranteed unless the Nagorno-Karabakh conflict is brought to a close.

[2] Malysheva, D., *Konflikty v Razvivayushchemsya Mire, Rossii i SNG* [Conflicts in the developing world, Russia and the CIS] (Russian Academy of Sciences, Institute of World Economy and International Relations (IMEMO): Moscow 1997), p. 31; and Oganesyan, N., 'Nagorno-Karabakhskiy konflikt i varianty ego resheniya' [Nagorno-Karabakh conflict and ways to resolve it], *Etnopoliticheskiye Konflikty v Zakavkazye: ikh Istoki i Puti Resheniya* [Ethno-political conflicts in Transcaucasus: their roots and ways to resolve them] (University of Maryland: College Park, Md., 1997), pp. 100–102.

[3] The cleansing was preceded by Armenian pogroms in Azerbaijan and by deportations of Armenians from Azerbaijan in 1988–91. For further detail see Chobanyan, S., *Gosudarstvenno-organizovanny Terrorizm* [State-sponsored terrorism] (Yerevan, 1992); and Babanov, I. and Voyevodskiy, K., *Karabakhskiy Krizis* [The Karabakh crisis] (St Petersburg, 1992), pp. 47–53.

[4] On the actual and projected pipeline routes see chapter 3 in this volume.

[5] For further detail see *Rossiya i Zakavkazye: Realii Nezavisimosti i Novoye Partnerstvo* [Russia and the Transcaucasus: the realities of independence and a new partnership] (Finstatinform: Moscow, 2000), pp. 63–75; and Bahgan, G., 'The Caspian Sea geopolitical game: prospect for the new millennium', *OPEC Review*, vol. 23, no. 3 (Sep. 1999), p. 205.

At the Summit Meeting of the Organization for Security and Co-operation in Europe (OCSE) in Istanbul on 18–19 November 1999, the presidents of Azerbaijan, Kazakhstan and Turkmenistan plus Georgia and Turkey achieved a breakthrough by signing a number of important documents on the transfer of oil and gas.[6] The implementation of these agreements could well change the geopolitical and geo-economic situation in the South Caucasus and the larger Caspian region. However, the struggle for the division of the region's oil resources is far from over, and it affects the course of the Nagorno-Karabakh conflict and the positions of the contending sides. The conflict, moreover, has a momentum of its own.

II. The positions of the contending parties

Azerbaijan

Azerbaijan, striving to uphold its territorial integrity, refuses to recognize the self-proclaimed Nagorno-Karabakh Republic or to regard it as a party in the conflict. It accuses the NKR leadership of separatism and Armenia of connivance. Azerbaijan is also striving to persuade world opinion that the Nagorno-Karabakh conflict is not a struggle for self-determination on the part of the Karabakh Armenians but a case of aggression by Armenia and the seizure of foreign territory, with all the liabilities and international sanctions that implies.

Azerbaijan is using the Caspian oil resources as its main lever to put pressure on Armenia. As the number of foreign companies taking an interest in extracting the Caspian oil rises, the stand taken by Azerbaijan on Nagorno-Karabakh and Armenia becomes less flexible: it 'punished' Armenia by a blockade of transport communication links with Russia running across Azerbaijani territory and, together with Turkey, by creating hurdles for Armenia's participation in the European Union (EU) TRACECA (Transport Corridor Europe Caucasus Asia) project (although some TRACECA programmes are being implemented on Armenian territory).[7] At the TRACECA conference held in Baku in September 1998 Armenia's proposals to route a railway from Kars to Tbilisi via Armenia and to construct a second rail link from the Georgian ports of Poti and Batumi via Armenia to Iran were rejected by Turkish Foreign Minister Ismail Cem on the grounds that the Nagorno-Karabakh conflict was not yet resolved.[8] Azerbaijan links the lifting of the blockade and Armenia's participation in TRACECA with its own demand for the return of its occupied land, which must also be de-mined.[9] The Western states, whose economic interests are more in

---

[6] Akhundova, E., 'Bol'shaya neft' potechet mimo nas' ['Big oil' will flow past us], *Obshchaya Gazeta*, no. 47 (30 Nov.–1 Dec. 1999), p. 8.

[7] On TRACECA see the Internet site, URL <http://www.traceca.org>.

[8] Martirosyan, A. and Petrosyan, D., 'Armeniya i proyekt vosstanovleniya "velikogo shelkovogo puti"' [Armenia and the 'Great Silk Road' project], *Tsentral'naya Aziya i Kavkaz* (Luleå), no. 1 (1998), p. 76.

[9] Shermatova, S., 'Karabakh uzhe podelen?' [Has Karabakh has already been divided?], *Moskovskiye Novosti*, no. 42 (2–8 Nov. 1999), p. 13.

line with those of Azerbaijan than with those of Armenia, support Azerbaijan, in this way bolstering the latter's position at the Karabakh negotiations.

The conditions set by Azerbaijan for a discussion of the status of Nagorno-Karabakh are that: (*a*) the legislation that changed its status must be abolished; (*b*) the seven districts adjacent to Nagorno-Karabakh presently occupied by the NKR Army, which Azerbaijan estimates at 20 per cent of its own territory, must be returned;[10] (*c*) the NKR Army must be disarmed and disbanded; and (*d*) Nagorno-Karabakh must be subject to the jurisdiction and legislation of Azerbaijan.[11]

In trying to resolve the Nagorno-Karabakh conflict, Azerbaijani President Heidar Aliyev has to be extremely cautious so as not to give his domestic opposition, which has long used the Karabakh issue as a bargaining chip,[12] arguments for charging him with betraying the national interests. As the hopes Azerbaijan placed on Turkish and Western capital have not been justified, and as Azerbaijan is gripped by a deepening economic crisis,[13] its ruling elite links the solution of the Karabakh problem to greater cooperation with Russia, although continuing to rely on Western support. Aliyev said on national television in June 2000 that 'the key to settling regional conflicts, such as the Karabakh conflict, is in Moscow'.[14]

Russia, in its turn, during President Vladimir Putin's visit to Baku in January 2001, tried to improve relations with Azerbaijan, which had remained cool over the previous decade. Holding talks with Aliyev, Putin strove to keep to the same line that he followed with Armenian President Robert Kocharian in the course of their dialogue on the Karabakh problem in September 2000. At that time Putin stated that he would not like 'anyone to believe that Russia owns the right or has exclusive opportunities to resolve any conflict, including in Karabakh'.[15] He also disavowed the view that 'everything could be changed overnight at Russia's bidding' and characterized this attitude as 'a manifestation of empire-oriented thinking'.[16] In Baku again Putin talked about maintaining equidistance (or 'equal nearness'), keeping in line with the official Russian stand: Russia was prepared to accept any solution of the Karabakh problem which was acceptable to both Armenia and Azerbaijan.[17] Putin affirmed that Russia was ready to promote further dialogue between the two sides and to help

[10] See, e.g., Pashaeva, G., 'Karabakhskiy konflikt: est' li vykhod iz tupika?' [The Karabakh conflict: is there an end to the deadlock?], *Tsentral'naya Aziya i Kavkaz* (Luleå), no. 5 (1999), p. 77.

[11] Oganesyan (note 2), pp. 108–109.

[12] Naumov, G., 'Azerbaijanskaya oppozitsiya protiv dogovora s Armeniey' [The Azerbaijani opposition is against a treaty with Armenia], *Nezavisimaya Gazeta*, 15 Oct. 1999; and Kyamal, 'Bol'she my ne ustupim' [We will concede no more], *Zerkalo* (Baku), no. 85 (6 June 2000), p. 8.

[13] For further detail see Malysheva, D., 'Nevoyennye vyzovy natsional'noy bezopasnosti v sovremennom Azerbaijane' [Non-military challenges to Azerbaijan's national security], *Regional'naya Bezopasnost' i Sotrudnichestvo v Tsentral'noy Asii i na Kavkaze* (Tsentrforum: Moscow, 1999), pp. 221–38.

[14] Sergeyev, D., 'Azerbaijan: novye nadezhdy' [Azerbaijan: new hopes], *Izvestiya*, 22 July 2000, p. 5.

[15] Khanbabyan, A., 'Moskva i Yerevan udovletvorennye urovnem politicheskikh otnoshenii' [Moscow and Yerevan are satisfied by the level of political relations], *Nezavisimaya Gazeta*, 27 Oct. 2000.

[16] Khanbabyan (note 15).

[17] Gajizade, A. and Kozyrev, D., 'Putin nachal god s Baku' [Putin begins the year with Baku], *Nezavisimaya Gazeta*, 10 Jan. 2001.

implement any agreement reached between Aliyev and Kocharian, both in its capacity as a co-chairman of the OSCE Minsk Group and acting independently.[18] Putin's visit to Baku resulted in proclamation of a strategic partnership recorded in the Baku Declaration of the principles of security and cooperation in the Caucasus.[19]

The leaders of Azerbaijan would undoubtedly like to secure Russia's support in reaching a peaceful resolution of the Karabakh conflict. The essential point is Aliyev's desire to maintain smooth relations with both the West and Russia. In order to achieve this he uses contacts with one side as a stimulus for facilitating contacts with the other. Besides, Aliyev is trying to secure Russian support in the domestic power struggle and to affirm the claims of his son Ilham in the anticipated redistribution of power. Russia's reaction to this has been aptly defined in the Baku weekly *Zerkalo*: 'Moscow is unlikely to trust implicitly the present leaders of Azerbaijan whose past was definitely pro-Western'.[20] Still, Moscow would like to see the 'Aliyev line' continued. Should a radically pro-Western and anti-Russian opposition come to power Russia would stand to lose important strategic positions in this key region of the South Caucasus.

Keeping in mind the speed of Azerbaijan's military build-up[21] and its rich oil and gas resources, the return of the lost territories would improve the image of the ruling elite at home and ensure the country's strategic preponderance over Armenia. That is why the option for Azerbaijan of resolving the Karabakh issue by force cannot be ruled out. Armenia and the NKR are both aware of this, and it impels them to intensify the build-up of their defence potentials.

Armenia

The issues that dominate Armenia's position are the security of the Armenian population of Nagorno-Karabakh and the settlement of the issue in a way that is acceptable to the NKR. Without having officially recognized the NKR, Armenia upholds its right of self-determination.[22] It agrees with the NKR in the assessment of the conflict and its participants and recognizes the NKR as a warring party in addition to Armenia and Azerbaijan. According to President

---

[18] 'Azerbaijani, Russian presidents pledge to build "strategic partnership"', Radio Free Europe/Radio Liberty (hereafter RFE/RL), *RFE/RL Newsline*, vol. 4, no. 2, Part 1 (11 Jan. 2001). The Minsk Group was set up by the Conference on Security and Co-operation in Europe (CSCE) in Mar. 1992 to monitor the situation in Nagorno-Karabakh. It is discussed further in section V of this chapter. The member countries at the time of writing (2000) were Armenia, Austria, Azerbaijan, Belarus, Finland, France, Germany, Italy, Norway, Russia, Sweden, Turkey and the USA. See, e.g,. Organization for Security and Co-operation in Europe, *OSCE Handbook* [2000], URL <http://www.osce.org/publications/handbook/index.htm>.

[19] ITAR-TASS (Moscow), 9 Jan. 2001, in 'Russian, Azeri presidents issue declaration on strategic cooperation', Foreign Broadcast Information Service, *Daily Report–Central Eurasia (FBIS-SOV)*, FBIS-SOV-2001-0109, 10 Jan. 2001.

[20] Nurani, A., 'Baku reshil "prodatsya" [Baku decides to 'sell itself'], *Zerkalo*, 27 Dec. 2000.

[21] Over the 6 years 1995–2000 Azerbaijan's military expenditure estimated in constant US dollars rose by 73%. See chapter 5 in this volume.

[22] Kaban, E., 'Davos: Azeri, Armenian leaders upbeat on peace', Reuters, 28 Jan. 2000.

Kocharian, 'it is essential that the solution of the Karabakh conflict is devised by the sides involved and not imposed by the international community'.[23]

Armenia does not rule out discussion about Nagorno-Karabakh becoming an administrative unit of the Republic of Armenia if the Karabakh ethnic Armenians address such a request to it.[24] However, it realizes that supporting an independent Karabakh or its incorporation into Armenia would inevitably be followed by international sanctions: UN Security Council resolutions 822, 853, 874 and 884, adopted during the 1993 offensive of the Armenian-Karabakh forces and urging the withdrawal of troops from the territory of Karabakh, are still in force.[25] Western attitudes towards the conflict and the part played by Armenia are also changing: there is no unanimous opinion in the West with regard to Armenia's unyielding stand on the issue of what Azerbaijan calls the 'occupied territories' (the territory of Azerbaijan which is presently under the control of the NKR Army), the patently pro-Russian slant of Armenia's policy, its good-neighbourly relations with Iran or the continued tensions in relations between Armenia and Turkey.

Russia, undoubtedly Armenia's strategic partner, nevertheless firmly supports the territorial integrity of Azerbaijan, and Armenia cannot expect Russia to change its stand during the settlement process.

Objectively Armenia is interested in peace with Azerbaijan. This would help it to break out of its isolation and normalize relations with all its neighbours and the international community; Armenia hopes to improve its very serious social and political situation; and it expects a share in the lucrative economic projects linked, among other things, to the export of Caspian oil. This last factor may lead to Armenia shifting its position on the Karabakh issue and becoming more tractable.

The Nagorno-Karabakh Republic

For the NKR the crucial issue is its status. In November 1993 then NKR Foreign Minister Arkadiy Gukasian linked the resolution of the Karabakh conflict and the withdrawal of the NKR armed formations from the Azerbaijani districts they held to the problem of determining the status of the NKR and the lifting of the blockade of Armenia.[26] Today, however, the Karabakh politicians prioritize the question of the safety of the NKR Armenian population. Thus Naira Melkumian, the present Foreign Minister of the NKR, believes that the republic's security can be guaranteed only if it is able to preserve its geo-

---

[23] 'Prezident Armenii storonnik mirnogo resheniya karabakhskoy problemy' [Armenia's president stands for a peaceful solution of the Karabakh issue], *Izvestiya*, 15 Feb. 2000.

[24] *Zerkalo* (Baku), no. 31 (16 Feb. 2000), p. 2.

[25] Oganesyan (note 2), p. 90.

[26] Mityaev, V. G., 'Karabakhskiy konflikt v kontekste mezhdunarodnykh otnoshenii' [The Karabakh conflict in the context of international relations], *Armeniya: Problemy Nezavisimogo Razvitiya* [Armenia: the problems of independent development] (Rossiyskiy Institut Strategicheskikh Issledovanii [Russian Institute of Strategic Studies]: Moscow, 1998), p. 513.

graphical connection with the outside world and retain the 'security belt' which can minimize 'the effect of a surprise attack with conventional weapons'.[27]

Over the past few years the Karabakh elite has been able to exert considerable influence on the position of Armenia. Experts have labelled this the 'Karabakhization' of Armenia's social and political life.[28] Citizens of the NKR have won high-level government posts in Armenia; Armenian government policy evinces a stronger tendency to prioritize relations with Russia, which is a characteristic feature of the political course of the NKR; and Armenia's attitude to the West is growing more wary, in line with the mind-set of the Karabakh elite.

The process of building an independent state is proceeding apace in the NKR itself. The republic has been an independent military–political factor in the Karabakh conflict for some time, which means that a political settlement will be difficult to carry out without direct negotiations between Baku and Stepanakert. The NKR won de facto recognition as a party to the conflict for the first time at the Commonwealth of Independent States (CIS) summit meeting held in Bishkek in May 1994,[29] but its representatives do not take part in the negotiations as a recognized party to the conflict. President Gukasian of the NKR believes that at the present stage Azerbaijan is not yet psychologically adjusted to negotiations with the Karabakh authorities, fearing that these might be interpreted as recognition of the NKR's independent status. In his opinion, 'the issue cannot be settled with Armenia alone, without our participation'.[30]

International recognition of the NKR as an independent entity is the long-term goal of the Karabakh elite, and there is no unanimous support inside the NKR for integration into Armenia. At this point in time, the NKR is eager to convince the world that it and the 'Karabakh people' are engaged in a national liberation struggle and should therefore be recognized as one of the conflicting parties, with direct participation in the settlement talks.

Recently instability in Nagorno-Karabakh and Armenia has increased. On 22 March 2000 the NKR Defence Minister, General Samvel Babayan, and his supporters made an attempt on President Gukasian's life. The attempt failed and its organizers were arrested and prosecuted.[31] On 18 June 2000 parliamentary elections were held in the NKR but they did not resolve the domestic conflict.[32] The Karabakh military elite which rose to power during the armed conflict with Azerbaijan, and was involved in internal feuding, did not savour the prospect of being sidelined by the more pragmatically-minded people who had come on to

[27] Melkumyan, N., 'Nagorny Karabakh: v poiskakh ustoichivogo mira' [Nagorno-Karabakh: in search of a stable peace], *Tsentral'naya Aziya i Kavkaz* (Luleå), no. 3 (1999), p. 61.

[28] For further detail see Avakyan, G., 'Vliyaniye Karabakhskogo faktora na formirovaniye politicheskoy identichnosti v Armenii' [The influence of the Karabakh factor on the development of a political identity in Armenia], *Severny Kavkaz–Zakavkazye: Problemy Stabil'nosti i Perspektivy Razvitiya* [The North Caucasus and trans-Caucasus: problems of stability and the prospects for development] (Grif-F: Moscow, 1997), pp. 166–80.

[29] *Spornye Granitsy na Kavkaze* [Contested frontiers in the Caucasus] (Ves Mir: Moscow, 1996), p. 37.

[30] 'Posledny shans ne dopustit' voiny' [The last chance to avoid war], *Obshchaya Gazeta*, no. 36 (9–15 Sep. 1999), p. 5.

[31] Maksimenko, O., 'Ministra oborony sudyat za pokusheniye na prezidenta' [Defence Minister under trial for attempt on president's life], *Kommersant* (Moscow), 19 Sep. 2000.

[32] Kachmazov, A., 'Vybory v tylu vraga' [Elections in the enemy's rear], *Izvestiya*, 20 June 2000.

the political scene in peacetime. The NKR military high command was also displeased by Gukasian's dismissal of the entire government of the republic and by his choice of Anushan Danielian, an outsider not connected with the Karabakh elite, as the new prime minister. According to President Kocharian a number of senior Karabakh officers who were dissatisfied with Gukasian's policy continued to challenge his authority.[33]

In Armenia, too, political tensions remained. On 2 May 2000 Kocharian dismissed the prime minister and defence minister, who criticized him severely.[34] Given those domestic changes there may also be changes in Armenia's approach to the Karabakh issue. Thus, Kocharian may agree to an exchange of territory that will give Armenia the Lachin corridor in exchange for the Megrin region being ceded to Azerbaijan. In fact this exchange has already been discussed in bilateral negotiations between Aliyev and Kocharian.[35]

The positions of all the sides are clearly affected by the internal political situation prevailing in each of them and by the fluctuating alignment of forces in the trans-Caucasus and Caspian regions, as well as in Russia, the CIS, the neighbouring countries of the Middle East and the world as a whole.

III. The positions of the regional countries

Georgia

Because of its proximity to the Karabakh conflict zone, Georgia is vitally concerned with the settlement of the conflict. It is officially Azerbaijan's strategic partner, upholds the preservation of Azerbaijan's territorial integrity and supports the latter in its conflict with Armenia on most contentious issues.

This standpoint is determined by several factors. First, there is concern for the security and integrity of Georgia itself, since the rekindling of the internal conflicts involving Abkhazia and South Ossetia is still a dangerous prospect, and strained relations with Adzharia and some other parts of the country still persist.[36] In such a setting there is no logic in supporting the Nagorno-Karabakh Armenians who are seeking self-determination. Second, the Georgian authorities suspect Armenia of encouraging secessionist tendencies among the ethnic Armenians who live in a compact group in Javaheti in southern Georgia and thus acting in the interests of Russia.[37] Relations between the latter and the Georgian leadership have lately been very tense. Third, Georgia's obviously pro-Azerbaijan approach to the Karabakh problem is accounted for by Georgia's plans to make its territory the main transit route for Caspian oil.

[33] Kocharian, R., 'My s Putinym myslim skhodnymi kategiriyami' [Putin and I think in the same way], *Izvestiya*, 22 Sep. 2000.

[34] Djivalian, A. and Khanbanyan, A., 'Pobeda Kochariana' [Kocharian's victory], *Nezavisimaya Gazeta*, 14 May 2000.

[35] Makunz, G., 'Sud'bu Karabakha reshat velikiye mira sego' [The mighty will determine Karabakh's fate], *Nezavisimaya Gazeta*, 9 June 2000.

[36] See also chapter 11 in this volume.

[37] Darchiashvili, D., 'Yuzhnaya Grusiya: vyzovy i zadachi bezopasnosti' [Southern Georgia: challenges to and the task of security], *Tsentral'naya Aziya i Kavkaz* (Luleå), no. 1 (2000), p. 181.

Fourth, Georgia, like Azerbaijan, is striving to come under the 'NATO umbrella': both countries hope for the support of NATO in maintaining peace and achieving national and regional security.

Any resumption of hostilities on the Karabakh front would be a most unwelcome development for Georgia since it would pose a serious challenge to its own security. Georgia therefore has a vital interest in peace between Armenia and Azerbaijan. Yet the weakness of its own economic potential, the absence of weighty geo-strategic arguments, internal instability (which places Georgia in the category of 'failed states') and its lack of political and military self-reliance all limit its ability to influence the resolution of the Karabakh conflict in any significant way, making it merely a 'concerned side'. It is not capable of making any serious impact on the course of the Karabakh settlement.

The Central Asian Caspian states

Like Georgia and Russia, the Central Asian Caspian states are concerned with the Karabakh conflict and have tried to act as mediators. In the early 1990s Kazakhstan attempted to help in working out a settlement following the failed mediation initiatives of Russia, Iran and the Conference on Security and Co-operation in Europe (the CSCE, forerunner of the Organization for Security and Co-operation in Europe, the OSCE). On the initiative of President Nursultan Nazarbayev of Kazakhstan, peace talks were held in Alma Ata in September 1992, but his peacemaking did not prove a success: having signed a ceasefire protocol to be valid until September 1999, the warring sides promptly resumed hostilities on the Armenian–Azerbaijani border.[38] At the beginning of March 1993 President Nazarbayev came out with the proposal that the Council of the CIS Heads of State should demand a ceasefire on the Karabakh front.[39] After that Kazakhstan, which is an active participant in all the Caspian oil ventures, never emerged as a peacemaker.

The position of Turkmenistan is determined by its basic approach to developments in the CIS: formally a CIS member, it prefers to avoid political initiatives in favour of bilateral relations with other post-Soviet states and it is not a signatory of the 1992 Treaty on Collective Security (the Tashkent Treaty).[40] It keeps an equal distance from all the participants in the Karabakh conflict, but its relations with Azerbaijan are overshadowed by the issue of four contested Caspian oil fields which are claimed by both Azerbaijan and Turkmenistan, as well as by problems related to the transfer of Turkmen gas via the Caucasus.

[38] Yemelyanenko, V., 'Kazakhstan v roli mirotvortsa' [Kazakhstan as a peacekeeper], *Moskovskiye Novosti*, no. 37 (13 Sep. 1992), p. 9.

[39] Amer, R. *et al.*, 'Major armed conflicts', *SIPRI Yearbook 1993: World Armaments and Disarmament* (Oxford University Press: Oxford, 1993), p. 97.

[40] On the Tashkent Treaty see chapter 5 in this volume. For the text see *Izvestiya*, 16 May 1992, p. 3.

Russia

Russia, the largest state on the territory of the former Soviet Union and the co-chairman of the OSCE Minsk Group, long ago assumed the role of mediator and 'third party' in the Karabakh conflict. Russia's national interests are directly involved, for the conflict destabilizes the situation on its southern borders, complicates its relations with the newly independent states of the South Caucasus, and disrupts stability in the region where Russia has important economic and political interests.

A summary of Russia's interests in the South Caucasus and the larger Caspian region illustrates what Russia aims to achieve first and foremost. It aims to preserve its political and military presence there, to extend its control over the extraction of Caspian oil and its transport routes and to restrain its potential geopolitical and economic rivals in the region, such as Turkey, the USA and other Western countries. Russia thus faces the difficult task of coordinating its domestic and foreign policy interests and the interests of the conflicting sides, as well as those of the countries concerned by, or involved in, the Karabakh conflict.

Since 1995 the Russian political elite has begun to define its foreign policy priorities. President Boris Yeltsin declared both the South Caucasus and the entire CIS space to be the sphere of Russia's top-priority interests.[41] Mediation in the Karabakh conflict enables Russia to maintain its presence in the South Caucasus and the Caspian region. Russia is trying to keep off international mediators or at least to force them to acknowledge that no settlement of the Karabakh conflict will be achieved without Russia as the principal peacemaker. Russia 'has more reasons to consider the Caspian a zone of its vital interests than any of the powers not belonging to that region'.[42]

In the past few years Russia has chosen to make Armenia its main ally in the region, but the oil factor and Azerbaijan's important geo-strategic position are major arguments in favour of closer ties with Azerbaijan, which keeps a jealous eye on the progress of the military and political alliance between Armenia and Russia. In 1991 they signed a Treaty of Friendship, Cooperation and Mutual Security, and on 29 August 1997 this was followed by a new treaty.[43] In order to keep up the system of 'checks and balances', on 3 July 1997 Russia signed the Treaty of Friendship, Cooperation and Mutual Security with Azerbaijan.[44] The treaty with Armenia made it incumbent on the two countries to assist each other in the event of armed aggression by a third country, whereas the Azerbaijani–Russian treaty merely provides for 'urgent consultations'.[45]

---

[41] Ukaz Prezidenta Rossiyskoy Federatsii [Presidential Edict] no. 940, 14 Sep. 1995.

[42] Tesyomnikova, E., 'Problema Kaspiya: ostorozhny optimizm Moskvy' [The Caspian problem: Moscow's cautious optimism], *Sodruzhestvo NG* [supplement to *Nezavisimaya Gazeta*], no. 5 (May 2000), p. 9.

[43] For the text of the treaty see *Diplomaticheskiy Vestnik*, no. 9 (1997), pp. 31–38.

[44] This did not prevent Azerbaijan from assessing the Armenian–Russian agreements as a 'military pact'. Baranovsky, V., 'Russia: conflicts and peaceful settlement of disputes', *SIPRI Yearbook 1998: Armaments, Disarmament and International Security* (Oxford University Press: Oxford, 1998), p. 128.

[45] *Diplomaticheskiy Vestnik*, no. 8 (1997), p. 41.

Clearly enough, the Armenian politicians, like their counterparts in Azerbaijan, are trying to play on the differences and rivalries between Russia and the USA so as to secure maximum advantage to themselves. Russia, which has no intention of being manipulated or saddled with someone else's problems, is well aware of this. It is the activities of the West, and primarily of the USA, that cause Russia to make more diplomatic efforts over the Karabakh settlement. The USA is active in the region, working along several lines, such as cultivating the local elites, getting footholds in the army and the frontier forces through the NATO Partnership for Peace (PFP) programme, and seeking to win control over the key sectors of the economy, in particular over the oil and gas sector. The USA is concentrating its efforts on redirecting all the communication lines of the Caspian Basin and the South Caucasus by means of TRACECA and the projects for the Baku–Ceyhan and trans-Caspian oil and gas pipelines. Russia is thus confronted with the very real threat of forfeiting its positions in the region.

Russia is trying to intercept the initiatives of Turkey and the USA in managing the conflict and to build up its influence in the South Caucasus, as testified by the programmatic statement made by Foreign Minister Igor Ivanov before his visit to the three South Caucasian capitals in the autumn of 1999: 'Russia was, is, and will be a Caucasian power, and we therefore want stability in this region and make no secret of our position: the "neither peace nor war" situation which prevails there today does not suit us'.[46] The importance Russia attaches to having a firm foothold in the Caspian region is exemplified by the discussion of Russia's strategic interests in the Caspian Sea area at the May 2000 meeting of the Russian Security Council directly after the discussion of the country's new military doctrine.[47] President Putin said at the time that the authorities must strive to consolidate the positions of the Russian companies in the Caspian.[48] Accordingly, on 25 July 2000 the Russian companies Lukoil, Yukos and Gazprom set up the Caspian Oil Company to develop the new oil and gas fields in the Caspian region;[49] Viktor Kalyuzhny, the newly appointed special representative of the Russian President for the Caspian region, met the heads of the Caspian states in July 2000. According to Kalyuzhny, Azerbaijan supported nearly all the new Russian proposals on the status of the Caspian Sea.[50]

Russia's increasing efforts to settle the conflict are also borne out by the Armenian–Azerbaijani talks it organized in January 2000. The Russian President said at that time, 'If the negotiations come to a successful end, Russia would act as a guarantor of a compromise solution'.[51] In the opinion of experts,

[46] Dubnov, A., 'Velikaya Kavkazskaya derzhava' [A great Caucasian power], *Vremya*, no. 160 (2 Sep. 1999).

[47] The new military doctrine as approved by President Vladimir Putin on 21 Apr. 2000 was published in *Nezavisimaya Gazeta*, 22 Apr. 2000. An unofficial translation into English was released by BBC Monitoring on 22 Apr. 2000.

[48] Amirov, A., 'Kaspiyskiy perekryostok' [The Caspian crossroads], *Russkaya Mysl'* (Paris), no. 4316 (4–10 May 2000), p. 7.

[49] Ignatova, M., 'Vmeste veselo burit'' [It's fun to drill together], *Izvestiya*, 26 July 2000, p. 6.

[50] Shermatova, S., 'Kaspiy plus Karabakh' [Caspian plus Karabakh], *Moskovskiye Novosti*, no. 28 (8–14 July 2000), p. 10.

[51] Amirov (note 48).

what he meant was first and foremost military guarantees. Russia is prepared to send peacekeeping forces to the region, including the neutral zone which would be established along the line of contact between the Armenian-Karabakh and Azerbaijani troops. The Russian peace contingent could be stationed on those territories of Azerbaijan which are presently under the control of the NKR Army. These territories are supposed to go back to Azerbaijan once a full-scale settlement has been achieved.[52]

In keeping with its approach of supporting Azerbaijan's territorial integrity, Russia, like Azerbaijan, does not regard Nagorno-Karabakh as a full negotiating partner. Its stand is in no small degree the result of its own experience in Chechnya. Armenia's geopolitical isolation and its need to find outside patronage make it easier for Russia to maintain its positions in the region and to counterbalance the influence of Turkey and the USA, which are on Azerbaijan's side. Russia wants a situation of military and political balance in the region, but this political line is not always pursued with adequate consistency, provoking criticism at home as well as from the sides in the Karabakh conflict.

The mechanisms to which Russia resorts in order to exert pressure on the conflicting sides are the CIS and the Tashkent Treaty, of which Russia is the clear leader. Registered at the UN Secretariat, the Tashkent Treaty provides (under article 51 of the UN Charter) the legal basis for a fully-fledged military alliance, granting its participants the right of collective defence. The Minsk summit meeting of the signatories to the treaty in 23–24 May 2000 issued a memorandum on increasing the efficiency of the treaty as well as some other documents.[53] This places the Karabakh situation in a new context, for it would enable Russia in case of need to provide the required support to Armenia as a signatory of the Tashkent Treaty and at the same time exert pressure on 'recalcitrant' Azerbaijan. Thus it enhanced the role of the Tashkent Treaty, to the potential detriment of NATO involvement in the management of the conflict.

Both Armenia and Azerbaijan signed the Tashkent Treaty, but in April 1999 Azerbaijan, together with Georgia and Uzbekistan, announced that it was withdrawing from it, explaining the decision by its disappointment over Russia's passivity on the Karabakh issue and over the deliveries of Russian weapons to Armenia.[54] Discernible behind this step, however, were those foreign policy and economic interests which at that time determined the logic of Azerbaijan's attitude: it was annoyed by Russia's increasing military presence in Armenia, by its efforts to restrict Western and Turkish economic and geopolitical expansion in the region, and by the persistence of Russian business circles and companies in the oil and gas sector.

[52] Dzhilavyan, A., 'Proryv v Karabakhskom uregulirovanii?' [A breakthrough in the Karabakh settlement?], *Nezavisimaya Gazeta*, 26 Jan. 2000.

[53] *Diplomaticheskiy Vestnik*, no. 6 (2000), pp. 30–31.

[54] Korbut, A., 'Krizis sistemy kollektivnoy bezopasnosti' [Crisis in the system of collective security], *Sodruzhestvo NG* [supplement to *Nezavisimaya Gazeta*], no. 5 (May 1999), p. 10.

The GUUAM group

On top of this, in the late 1990s Azerbaijan was active in launching the GUUAM political–economic group, which its participants came to regard as a kind of alternative to the CIS and its security system. Originally named GUAM, it was founded in 1997 by the presidents of Georgia, Ukraine, Azerbaijan and Moldova in Strasbourg during a conference of the heads of state and government of the Council of Europe. On 25 April 1999 in Washington during the NATO 50th anniversary session, which was attended by most of the CIS heads of state, Uzbekistan joined it and it became GUUAM.[55] In addition to cooperation over the transport of oil and gas and other economic matters, the GUUAM participants undertook to develop multilateral cooperation to facilitate conflict management and overcome separatism; they also agreed to interact with the UN, the OSCE, NATO and the PFP programme.[56] This was a clear sign that GUUAM hopes for NATO guarantees not only as regards conflict management and coping with crises but also as regards regional security. This is attested to by the members' discussion of plans for a permanent GUUAM peacekeeping battalion for maintaining peace and ensuring the safety of pipeline communications.[57] This project was considered at a meeting of the Azerbaijani, Georgian and Moldovan defence ministers in Baku in January 1999.[58] Characteristically enough, Armenia, eager to join the economic projects in the trans-Caucasus, has shown an interest in GUUAM.[59]

It seems, however, that the other members of GUUAM are not as deeply concerned as Azerbaijan and Georgia with the settlement of the Nagorno-Karabakh conflict. Their main purpose is to assert their presence on the energy markets. All kinds of means are being used to this end, including anti-Russian rhetoric, of which one example was the public statements of the GUUAM members at the Cisinau summit meeting of the CIS in October 1997.[60] On the whole, however, they have advanced no further than making declarations and have not been able to influence the Karabakh negotiating process. At this stage, GUUAM is not to be regarded as a significant factor of regional policy because of its weak economic potential and the disagreements between its members.

Far more noticeable have been other 'players' on the field of Transcaucasian politics, who are likewise attracted by the potential of the Caspian oil fields—namely, Iran and Turkey, the close neighbours of Armenia and Azerbaijan.

---

[55] Olegov, F., 'Zachem GUAMu yescho odna bukva "u"' [What about another 'U' in GUAM?], *Sodruzhestvo NG* [supplement to *Nezavisimaya Gazeta*], no. 5 (May 1999), p. 1. See also chapter 5, section V in this volume.

[56] Parakhonskiy, B., 'Formirovaniye modeli regional'nogo sotrudnichestva v sisteme GUUAM' [Forming a model for regional cooperation inside the GUUAM system], *Tsentral'naya Aziya i Kavkaz* (Luleå), no. 2 (2000), pp. 104–105.

[57] Useynov, A., 'Os Kiev–Baku' [The Kiev–Baku axis], *Vremya Novostei*, 22 Mar. 2000, p. 6.

[58] Parakhonskiy (note 56), p. 101.

[59] Ivanov, G., 'Kavkaz odin na vsekh' [The Caucasus is a single entity for all], *Izvestiya*, 30 Mar. 2000, p. 8.

[60] *Diplomaticheskiy Vestnik*, no. 11 (1997), p. 32; and Parakhonskiy (note 56), p. 100.

Iran

Iran regards the Karabakh conflict as the greatest danger to regional security. It upholds the territorial integrity of Azerbaijan and connects the causes of the conflict with the influence of the West.[61] A close look at Iran's policy on the Karabakh conflict reveals a well-calculated line: avowals of Islamic solidarity do not prevent Iran from supporting Armenia, a Christian country, rather than its Muslim brothers in Azerbaijan, for it is Armenia that stands in the way of the implementation of the Turkish route for the oil pipeline. Armenia, or rather the Armenian armed forces in Karabakh, also serve as a most effective means of pressuring Azerbaijan. At the same time Iran does not wish to see the continuation or expansion of Armenia's military presence on the territory of Azerbaijan as this could result in a flow of refugees into the Iranian provinces bordering on Azerbaijan, with the result that the Iranian authorities would face the same problems as Pakistan had to face during the war in Afghanistan. Iran has good reason to fear that the refugees might stir up separatist feelings in the Azeri-populated provinces of Iran.

Relations between Iran and Azerbaijan still evince a certain degree of tension engendered by historical, ethnic and religious contradictions. There is a feeling in Iran that Azerbaijan is committing an historic error by granting the USA access to the Caspian region. Iran is also strongly opposed to the rapprochement between Azerbaijan and Israel.[62] (President Kocharian of Armenia expresses concern at the prospect of Azerbaijan joining the Israeli–Turkish military alliance: this could have negative implications for Armenia as long as the Karabakh conflict remains unresolved.[63])

As for the Iranian–Russian alliance, its basis is too fragile. In the long history of Russia's relations with Iran, strategic alliances to ward off Turkish or Western threats were invariably reluctant on the part of Iran and short-lived. If Iran succeeds in improving its relations with the United States and attracting the transport of Azerbaijani oil through its own territory its interests will no longer coincide with Russia's.

Because of its advantageous geopolitical position, Iran is of vital importance for blockaded Armenia. In its turn Iran looks for opportunities to break out of its isolation by cooperating with Armenia and Russia. This kind of rapprochement, which does not run counter to Russia's strategy in the region, has emerged as an independent and significant factor of its policy aimed at opposing the growing 'Turkish expansion', which is a subject of equal concern to Iran and Armenia.

[61] Bigdeli, A., 'Overview of relations between the Islamic Republic of Iran and the Republic of Azerbaijan', *Amu Darya: the Iranian Journal of Central Asian Studies* (Center for the Study of Central Asia and the Caucasus, Tehran), vol. 4, no. 2 (summer 1999), p. 164.

[62] Maleki, M.-R., 'Turkish–Israeli relations: impact on Central Asia and the Caucasus', *Amu Darya* (Tehran), vol. 4, no. 2 (summer 1999), pp. 180–96.

[63] *Zerkalo*, no. 14 (22 Jan. 2000), p. 7.

Turkey

Turkey's interests and priorities are underpinned, just as is the case with Iran, by the urge to play a more active part in the post-Soviet south, where Turkey plans to set up an economic framework dependent on itself.[64] The main obstacle to these plans is the uncertain tenor of Turkish–Azerbaijani relations and the possible resumption of hostilities in the Karabakh conflict zone.

Having officially proclaimed its neutrality in the conflict, Turkey actually sides with Azerbaijan. In the early 1990s it closed its frontier with Armenia, but in the mid-1990s it did allow Armenia an air corridor. However, Turkey's functions in the region are mostly those of mediation, for it lacks a developed infrastructure and does not command the funds needed for investments in major projects. It can only rely on its advantageous geographical location in trying to steer through its own territory the communication lines from the Caspian zone and Central Asia.

The growing importance of the Iranian and Turkish factors is bound up with the struggle waged by the two countries for regional leadership and spheres of influence; this struggle naturally includes claims to the region's resources, vital communication lines, and energy and strategic centres. As they project their own interests and priorities, both Iran and Turkey realize their limitations and are therefore eager to coordinate their activities with those of the major states— either Russia or the USA. Barring either Iran or Turkey from participation in the regional process could prove counterproductive both in the context of political stabilization and the settlement of the Karabakh conflict, and in the context of integrative processes in the South Caucasus region.

IV. The stand of the Western countries

The Western states and the USA, as their leader, realize that the way the Karabakh conflict is resolved will in many respects determine the prospects of a new geopolitical configuration in the South Caucasus and in the Caspian region in general. Helping US and West European companies to have unimpeded access to the Caspian oil and gas resources would serve to minimize the West's dependence on Middle East oil and help to bring down world prices of fuel. According to former US Secretary of State James Baker, in the 21st century Caspian oil may become as vital to the industrial world as Persian Gulf oil is today.[65] Under these plans, Russia's role is relegated to that of a low-key partner of the West and not a dominant player in the region. US strategists also aim to minimize Iran's influence in the region.

Having in 1997 declared the Caspian to be a zone of its vital interests,[66] the USA heightened its activities, attempting, among other things, to act as an inde-

---

[64] See note 5.

[65] Orlov, A., 'Persidskiy zaliv v Kaspiyskom more' [Persian Gulf in the Caspian Sea], *Itogi* (Moscow), 16 Sep. 1997, p. 37.

[66] On US policy in the Caspian region see chapter 7 of this volume. See also Lieven, A., 'The (not so) Great Game', *National Interest* (Washington, DC), no. 58 (winter 1999/2000), pp. 69–70.

pendent mediator in the Karabakh settlement. At the OSCE Summit Meeting in Budapest on 5–6 December 1994, US diplomats succeeded in having a US representative made the third co-chairman of the Minsk Group,[67] thus winning direct access to the management of the conflict.

On the eve of the last US presidential election and with a view to removing the vexing threat of a new Karabakh war, the USA intensified its contacts not only with Azerbaijan, but also with Armenia and the NKR. One of the means of influencing these countries was the US economic aid programmes. Thus, the US Agency for International Development (USAID) released in April 2000 a special report on assistance to Nagorno-Karabakh and to the victims of the conflict.[68]

Azerbaijan views the development of contacts with the USA and NATO as an important factor for its own security and for the security of the entire Caucasian region. In the opinion of Rza Ibadov, chairman of a parliamentary commission, 'responsibility for the security of the Baku–Ceyhan main export pipeline should be assumed by NATO'.[69] Strengthening its ties with NATO, Azerbaijan signed an agreement in 1994 on participation in the PFP programme. It was also planning to set up a NATO information centre serving the entire region. This project was officially submitted for the consideration to NATO by Azerbaijan in December 1999.[70] In January 1999 the idea of moving, partially or fully, NATO's Injirlik military base[71] from Turkey to the Apsheron Peninsula in Azerbaijan was voiced by Azerbaijani foreign policy adviser Wafa Guluzade.[72] Guluzade said at the time: 'Seeing that Armenia harbours Russian military bases on its territory, why shouldn't Azerbaijan have US, Turkish or NATO military bases on its territory?'.[73] This move was made after the Azerbaijani media reported Russian plans to supply Armenia with S-300 surface-to-air missiles (SAMs),[74] even though that report was refuted by the Russian Ambassador to Armenia, Anatoliy Dryukov.

President Aliyev, however, preferred to distance himself from an outspoken advocate of NATO and in the autumn of 1999 dismissed Guluzade as well as Foreign Minister Tofik Zulfugarov and the head of the presidential secretariat, Eldar Namazov, all of whom were notorious for their pro-US leanings. This decision was attributed to the somewhat warmer climate in relations between

[67] See note 18.

[68] Dzhilavyan, A., 'Vashington aktiviziruyet programmy sodeystviya Stepanakerty' [Washington is reviving its programme of assistance to Stepanakert], *Nezavisimaya Gazeta*, 21 Apr. 2000.

[69] Useynov, A., 'Truba imeni Heidara' [The Heidar pipeline], *Vremya*, 24 Nov. 1999.

[70] Romanov, P., 'V Baku budet otkryt informatsionny tsentr NATO' [NATO's information centre to open in Baku], *Nezavisimaya Gazeta*, 22 Feb. 2000.

[71] Injirlik, incidentally, is the home base of the US and British aircraft patrolling the no-fly zones over Iraq and occasionally striking at the Iraqi air defence system.

[72] Nurani, A., 'Budut li v Azerbaijane voyennye bazy NATO?' [Will there be NATO military bases in Azerbaijan?], *Zerkalo*, no. 3 (23 Jan. 1999).

[73] Gajizade, A., 'Budet li na Apsherone razmeshchena amerikanskaya baza?' [Will a US base be settled in Apsheron?], *Nezavisimaya Gazeta*, 20 Jan. 1999.

[74] Useynov, A., 'Amerikanskikh voyennykh priglashayut v Azerbaijan' [Azerbaijan invites US military], *Vremya MN*, 2 Jan. 1999.

Azerbaijan and Russia which made itself felt at the close of 1999.[75] Nevertheless, a new switch in Azerbaijan's policy in favour of NATO cannot be excluded, especially given the strong partnership between Armenia and Russia.

V. Attempts at mediation

Mediation initiatives to achieve a Karabakh settlement have been offered at one time or another by different countries, political figures or international organizations. However, efforts to mediate in the conflict are complicated by the absence of 'a unified methodological approach to its solution', by the existence of several mediators acting at cross-purposes, and by an endless rotation of such mediators.[76] This also afflicts the OSCE and the Minsk Group, which has been handling the Karabakh settlement since 1992.

Initially the Minsk Group tried to achieve a 'package' resolution of several pivotal problems. This package deal envisaged simultaneous moves to define the political status of Karabakh, ensure the withdrawal of Armenian troops from the occupied territories and the return of refugees, and provide guarantees that would preclude the resumption of hostilities. The OSCE Budapest Summit Meeting of 5–6 December 1994 envisaged more energetic OSCE and Minsk Group efforts to launch a peacekeeping operation in the Karabakh conflict zone. It was decided to dispatch peacekeeping forces in accordance with a UN resolution as soon as the sides reached agreement on putting an end to the military conflict.[77] This decision was never realized because of the differences between the conflicting sides, as well as between the mediators. While neither the USA nor West European countries objected in principle to Russia's participation in the peacekeeping operation, they regarded its claims to a place in the peacekeeping process that would match its position and influence in the Caucasus as excessive.[78] There was also an extremely negative reaction in the NKR when it became known that Turkey intended to send troops to join the peacekeepers in Nagorno-Karabakh. The NKR Foreign Ministry declared that Stepanakert would never agree to that.[79]

The Minsk Group proposals feature the following key issues: (a) the security of Nagorno-Karabakh and the terms on which international peacekeeping forces would be stationed there; (b) troop withdrawal from the districts that are not the

[75] Gafarly, M., 'Stary drug luchshe novykh dvukh' [One old friend is better than two new ones], *Nezavisimaya Gazeta*, 16 Oct. 1999.

[76] Novikova, G., 'Palestinskiy i Nagorno-Karabakhskiy konflikty: v poiskhakh vykhoda' [The Palestinian and Nagorno-Karabakh conflicts: in search of a settlement], *Problemy Natsional'nogo Samoopredeleniya na Sovremennom Etape* [Problems of national self-determination at the present stage] (Tsentr Strategicheskikh Issledovanii [Centre for Strategic Studies]: Moscow, 2000), p. 55.

[77] Baranovsky, B., 'Russia and its neighbourhood: conflict developments and settlement efforts', *SIPRI Yearbook 1995: Armaments, Disarmament and International Security* (Oxford University Press: Oxford, 1995), p. 254.

[78] Remacle, E. and Paye, O., 'The conflict in Nagorno-Karabakh: a new pattern for cooperation between UN and OSCE', ed. R. Seidelman, *Crisis Policies in Eastern Europe: Imperatives, Problems and Perspectives* (Nomos: Baden-Baden, 1996), p. 174.

[79] Vinogradov, B., '3000 miritvortsev dolzhny sozdat' usloviya dlya uregulirovaniya v Karabakhe' [3000 peace-keepers to create conditions for a Karabakh settlement], *Izvestiya*, 9 Dec. 1994.

proper territory of Nagorno-Karabakh; (c) the Susha problem and the return of refugees, both Armenian and Azerbaijani; (d) the problem of the Lachin land corridor connecting the NKR and Armenia; (e) the possibility of some form of international control over the corridor as a possible compromise solution; and (f) the status of Nagorno-Karabakh.[80] Seeking to show that OSCE mediation was productive, the Minsk Group proposed a new plan in June 1997, the essence of which was the adoption of a step-by-step approach to tackling these problems. Azerbaijan accepted this plan and Armenia finally supported it, although with a number of reservations, but Nagorno-Karabakh was against it. Its position boiled down to the demand that either all aspects of the Minsk Group plan must be dealt with at the same time or the status of Karabakh must be the first to be determined. Azerbaijan, however, wants the withdrawal of troops and the resolution of the refugee problem to come first.

One of the latest proposals, made by Minsk Group co-chairman Carey Cavanaugh of the USA, features the 'common state' concept. This appears to take the talks back to 1998, when this concept, suggested by the Minsk Group mediators for the first time, won the support of the Karabakh and Armenian sides but was rejected by Azerbaijan. At its present stage the plan represents a package set of proposals: Nagorno-Karabakh would be nominally retained by Azerbaijan but granted de facto independence, allowing for the preservation of full-scale ties with Armenia.[81] The fate of this proposal is predictable: as before, both Karabakh and Azerbaijan take a rather sceptical view of it.[82]

Because the efforts of the OSCE Minsk Group have so far not been crowned with visible success, another idea was floated—that of a confidential meeting between the presidents of Armenia and Azerbaijan.[83] In 1999–2000 dialogues between Aliyev and Kocharian took place in Moscow, Nakhichevan, Davos and other places. Talks were also held in New York during the UN Millennium Summit. These negotiations probably brought the sides closer to a compromise solution: at the OSCE Istanbul Summit Meeting in November 1999 there were expectations that an agreement on Karabakh, allegedly coordinated at a confidential meeting between Aliyev and Kocharian held in Nakhichevan on 11 October 1999, would be signed.[84] Under this agreement Karabakh was to be de jure retained by Azerbaijan, while being granted the rights of an independent entity and preserving the Lachin connection with Armenia. According to Etibar Mamedov, leader of the Azerbaijani opposition Party of National Independence, who published a version of the projected peace agreement on the eve of the

[80] Tchilingirian, H., 'Nagorno Karabakh: transition and the elite', *Central Asian Survey*, no. 18 (1999), p. 449; and Shushetsi, A., 'Protsess uregulirovaniya kharabakhskho-azerbaijanskogo konflikta pod egidoy OBSE' [The settlement of the Karabakh–Azerbaijani conflict under the aegis of the OSCE], *Armyanskiy Vestnik* (Moscow), no. 1 (1998), pp. 16–19.

[81] Ali, K., 'Kavano vozrodil pokhoronennuyu bylo ideyu "obshchego gosudarstva"' [Cavanaugh revives the "common state" concept], *Zerkalo*, 13 May 2000, p. 8; and Radchenko, E., Balytnikov, V. and Radchenko, I., 'Nagorny-Karabakh kak sovmestnoye vladeniye' [Nagorno-Karabakh as a joint possession], *Sodruzhestvo NG* [supplement to *Nezavisimaya Gazeta*], 31 May 2000, p. 12.

[82] Ali (note 81).

[83] Tatevosyan, A., 'Koridor my ostavim sebe' [We'll leave the corridor for ourselves], *Moskovskiye Novosti*, no. 6 (5–21 Feb. 2000), p. 13.

[84] Shermatova (note 9), p. 13.

OSCE Istanbul meeting, the Azerbaijani side made the lifting of the blockade and Armenia's participation in TRACECA conditional on the return of three districts (Zangelan, Jebrail and Fizuli) and the clearing of landmines in those districts. Armenia, however, was only willing to vacate the Megri corridor along the entire length of the railway line. Mamedov also revealed that the agreement, drawn up in secrecy, included a statement about running the Baku–Ceyhan pipeline across Armenian territory to reach the Nakhichevan exclave, which belongs to Azerbaijan, and thence to Turkey. It was planned to put the blocked Yerevan–Nakhichevan–Baku railway line back into operation.[85]

This sensational revelation by Mamedov had strong repercussions in Baku and was followed by the dismissal of senior Azerbaijani officials in October 1999 and the shooting in the Armenian Parliament, when a terrorist group killed the prime minister, the speaker and several MPs. As a result of these developments no decision on Nagorno-Karabakh was reached at Istanbul and the negotiating process was deadlocked.

So far the Minsk Group's work, taken as a whole, has fallen short of a breakthrough. One reason for this may be that the Minsk Group, in contrast to the UN, lacks a mechanism for enforcing its peacemaking. Moreover, after the inclusion of a US co-chairman, the Minsk Group peacemakers' loyalties are divided between Russia and the USA, whose contending interests have long been admixed to the conflict. This lack of results sustains an alarming situation. Violence could erupt again as soon as one of the sides directly engaged in the conflict decides that it has gained enough strength to tip the scales in its favour.

This is all the more likely since all sides used the pause in the hostilities on the Karabakh front in 1994 to arm and rearm their military forces. A new threat to security has appeared, coming from the militarization of the region.

VI. The danger of armed conflict

Under the Agreement on the Principles and Procedures of the Implementation of the Treaty on Conventional Armed Forces in Europe (the Tashkent Document) signed at the meeting of the heads of CIS states on 15 May 1992, Armenia and Azerbaijan, which at the time were officially considered to possess no weapons, undertook to keep to the parameters prescribed by that agreement.[86] However, after both countries had received weapons from the former Soviet Transcaucasian Military Command, they went on to purchase arms, hardware and ammunition, Armenia procuring them mostly from Russia, and Azerbaijan from Turkey and Ukraine.[87]

In contravention of Yeltsin's 1993 decree forbidding deliveries of weapons to conflict zones, Armenia continued to receive them. The late General Lev

[85] Shermatova (note 9).

[86] Sharp, J. M. O., 'Conventional arms control in Europe', *SIPRI Yearbook 1993* (note 39), p. 596. An unofficial translation of the Tashkent Document is reproduced in *SIPRI Yearbook 1993*, pp. 671–77.

[87] Georgiev, V., 'Mezhetnicheskiye konflikty v byvshem SSSR porodila sama Rossiya' [It was Russia that gave rise to ethnic conflicts in the former USSR], *Nezavisimoye Voyennoye Obozreniye*, no. 39 (1997), p. 2. On the military build-up in the region see also chapter 5 in this volume.

Rokhlin, who was chairman of the Defence Committee of the Russian State Duma, maintained that the total value of Russian military supplies to Armenia in 1993–96 exceeded $1 billion.[88] Russia denies all such charges and maintains that arms supplies to Armenia and Azerbaijan were made on a parity basis and that those delivered to Armenia were legal and in full accord with an intergovernmental agreement of 6 July 1992 on the terms and schedules of the handing over of the weapons and equipment of the Russian military formations and units stationed in Armenia.[89]

Observers have pointed out that after the conclusion of the Bishkek ceasefire agreement in 1994 Azerbaijan exceeded the quotas imposed by the 1990 Treaty on Conventional Armed Forces in Europe (the CFE Treaty).[90] Towards the end of 1998 and in early 1999 its orientation towards stronger military cooperation with Turkey became clear. Azerbaijan also announced its intention to speed up the introduction of NATO standards in its own armed forces. More than 5000 Azerbaijani officers received training in Turkey, the USA and other countries.[91]

Russia's military cooperation with Armenia appears to be proceeding with considerable success. The Armenia Group of the Russian armed forces, belonging to the Federal Frontier Force of Russia, has been stationed in Armenia since 1992 in order to ensure the security of the latter's frontiers with Iran and Turkey.[92] The agreement on the Russian military base signed in Moscow on 16 March 1995 and ratified by the Russian Duma two years later (on 18 April 1997) enables Russia to keep such a base in Gyumri, with roughly 3000 men equipped with Su-27 combat aircraft, a squadron of MiG-29 fighter planes and S-300 SAMs.[93] Having signed the agreement on the adaptation of the CFE Treaty at the OSCE Istanbul meeting, Russia undertook to remove two of its military bases (in Vaziani and Gudauta) from the territory of Georgia by 1 July 2001.[94] When this withdrawal began the possibility of redeploying these bases in Armenia was discussed.[95]

[88] Livotkhin, V., 'U oruzheynogo skandala mogut byt' seryoznye politicheskiye posledstviya' [The arms scandal may have serious political consequences], *Izvestiya*, 15 Apr. 1997. See also Anthony, I. (ed.), SIPRI, *Russia and the Arms Trade* (Oxford University Press: Oxford, 1998), pp. 224–25.

[89] Meshcheryakov, V., 'Armeniya: strategiya vyzhivaniya' [Armenia: strategy of survival], *Asiya i Afrika Segodnya* (Moscow), no. 4 (1998), p. 15.

[90] Korbut, A., 'Baku gotov voyevat' za Karabakh' [Baku is ready to fight for Karabakh], *Nezavisimaya Gazeta*, 3 June 1999. On the CFE Treaty see, e.g., Lachowski, Z., 'Conventional arms control', *SIPRI Yearbook 1998* (note 44), pp. 503–504.

[91] Korbut (note 90).

[92] Golotyuk, Yu., 'Zakavkazskaya "gonka vooruzhenii"' [Transcaucasus 'arms race'], *Izvestiya*, 23 Jan. 1999; Meshcheryakov (note 89); and Tishchenko, G., 'Vooruzhennye sily i voyenno-politicheskiy kurs Armenii' [Armenia's armed forces and its military–political course], *Armeniya: Problemy Nezavisimogo Razvitiya* (note 26), pp. 558–60. See also chapter 5, section III in this volume.

[93] Yermolin, V., 'Ne Gruziey yedinoy: voyennoye prisutstviye Rossii v Zakavkazye prodolzhitsya' [Not only Georgia: Russia's military presence in the Transcaucasus continues], *Izvestiya*, 28 Apr. 2000, p. 2; and Tishchenko (note 92), p. 558.

[94] Shaburkin, A., 'Voyennye itogi Stambulskogo sammita' [The military results of the Istanbul summit], *Nezavisimaya Gazeta*, 23 Nov. 1999, p. 6; and Lachowski, Z., 'Conventional arms control', *SIPRI Yearbook 2000: Armaments, Disarmament an International Security* (Oxford University Press: Oxford, 2000), pp. 584–85.

[95] Yermolin (note 93).

Russia's military facilities in Armenia can hardly be regarded as a factor endangering relations between Armenia and Azerbaijan, yet in a crisis situation the stocks of equipment and ammunition would make it possible to quickly convert the existing forces into massive formations, such as military divisions and brigades. Russia's military presence in Armenia also enables it to influence the political situation in that country as well as many political processes in the Caucasus.

As for the NKR Army, many experts consider it to be one of the strongest forces from the point of combat readiness and efficiency on the territory of the former Soviet Union.[96]

Azerbaijan's modest economic and military potential, its so far ineffectual attempts to involve Western and NATO military systems on a large scale, and Russia's military presence in Armenia and in the North Caucasus—these are the factors that leave Azerbaijan without any realistic prospects of a military breakthrough should hostilities on the Karabakh front be resumed. However, a new attempt by Azerbaijan to regain by force the territories seized by the NKR Army cannot be completely excluded. Moreover, the number of those disenchanted by the negotiations around the conflict is rising, with the party of war in Azerbaijan growing ever more vociferous.

The conflicting sides realize that the front-line positions have been reinforced and that negotiating them will be a much harder task that it was at the outset or the peak of the conflict. The current ceasefire rests on a balance of forces, not on international guarantees. Kosovo-style direct military intervention by NATO appears to be out of the question. The dragging on of the conflict risks causing the militarization of the region, with the consequences of a humanitarian crisis in Armenia and Azerbaijan, slower economic growth and the increasing dependence of the participants in the conflict on external factors and forces.

The Karabakh problem can obviously be settled only by a compromise solution that would take into account the interests of Azerbaijan as well as those of Armenia and the NKR. In this respect, the worldwide experience of conflict resolution, both its positive and negative instances, could be quite useful.

The next section considers alternative scenarios of and models for coping with the Karabakh conflict.

VII. Scenarios for conflict resolution

The first is the 'Kosovo option'—a resolution of the Karabakh conflict modelled on the 'protectorate' set up in the Kosovo province of the Federal Republic of Yugoslavia, the security of which is guaranteed by the international community. This option is favoured by both Armenia and Azerbaijan, albeit for different reasons. Armenia favours the Western plan whereby the future status of Karabakh would depend on the organized expression of its people's will. Azerbaijan, with its clear-cut pro-NATO stand in the Kosovo conflict, would

[96] Avakyan (note 28), p. 171.

welcome a Kosovo-style peacekeeping operation in Karabakh. Yet the NATO scenario tried out in Kosovo is inapplicable in the case of Karabakh, not least because, unlike the Kosovo Albanians, the Karabakh Armenians have a very efficient army. Moreover, NATO is not likely to undertake an involvement in Russia's traditional geopolitical region, for this could lead to consequences that are hard to predict.

The second option is the 'Cyprus option', based on the concept that a state can exist and function de facto unrecognized by the outside world. In the Karabakh context this would imply recognition of the present status of the NKR—something Azerbaijan would not agree to under any circumstances. The division of Nagorno-Karabakh into Armenian and Azerbaijani sectors would give rise to near-insoluble problems, such as ensuring the safety of returning refugees, preventing clashes between them, bringing in peacekeeping forces and stationing them along the 'green line' dividing the two communities, not to mention the difficulties inherent in the demarcation of that line and the composition of the peace contingent.

The third, 'common state', scenario has been discussed for several years now and resembles in essence the Cyprus model. It would involve the setting up of a confederation-style condominium. This option would keep the NKR borders as they were when it was an autonomous region of Azerbaijan but make it a fully-fledged autonomous unit of Armenia. This would be tantamount to granting Nagorno-Karabakh the status of an independent state entity, which would be *de jure* (but not de facto) independent of Armenia, and de facto (but not *de jure*) independent of Azerbaijan. This arrangement would give dual citizenship to the people of the NKR. The defects of this option are: (*a*) that it would in an indirect way preserve the existing status of the NKR; and, far more important, (*b*) that there would be no way for Azerbaijan to repossess the territories seized in the course of hostilities. This scenario would suit Armenia well but is unacceptable to Azerbaijan, which will not forfeit its sovereignty over Nagorno-Karabakh. Moreover, it would not be to the liking of the NKR, which at present claims self-determination of a much higher order—that is, independent statehood.

The fourth option, an 'associated state' (proposed in 1994 by John Mareski, then US representative at the negotiations over Nagorno-Karabakh), is equally unacceptable to the NKR: the self-governing entity would still be under the jurisdiction of Azerbaijan, since the latter considers the NKR to be part of its own territory. The 'limited sovereignty' option, proposed by NKR President Gukasian in September 1997 to replace the Azerbaijani formula of 'broadest possible autonomy', provides for the return of the occupied territories in exchange for the establishment of federative relations between Azerbaijan and the NKR. Azerbaijan rejected this point-blank.

Fifth, the 'deferred status' model still merits consideration. Azerbaijan rejects it and Russia found it to be less than successful in Chechnya after it signed the 1996 Khasaviurt agreements, but this option still clearly has some advantages over the others. It could serve as the basis for a negotiating process during a period of transition, in the course of which a decision on the raw nerve of the conflict—the status of the NKR—would be relegated to a future date fixed by the sides. This would provide a breathing space as well as more favourable geo-political and economic conditions for a final settlement of the entire set of problems.

Sixth, the option of resolving the Karabakh problem by means of an exchange of territories was proposed by the US politician Paul Goble when the conflict was at its height. At that time it was rejected by the sides because each was still hopeful of winning by military means. Today this scenario seems to have a future. First, it has attracted a number of influential politicians in Armenia and Azerbaijan.[97] Second, the USA has joined the efforts to boost this option: there are some indications that the Armenian authorities would favour the plan if the USA undertook to invest $3 billion in the Armenian economy.[98]

The land exchange option would, however, be of no advantage to the NKR—in fact it would lose more than it would gain, for it would not be a party to the negotiations and its main goal, that of establishing itself as an independent state, would not be achieved. Pro-Russian politicians in Armenia, as well as Russia itself, might be among the losers: Russia would be deprived of its levers of influence. It would also face the very real threat of losing control over the routes for the transport of energy resources from the Caspian zone because the Baku–Novorossiysk pipeline would be made redundant; its strategy in the Caucasus, based on partnership with Armenia and arbitration of the Armenian–Azerbaijan conflict, might be disrupted; and the positions of the USA might be strengthened.

According to *Izvestiya*, in that case 'Russian influence in the Caucasus, of which Armenia is the last bulwark, would be destroyed, as well as Russia's plans to take part in the transfer of Azerbaijan's "big oil"'.[99] Russia, however, has repeatedly shown its talent for gaining direct or indirect influence over developments in the conflict zone—among other things, by means of backstage moves. It was able on several occasions to bring both sides closer to the point where it could manage the conflict to its own advantage. The part played by Russia in the region at this juncture cannot be compared to the unlimited influence formerly enjoyed by the USSR's central authority, but Russia is almost sure to make some future gains by playing on the existing contradictions and colliding interests.

VIII. Conclusions

It is evident that none of the above options for a settlement of the Karabakh issue can be mechanically applied to Caucasian realities today. Moreover, they

---

[97] Mamedov, M., 'Yerevan i Baku ischut kompromissa po Karabakhu' [Yerevan and Baku are searching for a compromise on Karabakh], *Kommersant*, 18 Feb. 2000.

[98] Koptev, D., 'Obmen s doplatoy' [An exchange with additional payment], *Izvestiya*, 17 May 2000, p. 3.

[99] Koptev (note 98).

are only a fraction of a great range of models, scenarios and political techniques proposed for negotiations on the issue. The main reason why most of them cannot be applied in working out a settlement is the proliferation of mediators. A creditable settlement process begins only when the conflicting sides respond to the influence of a single mediator.

The Karabakh conflict continues to be a factor destabilizing the situation in the region, and its continuation would have a vicious effect on all the people of the region. Can peace be expected to come to Karabakh in the near future? Are there any prospects of achieving regional security? The situation in the region may become more settled when major geopolitical actors resolve the key issues of the 'Great Pipeline Game', such as the legal status of the Caspian Sea, its actual hydrocarbon reserves, and oil and gas pipeline routes.

Attempts to normalize the situation in the South Caucasus by reaching a consensus on the principles of peaceful coexistence in the region are impeded by the great divergence of the interests of the regional countries and deeply affected by the attitudes the principal actors take in the geopolitical struggle going on in the region. At this point Armenia and Azerbaijan are unable to agree on any of the issues, including the prospects for settling the Karabakh conflict and the achievement of regional security. Far from helping to phase out the current confrontation in the Caucasus, this serves to enhance the trend towards polarization, with Armenia, Iran and Russia facing Azerbaijan, Georgia and Turkey, backed by the USA and NATO.

Both in Yerevan and in Baku the presidents' attempts to make mutual concessions provoked acute political crises. Even the conflicting sides' willingness to settle the conflict will not automatically result in its termination. A good deal of time is needed for the societies in the post-Soviet republics of South Caucasus to become internally 'self-organized' and for the contending sides to make up their minds about their primary concern—whether they want to achieve peace or to assert their own political ambitions. Only then it will it be possible to advance the negotiating process and to start building real peace.

16. The Georgian–Abkhazian conflict

Alexander Krylov

I. Introduction

The Abkhaz have long populated the western Caucasus. They currently number about 100 000 people, speak one of the languages of the Abkhazo-Adygeyan (west Caucasian) language group, and live in the coastal areas on the southern slopes of the Caucasian ridge and along the Black Sea coast. Together with closely related peoples of the western Caucasus (for example, the Abazins, Adygeyans and Kabardians (or Circassians)) they play an important role in the Caucasian ethno-cultural community and consider themselves an integral part of its future. At the same time, the people living in coastal areas on the southern slopes of the Caucasian ridge have achieved broader communication with Asia Minor and the Mediterranean civilizations than any other people of the Caucasus. The geographical position of Abkhazia on the Black Sea coast has made its people a major factor in the historical process of the western Caucasus, acting as an economic and cultural bridge with the outside world.

Georgians and Abkhaz have been neighbours from time immemorial. The Georgians currently number about 4 million people. The process of national consolidation of the Georgian nation is still far from complete: it includes some 20 subgroups, and the Megrelians (sometimes called Mingrelians) and Svans who live in western Georgia are so different in language and culture from other Georgians that it would be more correct to consider them as separate peoples. Some scholars, Hewitt, for example,[1] suggest calling the Georgian nation not 'Georgians' but by their own name, Kartvelians, which includes the Georgians, Megrelians and Svans.[2] To call all the different Kartvelian groups 'Georgians' obscures the true ethnic situation. Increasingly, scholars prefer to distinguish between Georgians, Megrelians and Svans, the Georgians being the population of eastern Georgia.[3]

Historically, Georgian–Abkhaz interaction has alternated between close cooperation and bitter fighting. The beginning of the current Georgian–Abkhaz

---

[1] Hewitt, G. (ed.), *The Abkhazians: A Handbook*, Peoples of the Caucasus Handbooks (St Martins Press: New York, 1999), pp. 13–16. See also Coppieters, B., Darchiashvili, D. and Akaba, N. (eds), *Praktika Federalizma: Poiski Alternativ dlya Gruzii i Abkhazii* [Practice of federalism: exploring alternatives for Georgia and Abkhazia] (Ves'mir: Moscow, 1999) p. 21.

[2] The names 'Georgia' and 'Georgian' most likely derive from the Persian 'Gurgistan' and 'Gurg' ('the country of wolves', 'wolf'). They first appear in Russian chronicles and documents in the 15th century. The Megrelians are the most numerous in the Kartvelian linguistic group: estimates range from 20% to 30% of the group. This is the primary factor which has prevented their rapid assimilation by Georgians.

[3] Mehtiev, A., 'Baku i Tbilisi nuzhny drug drugu' [Baku and Tbilisi need each other], *Nezavisimaya Gazeta*, 17 Sep. 1992; and Zhidkov, S., *Brosok Maloy Imperii* [The spurt of a small empire] (Adygeya: Maikop, 1996).

conflict can be traced back to the 1870s when, after the end of the Caucasian war, there was a mass resettlement of Abkhaz to Turkey (the Mahajeers). As a result the Abkhaz territory along the Black Sea—divided into two parts, the north-west (Bzibean) and the south-east (Abjuan)—has since been populated by various nationalities, including Armenians, Greeks, Megrelians and Russians, thus giving modern Abkhazia its multi-ethnic character.

The Georgian nationalist movement that emerged in the 19th century defined the 'primordial Georgian territory' as being that which lay within the borders of the medieval Georgian empire of the 10th–13th centuries. This ignored the initially multi-ethnic character of the state. The first attempts by the movement to base the development of the Georgian state on these 'historical lands' were made after the Russian Empire disintegrated, during the period of the independent Georgian republic (1918–21). In Abkhazia and other ethnic minority areas a policy of assimilation began, with the mass resettlement of Georgians to Abkhazia and the declaration of Georgian as the state language. This policy combined with acts of violence and robberies by the Georgian armies caused many protests among the population of Abkhazia, including some of the local Megrelians.[4] The establishment of Soviet rule in Abkhazia in March 1921 was, therefore, welcomed by the people and heralded as the end of national oppression and of the Georgian occupation.

In 1921 Abkhazia received the status of a Soviet Republic allied with Georgia by a special treaty, but its status was downgraded in February 1931 to that of an autonomous republic within Georgia with the aim of facilitating the assimilation of the Abkhaz by Georgians. Soviet Communist Party General Secretary Joseph Stalin (a Georgian) regarded the Abkhaz as a primitive people who were to be assimilated by the 'culturally advanced' Georgians.[5] The period from 1931 to the early 1950s was particularly tragic in the history of Abkhazia. It saw the 'Georgianization' of Abkhazia, which for all intents and purposes meant the genocide of its indigenous population and included the physical extermination of the Abkhaz intelligentsia, the expulsion of Abkhaz from the management of all administrative and public organizations and state enterprises, the closure of Abkhaz schools and the forcible enrolment of Abkhaz children into Georgian schools, the prohibition of teaching in the Abkhaz language in high schools, the replacement of Abkhaz names with Georgian ones, restricted social security for persons of Abkhaz ethnicity, unwritten privileges for Georgians, the massive resettlement of Georgians into Abkhazia, the persecution of Abkhaz culture and the falsification of Abkhaz history.[6]

All through the Soviet period the main goal of the Georgian leadership and of the Georgian nationalist movement as a whole was the creation of a con-

---

[4] Mescheryakov, N. V., 'Men'shevistskom rayu: iz vpechatlenii poezdki v Gruziyu' [In Menshevist paradise: from impressions of a trip to Georgia] (Gosizdat: Moscow, 1921); and Denikin, A., 'Ocherki russkoy smuty' [Studies in Russian troubled times] (Slovo: Berlin, 1925).

[5] Stalin, J., *Sochineniya* [Works] (Politizdat: Moscow, 1946), vol. 2, pp. 350–51.

[6] Russian Academy of Sciences, Institute of Sociopolitical Studies, *O Bezopasnosti Rossii v Svyazi s Sobytiyami v Abkhazii* [On Russia's security in connection with events in Abkhazia], Analytical paper (Russian Academy of Sciences: Moscow, 1993), pp. 3–4.

solidated Georgian nation in the shortest possible time. With Stalin in power, when the influence of the Georgian lobby in the Kremlin was at its greatest, this policy was carried out by repressive methods. Some peoples were deported from Georgia (Greeks, Kurds and Meskhetian Turks). Others, not even related to the Kartvelians, were declared part of the 'Georgian tribes' and along with Svans and Megrelians were quickly assimilated.

After Stalin's death the Georgian lobby in the central Soviet Government remained but was weakened. From the mid-1950s the Georgian republican authorities were forced by the Soviet Government to stop the worst forms of discrimination against the Abkhaz, but the mass resettlement of Georgians to Abkhazia continued. As a result, at the end of the 1980s the share of Abkhaz in the 525 000-strong population of Abkhazia was reduced to 17.8 per cent while the share of the Georgian population reached 45.7 per cent.[7] In the mid-1950s, in line with the ideological goals of the resettlement policy, a theory was fabricated declaring the true Abkhaz to be 'an ancient cultural Georgian tribe living on the territory of Abkhazia' and describing the modern Abkhaz as descendants of backward highlanders, Apsuaers,[8] who ostensibly moved into Abkhazia from the north in the 17th century.[9] The thesis of the 'resettlement of the Apsuaers' became part of a racist theory asserting a supposed primordial superiority of the 'civilized' Georgians over their neighbours—a theory which dominated in Georgian science and public consciousness. Widespread promotion of this theory caused sharp protests from the Abkhaz intelligentsia and aggravated inter-ethnic relations. Tensions between Abkhaz and Georgians became particularly evident in 1957, 1964, 1967 and 1978 when there were mass protest actions by the Abkhaz population and only emergency intervention by the central government prevented further escalation of the conflict.[10]

At the end of the 1980s, in conditions of a growing crisis of the central government, the contradictions between the Abkhaz and the Georgians assumed much sharper forms. The Georgian nationalist movement raised demands for national independence and the creation of a mono-ethnic Georgian state within its 'historical borders'. The Abkhaz actively opposed Georgian separatism. The 'Abkhaz letter' of 1988 formulated a demand for the restoration to Abkhazia of the status of Soviet Socialist republic it enjoyed in 1921–31.[11]

---

[7] *Belaya Kniga Abkhazii: Dokumenty, Materialy, Svidetel'stva* [White book of Abkhazia: documents, materials, evidence] (Vnekom: Moscow, 1993), p. 30. The remainder of the population was made up of Armenians, Greeks, Russians, Ukrainians and others.

[8] From the Abkhaz' own name for themselves, 'Apsua'.

[9] Zorzoliani., G., Lekishvili, S. and Toidze, L., *Istoricheskiye i Politiko-Pravovye Aspekty Konflikta v Abkhazii* [Historical and politico-legal aspects of the conflict in Abkhazia] (Metsniereba: Tbilisi, 1995), pp. 12–13; and Pipia, B. and Chikviladze, Z., *Raspyataya Gruziya* [Crucified Georgia] (Pechatny Dvor: St Petersburg, 1995), p. 9.

[10] Vasilyeva, O., *Gruziya kak Model' Postkommunisticheskoy Transformatsii* [Georgia as a model of post-communist transformation] (Gorbachev-Fond: Moscow, 1993), p. 31.

[11] *Abkhaziya v Sovetskuyu Epokhu: Abkhazskiye Pis'ma (1947–1989): Sbornik Dokumentov* [Abkhazia during the Soviet epoch: Abkhaz letters (1947–1989): Collection of documents] (El-Fa: Sukhumi, 1992), vol. 1, p. 435. The appeals by Abkhaz political and public figures to the central Soviet Government known as the 'Abkhaz letters' played an important role in the Abkhaz national movement and the history of inter-ethnic relations in Abkhazia. The story of the Abkhaz letters was published in this collection.

In 1989–91 a wave of inter-ethnic conflicts swept through Georgia, behind which Georgian radicals saw the 'hand of Moscow'. In fact the growth of inter-ethnic tensions could be attributed to the activists for Georgian independence, who called for policies of 'de-Armenianization' and 'de-Azerbaijanization', the abolition of all autonomies, and even a state birth control programme to limit the expansion of the non-Georgian population. In 1990 the ultra-radical (later President) Zviad Gamsakhurdia elevated the idea of a mono-ethnic Georgian state into official policy. The autonomy of South Ossetia was abolished and open persecution of the non-Georgian population began.[12]

In Abkhazia, following major clashes in 1989 between Abkhaz and Georgians, the conflict was reflected in legislation. Under the slogan of a return to the independent republic of 1918–21, Tbilisi annulled all legal acts of the Soviet period, including those on the allied status of Georgia and Abkhazia (1921) and on the autonomy of Abkhazia within the Georgian Soviet Socialist Republic (1931). In response, in August 1990, the Supreme Soviet of Abkhazia adopted a Declaration of the State Sovereignty of the Abkhazian Autonomous Soviet Socialist Republic. It declared Abkhazia a 'sovereign socialist state having all the power of authority on its territory except the rights voluntarily delegated by it to the USSR and Georgian Soviet Socialist Republic by the previous agreements'.[13] A 'war of laws' followed: all Abkhazian legislation was annulled by the Georgian Government. As a result authority was increasingly paralysed in Abkhazia and Tbilisi rapidly lost control of the situation.

After Gamsakhurdia's overthrow in January 1992 the situation in Abkhazia deteriorated further . The war which broke out in 1992–93 was the peak of the conflict between Abkhazia and Georgia, characterized by the aspirations of the Abkhaz to secure their national and physical survival and by the desire of the Georgians to achieve national consolidation on the basis of their own ethnos and to create a mono-ethnic Georgian state on a territory with a multinational population and within completely artificial borders.

Originally Georgian propaganda justified the military intervention in Abkhazia by the need to protect the safety of the railways and to free Georgian officials taken hostage by followers of Gamsakhurdia. Realizing the absurdity of these allegations, President Eduard Shevardnadze later laid the blame for starting the war on Tengiz Kitovani, Minister of Defence for Georgia and a member of the Military Council that had overthrown Gamsakhurdia, alleging that Kitovani had ordered the army into Abkhazia without Shevardnadze's knowledge. Shevardnadze described the Georgian Army's actions in Abkhazia as intolerable: 'I will not even mention the inadmissible methods they used. Tanks, armoured vehicles, removal of the flag from the House of Government

---

[12] Vasilyeva (note 10), pp. 29–46.

[13] 'Deklaratsiya o gosudarstvennom suverenitete Abkhazskoy Sovetskoy Sotsialisticheskoy respubliki: Prinyata X sessiyey Verkhovnogo Soveta Abkhazskoy ASSR 11 sozyva 25 avgusta 1990 goda' [The Declaration of the state sovereignty of the Abkhaz Soviet Socialist republic adopted by the 10th session of the 11th Supreme Soviet of the Abkhaz ASSR, 25 Aug. 1990], available at URL <http://www.apsny.org>; and *Abkhaziya: Khronika Neob'yavlennoy Voynu* [Abkhazia: chronicle of undeclared war] (Luch: Moscow, 1992), part 1, pp. 12–15.

as if it were a foreign country . . . Much of what was done then cannot be justified and cannot be regarded as normal'.[14]

In fact there is no doubt that the Georgian–Abkhazian war was provoked not by the situation in Abkhazia—the situation there was calmer than in neighbouring Megrelia, where numerous armed gangs of 'Zviadists'[15] were operating—but by the situation in Tbilisi following the overthrow of Gamsakhurdia. It was probably the personal interests of the members of the Military Council (later the State Council of Georgia) that were behind the military campaign in Abkhazia. For each of them: 'A victory over Abkhazia could be a new important step in his political career. For Shevardnadze, however, this war could open much broader prospects. For the "new opposition" he was a former opponent, a stranger; he was still a Russian citizen with a Moscow residence; his strength was the support he received from Moscow, but he could never achieve the admiration among the Georgian people that Gamsakhurdia enjoyed'.[16] For Shevardnadze therefore a war in Abkhazia was absolutely necessary: without it, the consolidation of his personal power and defeat of his political opponents were inconceivable. In fact it was the war in Abkhazia that allowed him to put down public discontent in Megrelia,[17] to strengthen his own position in Tbilisi, and to dismiss and then arrest those who had overthrown Gamsakhurdia and invited Shevardnadze himself to Georgia (for example, Djaba Ioseliani and Tengiz Kitovani). Thus the Georgian–Abkhazian war was the price which the population of Georgia paid for Shevardnadze's return to power.

Shevardnadze probably received approval for a military operation in Abkhazia from Russian President Boris Yeltsin. It was hardly coincidental that one day before fighting broke out Russia transferred tanks, helicopters, artillery pieces and other military equipment to the Georgian armed forces. However, in spite of its overwhelming superiority in arms and numbers over the Abkhaz militia, the Georgian Army failed to achieve a quick victory.

The massive and fierce resistance that the Georgian Army met came as a surprise for the Georgian leaders, but was completely natural: the Abkhaz population regarded the Georgian military intervention as a real threat to its very existence.[18] The Abkhazian leadership, relying on the support of the public, also succeeded in quickly creating Abkhazian territorial armed forces. They received fast and effective help from the neighbouring peoples of the North Caucasus as a result of the traditional ethnic solidarity among the Abkhaz–Adygeya peoples. Furthermore, the activities of the Georgian leadership appeared so scandalous

[14] Kalinin, Yu., 'Zerkala separatizma: Eduard Shevardnadze vpervuye rasskazal o taynakh nachala gruzino-abkhazskoy voyny' [Mirrors of separatism: Eduard Shevardnadze discloses for the first time mysteries of how the Georgian–Abkhazian war began], *Moskovskiy Komsomolets*, 10 Feb. 1996.

[15] Followers of Zviad Gamsakhurdia.

[16] Zhidkov (note 3).

[17] Gamsakhurdia was a Megrelian, and it is in Megrelia that the influence of his followers, the 'Zviadists', is strongest.

[18] One month after the hostilities began the Presidium of the Supreme Soviet of the Abkhaz Republic adopted a special resolution which described 'mass terror, physical extermination of people, torture of prisoners and hostages carried out by the State Council of Georgia in Abkhazia as an act of genocide of the Abkhaz nation'. 'On genocide of the Abkhaz nation', Resolution no. 10-127, Gudauta, 16 Sep. 1992.

and unfair that there was a large influx of volunteers from different parts of the former Soviet Union, including Chechens, Ossetians, Russians and Ukrainians, to fight the Georgian Army. Usually these volunteers formed international brigades but the Cossacks from southern Russia formed their own units.[19]

Initially the Abkhazian armed forces experienced an acute shortage of arms. There is widespread opinion in the West that they received their arms from the Russian military.[20] In the view of the present author, based on numerous interviews with local veterans of the Georgian–Abkhazian war, arms were indeed often purchased from the Russian military but this was the result of private deals, reflecting the progressive disintegration of government authority under Yeltsin, and did not represent a refined Byzantine approach to the conflict on the part of the Russian authorities. Moreover, when the Georgian Army was defeated at Gagra in 1992 the Abkhazian Army seized a large amount of modern military equipment, including tanks, surface-to-air missile systems and artillery pieces, which eased their arms and ammunition shortage.

The Georgian–Abkhazian war lasted over a year and was very bloody and destructive. About 20 000 civilians died in Abkhazia;[21] material damage was estimated at $11.5 billion.[22] The war resulted in a fundamental change in the ethnic groups in the Georgian–Abkhazian conflict. Although the attitudes of Georgians, Megrelians and Svans differed,[23] the local Georgian population on the whole supported the military action. Other ethnic groups, initially neutral in the conflict, later adopted a pro-Abkhaz position as a result of robberies and other excesses by the Georgian military. Thus, since 1992 the Georgian–Abkhazian conflict has assumed the character of a confrontation between the Georgian state and the local Georgian community, on the one hand, and the rest of the multi-ethnic population of Abkhazia, on the other hand.

II. The post-war situation

After the defeat of the Georgian Army and the flight of part of the local Georgian population from Abkhazia,[24] the political position of the Abkhazian leadership solidified. The overwhelming majority of the population consistently

[19] 'Konfederatsiya gorskikh narodov Kavkaza vstupayet v boy' [The Confederation of Caucasian Mountain Peoples joins the fight], *Krasnaya Zvezda*, 27 Aug. 1992, p. 1: and Leontyeva, L., 'The path of war', *Moscow News*, 6–13 Sep. 1992.

[20] *Gruziya/Abkhaziya: Narusheniya Zakonov Vedeniya Voyny i Rol' Rossii v Konflikte* [Georgia/Abkhazia: violations of the laws of war and Russia's role in the conflict] (Human Rights Watch: Helsinki, 1995).

[21] *Stabilizatsiya Mezhetnicheskikh i Sotsiokulturnykh Otnoshenii na Kavkaze* [Stabilization of interethnic and socio-cultural relations in the Caucasus] (Etnosfera: Moscow, 1999), p. 87.

[22] Mukhin, V., 'Abkhaziya nikogda ne stanet avtonomnoy edinitsey Gruzii' [Abkhazia will never become an autonomy of Georgia], *Nezavisimaya Gazeta*, 29 Sep. 2000.

[23] The attitude taken by Megrelians towards the war is described in Zhidkov (note 3), pp. 236–37.

[24] According to the Department of Statistics of the Government of Abkhazia, by 1995 the population of Abkhazia was reduced to 313 000, of which 29.1% were Abkhaz, 28.7% Georgians, 19.8% Armenians, 16.5% Russians, 2.6% Ukrainians, 1.1% Greeks and 2.2% others. Krylov, A., *Post-Sovetskaya Abkhaziya: Traditsii, Religii, Narod* [Post-Soviet Abkhazia: traditions, religions, people] (OOAgent: Moscow, 1999), p. 11.

supported independence and a strongly pro-Russian orientation. Internal political stability allowed Abkhazia's leaders to resolve the country's economic problems in spite of isolation from the outside world.

Abkhazia's economic achievements were especially evident in comparison with Georgia's. Its social and economic infrastructure was restored without foreign aid and relied entirely on Abkhazia's domestic potential. The greatest success was in the production of electric power. While in Georgia over the past eight years the energy crisis has resulted in restrictions on public electricity consumption (to six hours per day, and during the winter months of 2001 only one or two hours per day), in Abkhazia there were no such restrictions and electric power tariffs for ordinary consumers remained the lowest throughout the former Soviet Union. In 1999 Abkhazia harvested about 10 000 tons of tea and 1000 tons of tobacco, while exporting over 20 000 tons of citrus crops, achieving a positive trade balance for the first time since the end of the war.[25]

After the breakup of the Soviet Union the leaders of Abkhazia considered reunion with Russia a priority task. An appeal of the Supreme Soviet of Abkhazia to the Supreme Soviet of the Russian Federation dated 23 March 1993 asked it to 'return the Republic of Abkhazia into the Russian fold, or to place it under the protection of Russia in the appropriate international legal form'.[26] A resolution adopted at a mass meeting held in Abkhazia on 16 April 1995 repeated the request to the Russian Government for a reunion of Abkhazia and Russia.[27] However, there was no positive reaction to these requests. Russia's policy was clearly pro-Georgian policy at that time, and the Abkhazian leadership was forced to work towards legalizing the state's independence. On 3 October 1999, along with the presidential elections in Abkhazia, a referendum was held in the country in which the overwhelming majority of Abkhazians (97.7 per cent of voters) supported the creation of an independent and democratic Abkhazian state.[28] On the basis of the result, on 12 October 1999 Abkhazia adopted an Act of State Independence of the Republic of Abkhazia.[29]

Understanding that in the circumstances it would be impossible to achieve *de jure* recognition of Abkhazia's independence by the world community, the Abkhazian leadership agreed to possible coexistence with Georgia in a 'common state' within the borders of the former Georgian Soviet Socialist Republic. At the same time Abkhazia rejected the status of autonomy and agreed to build relations with Georgia only on the basis of equality within a common state whose functions would be limited to foreign policy, defence, finance, border

---

[25] Mukhin (note 22).

[26] *Gruzino-Abkhazskiy Konflikt: Proshloye, Nastoyascheye, Perspectivy Uregulirovaniya* [The Georgian–Abkhazian conflict: past, present and prospects of settlement] (Institute of Diaspora and Integration, Institute of the CIS Countries: Moscow, 1998), p. 27.

[27] 'Obrashcheniye skhoda mnogonatsional'nogo naroda Abkhazii, posvyashchennogo 185-letiyu dobrovol'nogo vkozhdeniya Abkhazii v sostav Rossii' [Appeal of the mass meeting of the multinational people of Abkhazia devoted to the 185th anniversary of the voluntary entry of Abkhazia into Russia], Sukhumi, 16 Apr. 1995 (copy in SIPRI archive).

[28] See the Internet site of the Republic of Abkhazia (Apsny), URL<http://www.apsny.org>.

[29] Akt Gosudarstvennoy Nezavisimosti Respubliki Abkhaziya [Act of state independence of the Republic of Abkhazia], Sukhumi, 12 Oct. 1999 (copy in SIPRI archive).

protection and customs services. Initially the Georgian leadership agreed with this approach. It was reflected in the joint Statement on Measures for a Political Settlement of 4 April 1994 in which Georgia and Abkhazia agreed to act as equal sides and pledged to resume official relations on this basis.[30] Later, however, the Georgian leadership changed its position and refused to build relations with Abkhazia on the basis of equality.

The Georgian leadership did not blame Abkhazia's secession on its own policies but interpreted it as an annexation and occupation of the primordial territory of Georgia and as 'aggression of international terrorism against a sovereign state'.[31] For Tbilisi the only acceptable resolution to the conflict was to grant Abkhazia the status of autonomy inside the unified Georgian state, and neither the future structure of the Georgian state nor a possible form of autonomy for Abkhazia were even discussed.

For the whole post-Soviet period Georgia's policy of state-building has been conducted on the basis of rigid unitarism. The result of this policy was a profound economic crisis and the progressive disintegration of Georgia. The government in Tbilisi lost control over all the autonomies that existed during the Soviet period (Abkhazia, Adzharia and South Ossetia), over Javaheti with its compact 130 000 Armenian population, and over many mountain areas such as Svanetia and the Pankisi gorge, which is populated by Chechen-Kistins.

The ruinous character of the policy of building a mono-ethnic state in a country where the share of ethnic minorities in the population is over 30 per cent was absolutely clear. However, the majority of Georgian legislators continued to take a negative attitude to any measures that might 'undermine the unity of the Georgian state'.[32] The 1995 constitution proclaimed Georgia 'an independent, unified and indivisible' state and the term 'federalism' is not used in it. The constitution proclaims that 'citizens of Georgia regulate matters of local importance through local self-government as long as it does not encroach upon national sovereignty'. It also states that 'when conditions are appropriate and self-government bodies have been established throughout the territory of Georgia, the parliament shall be formed with two chambers: the Council of the Republic and the Senate'. In the future the Senate will consist of 'members elected from Abkhazia, Adzharia and other territorial units of Georgia as well as five members appointed by the President'.[33]

Consisting exclusively of ethnic Georgians, the political leadership of Georgia[34] did not even consider the possibility of starting national construction on the basis of federalism rather than on the basis of a unitary state.

The Abkhazian problem remains the highest priority on Georgia's security agenda and it influences its approach to other conflicts. As one South Ossetian leader observed, 'a Georgian–Ossetian settlement will hardly be possible before a Georgian–Abkhazian settlement as South Ossetia does not anticipate having a

[30] The text of this Statement was published in Sukhumi on 5 Apr. 1994.
[31] *Gruzino-Abkhazskiy Konflikt* (note 26), p. 15.
[32] *Gruzino-Abkhazskiy Konflikt* (note 26), p. 15.
[33] The Constitution of Georgia, available at URL <http://www.apsny.org>.
[34] Coppieters *et al.* (note 1), p. 48.

status lower than that of Abkhazia'.[35] It is also clear that Adzharia will adopt a similar position. Although the Adzharian Government has not formally declared its intention to secede, it operates in a completely independent way and disregards the Tbilisi authorities. The customs, the office of the public prosecutor, the courts, the police and the coastguard are under its full control. Posts with armed units have been set up on the administrative borders of Adzharia to prevent any armed infiltration from Georgia. The authorities of Abkhazia and Adzharia maintain constant contact, and during the Georgian–Abkhazian war Adzharia declared its neutrality. The Adzharian authorities take their own position on the issue of the Russian military presence in the South Caucasus. They oppose the withdrawal of the Russian troops from the territory of Adzharia and have openly declared a pro-Russia policy.[36]

Tbilisi's control over Javaheti is similarly only nominal. Its Armenian population is pro-Russian and pro-Armenian, and is increasingly demanding autonomy.[37] With the progressive disintegration of the Georgian state, such compact national minorities living in Georgia as the Megrelians and Svans, and then Georgian sub-ethnic groups such as the Cahetians, Gurians, Khevsurs and Tushins, may also demand autonomy. The possibility of the country splitting into many different parts as it was in the 13th–18th centuries until Georgia became part of the Russian Empire may therefore again become a reality. This would mean not only the collapse of the Georgian state but also a tragedy for the Georgian people.

It is logical therefore that the Georgian Government is only ready to give Abkhazia autonomous status. It has concentrated all its diplomatic efforts on the Georgian refugee problem. The return of the Georgian population to Abkhazia, which the Georgian leaders insist on, will obviously result in a renewal of hostilities, as it is completely unacceptable for the people of Abkhazia and its leadership. Natella Akaba, an Abkhazian political analyst, writes that among those who fall under the definition of 'refugees':

There are many people who committed criminal and military offences in 1992–93. Abkhazia is a small country: everybody knows nearly everything about their neighbours; the names of those who in the late 1980s demanded the liquidation of the Abkhazian Autonomous Republic and who in August 1992 wrote to the Georgian leaders asking for Georgian troops (which ended in bloody clashes) are well known. If they come back, another war will be inevitable.[38]

---

[35] Hanbabjan, A., 'Gruziya–Abkhaziya . . . Obsuzhdeniye konstitutsionnogo statusa samoprovozglashennoy respubliki chrevato ser'yoznymi posledstviyami' [Georgia–Abkhazia . . . Discussion of the constitutional status of the self-proclaimed republic is fraught with serious consequences], *Nezavisimaya Gazeta*, 19 Sep. 2000.

[36] Soidze, O. and Berdzenishvili, D., 'Protivostoyaniye mezhdu Tbilisi i Batumi ili o problemakh sobrannosti natsii i polnote gosudarstva' [Confrontation between Tbilisi and Batumi, or on problems of consolidation of the nation and completeness of the state], *Tsentral'naya Aziya i Kavkaz* (Luleå), no. 2 (2000), p. 214. On the Russian military presence, see section III in this chapter.

[37] Soidze and Berdzenishvili (note 36), pp. 217–18.

[38] Akaba, N., 'Georgian–Abkhazian conflict: rooted in the past, resolved in future', *Central Asia and the Caucasus* (Luleå), no. 6 (2000), p. 119.

At the same time neither the population of Abkhazia nor its leaders object to a gradual, staged return of refugees, first of all to the Gali region. However, the leadership of Georgia is strongly against this mode of resolving the refugee problem. In the opinion of Russian political analysts these objections are raised because 'a staged return of refugees presents a threat [to Georgia] of their "political" assimilation and gradual integration into the Abkhazian state, in particular because the Sukhumi authorities are taking appropriate steps in this direction: among the deputies of the Abkhazian Parliament there are now two Georgians/Megrelians elected by the population of the Gali region'.[39]

The mass return of Georgian refugees on which the Georgian leadership insists does not mean a peaceful resolution of the Georgian–Abkhazian conflict but is actually intended to help to create favourable conditions for a new military campaign for the conquest of Abkhazia, and after that of other rebellious regions and peoples in Georgia.

III. The position of Russia

The official position of the Russian Federation on the Georgian–Abkhazian conflict is based on the recognition of the inviolability of Georgia's territorial integrity, inside which Abkhazia should be given broad political rights. On the basis of this position Russia has acted as an intermediary helping the conflicting sides conclude the Memorandum of Understanding (December 1993), the Agreement on Refugees and the Statement on Measures for Political Settlement of April 1993. At the request of both sides, in July 1994 a Russian peace-keeping force numbering about 2500 soldiers moved into a security zone along the Georgia–Abkhazia border.[40]

Soon after the deployment, Russian diplomacy ceased to take the interests of the Abkhazian side into account and began to act as a lobbyist for Georgian interests. The then Russian Minister of Foreign Affairs, Andrey Kozyrev, 'drew himself a plan for the economic suffocation of Abkhazia, having shown a good understanding for the specific features of its subtropical economy'.[41] Under this plan, in December 1994 the Russian Government established a 'special' regime of economic and political relations with Abkhazia which actually meant a blockade of Abkhazia and its isolation not only from Russia but also from the rest of the world.[42] The purpose of Russian diplomacy at that time was to force the Abkhazian Government to accept such conditions as would mean full capitulation to Tbilisi.[43] However, the economic and political blockade of

[39] *Gruzino-Abkhazskiy Konflikt* (note 26), pp. 19–20.

[40] The number of Russian peacekeepers in Abkhazia is not constant. Initially they numbered 2500, but by the end of 1996 that was reduced to 1500. By the end of 2000 the number of Russian peacekeepers in Abkhazia was 1747. Figure supplied by the Russian Embassy in Stockholm, 26 Feb. 2001.

[41] *Gruzino-Abkhazskiy Konflikt* (note 26), p. 25.

[42] Government of the Russian Federation Decree no. 1394, 19 Dec. 1994.

[43] The dominance of the Georgian lobby in the Russian Ministry of Foreign Affairs was largely explained by a 'personnel heritage' left by Eduard Shevardnadze, former Minister of Foreign Affairs of the USSR under Mikhail Gorbachev. Reflecting this, in the middle of 1990s a popular joke was to call the Russian Ministry of Foreign Affairs the Russian Ministry of Foreign Affairs of Georgia.

Abkhazia not only did not help resolve the Georgian–Abkhazian conflict; it strengthened the animosity of the population of Abkhazia towards Georgia. It did not, however, result in anti-Russian feelings: both the Abkhazian authorities and the general public viewed it as the result of diplomatic intrigues by Tbilisi with the Georgian lobby in Moscow and of Western pressure on Russia.

The blockade of Abkhazia completely contradicted Russia's national interests, and it was severely criticized in both houses of the Russian Parliament.[44] It could have meant the destabilization of the situation and the undermining of Russia's positions in the entire western Caucasus. However, it was never completely implemented because of the progressive crisis of the Yeltsin Administration and its inability to persuade the regions to implement decisions taken at the federal level. Many subjects of the Russian Federation—Bashkortostan, Tatarstan, Krasnodar Krai (territory) and the republics of the North Caucasus—continued political and economic relations with Abkhazia against the wishes of the central government.

Georgian–Russian cooperation did not bring either side the expected benefits. It did not protect Russia's geopolitical interests and did not guarantee the preservation of its military bases in Georgia. The Georgian Government was extremely disappointed that Russia did not expand the powers of its peacekeeping force by giving it police functions over the entire territory of Abkhazia: according to Tbilisi's plans, Russia should first pacify Abkhazia and then return it to Georgian rule.

Long before Yeltsin's departure from office in December 1999 the policy of Tbilisi turned anti-Russian. In the hope of military intervention by the West in the Georgian–Abkhazian conflict, Georgian diplomacy called for the creation around Russia of a 'belt of democratic states' and actively supported the idea of creating a uniform Caucasus (without the participation of Russia); the policy aimed to destabilize the situation in the North Caucasus and remove Russia from the South Caucasus.

Many Georgian leaders are convinced that after the disintegration of the Soviet Union the confrontation between Russia and the West continues. They therefore pin their hopes on military intervention by the West in the Abkhazian conflict since, in their opinion, the Abkhazian problem is not only Georgia's problem but 'is linked to those world processes of which we are eyewitnesses; that is, the collapse of the Soviet Union and the beginning of a new redistribution of the world . . . Georgia becomes a stable partner of the West which, in its turn, tries to complete the process which has been started—to crush the Russian Empire by all possible means'.[45]

Such a policy adopted by Tbilisi could only worsen relations with Russia. It is sharply criticised by the Georgian opposition who regard it as 'unceremoniously

[44] Resolution of the State Duma no. 1640, 2 June 1997; Appeal of the Federation Council to President Boris Yeltsin no. 166, 15 May 1997; and Appeal of the State Duma to the Government of the Russian Federation, 11 Jan. 1999.

[45] Nadareishvili, T., 'Ya ne nadeyus' chto abkhazskiy vopros reshitsya mirnym putyom' [I do not believe that the Abkhazian problem will be resolved peacefully], *Tsentral'naya Aziya i Kavkaz* (Luleå), no. 2 (2000), p. 27.

ignoring Russia's national interests' and as a manifestation of 'irrational Russophobia' on the part of the Georgian Government.[46]

With Vladimir Putin's rise to power, Russia ceased to consider Georgia as its political ally in the region. Its position on the Georgian–Abkhazian conflict also changed. In September 1999 Putin, then Russian Prime Minister, annulled the 'special' regime on the border with Abkhazia, thus lifting the economic blockade.[47] In November 2000, the President of Abkhazia, Vladislav Ardzinba, visited Moscow for the first time in several years for bilateral Abkhazian– Russian consultations on political and economic issues. In particular, discussions focused on the Abkhazian leadership's desire to maintain the Russian military presence in the South Caucasus as it is the one major factor for stability, and on its opposition to the proposed closure of the Russian military base at Gudauta in Abkhazia.[48]

When frontier areas of Georgia were transformed into rear bases for Chechen separatists and there were allegations that official Tbilisi was supporting them,[49] there was a crisis in Georgian–Russian relations. In December 2000 Russia (for the first time within the framework of the Commonwealth of Independent States, the CIS) introduced a visa regime for citizens of Georgia; however, the regime did not apply to Abkhazia and South Ossetia. The conclusion can be drawn that Russia has begun to develop a new system for addressing its interests in the South Caucasus. Active participants in this system are now not only Armenia, Azerbaijan and Georgia but also the unrecognized states in the region, including Abkhazia. Thus all the states in the South Caucasus that exist *de facto* may form important elements of stability and political balance in the region, which is a strategically important one for Russia.

IV. The position of the West

The Western countries support Georgia's territorial integrity and take a one-sidedly pro-Georgian position. During the Georgian–Abkhazian war the West did not condemn Georgia for excessive use of force and did not express concern over the violations of basic human rights and individual freedoms perpetrated by the Georgian military. It approved the introduction of repressive sanctions against Abkhazia as 'the most effective means of achieving political peace',[50]

---

[46] Kobalia, V., 'Rossiya zakhlopnula dver' k spaseniyu' [Russia slams the door to rescue], *Nezavisimaya Gazeta*, 24 Feb. 2001.

[47] Government of the Russian Federation Decree no. 1029, 9 Sep. 1999.

[48] 'O kharaktere rossiyskogo-abkhazskikh peregovorov' [The character of the Russian–Abkhazian negotiations], *Apsnipress* (Sukhumi), no. 225 (22 Nov. 2000). In June 2001 the Abkhazian leadership initiated a blockade of the base at Gudauta, thus preventing its closure and withdrawal of military equipment from the base. TV1 (Tbilisi), 14 June 2001, in 'Georgia: Abkhaz foreign minister says Russian hardware should remain in Abkhazia', Foreign Broadcast Information Service, *Daily Report–Central Eurasia (FBIS-SOV)*, FBIS-SOV-2001-0614, 14 June 2001; and Radio Free Europe/Radio Liberty (RFE/RL), *RFE/RL Newsline*, vol. 5, no. 127, Part I (9 July 2001).

[49] Broladze, N., 'Kuda ischezli narushiteli granitsy?' [Where have border infringers disappeared?], *Nezavisimaya Gazeta*, 23 Nov. 2000; and Aleksandrov, V., 'Na kholmakh Gruzii—bandity' [Gangsters on the hills of Georgia], *Trud*, 28 Nov. 2000.

[50] *Gruzino-Abkhazskiy Konflikt* (note 26), p. 25.

refused to consider the security needs of Abkhazia and concentrated all its criticism on the Abkhazian leadership.[51] This unbalanced position only increased the mistrust between the conflicting parties and caused the Abkhazian Government to take a negative attitude to any Western diplomatic initiative.

Meeting the leaders of the three South Caucasus states at the UN Millennium Summit in New York in September 2000, then US Secretary of State Madeleine Albright 'made it clear that all future American Administrations will continue to consider the post-Soviet space a zone of the US strategic and vital interests'.[52] NATO's adoption in April 1999 of the concept of humanitarian intervention, which meant that military intervention by NATO in the internal affairs of foreign states would be permissible, raised hopes in Georgia that a military action similar to that carried out by NATO in Yugoslavia might be taken in Abkhazia.

Georgia has expressed its interest in replacing the Russian peacekeeping force with other foreign forces.[53] Although this initiative found support in Turkey and Ukraine, the West refused to consider sending forces to Abkhazia as it could not risk 'sustaining losses there similar to those incurred in previous years by the Russian contingents participating in peace-making operations'.[54]

Hoping to attract the military intervention of the West in the conflict, Georgia expressed its determination to join NATO quickly.[55] This appeared impossible. Conditions for the acceptance of new members include economic stabilization, the resolution of conflicts on the territory of an applicant, the attainment of NATO standards of military equipment and training, and constructive relations with neighbours. As a result, despite the constant expansion of cooperation between Georgia and NATO in the military sphere, the West has limited its activity in the Georgia–Abkhazia conflict to sending military observers.[56]

In recent years the policy of Western countries in the Caucasian region has been increasingly influenced by the 'oil factor'. In the mid-1990s the Western countries adopted a new energy security doctrine which called for the diversification of energy transport routes to Europe. The European Union (EU) introduced the TRACECA (the Transport Corridor Europe Caucasus Asia) and INOGATE (Interstate Oil and Gas Transport to Europe) projects.[57] On this basis development began of a new system of transport routes for petroleum and gas to Europe from Central Asian and the South Caucasus. An oil pipeline from Baku to Supsa was laid through the territory of Georgia, its final section being

[51] Coppieters et al. (note 1), p. 63.

[52] Nuriev, E., 'No war, no peace in the Caucasus: the geopolitical game continues!', *Central Asia and the Caucasus* (Luleå), no. 6 (2000), p. 13.

[53] 'Gruziya predlagayet peresmotret' mandat mirotvortsev' [Georgia propose to review the peacekeepers' mandate], *Segodnya*, 24 Mar. 1997, p. 1. See also Lynch, D., *The Conflict in Abkhazia: Dilemmas in Russian 'Peacekeeping' Policy* (Royal Institute of International Affairs: London, 1998), pp. 31–36.

[54] Coppieters et al. (note 1), p. 58.

[55] Associated Press, 'Georgian leader hopes to join NATO', 29 Apr. 1999.

[56] In the UN Observer Mission in Georgia (UNOMIG), tasked with verifying the compliance of both sides with the ceasefire agreement.

[57] For details see the TRACECA Internet site, URL <http://www.traceca.org>; and the INOGATE Internet site, URL <http://www.inogate.com>.

close to the zone of the Georgian–Abkhazian conflict. The economic penetration of the West into the South Caucasus and Central Asia also led to an increase of its political influence in these regions.

The construction, with Western investment, of a new system of oil and gas pipelines that would bypass Iran and Russia was received with apprehension in Russia as it could deprive it of revenues from oil transit. Repeated statements made in Western countries to the effect that they 'refused to consider the region as part of the Russian sphere of influence',[58] while at the same time regarding it as a zone of NATO's strategic interests, were recognized by Russia as clear proof of the West's ambition to exclude it from the region.

V. Conclusions

At present the Georgian–Abkhazian conflict has little chance of being resolved politically: the interests of the conflicting sides are in complete contradiction. While political efforts to halt the fighting have so far been unsuccessful, the resumption of hostilities would cause the destabilization not only of Abkhazia but also of the entire west Caucasian region. It is unacceptable, therefore, either from the point of view of Russia's interests (the threat of destabilization in the North Caucasus) or from that of the West (the danger of military operations spreading to the systems of oil and gas pipelines between Central Asia, the Caucasus and the outside world).

The political normalization of the conflict is impossible unless Georgia puts an end to its policy of unitarism. A single Georgian state within the borders of the former Georgian Soviet Socialist Republic is possible only as a federation of equal peoples like Belgium or Switzerland. Each people must be granted its own form of statehood and representation in the central government. There should also be international guarantees of the rights of ethnic minorities and of the territorial integrity of Georgia. On the other hand, a continuation of the policy of unitarism may result in the further disintegration of the Georgian state; in that case Abkhazia may aspire to international recognition as an independent state.

Contradictions between Russia and the West in the South Caucasus present a serious potential danger. Under the existing conditions of general instability in the region, further escalation may be caused with the minimum of effort. Russia and the West should, therefore, be interested not in continuing their rivalry but in closer coordination of their regional policies. The basis of such cooperation might be mutual recognition of each other's strategic interests in the region. The development of a coordinated policy might be an effective means of stabilizing the entire Caucasian region and creating a basis for the resolution of local conflicts, including the Georgian–Abkhazian conflict.

[58] Coppieters *et al.* (note 1), p. 51.

17. The glitter and poverty of Chechen Islam

Aleksei Malashenko

I. Introduction

Originally the separatist movement in Chechnya was unrelated to Islam. Its ideology was ethnic nationalism and its goal was the establishment of an independent national state. The Chechen separatists' social base was limited: far from all members of Chechen society supported the idea of independence. Nor, it seems, did the leaders of the Chechen insurgents seriously believe that it was possible for Chechnya to attain true independence. The future president of the self-proclaimed Chechen Republic of Ichkeriya, Soviet Air Force Major-General Dzhokhar Dudayev, used to say that after Chechnya gained independence it would join the Commonwealth of Independent States (CIS) and preserve its close economic and political ties with Russia.

Before the beginning of the armed struggle for independence the Chechens aimed at maximum autonomy within the Russian Federation. The strategic tasks which the Chechen leaders set themselves were largely similar to those pursued, and realized for a period of time, by the ethno-political elite of Tatarstan.[1] In Chechnya, for a number of reasons (which are not the subject of the present study), the conflict between the centre and Grozny followed a different path—that of military–political confrontation, in which Islam became one of the main ideological and political vectors.

In the Russian scholarly literature and other publications much has been written about the important role of Islam in the events of the 1990s in Chechnya. The more convincing work is that of Vakhid Akaev (a Chechen researcher),[2] Alexei Kudryavtsev and Vladimir Bobrovnikov (two orientalists based in Moscow), and the journalist experts Ilya Maksakov and Igor Rotar.[3]

---

[1] In 1993 only 2 republics—Tatarstan and Chechnya—refused to sign the Federation Treaty. Later, in 1994, Tatarstan did sign an agreement with Moscow under which it received broad economic and even political autonomy. However, after the new Russian President, Vladimir Putin, restored the 'vertical line of power' Tatarstan's gains from the agreement were considerably reduced.

[2] Akaev, V., 'Chechnya: vozmozhen li afganskiy variant?' [Chechnya: is the Afghan variant possible?], *Central Asia and the Caucasus* (Luleå), no. 2 (1999); Akayev, V., 'Sufizm i vahhabizm na Severnom Kavkaze: issledovaniya po prikladnoy i neotlozhnoy etnologii' [Sufism and Wahhabism in the North Caucasus: studies in applied and actual ethnology], *Research in Applied and Actual Ethnology*, no. 127 (Russian Academy of Sciences, Institute of Ethnology and Anthropology: Moscow, 1999); and Akayev, V., *Sheikh Kunta-Hadji: Zhizn' i Ucheniye* [Sheikh Kunta-Hadji: his life and teaching] (Grozny, 1994).

[3] Among their publications on Chechnya are: Maksakov, I., 'Chto ozhidayet Chechnyu v novom godu' [What awaits Chechnya in the new year], *Nezavisimaya Gazeta*, 27 Dec. 2000; Maksakov, I., 'Chechenskiy sled' v terraktakh podtverzhdayetsya' ['Chechen hand' in terrorist acts confirmed], *Nezavisimaya Gazeta*, 28 Mar. 2001; Kudryavtsev, A., 'Islam i gosudarstvo v Chechenskoy respublike' [Islam and the state in the Chechen Republic], *Vostok*, no. 3 (1004), pp. 64–70; Kudryavtsev, A., 'Wahhabism: religious extremism in the northern Caucasus', *Central Asia and the Caucasus* (Luleå), no. 3 (2000); Bobrovnikov, V., 'Collective farm as a form of Islamic order in Muslim societies' in *Notions of*

Many of these interesting publications were prepared during the period when combat operations were going on in Chechnya, future relations between Moscow and Grozny were uncertain and it was not possible to draw far-reaching conclusions concerning the internal situation in Chechnya. Now that the large-scale operations there are over and attempts have been started to form a civil administration a whole stage has been completed and it is possible to evaluate its results. It is in this context that it is worthwhile to analyse the influence of the Islamic factor on events in Chechnya.

II. The influence of Islam on events in Chechnya

Islam has always been an ideology against Russian expansion in the North Caucasus. This was clear in particular in the 18th and 19th centuries when Russian expansion in the region was at its most intensive.[4] Chechnya offered especially stubborn resistance, conducted under religious slogans, to the Russian conquerors who, justifying their expansion, also used religious arguments relating to the Orthodox faith.

At the same time, the idea of jihad—holy war—in Chechnya and the rest of the North Caucasus went hand in hand with another, less popular idea, which tended to disunite the local Muslims rather than to consolidate their forces—that of establishing an Islamic state. Among the Chechens the most ardent supporter of this idea was Sheikh Mansur who, in pursuing his ends, destroyed whole villages which dared to disobey him.[5] In the opinion of the supporters of the Islamic state idea, only such a state could successfully oppose the Russian onslaught.

Islam was one of the factors which facilitated the formation of relations between Russia and the Caucasian peoples, including the Chechens. The Soviet period was no exception here. In relations between the communist government and the Chechens, Islam continued to play its peculiar, sometimes contradictory, part: at times the government flirted with the Muslims, pitting them against the anti-Soviet Cossack movement (as in the 1920s) and permitting, sometimes encouraging, the use of Islamic traditions, including Islamic legislation; at other times it declared Islam its enemy and destroyed mosques (in the 1930s and the 1980s). The religious 'thaw' of the 1940s, which started during the war years, had comparatively little effect on the Muslims of the Caucasus, especially the Chechens, Karachais and Balkars. Some of them collaborated with the Germans, and because of that entire peoples were later deported.

Law and Order in Muslim Societies, Papers of the Summer Academy of the Working Group on 'Modernity and Islam', Casablanca, 1999, pp. 25–40; and Rotar, I., Islam i Voyna [Islam and war] (AIRO-XX: Moscow, 1999).

[4] See, e.g., Gammer, M., Shamil: Musul'manskoye Soprotivleniye Tsarizmu: Zavoyevaniye Chechni i Dagestana [Shamil: Muslim resistance to tsarism: the conquest of Chechnya and Dagestan] (Kron Press: Moscow, 1998).

[5] Sheikh Mansur (his original name was Ushurma) was born in 1760. He became the first imam in the North Caucasus and promoted the Islamization of the local population. He was captured by Russian troops in 1791 and died in incarceration.

During World War II the German occupation forces tried, not without success, to play the Islamic card by encouraging the work of the Muslim clergy,
opening the mosques which had been closed by the Soviet authorities and
demonstrating their respect for Islam and its believers. The Germans reactivated
the slogan of anti-Russian (anti-Soviet) jihad—which was not difficult. Writing
about the anti-Soviet rebellions which erupted in the North Caucasus period-
ically before the war, Abdurrakhman Avtorkhanov, a Chechen journalist, notes
that 'whereas it is difficult to establish any organizational links between those
rebellions, the national–ideological links between them are perfectly clear: they
were provoked by the calls for jihad issued by the founders of the idea of
independence for the mountain peoples—Mansur, Gamzat-Bek, Kazimulla and
Shamil'.[6] The last Chechen armed insurrection, led by Hasan Israilov, was put
down in the spring of 1940. (In 1995 the present author was told in Grozny that
the last Chechen rebel was arrested by the authorities in 1972.)

Nevertheless, there is no direct connection between the 19th- and 20th-
century jihad (let alone attempts to establish an Islamic state) and the Chechen
separatist movement of the 1990s. Things are more complex than they seem.
The continuance of the Islamic tradition was interrupted by the deportations of
1944 and the dispersal of the Chechens across the vast expanses of the USSR.
As a result of that dispersal the influence of Islam on their minds and behaviour
was considerably reduced. Unlike their ethnic mountain peoples' solidarity,
Islam was not a decisive factor for the Chechens' survival in an alien environment. Much more effective was their adherence to national traditions, such as
the custom of burying their dead at all costs in their native land.[7]

The Chechen diaspora—the Chechens who later, in the 1950s, returned—
were largely indifferent towards Islam. To them it was, above all, a component
part of an ethnic culture many elements of which were in contradiction with
'orthodox' Islam. Lately, Chechen Islam has regressed towards its 18th-century
form, when it was a syncretist religious culture with rudiments of idolatry and
absolute domination of customary law, *adat*, over shariah, the Islamic canon
law. In other words, the Chechen Islam of the late 20th century has to a certain
extent been reconstituted into the variety which was opposed by Sheikh
Mansur.

As a result, Islam in Chechnya, particularly among the Chechen diaspora,
found itself on the periphery of the Chechens' social consciousness and was not
in demand at first as an ideological model of Chechen separatism. So, in the
Islamic tradition of the Chechen society, to use a well-known expression, 'the
time was out of joint'.

Why, then, was Islam once again 'in demand' in Chechnya and why did it
even claim (unsuccessfully, as it turned out) the role of a dominant ideological
model in the Chechen consciousness and even a factor of state development?

---

[6] Uralov, A. (pen name of Abdurrakhman Avtorkhanov), *Narodo-Ubiystvo v SSSR* [The murder of
peoples in the USSR] (Moscow, 1991), p. 24.
[7] Private communications of the author with Chechen colleagues.

In the first place, the Chechen conflict began amid a general 'Islamic renaissance' on the territory of the former USSR, including Russia. In the North Caucasus this process was particularly vigorous in Dagestan and Chechnya.[8] The Islamic rebirth facilitated the regeneration of the Chechens' historical memory in which jihad (*gazavat*) figured prominently. It revived in people's minds a sense of dignity, pride and belief in their ability to oppose any external enemy. It would be fair to say that the early 1990s were a brief period of emotional religious euphoria which was capitalized on by the then Chechen politicians, and above all by General Dzhokhar Dudayev, the first president of the self-proclaimed Chechen Republic, who at first had no intention of appealing to Islam for political purposes.

In the second place, if Moscow had not set out to suppress the Chechen separatists by military methods (whether this was justified or not) the Chechen Islamic rebirth would not have taken such radical, even extremist forms. It was only when the conflict between Moscow and Grozny became a military confrontation that the Islamic rebirth in Chechnya assumed the form of jihad. 'Russia . . . forced us to enter on the path of Islam, although we were not prepared well enough to accept the Islamic values', Dudayev said in 1996.[9]

The transformation of religious renaissance into a holy war made Islam one of the key factors in the Chechen conflict, as well as in the overall situation in the North Caucasus. Only after that did outside influence from radical Islamic organizations as well as certain Muslim states begin to be felt. (Jordan, Saudi Arabia, Syria and Turkey are the countries most often named in this connection. This overlooks the fact that initially this outside influence was generated by Chechen rather than Islamic solidarity, since there is a united and influential Chechen diaspora in those countries.)

III. The aims of the Chechen leaders in appealing to Islam

Dudayev and his associates were forced to turn to religion for their political purposes. Neither Dudayev nor his associates envisaged the consequences of this move, which, following Dudayev's death in 1996, led to a split in the Chechen society and its military–political leadership.

Of course, even before Dudayev turned to Islam there were in Chechnya various Islamic groups which called themselves Salafites and worked to spread 'pure' Islam, in contrast with traditional Caucasian Islam.[10] There also appeared in Chechnya a branch of the Islamic Rebirth Party (IRP), based on a quasi-Salafite ideology and headed by Islam Khalimov, who soon became one of Dudayev's advisers. Salafite preachers were active in Chechnya. However, compared with neighbouring Dagestan, their success in Chechnya was not significant. In Chechnya (as well as in the neighbouring republics of the North

---

[8] Malashenko, A. V., *Islamskoye Vozrozhdeniye v Sovremennoy Rossii* [Renaissance of Islam in modern Russia] (Moskovskiy Tsentr Karnegi: Moscow, 1998).

[9] 'Terms of war and peace', *Time*, Mar. 1996, p. 19.

[10] The Salafites are known as Wahhabites in Russia. The terms are used interchangeably here.

Caucasus) 'the IRP failed to become a fully-fledged opposition party. It refrained from any serious political actions and actually limited itself to "educational activity", that is, propaganda for pure Islam'.[11]

The majority of Chechen Muslims remained either indifferent to religion or oriented towards Tarikatism, a variety of Islam traditional for the Chechens. The Naqshbandi and Kadiri tarikats (brotherhoods) were active in the republic. Their members were the followers of Sheikh Kunta-Hadji.[12] Although the Kadirites competed among themselves, they were in a stable state of agreement.

In the form in which it existed in Chechnya, Tarikite Islam was not very suitable as a militant ideology, as a factor that would help to consolidate the society and its political forces for organizing resistance to the Russian centre. Nor could the religious authorities, whose prestige among the public was very limited, call for unity in the struggle against Moscow. In fact, the institutional clergy was dependent on secular politicians and played no role of its own.

The initiative of turning to Islam as an ideological and political means of struggle could only be taken by influential secular politicians in the pursuit of concrete pragmatic aims. In implementing those aims religion was expected to play an important but purely instrumental role. Symbolically, Dudayev did not consider himself an ardent Muslim believer. In fact, he could not have been one because of his upbringing, way of life and professional occupation. It is true that in one interview he asserted that he was 'a profoundly religious person from childhood',[13] but it is well known that people with a Muslim background seldom risk admitting to atheistic convictions publicly. (It will for ever remain a mystery what transformations took place in Dudayev's mind after his proclamation of jihad.)

In other words, the decision to proclaim jihad was made by Dudayev himself, and this could not have been otherwise, even if formally it was announced by others, including clergymen. Relevant in this connection is Decree no. 2, which was signed by Dudayev in November 1991 and which contained an appeal to all Muslims living in Moscow 'to turn Moscow into a disaster zone in the name of our freedom from kufr'.[14] Although the word 'jihad' is never mentioned in the text of the decree, its phraseology and rhetoric show that Dudayev was determined to make use of the religious factor.

As time went on, Dudayev and his associates became convinced that jihad was the most effective ideology in the Chechens' struggle for independence and that appeals for a holy war were capable of uniting the nation and raising the people's fighting spirit.

[11] Kudryavtsev, A. V., '"Vahhabizm": Problemy religioznogo ekstremizma na Severnom Kavkaze' [Wahhabism: problems of religious extremism in the North Caucasus], *Central Asia and the Caucasus* (Luleå), no. 9 (2000), p. 116.

[12] Sheikh Kunta-Hadji (Kishiev), 1830(?)–67, was one of the most prominent Chechen religious authorities whose followers are still influential in Chechnya. See also *Sheikh Kunta-Hadji: Zhizn' i Ucheniye* (note 2).

[13] Quoted from *Ternisty Put' k Svobode* [A thorny path to freedom] (Grozny, 1992), p. 50.

[14] *Sbornik Ukazov Prezidenta Chechenskoy Respubliki s 1 noyabrya 1991 goda po 30 iunya 1992 goda* [Collection of decrees by the President of the Chechen Republic from 1 November 1991 to 30 June 1992] (Grozny, 1992), p. 4.

For the Chechen military–political elite, jihad was a convenient justification of its actions since it gave them a sacral sanction: the struggle for independence was identified with a holy war. Thus the conflict took on a double identity—both national and religious. In an interview given in 1998 the Mufti of Chechnya, Akhmed-Hadji Kadyrov (a sworn enemy of Wahhabism—a term used for the fundamentalists in the Russian mass media) said that 'the Chechen resistance movement should be regarded as religious, in the first place, and as nationalist, in the second'.[15]

Jihad was associated with Islamic 'renaissance'. The well-known Chechen politician Zelimkhan Yandarbiyev, who was Chechen President for a few months after Dudayev's death, seems to have been right in saying that the process of Islamic rebirth in Chechnya 'is best described as *gazavat* or jihad'.[16] At any rate, such an assessment is quite applicable to the first half of the 1990s.

On the whole the use of the *gazavat* slogan proved quite productive for the Chechen resistance movement. Of course, it was not the Islamic ideology itself that ensured the Chechens' military successes against the Russian troops—there were many political and purely military reasons for that—but the jihad slogan had a definite mobilizing effect and boosted the fighting spirit of the Chechen militants, particularly among the young. The proclamation of jihad also to some extent promoted the internationalization of the conflict, encouraging religious fanatics from other Muslim countries to take part and enlisting the help of various Islamic organizations. In other words, thanks to the proclamation of jihad, the Chechens managed to activate the mechanism of Islamic solidarity. If this did not decide the outcome of military operations, it did enable the Chechens not to feel isolated from their fellow believers in the rest of the world.

However, the Chechen jihad received no serious support from Russia's Muslim community, most of which, including the political elites and leading clergy, regarded the Chechens' actions with apprehension and even disapproval, fearing quite justly that the Chechen conflict might result in an even more negative attitude among society towards Muslims and Islam in general. Ruslan Aushev, the President of Ingushetia, which has a common border with Chechnya, was the exception. His 'sympathies' for the Chechens, however, were due partly to his reluctance to prejudice Ingushetia's relations with its unpredictable neighbour and partly to the fact that from time to time Moscow used him as an unofficial go-between in its contacts with the separatists.

Some radical groups in Tatarstan and Bashkortostan did declare their solidarity with the Chechens and even sent some Muslim volunteers to the Chechen front. These actions, however, were of very limited scope and were resolutely checked by the Russian special services.

Thus, the Chechen separatist movement for the most part took the form of a jihad, which on the one hand was beneficial to it both internally and externally but on the other failed to prevent internecine wars inside Chechnya itself in the mid-1990s.

[15] Rotar (note 3).
[16] *Nezavisimaya Gazeta*, 20 Dec. 1996, p. 3.

The proclamation of the Chechen Republic of Ichkeriya, an Islamic state, was intended to be the finishing touch of the Chechen resistance movement in the form of a jihad. This idea was first voiced back in 1991 at the Second National Congress of the Chechen People. The documents of that congress stressed that an independent Chechen state must be an Islamic one. At the time, however, this idea was not developed further, perhaps because Dudayev himself held an entirely different view: he insisted that the Chechen republic should be 'a constitutional secular state'.[17] It is conceivable that Dudayev (who, despite the constantly growing ambitions of his associates, remained the leader of fighting Chechnya) was the chief obstacle to the establishment of an Islamic state. After its proclamation he would inevitably have to share power with someone else: being a national leader, he could hardly become a religious one as well. The establishment of an Islamic state would certainly require the formation of new autonomous structures, independent of the president, which would be headed by other people. The idea of national power might enter into contradiction with the idea of religious power.

However, 'great people know when to die', and Dudayev departed this life a national leader, never witnessing the fierce confrontation within the anti-Russian opposition.

The separatists subsequently split, mainly because of personal ambitions, an intention to be more respected by Moscow and lack of ideological integrity. More significant, however, is the part Islam played in shaping the internal political situation, especially during the attempt to establish a national state.

The reason why the Chechen politicians turned to Islam in the second half of the 1990s is formally consonant with the reason why this was done under Dudayev, but there is an essential difference.

Jihad was supposed to consolidate the Chechen nation in the face of the external enemy, and it did meet with a response and promote national consolidation in the face of external danger. The aim of the introduction of the shariah criminal code in 1996 was to establish order in the society, to create a basis for regulating the relations between the various groups of the population and to stem the growth of crime, but the introduction of shariah rather split the society into supporters and opponents of forced Islamization. Furthermore, whereas for some politicians the establishment of shariah was both an end and a means towards taking the next step—proclaiming an Islamic state in Chechnya—for others it was a forced move.

The idea of progressing towards an Islamic state was upheld by the Salafites. They advocated the priority of Islamic values over all others, including ethnic ones, the 'purging' of Islam of all pagan elements and the introduction of strict behavioural customs such as prayer five times a day and refusal of alcohol. They also rejected democracy as being alien to the Muslims. This paradigm of values is typically fundamentalist (described by the Arab term *usuliya*, a derivative of *usul ad-din*—the roots of faith) and is practically identical with

---

[17] *Literaturnaya Gazeta*, 12 Aug. 1992.

the requirements of fundamentalism in the Middle East and other parts of the Muslim world. (The advocates of such requirements prefer not to call themselves fundamentalists or Wahhabites and not even Salafites, but simply Muslims, implying that only they can be regarded as true believers.)

The question who in Chechnya (and elsewhere) can be considered a Salafite remains an open one. Some researchers and journalists believe that a Salafite is a person who knows Arabic, is familiar with the appropriate philosophy, has the necessary theological knowledge and is capable of arguing his position. On this view, no 'true' Salafites will be found in Chechnya or in the whole North Caucasus, where in the years of Soviet government high Muslim culture was almost completely destroyed, along with its bearers, the ulemas and other Muslim intellectuals. Others (including the present author) believe that all those who more or less share the principles of Islamic rebirth and are prepared to uphold them in practice in the present-day situation in Chechnya may be regarded as Salafites. Strictly speaking the term 'Salafite' is not applicable to people who finished Soviet schools and colleges, who have no regular religious education and whose knowledge of Arabic is poor or non-existent. They may be properly described as 'quasi-Salafites' or 'Salafitic Muslims'. By their practical actions, however, they strive to attain the aims contained in the philosophy of Salafiya. Thus such different people as Bagautdin Muhammad, an ideologist and preacher of Salafism, who is well know throughout the Caucasus and was invited by Yandarbiyev to Chechnya from Dagestan in 1997, Shamil Basayev, who carried out acts of terrorism and who held the post of Vice-Premier from 1996, and a rank-and-file Islamic militant who is unable to read the inscription in Arabic on the band round his head but is prepared to fight for the establishment of an Islamic state, all fall within the category of Salafites.

At any rate, it was this Salafite public which consciously supported the idea of rebuilding the Chechen state on an Islamic basis.

Of course, it should be borne in mind that quite often Islamic rhetoric conceals personal ambitions and that to many Chechen Salafites Islam has been primarily an instrument for attaining their selfish ends. However, once these people had adopted Islam as a weapon in their struggle, they all became hostages to religion, and once they summoned the name of Allah they could no longer depart from the chosen path without the risk of being accused of betrayal of the faith and losing their prestige for ever.[18]

Finally, it should be remembered that the spread of Salafism has been facilitated by the ever more active penetration into Chechnya of foreign Muslims, above all ethnic Chechens and Arabs from the Middle East. An example of this is the activity of Fatkha ash-Shashani, who returned to his historic homeland and not only headed an Islamic battalion called Dzhamaat but also did all he could to spread the idea of establishing an Islamic state in Chechnya. It was in

---

[18] It was certainly no accident that, realizing the futility of the struggle for an Islamic state in Chechnya, Shamil Basayev declared in Oct. 2000, at a moment when Palestinian–Israeli relations were seriously deteriorating, his readiness to send 150 fighters to support the Palestinians. Thereby he reminded the world once again that he was an Islamic politician who remained loyal to the principle of religious solidarity.

this battalion that Khattab (whose real name is Habib Abd ar-Rakhman), the most abhorrent foreign field commander in Chechnya, perfected his fighting skills. He is also a consistent proponent of the Islamic state idea.

After the shariah criminal code was introduced a corresponding shariah judicial system was instituted—'in rough form' as yet. The following two years saw a struggle for the establishment of an Islamic state. At the end of that struggle, in February 1999, full shariah rule was introduced, which was tantamount to the proclamation of an Islamic state. The fact that such the process took so long seems to indicate that the decision was not based on the wholehearted approval of the whole of Chechen society. Paradoxically, the decision was taken by Aslan Maskhadov, who was elected President of Chechnya in 1996 and had always opposed the Salafites. The sole purpose of his doing so was to wrest the initiative from his Salafite opponents.

The president and his associates, some of the field commanders and the Muslim clergy, including Kadyrov, opposed the Salafites in general. It is known that, in an attempt to postpone the introduction of shariah in Chechnya, Maskhadov and Kadyrov tried to enlist the support of some Arab and Malaysian leaders and theologians.[19] They and their numerous supporters realized that the introduction of shariah and the ensuing proclamation of an Islamic state would inevitably undermine their positions. In fact, the office of the first president to be elected in accordance with a secular constitution would be rendered illegitimate. A statement made by Abdul-Malik Medzhidov, commander of the Shariah Guard (whose appointment Maskhadov was compelled to approve) is typical: 'I do not consider Maskhadov a legitimate head of the Islamic state ... because in a Muslim state legitimacy can only be achieved under the shariah law, and it was not under this law that Maskhadov came to power'.[20]

The most important thing, however, is that far from all Chechens supported the introduction of shariah, let alone the establishment of an Islamic state. Shariah infringed on the mountain people's traditions, in which personal freedom plays an important role. It was unacceptable to many women, who worked as hard as men and took an active part in social life. It ran counter to the norms of behaviour which people had formed in Soviet times and the notions they had acquired in Soviet secondary and higher schools. Finally, many Chechens regarded shariah as an alien influence exerted by Arabs and foreign Muslims in general who were trying to force their philosophy and way of life on Chechens. A statement by Zia Susuev, a member of the Presidium of the Executive of the United Congress of the Chechen People, is expresses a view which is characteristic of part of Chechen society: 'We Chechens, the descendants of ancient Hurrite tribes and bearers of the Caucasian mountain people's traditions, confront the threat of being turned into a section of a faceless umma with the character and appearance of a Semitic tribe'.[21]

---

[19] *Kavkazskaya Konfederatsiya* [The Caucasian Confederation] (Grozny), no. 2(11) (1999), p. 2.

[20] *Golos Chechenskoy Respubliki* [Voice of the Chechen Republic] (Grozny), 25 Feb. 1999, p. 3.

[21] Susuev, Z., 'My narod bez prava vybora?' [Are we a people without the right of choice?], *Golos Chechenskoy Respubliki*, 25 Feb. 1999, p. 1.

It is difficult today to assess which sections of the Chechen population (including the Chechen diaspora) supported the Islamization of their country and which opposed it. However, it is clear that the supporters of Islamization were far more active than the opponents and even tried to use force in achieving their ends. Furthermore, the Salafites interfered in the everyday life of the Chechens: they forbade the sale and consumption of alcohol, compelled women to wear clothes that were more in keeping with Islamic ethics, and so on. They interfered in people's religious life, forbidding the observance of tarikat customs such as visiting the graves of holy sheikhs. (The height of the anti-tarikat campaign was an attempt by the Salafites in 1995 to destroy the grave of Kunta-Hadji's mother, Hedi. This led to a clash between the Salafites and the followers of Kunta-Hadji.)

It was in the struggle for power that the opposition between the Salafites and the supporters of Maskhadov and Kadyrov was the strongest. The question of introducing shariah and proclaiming Chechnya an Islamic state was above all a political one. In August 1997 opposition took the form of armed clashes in Gudermes between 'Wahhabite' detachments and the National Guard, which supported Maskhadov. The coup attempt was unsuccessful. Following it, the Shariah Guard was disbanded and several Salafite leaders and preachers, including Bagautdin Muhammad, were banished.

However, the success of Maskhadov and his allies was only partial: the Islamic radicals continued to enjoy the support of such politicians as Basayev and Yandarbiyev who did not want the 'Wahhabites' to be defeated either as a political force or as a religious trend. A stalemate had developed in the republic: while Maskhadov tried to regain the political initiative from the Islamic radicals, Mufti Kadyrov continued to criticize the Salafites/Wahhabites, stressing the incompatibility of their views not only with Caucasian Islamic tradition but also with Islam in general. Meanwhile, the Salafites continued to insist on the introduction of an Islamic mode of government.

Basayev's well-known raid into Dagestan in 1999 triggered off the second Chechen campaign, in the course of which his supporters suffered heavy losses and a pro-Moscow civil administration began to be formed on the part of the territory controlled by the federal forces. (Kadyrov, who resigned as Mufti of Chechnya in 2000, was appointed head of this administration.) Following the raid the idea of setting up an Islamic state was once again transformed into calls for a holy war.

IV. The failure of the 'Salafite project'

The idea of establishing an Islamic state in Chechnya (unlike the launching of jihad) seems to have been stillborn. It did not have the necessary social and religious basis; its advocates lacked the appropriate professional—theological, legal and administrative—training, and many 'Wahhabite' leaders had compromised themselves in the eyes of the Muslims by their misdeeds, acts of cruelty and an unquenchable thirst for power. While advocating 'pure Islam', they pursued 'only one purpose—to be the "fathers of the nation" and to get high posts—not for the sake of the Islamic idea but for the sake of acquiring creature comforts and earthly grandeur'.[22] That is how the 'Wahhabites' were characterized by their opponents among the participants in jihad.

One of the reasons, albeit not the main reason, for the failure of the idea was Moscow's total rejection of any form of Islamic statehood in Chechnya. Russian propaganda, both official and unofficial, did all it could to discredit shariah and its supporters and used the struggle against radical Islam as one of its main arguments for justifying before the rest of the world Moscow's policy in Chechnya and the North Caucasus as a whole. Indeed, the proclamation of shariah as the only law in Chechnya did nothing to help evoke Western sympathy for the Chechen resistance, which Maskhadov and some other Chechen leaders were constantly seeking.

The Chechen experiment of introducing shariah as a first stage in the formation of an Islamic statehood on the territory of the former USSR is far from unique. Efforts in this direction have already been made in Central Asia and in Dagestan. The 'Salafite project' is gradually becoming a pervasive—actual or latent—form of socio-political activity in the Muslim territories of the CIS.

It is an established view that the idea of Islamic government is a utopia supported almost exclusively by religious fanatics and political adventurers. The introduction of shariah does have the approval of all Muslims. Shariah enclaves exist today and will appear in the future. A case in point is the 'Kadar zone'—the villages of Karamakhi, Chabanmakhi and Kadar—in Dagestan, Tavildara in Tajikistan, and some regions in Uzbekistan and even in Kyrgyzstan, which in the autumn of 2000 found themselves under the control of the Islamists. In some cases an Islamic 'proto-state' has been known to exist for several months and even years. However, there is not a single Chechen village, let alone town or city, under shariah control. This is highly indicative: despite jihad, no stable Salafite enclaves where the bulk of the population favours the introduction of shariah have been formed in Chechnya. On the popular level, as it were, Salafism has proved incapable of providing the basis for the development of an eventual state. Moreover, the Salafites, having failed to secure their rear in the form of territories that they trusted, were compelled to shift their struggle abruptly to the national level where they no longer appeared as fighters for social justice and 'true Islam' but rather as ordinary political self-seekers, and at that level their struggle for an Islamic state was deprived of its would-be religious sanction.

In Chechnya the national Salafite project was doomed because it lacked a firm socio-cultural basis: it only existed on a verbal level. Besides, its implementation resulted in continuous confrontation between different military–political groupings. The Salafites turned out to be only one of the political

[22] 'Obrashcheniye k parlamentu Chechenskoy Respubliki Ichkeriya Soyuza veteranov Yugo-Zapadnogo napravleniya' [Address to the Parliament of the Chechen Republic of Ichkeria by the Veterans' Union of the South-Western Sector], *Jihad*, no. 3 (Jan. 1999), p. 1.

forces. Furthermore, they failed to impress the Muslims as fighters for the faith and for justice.[23]

Failure in Chechnya impelled the Chechen Salafites to try to construct the project elsewhere in the North Caucasus, above all in Dagestan, where Salafiya was particularly deep-rooted. It was there that they won their greatest social influence, organized appropriate groups and movements, and even introduced quasi-shariah government in territories under their control.[24] They were not, however, able to expand their influence any further. They were opposed by the entire administration of the republic and by the local clergy, who began to cooperate closely with the tarikat sheikhs, forming a united religious–political bloc against the Salafites. Thus in Dagestan the Salafites did not have reliable patronage or protection on the republican level. Meanwhile their opposite numbers in Chechnya held strong positions in the leadership of the republic but had no reliable social base and no serious religious prestige in the eyes of their fellow citizens.

Cooperation between the Salafites in Dagestan and the Salafitic Chechen politicians started in the mid-1990s, and on that basis there appeared what seemed a potentially powerful religious–political coalition whose purpose was to set up a common Islamic state on the territory of Chechnya and Dagestan. It was expected that this state would be joined by some other North Caucasian republics, primarily Ingushetia, Chechnya's neighbour, worn out by its long-lasting conflict with North Ossetia, a republic with a predominantly Christian population. The aims of the Chechen radicals were to spread their influence to new territories under the cover of Islamic phraseology. (Later, in 1999, these aims were modified, and Basayev's raid into Dagestan was meant as a kind of compensation for his rather ineffectual actions inside Chechnya, including the period when he was vice-premier under President Maskhadov.[25])

On the practical level these aims were promoted by various joint Dagestani–Chechen organizations, the largest being the Congress of the Peoples of Chechnya and Dagestan, formed in April 1998. Its stated strategic aim was the 'unification of the Caucasian peoples on the basis of the laws of Allah'.[26] The initiative of setting up the Congress belonged to such organizations, formerly influential on the Chechen political scene, as the Islamic Nation and the Socio-Political Union of the Caucasian Confederation. It is noteworthy that Dagestan

[23] There is abundant evidence that, while demanding that others observe the shariah norms, members of the Shariah Guard themselves consumed alcohol, used drugs and committed other acts incompatible with shariah.

[24] For more detail see Shikhsaidov, A., 'Islam v Dagestane, Tsentral'noy Azii i na Kavkaze' [Islam in Dagestan, Central Asia and the Caucasus], *Central Asia and the Caucasus* (Luleå), no. 5 (1999); Makarov, D., 'Ofitsial'ny i neofitsial'ny Islam v Dagestane' [Official and unofficial Islam in Dagestan] (manuscript), 1999; and Maksakov, I., 'Sootnosheniye islamskikh dvizhenii Dagestana' [The correlation of the Islamic movements in Dagestan], *NG-Religii* (supplement to *Nezavisimaya Gazeta*), 18 Mar. 1998.

[25] Many experts believe that Basayev's raid was a provocation engineered by the Russian special services in order to justify the resumption of military operations in Chechnya and defeat the local militants. This view is ignored here.

[26] Dzadziev, A., *Kongress Narodov Chechni i Dagestana: Set' Etnologicheskogo Monitoringa i Rannego Preduprezhdeniya Konfliktov* [Congress of the Peoples of Chechnya and Dagestan: a network of ethnological monitoring and early prevention of conflicts] (Moscow, June 1998), p. 19.

was represented only by the Supreme Council of the Lak People (a local ethnic group).

As the Congress was being created, it became clear that the idea of unifying Chechnya and Dagestan on an Islamic basis was not very popular in Dagestan because to its ruling republican elite and the local ethnic groups this would mean a redistribution of power and wealth in favour of the Chechens and their placemen—something no one in Dagestan could agree to. Furthermore, in Dagestan itself the Salafites, while active, are in a minority. Thus the idea of unification on an Islamic basis does not meet with understanding from the majority of Dagestanis.

Besides, the creation of an Islamic political alliance like that would never be allowed by Russia, which is very sensitive to the 'Islamic threat' and is waging a consistent, although poorly organized, struggle against it. The consolidation of such a union would lead to the expansion of the zone of separatism and to general destabilization in the North Caucasus, as well as in the entire southern macro-region of the Russian Federation comprising the Stavropol and Krasnodar territories, the Rostov and Astrakhan regions and the Republic of Kalmykia. The appearance of a Dagestani–Chechen state would mean the emergence of the Islamic radicals onto the Caspian seaboard, which would affect the correlation of forces in that oil-producing region. This would upset, with unpredictable consequences, the already unstable balance of interests and forces there.

The Chechen politicians who talk about the prospects of establishing an Islamic state in the North Caucasus must be aware of all these circumstances which make it impossible to realize their project. Shamil Basayev, head of the Congress of the Peoples of Chechnya and Dagestan, became convinced of that after his detachments were routed and driven out of Dagestan.

(In spite of this, a community of interests between the Dagestanis and the Chechens has been demonstrated on the path of Islam: the Chechen and Dagestani Salafites fought shoulder to shoulder both in Chechnya and in Dagestan against the Russian federal troops and Interior Ministry detachments which, it should be noted, included Dagestani natives. Some believe that the majority of Basayev's fighters who invaded Dagestan in 1999 were Dagestanis. Hundreds of them today are members of the fighting Chechen detachments and they are said to be the most ardent advocates of jihad.)

The failure of the Islam-based Chechen–Dagestani unity project, coupled with the relative successes of the federal forces in Chechnya in 1999–2000, put an end to the Chechen radicals' hopes of creating a union of the peoples of the North Caucasus (with implied Chechen leadership). Evidently, belief in the success of the project existed only in the minds of Muslim fanatics who had lost touch with reality and political demagogues such as Movladi Udugov, former Chechen Foreign Minister and Vice-Premier.[27]

Russian politicians, most of whom reacted with pain to the radical Islamic slogans, found the propaganda of the idea of an Islamic state to their advantage:

[27] It is doubtful that, while stressing his loyalty to the idea of establishing an Islamic state in the North Caucasus, Udugov seriously believed it to be feasible, for he has always been a pragmatist.

to the nationalists it furnished a convenient pretext for demonstrating their xenophobia and 'Islamophobia', while the democrats criticized the very combination of religion and politics as medieval. The Russian leadership identified ethnic separatism more and more with Wahhabite ideology.

The Russian military are interested in keeping up the 'Islamic threat' propaganda since it enables them to maintain their importance in the public eye as the chief barrier in the way of religious extremism and terrorism. This goes for both local Chechen and general international Islamic extremism. Russia's military and political elites see eye to eye on this matter. Russia regards the struggle against international Islamic extremism as confirmation that it and the world democratic community have common positions and that Russia takes an active part in world affairs. (This attitude is confirmed by its activity in Central Asia in the spring and summer of 2000, where it sided more or less successfully with the local ruling regimes against the militants of Uzbekistan's Islamic movement.)

V. External influences

In this connection how strong is the influence of external forces on events in Chechnya and on the efforts of the local Salafites to create an Islamic state?

In the 1990s Russian politicians and the mass media gave a good deal of attention to this question. Their main effort was aimed at proving that there was continuous coordination of actions between different Islamic forces, including radical religious–political organizations and even some state structures. Moreover, it was asserted that some Western intelligence services were implicated in the activity of the Islamic radicals: 'certain Western and Islamic special services plan to spread instability and Wahhabism in Central Asia and the North Caucasus'.[28] This view would have been completely justified at the time of the Soviet military presence in Afghanistan. Its application to the present-day situation, however, indicates partiality and impedes a true understanding of the motivation of the Islamic movement and the course its development is likely to take, including in the North Caucasus. It is rooted in a conspiracy theory and its exponents often ignore the internal reasons for the appearance of radical Islam in a aprticular region, including Chechnya. While there is no denying that Islamic radicals have offered cooperation or that the Chechen Wahhabites have received outside financial assistance, it must be admitted that they act in accordance with an inner logic of their own. It is well know that the Chechens are dissatisfied with the extent of Islamic solidarity shown in their conflict with Moscow, especially in the late 1990s, and that they have expressed disappointment at the fact that not a single Muslim state has yet recognized Chechnya as an independent entity.[29]

---

[28] Surikov, A. and Baranov, A., 'Vahhabity kak kontseptual'naya ugroza' [Wahhabites as a conceptual threat], *Pravda*, 5 Feb. 1998.

[29] The Chechen Republic was recognized by Bosnia and Herzegovina, the Turkish part of Cyprus and the Taliban movement in Afghanistan.

A Russian researcher, Alexander Ignatenko, has expressed an opinion that is very difficult to agree with but also not easy to argue against. 'It is possible', he has said, 'to trace a process, directed from the outside, whereby the Chechen autonomist movement is being Islamized and its detachments are being turned into units of the worldwide Islamist (Wahhabite) movement'.[30] It is, however, not quite correct to consider the events in Chechnya and the related attempts to create an Islamic state in the North Caucasus as part of some kind of geo-political project conceived at the headquarters of Islamic organizations and deliberately supported by united Islamic capital, particularly in view of the fact that after the Chechens suffered their first major setbacks external sources of support began to dry up. (This was the reason for a statement made by Khattab at the end of 1999 to the effect that the mission assigned to him by Allah had been completed and that he was leaving Chechnya.)

It should be remembered that to many Muslim countries the problem of sep-aratism is also sensitive. North Caucasian separatism, even under the banner of Islam, could touch off a chain reaction in the neighbouring regions—in Turkey and Iraq, for instance, where there are Kurdish populations struggling for inde-pendence. The appearance of a new Islamic state in the south of Russia would be of questionable benefit to the Muslim world and would pose new, very complex problems to the Muslim community. For instance, this community would have to take partial responsibility for such actions carried out by Chechen Muslims as the taking of hostages, terrorist attacks and much else.[31]

A distinction should be made between the anti-Russian rhetoric that has become widespread in many Muslim countries and the concrete actions of their governments. It is noteworthy that throughout the Chechen conflict there has been no sudden deterioration of Russia's relations with any of the Muslim states. Moreover, criticism of Russian policy in the North Caucasus expressed by the Organization of the Islamic Conference (OIC), the most influential org-anization in the Muslim world, has been much more restrained than that which came from the Organization for Security and Co-operation in Europe (OSCE).

All this point to the conclusion that on the national (Chechen) and the regional (North Caucasian) levels the 'Salafite (Islamic) project' has not had any significant outside support. The external factor has not, nor could it have, played a decisive role in the Chechen jihad, nor has it succeeded in establishing an Islamic state. This is the principal difference between the situation in the North Caucasus and that in Central Asia where a similar project, despite strong opposition, has a chance of being realized on a national level, and will inevitably affect the general situation in the Caspian region.

---

[30] Ignatenko, A., 'Ot Filippin do Kosovo: Islamizm kak global'ny destabiliziruyushchiy faktor' [From the Philippines to Kosovo: Islamism as a global destabilizing factor], *Nezavisimaya Gazeta*, 12 Oct. 2000, p. 8.

[31] Such actions were often sanctioned by clergymen who came to Chechnya from the Middle East and who cooperated with the radicals. However, it should be taken into account that, according to the Islamic canons, practically any Muslim who is at the moment recognized as a religious authority by other Muslims can utter fatwa (judgement in the name of Islam). In Chechnya, any man who knew Arabic and could interpret the Koran, especially if he had distinguished himself in military operations, was regarded as such an authority.

The fact that it was impossible to realize the 'Salafite project' in Chechnya, even on the scale of village or district and its failure on the national and North Caucasian level (with Chechnya as the nucleus) show that Chechnya cannot and will not become the main centre for the spread of the Salafite ideology and related political practice.

The popularity of the idea of jihad in the first half of the 1990s is explained above all by the fact that it was an ideology of national resistance, a factor for unification on an ethnic basis, not a religious one. When it came to introducing Islamic norms into the legislative process, let alone into the process of state development, Chechen society split, the bulk of it rejecting the idea of state development on a religious basis.

Even the affluent, radically thinking believers abroad proved to be powerless to do anything about it. The threat of 'Wahhabism winning victory in the North Caucasus'[32] which is used to scare the Russian 'man in the street' is ephemeral.

However, the limited extent of the re-Islamization of Chechen society and the failure to Islamize its administrative structures do not mean that Islam has withdrawn from the socio-political life of Chechnya or the North Caucasus as a whole. Its influence on the society will continue, although it will have its ups and downs. It may grow whenever the forces in power—in Chechnya and the North Caucasus in general—are unable to resolve complex economic and social problems. In such cases the attractiveness of the 'Islamic alternative' will grow again, and the experience of the Islamic radical forces will again be in demand.

[32] Gapbaev, A., 'Vahhabizm na Kavkaze' [Wahhabism in the Caucasus], *Den' Respubliki* (Cherkessk), 19 Aug. 2000, p. 2.

18. Radical Islam as a threat to the security of the Central Asian states: a view from Uzbekistan

Farkhad Khamraev

I. Introduction

The changes in the former Soviet Union that took place at the beginning of the 1990s radically transformed the global geopolitical structure. Fifteen former Soviet republics, now independent states, set out on a course of independent development and transformation of their societies. Among them were the republics of Central Asia, whose subsequent development became dependent on the identification and effective use of factors that would preserve national stability and on the timely identification of threats to this stability, their sources and interrelationships.

The post-cold war world remains highly complex and contradictory. It has become highly interdependent, and autarky is therefore not a viable option. International relations in the 21st century will be increasingly affected by the emerging influences of globalization. The active participation and integration of the sovereign states of Central Asia in international institutions will be an important factor for the stable development of the entire region.

A 'Great Game' has resumed in Central Asia between the world's great powers. In contrast to the experience here during the 19th and the greater part of the 20th centuries, the major factors influencing this are now geo-economic rather than geopolitical—the struggle is now over energy resources. In this regard, the availability of and existing plans for the exploitation of the large deposits of oil and gas in the Central Asian region create serious preconditions for the region to become one of the most important centres of world politics in the years to come.

It might be expected that in the process of exploring the raw material potential of the region there will be close cooperation between US, European and Japanese corporations. That cooperation already exists and there is consequently increasing coordination of interests and actions between the USA, the European Union (EU) and Japan in the region. If China offers necessary guarantees and opens up its territory for pipelines to be laid and energy to be delivered to Japan, political consolidation in the China–Japan–USA triangle can also be expected.

These two processes are helping to intensify the integration of the Central Asian states into the global economy and therefore into global politics. They will not, however, develop as quickly or as smoothly as many hope they will, and may therefore provoke serious conflicts.

Such conflicts and crises may be serious in the event of the interests of Russian and Western corporations clashing. The USA has already taken action to establish its influence in the Caspian Sea region and is interested in enhancing its role there. The Kazakh political scientist Nikolay Masanov has written:

US and Western trans-national corporations are active in the exploration of Central Asian resources and they are particularly interested in reducing Russia's influence in the region. When new transport routes, such as the trans-Caucasus corridor, become operational, Russia is expected to experience serious negative consequences. The point is that the flow of export goods from Central Asia across Russia unites the Urals, the Volga region, western Siberia and the Far East into a single complex. If this flow takes alternative routes *it is quite possible that the territorial integrity of Russia will be endangered.*[1]

Under these conditions, the Central Asian states should show their consistent interest in strengthening the geo-economic presence of the West in the region while also taking Russia's interests and ambitions into account. The transformation of the region into an integral part of the global economy and politics will not, of course, reduce genuine and objective contradictions, but it will help to promote economic development and transparent government. The emergence of zones of competing economic interests in Central Asia also increases the need for national and regional stability.

Analysis of the main factors influencing Central Asia's strategic development reveals that there are serious problems and contradictions blocking the creation of regional stability and security systems. In spite of efforts by the regional states there continue to be deep disparities in their domestic development which must be overcome in order to consolidate their national sovereignty. The economies of most of the regional countries remain unstable. These countries will also continue to be vulnerable to negative tendencies which are initiated from outside the region and which remain outside their control.

Different countries in the region experience different tensions and challenges. In spite of all they have in common, particularly in culture and history, their geopolitical conditions are quite diverse. Tensions exist between regional countries which will most likely remain in the near future. The potential for conflict in Central Asia is influenced by many different factors, such as ethnicity, territorial disputes, disputes over access to water and natural resources, ideology and religion, as well as by Russia. The security of the new sovereign Caspian states is also highly dependent on external factors, both regional and global.

---

[1] Masanov, N., 'Podbryushye Rossii yzhe ne myagkoye' [Russia's underbelly is no longer soft], *Novaya Gazeta* (Moscow), 6–12 Apr. 1998. Emphasis in original.

II. Threats to security

As a result, the situation in Central Asia is characterized above all by: (a) the creation of democratic institutions in the regional countries at a time of intense domestic political struggle; (b) the existence of inter-ethnic conflicts; (c) the growth of political and religious extremism in different forms against the backdrop of the collapse of former ideological dogmas; (d) poorly developed economies and widespread suffering among the common people in most of these countries; and (e) the growth of economic and social disparities between the regional states and between different social groups within each state.

The Afghan source of instability in the 'Islamic arc' formed during the global confrontation between the superpowers is spreading to the north. It is as if the arc is now extending into the Central Asian states. The escalation of the Afghan conflict is creating the conditions for a progressive escalation of instability in the region. This is the most dangerous threat to national and regional security, as was seen in the Batken region of Kyrgyzstan in the summer and autumn of 1999 and the summer of 2000; in Tashkent in February 1999; in the Tashkent region in the autumn of 1999; and in the Surkandarya region of Uzbekistan in the summer of 2000.

The five Central Asian states—Kazakhstan, Kyrgyzstan, Tajikistan, Turkmenistan and Uzbekistan—occupy 4 million square kilometres (km[2]) of territory, and of their combined population of over 53 million people approximately 75 per cent are Islamic peoples which are culturally close.[2] Naturally, when the communist ideology collapsed the processes of national revivalism began in the regional countries. Equally naturally, a significant proportion of the local populations reverted to Islamic values and stronger religious identities. These were logical processes, influenced by the natural and understandable desire of Islamic nations to re-establish their historical, cultural and political identities: Islam presents a system of values that was formed and existed over several centuries, emphasizing justice, empathy with one's neighbours and the desire to help others (with the expectation of rewards in the afterlife). For many generations, and for Islamic peoples in different countries, the Koran was and will remain the sacred code of the basic laws of life.

At the end of the 1980s and the beginning of the 1990s, the religious revival in the Central Asian republics intensified significantly. It was characterized by: a substantial increase in the number of mosques in all the Central Asian republics (recently the uncontrolled construction of both large and small mosques has been stopped, for instance, in Uzbekistan[3]); zealous observance of ancient traditions and ceremonies, especially of a ritual nature; a many-fold increase in

---

[2] On the populations of the Central Asian states see Khamraev, F. M., 'Tsentral'naya Aziya: problema razdelyonnykh natsii' [Central Asia: problem of divided nations] in *Gosudarstvo i Obshchestvo v Stranakh Postsovetskogo Vostoka: Istoriya, Sovremennost', Perspektivy* [State and society in post-Soviet Oriental countries: history, modern times, prospects], proceedings of a conference (Daik Press: Almaty, 1999), pp. 146–47.

[3] In Kyrgyzstan the government decided that all the country's estimated 1300 mosques must be re-registered with the Ministry of Justice and the qualifications of all imams re-evaluated during 2001. Radio Free Europe/Radio Liberty (RFE/RL), *RFE/RL Newsline*, vol. 4, no. 213, Part 1 (2 Nov. 2000).

the number of students in religious schools and institutions, even in those republics where Islam has never played a significant role in public life, such as Kazakhstan; the opening of institutions of higher learning where the rich historical and cultural heritage of the regional peoples is studied, with priority being given to Islam, and the creation of specialized universities for the study of Islam, such as the Islamic University in Tashkent; the declaration of Islamic holidays as state holidays and the official celebration of important dates connected with outstanding religious leaders; the (now lawful) publication of material and the launching of television and radio programmes propagating Islamic norms and values; the expansion of contacts with other Islamic countries, including membership in different international Islamic organizations; and the development of official and unofficial activities on the part of political movements using Islamic slogans.

Each Central Asian republic has moved along the road of Islamic revival in its own way. This as a necessary and indispensable process, and the peoples of Central Asia cannot and should not disregard their past. They remember and esteem their ancestors and are proud to be the descendants of Imam al-Bukhari, Naqshbandi and Akhmet Yassavi, for example. Without historical memory there can be no future for a civilized people. Islam Karimov, President of Uzbekistan, has pointed out that during its independence his country has succeeded in 'reviving in our life the historical national and spiritual values and traditions and re-establishing our sacred religion in the spiritual development of the society'.[4]

However, to revive classical Islam and establish its proper role and place in the modern world is not a simple matter. The road from accepting the need for it to implementing it is difficult because Islam is not being and should not be forced onto the citizens of these countries. The acceptance of a religion and its basic values is individual. The Central Asian peoples have passed through a period of atheism and the loss of their history—mistakes that must not be repeated. There are destructive forces that interpret the Islamic revival in their own militant way. Although many peoples living in this region follow the same religion, their social perceptions, values, frame of mind and attitudes towards the modern world are far from uniform. Moreover, in accordance with their social and political views, different Islamic groups interpret the sacred religious texts differently. Sometimes these variations in interpretation cause irreparable damage to human relationships and even loss of life.

The Islamization of Central Asia came in two stages, an early and a later one. The early phase, which started in the 7th, 8th and 9th centuries, involved the peoples living settled agricultural lives in what are now Tajikistan and Uzbekistan, and in south-western Kyrgyzstan. The later phase, which covered the period up to the 16th century, affected the nomads on the territory of modern Kazakhstan, Kyrgyzstan and Turkmenistan. This influenced the role Islam plays in the lives of various populations of Central Asia. Generally, the level of

⁴ Karimov, I., *Uzbekistan Ustremlyonny v 21 Vek* [Uzbekistan aspiring for the 21st century] (Tashkent, 1999), p. 8.

sustainability of Islam and its norms in different spheres of life, including the political, cultural and legal, varied throughout the region. In the areas Islam influenced first its norms and laws have become an integral part of the lifestyle of local populations. In the former nomadic regions of Central Asia, however, its role is more superficial and is intertwined with the pre-Islamic traditions of the local populations.[5] However, in spite of these differences all the regional peoples view Islam as one of the basic world religions which has played a significant role in the history of civilization and continues to influence different spheres of public and private life in Central Asia.

Much can be said about the positive role of Islam and about its past and current influence. In August 1996 at a regional conference on security problems participants from both regional and international organizations were united in the opinion that Islamization did not pose a threat to the security of the Central Asian region.[6] However, in only a few years the situation has changed radically. The strengthening of the Islamic opposition in Tajikistan, the advance of the Taliban movement to the north of Afghanistan and the explosions in Tashkent in February 1999 have resulted in Islamic revivalism coming to be seen as a movement that aims to create a new Islamic political regime or regimes. Islamic radicalism has thus become the primary regional security threat, not just in individual countries but for the region as a whole.

In the political sense, this threat is reflected in attempts to undermine the trust of Islamic believers in their governments, which are undertaking reform, by destroying stability and disturbing national, civic and inter-ethnic harmony, all of which are indispensable conditions for the implementation and success of reforms. The activities of radical Islamists are aimed at discrediting democracy, the secular state, and multi-ethnic and multi-confessional societies. Simultaneously, radical Islamists are trying to provoke confrontation between different regions within countries and among different social groups that lead 'true' or 'false' lives from the point of view of radical Islam. They are also trying to create a negative image of the Central Asian republics, Tajikistan and Uzbekistan in particular, in the wider Islamic world.

The strengthening of radical Islam in the region is in most instances connected with a serious deterioration in the socio-economic situation in the different countries. They are still experiencing deep crises which affect the lives of their populations in different ways. The crisis has become so fundamental and has so undermined development that the situation is barely controllable. One of the most complex issues, which requires immediate and constant attention, is the preservation of civil peace and harmony. The populations are becoming increasingly impoverished and the rate of unemployment is rising. Factories, plants and offices are being privatized and transformed into commercial structures, and are often used only as storage facilities. As a rule, the salaries of civil

---

[5] Sultangalieva, A., *Islam v Kazakhstane: Istoriya, Etnichnost', Obshchestvo* [Islam in Kazakhstan: history, ethnicity, society] (Kazakhstan Institute for Strategic Studies: Almaty, 1998), pp. 89–90.

[6] Conference on Democratic Civilian Control of the Military, Defense Planning and Management, and Regional Security in Central Asia, Tashkent, 12–16 Aug. 1996, co-sponsored by the George C. Marshall Center and the Uzbekistan International Institute for Strategic Studies.

servants only marginally exceed subsistence level. People's purchasing power has fallen considerably while consumer prices, especially food prices, have increased substantially. Living conditions have deteriorated, especially in the small towns and rural areas. Systematic or chronic underpayment and late payment of salaries are contributing to a rapid decline in the quality of life and living standards. On the other hand, there is a growing disparity between the rich and poor people of the regional countries, while the middle class remains insignificant in both numbers and influence.[7]

All these factors contribute to the growing dissatisfaction among various sections of the regional populations, and as a consequence opposition is emerging, sometimes functioning officially and sometimes underground, using all the means at its disposal, including religious ones. In the opinion of some experts, an additional cause for the emergence of radical Islam is the rigid and even cruel suppression of opposition elements in the early years of independence (1992–94). The secular opposition, deprived of the right to oppose the government authorities openly, emigrated for the most part and continued its involvement in regional domestic affairs from abroad. Initially this opposition took the form of ideological confrontation, but later opposition forces turned to the use of violence. These observations are relevant above all to the case of Uzbekistan, where the government accused the opposition of maintaining ties with 'Tajik nationalists and Islamic fundamentalists' and mercilessly suppressed it.[8] Regional leaders are also convinced that the lessons of Tajikistan and the events in neighbouring Afghanistan 'legitimize' authoritarian rule, which is allegedly required during the current transitional period in order to avoid bloodshed and to preserve ethnic and civil harmony, peace and stability.

However, the basic causes of the strengthening of radical Islam in Central Asia are external, and they have recently become even more important. Islam is increasingly considered by a number of foreign countries as a force which may help (or prevent) the realization of their own goals in the region. One group of such countries is interested in the total Islamization of the Central Asian states and striving to achieve this goal using every available weapon. There is, however, a second group of countries which share the fears and concerns of the regional states that a further strengthening of Islam in Central Asia may produce unwelcome geopolitical and geo-economic changes.

Iran, Pakistan, Saudi Arabia, Turkey and (obviously) Afghanistan belong to the first group. Although their activities differ they usually take the form of financial assistance and the supply of religious literature to religious and political organizations or the training and upgrading of 'religious' cadres capable of launching a jihad in different forms. The second group of countries includes Russia, the USA, the developed European countries, China and India. Each of

---

[7] These conclusions are based on a survey conducted by the Institute of Kazakhstan's Development in 1996 and published in *Ustoychivo li Razvitiye Kazakhstana? Otsenka Potentsiala Napryazhonnosti v Obshchestve* [Is Kazakhstan's development stable? Evaluation of tension potential in society] (Almaty, 1996), pp. 49–51.

[8] Horsman, S., 'Uzbekistan's involvement in the Tajik civil war 1992–1997: domestic considerations', *Central Asian Survey* (Oxford), vol. 18, no. 1 (1999), p. 43.

these is no doubt pursuing its own political goals, but in general all are interested in a secular development of the Central Asian states, thus creating a counterbalance to the activities of the first group of countries.

Today as never before Central Asian leaders face the problem of maintaining regional stability. They have to avert the threat of fragmentation of the Ferghana Valley, which is shared by Kyrgyzstan and Uzbekistan, in the same way as happened in Afghanistan and Tajikistan. This threat is very real. The Central Asian republics are today making maximum efforts to prevent violence and extremism, using for this purpose all available domestic means. However, the scope of the threat is such that difficult situations are emerging in one part of Central Asia after another. The regional countries are therefore striving to increase their cooperation in order to fight these local conflicts.

Uzbekistan has launched several initiatives in different international forums aimed at strengthening global and especially regional security. These include proposals to create a nuclear-weapon-free zone in Central Asia, to establish an embargo on arms deliveries to zones of local conflict (especially in Afghanistan), to activate the 'Six Plus Two' Group in order to reach a peaceful resolution of the Afghan conflict and to support the activities of the Shanghai Forum,[9] and the latest initiative of President Karimov for the creation of an international anti-terrorist centre.[10]

This last initiative is aimed at fighting transnational terrorism and fostering global and regional security. The basic task of the new anti-terrorist centre, with its headquarters in Vienna, would be to coordinate appropriate measures within the framework of the United Nations, using for these purposes the tried and tested forms of international cooperation. Special importance should be accorded to the implementation of decisions taken by the UN. The proposed centre will not duplicate the activities of the administrations and security agencies of the individual Central Asian states or of the Commonwealth of Independent States (CIS) anti-terrorist centre in Moscow. It may include several groups that would monitor the implementation of existing conventions and other international agreements on the struggle against terrorism, monitor and evaluate national legislation in this area, prepare information and analytical materials, and so on. However, Uzbekistan's proposal encountered serious procedural and financial difficulties in the UN. The support of the major world powers, the USA in particular, who are interested in creating a reliable security system in Central Asia could be critical to the future of the proposed centre. The CIS anti-terrorist centre in Moscow plans to establish a branch office in Central Asia, either in Tashkent or in Almaty. This may become one of the positive factors in the collective effort of regional countries in the fight against radical Islamic organizations.

---

[9] The 'Six Plus Two' Group consists of China, Iran, Pakistan, Russia, the USA, the UN and 2 Central Asian states, Tajikistan and Uzbekistan (signatories of the 1996 Tashkent Declaration on the Fundamental Principles of a Peaceful Settlement of the Conflict in Afghanistan). On the Shanghai Forum (since June 2001 called the Shanghai Cooperation Organization) see chapter 5, section V in this volume.

[10] *Narodnoye Slovo* (Tashkent), 19 Nov. 2000.

Diverse as they are socially, politically, ethnically and culturally, the regional countries may collectively succeed in creating a favourable environment for fighting external threats and for the stable development of the region. It must be admitted, however, that so far there is no regional security system in Central Asia and there are only a few elements of such a system currently in place.

When terrorists invaded southern Kyrgyzstan at the end of July 1999, the regional countries failed to develop a mechanism for coordinating their activities against such incursions. As a result, and because there was a great degree of complacency, the region soon faced tragic consequences. It has become clear that the armed forces of the regional countries are incapable of repulsing such invasions individually. However, it did seem that the proper lessons were drawn from this experience, as over the next six months substantial efforts were made to prepare to fight similar threats. As a result there was a more effective response to the more powerful groups of Islamic militants which penetrated the territory of Kyrgyzstan and Uzbekistan in the summer of 2000.

On 21 April 2000 the presidents of Kazakhstan, Kyrgyzstan, Tajikistan and Uzbekistan, meeting in Tashkent, signed a four-party treaty on the collective struggle against the international terrorism, religious and political extremism and organized crime that are threatening stability in the region.[11] A meeting in Bishkek on 20 August 2000 was a logical continuation of the Tashkent talks and was particularly important, first, because it was held at a time when hostilities against Islamic militants were going on in the south of Kyrgyzstan and Uzbekistan, and, second, because it was attended by Sergey Ivanov, then Secretary of the Russian Security Council. The close relationship between developments in the North Caucasus, Central Asia and Afghanistan was thus underlined. The participants at the Bishkek meeting adopted a declaration which reflected their serious concern over the developments in Central Asia. They confirmed 'their firm resolution to respond adequately to the arrogant activities of bandits'.[12]

III. The future of security relations in Central Asia

This section discusses in greater detail the state of cooperation between the Central Asian countries and Russia. Russia is now the principal guarantor of regional security and only with its help will the Central Asian republics be able to withstand incursions by major Islamic formations crossing over the Afghan border.

Until recently, some regional countries did not consider the possibility of such assistance realistic. However, the ongoing changes in the balance of external forces influencing the internal situation in Central Asia made fundamental changes in regional governments' foreign policy strategies unavoidable. Until recently the regional states based their foreign policies mainly on the principle

---

[11] *Narodnoye Slovo*, 21 Apr. 2000.
[12] *Narodnoye Slovo*, 22 Aug. 2000. See also the text of the Bishkek Declaration in *Diplomaticheskiy Vestnik*, no. 9 (Sep. 2000), p. 23.

of equidistance from the major powers—Russia and the USA—but current realities have forced them to review their policies seriously. To a certain extent the change in their outlook has been also encouraged by the rise to power of a new generation of politicians in Russia.

Given the new geopolitical realities in Central Asia, special significance must be given to reforming the relations of the regional countries, and especially of Uzbekistan, with Russia. Otherwise the region may face irreversibly negative consequences. Russia is currently increasing its political and military presence in the region following the emergence of serious security threats coming from the southern CIS borders. It is also generally redirecting much of its foreign policy efforts in a southerly direction, to countries of the Middle East and North Africa, and to the so-called rogue states—Iran, Iraq and North Korea—which may be interpreted as a thinly disguised warning to the USA not to increase its presence and/or influence in CIS countries. In relations between the Central Asian countries and Russia, the transition is now nearly complete and the participants are actively seeking avenues for cooperation on an equal basis, critically taking their past experiences into account. A new stage in relations between the regional countries and Russia is emerging, which needs to be based on new approaches and initiatives, with the Russian leadership building partnership with all the regional countries on the basis of equality.

These new developments in the Central Asian geopolitical situation mean that a Russian presence in the region is no longer at issue. It is without question in the interest of the regional countries to have a continued Russian presence in Central Asia as one of the principal guarantors of regional security and stability, as one participant in regional economic integration, and as a partner against such global threats as international terrorism, drug trafficking and the illegal arms trade.[13]

---

[13] These changes in geopolitical realities in Central Asia resulted in military and security cooperation between the regional states and Russia being stepped up. In response to the concerns of Kazakhstan, Kyrgyzstan and Tajikistan over the growing threat posed to their security by international terrorism and political and religious extremism, at the summit meeting of the 1992 Treaty on Collective Security (the Tashkent Treaty), held in Bishkek in Oct. 2000, Russia signed an agreement on increasing its military assistance to these countries, including arms sales and the creation of a joint rapid-deployment force that could be sent to any of those states to help them counter a threat of external aggression or terrorism. Also in 2000 Uzbekistan (no longer a party to the Tashkent Treaty) signed a number of bilateral agreements with Russia that included increased procurement of Russian arms and training of Uzbek military personnel in Russia. In June 2000 Uzbekistan also agreed to join Russia in establishing a common anti-aircraft defence in Central Asia. ITAR-TASS, 11 Oct. 2000, in 'CIS leaders sign security agreements', Foreign Broadcast Information Service, *Daily Report–Central Eurasia (FBIS-SOV)*, FBIS-SOV-2000-1012, 11 Oct. 2000; and Interfax, 20 June 2000, in 'Russia, Uzbekistan begin joint anti-aircraft defense service duty', in FBIS-SOV-2000-0620, 20 June 2000.

During Karimov's visit to Russia on 3–5 May 2001 several economic and military issues were discussed. The 2 countries pledged to increase bilateral trade and enhance military–technical cooperation with the creation of working groups within the Russian and Uzbek national security systems to coordinate the military–technical cooperation called for in agreements signed in 1999 and 2000. See also chapter 5 in this volume. According to Karimov, this cooperation is essential as Russia 'is, for us, not only a guarantor of security but also a strategic partner'. Uzbek Television first channel/BBC Monitoring Service, 'Uzbekistan, Russia agree to set up military cooperation groups', 6 May 2001, URL <http://www. eurasianet.org/resource/uzbekistan/hypermail/news/ooo7.html>: and ITAR-TASS (Moscow), 4 May 2001, in 'Uzbekistani President says no disagreements between Russia and Uzbekistan', FBIS-SOV-2001-0504, 7 May 2001.

However, the development of cooperation with Russia on issues of regional security does not necessarily preclude Central Asian states' diversifying their security ties with other countries and international organizations. Uzbekistan therefore intends to develop cooperation with the NATO member states, including the USA, in order to strengthen its national security and enhance its capability to combat terrorism, drug trafficking and organized crime. This was stated by President Karimov during his meeting with the then US Secretary of State, Madeleine Albright, at the UN Millennium Summit in New York in September 2000.[14] Uzbekistan also welcomed an offer of political and military assistance from Turkey made by President Ahmet Sezer during his visit to Tashkent in October 2000[15] and joined the Shanghai Forum in June 2001 as a full member. This regional organization, now renamed the Shanghai Cooperation Organization, is gaining in strength and authority in the security affairs of Central Asia.

Uzbekistan is adapting its policy to the concrete security realities developing in Central Asia. Following the military gains achieved by the Taliban in Afghanistan in late 2000, which turned the course of the civil war there irreversibly in the Taliban's favour, Uzbekistan decided to establish limited contacts with the leaders of the Taliban in order to ensure the security of its southern borders. This decision was partly taken because military assistance from Russia and its allies to the opposition Northern Alliance in Afghanistan was being either discontinued or sharply reduced. There were also reasons to believe that the extremist Islamic Movement of Uzbekistan (IMU) was receiving large-scale assistance not from the Taliban but from the Northern Alliance via the territory of Tajikistan. (This, incidentally, explains the chilling of relations between Tajikistan and Uzbekistan.)

The creation of a new system of international relations in the 21st century, especially on the territory of the former Soviet Union, will depend to a significant extent on how the new sovereign states of Central Asia develop. It is against the interests of the regional countries to create a system of international relations that is of a confrontational nature. Their stability and security must create a basis for the dynamic and sustainable development of the region and for the prevention of conflicts. It may also be one of the preconditions of ensuring global security. In this regard, the interests of the Central Asian countries in international relations can be said to involve: (*a*) the preservation of global stability and avoidance of regional conflicts; (*b*) the resolution of tensions and armed conflicts on regional borders, above all in connection with the threat of radical Islam; (*c*) the development of normal, constructive relations with all countries, giving priority to developing such relations at the regional level; (*d*) the strengthening and development of the peacekeeping activities of the UN, the Organization for Security and Co-operation in Europe (OSCE) and other international organizations in order to achieve early political resolutions of

[14] Interfax, 11 Sep. 2000, in 'Karimov says US ready to help Uzbekistan to fight against Islamic militants', FBIS-SOV-2000-0911, 11 Sep. 2000.
[15] *Narodnoye Slovo*, 18 Oct. 2000.

regional armed conflicts. In this connection, regional countries should strive to preserve their domestic stability and normalize and stabilize the situation on the regional level; (*e*) the end of the civil war and achievement of peace in Afghanistan; (*f*) the stabilization of the national reconciliation process and the establishment of a durable peace in Tajikistan; (*g*) the strengthening and deepening of processes of cooperation and integration in Central Asia; (*h*) the active involvement of the Central Asian states in international security structures and the development of close cooperation with international organizations by all regional countries; (*i*) the development of mutually beneficial and equal relations with Russia and other post-Soviet states; (*j*) the maintenance of constructive and beneficial relations with China; and (*k*) the development of normal pragmatic relations with the Central Asian states' southern neighbours, in particular in connection with ensuring the security of the transport systems of individual regional countries and of the region as a whole.

In the near future the destabilizing role of radical Islam is likely to remain. A serious security threat to all regional countries therefore persists. This being the case, two scenarios of regional cooperation aimed at combating this threat are worth considering.

The first is for the regional states to agree to terminate Russia's role as a guarantor of regional security on the assumption that they are themselves now capable of independently ensuring their own domestic and external security. In the foreseeable future this scenario is highly unlikely. On the contrary, it is only with Russia that a realistic regional security system can now be created.

The second scenario involves the creation of new forms of cooperation and trust among the regional countries in addition to those already established between them on a bilateral basis (including in the sphere of security) with the ultimate goal of creating a new community of nations. Such a supranational community would be able to contribute to the effective resolution of the domestic problems of its members as well as protecting the common interests of the region in international relations. Such a community, in this author's opinion, will eventually be capable of forming the basis for an effective regional security system in Central Asia.

Part IV

Competition and cooperation in the Caspian Sea region

19. The Caspian Sea region: towards an unstable future

Gennady Chufrin

I. Introduction

Analysis of the evolving security environment in the Caspian Sea region clearly demonstrates its multidimensional character. It is profoundly influenced (*a*) by domestic developments in the Caspian states, which are passing through a dramatic process of political, social and economic change, and (*b*) by the different, sometimes sharply competing, national interests of various international actors in the region. The interaction of these factors over the past decade has been mostly destabilizing, and there is little evidence that in the foreseeable future the security situation in the region will improve in any substantial way. On the contrary, the analyses of the prevailing current social, political and economic trends by the authors of this volume lead to the unhappy conclusion that the attainment of political stability and economic progress for most of the regional states remains an elusive goal.

II. The regional states

The new Caspian states

Political stability and economic progress are particularly elusive in the case of former Soviet republics of Central Asia and the South Caucasus, where continuity and changes in their security policies are closely linked to their highly volatile internal situations, which are characterized by lack of political stability and dangerous social and economic strains. The state of their economies worsened considerably during the greater part of the 1990s. According to data released by the Interstate Statistical Committee of the Commonwealth of Independent States (CIS), gross domestic product (GDP) measured in constant US dollars fell over the nine years 1991–99 in Armenia by 27.5 per cent, in Azerbaijan by 46.6 per cent, in Georgia by 53.7 per cent, in Kazakhstan by 29.6 per cent, in Kyrgyzstan by 31.5 per cent, and in Uzbekistan by 4.8 per cent.[1] As a result of this sharp decline living standards in the Caspian states plummeted and over one-third of their populations found themselves living below the poverty line.[2] Even though the first signs of recovery appeared at the

---

[1] *Sodruzhestvo Nezavisimykh Gosudarstv v 1999 Godu: Statisticheskiy Ezhegodnik* [Commonwealth of Independent States 1999: statistical yearbook] (CIS Interstate Statistical Committee: Moscow, 2000), p. 18.

[2] According to the World Bank's report for 1999/2000, by the mid-1990s the percentage of the population living below the poverty line was 34.6% in Kazakhstan and 40% in Kyrgyzstan. World

end of the 1990s, none of the Caspian states has succeeded so far in creating the conditions for sustainable economic growth that would mitigate political and social discontent among the general population.

The unresolved economic and social problems in their turn continue to breed ethno-political conflicts, which are being used by radical religious and nationalist elements to encourage new and strengthen existing secessionist tendencies in the region.

In the South Caucasus the threat of secession continues to be most prominent in Abkhazia, Nagorno-Karabakh and South Ossetia. In spite of repeated efforts undertaken at the national and international levels over the past decade, the political status of all these three territories which aspire to independence remains unresolved. Even though hostilities there are stopped or reduced to occasional incidents, tensions run high along the ceasefire lines, keeping alive the possibility of a resumption of large-scale armed confrontation. In Central Asia the ethno-political situation also remains unstable as religious and nationalist radicals, receiving ideological guidance as well as political and military support from abroad channelled through Afghanistan, intend to form an Islamic state in the Ferghana Valley, which runs through Kyrgyzstan, Tajikistan and Uzbekistan, resorting to violence for that purpose.

As a consequence not only is the process of nation-building in the new sovereign regional states seriously impaired, but even the very existence of some of them, at least within their present borders, remains in serious doubt, which means that most if not all of them are likely to remain in a state of acute political and social instability for many years to come.

In order to overcome their social and political crisis and to stop destructive domestic processes, the new Caspian states desperately need a major break-through in their economic development. For most of them the principal sustainable source of economic prosperity is oil—the exploration and export of their energy resources or revenue from the transport of oil and gas across their territories, or both. As none of these countries can expect any other economic sector to offer real prospects for development in the foreseeable future, it is quite logical for them to orient their domestic economic strategies and foreign policies towards these goals. Since Russia, their main economic partner within the former Soviet Union, has until recently been either unable or unwilling to assist them in the rapid and massive development of their oil and gas resources it has become quite natural for these countries to seek new political and economic partners. However, the new Caspian states' initial expectations of rapid prosperity thanks to the 'oil factor' have been shown to be over-optimistic. Moreover, they find themselves in a new political and security situation in the Caspian region, which is increasingly threatened by deepening conflict over their very interests in the oil and gas reserves there.

In the absence of a new, mutually agreed legal regime of the Caspian Sea, there are mounting disputes between the littoral states over ownership rights to the

Bank, *Entering the 21st Century: World Development Report 1999/2000* (Oxford University Press: Washington, DC, 2000), pp. 236–37.

existing and prospective oil and gas deposits which create a dangerous potential for new and more serious conflicts. A comprehensive agreement on the legal status of the sea that was acceptable to all the littoral states could have been a fundamental condition for preventing the further escalation of these tensions. Even though the differences on the legal status of the sea were narrowed as a result of intensive negotiations between the littoral states in 2000–2001, there has so far not been sufficient progress in this direction.

The choice of oil and gas routes from the Caspian Basin to the world market continues to be another sore point in relations between the littoral states. The nature of the debates on this issue reflects the increasing polarization of the positions taken by the individual Caspian states. On top of this the security of oil and gas transport routes is threatened by a number of local conflicts. Although such conflicts as those in Abkhazia or Nagorno-Karabakh have their own dynamics, they have become increasingly linked to the oil factor, since their settlement is regarded as a necessary condition for ensuring the security of both existing and planned oil and gas routes in the region. Here again there has been no substantial progress.

As a result of continued domestic instability in the regional countries and lack of progress in interstate relations on major issues, a new security agenda has taken shape in the Caspian region over the past decade.

Responding to growing domestic and external security threats, the new Caspian states (with the exception of Georgia) are actively building up their national special security and regular armed forces and continuing to increase their military budgets and arms acquisitions.[3] In their foreign relations, including those with their Caspian neighbours, they have been trying to establish a safe security environment and create effective security mechanisms that would help to de-escalate existing tensions and prevent new conflicts in the region.

Their concrete security strategies have, predictably, been different depending on their individual threat assessments, indigenous defence capabilities, the combat readiness of their national armed forces and so on. Armenia, Kazakhstan, Kyrgyzstan and Tajikistan, although they participate (with the exception of Tajikistan) in the NATO Partnership for Peace (PFP) programme, basically rely on security cooperation within the 1992 Collective Security Treaty (the Tashkent Treaty), led by Russia.[4] Turkmenistan has opted for neutral status as the best response to security threats.[5] Azerbaijan and Uzbekistan are pursuing their security policies by simultaneously building up security relations with NATO countries and maintaining limited military cooperation with Russia on a bilateral basis. A consistently prominent role in regional security affairs is

---

[3] For details see chapter 5 in this volume.

[4] On the membership of the Tashkent Treaty see chapter 5, section V in this volume.

[5] According to President Eduard Shevardnadze, Georgia is also considering adopting neutral status instead of its earlier plans to join NATO. Georgia Radio, Tbilisi, 12 Feb. 2001. See also Broladze, N., 'Sredstvo protsvetaniya—neytralitet' [The means to prosperity is neutrality], *Nezavisimaya Gazeta*, 29 Mar. 2001. This may reflect not only an admission that it cannot meet the economic, political and military standards of NATO but also the impossibility of adopting policies that would further antagonize Russia.

played by multilateral alliances involving the active participation of extra-regional countries. An outstanding example of one already fully formalized alliance is the Shanghai Forum, which includes China as well as Kazakhstan, Kyrgyzstan, Russia and Tajikistan. Meeting for the first time in Shanghai in 1996 to discuss the demilitarization of the CIS–Chinese border, the presidents of these countries gradually shifted the emphasis at subsequent annual meetings to the pressing security threats posed by separatism and Islamic extremism. Uzbekistan joined the forum in June 2001, stating its interest in participation in joint anti-terrorist and anti-separatist activities,[6] and it was later renamed the Shanghai Cooperation Organization.

However, as the existing security arrangements, whether bilateral or multi-lateral, have proved to be partly or even totally ineffective in coping with their domestic and external security concerns,[7] the new Caspian states have continued their search for new security schemes. Some of their initiatives, such as the formation of the Central Asian Battalion (CentrasBat) in May 1996 and its annual exercises since 1997 with the participation of NATO units, have already become part of the new security environment in the Caspian region. Others, given the extent of the differences between the countries covered by such proposals and the lack of mutual trust, will need a great deal of effort before they can be accepted and put into practice.

Thus, in the South Caucasus the presidents of Armenia and Azerbaijan, Robert Kocharian and Heidar Aliyev, respectively, addressing the Summit Meeting of the Organization for Security and Co-operation in Europe (OSCE) in Istanbul in November 1999, proposed the creation of a South Caucasus security system. However, although agreeing on the ultimate goal of strengthening regional security, they had different perceptions of future security arrangements.

According to President Kocharian a future regional security pact should not only address issues of military security and conflict resolution but also provide a basis for regional economic cooperation. As to the membership of the pact, he suggested that it should be based on a 'three plus three plus two' formula, with Armenia, Azerbaijan and Georgia as its core members, Iran, Russia and Turkey as guarantors, and the USA and the European Union (EU) as sponsors.[8] Addressing the Georgian Parliament in March 2000, Kocharian expanded on this proposal, saying that without the involvement of all the powers which have influence in the region any future security pact would fail. In this regard, he

---

[6] 'Shankhayskaya pyatyorka rasshiryayetsya' [The Shanghai Five expand], *Nezavisimaya Gazeta*, 5 July 2000. On the Shanghai Cooperation Organization see also chapter 5, section V in this volume.

[7] Thus, in May 1998 a union of Russia, Tajikistan and Uzbekistan was declared with the aim of preventing the spread of Islamic extremism onto the territory of Central Asia from Afghanistan. In Oct. 1998 the presidents of these states signed a trilateral agreement promising mutual assistance in the event of one of them being seriously threatened by militant Islamic forces. However, the interaction among the parties in combating the threat of Islamic extremism proved very inefficient. This provoked deep dissatisfaction with its partners on the part of Uzbekistan, which in Apr. 1999 withdrew from the Tashkent Treaty.

[8] 'Address by H. E. Robert Kocharyan at the OSCE Summit in Istanbul, 19 November 1999', URL <http://www.armeniaforeignministry.com/htms/speeches/rk_osce1_1999.html>.

stressed that 'stability will not rest on any solid basis if we ignore the need to cooperate with Russia. The region cannot fail to take account of Russia's fundamental interests'. He also stated that the Russian military bases in Armenia and Georgia must be incorporated into any future regional security plan.[9]

In contrast, President Aliyev placed issues of military security at the centre of his proposal.[10] He also insisted that under the terms of the proposed security system in the South Caucasus all foreign troops should be withdrawn from the region. Moreover, according to his proposal the status of Russia, Turkey and the USA as parties to a future security pact should be equal to that of the three South Caucasus states. Clarifying Aliyev's proposal, his Foreign Minister, Vilayet Guliyev, stated in February 2000 that a future regional security system 'should pursue a strengthening and an expansion of international relations, of peaceful conflict resolution, of foreign troop withdrawals from the region, the elimination of regional dividing lines, the prevention of aggression and ethnic cleansing, the combat of terrorism, the abandonment of double-standards and the prevention of ultimatums backed by force'. For Azerbaijan the prerequisites for such a pact being realized included the resolution of regional conflicts, including its conflict with Armenia over Nagorno-Karabakh.[11]

Both proposals appeared to be stillborn because of the serious reservations of and objections from other regional states. While Armenia seemed to prefer the maintenance of the status quo in the region, Azerbaijan and Georgia[12] supported a regional security pact that would focus on restoring the territorial integrity of the regional states. Iran objected to Turkey and the USA being included as fully-fledged members in the proposed security system: 'At the initial stage such a system should include only the countries of the region but that once that system has developed other states could join'.[13] Russia's (and Armenia's) attitudes to Aliyev's proposal for the withdrawal of foreign troops were predictably negative as it was clearly aimed at forcing the Russian military presence out of Armenia.[14] These contradictions became so strong that, in parallel to considering inclusive regional security arrangements, Azerbaijan and Georgia did not exclude the possibility of an exclusive tripartite security pact with Turkey.[15] All this makes agreement on a single plan for the South Caucasus security system unlikely, at least in the near future.

[9] Radio Free Europe/Radio Liberty (RFE/RL), *RFE/RL Newsline*, vol. 4, no. 65, Part I (30 Mar. 2000).

[10] 'Azerbaijani delegation in Istanbul', *Azerbaijan Newsletter* (Embassy of the Republic of Azerbaijan, Washington, DC), 19 Nov. 1999, URL <http://www.azembassy.com/letters/19nov99.html>.

[11] Interfax, 'Azerbaijan advocates wide participation in South Caucasus pact', 22 Feb. 2000.

[12] Interfax, 'President Shevardnadze calls for signing pact on peace and stability in the Caucasus', 17 July 2000.

[13] *RFE/RL Newsline*, vol. 4, no. 99, Part 1 (23 May 2000).

[14] Indeed, in the opinion of President Aliyev it was the continuing Russian military presence in Armenia that could lead 'to the militarization of the South Caucasus'. ITAR-TASS, 15 Feb. 2000, in Foreign Broadcast Information Service, *Daily Report–Central Eurasia (FBIS-SOV)*, FBIS-SOV-2000-0215, 15 Feb. 2000.

[15] *Istanbul Milliyet*, 12 Feb. 2000, in 'Turkey: Azerbaijan, Georgia, Armenia view Caucasus pact', FBIS-SOV-2000-0216, 18 Feb. 2000.

Iran

In the case of Iran, another regional state with good human and abundant natural resources strategically located on the southern trade and transport routes from the Caspian region to the outside world, there is also a strong relationship between domestic developments and Caspian security policy. The strengthening of the reform processes which are under way in Iran is having a profound impact not only on its domestic affairs but also on its foreign and security policy. The liberalization of Iranian political life may speed up the normalization of relations with the USA. The lifting of US political and economic sanctions as a result of this rapprochement will undoubtedly improve Iran's international standing and strengthen its role in Caspian regional affairs.

While continuing to resolutely oppose the trans-Caspian pipeline project—which it believes is politically, not economically, motivated—Iran displays a distinct interest in establishing direct oil and gas transport links with the land-locked Caspian states and in becoming a bridge between them and the outside world. Other littoral states, Kazakhstan and Turkmenistan in particular, also regard the Iranian route as very attractive both logistically and commercially. Iran's proximity to major oil and gas deposits in the new Caspian states combined with access to the pipeline network on Iranian territory and Iranian oil terminals in the Persian Gulf certainly makes the costs of transporting their oil and gas via Iran comparatively low. If, following rapprochement between Iran and the USA, US financial resources and technical expertise begin to be invested in the development of this transport network this will further enhance its commercial competitiveness, which is already high compared both with the planned Baku–Ceyhan pipeline and with the Russia-bound northern oil and gas routes. This may result not only in economic but also in larger strategic consequences for Iran, its Caspian neighbours, Turkey and the West. Rapprochement with Iran may be in the USA's interests as well as it will help it to re-establish the political influence in Iran which it once enjoyed but lost after the revolution of 1979 and to gain access to rich Iranian (or expand to Central Asian) energy resources.

However, in spite of the seemingly obvious mutual economic and strategic advantages, this rapprochement will be rather difficult to achieve, at least in the near future, mainly because of strong domestic opposition among the radical sections of both the Iranian and the US political elites. A more likely scenario in Iranian–US relations will be a cautious probing amid continuing strains and mutual mistrust. In this situation Russia's readiness to actively assist Iran in its long-term economic development programme—and, what may be especially important, in the construction of nuclear power plants, as reflected in the first broad Iranian–Russian treaty since the Iranian Revolution, signed when President Mohammad Khatami visited Moscow in March 2001[16]—makes Russia a priority partner for Iran. Another important factor which further boosted

[16] ITAR-TASS, 12 Mar. 2001, in 'Russia, Iran sign treaty on relations, cooperation', FBIS-SOV-2001-0312, 12 Mar. 2001.

Iranian–Russian relations was Russia's positive response to Iran's requests that sales of conventional arms, suspended in 1995 following an agreement between Russian Prime Minister Viktor Chernomyrdin and US Vice-President Al Gore, be resumed.[17]

This notable progress cannot, however, overshadow the differences between Russia and Iran over the future of the legal status of the Caspian Sea. The best they were able to achieve during Khatami's visit was a declaration in their joint statement on the Caspian Sea that 'until the perfection of the legal regime for the Caspian Sea they do not officially recognise any borders in that Sea'. However, on other important issues related to the sea their positions were more convergent. They declared their opposition 'to the laying of any ecologically unsound trans-Caspian oil or gas pipelines' and affirmed that it was inadmissible for non-Caspian states to have a military presence on the Caspian.[18]

Iran's strategic role in Caspian affairs may be further enhanced when it completes the construction of a gas pipeline to Armenia. With the commissioning of this pipeline Armenia is expected to reduce its dependence on gas imports from Russia and to meet most of its requirements with supplies from Iran. Armenia and Iran also plan other joint projects, including an oil refinery in Meghru and a tunnel under the Kajaran mountain pass along the main highway from Armenia to Iran. By helping Armenia to resolve its acute energy problems Iran is paving the way for closer political and strategic cooperation with this country.

Although the oil factor is now and will certainly continue to be extremely important in Iran's regional politics, it is far from being the only one that helps Iran exercise a profound influence on Caspian affairs. Its geographical proximity to the South Caucasus and Central Asia and its diverse and deep historic, religious, cultural and ethnic ties with the new sovereign states there make Iran a natural and very important participant in building any regional security schemes.

III. Non-regional actors

Conflictual internal processes in the Caspian region and the many economic, social, ethnic and religious problems and conflicts will without doubt continue to have a profound influence on its security. However, this is not to say that the role of external factors in its security is of no or of minor importance. On the contrary, analysis of regional politics testifies to the obvious and even growing involvement of extra-regional countries in regional affairs. Their interests in Caspian regional security are motivated by a wide range of factors, from mainly economic to political, military or ideological ones. The questions remain, however, exactly what those interests are, whether and how far they are sustainable

[17] Chudodeyev, A., 'Nesmotrya na protesty SSHA Rossiya gotova postavlyat' oruzhiye Iranu' [In spite of US protests Russia is ready to supply arms to Iran], *Segodnya*, 13 Mar. 2001.

[18] Interfax, 12 Mar. 2001, in 'Russia and Iran sign a joint statement on the Caspian Sea', FBIS-SOV-2001-0312, 12 Mar. 2001; and Reutov, A., 'Rossiya i Iran ne stali ssorit'sya: Vopros o razdele Kaspiyskogo morya otlozhen' [Russia and Iran decide not to quarrel: division of the Caspian Sea is postponed], *Kommersant*, 13 Mar. 2001.

in the long run, and how these extra-regional countries are prepared to respond to the host of political, economic and military challenges to these interests.

Turkey

The first among these international actors is Turkey, which enjoys long-standing historical, cultural and ethnic links with a number of regional countries and at one time (at the beginning of the 1990s) even considered using these links and affinities to establish a dominant political and ideological position in the region. Although this euphoria ended quite quickly, if only because Turkey was economically unable to sustain such an ambitious regional policy, Turkey's goals in the region clearly go beyond promoting its economic interests and include enhancing its political and security role there. For these purposes Turkey proposed a Stability Pact for the South Caucasus states[19] or the creation of a Caspian political group aligned on ethnic grounds and consisting of Azerbaijan, Turkey and the four Turkic-speaking states of Central Asia (Kazakhstan, Kyrgyzstan, Turkmenistan and Uzbekistan).[20]

Neither of these initiatives has much chance of being implemented, at least in its original form, as both met serious doubts and objections from such major players in the Caspian Sea basin as Armenia, Iran and Russia. Indeed, both initiatives excluded Iran from any active participation in regional security arrangements,[21] while Russia formally rejected as completely unacceptable Turkey's proposal that security in the region should be built on ethnic grounds.[22] Russia also saw Turkey's proposal that not only regional states but also the major world powers should sign the Caucasus Peace and Stability Pact[23] as a challenge to its own position in the region and an intention to increase Western, and particularly US, influence there.

Part of the Turkish political elite sees Turkey's role in the Caspian Basin as that of a guarantor of the independence of the new sovereign states there.[24] It is not clear how Turkey intends realistically to pursue this role or whether among different options it will consider establishing a military presence of its own in the region, possibly in Azerbaijan. Should that happen it would certainly escalate tensions in the region as it would be regarded as an unfriendly act both in Russia and in Armenia and would impel them to step up their military cooperation. Also, as some Western security analysts suggest, any deployment of Turkish troops in Azerbaijan would threaten to draw NATO into regional conflicts and confrontation with 'the interests of Russia, Iran and China either in

---

[19] *RFE/RL Newsline*, vol. 4, no. 11, Part 1 (17 Jan. 2000).

[20] *RFE/RL Newsline*, vol. 4, no. 21, Part 1 (31 Jan. 2000).

[21] Tamrazian, H., 'Which formula can guarantee security for the South Caucasus?', *RFE/RL Newsline*, vol. 4, no. 112, Part 1 (9 June 2000).

[22] *Diplomaticheskiy Vestnik*, no. 2 (2000), p. 43; and Snark (Yerevan), 22 Apr. 2000, in 'Armenian, Russian foreign ministers discuss issues', FBIS-SOV-2000-0422, 2 Apr. 2000.

[23] *RFE/RL Newsline*, vol. 4, no. 11, Part 1 (17 Jan. 2000) (note 19).

[24] See, e.g., the statement of Turkey's Foreign Minister Ismail Cem issued by Anatolia (Ankara), 28 May 2000, in 'Cem comments on relations with Caucasus, Central Asia, EU', Foreign Broadcast Information Service, *Daily Report–West Europe (FBIS-WEU)*, FBIS-WEU-2000-0528, 28 May 2000.

the Caucasus–Caspian region or further east in Central Asia'.[25] However, this scenario of confrontation seems unlikely. Turkey seems more likely to assess its current political, economic and military potential realistically and turn for the foreseeable future to low-key activities mostly confined to the development of economic and cultural relations with the new sovereign states in the region, hoping that in time this will create a beneficial environment in which it can reassert itself as a key power in the Caspian Basin.[26]

Nevertheless, Turkey continues actively to develop military cooperation with the new Caspian states. In March 1999 it signed a five-year military coopera-tion agreement with Georgia providing for financial assistance in the moderniza-tion of the Georgian armed forces, and in January 2001 it concluded two more agreements with Georgia on defence industry cooperation and training of military personnel.[27] In October 2000 Turkey signed a military cooperation agreement with Uzbekistan giving it support in combating terrorism and extrem-ism and providing with military technology.[28] At the end of 2000 Turkey also began an extensive training programme of officers for the Kyrgyz Army and its National Guard[29] and in February 2001 it concluded two agreements with Azerbaijan on financial assistance to the Azerbaijani Armed Forces.[30]

A pragmatic and constructive approach by Turkey to Caspian regional affairs may be facilitated by the realization of the Blue Stream project, which envisages the delivery of 365 billion cubic metres (bcm) of natural gas by an underwater pipeline across the Black Sea from Russia over the next 25 years. Deliveries are expected to begin by the first quarter of 2002.[31] The economic advantages of the project for both Russia and Turkey may be substantial: Turkey will be able to balance a large part of its energy deficit with Russian gas, while Russia expects to earn up to $7 billion annually in gas sales.[32] The political merits of Blue Stream—which is vital for both Russia's and Turkey's national interests—may be even greater because its implementation may prelude a better understanding between the two countries on other issues. However, the project remains under heavy criticism from an influential lobby in Turkey among the military and from part of the political elite. They maintain a deep-rooted suspicion of Russia and

[25] Blandy, C., *The Caucasus–Caspian Region: Cardinal Changes to the Military Balance*, Conflict Studies Research Centre, S64 (Royal Military Academy: Sandhurst, Mar. 1999), pp. 3, 4.

[26] Cornell, S., *The Nagorno-Karabakh Conflict*, Arbetsrapporter 46 (Uppsala University: Uppsala, Apr. 1999), pp. 78–79 (in English).

[27] *Jane's Defence Weekly*, 17 Mar. 1999, p. 13; and ITAR-TASS, 29 Jan. 2001, in 'Turkey, Georgia sign declaration on cooperation', FBIS-SOV-2001-0129, 29 Jan. 2001.

[28] 'Uzbekistan, Turkey to join forces against terrorism, crime', URL <http:www.eurasianet. org/resource/uzbekistan/hypermail/200010/0026.html>.

[29] Kyrgyz Press International News Agency (Bishkek), 'Turkish military specialists help Kyrgyzstan train officers', BBC Monitoring Service, 4 Feb. 2001.

[30] Turan (Baku), 28 Feb. 2001, in 'Azeri defence minister, Turkish military delegation discuss cooperation', FBIS-SOV-2001-0301, 28 Feb. 2001.

[31] Interfax, 25 June 2000, in 'Russian Gazprom official cited on date for joining Turkish pipeline segments', FBIS-SOV-2001-0629, 29 June 2001. On the Blue Stream project see also chapter 3 in this volume.

[32] Novopashin, A., 'Gas—toplivo rossiyskikh reform' [Gas is the fuel of Russian reforms], *Neza-visimaya Gazeta*, 26 Oct. 2000.

are strongly opposed for strategic reasons to Turkey depending on Russian energy supplies.[33]

Taking into account Turkey's rapidly growing dependence on energy imports and the role accorded to the Caspian region's hydrocarbon resources in its energy supply strategies,[34] it seems that the controversies between Russia and Turkey over the oil and gas routes from the Caspian region—the future of the Baku–Ceyhan pipeline and the mounting problem of oil tankers passing through the Bosporus and Dardanelles—will loom large in their relations in the years to come. They may even overshadow other political and economic bilateral issues.

China

Another important international actor whose presence in the Caspian region has grown constantly over the past decade is China. There is little doubt that its interests in the Caspian Basin, in particular in its eastern part, where the five former Soviet Central Asian states are situated, are both diverse and strong. They include the need to ensure strategic stability along its long borders with Kazakhstan, Kyrgyzstan and Tajikistan, and the need to maintain active cooperation with these countries in fighting common threats to their national security. They are also related to China's economic requirements, in particular its growing need for energy: China has been a net energy importer since 1993.

It is important to stress that so far China has been pursuing these interests in a non-confrontational and cooperative manner, avoiding conflicts with the Central Asian states or rivalry with Russia as their long-standing patron and ally, and has been working to establish mutually beneficial relationships with the regional states. To ensure its political and security interests in the Caspian Basin, China conducted intensive negotiations with the eastern Caspian Central Asian states during the 1990s and concluded with them a number of important bilateral and multilateral agreements on confidence-building measures, thus creating a favourable climate for a broader security relationship. Among those agreements the most important were those on arms control in the region, on the settlement of some border issues, and on the joint fight against international terrorism and ethnic separatism, religious extremism, large-scale drug trafficking, arms smuggling, illegal immigration and other forms of cross-border criminal activities.

These issues form the agenda of the Shanghai Forum (now the Shanghai Cooperation Organization), which was founded on China's initiative in 1996. Participation in the forum enhanced China's role in regional security affairs considerably, paving the way for a strengthening of its military and security cooperation with the regional states on a multilateral and also a bilateral basis. It

[33] Winrow, G., *Turkey and Caspian Energy* (Emirates Center for Strategic Studies and Research: Abu Dhabi, 1999), p. 15; Pamir, N., 'Is there a future for the Eurasian corridor?', *Insight Turkey*, vol. 2, no. 3 (July/Sep. 2000), pp. 37–38; and Djilavyan, A., '"Goluboy potok" pod ugrozoy sryva' [Blue Stream threatened with collapse], *Nezavisimaya Gazeta*, 2 June 2000.

[34] Pamir (note 33), pp. 32, 33, 35, 36.

also helped China among other things to create a political environment conducive to promoting economic cooperation with the Central Asian states. In the 1990s China concluded a number of agreements with them that were intended to help it establish a solid economic presence in the region favourable to its long-term interests. Those agreements envisaged the promotion of bilateral and multilateral cooperation between China and the five Central Asian states in commerce, finance, and science and technology, as well as in developing such crucial areas of the Central Asian economy as agriculture, animal husbandry, and energy and mineral resources.[35] A strategically important agreement was signed with Tajikistan on the construction of a road that would link China with this landlocked country and help to divert part of the latter's trade in a southerly direction.[36] A railway line between the Xinjiang Uighur Autonomous Region of China and Kazakhstan was also completed in 2000 as part of the international Transport Corridor Europe Caucasus Asia (TRACECA) project.[37]

These agreements cover broad areas but they have not so far brought about a significant breakthrough in the scope of economic and trade relations between China and Central Asia. Since 1991 China has become the Central Asian states' second-largest trading partner after Russia, but the value of its trade with them never exceeded $1 billion per year during the whole of the 1990s.[38]

However, the situation may change substantially if and when China builds a 2800-km oil pipeline with an annual capacity of 20 million tonnes connecting it with oilfields in western Kazakhstan. The contract for this was signed with Kazakhstan as early as in September 1997. The construction of the pipeline faces serious difficulties because of major technical problems involved in laying it over a long distance in sparsely populated areas and because of the cost, which may run into several billion dollars. The security of the pipeline may also be threatened by Uighur separatists and extremists where it crosses Xinjiang. Whether China is prepared to take all these risks and challenges remains to be seen and will depend on whether Chinese strategic planners consider the Caspian oil- and gas-producing countries as a potential important alternative source of energy supply for the Chinese economy. If China finally decides in

---

[35] *Xingang Ribao* (Urumqi), 28 Sep. 1998, in 'China: Agreement signed with five former USSR nations', Foreign Broadcast Information Service, *Daily Report–China (FBIS-CHI)*, FBIS-CHI-98-287, 14 Oct. 1998. For more information on China's economic cooperation with Central Asia see also Khamraev, F., 'Politika Kitaya v Tsentral'noy Azii' [China's policy in Central Asia] in *Kitay na Puti Modernizatsii i Reform* [China on the road to modernization and reform], Proceedings of a conference organized by the Institute of the Far East, Moscow, 22–24 Sep. 1999 (Institute of the Far East: Moscow, 1999); and Yang Shu, 'Neft' Kaspiyskogo morya i KNR' [Caspian Sea oil and the PRC] in *Natsional'naya i Regional'naya Bezopasnost' Tsentral'noaziatsikh Stran v Basseyne Kaspiyskogo Regiona* [National and regional security of the Central Asian states in the Caspian Basin region], Proceedings of a conference organized by SIPRI and the Kazakhstan Institute for Strategic Studies, Almaty, 22–23 Sep. 2000 (Kazakhstan Institute for Strategic Studies: Almaty, 2000).

[36] *RFE/RL Newsline*, vol. 3, no. 111, Part I (8 June 1999).

[37] Zhongguo Xinwen She (Beijing), 22 June 2000, in 'Li Peng discusses "New Silk Road", other business projects with Azerbaijan PM', FBIS-SOV-2000-0622, 22 June 2000. On the TRACECA project see, e.g., the TRACECA Internet site, URL <http://www.traceca.org>.

[38] Burles, M., *Chinese Policy toward Russia and the Central Asian Republics* (RAND: Santa Monica, Calif., 1999), pp. 20–21.

favour of constructing the pipeline it will be because it believes that its long-term interests will be best served by reducing its dependence on energy imports via sea routes from the Middle East, which can easily be disrupted in the event of a conflict in the Persian Gulf, in the South China Sea or in the Taiwan Straits.

In geopolitical terms the construction of the Kazakhstan–China oil pipeline will support the Central Asian states' multi-route energy transport policies and may become an important factor in regional political security as it will increase China's interest in cooperation with local countries in safeguarding peace and stability in the eastern Caspian region.

IV. Global powers

The USA

Over the past decade the USA has become one of the principal actors in the Caspian region and its policies are without any doubt crucial to the future of Caspian regional affairs. By declaring this region strategically important for its national interests,[39] the USA clearly stated its intention to pursue an activist policy there that would enhance its engagement with the Caspian Basin countries. From the very start the USA's objectives in the region were above all political and were aimed at safeguarding the new geopolitical realities in the region that had developed after the breakup of the Soviet Union and the emergence of a group of new sovereign states in Central Asia and the South Caucasus. Some of these states, Azerbaijan and Georgia in particular, started to distance themselves politically from Russia and orient themselves towards the West almost immediately after gaining independence. Others—all the Central Asian states except Tajikistan—did so after a short initial period of hesitation and uncertainty. As a result a 'window of opportunity' was created for the USA to establish its influence in this vast region that had been closed to the West for the greater part of the 20th century.

Responding to this historic opportunity, the USA started from the mid-1990s to become actively involved in regional affairs. Apart from pursuing political goals, the US involvement at the time was also increasingly influenced by expectations of rich energy reserves in the Caspian Basin. Consequently, a second set of US policy objectives in the region was formulated in terms of national energy security, which reflected the need for the USA to diversify its sources of energy supply and to reduce its dependence on Persian Gulf oil.

More recent and more modest estimates of recoverable oil reserves in the Caspian Basin have considerably reduced the interest of US businesses in the

[39] See, e.g., the statement of Under Secretary of State Stuart Eizenstat before the US Senate Committee on Foreign Relations on 23 Oct. 1997, 'US economic and strategic interests in the Caspian Sea region: policies and implications', Washington, DC, 1998; and the statement of Special Adviser to the Secretary of State, Ambassador Stephen Sestanovich, made in the US Congress International Relations Committee on 30 Apr. 1998, 'US policy toward the Caucasus and Central Asia', US Department of State International Information Programs, Washington, DC, 1998, URL <http://www.state.gov/www/policy-remarks/1998/980430-sestan-hirc.html>.

region and raised the need to reappraise US policy priorities there as well. Arguments against any excessive US engagement in Caspian energy affairs included uncertainties about regional stability, the Caspian Sea legal regime, world oil and gas prices, and the size of regional energy reserves. Questions were raised as to whether the Caspian reserves were in fact vital to US energy security, since for the most part they would not be available on the world market for many years. It was also claimed that by opposing oil routes through Iran the USA was pushing regional states into closer cooperation with Russia. Consequently, after George W. Bush was elected US President, even though the US Government continued to support the Baku–Ceyhan and trans-Caspian pipeline projects, it did so largely as a political commitment to the principles of a multi-route energy transport strategy rather than as part of its national economic policy. In the opinion of some US experts, however, the USA should continue to pursue direct access to Caspian energy resources, which, although only a small percentage of total world production, may nevertheless erode some of the market power of the Organization of the Petroleum Exporting Countries (OPEC) states and at least modestly reduce world oil prices.[40]

In practical terms, after the change of administration in Washington US policy in the Caspian region continued to focus largely on political rather than economic goals and concentrated on promoting political and security relations with the 'key' regional players, such as Azerbaijan, Georgia and Uzbekistan.[41] Relations with regional countries in the field of security continued to focus on the development of their national armed forces through the PFP and International Military Education and Training (IMET) programmes. Priority was given to establishing the capacity of the national armed forces to respond effectively to regional security threats such as international terrorism and extremism. To support its policy in the region the USA provided security assistance to national armed forces, border forces and anti-narcotics forces.

Preventing the illicit transfer from the Caspian countries of strategic missiles, and nuclear, biological and chemical weapons, technologies, materials and expertise to the 'rogue' states also remained high on the list of US policy objectives in the region. Although nuclear weapons had been withdrawn from the region, proponents of a prominent US role in the Caspian region pointed out that nuclear weapon-related materials and facilities were still there and could fall into the hands of actors unfriendly to the USA.

---

[40] See, e.g., Pugliaresi, L., *Energy Security: How Valuable is Caspian Oil?*, Caspian Studies Program Policy Brief no. 3 (Harvard University: Cambridge, Mass., Jan. 2001). Pugliaresi writes: 'Even a modest reduction in world oil prices offers large-scale benefits to a major oil-importing country like the United States, which is likely to be importing 15 million barrels per day in 2020'.

[41] This approach was manifested when Georgian Defence Minister Lt-Gen. David Tevzadze visited the USA in Mar. 2001 with promises of intensified US assistance in organizing the Georgian armed forces. Also in Mar. 2001 Gen. Carlton W. Fulford, Deputy Commander-in-Chief, US European Command, while on a visit to Azerbaijan, welcomed the idea of NATO bases being deployed in the South Caucasus. ITAR-TASS, 7 Apr. 2001, in 'Georgian Defense Minister satisfied with US talks', FBIS-SOV-2001-0407, 7 Apr. 2001; and ITAR-TASS, 24 Mar. 2001, in 'Azerbaijan: officials welcome foreign military presence', FBIS-SOV-2001-0324, 24 Mar. 2001.

Another important aspect of the US Caspian policy continued to be support for the efforts of Turkey, a NATO ally, to enhance its role in the Caspian Basin.

This multi-directional policy undoubtedly helped the USA to secure a strong foothold in the region in spite of the relative decline of its interest in Caspian energy affairs. Yet it is and will most likely continue to be insufficient to establish unassailable political and security leadership in the Caspian region.

Russia

Russia remains another contender for a leadership role in the Caspian region. It maintains major political, economic and security interests in a part of the world which it dominated for several centuries and which was until recently an integral part of the Soviet Union. However, the dismal record of the 1990s, when Russia was in continuous strategic retreat from the Caspian region, put in serious doubt its ability to reverse this trend and to pursue a sustainable strategy there. In order to change this Russia needed both to formulate its short- and long-term goals and priorities in the region clearly and realistically and to demonstrate the will and capacity to implement them.

The new administration of President Vladimir Putin, which came to power in March 2000, appeared to have risen to these challenges when it came forward with what may be termed a Caspian strategic initiative. It included a package of administrative, political, security and economic measures aimed at reasserting Russia's influence in the strategically important and resource-rich Caspian region. While this initiative was being conceptualized it was realized in Moscow that Russia's policy in the Caspian region was unlikely to be effective, especially in the long run, if Russia continued to limit it to cooperation with regional states solely or primarily in military security matters. Unless Russia increased its economic engagement in the region and reversed the negative trends that had dominated its trade with the Caspian states in the 1990s,[42] it was bound to continue to lose ground there not only in economic terms but also politically. It would have little chance to withstand growing pro-Western and pro-NATO tendencies in the region unless it used the whole range of both political and economic methods to support its policy goals. Besides, in order to re-establish its substantially diminished influence in the region, Russia had to shift the emphasis from its 'policy of denial' in regional economic affairs to a more constructive 'policy of engagement'. Indeed, merely opposing the implementation of the trans-Caspian transport project or demanding high transit fees for the transport of Caspian oil and gas across its territory had in the past and may have in the future only a temporary positive effect, if it has any effect at all. It

---

[42] Over the 6 years 1994–99 the value of Russia's trade with the new Caspian states (in current prices and US dollars) fell by 51.7%. *Rossiyskiy Statististichesky Ezhegodnik, 1999* [Russian statistical yearbook, 1999] (Goskomstat Rossii: Moscow, 1999), p. 567; and *Vneshnyaya Torgovlya*, no. 3 (2000), p. 51.

is more likely that such policies will only alienate local actors and encourage them to search for alternative solutions.

Building on these assumptions, the new Russian initiative included among its main directions, first, the need to strengthen coordination between the different government agencies involved in Caspian affairs and to enhance coordination between Russian commercial organizations operating in the Caspian region. Second, it was decided to step up economic cooperation with the energy-rich CIS Caspian states by offering to buy from them or transport across Russia's own territory vast volumes of oil and gas, using for this purpose existing pipelines, upgrading them if necessary, or building new ones. Third, in order to engage the CIS Caspian states more actively in joint security and defence programmes it was necessary to undertake a fundamental reassessment of the security situation in the Caspian region, to identify common security threats with the Caspian states and to adjust the Tashkent Treaty to the new geopolitical realities there.

The success of this complex, multidimensional strategic initiative is by no means certain and will depend on many internal as well as external factors. Most important among them will be Russia's ability to mobilize sufficient financial and economic resources to support its policy goals. Concrete steps undertaken so far and described in previous chapters of this volume include: (a) the construction of a 1500-km pipeline with an annual capacity of up to 28 million tonnes of oil linking the Tengiz oil deposit in Kazakhstan with the sea terminal in Novorossiysk; (b) the construction of a 315-km section of the Baku–Tikhoretsk–Novorossiysk oil pipeline bypassing Chechnya; (c) an agreement with Kazakhstan to step up transit of its oil across Russian territory from 9.5 up to 15 million tonnes per year through the pipeline linking Atyrau and Samara; and (d) an agreement with Turkmenistan to radically increase gas exports to Russia over the next 30 years.

If and when these plans and agreements are put into practice Russia will be able to significantly boost its influence in Caspian energy affairs and by implication in Caspian economic and political security, and the future of the US- and Turkish-supported trans-Caspian transport project will then be highly problematic, not only because of Russia's political opposition to it but also because, at least for the next several years, the Central Asian states will probably not be able to produce enough oil and natural gas—in addition to what they will transport to Russia—to make the trans-Caspian pipelines economic.

Also, in order to counterbalance the Western-promoted transport projects from the Caspian Sea basin, such as TRACECA, which was regarded as undermining the role of the Russian Trans-Siberian and Baikal–Amur railways, Russia came forward with several projects of its own. One was for the construction of a road and railway network that would link China, Japan and the Russian far east with the Middle East via the South Caucasus states and the Russian North Caucasus.[43] Another, equally ambitious, project, on which Russian Prime

---

[43] Khabitsov, B., '"Transkam"—otechestvennaya versiya Shelkopvogo puti' [Transcam is a national version of the Great Silk Road], *Nezavisimaya Gazeta*, 6 Mar. 2000.

Minister Mikhail Kasyanov announced agreement between Russia, Iran and India in September 2000, was to build a north–south international transport corridor via the Caspian region that would connect Central and Northern Europe across the territory of Russia and Iran with India and the Gulf states and radically speed cargo traffic between Asia and Europe.[44]

Building on growing tensions in Central Asia in connection with the activities of the extremist Islamic Movement of Uzbekistan (IMU) in southern Kyrgyzstan and Uzbekistan, and of the Khizbi al Takhri (Party of Correction) in Kyrgyzstan and Tajikistan, and following the military successes of the Taliban in neighbouring Afghanistan, Russia stepped up its cooperation with the Caspian states which are signatories of the Tashkent Treaty. Registering their concern at the increased threat posed to Central Asia by international terrorism and religious extremism, signatories of the treaty concluded an agreement at their summit meeting in Bishkek in October 2000 on the creation of a joint rapid-deployment force as well as on increased Russian arms sales to upgrade the combat-readiness of their armed forces.[45] The renewed threats to stability and security in Central Asia also helped Russia to revitalize its military cooperation with Uzbekistan, which had been significantly undermined by the latter's withdrawal from the Tashkent Treaty in April 1999. Even though Uzbekistan refused to rejoin the treaty, it decided to step up its military and security ties with Russia by concluding with it a number of bilateral agreements that provided for the delivery of advanced Russian weapons, matériel and accessories to enhance the combat-readiness of the Uzbek national armed forces, and for training of Uzbek military personnel and repair of all Uzbek military equipment in Russia.[46] A new impulse was given to bilateral relations when Uzbek President Islam Karimov paid a state visit to Moscow in May 2001. Both sides stressed the importance of implementing military and military–technical agreements, and statements by Karimov show that Russia has succeeded in convincing Uzbekistan that security cooperation with Russia is essential for regional stability.[47]

In an effort to build up its influence in the South Caucasus, Russia, while continuing to maintain a high level of political and military cooperation with Armenia, sought to improve its relations with Azerbaijan as well. Trying to stop or at least to slow down Azerbaijan's drift towards the West and to bridge differences with it on the legal status of the Caspian Sea, President Putin paid a visit to Baku in January 2001, signing there with President Aliyev a number of documents including a joint statement on principles of cooperation in the Caspian Sea zone and the Baku Declaration, which outlined the foundations for

---

[44] *RFE/RL Newsline*, vol. 4, no. 170, Part 1 (13 Sep. 2000).

[45] Romanova, L., 'Sozdayutsya sily bystrogo reagirovaniya' [Rapid-reaction force created], *Nezavisimaya Gazeta*, 12 Oct. 2000.

[46] *Diplomaticheskiy Vestnik*, no. 6 (2000), p. 29; Interfax, 18 May 2000, in 'Putin informs Duma of Uzbek military agreement', FBIS-SOV-2000-0518, 18 May 2000; and *RFE/RL Newsline*, vol. 4, no. 124, Part 1 (27 June 2000).

[47] Interfax (Moscow), 4 May 2001, in 'Uzbekistan President hails Russia's contribution to Central Asian security', FBIS-SOV-2001-0504, 7 May 2001. See also chapter 5 in this volume for detail on Russian–Uzbek bilateral military and military–technical cooperation.

expanding bilateral political and economic relations and stressed the readiness of both states to develop long-term military cooperation.[48] However, the strategic achievements of Putin's visit to Azerbaijan were put in doubt as early as March 2001 when Azerbaijani Defence Minister Safar Abiyev and Foreign Minister Guliyev reiterated that Azerbaijan should host either a NATO or a Turkish military base on its soil in order to balance the Russian military presence in Armenia and strengthen its security.[49]

In promoting relations with Iran, another Caspian state, Russia seemed to be more successful, entering large-scale political and economic cooperation with Iran (discussed above) and deciding, even at the risk of straining relations with the USA, to sell nuclear technologies to and step up military cooperation with Iran.

These initiatives in economic and military cooperation with regional states notwithstanding, if it is to succeed in Caspian affairs Russia will also have to demonstrate its ability to effectively stabilize the security situation in its own regions of the North Caucasus, which are suffering the most profound economic and social crisis in their modern history, exacerbated by growing differences in a multi-ethnic society.

Finally, success in regional security affairs and the ability to gain political goodwill and trust among the countries of the Caspian Basin will depend to a very significant degree on Russia's resolve to contribute decisively to the resolution of the long-standing regional conflicts there and on its assisting its friends and allies in a meaningful way in countering threats to their security. That will be particularly difficult to do, since Russia will have either to adhere consistently to the principle of territorial integrity or to apply a more flexible approach to the resolution of existing conflicts, such as those in Abkhazia, Nagorno-Karabakh or South Ossetia, on a case-by-case basis. In either case Russia risks antagonizing the parties involved in these conflicts.[50] Trying to mend fences or build up a lasting relationship with regional critics or opponents, such as Azerbaijan or Uzbekistan, Russia is walking a thin line and risks antagonizing its friends and allies in the area, such as Armenia.

V. Russian–US interaction in the Caspian region

While it must be recognized that over the past decade the number of international actors in the Caspian region has increased dramatically, it is equally true that it is Russia and the USA that play now and will continue to play in

---

[48] For a detailed analysis of President Putin's visit to Azerbaijan see chapter 10, section IV of this volume.

[49] ITAR-TASS, 24 Mar. 2001, in 'Azerbaijan: Foreign minister sees possible deployment of NATO, Turkish base', FBIS-SOV-200-0324, 24 Mar 2001; and Khanbanyan, A., 'Aliyev okonchatel'no opredelilsya? Voyennye bazy NATO v Azerbaijane mogut stat' real'nost'yu' [Has Aliyev decided his final position? NATO military bases in Azerbaijan may become a reality], *Nezavisimaya Gazeta*, 29 Mar. 2001.

[50] Relations between Georgia and Russia took another downturn when Russia exempted residents of Abkhazia and South Ossetia from the visa regime it introduced with Georgia in Dec. 2000.

the future the leading roles in regional affairs. Because of this, and depending on what kind of Russian–US interaction in the region develops, their individual or combined influence on the future of regional security and stability will be of crucial importance.

After the change of their respective political leaderships, relations between Russia and the USA stand at a crossroads. The direction they take on a number of highly important issues of national and global security, including arms control, national missile defence (NMD), the future of the 1972 Anti-Ballistic Missile (ABM) Treaty and NATO expansion eastwards, will be decided over the next few years and will constitute the mainstream of the Russian–US security agenda. However, on the issue of Russian–US interaction in the Caspian Sea region it seems that the best strategy for both countries to pursue their national interests will be to avoid unnecessary confrontation and seek instead some form of strategic understanding and cooperation.

The reasons for this conclusion can be derived from the analyses in the previous chapters of this study, which show convincingly that the Caspian region is and will remain high on the agenda of both Russian and US foreign and security policy. Their national interests in the region are highly competitive but not necessarily incompatible or antagonistic—including in the economic area, although here the level of competition is understandably higher. One of the most visible areas of Russian–US controversy is the oil and gas routes from the region. Nevertheless, even here there are already examples of mutually beneficial commercial cooperation, such as the construction of the pipeline from the Tengiz oil field in Kazakhstan to the Russian port of Novorossiysk by the Caspian Pipeline Consortium in which Russian and US companies are the major shareholders.[51]

There is an obvious asymmetry in the relative importance of the region for Russia and the USA. Political and security developments in the region are of vital importance for Russia's national interests, if only because of its geographical proximity, but not for the USA. Not only this; their capabilities to pursue them are also asymmetrical. Russia has a clear advantage when it comes to military and security cooperation with regional states, while the USA has obvious economic advantages. Often Russian and US interests in the region are threatened by similar challenges such as religious extremism, political extremism and international terrorism; this opens a realistic possibility for broad Russian–US cooperation or coordinated activities.[52]

Other important causes of regional conflicts include such social factors as the dramatic fall in living standards over the past decade and widespread poverty and unemployment in the new Caspian states. These are causing increasing public discontent with the current governing regimes there. Radical forces in the region, Islamic parties or groups in particular, are gaining support as a result of

[51] For details see chapter 3 in this volume.

[52] The realization that there are common threats to their interests in this part of the world brought Russia and the USA to jointly sponsor UN Security Council Resolution 1333, adopted on 19 Dec. 2000, which condemned the Taliban regime in Afghanistan for its support of international terrorism and imposed economic sanctions against it.

these social problems and the failure of economic and social reforms. The economic development of regional states is therefore another potential area of cooperation between Russia and the USA. The already existing practice of exchanging views on the situation in the Caspian region between the US State Department and the Russian Foreign Ministry may be a particularly useful instrument for exploring other areas and ways of promoting Russian–US cooperation there.

Neither Russia nor the USA can play a dominant role in the region unilaterally. The USA is already firmly accepted in the region as its major economic partner and an important guarantor of the national sovereignty of the regional states, and it cannot be excluded from regional affairs. Nor can Russia be expected to turn its back on its fundamental political, economic and security interests in the Caspian or agree to be squeezed out from the region. On their part the Caspian states, taking into account these realities, favour the balancing presence of Russia and the USA in the region and do not wish either of them to play a dominant role there. In their turn Russia and the USA must avoid the very real possibility that unilateral involvement in regional affairs may adversely affect their overall bilateral relations.

The alternative to Russian–US cooperation on Caspian regional security may be a deepening of the already existing dividing lines in the region, which rivalry between Russia and the USA would further exacerbate. Undoubtedly, both in Russia and in the USA there are influential groups that would prefer to see the future Russian–US relationship in the Caspian region in terms of a 'zero-sum' game. In this they are encouraged by various regional actors who expect to obtain maximum gains by playing Moscow against Washington and vice versa. Such a scenario will run counter to the larger national interests not only of Russia and the USA and but also of the Caspian regional states.

Appendix. Chronology of defence and security-related declarations and agreements involving the countries of the Caspian region, 1991–2001

Mark Eaton

1991

31 Mar.	Georgia declares its independence.
31 Aug.	Kyrgyzstan and Uzbekistan declare their independence.
9 Sep.	Tajikistan declares its independence.
23 Sep.	Armenia declares its independence.
18 Oct.	Azerbaijan declares its independence.
26 Oct.	Turkmenistan declares its independence.
8 Dec.	In Belavezh (USSR), the leaders of Belarus, Russia and Ukraine sign an agreement establishing the Commonwealth of Independent States (CIS), thereby recognizing that the USSR has ceased to exist as an international entity. The states agree to maintain a common military–strategic space under a unified command. The signatories furthermore agree that CIS membership will be available to all former Soviet republics and any other like-minded states.
13 Dec.	Meeting in Ashkhabad (Turkmenistan), the leaders of Kazakhstan, Kyrgyzstan, Tajikistan, Turkmenistan and Uzbekistan state their desire to join the CIS as equal (co-founding) members.
16 Dec.	Kazakhstan declares its independence.
21 Dec.	In Almaty (Kazakhstan), the leaders of Armenia, Azerbaijan, Belarus, Kazakhstan, Kyrgyzstan, Moldova, Russia, Tajikistan, Turkmenistan, Uzbekistan and Ukraine sign a protocol to the agreement of 8 Dec. establishing the CIS, making the agreement valid for each state upon ratification by its national legislature. They also sign a separate declaration agreeing to the maintenance of a unified command structure for military/strategic forces and single control over nuclear weapons, as stipulated in the 8 Dec. agreement.
21 Dec.	Belarus, Kazakhstan, Russia and Ukraine sign an agreement on joint measures regarding nuclear weapons. Under the agreement, Kazakhstan undertakes that by 1 July 1992 all tactical nuclear weapons stationed on its territory will be transferred to 'central factory premises' for dismantling under joint supervision. Kazakhstan also agrees to submit the Strategic Arms Reduction Treaty (START I) to its Supreme Soviet for ratification.
30 Dec.	The CIS member states agree to recognize and adhere to international treaties concluded by the USSR and to support coordinated international

arms control policies. In a separate agreement the CIS states confirm their right to create their own national armed forces.

1992

30 Jan.   All member countries of the CIS are admitted to the Conference on Security and Co-operation in Europe (CSCE).

14 Feb.   In Minsk (Belarus), nine CIS member states sign an agreement placing all CIS conventional (non-nuclear) forces under a joint central command (the CIS Joint Force) for an interim period of at least two years. (Azerbaijan, Moldova and Ukraine opt to develop their own national armed forces.)

24 Mar.   The CSCE Minsk Group, composed of Belarus, Czechoslovakia, France, Germany, Italy, Russia, Sweden, Turkey and the USA, is created and tasked with facilitating a return to peace in the Armenian-populated exclave of Nagorno-Karabakh in Azerbaijan.

20 Mar.   The CIS member states sign an agreement pledging not to use or threaten to use force against each other. An Agreement on Groups of Military Observers and Collective Peacekeeping Forces in the CIS is also signed (not including Turkmenistan). It allows for the creation of voluntary peacekeeping forces to aid in the implementation of ceasefire agreements.

15 May   CIS member states Armenia, Kazakhstan, Kyrgyzstan, Russia, Tajikistan and Uzbekistan meet in Tashkent (Uzbekistan) and sign a five-year Treaty on Collective Security (the Tashkent Treaty). (Azerbaijan, Belarus and Georgia had also signed the treaty by the spring of 1994.) The parties to the treaty agree to provide mutual military aid to fellow signatories in the event of aggression. In 1999, Azerbaijan, Georgia and Uzbekistan failed to renew their participation in the treaty. Armenia, Azerbaijan, Belarus, Georgia, Kazakhstan, Moldova, Russia and Ukraine also agree to adhere to the limitations on personnel and conventional arms agreed in the 1990 Conventional Forces in Europe Treaty (the CFE Treaty).

25 May   A Treaty on Friendship, Cooperation and Mutual Assistance is concluded by presidents Boris Yeltsin of Russia and Nursultan Nazarbayev of Kazakhstan. The two countries agree to form common military and economic zones.

5 June   At the Extraordinary Conference of the states parties to the CFE Treaty, Armenia, Azerbaijan, Georgia, Kazakhstan and Russia join NATO member states and others in signing the Oslo Document which modifies the CFE Treaty in order to make these newly independent states of the former USSR parties to it.

10 June   An Agreement on Friendship, Co-operation and Mutual Assistance is signed between the Republic of Kyrgyzstan and the Russian Federation. Each recognizes the sovereignty and territorial integrity of the other and pledges to resolve disputes peacefully.

24 June   Presidents Eduard Shevardnadze of Georgia and Boris Yeltsin of Russia sign the Agreement on the Principles Governing the Peaceful Settlement of the Conflict in South Ossetia. Under the agreement, a Joint Monitor-

ing Commission is established composed of Russian, Georgian and North and South Ossetian members and tasked with maintaining a buffer zone between the opposing sides and overseeing the implementation of ceasefire agreements.

2 July   Kazakhstan ratifies the START I Treaty.

15 July   CIS foreign and defence ministers agree on principles for the creation of CIS peacekeeping forces to be sent to areas of ethnic conflict. All parties to a conflict must agree to the presence of any CIS peacekeeping force.

31 July   A Treaty on Friendship and Co-operation is signed between Russia and Turkmenistan.

19 Sep.   A ceasefire agreement is signed by the defence ministers of Armenia, Azerbaijan, Georgia and Russia concerning the protracted conflict between Armenia and Azerbaijan over Nagorno-Karabakh.

12 Oct.   An Azerbaijani–Russian mutual security agreement is signed in Moscow (Russia) by President Boris Yeltsin and Azerbaijani President Ebulfez Elcibey.

4 Nov.   Meeting in Almaty (Kazakhstan), the leaders of Kazakhstan, Kyrgyzstan, Russia and Uzbekistan agree that the Russian 201st Motorized Rifle Division (MRD) already stationed in Tajikistan should form the nucleus of the proposed CIS peacekeeping force in Tajikistan.

6 Nov.   The CSCE creates a mission to be sent to Georgia to monitor the peace process in South Ossetia.

1993

25 May   In Moscow, Russian President Boris Yeltsin and Tajik President Imomali Rakhmonov conclude a bilateral Treaty of Friendship, Cooperation and Mutual Assistance and an agreement on the status of Russian forces based in Tajikistan.

15 June   At a meeting of the CIS defence ministers in Moscow, the CIS High Command is abolished and replaced by a new, largely consultative body, the Staff for Co-ordination of Military Co-operation of CIS Member States.

27 July   The leaders of Abkhazia and Georgia sign a ceasefire agreement with the aid of Russian mediation.

24 Aug.   The UN Security Council adopts Resolution 858 establishing the UN Observer Mission in Georgia (UNOMIG).

24 Sep.   The foreign and defence ministers of Kazakhstan, Kyrgyzstan, Russia, Tajikistan and Uzbekistan meet in Moscow and formally establish the CIS peacekeeping force for Tajikistan, to be jointly funded, with Russia contributing 50 per cent, Kazakhstan and Uzbekistan 15 per cent each, and Tajikistan and Kyrgyzstan 10 per cent each.

9 Oct.   The Russian military presence in Georgia is formally legalized with the conclusion of a Georgian–Russian military cooperation agreement. Under the agreement Russia may maintain garrisons in Tbilisi and two other cities, and rent the naval base at Poti and several airfields.

1994

3 Feb. During an official visit by Russian President Boris Yeltsin to Georgia, the Georgian–Russian Treaty of Friendship, Neighbourly Relations and Cooperation is signed, along with numerous military-related agreements. Under the agreements the signatories agree to ensure their mutual security and defence and to jointly protect Georgia's external borders.

23 Mar. Georgia signs the Partnership for Peace Framework Document.

28 Mar. The Agreement between the Republic of Kazakhstan and the Russian Federation on the Major Principles and Conditions for using the Baikonur Cosmodrome is signed at a Kazakh–Russian presidential summit meeting. Under the agreement Russia will lease Baikonur for 20 years and Russian Military Space Forces (MSF) will operate the complex. The commander of the complex will be appointed by the Russian President and approved by the President of Kazakhstan, and the legislation of the Russian Federation will prevail on the territory of the complex.

28 Mar. Presidents Boris Yeltsin of Russia and Nursultan Nazarbayev of Kazakhstan sign a Treaty on Military Cooperation. They agree to lease military facilities to each other, coordinate their military intelligence activities and not conduct military or intelligence operations against each other. They also agree on the joint use of their Caspian Sea naval forces.

28 Mar. Russian Prime Minister Viktor Chernomyrdin and his Kazakh counterpart Viktor Tereshchenko sign the Agreement between the Government of the Republic of Kazakhstan and the Government of the Russian Federation on Military and Technological Co-operation which includes such provisions as increasing the scope of bilateral military and technological cooperation, expanding cooperation between national arms manufacturers, increasing bilateral trade in military products deemed necessary for national security and coordinating mobilization plans.

4 Apr. Meeting in Moscow, representatives of Georgia and Abkhazia agree to an immediate ceasefire and renounce the use of force.

14 Apr. Meeting in Moscow, the CIS defence ministers sign a Declaration on Collective Security aimed at the development of a new security structure operating as a defensive alliance in the Euro-Asian region.

15 Apr. The CIS Council of Heads of State agrees in principle to the creation of a peacekeeping force to be stationed on the Georgian–Abkhaz border and composed of forces from interested signatories to the Tashkent Treaty.

4 May Azerbaijan signs the Partnership for Peace Framework Document.

10 May Turkmenistan signs the Partnership for Peace Framework Document.

14 May Georgian and Abkhazian officials meet in Moscow and sign an Agreement on a Cease-fire and Separation of Forces, thereby agreeing in principle to the deployment of a CIS peacekeeping force.

16 May Representatives of Armenia, Azerbaijan and Nagorno-Karabakh sign a Russian-mediated ceasefire agreement.

27 May Kazakhstan signs the Partnership for Peace Framework Document.

1 June Kyrgyzstan signs the Partnership for Peace Framework Document.

Early July	The leaders of Kazakhstan, Kyrgyzstan and Uzbekistan sign a document creating the Central Asian Union (CAU) aimed at strengthening economic ties between the member states. Russia received observer status to the union in 1996 and Tajikistan joined in 1999.
13 July	Uzbekistan signs the Partnership for Peace Framework Document.
27 July	A ceasefire agreement is signed by the Armenian and Azerbaijani defence ministers and the commander of the Nagorno-Karabakh Army.
5 Oct.	Armenia signs the Partnership for Peace Framework Document.

1995

10 Feb.	At a summit meeting in Almaty (Kazakhstan), CIS member states reach agreement on the creation of a joint air defence system and approve the continued operation of the CIS peacekeeping forces in Tajikistan.
16 Mar.	Presidents Boris Yeltsin of Russia and Levon Ter-Petrosian of Armenia conclude an agreement on the deployment of Russian military formations in the Armenian towns of Gyumri and Yerevan.
25 May	In Moscow, Russia and Tajikistan sign an Agreement on Friendship, Cooperation and Mutual Assistance. They agree that their relations should be based on certain principles, including mutual respect for each other's national sovereignty and territorial integrity, and the peaceful resolution of conflict.
15 Sep.	Russia and Georgia reach an agreement on the deployment of Russian military bases in Georgia. According to the agreement, Russia is entitled to maintain four bases in Georgia for up to 25 years. It is further agreed that no more than 25 000 Russian servicemen are permitted on Georgian soil.
5 Nov.	President Saparmurat Niyazov of Turkmenistan and the Ukrainian Defence Minister sign a Military Co-operation Treaty under which a wide range of military–technical cooperation is envisaged.
18 Dec.	A joint council of defence ministers is established by the governments of Kazakhstan, Kyrgyzstan and Uzbekistan to coordinate military exercises, air defence and arms procurement.

1996

26 Jan.	Russian and Kazakh defence officials conclude 16 military cooperation agreements covering joint communications, joint air defence and national defence industry collaboration, among other issues. Russia also pledges to aid Kazakhstan in the establishment of a Caspian Sea navy and to train its military personnel.
26 Feb.	A Joint Statement on Future US–Kazakhstan Defense and Military Relations is issued, stating that Kazakhstan's armed forces would receive an unspecified amount of US financial aid.
26 Apr.	The leaders of China, Kazakhstan, Kyrgyzstan, Russia and Tajikistan meet in Shanghai (China) to discuss military confidence-building measures (CBMs). The participants agree to several military CBMs within a 100 km-wide zone along their common borders. They further agree to limit the number of military exercises within the 100-km zone, to

increase bilateral cooperation between their armed forces and to resolve mutual conflicts peacefully.

5 May   The presidents of Kazakhstan, Kyrgyzstan and Uzbekistan agree to create a 500-strong Central Asian Battalion (CentrasBat) to be trained under the NATO Partnership for Peace (PFP) programme. It is envisaged that the force will perform peacekeeping duties on the territory of the participating states and even under UN auspices abroad.

10 June   The Azerbaijani and Turkish defence ministers sign a bilateral Agreement on Co-operation in the Military Field.

5 July   A Joint Declaration is signed by Chinese President Jiang Zemin and Kazakh President Nursultan Nazarbayev. In the declaration, Kazakhstan recognizes Taiwan as an inalienable part of China, China reiterates security guarantees for Kazakhstan and supports Kazakhstan's right to protect its independence, territorial integrity and national sovereignty, and both sides state the importance of enhancing bilateral cooperation in the fight against international terrorism, organized crime, drug trafficking, smuggling and other criminal activities.

31 Oct.   The deputy chief of the Turkish Armed Forces General Headquarters and Azerbaijan's Defence Minister meet in Baku (Azerbaijan) and sign two protocols, one on cooperation between their respective defence ministries and the other on cooperation on military health issues.

27 Nov.   Presidents Islam Karimov of Uzbekistan and Saparmurat Niyazov of Turkmenistan sign several bilateral agreements, including one on military–technical cooperation.

1997

10 Jan.   Kazakhstan, Kyrgyzstan and Uzbekistan sign a trilateral Treaty on Eternal Friendship, thereby agreeing not to allow their territories to be used as staging points for armed aggression against each other.

27 Feb.   During a visit to Baku (Azerbaijan) by President Eduard Shevardnadze of Georgia, Azerbaijan and Georgia conclude bilateral agreements calling for a closer strategic partnership and cooperation between the two countries.

28 Feb.   The heads of state of Kazakhstan, Kyrgyzstan, Tajikistan, Turkmenistan and Uzbekistan issue the Almaty Declaration, effectively calling for the establishment of a nuclear weapon-free zone open to all Central Asian states.

8 Apr.   Presidents Nursultan Nazarbayev of Kazakhstan and Askar Akayev of Kyrgyzstan sign an eternal friendship agreement and a military cooperation agreement.

24 Apr.   Building on the agreement signed on 26 Apr. 1996 on military CBMs in border areas, a Treaty on Mutual Reduction of Military Forces in Border Areas is signed by the presidents of the 'Shanghai Five' states—China, Kazakhstan, Kyrgyzstan, Russia and Tajikistan. They agree to observe armament and personnel limitations in a 100 km-wide zone on each side of their common borders.

16 May	A military cooperation agreement is reached between Georgia and Italy and signed by President Eduard Shevardnadze in Rome (Italy). This is the first such agreement between Georgia and a NATO member country.
27 May	Georgia and Ukraine sign six military cooperation agreements on issues such as cooperation in air defence and military training.
27 June	A Peace and Reconciliation Accord is signed in Moscow by Tajik President Imomali Rakhmonov, the United Tajik Opposition leader Said Abdullo Nuri and the UN special envoy to Tajikistan. The agreement marks an official end to the country's civil war.
3 July	Meeting in Moscow, Russian President Boris Yeltsin and Azerbaijani President Heidar Aliyev sign a Treaty of Friendship, Co-operation and Mutual Security. The parties to the treaty jointly denounce all forms of separatism and agree to abstain from military or economic actions aimed against each other. They also agree to recognize and respect the right of each to independently defend its sovereignty and territorial integrity. The Russian State Duma ratified this agreement on 23 Jan. 1998.
17 July	Presidents Eduard Shevardnadze of Georgia and Suleyman Demirel of Turkey sign several agreements, including an agreement on sea borders and on cooperation in training military personnel.
29 Aug.	A Treaty of Friendship, Cooperation and Mutual Assistance is signed in Moscow by presidents Boris Yeltsin of Russia and Levon Ter-Petrosian of Armenia. According to the treaty, the parties agree to interact closely in their mutual defence against external aggression and expand interaction between their respective armed forces. The Armenian National Assembly ratified this agreement on 2 Feb. 1998. The Russian State Duma ratified the agreement on 23 Jan. 1998.
10 Oct.	Azerbaijan, Georgia, Moldova and Ukraine sign a treaty creating the informal GUAM association with the goal of increasing economic, political and military cooperation among the signatories. Uzbekistan joined the association in Apr. 1999.
10 Oct.	The defence ministers of Russia and Kyrgyzstan sign an agreement on the lease of four Kyrgyz military installations to Russia. Under the same agreement, Russia is to provide military training and spare weapons parts to the Kyrgyz Army.
17–18 Nov.	President Nursultan Nazarbayev of Kazakhstan visits the United States and concludes numerous military cooperation agreements.

1998

5 Feb.	Tajikistan and Uzbekistan conclude several cooperation agreements, including one between the Tajik Ministry of Security and Uzbekistan's National Security Service, one between the interior ministries of the two countries, and one between their interior ministry bodies in border regions.
15 Apr.	A memorandum of mutual understanding in the sphere of military cooperation is signed between the Georgian Defence Ministry and the General Staff of the Turkish Armed Forces. Joint military exercises are held within the framework of this memorandum in Apr. 1998.

6 May   An agreement is signed in Moscow by presidents Boris Yeltsin of Russia
               and Islam Karimov of Uzbekistan acknowledging their shared interest in
               resisting the advance of Islamic fundamentalism. The agreement is
               aimed primarily against Afghanistan as a source of regional instability.
               Tajikistan signed the agreement a short time thereafter.

3 July   The leaders of the 'Shanghai Five' countries agree to implement troop
               reductions along their common borders according to the agreement of
               24 Apr. 1997. They issue a joint statement calling for increased bilateral
               and multilateral cooperation in the name of regional security and
               stability, and further support calls for the creation of a nuclear weapon-
               free zone in Central Asia.

7 July   Presidents Boris Yeltsin of Russia and Nursultan Nazarbayev of Kazakh-
               stan sign a declaration of 'eternal friendship and alliance' and in doing so
               agree to aid each other militarily in the event of aggression from a third
               state.

2 Nov.   Presidents Nursultan Nazarbayev of Kazakhstan and Islam Karimov of
               Uzbekistan sign a treaty of eternal friendship and a treaty of economic
               cooperation for the period 1998–2005.

18 Nov.   The defence ministers of Greece and Uzbekistan sign a military
               cooperation agreement.

19 Dec.   The Georgian Defence Ministry and US Department of Defense sign an
               agreement on military cooperation for 1999. US Secretary of Defense
               William Cohen also pledges continued US support in the development of
               Georgia's armed forces.

1999

21 Jan.   Within the framework of the GUAM grouping, the defence ministers of
               Azerbaijan, Georgia and Ukraine sign a communiqué on enhancing
               military cooperation.

4 Mar.   Turkey and Georgia sign a five-year military cooperation agreement
               under which Georgian officers may receive training in Turkish schools
               and Turkey offers financial support to efforts to modernize Georgia's
               armed forces.

16 Apr.   On an official visit to Russia by Tajik President Imomali Rakhmonov,
               several documents are signed, including the Treaty of Alliance and
               Co-operation between the Republic of Tajikistan and the Russian
               Federation, and the Treaty on the Status and Conditions of Presence of
               the Russian Military Base on the Territory of Tajikistan. The Russian
               Federation Council (the upper house of the Russian Parliament) ratified
               this agreement on 14 Mar. 2001.

20 May   The defence ministers of Armenia and Belarus sign an intergovernmental
               agreement on bilateral military and military–technical cooperation in
               Yerevan. The agreement envisages that when one party to the agreement
               is threatened the other will provide military aid. It is valid for five years
               and may be extended for an additional five years.

21 May   The US Special Advisor to the Secretary of State for the New Inde-
               pendent States, Stephen Sestanovich, signs a series of documents on
               military–technical cooperation with Uzbekistan. A cooperation plan for

the defence ministries of the two countries for 1999–2000 is also signed, which includes bilateral cooperation in the prevention of chemical weapons proliferation.

26 May The foreign ministers of Tajikistan and Uzbekistan meet in Khojand (Tajikistan) and sign an agreement on bilateral cooperation against international terrorism, political and religious extremism, and drug trafficking.

19 July The 'Six Plus Two' group on Afghanistan meet in Tashkent where the deputy foreign ministers of China, Iran, Pakistan, Russia, Tajikistan, Turkmenistan, Uzbekistan and the USA, together with the UN Secretary-General's special envoy on Afghanistan, sign the Tashkent Declaration on the Fundamental Principles of a Peaceful Settlement of the Conflict in Afghanistan. The signatories agree not to provide military aid to the conflicting parties and call on the international community to take measures to prevent weapon deliveries to Afghanistan. They also support UN-directed negotiations between the conflicting Afghan parties.

25 Aug. In Bishkek (Kyrgyzstan), two agreements are signed between Kyrgyzstan and Russia—on military technical cooperation, and on the procedures for the use of Russian military facilities in Kyrgyzstan and the status of Russian armed forces personnel in Kyrgyzstan.

28 Sep. Azerbaijan and the USA sign an agreement on cooperation in the counterproliferation of nuclear, chemical and biological weapons, and related materials.

2 Oct. Kyrgyz President Askar Akayev and the Secretary General of the Collective Security Council of the Tashkent Treaty, Vladimir Zemskiy, sign an agreement on military assistance to Kyrgyzstan for its armed forces engaged in combat against Islamic forces.

18 Oct. The Armenian and Greek defence ministers sign a defence cooperation pact. The agreement deals mainly with enhancing bilateral cooperation in military training, research, information exchange and cooperation between the national defence industries.

18–19 Nov. During the Nov. Organization for Security and Co-operation in Europe (OSCE) Summit Meeting in Istanbul (Turkey), Georgia and Russia agree on the gradual withdrawal of Russian military forces in Georgia. Russia agrees to reduce its military equipment in Georgia by 31 Dec. 2000 and to close its bases at Vaziani and Gudauta by 1 July 2001.

1 Dec. US Secretary of State's envoy Anthony Zinni signs a programme for military cooperation with Kazakhstan in Almaty (Kazakhstan). Under the programme, the USA will help Kazakhstan reorganize its military forces and provide training for its servicemen in the USA.

11 Dec. During a visit to Tashkent (Uzbekistan) by Russian Prime Minister Vladimir Putin, a Treaty on the Further Deepening of All-Round Cooperation in the Military and Military–Technical spheres between the Russian Federation and the Republic of Uzbekistan is signed. It calls for enhanced cooperation between the two countries' defence ministries against international terrorism, cooperation in the production and development of weapons, and joint training of military personnel. The Russian Federation Council ratified the agreement on 14 Mar. 2001.

17 Dec.	US Secretary of Defense William Cohen and his Kazakh counterpart sign the US–Kazakh Defense Co-operation Plan for 2000. It envisages greater cooperation towards the development of a modern and effective military force in Kazakhstan. It also covers Kazakhstan's continued participation in the US Individual Military Education and Training (IMET) programme and NATO's PFP programme.

2000

10–13 Mar.	Tajikistan and Uzbekistan agree to join the CIS Integrated Air Defence System (IADS). They thus join Armenia, Belarus, Kazakhstan, Kyrgyzstan and Russia as members of the joint air defence system.
16 Mar.	CIS defence ministers sign 10 cooperation agreements, including several on peacekeeping and anti-terrorist issues.
16 Mar.	Presidents Heidar Aliyev of Azerbaijan and Leonid Kuchma of Ukraine sign a treaty on friendship, cooperation and partnership which describes their relationship as a 'strategic partnership'.
30 Mar.	The defence ministers of the 'Shanghai Five' member states sign the Astana Communiqué, reinforcing their commitment to cooperative relations and CBMs in the military sphere. The defence ministers also state their wish to consolidate cooperation between their national border forces and structures, particularly against international terrorism and separatism.
3 Apr.	Georgian and Greek defence ministry officials sign a military cooperation plan for 2000 within the PFP and agree to allow members of each other's armed forces to observe military exercises.
8 Apr.	Secretary of the Russian Security Council Sergey Ivanov and his Tajik counterpart sign a protocol on bilateral cooperation against international terrorism, drug smuggling and illegal immigration.
15 Apr.	US Secretary of State Madeleine Albright meets President Nursultan Nazarbayev in Astana (Kazakhstan) to discuss regional security issues. She offers $3 million to support Kazakhstan's armed forces. Also in April, Albright makes similar offers during meetings with the presidents of Kyrgyzstan and Uzbekistan.
21 Apr.	The presidents of Kazakhstan, Kyrgyzstan, Tajikistan and Uzbekistan sign a 10-year agreement in Tashkent on joint efforts against the spread of Islamic militancy in Central Asia, as well as against the drug trade, organized crime, and other threats to regional stability and security. The security pact aims to coordinate the intelligence and security services of the signatories, who furthermore pledge joint military action if one party comes under attack.
19 May	The heads of the security and special services of the CIS states meet in Astana (Kazakhstan) to discuss the joint fight against organized crime, drug trafficking and terrorism.
24 May	In Minsk (Belarus), the leaders of the signatories of the 1992 Tashkent Treaty—Armenia, Belarus, Kazakhstan, Kyrgyzstan, Russia and Tajikistan—adopt nine documents dealing mainly with the growing threat to regional security posed by international terrorism and extremism.

15 June	Secretary of the Russian Security Council Sergey Ivanov and his Georgian counterpart sign a joint statement on security issues, including expanding bilateral political, economic and military ties, and cooperation against international terrorism, organized crime, and arms and drug trafficking.
15 June	Presidents Imomali Rakhmonov of Tajikistan and Islam Karimov of Uzbekistan sign a treaty of eternal friendship in Dushanbe (Tajikistan). They also sign a memorandum delimiting their common border.
20 June	The CIS Council of Foreign Ministers decides not to renew the mandate of the CIS Peacekeeping Force in Tajikistan.
20 June	CIS prime ministers, meeting in Moscow, approve plans for the establishment of an international anti-terrorist centre to be based in Moscow.
24 June	The Russian and Uzbek defence ministers sign bilateral agreements on military cooperation and draft further agreements on the training of Uzbek servicemen in Russian academies, the repairing of Uzbek weapons in Russian facilities and the joint manufacture of explosives.
5 July	The heads of member states of the Shanghai Forum—China, Kazakhstan, Kyrgyzstan, Russia and Tajikistan, formerly the 'Shanghai Five'— issue a joint declaration following a meeting in Dushanbe (Tajikistan). The declaration stresses the growing importance of the Shanghai Forum in ensuring regional stability and security, and expresses the need to jointly fight religious extremism, international terrorism and national separatism. The participants support the Kyrgyz proposal for the creation of a 'regional anti-terrorist structure'. For the first time, Uzbekistan participates as an observer. The Shanghai Five become the Shanghai Forum with the granting of observer status to Uzbekistan at this meeting.
27 July	In Moscow, Presidents Vladimir Putin of Russia and Askar Akayev of Kyrgyzstan sign a declaration on eternal friendship and a 10-year economic cooperation plan.
Late July	Armenian Defence Minister Serzh Sarkisian and US Defense Secretary William Cohen sign an agreement on cooperation in preventing the proliferation of weapons of mass destruction.
24 Aug.	The defence ministers of China and Uzbekistan sign a defence cooperation agreement.
20 Sep.	The defence ministers of Azerbaijan and Turkey sign a military–industrial cooperation agreement in Baku (Azerbaijan).
27 Sep.	The Armenian and Russian defence ministers sign three agreements, including one on the joint planning of armed forces activities. Other documents signed include a protocol on amendments to a 26 Sep. 1996 agreement regulating the Russian military presence in Armenia and an agreement on the joint use of Armenian and Russian airspace.
1 Oct.	The Armenian, Azerbaijani, Georgian and Russian interior ministers sign three documents aimed at enhancing cooperation in the fight against terrorism and in maintaining regional stability. The documents call for the exchange of information on individual terrorists and terrorist organizations active in the region, and on the illegal trade in arms and drugs.
9 Oct.	Presidents Vladimir Putin of Russia and Nursultan Nazarbayev of Kazakhstan sign a joint communiqué stressing the importance of multi-

lateral cooperation under existing CIS agreements and the Tashkent Treaty, particularly for ensuring the security of the southern borders of the CIS.

11 Oct.   The presidents of the six Tashkent Treaty countries sign the Bishkek Agreement on the Status of Forces and Means of Collective Security Systems, thus allowing for the dispatch of troops to the territory of parties to the agreement, cooperation in repelling external aggression, and joint anti-terrorist operations and military exercises.

16 Oct.   Presidents Islam Karimov of Uzbekistan and Ahmet Sezer of Turkey pledge to cooperate in fighting terrorism, drug trafficking and organized crime. The Uzbek Defence Minister and a representative of the Turkish General Staff sign a military cooperation agreement.

18 Oct.   Presidents Askar Akayev of Kyrgyzstan and Ahmet Sezer of Turkey sign a joint declaration on cooperation against terrorism.

19 Oct.   Presidents Nursultan Nazarbayev of Kazakhstan and Ahmet Sezer of Turkey sign a joint declaration on cooperation against terrorism.

31 Oct.   Armenian Prime Minister Andranik Markaryan and Belarussian Prime Minister Uladzimir Yarmoshyn sign a treaty on friendship and cooperation. The document addresses many aspects of bilateral cooperation, including military–technical cooperation.

1 Dec.   During a CIS summit meeting in Minsk (Belarus), CIS leaders approve the statute for the proposed CIS anti-terrorist centre and extend the mandate of the Russian peacekeeping force in the Georgian–Abkhazian conflict.

13 Dec.   A military cooperation agreement is signed in Yerevan between the US Armed Forces in Europe and the Armenian Ministry of Defence. The agreement addresses several forms of cooperation including military training and bilateral interaction in cases of emergency.

2001

5 Jan.   The leaders of Kazakhstan, Kyrgyzstan, Tajikistan and Uzbekistan, and the Russian Deputy Foreign Minister meet in Almaty (Kazakhstan) to discuss regional security issues, including drug trafficking and cross-border terrorism.

9 Jan.   Presidents Vladimir Putin of Russia and Heidar Aliyev of Azerbaijan sign a joint declaration on the principles of cooperation on Caspian Sea issues and the Baku Declaration on the principles of ensuring security and developing cooperation in the Caucasus. The latter document contains provisions for the development of military cooperation between Azerbaijan and Russia not aimed against any third country.

28 Feb.   Azerbaijani and Turkish defence and military officials sign two inter-governmental agreements—an Agreement on Free Military Assistance and a Protocol on Financial Assistance between the Azerbaijani Defence Ministry and the General Staff of the Turkish Armed Forces.

1 Mar.   A military cooperation agreement is signed by the defence ministers of Kazakhstan and Kyrgyzstan. The Kazakh Defence Minister, Sat Tokpakbayev, states that if Islamic extremists invade Kyrgyzstan in the future Kazakhstan will provide the 'necessary' assistance.

11 Mar.   The Special Representative of the Russian President for the Caspian Sea region, Viktor Kalyuzhny, and the US Caspian Envoy Ambassador Elizabeth Jones agree that the Russian Foreign Ministry and the US Department of State will continue a dialogue promoting bilateral interaction in the Caspian region.

12 Mar.   Presidents Vladimir Putin of Russia and Mohammad Khatami of Iran sign a 10-year Treaty on the Foundations of Relations and Principles of Cooperation between the Russian Federation and the Islamic Republic of Iran. Under the treaty, both sides agree to enhance bilateral cooperation in the fields of industry, science and technology, agriculture and nuclear energy, as well as in the fight against international terrorism.

13 Mar.   A Russian Defence ministry delegation visits Tajikistan to discuss future Russian–Tajik military–technical cooperation.

16 Mar.   Georgian Defence Minister David Tevzadze and US Defense Secretary Donald Rumsfeld meet in Washington, DC (USA) to discuss bilateral military cooperation.

22 Mar.   During the visit of the head of the US Federal Bureau of Investigation (FBI), Louis Freeh, to Georgia, an agreement is reached on opening a permanent FBI office in Tbilisi (Georgia). Under the agreement the office will contribute to the protection of energy pipelines crossing Georgian territory.

22 Mar.   A protocol on military cooperation is signed in Baku (Azerbaijan) between the Azerbaijani Defence Ministry and Turkey's General Staff.

14 Apr.   Russia and Armenia agree to create a joint military contingent for the purpose of ensuring regional security.

28 Apr.   The foreign ministers of the Shanghai Forum countries meet in Moscow and release a communiqué expressing their shared concern over growing international terrorism, religious and political extremism, and drug trafficking in the region.

28 Apr.   Azerbaijani and Turkish defence officials sign a protocol on cooperation in the sphere of military–technical supply between the Azerbaijani Defence Ministry and the Turkish General Staff.

4 May   During a state visit by President Islam Karimov of Uzbekistan to Russia the two sides sign numerous agreements, including a protocol on exchanging instruments of ratification of the Dec. 1999 Treaty on the Further Deepening of All-Round Cooperation in the Military and Military–Technical Spheres between the Russian Federation and the Republic of Uzbekistan and agree to create working groups within their national security systems to implement and regulate the military–technical cooperation called for in the agreement.

14 June   Uzbekistan is admitted as a full member of the Shanghai Forum at the summit meeting of the organization in Shanghai. The participants at the meeting decide to change the name of the forum to the Shanghai Cooperation Organization.

About the authors

Najia Badykova (Turkmenistan) is Chief of the Foreign Economic Relations Department at the National Institute of Statistics and Forecasting (Ashkhabad). Her recent publications include *Iran i Perspektivy Eksporta iz Kaspiyskogo Regiona* [Iran and prospects of gas export from the Caspian region], Occasional Papers no. 61 (Slavic Research Centre/Hokkaido University: Sapporo, Tokyo, 1998); and *The Opportunities for Attracting Japanese Capital in Turkmenistan and Other Central Asian Countries* (Institute of Developing Economies: Tokyo, 1999).

Sabit Bagirov (Azerbaijan) is President of the Center for Political and Economic Research. He is also President of the Entrepreneurship Development Foundation which aims to create a favourable business environment in Azerbaijan. Formerly he was the President of Azerbaijan's State Oil Company (SOCAR). He has published many articles on energy and political issues in English, Azeri and Russian, and is currently working on a book entitled *Azerbaijan in Transition*.

Gennady Chufrin (Russia), Associate Member of the Russian Academy of Sciences, is Project Leader of the SIPRI project on the Security of the Caspian Sea Region. He recently published 'The Caspian Sea Basin: the security dimensions', *SIPRI Yearbook 1999: Armaments, Disarmament and International Security* (Oxford University Press: Oxford, 1999): and 'Russia: separatism and conflicts in the North Caucasus', *SIPRI Yearbook 2000*. He also edited *Russia and Asia–Pacific Security* (SIPRI, 1999); and *Russia and Asia: The Emerging Security Agenda* (Oxford University Press, 1999).

Mark Eaton (Canada) is Research Assistant for the SIPRI project on the Security of the Caspian Sea Region.

Murad Esenov (Sweden) is Director of the Central Asia and the Caucasus Information and Analysis Center and Editor-in-Chief of the journal *Central Asia and the Caucasus* (Luleå, Sweden). His recent publications include *Political Islam and Conflicts in Russia and Central Asia* (co-edited with Lena Jonson) (Swedish Institute of International Affairs: Stockholm, 1999); *Chechnya: The International Community and Strategies for Peace and Stability* (co-edited with Lena Jonson) (Swedish Institute of International Affairs: Stockholm, 2000); and '"The Turkmen model of democracy": specific features', *Central Asia and the Caucasus*, no. 2 (2000).

Amy Myers Jaffe (USA) is Senior Energy Advisor and Program Co-ordinator for the Energy Forum of the James A. Baker III Institute for Public Policy at Rice University (Houston, Texas). Her recent publications include 'The myth of the Caspian "Great Game": the real geopolitics of energy', co-author with R. Manning, *Survival*, vol. 40, no. 4 (winter 1998); (with R. Manning), 'The shocks of a world of cheap oil', *Foreign Affairs*, vol. 79, no. 1 (Jan./Feb. 2000); and (with Martha Brill Olcott) 'The geopolitics of Caspian energy', eds E. Kalyuzhnova and D. Lynch, *The Euro-Asian World: A Period of Transition* (St Martins Press: New York, 2000).

Lena Jonson (Sweden) is Associate Professor and Senior Research Fellow at the Swedish Institute of International Affairs. She has published extensively in the field of Russian foreign and security policies. Among her latest publications are *Russia and Central Asia: A New Web of Relations* (Royal Institute of International Affairs: London, 1998); *The Tajik War: A Challenge to Russian Policy* (RIIA: London, 1998); *Keeping the Peace on CIS Territory: The Evolution of Russian Policy* (RIIA: London, 1999); and *Central Asian Security: The New International Context,* co-edited together with Roy Allison (Brookings Institution/RIIA: Washington, DC, and London, 2001).

Ali Karaosmanoglu (Turkey) is Chairman of the Department of International Relations at Bilkent University in Ankara. His recent publications include 'NATO enlargement and the South', *Security Dialogue,* vol. 30, no. 2 (June 1999); and 'The evolution of the national security culture and the military in Turkey', *Journal of International Affairs,* vol. 54, no. 1 (fall 2000).

Farkhad Khamraev (Uzbekistan) is Assistant Professor at the University of World Economy and Diplomacy in Tashkent. He was previously Head of Department at the Division of Political Analysis in the Ministry of Foreign Affairs of Uzbekistan. His recent publications include 'Tsentral'naya Aziya: problemy razdelyonnykh natsii' [Central Asia: problems of divided nations] in *Gosudarstvo i Obshchestvo v Stranakh Post-Sovetskogo Vostoka* [State and society in the post-Soviet oriental countries] (Almaty, 1999); and 'Afghanskiy uzel i problemy bezopasnosti Tsentral'noy Azii' [The Afghan knot and Central Asian security problems], *Vostok* (Moscow), no. 1 (2000).

Alexander Krylov (Russia) is a Senior Research Fellow at the Institute of Oriental Studies, Russian Academy of Sciences. He is the author of over 70 publications, including *Separatizm v Stranakh Vostoka* [Separatism in the countries of the East] (GRVL: Moscow, 1992); and *Post-Sovetskaya Abkhaziya: Traditsii, Religii, Lyudi* [Post-Soviet Abkhazia: traditions, religions, people] (OOAgent: Moscow, 1999).

Aleksei Malashenko (Russia) is Scholar-in-Residence, Ethnicity and Nation-Building Program Co-Chair, Carnegie Endowment for International Peace (Carnegie Moscow Center). He is the author of numerous monographs on contemporary Islam and the Muslim mentality. His recent publications include *Islamskoye Vozrozhdeniye v Sovremennoy Rossii* [Islamic renaissance in Modern Russia] (Moscow Carnegie Center: Moscow, 1998); and (co-editor with Martha Brill Olcott) *Faktory Etno-konfessional'noy Samobytnosti v Postsovetskom Obshchestve* [Factors of ethno-confessional identification in post-Soviet society] (Moscow Carnegie Center: Moscow, 1998).

Dina Malysheva (Russia) is a Senior Research Fellow at the Institute of World Economy and International Relations (IMEMO) of the Russian Academy of Sciences. Her recent publications include 'Rossiya i Zakavkaz'ye: realii nezavisimosti i novoye partnyorstvo' [Russia and the trans-Caucasus: realities of independence and the new partnership] (co-author) (Finstatinform: Moscow, 2000); and 'Iran i problemy regional'noy bezopasnosti Zakavkaz'ya' (Iran and problems of regional security of the trans-Caucasus', in *Blizhniy Vostok i Sovremennost'*, issue no. 9 (Institute of Israel and Middle East, Moscow, 2000).

Mehrdad Mohsenin (Iran) is Senior Research Fellow at the Center for the Study of Central Asia and the Caucasus at the Institute for Political and International Studies (IPIS) in Tehran. His recent publications include 'Regional role of Iran in the development of Central Asia', *Amu Darya,* vol. 2, no. 1 (1997); and 'Pipeline options for exporting oil and gas from the Caspian basin', *Relazioni Internazionali* (Institute for the Study of International Politics, Milan), no. 47 (Nov./Dec. 1998).

Vitaly Naumkin (Russia) is President of the Russian Centre for Strategic Research and International Studies, Head of the Arabic Department of the Institute of Oriental Studies (IOS) of the Russian Academy of Sciences, and Editor-in-Chief of the journal *Vostok,* published by the Russian Academy of Sciences. His recent publications include *Ethnic Conflict in the Former Soviet Union* (Moscow, 1997); and 'The emerging geopolitical balance in Central Asia: a Russian view', ed. G. Chufrin, SIPRI, *Russia and Asia: The Emerging Security Agenda* (Oxford University Press: Oxford, 1999).

John Roberts (UK) is a consultant specializing in the relationship between energy, economic development and politics and a senior partner in Methinks Ltd (Edinburgh), a consultancy focusing on Central Asian, Middle Eastern and development issues. He has written and lectured extensively on Caspian energy issues, notably pipelines. His recent publications include *Visions and Mirages: The Middle East in a New Era* (Mainstream: Edinburgh, 1995) and *Caspian Pipelines* (RIIA: London, 1996).

Alexander Rondeli (Georgia) is Director of the Foreign Policy Research and Analysis Center at the Ministry of Foreign Affairs of Georgia. Formerly he was Professor and Chair of the Department of International Relations at Tbilisi State University. His recent publications include 'The nature of the security problematique in the CIS', eds N. MacFarlane and O. Thränert, *Balancing Hegemony: The OSCE in the CIS* (Centre for International Relations, Queens University: Kingston, Ontario, 1997); *Georgia: Foreign Policy and National Security Priorities*, Discussion Paper Series no. 3 (UNDP Country Office in Georgia: Tbilisi, 1998); and 'Security problems in the Caucasus', eds W. Asher and N. Mirovitskaia, *The Caspian Sea: A Quest for Environmental Security* (Kluwer: Dordrecht, 2000).

Konstantin Syroezhkin (Kazakhstan) is Political Observer for *Continent Magazine* (Almaty) and was formerly Deputy Director of the Kazakhstan Institute of Strategic Studies (KISS). His recent publications include *Natsional'no-Gosudarstvennoye Stroitel'stvo v KNR: Teoriya i Praktika* [Nation-state building in the PRC: theory and practice] (Almaty, 1998); 'Politika Rossii v Tsentral'noy Azii i Kazakhstanskaya perspektiva' [The policy of Russia in Central Asia and Kazakhstan's perspective], *Kazakhstan Spectrum*, no. 2 (1999); and 'Vzaimootnosheniya Kitaya s gosudarstvami Tsentral'noy Azii' [The relations of China with the states of Central Asia], *Kazakhstan Spectrum*, no. 2 (2000).

Igor Zonn (Russia) is Professor of Geography, member of the Russian Academy of Natural Sciences, and Editor-in-Chief of the *Caspian Sea Bulletin*. His recent publications include *Kaspiy: Illyuzii i Real'nost'* [The Caspian: myths and realities] (Korkis: Moscow, 1999); and *Trista Let na Kaspii* [Three centuries in the Caspian] (Edel-M: Moscow, 2000).

Index

Abiyev, Safar 341
Abkhazia:
　armed forces 94
　conflict in 93, 197, 199, 201, 202, 211, 264,
　　281–94, 284–86, 294:
　　background to 281–83
　　ceasefire 347, 348
　　ethnic factors 282, 283, 284, 288
　　oil and 327
　　situation after 286–90
　cconomy 287, 288
　Russia and 15, 94, 197, 204, 205, 207, 209,
　　287, 290–92, 356
　Russian forces in 94, 290, 292
　status of 288, 289
　West and 292–94
ACG see Azerbaijan: Azeri–Chirag–
　deepwater Guneshli field complex
Adams, Terry 54, 55
Adzharia 264, 289
Afghanistan:
　drug trade and 63, 224, 227, 249, 251, 252
　instability 63
　Islamic extremists and 121
　Islamic radicalism and 316, 326
　Kazakhstan and 213, 219, 224
　Mujahideen 247
　Northern Alliance 213, 250, 320
　oil and 172
　pipelines across 62–63, 246, 247
　'Six Plus Two' group 32, 317, 353
　Tajikistan and 104, 105
　Taliban:
　　coalition against 213
　　emergence of 247
　　instability and 21, 172
　　Russia and 147
　　successes 3, 122, 320
　　terrorism and 227, 250, 251
　　threat from 213, 227
　　Turkey and 147
　　USA and 147, 250, 251
　Turkmenistan and 227, 246–51, 252
　USA and 146, 147, 227, 250
　Uzbekistan and 227
Agip 49, 123

AIOC see Azerbaijan International Operating
　Company
Akayev, President Askar 101–2
Akmazov, Lieutenant-General Yuriy 109
Albright, Madeleine 29, 100, 103, 110, 137
　and fn, 143, 228, 293, 320, 354
Alexandroupolis 171
Alikperov, Vagit 183
Aliyev, Ilham 129
Aliyev, Natiq 36, 66, 235
Aliyev, President Heidar 137fn, 181:
　Caspian Sea and 65, 67, 132
　gas and 37
　Iran and 178–79
　Kocharian, dialogue with 274–75
　Nagorno-Karabakh and 260, 261
　NATO and 92, 272
　Russia and 92, 133, 178–79, 182, 340
　security and 328, 329
Alma Ata Declaration (1991) 169
Almaty Declaration (1997) 350
Amerada Hess 193
Amoco 36, 53, 123, 180, 190 see also
　BP Amoco
Ankara Declaration (1998) 139, 156, 158, 192
Apsheron Peninsula 75, 76
Arak 57, 58
Aral Sea 41
Arazov, Regepbay 39
Ardebili, Hosein Kazempur 132
Ardzinba, President Vladislav 94, 292
Armenia:
　armed forces 89
　arms imports 3–4, 83, 90, 91, 272, 275, 276
　arms industry 115
　Azerbaijan and 179, 262, 274
　Belarus and 352, 356
　China and 91
　EU and 259
　GDP 325
　Greece and 90, 353
　Iran and 20, 187, 262, 270, 331
　military expenditure 84, 85, 86, 88–89
　NATO and 28–29, 89, 90
　Partnership for Peace and 28–29, 349
　railways 259

Russia and 14, 89, 134, 144, 179, 182, 183,
  262, 266–68, 276, 277, 329, 340, 349,
  351, 355, 357
  arms deliveries 90, 268, 272, 275–76
Russian forces in 89–90, 183, 276
Turkey and 89, 164, 262, 350
USA and 89, 90, 158, 272, 355, 356
West and 263
see also Nagorno-Karabakh
Astana Communiqué (2000) 112, 121, 354
Astrakhan 78, 141
Atyrau–Karakoin pipeline 60
Atyrau–Novorossiysk pipeline 33–34
Atyrau–Samara pipeline 22, 44, 339
Aushev, President Ruslan 300
Azerbaijan:
  aid to 93
  armed forces 91, 185
  Armenia and 179, 183, 187–88, 259, 274
  arms imports 79, 92, 275, 276
  Azeri–Chirag–deepwater Guneshli field
    complex (ACG) 33, 36, 45, 51, 55, 65,
    180, 181, 192
  Caspian Sea and 75, 178–94:
    legal regime and 64, 65, 169–70, 188–89
  Chirag oilfield 65, 142, 180, 181
  CIS and 4, 91, 179, 185
  condensate 193
  Dan Uludzu prospect 36
  economy 260
  energy deposits 22, 36
  energy needs 190
  ethnic minorities 185
  foreign investment 181
  foreign policy 178–88
  Gabala radio location station 185
  gas 35, 36, 37, 140, 193
  GDP 325
  Georgia and 264–65, 350
  GUUAM and 4, 113, 178
  importance of 16
  Iran and 182, 186–88, 270
  Karabakh oilfield 36, 123
  Kazakhstan and 92
  military build-up 261
  military expenditure 84, 85, 86, 88, 91
  military weakness 277
  NATO and 4, 92, 112, 162, 272, 276, 327,
    341
  occupied land 258, 259, 273, 277, 278

oil 22, 25, 33, 43, 44, 45, 47, 48, 50, 51, 55,
  58, 65, 123, 129, 179, 180, 236:
  export routes 187, 190–94, 243
  foreign investment in 129, 179, 181fn,
    186
  production 35, 36, 51, 141, 181
  reserves 36–37, 140, 157, 193, 235
  transit revenues 50
oil companies and 36, 181–82, 188, 190
Oil Rocks field 180
Partnership for Peace and 92, 272, 348
refugees 270
Russia and 14, 16, 92, 129, 133–35, 182–86,
  189, 260, 261, 262, 266–68, 273, 336,
  340–41, 347, 351, 356:
  troop withdrawal 185
Russian population 183–84
Shah Deniz 36, 37, 131, 144, 149, 168, 180,
  235, 239
strategic choice 178–94
Tashkent Treaty and 4, 92, 268, 346
Turkey and 19, 20, 93, 112, 144, 151–52,
  164, 179, 182, 187, 271, 276, 332, 333,
  350, 355, 356, 357
Turkmenistan, disputes with 65, 106, 131,
  134, 144, 236, 238, 243
Ukraine and 92, 114, 178
unification 187
USA and 18, 92–93, 129, 133, 158, 178,
  179, 272, 337, 353
West and 4, 14, 88, 178, 179–82, 259–60,
  340
see also Nagorno-Karabakh
Azerbaijan International Operating Company
  (AIOC) 36, 49, 51, 52, 53, 54, 55, 56, 65,
  131, 190, 191, 193, 194, 243

Babayan, General Samvel 263
Baigarin, Bekbulat 99
Baker, James 29, 271
Baku Declaration (2001) 92, 261, 340, 356
Baku–Ceyhan pipeline 19, 20, 22, 23, 45,
  49–53, 54–55, 68, 77, 123, 125, 126, 130,
  139–40, 142, 148, 149, 171, 190, 258, 267,
  272, 275, 337
Baku–Erzurum gas pipeline 62
Baku–Novorossiysk pipeline 22, 23, 24, 34,
  44, 47, 53, 55, 56, 79, 142, 157, 191, 279:
  Chechnya and 15, 23, 24, 44, 142
  Grozny Bypass 22–23, 56, 339
  see also Baku–Tikhoretsk–Novorossiysk

Baku–Supsa pipeline 22, 44, 45, 52, 53, 54–55, 56, 114, 123, 142, 171, 190, 191, 293–94

Baku–Tbilisi–Ceyhan (BTC) pipeline 131, 155, 156, 157, 158, 192, 193, 194, 199

Baku–Tikhoretsk–Novorossiysk pipeline 56, 339

Balgimbayev, Nurlan 37

Balkis, Taner 93

Basayev, Shamil 302, 304, 306, 307

Bashkortostan 300

Bechtel 144

Belarus:
  Armenia and 352
  arms imports 105
  nuclear weapons and 345

Berger, Sandy 19

Bhutto, Benazir 247

Bishkek agreement (2000) 356

Black Sea:
  NATO and 159
  naval presence in 159, 161
  oil tankers 68, 156
  pollution 156
  see also Blue Stream underwater pipeline

Black Sea Economic Cooperation scheme (BSEC) 161, 210

Blue Stream underwater pipeline 20, 23, 34, 61–62, 131, 144, 153, 154, 159, 194, 234, 333

'Borzhomi Four' 92

Bosporus 50, 55, 67, 68, 130, 137, 139, 142, 149, 152, 171, 190, 192

Botas 63, 192, 237

Bouygues 49

BP (British Petroleum) 37, 41, 123, 142, 180, 181, 190, 193

BP Amoco 38, 123, 131, 149

BP–Statoil 180

Brazil: arms exports 88

Bridas 39

British Gas 49

Burgas 171

Bush, President George W. 124, 148, 337

Caspian International Petroleum Co. 123

Caspian Oil Company 42, 132, 267

Caspian Pipeline Consortium (CPC) 22, 23, 33, 44, 48–49, 56, 143, 193, 227, 342
  see also Tengiz–Novorossiysk pipeline

Caspian Sea:
  Baku Bay 75–76

biological resources 69, 70–74, 81, 125

demilitarization 120, 132, 170, 175, 176

environmental degradation 64, 69–83

fish 69–70, 71, 72, 73, 74, 81, 131

future of 80–82

legal regime 2, 64–67, 169–70:
  Azerbaijan–Russia agreement on 189
  bilateral agreements on 133, 236
  condominium 175, 189
  disputes mounting 326–27
  division 64, 80, 127, 132, 134, 169–70, 188–89
  fisheries and 64, 69
  Kazakhstan–Russia agreement on 127, 133, 189
  Kazakhstan–US agreement 217
  median line 64–65, 127, 189
  mineral wealth exploited before decision on 133
  need for 2

military exercises 4

national sectors 16, 25, 189

Neftyanye Kamni oilfield 75–76

oil and 69, 74–79, 134

pipelines across 2, 20, 24, 77–79, 144

pollution 69, 70, 72, 74–76, 78, 79, 80

sea level fluctuations 69, 76–77, 125

seismicity 77–79

sturgeon 69, 70, 71, 72–73, 81, 131

tankers and 79

see also under Azerbaijan; Iran; Kazakhstan; Russia; Turkey; and Turkmenistan; and following entries

Caspian Sea Cooperation Organization (CASCO) 170, 175

Caspian Sea region:
  aid to 115
  armed forces 3, 4, 83–84, 114–15, 327
  arms imports 3, 83, 84–116, 327
  conflicts in 3, 31, 120
  corruption 129
  definition 1, 119
  drug trade 143 see also under Central Asia and under names of countries
  economies 128–32, 325–26, 342–43 see also under names of countries
  energy:
    development, factors affecting 25–26, 33–34
    importance of 12, 17, 326
    pipeline development 25–26, 33–34
    potential 2, 123, 128

production 35
  reserves 1–2, 17, 33–44, 123, 124,
    336–37
  transport 12
  see also gas; oil; oil pipelines
foreign investment 14, 32
future of 325–43
geology of 33
geopolitical situation 11–32
international actors and 1, 5, 11, 12, 16–21,
    43, 135, 257, 280, 331–36
military build-up 3, 83–84, 275–77, 327
  external aid and 84, 115
military expenditure 3, 83, 84–116, 327
NATO and 4, 162
nuclear weapons 337
security 3:
  arrangements 12, 26–30, 31, 111–14,
    143, 244, 327, 328, 329
  cooperation 4, 12, 111–14, 147
  international community and 28
  threats 3, 27, 30, 327, 328
  vulnerability 12
strategic rivalry 11
see also Caucasus; Central Asia; South
  Caucasus
Caspian seal 71, 80
Caucasus:
  definition 167
  Iran and 167
  NATO and 167
  regional cooperation 209–10
  Russia and 204, 205, 207, 267, 279
  Turkey and 162–63
  USA and 137, 205
Cavanaugh, Carey 274
CCC–Saipem 49
Cem, Ismail 96, 259
Central Asia:
  area 313
  balance of forces in 215–20
  China and 24, 30, 31, 97, 215, 216, 217,
    218–19, 220, 226, 321, 334–36
  corruption 129, 224, 228
  defence structures and 31
  definition 1, 167
  drugs trade 224, 228
  Europe and 216
  extremism in 27, 83 228, 230
  India and 97
  Iran and 167, 173–74, 216, 218, 219
  Kazakhstan and 214

military expenditure 3, 83, 97–111
Nagorno-Karabakh and 265
NATO and 4, 31, 167, 252
nuclear-weapon-free zone 317, 350, 352
Pakistan and 97, 219
population 313
Russia and 97, 215–16, 218–19, 220, 226,
    228, 229, 239, 243, 318–21, 321
security 244–53, 311–21
  regional security system 318
  threats 313–38
socio-economic conditions 30, 31, 315–16,
    325–26, 342–43
terrorism and 30, 97, 121, 228, 230, 317,
    319, 340
Turkey and 216, 219, 332
USA and 29, 137, 146, 215, 216–17, 218,
    220, 228–29, 336–38
West and 215, 252, 312
see also under names of individual countries
Central Asian Battalion (CentrasBat) 29, 100,
    113, 146, 328, 350
Central Asian Oil Pipeline (CAOP) 45
Central Asian Union (CAU) 4–5, 113, 213–14,
  349
Ceyhan see Baku–Ceyhan pipeline
CFE Treaty (Treaty on Conventional Armed
  Forces in Europe, 1990) 147, 275, 346:
  Azerbaijan and 276
  Georgia and 198
  Kazakhstan and 99
  Oslo Document 346
Chechnya 41:
  Congress of the Peoples of Chechnya and
    Dagestan 306–7
  deportations 296, 297
  external influences 308–10
  Federation Treaty and 295fn
  fundamentalism 301–2
  Germany and 296–97
  independence 14, 308
  Islam and 295, 296–304, 310
  Islamic Nation and 306
  Islamic Rebirth Party 298–99
  jihad 296, 297, 298, 299, 300, 301, 305, 310
  Khasaviurt Agreement (1996) 14, 28
  military successes 300
  oil and 22–23, 56, 171
  OSCE and 28
  Republic of Ichkeriya 295, 301
  Salafites 298, 301, 302, 303, 304, 305, 306,
    307, 308, 309, 310

separatist movement 295, 297, 301
shariah 297, 301, 303, 304, 305
Tarikatism 299, 304
Wahhabites 298fn, 300, 304, 308 *see also*
  Salafites
wars 14, 15, 22–23, 304, 307
World War II 296–97
Cheleken 76
Chernomyrdin, Viktor 248, 331
Chevron 45, 52, 124
Chi Haotian 101
Chicago Bridge and Iron 49
China:
  arms exports 87, 91, 115
  Caspian Sea region and 18:
    economic factors 24, 335
    security concerns 17, 21, 30, 334–36
  Central Asia and 24, 30, 31, 84, 215, 216,
    217, 218–19, 220, 226, 231, 334–36
  energy needs 2, 21, 25–26, 60, 63, 334
  gas and 17, 63, 234
  Iran and 87, 115
  Islam and 21, 31, 219, 316
  Kazakhstan and 21, 24, 30, 31, 101, 214,
    335–36, 350
  Kyrgyzstan and 21, 24, 30, 104,
  oil and 17, 44, 47, 48, 57, 58–60, 171,
    335–36
  Russia and 21
  separatism in 21, 31, 335
  Tajikistan and 21, 106, 335
  Turkmenistan and 63
  Uighurs 21, 31
  USA and 139
  Uzbekistan and 30, 110–11, 355
  Xinjiang 21, 217, 219, 335
China National Petroleum Corporation
  (CNPC) 24, 58, 59, 60, 63
Christopher, Warren 218
CIS (Commonwealth of Independent States) 4,
  111–12:
  Afghanistan and 248
  anti-terrorism centre 27, 28, 111, 126, 143,
    317, 355, 356
  Integrated Air Defence System 109, 111,
    185, 349, 354
  joint force 346, 347
  military cooperation 27
  peacekeeping and 26, 104–5, 111, 347, 355
  Russia and 14, 16, 26, 210
  see also Tashkent Treaty; terrorism; *and*
    under Tajikistan

Clinton, President Bill: Caspian Sea region
  and 19, 140, 217, 228, 251
companies:
  Russia 25, 32, 267
  UK 25
  USA 19, 25, 138, 148
  Western 18, 25, 32, 35, 60, 131, 148, 149
Cossacks 286, 296
Council of Europe 97, 198
CPC *see* Caspian Pipeline Consortium
CSCE (Conference on Security and
  Co-operation in Europe) 162
Czech Republic 96, 97

Dagestan 41:
  Chechen raid into 26, 121, 304, 306
  Chechen rebels and 15, 26
  Congress of the Peoples of Chechnya and
    Dagestan 306–7
  Federation Treaty and 295fn
  Islam and 121, 298, 305, 306–7
  oil and 23, 171
  Russian military base 132
  Salafites 298, 306, 307
Dagneft 43
Danielian, Anushan 264
Dardanelles 50, 139, 152, 190, 192
Delta Oil 48, 63, 123, 181, 193
Delta Hess 131
Demirel, President Suleyman 162
Devon 193
Dostum, General Abdul Rashid 248
Dragon Oil 39, 123
Dryukov, Anatoliy 272
Dudayev, Major-General Dzhokhar 295, 298,
  299, 301
Dyubendi–Batumi pipeline 45
Dzhamaat 302

Economic Cooperation Organization (ECO)
  173–74
Elcibey, President Ebulfez 178, 180, 181, 187
ENI 124, 144, 153
Enron 41
Erzurum–Ankara–Konya pipeline 62
EU (European Union):
  Central Asia and 163
  conflict prevention 30
  oil and 17, 79, 157
  Russia and 17
  South Caucasus and 163
  see also TRACECA; INOGATE

Exxon 63
ExxonMobil 39, 131, 149, 193

Ferghana Valley 121, 317, 326
Finland 44
Fluor Daniel 49, 53
Freeh, Louis 228

Gamsakhurdia, President Zviad 197, 200, 201,
    202, 207, 284, 285
Gamzat-Bek 297
gas:
    foreign investment and 1–2
    production 35
    reserves 1, 34–35
    see also under names of countries
gas pipelines 61–64, 144
    existing 61–62
    Iranian route 158
    Russia and 23
    Trans-Caspian Gas Pipeline (TCGP) 39, 40,
        65, 144
    Turkey and 153
    Turkmenistan–Iran 2
    Turkmenistan–Pakistan 246–47, 249,
        250–51
    USA and 5, 144
    see also Blue Stream and under names of
        pipelines
GazExport 61
Gazprom 25, 40, 42, 61, 132, 144, 149, 153,
    234, 235, 239, 250, 267
General Electric 144
Georgia:
    armed forces 93–94
        foreign aid to 93–94
    arms imports 94–95
    arms industry 94–95
    Azerbaijan and 264–65, 350, 352
    as buffer state 207–8
    Caspian Sea region and 134, 195–211
    CIS and 4, 94, 197, 202, 204, 207, 210
    corruption 203, 209
    Czech Republic and 96, 97
    economy 199, 209
    ethnic composition 281
    EU and 97, 206, 208, 210
    Europe and 207, 208, 210–11
    foreign aid to 83, 93–94, 95, 96
    foreign policy 200–3, 205, 206–11
    GDP 325
    Georgia and its Partners conference 196

Germany and 96, 97
Greece and 354
GUAM 198
GUUAM and 4, 113, 198, 210
    independence 197
    internal problems 199–200, 202
    Italy and 351
    Marneuli Military Airport 96
    military expenditure 83, 84, 85, 86, 93, 114
    Nagorno-Karabakh and 264–65
    NATO and 4, 29, 88, 95, 112, 162, 198,
        265, 293
    oil and 44, 45, 50, 52, 209
    Partnership for Peace and 95, 348
    refugees 289–90
    regional cooperation and 209–10
    Russia and 14, 94, 144, 160, 196–97, 202,
        203–6, 207, 209, 210, 264, 287, 292, 293,
        336, 346, 347, 348, 355
    Russian military bases in 4, 94, 135, 163fn,
        196, 197, 198, 201, 276, 291, 292, 349
        Abkhazia and 94, 290, 292 and fn
    Russian troops withdrawal 4, 31, 95, 96,
        199, 276, 353
    security and 196
    strategic idealism 195–96
    Tashkent Treaty and 2, 4, 94, 198, 204
    Turkey and 19, 20, 96, 151–52, 162, 333,
        351, 352
    UK and 96
    Ukraine and 95, 351
    USA and 95–96, 197, 198, 204, 337, 352,
        357
    West and 4, 14, 88, 196, 197, 204, 206–9,
        211
    see also Abkhazia; South Ossetia
Georgian Pipeline Company 54
Germany 96, 97, 296–97
Goble, Paul 279
Gore, Al 331
Gore–Chernomyrdin memorandum (1995) 86
Great Game 12, 32, 168, 311
Greece 91, 352, 353, 354
Grozny 56, 142
GUAM:
    creation 14, 351
    see also GUUAM
Gukasian, Arkadiy 262, 263, 264, 278
Guliyev, Vilayet 92, 329, 341
Guluzade, Wafa 272
GUUAM:
    creation 4, 14, 113

membership 113
Nagorno-Karabakh and 269
NATO and 269
peacekeeping unit 29, 269
pipelines and 114
purposes 113–14
*for relations with individual countries see
under names of countries*

Haider, Vice-Marshal Farug Usman 247
Hawes 95
Hormuz, Strait of 137
Hu Jintao 110
Husseinov, Colonel Surat 181

Idrisov, Yerlan 66
ILF Consulting Engineers 60
IMF (International Monetary Fund) 198, 203,
214
India: Islam and 316
Ingushetia 300, 306
INOGATE (Interstate Oil and Gas Transport
to Europe) project 293
Integral Azerbaijan Union 187
International Energy Agency (IEA) 63, 68
International Maritime Organization (IMO)
139, 156
Ioseliani, Djaba 285
Iran:
   armed forces 85
   Armenia and 20, 25, 187–88, 270, 331
   arms imports 4, 83, 86–88
   arms industry 86, 87, 88, 115
   Azerbaijan and 186–88, 270
   Azeri population 20, 186–87, 188
   Caspian Sea and 78
   Caspian Sea legal regime and 7, 20, 65,
      66–67, 127–28, 135, 169–70, 175, 188,
      189, 241, 331
      resource exploitation and 127, 175
   Caspian Sea region and 166–77, 330–31
   China and 87, 115
   conflict resolution 20–21
   culture 174
   foreign investment 43, 57
   France and 88
   gas 234–35
   gas pipelines and 22, 25, 330, 331:
      USA and 23
   gas transport and 88
   importance of 7, 20–21
   Islamic radicalism and 316

Kazakhstan and 20
Korea, North and 86–87
military expenditure 3, 84, 85–86
missiles and 87
Nagorno-Karabakh and 20, 270
NBC weapons and 86
oil:
   1998 Agreement 43
   imports 51, 130
   swaps system 44, 56, 60, 130, 172
oil pipelines and 24–25, 45, 51, 56–58, 88,
   124, 168, 172, 330, 331:
   USA and 25, 31, 130
oil reserves 43
oil transport and 88
railways 173
revolution, export of 20
Russia and 20, 21, 86–87, 132, 133, 134,
   270, 330–31, 341, 356
security concerns 17, 18, 20–21, 166–77,
   330–31
Tajikistan and 20, 174
terrorism and 148, 149
Turkey and 154
Turkmenistan and 20, 24–25, 174
Ukraine and 87
USA and 258:
   containment 5, 20, 21, 88, 138, 151, 172,
      176, 271
   rapprochement 23, 124, 130, 138,
      148–49, 270, 330
USSR, treaties, 1921 2, 169, 170, 188, 189,
   242
USSR's collapse and 166
Iraq:
   Kurdish people 309
   oil 125
Isfahan 57, 58
Islam:
   fear of 27, 219
   growing influence 3, 27
   Islamic extremism 121–22, 224
   Islamic radicalism 315–16, 326
   renaissance 298, 299
   revivalism 313–14
   see also under names of countries
Israel 270
Israilov, Hasan 297
Istanbul 67, 139
Istanbul Declaration (1999) 192
Italy 351
Itera 61, 234

Itochu 123, 131, 193
Ivanov, Igor 267
Ivanov, Sergey 16, 121, 122, 226–27, 318
Ivashov, Colonel-General Leonid 120

J. P. Kenny 190
Japan: gas and 63–64, 234
Javadov, Mahir 188
Javaheti 264, 288, 289
JKX 43

Kabul 213, 248
Kadyrov, Akhmed-Hadji 300, 303, 304
Kalmykia 41
Kalyuzhny, Viktor 16, 23, 66, 80, 133, 134, 170, 267
Karachaganak Petroleum Operating group 49
Karimov, President Islam 28, 108, 110, 137fn, 143, 314, 317, 320, 340
Kasyanov, Mikhail 61–62, 160, 339
Kazakhstan:
    Afghanistan and 213, 219, 224
    Aktyubinsk 24
    Aktyubinsk field 38
    armed forces 97
        reform 98
    arms exports 92, 99
    arms imports 4, 79, 83, 99, 227
    arms industry 99, 115
    Caspian Sea:
        legal regime and 64, 65, 66, 127, 170, 189
        security and 212–30
    CAU and 4, 212, 213–14
    China and 21, 24, 30, 31, 101, 214, 335–36, 350
    CIS and 98, 99, 212
    condensate 37
    corruption 221, 224–25
    criminalization 224–25
    demographic policy 214, 224
    drug trade 223–24, 229
    economy 128–29, 212, 220–23
    emigration 223, 224
    energy deposits 22
    extremism and 230
    foreign companies in 221, 222
    gas, deposits 235
    GDP 325
    immigration 223
    Iran and 138
    Karachaganak oilfield 37, 38, 45, 49

Kashagan oilfield 24, 37, 38, 55, 123–24, 140, 141, 157
Kyrgyzstan and 103, 350, 356
Mangystau 38
military doctrine 98, 229
military expenditure 84, 85, 86, 97–98, 114
Nagorno-Karabakh and 265
NATO and 4, 100–1
North Buzachi oilfield 38, 45
nuclear weapons and 213, 217, 345
oil 22, 23, 24, 31, 35, 44, 45, 47, 48–49, 50, 51, 52, 53, 56, 123–24:
    drilling for 141
    economic development and 128–29
    exploration 217
    production 35, 37, 38, 60, 141, 217
    reserves 129, 140
    swap arrangements 58
oil pipelines and 56–58, 143, 193, 339
oil transit fees 49
Partnership for Peace and 348
political situation 225
poverty 221
reform and 220–25
Russia and 14, 23, 31, 81, 98–99, 100, 121, 127, 132, 133, 142, 189, 214, 226, 339, 348, 349, 352, 353, 355
Russian population 19, 121
security policy 212–30
Strategy of National Economic Security 229–30
Tashkent Treaty and 111, 212–12, 229
Tengiz oilfield 22, 37, 45, 48, 124
terrorism and 98, 230
Turkey and 100–1, 356
USA and 19, 29, 100, 138, 214, 217–18, 349, 351, 353, 354
Uzbekistan and 352
Uzen oilfield 24, 38
Kazakoil 37
Kazimulla 297
KazNipiNeft 60
KazTransoil 79
Kelimbetov, Kairat 222
Khalimov, Islam 298
Kharazzi, Kamal 130, 170
Kharg Island 57, 172
Khasaviurt Agreement (1996) 14, 28, 278
Khatami, President Mohammad 57, 87, 177, 330, 331
Khattab 303, 309
Khizbi al Takhri 340

Kitovani, Tengiz 284–85
Kocharian, President Robert 260, 261–62, 264, 270, 274–75, 328–29
Komsomol'skaya 48
Korea, North: missiles and 87
Korpedze–Kurt–Kui (KKK) pipeline 22, 57, 61, 62, 238
Kosovo 15, 198, 278
Kozyrev, Andrey 226, 290
Krasnovodsk 106
KTI line see oil pipelines: Kazakhstan–Turkmenistan–Iran
Kubanneftegastroi 49
Kuchma, President Leonid 240
Kumkol 49
Kunta-Hadji, Sheikh 299, 304
Kyapaz oilfield 65, 67
Kyrgyzstan:
 aid to 102–3
 armed forces 101, 102
 Batken region 101, 102, 313
 CAU and 4
 China and 21, 24, 30, 104
 GDP 325
 Islam and 314
 Islamist incursions into 26, 30, 98, 101, 102–3, 121, 226, 253, 313, 318
 Kazakhstan and 103, 350, 356
 military expenditure 84, 85, 86, 101, 102
 NATO and 103
 Partnership for Peace and 103, 348
 Russia and 14, 27, 31, 101–2, 103, 346, 351, 353, 355:
  troops withdrawn 4, 102
 Turkey and 30, 103, 333, 356
 USA and 29, 103, 354
 Uzbekistan and 102

Laden, Usama bin 251
Larmag 39
Lasmo 39, 43
Lebedev, Alexander 160
Leggate, John 55
Lezgins 185
Libya 153
Lockheed Maritime Overseas 156
LukAgip 123
Lukarco 193
Lukoil 25, 41, 42–43, 49, 123, 132, 179, 181, 183, 186, 193–94, 267

Macdermott 181
Mackinder, Halford 18, 167
Main Export Pipeline Company (MEPC) 193
Makhachkala 79, 142
Mamedov, Etibar 274–75
Mansur, Sheikh 296, 297
Mapna 57
Mareski, John 278
Maskhadov, Aslan 303, 304, 305
Massoud, Ahmad Shah 248
Medzhidov, Abdul-Malik 303
Melkumian, Naira 262–63
Menagarishvili, Irakli 208
Mi-8 helicopter 105, 109
Mi-24 helicopter 105
MiG-23 aircraft 89
MiG-25 aircraft 92
MiG-29 aircraft 87, 89, 90, 99
Mir-Moezzi, Mehdi 43
Mitsubishi 39, 63
Mobil 123
Moldova: GUUAM and 4, 113, 114
Montreux Convention (1936) 67, 139, 155
Monument Oil 123
Morningstar, Richard 124, 137fn, 158
Muhammad, Bagautdin 302, 304
Musharraf, General Pervez 251
Mutalibov, Ayaz 178
Muttaki, Amir Han 250

Nagorno-Karabakh:
 armed forces 277, 278
 Armenia and 257, 258, 261–62, 263, 273–75, 277–80
 Armenian population 257, 262
 Armenian troops in 89
 Azerbaijan and 91, 179, 257, 259, 259–61, 273–75, 277–80
 Caspian region security and 257–80
 CIS and 263, 268
 conflict in 257–58, 275–77:
  background 257–59
  ceasefires 258, 265, 276, 347, 348, 349
  resolution scenarios 277–80
 elections 263
 external interests and 257, 280
 Georgia and 264–65
 GUUAM group and 269
 independence proclaimed 258
 Iran and 270

Kazakhstan and 265
Lachin corridor 264, 274
mediation attempts 273–75
military elite 263–64
oil and 258, 259, 327
OSCE and 161, 273–74
peacekeeping in 273
pipelines and 258
refugees 273, 274, 278
Republic 257, 258, 259, 261, 262–64, 268,
   277, 279
Russia and 15, 183, 265, 266–68
status of 263, 274, 278–79
Susha problem 274
Tashkent Treaty and 204, 268
Turkey and 19, 164, 271, 273
Turkmenistan and 265
USA and 267, 271–72, 279
West and 260, 262, 263, 267, 271–73
Namazov, Eldar 272
National Iranian Oil Company (NIOC) 43, 138
NATO (North Atlantic Treaty Organization):
   Caspian Sea region and 4, 15, 26, 28–30, 31,
      112, 143, 145
   eastward expansion 121
   KFOR 92, 95, 161
   Kosovo and 15, 92
   new members 167
   Partnership for Peace 4, 26, 28–29, 97, 105,
      112, 113, 137, 161–62, 267, 327, 337
   for relations with individual countries see
      under names of countries
Nazarbayev, President Nursultan 37, 51, 78,
   100, 123, 137fn, 157, 213, 229, 248, 265
Neka–Tehran pipeline 45, 57, 58
Netherlands: arms exports 88
Niyazov, President Saparmurat 137fn, 148:
   Afghanistan and 107
   Caspian's status and 66, 236, 241, 242
   gas sales and 237, 239
   neutrality and 246, 248–49
   Pakistan and 247
   pipelines and 24, 238, 249–50
   unreliability 40, 62
North Apsheron Operating Company (NAOC)
   123
North Caucasus:
   oil and 23
   Russia and 341
North Ossetia 306
North Sea 34, 168

Novorossiysk 22, 54 see also Baku–
   Novorossiysk pipeline
Novorossiysk–Komsomol'skaya pipeline 48

Öcalan, Abdullah 160
Offshore Kazakhstan International Operating
   Company (OKIOC) 37, 222
oil:
   cost of exploiting 17
   early 154, 190, 191
   foreign investment 1–2, 35, 122, 326
   importance of 12
   main 155
   myths and realities 125, 140–44
   Persian Gulf oil and 123–25, 140
   production 35
   prospecting for, difficulties of 140
   reserves 1–2, 17, 34–44, 123, 124, 140, 168
   transporting 22–26, 35, 44–64, 129, 141–44,
      327, 327:
      costs 52, 54, 128
      environmental risks 125, 154–56
   see also oil pipelines; oil prices
oil pipelines 44–60, 141–42, 154–55, 171–72:
   Albania–Macedonia–Bulgaria 191, 192
   Azerbaijan–Georgia 2, 155
   Bulgaria–Greece 191, 192
   Caspian Sea legal regime and 127
   geopolitics of 156–59
   Iranian routes 24–25, 53, 56–58, 124, 130,
      138, 172, 330
   Kazakhstan–China 47, 58–60
   Kazakhstan–Turkmenistan–Iran (KTI) 45,
      56–58, 60
   multiple necessary 126, 131, 158
   proposals 45–47
   routes for, disputes over 2, 12, 129–30, 327
   Russian routes 22, 23, 24, 53, 142, 143
   trans-Caspian 193
   Turkmenistan–Pakistan 249, 250–51
   Ukrainian route 2
   uncertainty over 24, 125, 126, 171–72
   see also under names of pipelines
oil prices 17, 33, 35, 55, 124, 125, 157, 193,
   194, 337
Olya 79
Oman Oil Company 190
Omar, Mullah Muhammad 247, 250
Omsk–Chardzhou pipeline 59
Organization of the Islamic Conference (OIC)
   174–75, 188, 309

OSCE (Organization for Security and
Co-operation in Europe) 28:
Baku–Ceyhan pipeline and 22, 51
Budapest summit meeting 272
Caspian Sea region and 28
Chechnya and 309
Istanbul summit meeting 22, 31, 51, 94, 115,
139–40, 192, 236, 259, 274, 328
Minsk Group 161, 183, 261, 272, 273, 274
Oslo Document *see under* CFE Treaty

Pakistan:
arms exports 88
gas and 62–63
Islamic radicalism and 316
oil and 47
Turkmenistan and 247, 251
Partnership for Peace *see under* NATO *and
under names of individual countries*
Pennzoil 36, 123, 181, 190
Pennzoil–Ramco 180
Persian culture 174
Persian Gulf: oil 35, 140, 151, 168
Petronas 39
Pickering, Thomas 227
Poland: arms exports 88
Primorsk 141
PSG 237
Putin, President Vladimir:
Azerbaijan and 92, 185–86, 189, 260, 340
Caspian Sea and 67
Caspian Sea region and 5, 15, 16, 23, 30–31,
133, 267, 338
gas imports 24
Georgia and 292
Iran and 87
Kazakhstan and 31, 99, 100, 226
Kyrgyzstan and 31, 102
Nagorno-Karabakh and 260–61
oil and 142
terrorism and 15, 27
Turkmenistan and 240
Uzbekistan and 31, 108

Rabbani, President Burhanuddin 247
Rakhman, Habib Abd ar- (Khattab) 303, 309
Rakhmonov, President Imomali 105
Ramco 131, 181, 193
Ramsar Convention (1971) 71
Rice, Condoleezza 148
Rich, Greg 54
Robertson, Lord 29, 103

Rokhlin, General Lev 275–76
Romania: arms exports 88
Rosneft 25, 43
Royal Dutch/Shell 39, 43, 144 *see also* Shell
Russia:
arms exports 86–87, 90, 92, 95, 105, 111,
160, 227, 268, 272, 276, 340
Azerbaijanis in 184
Caspian Sea and 73, 78, 80, 132–35:
biological disaster and 134
demilitarization 120, 132
legal regime and 16, 23, 64–65, 66, 78,
80, 81, 127, 132–35, 169–70, 188–89,
241, 242, 331
pipeline across 131
Caspian Sea region and 5, 13–16, 132–35,
145, 266:
allies in 14
dependence on 11
economic interests 122–23, 338, 339, 340
geopolitical interests 120, 130
importance of 5, 13
military presence 132, 135
oil production 52
oil reserves 34, 35, 41–43
retreat from 5, 30–31
security and 17, 18, 26–28, 119–35,
338–41
security threats 120–22
Special Representative 23
USA and 5, 11, 15, 19, 21, 125, 126–28,
146, 147, 206, 219, 341–43
Central Asia and 11, 15
CentrasBat and 29
CIS and 14, 16, 26, 210
companies 25, 32, 267
Druzhba pipeline system 44, 53
economy 159, 160
Federation Treaty 295fn.
foreign investment 42
foreign policy concept 15
gas:
companies 15, 42
exports 153, 234
imports 239, 339
outlets, dominance of 23, 234
pipelines 22, 61, 131, 194, 238–40
production 42, 238, 240
reserves 42, 234
GUUAM and 198, 217, 269
InchkeMore field 43
Islam and 296, 305, 307–8, 316, 318

Islamic extremism and 121, 143
as mediator 15
military doctrine 15
Muslim population 300
Muslim states and 309
national security doctrine 15, 119–20
NATO and 5, 11, 162
oil:
   companies 15
   outlets, dominance of 22, 24, 171, 227,
   234
   reserves 17, 145
   transit fees 49, 339–40
oil pipelines and 2, 12, 22, 53, 56, 131,
   142–43, 171, 194, 227
peacekeeping troops 26, 28, 268, 273, 290,
   293
railways and 339
Security Council 16, 23
separatism 307
Severny prospect 42
status of 13, 145, 146
terrorism and 15, 27, 32, 119, 121
trade 14
USA, relations with 5, 15, 125, 126, 147
West and 11
see also under names of successor countries

S-300 air defence system 87, 90, 97, 99, 100,
   272
SACE 62
Salafism see under Chechnya and Dagestan
Sangachali–Ceyhan pipeline 50
Sarkisian, Serzh 90
Sarmadi, Morteza 66
Saudi Arabia: Islamic radicalism and 316
Sea of Marmara 50, 67, 155, 156
Serdar oilfield 65, 66
Sergeyev, Igor 103, 109
Sestanovich, Stephen 52
Sezer, President Ahmet Necdet 157, 320
Shahab missiles 86
Shanghai Five/Forum/Cooperation
   Organization:
   anti-terrorism centre 30, 101, 355
   confidence-building measures 350, 352, 354
   membership 30, 32, 112, 214, 320, 328, 350,
   355, 357
   name changes 30, 113, 328, 357
   purposes of 112–13, 121, 230, 328, 334–35,
   350
Sharif, Nawaz 247

Shashani, Fatkha ash- 302
Shell 62, 237
Shevardnadze, President Eduard:
   Abkhazia and 284, 285
   foreign policy 200, 208, 211
   NATO and 29, 95
   return of 196, 197, 200, 201
   stability and 199
Shikhmuradov, Boris 250
Simpson, Thomas 126
Slavneft 25
SOCAR see State Oil Company of Azerbaijan
Socio-Political Union of the Caucasian
   Confederation 306
South Caucasus:
   military expenditure 3, 83, 88–97
   pipelines across 2
   Russia and 205, 266, 267, 291, 292, 328–29:
      retreat from 31
   secessionism 326
   security system 328–29
   Turkey and 151
   USA and 125
South Ossetia:
   conflict in 93, 197, 199, 201, 211, 264,
      288–89
   Russia and 15, 197, 204, 205, 207, 209, 292,
      346–47
Spie-Capag 49
Stability Pact for the Caucasus 134, 162–63,
   332
Stalin, Joseph 282, 283
Starstroi 49
State Oil Company of Azerbaijan (SOCAR)
   36, 56, 65, 123, 129, 156, 181, 190, 191,
   192, 193, 235
Statoil 131, 181, 193
Stavropoltruboprovodstroi 49
sturgeon 69, 70, 71, 72–73, 81, 131
Su-24 aircraft 87
Su-25 aircraft 94, 99, 105, 107
Su-27 aircraft 99, 276
Supsa 22 see also Baku–Supsa pipeline
Susuev, Zia 303

Tabriz 57, 58
Tabriz–Erzurum gas pipeline 61
Tajikistan:
   Afghanistan and 104, 105
   armed forces 104–5
   arms imports 105, 106
   arms industry 105

CAU and 4
China and 21, 105, 335
CIS peacekeeping forces in 104, 347, 355
civil war 21, 104, 105, 320
Iran and 106, 174
Islam and 305, 314, 315, 316
Islamic incursions into 121
military expenditure 84, 85, 86, 104
NATO and 105
Peace and Reconciliation Accord (1997)
    351
Russia and 14, 21, 104–5, 349, 352:
    military bases 104, 352
    Russian forces in 105, 347
United Tajik Opposition (UTO) 104
Uzbekistan and 320, 351, 353
Talbott, Strobe 17–18, 19
Tashkent Treaty (Treaty on Collective
  Security, 1992) 4, 14, 26, 111, 122, 327,
  346:
  Armenia and 90, 111, 268, 327, 346
  Azerbaijan and 4, 92, 265, 268, 346
  Belarus and 111, 346
  Bishkek summit meeting 111, 122, 319fn,
    340
  Collective Security Council 226, 227, 353
  Committee of Secretaries of the Security
    Councils 122
  Georgia and 2, 94, 198, 204, 346
  Kazakhstan and 111, 212–13, 226–27, 229,
    327, 346
  Kyrgyzstan and 27, 102, 105, 111, 327, 346
  membership 14, 26, 346
  purposes of 111–12
  rapid-deployment force 27, 122, 340
  Russia and 111, 268, 346
  Tajikistan and 105, 111, 327, 346
  Turkmenistan and 265
  Uzbekistan and 346, 355
  terrorism and 27, 122, 340, 354
Tatarstan 295fn, 300
Tbilisi Aircraft Works (TAW) 94, 107
TCG1 62
TCGP see Trans-Caspian Gas Pipeline
Tehran 57
Tenet, George 228
Tengiz 76, 77, 79, 124
Tengiz–Novorossiysk pipeline 22, 23, 44, 48,
  49, 79, 123, 131, 143, 227, 339, 342 see also
  Caspian Pipeline Consortium
Tengizchevronoil (TCO) 52, 124

terrorism 15, 27, 30, 97, 111, 112, 121, 228,
  230, 319, 334:
  anti-terrorism centres 27, 28, 30, 101, 111,
    121, 126, 143, 221, 230, 317, 355, 356
  interior ministry forces and 83
  military expenditure and 84
  see also under names of countries
    concerned
Tevzadze, David 95
Texaco 38, 45, 49
Thatcher, Margaret 180
Tikhoretsk 56, 79
Tokayev, Kassymzhomart 24
Total 58, 62
TPAO 131, 193
TRACECA (Transport Corridor Europe
  Caucasus Asia) 79, 163, 178, 198, 217, 259,
  267, 275, 293, 334, 339
Trans-Caspian Gas Pipeline (TCGP) 20, 23,
  39, 40, 62, 65, 130, 131, 144, 154, 236–38,
  330, 337, 339
Transneft 56, 142
Turkey:
  Armenia and 19, 164, 262
  Azerbaijan and 19, 20, 93, 112, 144,
    151–52, 164, 187, 270, 276, 332, 333,
    350, 356, 357
  Caspian Sea legal regime and 170
  Caspian Sea region and 7, 17, 18, 19–20,
    145, 151–65, 332–34:
      multilateralism 161–63
      West and 161–63
  Caucasus Stability Pact and 162–63
  Central Asia and 151
  Chechnya and 160
  constraints on 163–64
  economy 152–54, 231–53
  energy needs 2, 25, 63, 152–54, 334
  EU and 152, 157, 161
  future trends 164–65
  gas and 20, 23, 34, 61, 63, 153–54, 231–34,
    237
  Georgia and 19, 20, 96, 151–52, 160, 162,
    333, 351
  human rights and 163
  Iran and 154, 158
  Islamic radicalism and 316
  Israel and 270
  Kazakhstan and 100–1, 356
  Kurdish people 309
  Kyrgyzstan and 30, 103–4, 333, 356

Nagorno-Karabakh and 19, 164, 271, 273
NATO and 161–62
oil and 17, 20, 65, 152–54, 231–34
oil tankers and 2, 67–68, 130, 139, 152,
    155–56
pipelines and 7, 34, 40, 51, 131, 139, 142,
    154, 156–59
PKK 160
Russia and 139, 142, 154, 156, 159–60,
    163–65, 234, 239, 240, 332, 333–34:
trade 159–60
South Caucasus and 19–20, 151–52
terrorism and 145
Turkestan and 39
USA and 126, 130, 139, 158, 338
Uzbekistan and 110, 320, 333, 356
    see also following entries
Turkish Petroleum Corporation (TPAO) 156,
    181
Turkish Straits:
    tankers and 50, 67–68, 139, 155–56,
    171
    see also Bosporus; Dardanelles; Montreux
    Convention; Sea of Marmara
Turkmengas State Gas Company 39
Turkmenistan:
    Afghanistan and 227, 246–51, 252
    Amu Darya Basin 39
    armed forces 106, 107
    arms imports 106, 107
    Azerbaijan and 65, 106, 131, 134, 144, 236,
    238, 243
    borders 4, 106, 245
    Caspian Sea legal regime and 65, 170, 189,
    236, 241–42, 243
    drug trade 249, 252
    energy deposits 22
    Garashsizlik field 123
    gas 22, 34, 61, 62, 140, 154, 236:
        exports 24, 154, 232–33, 237, 240–41,
        339
        production 232, 233
        reserves 38, 39, 232–33, 245
    gas pipelines and 23, 24, 233, 234, 238–41
    Georgia and 107
    Iran and 5, 20, 24–25, 138, 174
    Islam and 314
    military expenditure 84, 85, 86, 106
    Nagorno-Karabakh and 265
    NATO and 107
    neutrality 26, 243–46, 252–53

oil:
    companies and 39–40, 123
    exports 44, 232–33
    production 35, 38–39, 232
    reserves 38, 39, 140, 232–33, 233, 245
oil pipelines and 24, 34, 39, 45, 56–58, 233,
    234
Pakistan and 107, 247, 251
Partnership for Peace and 28, 107, 348
Russia and 40, 106–7, 133, 134, 237,
    238–40, 243, 347
Russian forces in 215:
    troop withdrawal 4, 106
state, nature of 245
Taliban and 246–51
Turkey and 39, 107
Turkmenbashi refinery 233
Ukraine and 40, 106, 107, 349
USA and 107, 239–40
Uzbekistan and 245, 350
Turkmenneft State Oil Company 39
Typhoon missile 91

Udugov, Movladi 307
Ukraine:
    arms exports 87, 92, 95, 109
    Azerbaijan and 114
    energy needs 2
    gas imports 240–41
    Georgia and 351
    GUUAM and 4, 113
    pipelines across 2
    Turkmenistan and 40
Union of Soviet Socialist Republics:
    breakup, Caspian Sea region and 1, 7, 11,
    168
United Arab Emirates 39
United Nations:
    Caspian Sea region and 28
    Millennium Summit 274, 293, 320
United States of America:
    Caspian Sea region and 4, 5, 18–19, 31, 125,
    126, 136–50, 271–72, 336–38, 343:
        anti-terrorism and 29
        military cooperation 137
        oil and 34, 35, 137–38, 336, 336–37
        policy change expected 147–49
        Russia and 5, 11, 15, 19, 21, 125,
        126–28, 146, 147, 206, 219, 341–43,
        357
        security concerns 136–50, 158, 336

special envoy 137
strategic interests 17–18, 145–46
Central Command (CENTCOM) 217
Congress 5, 29
Cooperation Threat Reduction Programme 137
energy security 137
Energy Information Administration 41–42
Eximbank 236
Foreign Military Financing (FMF) 96, 110, 137
Freedom Support Act (1992) 137
GUUAM and 114
Iran and Libya Sanctions Act (1996) 172
oil pipeline security and 143–44
oil pipelines and 2, 5, 19, 52, 158
Silk Road Strategy Act (1999) 5
USAID 272
for relations with other countries see under names of
Unocal 41, 47–48, 63, 123, 131, 172, 181, 190, 193, 249
Uzbekistan:
Afghanistan and 227
aid to 109, 110–11
anti-terrorism centre and 317
armed forces 107
reform 108, 109
arms imports 108, 109, 340
arms industry 115
CAU and 4
China and 30, 110–11, 355
CIS and 4, 28
condensate, reserves 41
EU and 311
France and 110
gas:
exports 41
production 41
reserves 41, 235
GDP 325
Germany and 110
Greece and 110, 352
GUUAM and 4, 19, 108, 113
investment 41
Islamic Movement of Uzbekistan (IMU) 320, 340
Islamic radicalism and 314, 315, 316, 320, 340
Islamist incursions into 98, 110, 121, 122, 226, 253, 318
Japan and 311

Kazakhstan and 352
Kokdulamak oilfield 41, 235
Kyrgyzstan and 102
military expenditure 84, 85, 86, 107–8
NATO and 4, 109–10, 320, 327
nuclear weapons 345
oil:
production 35, 41
reserves 41
Partnership for Peace and 109, 349
regional security and 317
Russia and 14, 16, 27, 28, 31, 108–9, 319, 340, 352, 355, 357
Tajikistan and 320, 351, 353, 355
Taliban and 320
Tashkent Treaty and 4, 27, 108
Turkey and 110, 320, 333, 356
Turkmenistan and 245, 350
Ukraine and 109
USA and 18, 29, 110, 146, 311, 312, 337, 352, 354
West and 14, 108, 312
Uzbekneftegas 41

Velayati, Ali Akbar 186
Volzhskiy Pipe Works 49
Vyakhirev, Rem 239

Wahhabism *see under* Chechnya
Wood Mackenzie 141
World Bank 63, 198, 203, 214

Xinjiang *see under* China
XXI Asyr Turkmenin Altyn Asyry 237

Yandarbiyev, President Zelimkhan 300, 302, 304
Yeltsin, President Boris 5, 266, 275, 285, 286, 291
Yukos 25, 42, 132, 267

Zahid, Abdur Rahmad 251
Zaidi, Iglal Haider 250
Zemskiy, Vladimir 353
'zero-sum approach' 4, 12–13, 16, 32, 343
Zhvania, Zurab 208
Zulfugarov, Tofik 272

MAY 2 3 2002